D0787829

The Mind within the Brain

The Mind within the Brain

How We Make Decisions and How Those Decisions Go Wrong

A. DAVID REDISH

OXFORD
UNIVERSITY PRESS

OXFORD
UNIVERSITY PRESS

Oxford University Press is a department of the University of Oxford.
It furthers the University's objective of excellence in research, scholarship,
and education by publishing worldwide.

Oxford   New York
Auckland   Cape Town   Dar es Salaam   Hong Kong   Karachi
Kuala Lumpur   Madrid   Melbourne   Mexico City   Nairobi
New Delhi   Shanghai   Taipei   Toronto

With offices in
Argentina   Austria   Brazil   Chile   Czech Republic   France   Greece
Guatemala   Hungary   Italy   Japan   Poland   Portugal   Singapore
South Korea   Switzerland   Thailand   Turkey   Ukraine   Vietnam

Oxford is a registered trademark of Oxford University Press
in the UK and certain other countries.

Published in the United States of America by
Oxford University Press
198 Madison Avenue, New York, NY 10016

Library of Congress Cataloging-in-Publication Data
Redish, A. David.
The mind within the brain : how we make decisions and how those decisions go wrong / A. David Redish.
pages cm
Includes bibliographical references.
Summary: In The Mind within the Brain, A. David Redish brings together cutting-edge research in psychology,
robotics, economics, neuroscience, and the new fields of neuroeconomics and computational psychiatry,
to offer a unified theory of human decision-making. Most importantly, Redish shows how vulnerabilities, or
"failure modes," in the decision-making system can lead to serious dysfunctions, such as irrational behavior,
addictions, problem gambling, and post-traumatic stress disorder. Ranging widely from the surprising
roles of emotion, habit, and narrative in decision-making to the larger philosophical questions of how
mind and brain are related, what makes us human, the nature of morality, free will, and the conundrum
of robotics and consciousness, The Mind within the Brain offers fresh insight into some of the most
complex aspects of human behavior.—Provided by publisher.
ISBN 978–0–19–989188–7 (hardback)
1. Decision making. I. Title.
BF448.R43 2013
153.8'3—dc23*   2012046214

3 5 7 9 8 6 4 2
Printed in the United States of America
on acid-free paper

For Laura, Jay, Danny, and Sylvia,
the best decisions I ever made.

CONTENTS

PREFACE

If I could, I would reach beyond the cage of bone,
to touch the mind within the brain,
to reach the frightened nerves that wrap the heart;
I would speak your name there.

Our decisions make us who we are. Although we would like to think that our decisions are made rationally, deliberatively, many decisions are not. We all know that some of our decisions are made emotionally, and some are made reactively. Some have their intended consequences, and some have consequences we never imagined possible.

We are physical beings. The human brain is a complex network of neurons and other cells that takes information in from the world through its sensory systems and acts on the world through its motor systems. But how does that network of cells, in constant dynamic flux, become the person you are? How does the mind fit into that small place in the cage of bone that is our skull? How does it process information? How does it perceive the world, determine the best option, select an action, and take that action? How does it fall in love? Laugh at the overwhelming emotion of holding an infant? How does it create great art or great music? How does it feel the triumphant emotion of Beethoven's *Ode to Joy* or the devastating pathos of Bob Dylan's *Knock Knock Knocking on Heaven's Door*? Just how does the lady sing the blues? How does it get addicted and how does it break that addiction? How does it have a personality? What makes you you and me me?

Fundamentally, all of these questions are about how the being that you recognize as yourself fits into this physical brain nestled in your skull. Fundamentally, these questions are about how that brain makes decisions. This book is an attempt to answer that question.

Where this book came from

A few years ago, John Gessner, who runs a local program for people with gambling problems and their families, asked me if I would be willing to give a talk to his clients on decision-making. I had been giving talks to Jan Dubinsky's *BrainU* program for high school teachers interested in neuroscience and had recently given a talk to frontline medical professionals (doctors, nurses, and addiction social workers) on my laboratory's work identifying vulnerabilities in decision-making systems. John had heard of this talk and wanted me to present this work to his clients.

I protested that I was not a medical professional and that I could not tell them how to fix what was broken. He said that they had lots of people to tell them that, what they wanted was someone to tell them *why—Why do we make the choices we do?* He said they wanted to know why those decisions get made wrong, especially when they knew what the right choices were.

The lecture itself went very well. There were several dozen people in the audience, and they were involved and asking questions throughout. And then, afterwards, they had so many questions that I stayed there answering questions for hours. There was a hunger there that I had not appreciated until I met those gamblers and their families, an almost desperate desire to understand how the brain works. They had seen how things can go wrong and needed an explanation, particularly one that could explain how they could both be conscious beings making decisions and yet still feel trapped. Somehow, that science lecture on how the multiple decision-making systems interact reached them. I realized then that there was a book I had to write.

Over the past three years, this book has morphed and grown. My goal, however, remains to explain the science of how we make decisions. As such, an important part of this book will be to identify what questions remain.[1] My goal is not to provide a self-help book to help you make better decisions. I am not going to tell you what you should do. Nor are the answers to curing addiction or poor decisions herein. You should check with your own medical professionals for treatment. Every individual is unique, and your needs should be addressed by someone directly familiar with them. Nevertheless, I hope that you find the book illuminating. I hope you enjoy reading it. It has been tremendously fun to write.

The structure of the book

One of the remarkable things that has occurred over the past several decades is the convergence of different fields on the mechanisms of decision-making. Scientific fields as diverse as psychology, robotics, economics, neuroscience, and the new fields of neuro-economics and computational psychiatry have all been converging on the recognition that decision-making arises from a complex interaction of multiple subsystems. In fact, these fields have converged on a similar categorization of the differences between the subsystems. In this book, we will explore how this convergence explains the decision-making that we (as humans) do.

I have divided this book into four sections. The first sections (*Decisions and the Brain* and *The Decision-Making System*) will lay out the work that has been done on the basic mechanisms—*What is a decision? How does the brain's decision-making system work? What are the components that make up that decision-making system?* And then, the third and fourth sections will explore the consequences of that system.

The first section consists of five chapters, two chapters to set the stage (1: *What Is a Decision?* and 2: *The Tale of the Thermostat*) and three chapters to introduce the basic neuroeconomics of decision-making (3: *The Definition of Value*, 4: *Value, Euphoria, and the Do-It-Again Signal*, and 5: *Risk and Reward*). In the second section, we will start with the results that the decision-making system is made up of multiple modules or subsystems (Chapter 6), and then spend a chapter each on the component systems (Chapters 7 through 15).

In the third section (*The Brain With a Mind of Its Own*), we will explore the consequences of the physical nature of the brain, how mind and brain are related, and how vulnerabilities in the decision-making system can lead to dysfunction, such as addiction (Chapter 18), problem gambling (Chapter 19), and post-traumatic stress disorder (Chapter 20).

Finally, in the fourth section (*The Human Condition*), we will explore the philosophical questions of what makes us human (Chapter 22), of morality (Chapter 23), and of free will and consciousness (24: *The Conundrum of Robotics*) in the light of the new work on decision-making systems discussed in the previous sections.

I've tried to write the book so that it can be read straight through from start to finish by a reader with only a basic knowledge of neuroscience and computers; however, some readers may feel that they want a more detailed introduction to the concepts that are being discussed in this book. For those readers, I've included three chapters in an appendix, including *What is information processing* and *How neurons process information* (Appendix A), *How we can read that information from neural signals* (Appendix B), and *How memories are stored* (by content, not by index, Appendix C).

Throughout the book, every statement is backed up with citations. These citations will be marked with superscript numbers, matching the list in the bibliographic notes, which will then reference the actual list of citations.[2] These numbers are not endnotes and will not be used to refer to any additional text; they are there only to back up the claims in the book. Instead, extra information and discussion that could distract from the flow will be put into footnotes, marked with superscript letters.[A]

Each chapter begins with a short poem and ends with a set of follow-up readings. In my mind, I think of the poems as contemplative moments that can be used to shape one's perspective when reading the chapter. As a friend recovering from cancer in his hospital bed recently told me, "Sometimes you need the poetry to get to the heart of the science." The follow-up readings at the end of each chapter are books, review articles, starting points for those who want to pursue a topic in depth. While the superscript citations will refer to the primary literature, some of which can be quite difficult to understand, the follow-up readings should be understandable by anyone reading this book.

[A] I prefer footnotes to endnotes because footnotes allow you to glance at the text without having to lose your place in the book. I will generally be including three kinds of information in footnotes: (1) parenthetical comments that are too long to be included in parentheses (such as the etymology and location of brain structures); (2) cheeky jokes and stories that I can't resist including but would disrupt the flow of the book if I included them in the main text; and (3) technical details when there are subtle, second-order effects that need to be noted but are too complicated for those without the necessary background. The book should be readable without the footnotes, but I hope the footnotes will add an extra dimension for those who want more depth.

ACKNOWLEDGMENTS

Any project of this magnitude depends on many people. The results presented in this book include work by a host of scientists working in a number of fields over the past hundred years. Throughout, I have tried my best to acknowledge and cite the papers in which these ideas first appeared. I am sure that I have missed some, and apologize here to my colleagues for any omissions.

This work would never have been possible without the amazing and wonderful students and postdocs who have come through my lab, particularly Adam Johnson, Steve Jensen, Matthijs van der Meer, and Zeb Kurth-Nelson, with whom I have worked directly on these ideas, as well as Neil Schmitzer-Torbert, Jadin Jackson, John Ferguson, Anoopum Gupta, Beth Masimore, Andy Papale, Nate Powell, Paul Regier, Adam Steiner, Jeff Stott, Brandy Schmidt, and Andrew Wikenheiser. I am also indebted to Kelsey Seeland and Chris Boldt, without whom my laboratory would not function as it does and I would not have had the freedom to write this book.

Many of the ideas presented here have been worked out in conversations with colleagues. And so I need to thank those colleagues for the invigorating discussions we have had at conferences and workshops over the years, including Peter Dayan, Read Montague, Larry Amsel, Nathaniel Daw, Yael Niv, Warren Bickel, Jon Grant, Bernard Balleine, Dave Stephens, John O'Doherty, Antonio Rangel, Cliff Kentros, Andre Fenton, and many others too numerous to mention. I want to take the time here to thank my friends and colleagues who read drafts of part or all of this book, particularly Jan Dubinsky, Matthijs van der Meer, and John Gessner, as well as my editor Joan Bossert.

Much of the work presented in this book has been funded by the National Institutes of Health, particularly by grants for the study of decision-making from NIMH and NIDA. My first foray into decision-making was funded by a Fellowship from the Sloan Foundation, and from a McKnight Land-Grant Fellowship from the University of Minnesota. Students were funded by training grants from the National Science Foundation and the National Institutes for Health. This work would have been impossible without their generous support.

Finally, this book is dedicated to my wife Laura, my first reader, who read every chapter, before the first draft, after it, and then again, when the book was done, who has put up with the time and stress this book put on me, who inspires my poetry, and who doesn't let me get away with anything less than the best I can do. This book, all the work I have done, is for her.

PART ONE

DECISIONS AND THE BRAIN

1

What Is a Decision?

> snow flurries fall from the roof
> a squirrel skids to a stop
> Leap! into the unknown

In order to be able to scientifically measure decision-making, we define decisions as "taking an action." There are multiple decision-making systems within each of us. The actions we take are a consequence of the interactions of those systems. Our irrationality occurs when those multiple systems disagree with each other.

Because we like to think of ourselves as rational creatures, we like to define decision as the conscious deliberation over multiple choices. But this presumes a mechanism that might or might not be correct. If we are such rational creatures, why do we make such irrational decisions? Whether it be eating that last French fry that's just one more than we wanted or saying something we shouldn't have at the faculty meeting or the things we did that time we were drunk in college, we have all said and done things that we regret. Many a novel is based on a character having to overcome an irrational fear. Many an alcoholic has sworn not to drink, only to be found a few days later, in the bar, drink in hand.

We will see later in this book that the decisions that we make arise from an interaction of multiple decision-making systems. We love because we have emotional reactions borne of intrinsic social needs and evolutionary drives (the *Pavlovian* system, Chapter 8). We decide what job to take through consideration of the pros and cons of the imagined possibilities (*episodic future thinking* and the *Deliberative* system, Chapter 9). We can ride a bike because we have trained up our *Procedural* learning system (Chapter 10), but it can also be hard to break bad habits that we've learned too well (Chapter 15). We will see that these are only a few of the separable systems that we can identify. All of these different decision-making systems make up the person you are.

The idea that our actions arise from multiple, separably identifiable components has a long history in psychology, going back to Freud, or earlier, and has gained recent traction with theories of distributed computing, evolutionary psychology, and behavioral economics.[1] Obviously, in the end, there is a single being that takes an action, but sometimes it's helpful to understand that being in terms of its subsystems. The analogy that I like, which I will use several times in this book, is that of a car. The car has a drive train, a steering system, brakes. Cars often have multiple systems to accomplish the same goal (the foot-pedal brake and the emergency/parking brake, or the electric and gasoline engines in a hybrid like the Toyota Prius).

The psychologist Jonathan Haidt likes to talk of a rider and an elephant as a metaphor for the conscious and unconscious minds both making decisions,[2] but I find this analogy unsuitable because it separates the "self" from the "other" decision-making systems. As is recognized by Haidt at the end of his book, you are both the rider *and* the elephant. When a football star talks about being "in the zone," he's not talking about being out of his body and letting some other being take over—he feels that he is making the right decisions. (In fact, he's noticing that his procedural/habit system is working perfectly and is making the right decisions quickly and easily.) When you are walking through a dark forest and you start to get afraid and you jump at the slightest sound, that's not some animal reacting—that's you. (It's a classic example of the Pavlovian action-selection system.) Sometimes these systems work together. Sometimes they work at cross purposes. In either case, they are all still *you*. "Do I contradict myself?" asks Walt Whitman in his long poem *Song of Myself*. "Then I contradict myself. I am large. I contain multitudes."

So how do we determine how these multiple systems work? How do we determine when they are working together and when they are at cross-purposes? How do we identify the mechanisms of Whitman's multitudes?

To study something scientifically, we need to define our question in a way that we can measure and quantify it. Thus, we need a measure of decision-making that we can observe, so we can compare the predictions that arise from our hypotheses with actual data. This is the key to the scientific process: there must be a comparison to reality. If the hypothesis doesn't fit that reality, we must reject the hypothesis, no matter how much we like it.

One option is to simply to ask people what they want. But, of course, the idea that we always do what we say we want makes very strong assumptions about how we make decisions, and anyone who has regretted a decision knows that we don't always decide to do what we want. Some readers may take issue with this statement, saying that you wanted that decision when you took the action. Just because you regret that night of binge drinking when you have a hangover in the morning doesn't mean you didn't want all those drinks the night before. Other readers may argue that a part of you wanted that decision, even if another part didn't. We will come to a conclusion very similar to this, that there are multiple decision-making modules, and that the members of Whitman's multitudes do not always agree with each other. Much of this book will be about determining who those multitudes are and what happens when they disagree with each other.

As a first step in this identification of the multitudes, careful scientific studies have revealed that a lot of conscious "decisions" that we think we make are actually rationalizations after the fact.[3] For example, the time at which we think we decided to start an action is often after the action has already begun.

In what are now considered classic studies of consciousness, Benjamin Libet asked people to perform an action (such as tapping a finger whenever they wanted to) while watching a dot move around a circle.[4] The people were asked to report the position of the dot when they decided to act. Meanwhile, Libet and his colleagues recorded electrical signals from the brain and the muscles. Libet found that these signals preceded the conscious decision to act by several hundred milliseconds. Both the brain and muscles work by manipulating electricity, which we can measure with appropriate technologies. With the appropriate mathematics, we can decode those signals and determine what is happening within the brain. Libet decoded when the action could be determined from signals in the motor areas of the brain and compared it to when consciousness thought the action had occurred. Libet found that the conscious decision to take an action was delayed, almost as if consciousness was perceiving the action, rather than instigating it. Several researchers have suggested that much of consciousness is a monitoring process, allowing it to keep track of things and step in if there are problems.[5]

Much of the brain's machinery is doing this sort of filling-in, of making good guesses about the world. Our eyes can focus on only a small area of our visual field at a time. Our best visual sensors are an area of our retina that has a concentration of cells tuned to color and specificity in a location called the *fovea*. This concentration of detectors at the fovea means that we're much better at seeing something if we focus our eyes on it. Our vision focuses on a new area of the visual world every third of a second or so. The journeys between visual focusings are called *saccades*. Even while we think we are focusing our attention on a small location, our eyes are making very small shifts called *microsaccades*. If the visual world is aligned to our microsaccades so that it shifts when we do,[A] the cells adapt to the constant picture and the visual image "grays out" and vanishes. This means that most of our understanding of the visual world is made from combining and interpreting short-term visual memories. We are inferring the shape of the world, not observing it.

In a simple case familiar to many people, there's a small location on our retina where the axons from the output cells have to pass through to form the optic nerve sending the visual signals to the rest of our brain. This leaves us with a "blind spot" that must be filled in by the retina and visual processing system.[B] Our brain normally fills in the "blind spot" from memories and expectations from the surrounding patterns.[7]

In a similar way, we don't always notice what actually drives our decision-making process. We rationalize it, filling in our reasons from logical perspectives. Some of my favorite examples of this come from the work of V. S. Ramachandran,[8] who has studied patients with damage to parts of the brain that represent the body. A patient who is

---

[A] The visual world can be aligned to our microsaccades by tracking the movement of the eyes and shifting a video display very quickly. This is feasible with modern computer technology.

[B] The wires (axons) of our optic nerve have to pass through the retina because the retina is built backwards, with the processing cells on top and the light-detecting cells on the bottom. The processing cells are generally transparent, so light passes through them and the light-detecting cells can still see, but at some point the axons have to leave the processing cells to travel to the brain. There are no light-detecting cells at the point where the axons pass through, leaving a blind spot. This is a relic of the evolutionary past of the human species. Eyes do not have to be built this way—the octopus eye, with a different evolutionary history, is oriented correctly, with the light-detecting cells on top and the processing cells below. Octopi therefore do not have a blind spot that needs to be filled in.[6]

physically unable to lift her arm denies that she has a problem and merely states that she does not want to. When her arm was made to rise by stimulating her muscles directly, she claimed that she had changed her mind and raised her arm because she wanted to, even though she had no direct control of the arm. In a wonderful story (told by Oliver Sacks in *A Leg to Stand On*), a patient claims that his right hand is not his own. When confronted with the fact that there are four hands on the table (two of his and the two of the doctor's), the patient says that three of the hands belong to the doctor. "How can I have three hands?" asks the doctor. "Why not? You have three arms." replies the patient.

In his book *Surely You're Joking, Mr. Feynman*, the famous physicist Richard Feynman described being hypnotized. He wrote about how he was sure he could take the action (in this case opening his eyes) even though he had been hypnotized not to, but he decided not to in order to see what would happen. So he didn't, which was what he had been asked to do under hypnosis. Notice that he has rationalized his decision. As Feynman himself recognized, even if he said "I could have opened my eyes," he didn't. So what made the decision? Was it some effect of the hypnosis on his brain or was it that he didn't want to? How could we tell? Can we tell?

Many of the experiments we're going to talk about in this book are drawn from animals making decisions. If we're going to say that animals make decisions, we need to have a way of operationalizing that decision—it's hard to ask animals what they think. There are methods that allow us to decode information represented within specific parts of the brain, which could be interpreted as a means of asking an animal what it thinks (see Appendix B). However, unlike asking humans linguistically, where one is asking the overall being what it thinks, decoding is asking a specific brain structure what it is representing. Of course, one could argue that assuming what people say is what they think assumes that humans are unified beings. As we will see as we delve deeper into how decisions are made, humans (like other mammals) are mixtures of many decision-making systems, not all of which always agree with each other.

Just as the Libet experiments suggest that parts of the brain can act without consciousness, there are representations in the brain that are unable to affect behavior. In a remarkable experiment, Pearl Chiu, Terry Lohrenz, and Read Montague found signals in both smokers' and nonsmokers' brains that represented not only the success of decisions made but also what they could have done if they had made a better choice.[9] This recognition of what they could have done is called a *counterfactual* (an imagination of what might have been) and enables enhanced learning. (It is now known that both rats and monkeys can represent counterfactual reward information as well. These signals appear to use the same brain structures that Chiu, Lohrenz, and Montague were studying, and to be the same structures involved when humans express regret.[10]) Counterfactuals enhance learning by allowing one to learn from imagined possibilities. For example, by watching someone else make a mistake. Or (in the example used by Chiu, Lohrenz, and Montague) "if I had taken my money out of the stock market last week, I wouldn't have lost all that money when it crashed." While signals in both groups' brains reflected this counterfactual information, only nonsmokers' behavior took that information into account. If we want to understand how decisions are made and how they go wrong, we are going to need a way to determine not only the actions taken by the subject but also the information processing happening in his or her brain.

Certainly, most nonhuman animals don't have language, although there may be some exceptions.[c] Nevertheless, it would be hard to ask rats, pigeons, or monkeys (all of which we will see making decisions later in the book) what they want linguistically. Given that it is also hard to ask humans what they really want, we will avoid this language problem altogether and operationalize making a decision as *taking an action*, because taking an action is an observable response.

This is very similar to what is known in behavioral economics as *revealed preferences*.[13] Economic theory (and the concomitant new field of neuroeconomics) generally assumes that those revealed preferences maintain a rational ordering such that if you prefer one thing (say chocolate ice cream) to another (say vanilla ice cream), then you will always prefer chocolate ice cream to vanilla if you are ever in the same situation. We will not make that assumption.

Similarly, we do not want to assume that a person telling you what he or she wants actually reflects the choices a person will make when faced with the actual decision.[14] Given the data that our conscious observations of the world are inferred and the data that our spoken explanations are rationalizations,[15] some researchers have suggested that our linguistic explanations of our desires are better thought of as the speech of a "press secretary" than the actions of an executive.[16] Thus, rather than asking what someone wants, we should measure decisions by giving people explicit choices and asking them to actually choose. We will encounter some of the strangenesses discovered by these experiments in subsequent chapters.

Often, experimentalists will offer people hypothetical choices. It is particularly difficult to get funding to provide people a real choice between $10,000 and $100,000, or to give them a real choice whether or not to kill one person to save five. Instead, subjects are asked to imagine a situation and pretend it was real. In practice, in the few cases where they have been directly compared, hypothetical and real decision-making choices tend to match closely.[17] But there are some examples where hypothetical and real decisions diverge.[18] These tend to be with rewards or punishments that are sensory, immediate, and what we will recognize later as *Pavlovian* (Chapter 8).

A classic example of this I call *the parable of the jellybeans*. Sarah Boysen and Gary Berntson tried to train chimpanzees to choose the humble portion.[19] They offered the subject two trays of jellybeans. If he reached for the larger tray, he got the smaller one and the larger one was given to another chimpanzee; however, if the deciding chimpanzee reached for the smaller tray, he got the larger tray and the smaller one was given to another chimpanzee. When presented with symbols (Arabic numerals that they had previously been trained to associate with numbers of jellybeans), subjects were able

---

[c] The extent to which animals can acquire human-level languages is not without its controversies. Since we're not going to trust human language either,[11] this issue is actually irrelevant to our question of decision-making. For those interested in the question of animals learning language, I recommend one of the excellent books written by the various researchers who have tried to teach language to nonhuman animals, such as Daniel Fouts teaching Washoe the chimpanzee, Penny Patterson teaching Koko the gorilla, Sue Savage-Rumbaugh teaching Kanzi the bonobo, or Irene Pepperberg teaching Alex the parrot.[12]

to choose the smaller group, but when the choices were physical jellybeans, they were unable to prevent themselves from reaching for the larger group of jellybeans. Other experiments have found that more linguistically capable animals are more able to perform these self-control behaviors.[20] This may be akin to our ability to talk ourselves out of doing things that we feel we really want: "I know I'm craving that cigarette. But I don't want it. I really don't."

A similar experiment is known colloquially as *the marshmallow experiment*.[21] Put a single marshmallow in front of a child sitting down at the kitchen table. Tell the child that if the marshmallow is still sitting there in five minutes, you'll add a second marshmallow to it. Then leave the room. It is very, very difficult for children not to reach for the marshmallow. It is much easier for children to wait for two pennies or two tokens than for two marshmallows. We will discuss the marshmallow experiment in detail in the chapter on self-control (Chapter 15).

Studies of decision-making in psychology (such as the marshmallow experiment) as well as studies in behavioral economics and the new field of neuroeconomics tend to measure choices within the limitation of discrete options. In the real world, we are rarely faced with a discrete set of options. Whether it be deciding when to swing the bat to hit a baseball or deciding where to run to on a playground, we are always continuously interacting with the world.[22] As we will see later, some of the mechanisms that select the actions we take are not always deliberative, and do not always entail discrete choices.

So where does that leave us in our search for a definition of decision-making? We will not assume that all decision-making is rational. We will not assume that all decision-making is deliberative. We will not assume that decision-making requires language. Instead, we define decision-making as *the selection of an action*. Obviously, many of the decisions we take (such as pushing a lever or button—say on a soda machine) are actual actions. But note that even complex decisions always end in taking an action. For example, buying a house entails signing a form. Getting married entails making a physical statement (saying "I do"). We are going to be less concerned about the physical muscle movements of the action than about the selection process that decided on which action to take. Nevertheless, defining "decision-making" as "action-selection" will force us to directly observe the decisions made. It will allow us to ask *why we take the actual actions we do*. Why don't those actions always match our stated intentions? How do we choose those actions over other potential actions? What are the systems that select actions, and how do those systems interact with the world? How do they break down? What are their vulnerabilities and failure-modes? That is what the rest of this book is about.

2

The Tale of the Thermostat

> jet exhaust shimmers above the tarmac
>
> I remember the strength of swans
> on the lake up North, their wings
> stretching forward, beating back…
>
> acceleration pushes us into our seats
> and we lift into the sky

Your brain is a decision-making machine, a complex but physical thing. Like any physical process, there are multiple ways in which decisions can go wrong. Being a physical being does not diminish who you are, but it can explain some of the irrational choices you make.

The decision-making that you do arises from the physical processes that occur in your brain. Because your brain is a physical thing, it has *vulnerabilities*, what one might call "failure-modes" in the engineering world. We see these vulnerabilities in our susceptibility to bad choices (*Do you really need a new sports car?*), in our susceptibility to addictions (*Why can't you just quit smoking those cigarettes?*), in our inability to control our emotions or our habits (*Why do you get so angry about things you can't change?*). We would like to believe that we are rational creatures, capable of logic, always choosing what's best for us. But anyone who has observed their own decisions (or those of their friends) will recognize that this is simply not correct. We are very complex decision-making machines, and sometimes those decision-making processes perplex us. Understanding how the brain makes decisions will help us understand ourselves. To understand those vulnerabilities, we need to understand the mechanism of decision-making in our brains.

Today, we are all familiar with complex machines, even complex machines that make decisions. The simplest machine that makes a decision is the thermostat—when the house is too hot, the thermostat turns on the air conditioning to cool it down, and when the house is too cold, the thermostat turns on the furnace to heat it up. This process is called *negative feedback*—the thermostat's actions are inversely related to the difference between the temperature of the room and the temperature you'd like it to be (the *set-point*). But is the process really so simple? Taking the decision-making process of the thermostat apart suggests that even the simple decision-making process of the thermostat is not so simple.

The thermostat has three key components of decision-making that we will come back to again and again in this book. First, it *perceives the world*—the thermostat has a sensor that detects the temperature. Second, it *determines what needs to be done*—it compares that sensor to the set-point and needs to increase the temperature because it is too cold, needs to decrease the temperature because it is too hot, or doesn't need to do anything because the temperature is just right. Finally, it *takes an action*—it turns on either the furnace or the air conditioning.

In the artificial intelligence literature, there was an argument through much of the 1980s about whether a thermostat could have a "belief."[1] Fundamentally, a belief is a (potentially incorrect) representation about the world. Clearly, a working thermostat requires a representation of the target temperature in order to take actions reflecting the temperature of the outside world. But can we really say that the thermostat "recognizes" the temperature of the outside world? The key to answering this question is that the thermostat does not take actions based on the temperature of the world, but rather on its internal representation of the temperature of the world. Notice that the internal representation might differ from the real temperature of the room. If the sensor is wrong, the thermostat could believe that the room is warmer or cooler than it really is and take the wrong action.

One of the key points in this book is that knowing how the brain works allows us a better perception of what happens when something goes wrong. I live in Minnesota. In the middle of winter, it can get very cold outside. Imagine you wake up one morning to find your bedroom is cold. Something is wrong. But simply saying that the thermostat is broken won't help you fix the problem. We need to identify the problem, to *diagnose* it, if you will.

Maybe something is wrong with the thermostat's perception. Perhaps the sensor is broken and is perceiving the wrong temperature. In this case, the thermostat could think that the house is fine even though it is too cold. (Notice the importance of belief here—the difference between the thermostat's internal representation and the actual temperature can have a big impact on how well the thermostat makes its decision!) Maybe the set-point is set to the wrong temperature. This means that the thermostat is working properly—it has correctly moved the temperature of your house to the set-point, but that's not what you wanted. Or, maybe there's something wrong with the actions available to the thermostat. If the furnace is broken, the thermostat may be sending the signal saying "heat the house" but the house would not be heating correctly. Each of these problems requires a different solution. Just as there are many potential reasons why your bedroom is too cold and knowing how a thermostat works is critical to understanding how to fix it, when smokers say that they really want to quit smoking, but can't, we need to know where each individual's decision-making process has gone wrong or we won't be able to help. Before we can identify where the decision-making process has broken down, we're going to need to understand how the different parts of the brain work together to make decisions.

Many readers will object at this point that people are much more complicated than thermostats. (And we are.) Many readers will then conclude that people are not machines. Back when negative feedback like the thermostat was the most complicated machine mechanism that made decisions, it was easy to dismiss negative feedback as too simple a model for understanding people. However, as we will see later in the book, we now know of much more complicated mechanisms that can make decisions. Are these more complicated mechanisms capable of explaining human decision-making? (I will argue that they are.) This leaves open some difficult questions: Can we be machines and still be conscious? Can we be machines and still be human?

The concept of conscious machines making decisions pervades modern science fiction, including the droids C3P0 and R2D2 in *Star Wars*, the android Data of *Star Trek: The Next Generation*, the desperate Replicants of Ridley Scott's *Blade Runner*, and the emotionally troubled Cylons of *Battlestar Galactica*. *Star Trek: The Next Generation* spent an entire episode (*The Measure of a Man*) on the question of how the fact that Data was a machine affected his ability to decide for himself whether or not to allow himself to be disassembled. In the episode, the judge concludes the trial with a speech that directly addresses this question—"Is Data a machine? Yes. Is he the property of Starfleet? No. We have all been dancing around the basic issue: does Data have a soul? I don't know that he has. I don't know that I have. But I have got to give him the freedom to explore that question himself. It is the ruling of this court that Lieutenant Commander Data has the freedom to choose."[2] We will examine the complex questions of self and consciousness in detail at the end of the book (*The Conundrum of Robotics*, Chapter 24), after we have discussed the mechanisms of decision-making. In the interim, I aim to convince you that we can understand the mechanisms of our decision-making process without losing the freedom to choose.

I don't want you to take the actual process of the thermostat as the key to the story here, anymore than we would take jet planes as good models of how swans fly. And yet, both planes and swans fly through physical forces generated by the flow of air over their specially shaped wings. Even though bird wings are bone, muscle, and feathers, while airplane wings are metal, for both birds and planes, lift is generated by airflow over the wings, and airflow is generated by speed through the air. If we can understand what enables a 30-ton airplane to fly, we will have a better understanding of how a 30-pound swan can fly. Even though the forward push through the air is generated differently, both birds and planes fly through physical interactions with the air. We will use analogous methods of understanding decision-making processes to identify and fix problems in thermostats and in ourselves, because both use identifiable computational decision-making processes.

A good way to identify where a system (like a thermostat) has broken down is a process called "differential diagnosis," as in *What are the questions that will differentiate the possible diagnoses?* My favorite example of this is the show *CarTalk* on National Public Radio, in which a pair of MIT-trained auto mechanics (Tom and Ray Magliozzi) diagnose car troubles. When a caller calls in with a problem, the first things they discuss are the basics of the problem. (Anyone who has actually listened to *CarTalk* will know that the first things Tom and Ray discuss are the person's name, where the caller is from, and some completely unrelated jokes. But once they get down to discussing cars, they follow a very clear process of differential diagnosis.) A typical call might start with the caller providing a description of the problem—"I hear a nasty sound when I'm driving." And then Tom and Ray will get down to business—they'll ask questions about the sound: "What is the sound? Where is it coming from? Does it get faster as you go faster? Does it still happen when the engine is on but the car is not moving?" Each question limits the set of possible problems. By asking the right series of questions, one can progressively work one's way to identifying what's wrong with the car. If we could organize these questions into a series of rules, then we could write a computer program to solve our car problems. (Of course, then we wouldn't get to hear all the *CarTalk* jokes. Whether this is good or bad is a question of taste.)

In the 1980s, the field of artificial intelligence developed "expert systems" that codified how to arrange these sorts of question-and-answer rules to perform differential diagnosis.[3] At the time, expert systems were hailed as the answer to intelligence—they could make decisions as well as (or better than) experts. But it turns out that most humans don't make decisions using differential diagnoses. In a lot of fields (including, for example, medicine), a large part of the training entails trying to teach people to make decisions by these highly rational rules.[4] However, just because it is hard for people to make decisions by rule-based differential diagnoses does not mean that humans don't have a mechanism for making decisions. In fact, critics complained that the expert systems developed by artificial intelligence were not getting at the real question of what it means to be "intelligent" long before it was known that humans didn't work this way.[5] People felt that we understood how expert systems work and thus they could not be intelligent. A classmate in college once said to me that "we would never develop an artificial intelligence. Instead, we will recognize that humans are not intelligent." One goal of this book is to argue that we can recognize the mechanisms of human decision-making without losing our sense of wonder at the marvel that is human intelligence.

Some readers will complain that people are not machines; they have goals, they have plans, they have personalities. Because we are social creatures and much of our intelligence is dedicated to understanding each other, we have a tendency to attribute agency to any object that behaves in a complex manner.[6] Many of my friends name their cars and talk about the personality of their cars. My son named our new GPS navigation system "Dot." When asked why he named the GPS (the voice is definitely a woman's), he said, "So we can complain to her when she gets lost—'Darn you, Dot!'"

A GPS navigator has goals. (These are goals we've programmed in, but they are goals nonetheless.) Dot's internal computer uses her knowledge of maps and her calculation of the current location to make plans to achieve those goals. You can even tell Dot whether you prefer the plans to include more highways or more back-country scenic roads. If Dot were prewired to prefer highways or back-country scenic roads, we would say she has a clear personality. In fact, I wish I had some of Dot's personality—when we miss an exit, Dot doesn't complain or curse, she just says "recalculating" and plans a new route to her goal.

The claim that computers can have goals and that differences in how they reach those goals reflects their personality suggests that goals and plans are simple to construct and that personality is simply a difference in underlying behavioral variables and preferences. We explain complex machines by thinking they're like people. Is it fair to turn that on its head and explain people as complex machines?

In this book, I'm going to argue that the answer to this question is "yes"—*your brain is a decision-making machine*, albeit a very complex one. You are that decision-making machine. This doesn't mean you're not conscious. This doesn't mean you're not *you*. But it can explain some of the irrational things that you do.

Understanding how the human decision-making system works has enormous implications for understanding who we are, what we do, and why we do what we do. Scientists study brains, they study decision-making, and they study machines. By bringing these three things together, we will begin to get a sense of ourselves. In this book, I will discuss what we know about how brains work, what we know about how we make decisions, and what we know about how that decision-making machine can break down under certain conditions to explain irrationality, impulsivity, and even addiction.

3

The Definition of Value

diamond stars in a circle of gold
declare your love
with two months salary

Value measures how much one is willing to pay, trade, or work for a reward, or to work to avoid a punishment. Value is not intrinsic to an object, but must be calculated anew each time. This produces inconsistencies, in which different ways of measuring value can produce different orderings of one's preferences.

What is "value"? What does it mean to value something? In psychological theories, value is thought of as that which reduces needs or which alleviates negative prospects[1]—when you are hungry, food has value; when you are thirsty, water has value. Pain signals a negative situation that must be alleviated for survival. In economics, the concept of *revealed preferences* says that we value the things we choose, and make decisions to maximize value.[2] Although this is a circular definition, we will use it later to help us understand how the decision-making process operates. In the robotics and computer simulation worlds where many of the mechanisms that we will look at later have been worked out, value is simply a number r for reward or $-r$ for punishment.[3] The robotics and computer science models simply try to maximize r (or minimize $-r$).

In many experiments that study decision-making, value is measured in terms of money. But of course, money has true value only in terms of what it can buy.[4] Economists will often tell us that money is an agreed-upon fiction—I am willing to sell you this apple for a green piece of paper that we both agree is worth $1 because I am confident that I can then use the paper later to buy something that I want. The statement that money is valuable only in terms of what it can buy is not entirely true either: money can also have value as a symbol of what it implies for our place in the social network.[5] This is one reason why extremely well-paid professional athletes fight for an extra dollar on their multimillion dollar salaries—they want to be known as the "best-paid wide receiver" because that identification carries social value. Money and value are complex concepts that interact in difficult ways.

Part of the problem is that you cannot just ask people *How much do you value this thing?* We don't have units to measure it in. Instead, value is usually measured in what people will trade for something and in the decisions they make.[6] This is the concept called *revealed preferences*—by examining your decisions, we can decide what you value. Theoretically, this is very simple: one asks *How much will you pay for this coffee mug?* The price you'll pay is the value of the coffee mug. If we measure things at the same time, in the same experiment, we shouldn't have to worry about inflation or changes in the value of the money itself.

The problem is that people are inconsistent in their decisions. In a famous experiment, Daniel Kahneman and his colleagues Jack Knetsch and Richard Thaler divided their subjects into two groups: one group was asked how much money they would pay for a \$6 (in 1990) Cornell University coffee mug and the other group was first given the coffee mug and then asked how much money they would accept for the mug. The first group was willing to pay much less on average (\$3) than the second group was willing to accept for it (\$7). This is called *the endowment effect* and is a preference for things you already own.[7]

Simply phrasing decisions in terms of wins or losses changes what people choose.[8] The interesting thing about this is that even once one is shown the irrationality, it still feels right. This effect was first found by Daniel Kahneman and Amos Tversky, who made this discovery sitting in a coffee shop in Israel, asking themselves what they would do in certain situations. When they found themselves making irrational decisions, they took their questions to students in their college classes and measured, quantitatively, what proportion made each decision in each condition.

In the classic case from their 1981 paper published in the journal *Science*:[9]

> Imagine that the U.S. is preparing for the outbreak of an unusual Asian disease, which is expected to kill 600 people. Two alternative programs to combat the disease have been proposed. Assume that the exact scientific estimate of the consequences of the programs are as follows:
>
> Problem 1: If Program A is adopted, 200 people will be saved. If Program B is adopted, there is 1/3 probability that 600 people will be saved, and 2/3 probability that no people will be saved. Which of the two programs would you favor?
>
> Problem 2: If Program C is adopted, 400 people will die. If Program D is adopted, there is 1/3 probability that nobody will die, and 2/3 probability that 600 people will die. Which of the two programs would you favor?

A careful reading of the two conditions shows that Program *C* is identical to Program *A*, while Program *D* is identical to Program *B*. Yet, 72% of the first group chose program *A* and 28% chose program *B*, while only 22% of the second group chose program *C* and 78% chose program *D*! Kahneman and Tversky interpret this as implying that we are more sensitive to losses than to gains—we would rather risk not gaining something than we would risk losing something. This is clearly a part of the story, but I will argue that there is a deeper issue here. I will argue that "value" is something that we calculate each time, and that the calculation process doesn't always come up with the same "rational" answer.

Illogical value calculations

The most interesting thing about these results (of which there are many) is that even when they are illogical (like the disease example above), they often still sound right. There are other examples where we can see that decisions are irrational, and don't sound right when they are pointed out to us, but which humans definitely show when tested. The best examples of most of these come from the advertising and marketing worlds.

A person goes into an electronics store to buy a television and finds three televisions on sale, one for $100, one for $200, and one for $300. Imagine that the three televisions have different features, such that these are reasonable prices for these three TVs. People are much more likely to buy the $200 TV than either of the other two. If, in contrast, the person goes into the store and finds three televisions on sale, the same $200 TV, the same $300 TV, and now a fancier $400 TV, the person is more likely to buy the $300 TV. In the first case, the person is saying that the $200 TV is a better deal than the $300 one, but in the second case, the person is saying that the $300 TV is the better deal. Even though they've been offered the same televisions for the same prices, the decision changed depending on whether there is a $100 TV or a $400 TV in the mix. This is called *extremeness aversion* and is a component of a more general process called *framing*. In short, the set of available options changes your valuation of the options. This is completely irrational and (unlike the other examples above) seems unreasonable (at least to me). Yet it is one of the most reliable results in marketing and has probably been used since the first markets in ancient times through to the modern digital age.[10]

Products in advertisements used to compare themselves to each other. Tylenol would say it was better than aspirin and Coke would say it was better than Pepsi. I remember an RC Cola commercial with two opposing teams fighting about which drink they preferred, Coke or Pepsi, while a third person sits on the sidelines drinking an RC Cola, out of the fray, smiling. Advertisements today rarely mention the competition. This is because one of the heuristics we use is simply whether we recognize the name or not.[11] So although RC Cola was trying to communicate that Coke and Pepsi were the same, while RC Cola was different, what people took from the advertisement was a reminder that everyone drank Coke and Pepsi. Just mentioning the name reminds people that it exists and reinforces the decision to choose it. Familiarity with a brand name increases the likelihood that one will select it.

It is election season as I write this. All around my neighborhood, people have put out signs for their candidates. The signs don't say anything about the candidates. Often they don't even have the party the candidates belong to. Usually, it's just the name of the candidate, and sometimes, an appeal to "vote for" the candidate. What information do I get from seeing a sign that says nothing other than "Vote for X"? I suppose that one may need to be reminded to vote at all, but then why does the sign include "for X" on it? (One of my neighbors does have a large handmade sign she puts out every election season that just says "VOTE!" on it.) It is true that one can get a sense of the grouping of candidates from people who put out multiple signs: given that I like person X for state representative, seeing that all the people with person X also have person Y for county prosecutor, while all the people who have person X's opponent have person Z for county prosecutor, might suggest to me that I would like person Y over person Z for county prosecutor. But lots of people have just one sign out. All that tells me is that lots of people like person X. Why would knowing that lots of people like something suggest that I would too?

There are actually three things that these single-sign houses are doing. First, they are increasing my familiarity with that name. As with the products, just knowing the name increases one's likelihood of voting for someone. Second, if lots of people like a movie, it's more likely to be a good movie than one everybody hated. Using the same heuristic, if everyone likes a candidate, isn't that candidate more likely to be a good choice? And third, we like to be on the winning team. If everyone else is going to vote for someone, he or she is likely to win. Of course, we're supposed to be voting based on who we think is a better choice to govern, not who is most popular. But it's pretty clear that a lot of people don't vote that way.

These effects occur because we don't actually calculate the true value of things. Instead, we use rules of thumb, called *heuristics*, that allow us to make pretty good guesses at how we value things.[12] If you like all the choices, picking the middle one is a pretty good guess at good value for your money. If you're making a decision, familiarity is a pretty good guess. (Something you're familiar with is likely to be something you've seen before. If you remember it, but don't remember it being bad, how bad could it have been?)

Some economists have argued that evolutionarily, heuristics are better than actually trying to calculate the true value of things because calculating value takes time and heuristics are good enough to get us by.[13] But a lot of these nonoptimal decisions that we're making are taking time. Knowing that Programs A and C are the same and that programs B and D are the same in the Kahneman and Tversky flu example above doesn't change our minds. This makes me suspect that something else is going on. It's not that heuristics are faster and we are making do with "good enough." I suspect that these effects have to do with how we calculate value. We cannot determine how humans calculate value unless we can measure it. So, again, we come back to the question of how we measure value.

Measuring value

With animals, we can't ask them how much they value something; we can only offer them something and determine how much they'll pay for it. Usually, this is measured in terms of the amount of effort an animal will expend to get the reward.[14] *How many lever presses is the animal willing to make for each reward?*

Alternatively, we can give the animal a direct choice between two options:[15] *Would the animal rather have two apple-flavored food pellets or one orange-flavored food pellet? Would it rather have juice or water?* We can also titrate how much of one choice needs to be offered to make the animal switch—if the animal likes apple flavor better than orange flavor, would it still prefer half as much apple to the same amount of orange?

Finally, we can also measure the negative consequences an animal will put up with to get to a reward.[16] Usually, this is measured by putting a negative effect (a small shock or a hot plate) in between the animal and the reward, which it has to cross to get to the reward. (It is important to note that crossing the shock or hot plate is entirely up to the animal. It can choose not to cross the punishment if it feels the reward is not valuable enough.) A common experiment is to balance a less-appealing reward with a more-appealing reward that is given only after a delay.[17] Because animals are usually hungry (or thirsty) when running these experiments, they don't want to wait for reward. Thus delay becomes a very simple and measurable punishment to use—*how long will the animal wait for the reward?*

Of course, humans are animals as well and all of these experiments work well in humans: How much effort would a smoker spend to get a puff of a cigarette?[18] How much money will you trade for that coffee mug?[19] What negative consequences will you put up with to achieve your reward?[20] How long will you wait for that larger reward?[21] Will you wait for a lesser punishment, knowing that it's coming?[22]

These four ways of measuring value all come down to quantifiable observations, which makes them experimentally (and scientifically) viable. Economists, who study humans, typically use hypothetical choices ("What would you do if...?") rather than real circumstances, which, as we will see later, may not access the same decision-making systems. It has been hard to test animals with hypothetical choices (because hypothetical choices are difficult to construct without language), but there is some evidence that chimpanzees with linguistic training will wait longer for rewards described by symbols than for immediately presented real rewards.[23] (Remember the chimpanzees and the jellybeans?) This, again, suggests that language changes the decision-making machinery. More general tests of hypothetical rewards in animals have been limited by our ability to train animals to work for tokens. Recent experiments by Daeyeol Lee and his colleagues getting monkeys to work for tokens may open up possibilities, but the critical experiments have not yet been done.[24]

One of the most common ways to measure willingness to pay for something is a procedure called the *progressive ratio*—the subject (whether it be human or not) has to press a lever for a reward, and each time it receives the reward, the number of times it has to press the lever for reward increases, often exponentially. The first reward costs one press, the second two, the third four, the fourth eight, and so on. Pretty soon, the subject has to press the lever a thousand times for one more reward. Eventually, the animal decides that the reward isn't worth that much effort, and the animal stops pressing the lever. This is called the *break point*. Things that seem like they would be more valuable to an animal have higher break points than things that seem like they would be less valuable. Hungry animals will work harder for food than satiated animals.[25] Cocaine-addicted animals will work harder for cocaine than for food.[26] A colleague of mine (Warren Bickel, now at Virginia Tech) told me of an experimental (human) subject in one of his experiments who pulled a little lever back and forth tens of thousands of times over the course of two hours for one puff of nicotine!

It's been known for a long time that drugs are not infinitely valuable. When given the choice between drugs and other options, both human addicts and animals self-administering drugs[A] will decrease the amount of drug taken as it gets more expensive relative to the other options.[27] Drugs do show what economists call *elasticity*: the more expensive they get, the less people take. This is why one way to reduce smoking in a population is to increase the tax on cigarettes.

[A] The animal experimental literature is generally unwilling to call animals "addicts" and instead refers to their behavioral actions as "self-administering drugs." As we will see later in the book, animals self-administer the same drugs that humans do, and animals self-administering drugs show most of the same behaviors that humans self-administering drugs do.

Elasticity measures how much the decision to do something decreases in response to increases in cost. Luxuries are highly elastic; nonluxuries are highly inelastic. As the costs of going to a movie or a ballgame increase, the likelihood that people will go decreases quickly. On the other hand, even if the cost of food goes up, people aren't about to stop buying food. Some economists have argued that a good definition of addiction is that things we are addicted to are inelastic. This allows them to say that the United States is "addicted to oil" because we are so highly dependent on driving that our automobile use is generally inelastic to the price of oil. However, again, we face an interesting irrationality. The elasticity of automobile use is not linear[28]—raising the price of gasoline from $1 per gallon to $2 had little to no effect on the number of miles driven, but when a gallon of gasoline crossed the $3 mark, there was a sudden and dramatic drop in the number of miles driven in 2005. People suddenly said, "That's not worth it anymore." Of course, people then got used to seeing $3 per gallon gasoline and the number of miles driven has begun to increase again.

This irrationality is where the attempt to measure value gets interesting. In a recent set of experiments, Serge Ahmed and his colleagues found that even though the break point for cocaine was much higher than for sweetened water,[B] when given the choice between cocaine and sweetened water, almost all of the animals chose the sweetened water.[29] (Lest readers think this is something special about cocaine, the same effects occur when examining animals self-administering heroin.[30]) Measuring value by how much the animal was willing to pay said that cocaine was more valuable than sweetened water. (Cocaine had a higher break point than the sweetened water did.) But measuring value by giving the animals a choice said that the sweetened water was more valuable. (They consistently chose the sweetened water over the cocaine.) The two measures gave completely different results as to which was more valuable.

One of my favorite examples of this irrationality is a treatment for addiction called *Contingency Management*, where addicts are offered vouchers to stay off drugs.[31] If addicts come into the clinic and provide a clean urine or blood sample, showing that they have remained clean for the last few days, they get a voucher for something small—a movie rental or a gift certificate. Even very small vouchers can have dramatic effects. What's interesting about this is that raising the cost of a drug by $3 would have very little effect on the amount of drug an addict takes (because drugs are inelastic to addicts), but providing a $3 voucher option can be enough to keep an addict clean, straight, and sober. Some people have argued that this is one of the reasons that Alcoholics Anonymous and its 12-step cousins work.[C] It provides an option (going to meetings and getting praised for staying sober) that works like a voucher; it's a social reward that can provide an alternative to drug-taking.[32]

So why is it so hard to measure value? Why are we so irrational about value? I'm going to argue that value is hard to measure because value is not something intrinsic to an object.

[B] Ahmed and colleagues used saccharin in the water rather than sugar because saccharin has no direct nutritive value but tastes sweet to both rats and humans.

[C] The Anonymous meetings (AA, Narcotics Anonymous, Gamblers Anonymous, etc.) and their 12-step cousins also include additional elements that seem to access important decision-making components. One example is the presence of a "sponsor" (someone you can call 24/7), who provides a low-cost option to pull one away from the high-value drug-taking option. Suicide hotlines also work this way, providing a very low-cost option (a phone call) that can short-circuit a dangerous path.

First, I'm going to argue in this book that there are multiple decision-making systems, each of which has its own method of action-selection,[33] which means there are multiple values that can be assigned to any given choice. Second, in the deliberative experiments we've been looking at, we have to calculate the value of the available options each time.[34] (Even recognizing that options are available can be a complex process involving memory and calculation.) The value of a thing depends on your needs, desires, and expectations, as well as the situation you are in. By framing the question in different ways, we can guide people's attention to different aspects of a question and change their valuation of it. In part, this dependence on attention is due to the fact that we don't know what's important. A minivan can carry the whole family, but the hybrid Prius gets better gas mileage, and that convertible BMW looks cooler. It's hard to compare them.

This means that determining the true value of something depends on a lot of factors, only some of which relate to the thing itself. We'll see later that value can depend on how tired you are, on your emotional state, and on how willing you are to deliberate over the available options.[35] It can even be manipulated by changing unrelated cues, such as in the *anchor effect*, in which unrelated numbers (like your address!) can make you more likely to converge to a higher or lower value closer to that number.[36]

Economists argue that we should measure value by the reward we expect to get, taking into account the probability that we will actually get the reward, and the expected investment opportunities and risks.[37] If we tried to explore all possibilities and integrate all of this, we could sit forever mulling over possibilities. This leads us to the concept of *bounded rationality*, introduced by Herb Simon in the 1950s, which suggests that the calculation takes time, that sometimes it's better to get to the answer quickly by being less complete about the full calculation, and that sometimes a pretty good job is good enough.[38] Instead, we use heuristics, little algorithms that work most of the time.

The problem with this theory is that even when we are given enough time, we continue to use these heuristics. Economists and psychologists who argue for bounded rationality (such as Gerd Gigerenzer[39]) argue that evolution never gives us time. But if the issue were one of time, one would expect that the longer one was given, the more rational one would be. This isn't what is seen. People don't change their minds about taking the middle-value television if they are given more time; in fact, they become *more* likely to pick the middle television, not less, with more time.[40]

We pick the middle television in the three-television example because one of the algorithms we use when we want to compare the choices immediately available to us is to find the middle one. Another example is that we tend to round numbers off by recognizing the digits.[41] $3.99 looks like a lot less than $4.00. Think about your "willingness to pay" $3.75 per gallon for gasoline relative to $3.50 per gallon. If both options are available, obviously, you'll go to the station selling it for $3.50. But if it goes up from $3.50 to $3.75 from one day to the next, do you really stop buying gasoline? Now, imagine that the price goes up from $3.75 to $4.00. Suddenly, it feels like that gasoline just got too expensive. We saw a similar thing at the soda machine by my office. When the cost went up from 75¢ to $1, people kept buying sodas. But then one day it went up from $1 to $1.25, and people said, "It's not worth it" and stopped. (It's now $1.50 and no one ever buys sodas there anymore.) Sometimes the cost crosses a line that we simply won't put up with anymore.

Part of this is due to the mechanisms by which we categorize things. Whole dollar amounts draw our attention and we are more likely to pick them. In a recent experiment, Kacey Ballard, Sam McClure, and their colleagues asked people which they would prefer, $7 today or $20 in a week.[42] (This is a question called *delay-discounting*, which we will examine in detail later in our chapter on impulsivity [Chapter 5].) But then they asked the subjects to decide between $7.03 today and $20 in a week. People were more likely to pick the $20 over $7.03 than $20 over $7 even. In a wonderful control, they then asked the subjects to decide between $7 today and $20.03 in a week. This time, people were more likely to pick the $7. There is no way that these decisions are rational, but they do make sense when we realize (1) that making the decision requires determining the value of the two options anew each time and comparing them, and (2) that we use heuristics that prefer even dollar amounts to compare them.[D]

Value is an important concept to understanding decision-making, but our brains have to calculate how much we value a choice. That calculation is based on heuristics and simple algorithms that work pretty well most of the time but can be irrational under certain conditions. How do we actually, physically determine value? What are the neurophysiological mechanisms? That brings us to the differences between pleasure, pain, and the do-it-again signal.

Books and papers for further reading

- Daniel Ariely (2008). *Predictably Irrational: The Hidden Forces that Shape Our Decisions.* New York: HarperCollins.
- Daniel Kahneman (2011). *Thinking, Fast and Slow.* New York: Farrar, Straus and Giroux.
- Scott Plous (1993). *The Psychology of Judgment and Decision-Making.* New York: McGraw-Hill.

[D] Why people prefer even dollar amounts is not known. Perhaps even dollar amounts are easier to calculate with. Perhaps people are suspicious of odd amounts because they are concerned that there's a trick being pulled (like the extra $\frac{9}{10}$¢ used by American gas stations). Perhaps people can measure the even dollar amounts more easily, which may draw their attention. Whatever the heuristic, people do prefer even dollar amounts.[43]

4

Value, Euphoria, and the Do-It-Again Signal

> At the base of *dead man's hill*,
> sled toppled in a mound of snow,
> exhilaration lights up his face.
> Let's do that again!

Pleasure and value are different things. One can have pleasure without value and value without pleasure. They are signaled by different chemicals in the brain. In particular, the brain contains a signal for "better than expected," which can be used to learn to predict value. The lack of expected reward and the lack of expected punishment are separate processes (disappointment, relief) that require additional neural mechanisms.

Euphoria and dysphoria

It is commonly assumed that pleasure is our interpretation of the things we have to do again. "People seek pleasure and avoid pain." While this is often true, a better description is that people seek things that they recognize will have high value. As we will see below, pleasure is dissociable from value.

Although the saying is "pleasure and pain," pain is not the opposite of pleasure. Pain is actually a sensory system, like any of the other sensory systems (visual, auditory, etc.).[1] Pain measures damage to tissues and things that are likely to damage tissues. It includes specific receptors that project up to mid-brain sensory structures that project to cortical interpretation areas. The sensation of pain depends on cortical activation in response to the pain sensors, but this is true of the other sensory systems as well. The retina in your eyes detects photons, but you don't see photons—you see the objects that are interpreted from photons. Pleasure, in contrast, is not a sensation, but an evaluation of a sensation.

Euphoria, from the Greek word φορία (*phoria*, meaning "bearing" or "feeling") and the Greek root εὐ- (*eu-*, meaning "good"), is probably a better word than "pleasure" for the brain signal we are discussing. And, of course, euphoria has a clear antonym in *dysphoria*, meaning "discomfort," deriving from the Greek root δυσ- (*dys-*, bad). The terms *euphoria* and *dysphoria* represent calculations in the brain of how good or bad something is.

Differences between euphoria and reinforcement

Watching animals move toward a reward, early psychologists were uncomfortable attributing emotions to the animal, saying that it "wanted the reward" or that it felt "pleasure" at getting the reward. Instead they defined something that made the animal more likely to approach it as *reinforcement* (because it *reinforced* the animal's actions).

Experiments in the 1950s began to identify that there was a difference between euphoria and reinforcement in humans as well. In the 1950s, it was found that an electrode placed into a certain area of the brain (called the medial forebrain bundle) would, when stimulated, lead to near-perfect reinforcement.[2] Animals with these stimulations would forego food, sex, and sleep to continue pressing levers to produce this brain stimulation.

From this, the medial forebrain bundle became popularly known as "the pleasure center."[3] But even in these early experiments, the difference between euphoria and reinforcement was becoming clear. Robert Heath and his colleagues implanted several stimulating electrodes into the brain of a patient (for the treatment of epilepsy), and then offered the patient different buttons to stimulate each of the electrodes. On stimulation from pressing one button, the patient reported orgasmic euphoria. On stimulation from the second button, the patient reported mild discomfort. However, the patient continued pressing the second button over and over again, much more than the first. Euphoria and reinforcement are different.[4]

It turns out that the key to the reinforcement from medial forebrain bundle stimulation is a brain neurotransmitter called *dopamine*.[5] Dopamine is chemically constructed out of precursors[A] in a small area of the brain located deep in the base of the midbrain called the *ventral tegmental area* and the *substantia nigra*.[B]

[A] The pharmacology term "precursors" is used to identify molecules that are converted into the molecule being studied.[6] Your cells are, in a sense, chemical factories that convert molecules to other molecules, using specialized molecules called *enzymes*. For example, the chemical levodopa (L-dopa) is a precursor for dopamine, which means that if you had extra levodopa in your system, your cells would have more building blocks with which to make more dopamine, and you would find that your cells had more dopamine to use. This is why levodopa forms a good treatment for Parkinson's disease, since Parkinson's disease is, in fact, a diminishment of dopamine production in certain areas of the brain.[7]

[B] The ventral tegmental area is so called because it is *ventral* (near the base of the brain) in the *tegmentum* (Latin for "covering"), an area that covers the brain stem. *Substantia nigra* is Latin for "black stuff," so named because it contains melatonin, which makes the area appear black on a histological slice.

Melatonin is a chemical used by the body to signal the nighttime component of day/night cycles.[8] This is why it is sometimes used to reset circadian rhythm problems. It interacts with dopamine, particularly the release of dopamine in the brain, which means that manipulations of melatonin (say for jetlag) can affect learning and cognition. This is why pharmacology is so complex:[9] manipulating one thing often produces lots of other effects.

An early theory of dopamine was that it was the representation of pleasure in the brain.[10] Stimulating the medial forebrain bundle makes dopamine cells release their dopamine.[11] (Remember that these stimulating electrodes were [incorrectly] hypothesized to be stimulating the "pleasure center.") In animal studies, blocking dopamine blocked reinforcement.[12] Although one could not definitively show that animals felt "pleasure," the assumption was that reinforcement in animals translated to pleasure in humans. Most drugs of abuse produce a release of dopamine in the brain.[13] And, of course, most drugs of abuse produce euphoria, at least on early use.[C] Since some of the largest pharmacological effects of drugs of abuse are on dopamine, it was assumed that dopamine was the "pleasure" signal. This theory turned out to be wrong.

In a remarkable set of experiments, Kent Berridge at the University of Michigan set out to test this theory that dopamine signaled pleasure.[15] He first developed a way of measuring euphoria and dysphoria in animals—he watched their facial expressions. The idea that animals and humans share facial expressions was first proposed by Charles Darwin in his book *The Expression of the Emotions in Man and Animals*. Berridge and his colleagues used cameras tightly focused on the faces of animals, particularly rats, to identify that sweet tastes (such as sugar or saccharin) were accompanied by a licking of the lips, while bitter tastes (such as quinine) were accompanied by a projection of the tongue, matching the classic "yuck" face all parents have seen in their kids being forced to eat vegetables.

What is interesting is that Berridge and his colleagues (particularly Terry Robinson, also at the University of Michigan) were able to manipulate these expressions, but not with manipulations of dopamine. Manipulations of dopamine changed whether an animal would work for, learn to look for, or approach a reward, but if the reward was placed in the animal's mouth or even right in front of the animal, it would eat the reward and show the same facial expressions. What did change the facial expressions were manipulations of the animal's *opioid* system. The opioid system is another set of neurotransmitters in the brain, which we will see are very important to decision-making. They are mimicked by opiates—opium, morphine, heroin. Berridge and Robinson suggested that there is a distinction between "wanting something" and "liking it." Dopamine affects the wanting, while opioids affect the liking.

Opioids

The endogenous opioid system includes three types of opioid signals and receptors in the nucleus accumbens, hypothalamus, amygdala, and other related areas.[16] Neuroscientists have labeled them by three Greek letters (mu [μ], kappa [κ], and delta [δ]). Each of these receptors has a paired endogenous chemical (called a ligand) that attaches to it (*endorphins* associated with the μ-opioid receptors, *dynorphin* associated with the κ-opioid receptors, and *enkephalins* associated with the δ-opioid receptors). Current work suggests that activation of the μ-opioid receptors signals euphoria, and activation of the κ-opioid receptors signals dysphoria. The functionality of the δ-opioid

---

[C] Not all abused drugs are euphoric. Nicotine, for example, is often highly dysphoric on initial use, even though it is one of the most reinforcing of all drugs.[14]

receptors is less clear but seems to be involved in analgesia (the suppression of pain), the relief of anxiety, and the induction of craving. Chemicals that stimulate μ-opioid receptors (called *agonists*) are generally rewarding, reinforcing, and euphorigenic. The classic μ-opioid receptor agonist is the opium poppy, particularly after it is refined into morphine or heroin. μ-opioid receptor agonists are reliably self-administered when given the opportunity, whether by humans or other animals. In contrast, chemicals that block μ-opioid receptors (called *antagonists*) are aversive and dysphoric and interfere with self-administration. On the opposite side, κ-opioid receptor agonists are also aversive and dysphoric.

When Kent Berridge and his colleagues manipulated the opioid system in their animals, they found that they could change the animals' facial responses to positive (sweet) and negative (bitter) things. Stimulating κ-opioid receptors when animals were fed the sweet solution led to the yuck face, while stimulating μ-opioid receptors when animals were fed the bitter solution led to licking the lips. This hypothesis is further supported by introspective manipulations in humans as well. Naltrexone, a general opioid antagonist, has been shown to block the feeling of pleasure on eating sugar—subjects say that they can taste the sweetness, but they don't "care" about it.[17]

If pleasure or euphoria in the brain really is activation of μ-opioid receptors, then this is a great example of the importance of recognizing our physical nature. Euphoria is not a mental construct divorced from the physical neural system—it is instantiated as a physical effect in our brains. That means that a chemical that accesses that physical effect (in this case the μ-opioid receptors) can create euphoria directly. This also brings up a concept we will return to again and again in this book—the idea of a *vulnerability* or *failure mode*. We did not evolve μ-opioid receptors to take heroin; we evolved μ-opioid receptors so that we could recognize things in our lives that have value and thus give us pleasure. But heroin stimulates the μ-opioid receptors directly and produces feelings of euphoria. Heroin accesses a potential failure mode of our brains—it tricks us into feeling euphoria when we shouldn't. At least, it does so until the body gets used to it and dials down the μ-opioid receptor, leading to the user needing to take more and more heroin to achieve the same euphoria, until eventually even massive doses of heroin don't produce euphoria anymore, they just relieve the persistent dysphoria left behind.

Reinforcement

So if euphoria and dysphoria are the opioid receptors, then what is *reinforcement*, and what is its negative twin, *aversion*? According to the original scientific definitions first put forward by the animal learning theorists (for example by John Watson, Ivan Pavlov, and Edward Thorndike in the first decades of the 20th century, and Clark Hull and B. F. Skinner in the 1940s and 1950s), reinforcement is the process by which a reward (such as food to a hungry animal) increases responding, while aversion is the process by which a penalty decreases responding.[18] (Notice how this definition is defined operationally—in terms of directly observable behavioral phenomena. We will break open the decision-making mechanism in the next section and move beyond these simple behavioral limitations. For now, let us be content with observing behavior.)

When phrased in terms of reinforcement, the question becomes *When does a reward reinforce behavior?* In the 1960s, Leon Kamin showed that a stimulus reinforced a behavior only if another stimulus had not already reinforced it.[19] He called this *blocking* because the first stimulus "blocked" the second. In its simplest form, if you trained an animal to push a lever to get a reward in response to a tone and then tried to train the animal to respond to both the tone and a light presented together, the light would never become associated with the reward. You can test this by asking whether the animal presses the lever in response to the light alone. It won't. In contrast, if you had started training with both the tone and the light at the same time (that is, if you had not pretrained the animal with the tone), then it would have learned to respond to both the tone and the light when they were presented together. Learning occurs only when something has changed.

In 1972, Robert Rescorla and Allan Wagner proposed a mathematical theory based on the idea that reinforcement was about surprise and predictability.[20] They proposed that an animal learned to predict that a reward was coming, and that it learned based on the difference between the expectation and the observation. The light was blocked by the tone because the tone already completely predicted the reward. This theory is supported by more complicated versions of Kamin's blocking task, where the reward is changed during the tone + light training.[21] If the delivered reward or punishment is larger after tone + light than after just the tone, then the animal will learn to associate the changed reward with the light. If the delivered reward is smaller after tone + light than after just the tone, then the animal will learn that the light is a "negative" predictor. Testing this gets complicated—one needs a third cue (say a different sound): train the animal to respond to the third cue, then present the third cue with the light, and the animal responds less because the light predicts that the animal will receive less reward than expected from the other cues alone. Learning can also reappear if other things change, such as the actual reward given (apples instead of raisins), even when one controls for the value of the reward (by ensuring that the animal would work at similar levels for both rewards).

In the 1980s, two computer scientists, Richard Sutton and Andy Barto, laid out a new mathematical theory called *temporal difference reinforcement learning*, which built in part on the work of Rescorla and Wagner, but also on earlier work in control theory and "operations research"[D] from the 1950s, particularly that of Richard Bellman.[22] Bellman originally showed that one can learn an optimal strategy by measuring the difference between the observed value and the expected value and learning to take actions to reduce that difference. Sutton and Barto recognized the similarity between Bellman's operations research work and the Rescorla-Wagner psychology model. They derived an algorithm that was mathematically powerful enough that it could be used to actually train robots and other control systems.

[D] *Control theory* uses equations to determine how to change variables in response to stimuli so as to have desired effects. The thermostat (negative feedback) that we saw at the very beginning of the book is often the first example used in control theory textbooks. Cruise control in your car and the stability maintained by current fighter jets are both derived from modern control theory mechanisms. *Operations research* is the term often used for university departments studying these questions.

There were two major differences between the Sutton and Barto equations and the Rescorla and Wagner theory. First, Rescorla and Wagner assumed that predictions about reward were derived from single, individual cues. In contrast, decisions in the Sutton and Barto theory were based on categorizations of the situation of the world (which they called the "state" of the world).[23;E]

Second, while Rescorla and Wagner's theory learned to predict *reward*, Sutton and Barto's learning system learned to predict *value*.[24] Each potential situation was associated with a value. Actions of the agent (the computer program or the animal) and events in the world could change the situation. Once the expected value of each situation was known, the agent could decide the best thing to do (take the action leading to the situation with the highest expected value). The key was that Sutton and Barto showed that you could learn the value function (what the value of each situation was) at the same time that you were taking actions.[F]

Sutton and Barto called this the *actor-critic architecture*, because it required two components—an *actor* to take actions based on the current estimation of the value function and a *critic* to compare the current estimation of the value function with the observed outcomes. The critic calculated the difference between the value you actually got and the value you expected to get, which Sutton and Barto called *value-prediction error* and labeled as delta (δ), from the analogy to the common physics and mathematical use of the term Δ (delta) meaning "difference."[G]

Value-prediction error

The concept of value-prediction error (δ) is easiest to understand by an example. Imagine that there is a soda machine in the hallway outside your office, and the soda is supposed to cost \$1. You put your dollar in the machine, and you get two sodas out

---

[E] I prefer to use the term *situation* rather than the typical computer science term *state* (or the term preferred by psychology—*stimulus set*). *State* is used in many other literatures to refer to things like "internal state" (such as being under the influence of a drug, or not being under the influence of the drug), so overloaded terms like *state* can be confusing. Although many animal psychology experiments do use a single stimulus, look around you—what is the stimulus that is driving your behavior? I am currently listening to music and watching the sun rise above the snow outside my house, my feet are in fuzzy slippers, but my ankles are chilly—which of these stimuli are important? As we will see in Chapter 12, how we identify the important stimuli is a critical component of the decision-making system, so simply saying *stimulus* is incomplete. However, conveniently, *state*, *stimulus*, and *situation* all start with *S*, so if we wanted to write equations (as scientists are wont to do), we don't have to change our variables.

[F] There is a tradeoff between *exploration* and *exploitation*. If you take only the best choice, you might miss opportunities. If you go exploring, you might make mistakes. For our discussion here, we will assume that there is enough exploration not to get trapped in a situation where you know a good answer but haven't found the best one yet. We will explore the exploration–exploitation tradeoff in depth in its own chapter (Chapter 14).

[G] One of the problems with the science of decision-making is that it draws from lots of fields, each of which has its own terminology. The δ used in computer science to represent the value-prediction error is unrelated to the δ used to differentiate types of opioid receptors.

instead of one. Whatever the reason, this result was better than expected (δ, the difference between what you observed and what you expected, is positive) and you are likely to *increase your willingness* to put money into this machine. If, in contrast, you put your dollar in and get nothing out, then δ is negative and you are likely to *decrease your willingness* to put money into this machine. If, as expected, you put your dollar in and you get your soda out, your observations match your expectations, δ is zero, and you don't need to learn anything about this soda machine. Notice that you still get the nutrients (such as they are) from the soda. You still get the pleasure of drinking the soda. You still know what actions to take to get a soda from the soda machine. But you don't need to learn anything more about the machine.

In what I still feel is one of the most remarkable discoveries in neuroscience, in the early 1990s, Wolfram Schultz and his colleagues found that the transient bursts of firing in dopamine neurons increase with unexpected increases in value, decrease with unexpected decreases in value, and generally track the prediction-error signals proposed by Rescorla and Wagner and by Sutton and Barto.[25] At the time (the late 1980s and early 1990s), dopamine was primarily known as a reward or pleasure signal (remember, this is wrong!) in the animal behavior literature and as a motor-enabling signal in the Parkinson's disease literature.[H]

Schultz was looking at dopamine in animals learning to make associations of stimuli to reward under the expectation that he would then go on to look at its role in Parkinson's disease. The first step was to examine the firing of dopamine cells in response

---

[H] Parkinson's disease was first identified in the 1800s by James Parkinson, who wrote a monograph called *An Essay on the Shaking Palsy*. It is not uncommon in modern societies, but descriptions consistent with Parkinson's go back to ancient times.[26] For example, a description exists in Indian Ayurvedic texts that is likely Parkinson's disease, and it was treated with a medicinal plant that is now known to contain levodopa (a common modern treatment for Parkinson's disease). Throughout most of the 20th century, Parkinson's disease has been thought of as a dysfunction in the motor system—most patients with Parkinson's show an inability to initiate movement (akinesia) or a slowing of the initiation of movement (bradykinesia).[27] For example, patients with the disease develop posture problems and tremors in their limbs both before and during movement. Parkinson's disease, however, is not a disorder of the muscles or the actual motor system—there are situations where a Parkinson's patient can react surprisingly well.[28] This is nicely shown in the movie *Awakenings*, where Rose is able to walk to the window once the floor tiles are painted black and white. We will see later in this book that these are due to the intact nature of other decision-making systems in Parkinson's patients. Whether these are due to emotional reactions (running from a room during a fire, Chapter 8), to simple, long-stored reflexive action sequences (surprised by a thrown ball and "Catch!," Chapter 10), or to the presence of explicit visual cues (lines on the floor enabling access of Deliberative systems, Chapter 9) is still unknown.[29]

Neurophysiologically, Parkinson's disease is due to the loss of dopamine neurons.[30] How the effects of dopamine loss in Parkinson's disease are related to the issues of dopamine as a δ signal is complex. The δ signal observed by Schultz and colleagues is related to fast changes in dopamine firing (bursts, called *phasic* signaling). Dopamine cells also fire at a regular baseline rate (called *tonic* firing).[31] The relationship between the phasic bursts, the tonic firing, Parkinson's disease, and decision-making is still unknown, but it is known that decision-making is impaired in Parkinson's disease,[32] and several hypotheses have been proposed.[33] Tonic levels of dopamine have been suggested to play roles in the recognition of situations[34] (this chapter, below, and Chapter 12) and in the invigoration of movement[35] (motivation, Chapter 13).

to a reward. In these first experiments, Schultz and his colleagues found that dopamine neurons would respond whenever the thirsty animal received a juice reward. But in this first experiment, the reward was just delivered at random times; when Schultz and his colleagues provided a cue that predicted the reward, to their surprise, the dopamine neurons no longer responded to the reward. Instead, the cells responded to the cue that predicted the reward.[36]

These experimental results were unified with the theoretical work by Read Montague, Peter Dayan, and Terry Sejnowski, who showed that the unexpected-reward neurons reported by Wolfram Schultz and his colleagues were exactly the "delta" δ signal needed by the Sutton and Barto temporal difference learning algorithm. Over three years (1995, 1996, and 1997), they published three papers suggesting that the monkey dopamine cell data matched the value-prediction error signals needed for the temporal difference reinforcement learning theory.[37]

To really understand how dopamine tracks the delta signal, one can ask *Why do the dopamine neurons increase their responding to the cue?* Before the cue, the animal has no immediate expectation of reward. (For all it knows, the day's session is about to end.) It is in a low-value situation. When the cue is shown to the animal, it realizes that it is going to get a reward soon, so it is now in a higher-value situation. The change from low-value "waiting" to high-value "going to get reward" is an unexpected change in value and produces a delta signal of "better than expected." If the animal has learned that an instruction stimulus predicts the cue, saying that a cue will be arriving soon, then the dopamine signal will appear at the earlier instruction signal rather than at the cue (because the instruction signal is now the unexpected increase in value). If the cue then doesn't arrive, you get a decrease in dopamine because the cue was expected but not delivered and you have an unexpected decrease in value.

Subsequent experiments have found that the signal does track the δ value-prediction error signal remarkably well. If the reward was larger than the cue predicted, dopamine neurons increase responding again, while if the reward was not delivered when expected, the dopamine neurons decrease responding. Dopamine neurons have a small baseline firing rate of a few spikes per second. Positive responses entail a burst of spikes, while negative responses entail a cessation of spikes.[38] This allows dopamine neurons to signal both "better-than-expected" and "worse-than-expected." Dopamine even tracks the value-prediction error signals in Kamin blocking paradigms.[39] These results have since been replicated in rats, monkeys, and humans.[40]

Reinforcement and aversion, disappointment and relief

In the computer models, penalties are generally written as negative rewards and aversion is written as negative reinforcement. However, the examples of "worse-than-expected" used in the experimental data described above are not actually punishments, nor do they produce actual aversion. Rather, they are examples of *disappointment*—a lack of delivery of an expected reward.[41] When researchers have examined actual aversive events, the dopamine response to those events has turned out to be very complicated.[42;I]

As we will see below, aversion and disappointment are actually different phenomena and cannot work by a shared mechanism. Some researchers have suggested that there is another neurotransmitter signal analogous to dopamine that can serve as the aversion signal (in parallel to the reinforcement signal of dopamine),[47] but no one has (as yet) found it.[J] Responses to punishments (like retreating from painful stimuli) entail a different neural circuitry than responses to positive rewards, in part because the responses to punishment are an evolutionarily older circuit.[54] Learning not to do something (aversion) uses a different set of neural systems than learning to do something (reinforcement).[55]

[I] Just how well the value-prediction error (δ) theory explains the dopamine data is a point of much controversy today. Part of the problem is that all experiments require behavior, mammalian behavior is a complex process, and we often need to run computer simulations of the behavior itself to determine what a value-prediction error signal would look like in a given behavioral experiment.

For example, Sham Kakade and Peter Dayan showed that if two signals, one positive and one neutral, are provided to the agent, and the sensory cues from the two signals are similar, then one can see "generalization effects" where there is an illusory positive δ signal to the neutral stimulus that is followed quickly by a less-than-expected negative δ signal.[43] Imagine two doors, one that leads to food and one that doesn't. At the sound of a door opening, you might look to the two doors, getting a positive δ signal, but then when you realize that the neutral (nonrewarded) door was the one that was opened, you would be disappointed (giving you a negative δ).

As another example, Patryk Laurent has shown that an agent with limited sensory resources is evolutionarily well served by a positive orienting signal, even to potentially aversive events.[44] Essentially, this orienting signal allows the agent to do better than expected at avoiding those aversive events.

Both of these examples would provide complex dopamine signals to aversive events, explaining some of the dopamine signals seen to neutral and aversive events. However, they make specific predictions about how dopamine should respond to those events. Schultz and colleagues have found that the predicted less-than-expected reaction after generalization dopamine signals occurs.[45] Although the Laurent hypothesis has not been explicitly tested, it may explain the very fast response signals seen by Peter Redgrave and colleagues.[46]

[J] Some researchers have suggested that *serotonin* might play the role of the negative (aversive) signal,[48] but recent experiments have shown that not to be the case.[49] Another interesting potential candidate is *norepinephrine* (called *noradrenalin* in Europe). Norepinephrine is a chemical modification of dopamine, making dopamine a precursor to it.[50] In invertebrates, the norepinephrine analogue *octopamine* serves as the positive error signal, while dopamine serves as the negative error signal.[51] All of these molecules (serotonin, norepinephrine, octopamine, and dopamine) are very similar in their molecular structure,[52] making them plausible candidates, given the copy-and-modify process often seen in evolution.

Additionally, some recent very exciting work has found that neurons in another neural structure, the *habenula* (which projects to the dopamine neurons in the ventral tegmental area), increase their firing with aversion and decrease their firing with reinforcement.[53] It is still unclear whether these habenula neurons are the long-sought aversion neurons or if they are part of the brain's calculation of δ. Remember, δ is a mathematical term. Dopamine reflects δ, therefore, the brain calculates δ...somehow.

object provided	evaluation	effect	lack of delivery
reward	euphoria	reinforcement	disappointment
punishment	dysphoria	aversion	relief

Figure 4.1 Providing a positive thing (a *reward*, leading to *euphoria*) produces *reinforcement*, while the lack of delivery of an expected reward leads to *disappointment*. Similarly, providing a negative thing (a *punishment*, leading to *dysphoria*) produces *aversion*, while the lack of delivery of an expected punishment leads to *relief*.

From the very beginning of animal learning experiments, it has been known that the process of recognizing that a cue no longer predicts reward does not mean that the animal has forgotten the association.[56] This goes all the way back to Pavlov and his famous dogs learning to associate bells with food. Once the dogs had learned to salivate in response to the bell (in anticipation of the food), when the food was not presented to them, they showed frustration and anger, and they searched for the food. Eventually, however, they recognized that the bell no longer implied food and learned to ignore the bell. If, however, they were given food again just once after the bell was rung, they immediately started salivating for food the next time. Because learning was much faster afterward than before, Pavlov knew that the dog had not forgotten the original association.

This means that there must be a second process. In the literature, this process is usually called *extinction* because the lack of delivered reward has "extinguished" the response.[K] In fact, the exact same effects occur with aversion. If an animal is trained to associate a cue with a negative event (say an electric shock), and this association is extinguished (by providing the cue without the shock), then it can be reminded of the association (one pair of cue + shock) and the response will reappear without additional training. *Disappointment* is not the forgetting of reinforcement and *relief* is not the forgetting of aversion. Because both reinforcement and aversion have corresponding secondary processes (disappointment and relief), disappointment cannot be the same process as aversion and relief cannot be the same process as reinforcement. See Figure 4.1.

Neural mechanisms of extinction

As this point, scientists are not completely sure what the neural mechanisms are that underlie the secondary process of extinction that follows from disappointment or relief. There are two prominent theories to explain this secondary process. One is that there is a specific second inhibition process, such that neurons in this secondary area inhibit neurons in the primary association area.[57] It is known, for example, that synapses in the amygdala are critical to the initial learning of an aversive association (lesions of the amygdala prevent such associations, the creation of such associations changes firing patterns in the amygdala, and the creation of such associations occurs with and depends on synaptic plasticity in the amygdala). However, neurons in the central prefrontal cortex (the infralimbic cortex in the rat, the central anterior cingulate cortex in the human)

[K] Using the word *extinction* for this process is unfortunate because it has no relation to the evolutionary term *extinction*, meaning the ending of a species.

start firing after extinction and project to inhibitory neurons in the amygdala, which stop the firing of the original association cells. Yadin Dudai and his colleagues recently found that in humans, these areas are active when people with a phobia of snakes show courage and override their fear to perform a task in which they pull the snake toward themselves.[58] However, this theory implies that there is only one level of recursion—that one can only have an association and a stopping of that association.

The other theory starts from the assumption that you are not provided a definition of the situation you are in, but instead that you have to infer that situation from the available cues.[59] Look around you: there are millions of cues. How many of them are important to your ability to learn from this book? Around me right now, I am looking at windows, trees, an empty coffee cup, squirrels chasing each other. There is the sound of birds, a chickadee, a crow. There is the rumble of cars in the distance. There is the feel of the chair I am sitting in, the heat of my laptop (which gets uncomfortably hot when I work on it too long). Which of these cues are important? Most animal experiments are done in very limited environments with few obvious cues except for the tones and lights that are to be associated with the rewards and penalties. Animals didn't evolve to live in these empty environments.

This second theory says that before one can associate a situation with a reward or a penalty, one needs to define the set of stimuli that will identify that situation. Any situation definition will attend to some cues that are present in the environment and ignore others. We (myself and my colleagues Adam Johnson, Steve Jensen, and Zeb Kurth-Nelson) called this process "situation-recognition" and suggested that disappointment and relief produce a narrowing of the definition of the situation such that the agent would begin to pay attention to additional cues and begin to differentiate the new situation from the old one.[60] When animals no longer receive rewards or penalties (that is, they are disappointed or relieved), they begin "searching for the cue" that differentiates the two situations.[61] Imagine the soda machine we talked about when we first encountered the value-prediction error δ signal. If you put your money in and get nothing out, you aren't going to forget that putting money in soda machines can get you soda; you are going to look for what's different about this machine. Maybe there's a light that says "out of order" or "out of stock." Maybe the machine is off. Once you identify the difference, your definition of the soda-machine-available situation has changed, and you can go find a soda machine that works.

The second theory suggests that the additional signals being provided from the prefrontal cortex are providing additional dimensions on which to categorize the situation. It provides explanations for a number of specific phenomena seen in the extinction literature. For example, there is extensive evidence that extinction is about the recognition of a change.[62] Animals show much slower extinction after a variable (probabilistic) reward-delivery contingency than after a regular (being sure of always getting reward) reward contingency. If an animal is provided with a reward only half the time after the cue, it will still learn to respond, but it will be slower to stop when the reward is no longer delivered. On the other hand, if it is always provided with a reward, then it will quickly stop responding when the reward is no longer delivered. However, this is not simply a question of counting, because, as shown in Figure 4.2, if there is a pattern, then even with only a 50/50 chance of getting a reward, one can easily determine the pattern, and animals stop responding as soon as the pattern is disrupted.

R R R R R R R R R N N N N N N N N N

R R N N R R R R N N N N N N N N N N

R N R N R N R N R N N N N N N N N N

Figure 4.2 Sequences of reward and punishment. Imagine you are a subject in an experiment faced with one of these sequences of reward delivery. (**R** means you get the reward and **N** means you don't.) Imagine seeing the sequence from left to right. (Trace your finger across to provide yourself a sequence.) When would you stop responding? Try each line separately. You will probably find yourself trying to predict whether you get a reward or not. When the observations no longer match your predictions, that's when you recognize a change.

As we saw in Chapter 3, "value" is a complex thing. We have seen in this chapter how the calculation of value and the learning to predict value depend on multiple, interacting systems. There is a system measuring the pleasure of a thing (euphoria), a system learning the usefulness of repeating actions (reinforcement), and a system recognizing change (disappointment). In parallel, there are the dysphoria, aversion, and relief systems. As we will see in the next chapters, these value-learning components form the bases of multiple decision-making systems that interact to drive our actions. The fact that there are multiple systems interacting makes the detection and actual definition of value difficult.

Books and papers for further reading

- Kent C. Berridge and Terry E. Robinson (2003). Parsing reward. *Trends in Neurosciences, 26,* 507–513.
- P. Read Montague (2006). *Why Choose This Book?* New York: Penguin.
- Wolfram Schultz (1998). Predictive reward signal of dopamine neurons. *Journal of Neurophysiology, 80,* 1–27.
- A. David Redish, Steve Jensen, Adam Johnson, and Zeb Kurth-Nelson (2007). Reconciling reinforcement learning models with behavioral extinction and renewal: Implications for addiction, relapse, and problem gambling. *Psychological Review, 114,* 784–805.
- Richard S. Sutton and Andy G. Barto (1998). *Reinforcement Learning: An Introduction.* Cambridge, MA: MIT Press.

5

Risk and Reward

> *"Carpe diem,"* they say,
> but you don't get a day,
> you get a moment,
> a moment to hesitate....
> or to act.

Defining decision-making in terms of action-selection creates the potential for decisions that are illogical from a value-based perspective. The mammalian decision-making system includes multiple decision-making components, which can produce conflict between action options.

A teenager floors the accelerator as he navigates the winding curves of a wooded road; the car skids at each turn, barely containing its acceleration. A college student spends thousands of dollars on clothes and doesn't have enough money to pay for rent. An alcoholic stops by the bar on the way home. "Just one drink," he says. Hours later, his kids come to take him home. A firefighter stands frozen a moment before a burning building, but then gathers her courage and rushes into the building to pull a child to safety. Each of these examples is a commonly cited case of a conflict between decision-making systems.

The teenager is balancing the thrill of speed with the risk of losing any potential future he might have. The college student spends the money now for the short-term gain of having clothes and ignores (or forgets) the long-term gain of actually staying in her apartment. The alcoholic risks his family, his happiness, and often his job and livelihood for the simple, immediate pleasures of a drink. (Of course, the problem is that the one drink turns into two and then three and then more.) The firefighter must overcome emotional fear reactions that say "don't go in there." These are all conflicts between decision-making systems.

Risk-seeking behavior

Colloquially, risk entails the potential for loss in the face of potential gains. (Our hypothetical teenager is risking his life driving too fast.) In economics, the term *risk* is defined as the variability in the outcome[1]—the stock market has more risk than an FDIC-insured savings account. This is a form of uncertainty, and it is now known that there are representations of risk and uncertainty in our brains.[2] As we will discuss in depth in Chapter 14, there are differences between *expected variability* (a known probability, such as the chance of rain), *unexpected variability* (a surprise, such as when something that has been working suddenly breaks), and *unknown variability* (ambiguity, when you know that you don't know the probabilities). Animals will expend energy to translate unknown variability into expected variability and to reduce expected variability.[3]

Imagine you are an animal, entering a new environment. You don't know what dangers lurk out there. You don't know what rewards are available. Before you can make yourself safe from those dangers and before you can gain those rewards, you have to explore the environment.[4] Imagine that you have explored part of the environment. Now you have a choice: *Do you stay and use the rewards you've already found, or do you go looking for better ones?*

Animals tend to be risk-averse with gains and risk-seeking with losses. This is the source of the difference in the Asian flu example in Chapter 3—phrased in terms of saving lives, people take the safe option, but phrased in terms of losses, people take the risky option.[5] But this isn't the whole story either, because risk and reward interact with exploration and uncertainty.

Interestingly, the most risk-seeking behavior tends to occur in adolescents.[6] Adolescents are at that transition from dependence to independence. Humans first develop through a youth stage during which they are protected and trained. At the subsequent adolescent stage, humans go exploring to see what the parameters of the world are. As they age out of adolescence, humans tend to settle down and be less risk-seeking. This ability to learn the parameters of the world after a long training period makes humans particularly flexible in their ability to interact with the world.

An interesting question is then to ask *What drives exploration?* Animals, including humans, have an innate curiosity that drives us to explore the world. But as the proverb says, "curiosity killed the cat." Exploring is dangerous. A fair assessment of the dangers could lead us to be unwilling to take a chance. On average, however, people tend to underestimate dangers and to be overoptimistic about unknowns,[7] which tends to drive exploration, while still maintaining intelligent behavior in the parts of the world we do know. (Remember, "the grass is always greener on the other side of the hill"—except when you get there, and it's not.)

So how is the teenager speeding down a road an example of exploration overwhelming exploitation? Our hypothetical teenager is unlikely to be speeding down an untraveled road. When animals are exploring new territory, they tend to travel very slowly, observing everything around them.[8] But our hypothetical teenager is testing his limits, trying to figure out how good his reaction times are, how fast he can go while still maintaining control of the car. If the teenager is overestimating his abilities or underestimating the likelihood of meeting an oncoming car on that windy, dark road that late at night, the consequences can be tragic.

We will see throughout this book that personality entails differences in the parameters underlying the decision-making system. Here we have two parameters and an interaction: *How curious are you? How overoptimistic in the face of the unknown? How willing are you to risk danger for those new answers?* (Adolescents, of course, are notorious for both of these properties—risk-taking behavior driven by curiosity and overoptimism.) But each individual, even in both youth and adulthood, has a different take on these parameters,[9] and thus each of us has our own level of risk-seeking and overoptimism, our own threshold of what risks we will tolerate, and how badly we estimate those risks. Balancing risk and reward can be the difference between success and failure, and finding that right balance is not always easy.

Waiting for a reward

Which would you rather have, $10 today or $10 in a week? Barring some really strange situations, pretty much everyone would want the $10 today. What this means is that $10 in a week is worth less to you than $10 today. We say that rewards delivered in the future are *discounted*.[10] Logically, discounting future rewards makes sense because things can happen between now and then; waiting for the future is risky.[11] If you get hit by a bus or win the lottery or the world explodes in thermonuclear war, that $10 in a week just isn't worth as much as it was today.

$10 today can also be invested,[12] so in a week, you could have more than $10. This of course works with nonmonetary rewards as well (food, mates, etc.)[13] To a starving animal, food now is worth a lot more than food in a week. If you starve to death now, food next week just isn't that valuable. And, of course, in the long term, food now will lead to a stronger body, more energy, and more ability to find food later.

So rewards now are worth more than rewards in the future. By asking people a series of these money-now-or-money-later questions (*Which would you rather have, $9 now or $10 next week?*), we can determine how valuable $10 in a week actually is. If we were to plot this as a function of the delay, we can derive a *discounting curve* and measure how value decreases with delay.[14]

Of course, we can't ask animals this question,[A] but we can offer them a choice between a small amount of food now and a large amount of food later.[15] For example, in a typical experiment, a rat or monkey or pigeon is offered two options (levers[16] or paths leading to a food location[17]): taking the first option provides one food pellet immediately, but taking the second option provides more (say three) food pellets after a delay. By observing the animal's choices, we can again determine the discounting curve.

If discounting were simply due to inflation or the ability to invest money, we would expect it to follow an *exponential* function of time.[18] In an exponential function, the value decreases by the same percentage every unit of time.[B] So if your discounting function were an exponential with a half-life of a year, you would be equally happy with $5 now and $10 in a year or $2.50 now and $10 in two years. Exponential discounting curves

---

[A] We can ask them. But they are unlikely to give us a meaningful answer.

[B] Examples of exponential functions include bank accounts and population growth. When a bank says that it will pay you a percentage interest each year, the total amount of money in your account will increase by that percentage each year. Since the money goes back into your account, you are effectively multiplying your savings account by a number greater than 1 each year. Even a small number can build up quickly: a 5% interest rate will double in 15 years. Here, we are talking about exponential decay, which is like multiplying the value by a number a little less than 1 each year.

A good example of exponential decay is the decay of radioactive material: after a given number of years, half the material will have decayed. This is where the term *half-life* comes from. For example, plutonium-238 has a half-life of 88 years. So if you have a pound of plutonium-238, after 88 years, you would have half a pound. After another 88 years (176 years total), you would have a quarter of a pound, etc.

have a very useful property, which is that they are self-similar: your choices now are the same choices you would make in a year.

But neither humans answering questionnaires nor animals pressing levers show exponential discounting curves.[19] In fact, humans answering questionnaires, animals pressing levers for food, and humans pressing levers for food all show a discounting curve best described as a *hyperbolic* function, which drops off very quickly but then becomes more flat with time.

Any nonexponential discounting curve (including hyperbolic ones) will show a property called *preference reversal*, in which the choices change depending on your temporal vantage point.[20] You can convince yourself that you too show preference reversal. Ask yourself which you would rather have, $10 today or $11 in a week? Then ask yourself which you would rather have, $10 in a year or $11 in a year and a week? Each person has a different reversal point, so you may have to find a slightly different set of numbers for yourself, but you will almost certainly be able to find a pair of numbers such that you won't wait now, but will wait next year. Notice that this doesn't make any sense rationally. Today, you say it's not worth waiting for that extra dollar, but for a year from now, when faced with what is really the same choice, you say you'll wait. Presumably, if you ask yourself next year, you'll say it's not worth waiting—you'll have changed your mind and reversed your preferences. Even though this is irrational, it feels right to most people.

This is the mistake being made by our hypothetical extravagant student, who is saying she would prefer to spend the money now on the immediately available reward (new clothes) rather than waiting for the larger reward (paying rent) later. In fact, when her parents ask her at the beginning of the school year whether she's going to pay her rent or buy new clothes, she's likely to tell them (we'll assume honestly) that she's going to pay the rent. This switch (between wanting to pay the rent early and buying clothes) is an example of the preference reversal that we're talking about.

Preference reversal can also be seen in the opposite direction. This might be called the *Cathy effect*, after the comic strip *Cathy* by Cathy Guisewite, which has a regular motif of Cathy's inability to resist high-sugar[C] treats like Halloween candy or birthday cake. (In panel 1, Cathy says she won't eat the cake this time, but in panel 3, when faced with the actual cake, we find her eating it.) From a distance, the chocolate is discounted and has low value and the long-term value of keeping to her diet is preferred, but when the chocolate is immediately available, it is discounted less, and poor Cathy makes the wrong choice.

In part, Cathy's dilemma comes from an interaction between decision-making systems: from a distance, one system wants to stay on her diet, but from close up, another system reaches for the cake. This is the Parable of the Jellybeans that we saw in Chapter 1—it is hard to reject the physical reward in front of you for an abstract reward later.[22] One possible explanation for the success of Contingency Management (which offers concrete rewards to addicts for staying clean of drugs) in addiction and behavioral modification is that it offers a concrete alternative option, which allows the subject to attend to other options rather than the drug.[23]

In a positive light, preference reversal also allows for an interesting phenomenon called precommitment, in which a person or an animal sets things up so that it is not

---

[C] Processed sugar is far sweeter than most foods that we have evolved to eat, so it is a substance that overstimulates sensory systems, making intake particularly difficult to control.[21]

given the choice in the future.[24] For example, an alcoholic who knows that he will drink if he goes to the bar can decide not to drive by the bar in the first place. From a distance, he makes one choice, knowing that he will make the wrong choice if given an opportunity later. If our hypothetical extravagant student is smart and knows herself well, then she might put the money away in a prepaid escrow account that can be used only for rent. The two selves (the student at the beginning of the school year who wants to pay rent and the student midyear who wants to buy clothes) are in conflict with each other.[25] If she's smart, she can precommit herself when she's that early, thrifty student to prevent herself from wasting the money when she's that later, extravagant student. As we explore the actual components of the decision-making system, we will find that precommitment involves an interaction among Deliberative (Chapter 9) and Self-Control (Chapter 15) systems.[26] The ability to precommit to one option over another remains one of the most powerful tools in our decision-making arsenal.[27]

Stopping a prepotent action

The interaction between multiple decision systems can also produce conflict directly. Only some of the multiple decision-making systems that drive actions are reflected in our consideration of consciousness. This means that there can be actions taken, after which we find ourselves saying, "Now why did I do that?"

Other examples of conflict (such as the firefighter) come from one system wanting to approach or flee a stimulus and another component telling it to hold still.[28] In Chapter 6, we will see that there are emotional components that depend on the amygdala (a deep, limbic brain structure involved in simple approach-and-retreat cue–response phenomena[29]), learned-action components that depend on the basal ganglia (other neural structures that learn situation–action pairs[30]), and deliberative components that depend on the prefrontal cortex and the hippocampus (cognitive structures that enable the imagination of future possibilities[31]). When these three systems select different actions, we have a conflict.

Classic experiments on rats and other animals have studied a simple process called *fear conditioning*.[32] In a typical experiment, a rat would be placed in a box, and, at irregular intervals, a tone would be played and then the rat would receive a mild shock.[D] In modern experiments, the shock is never enough to hurt the animal, just enough to be unpleasant. Similar experiments can be done on humans, where they get a mild shock after a cue.[33] What happens is that the rat begins to fear the tone that predicts that a shock is coming. Humans explicitly describe dreading the oncoming shock and describe how unpleasant the expectation of a shock is. In fact, Greg Berns and his colleagues found that the dread of waiting for a shock was so unpleasant that people would choose to have

---

[D] It is important to note that both the animal and human experiments are highly regulated. To ensure that these experiments are humane and safe, the scientists have to get permission from the university's IRB (internal review board, for human experiments) or the university's IACUC (internal animal care and use committee, for animal experiments). Both of these boards include scientists, medical professionals (vets for animals, MDs for humans), and local community members (often including animal rights activists on IACUC boards). If the committee doesn't think the experiment is humane, safe, and likely to be important scientifically, then the experiment can't go forward.

a larger shock quickly rather than have to wait for a smaller one later.[34;E] Rats cannot, of course, tell us that they are fearful and nervous about the shock, but they freeze in fear and startle more in response to an unexpected event. If you are tense, waiting for a shock, then a loud noise will make you jump. Rats do the same thing.

This brings us to tone–fear conditioning, in which a rat learns to expect a shock after a tone is played. Fear conditioning can then be extinguished by subsequently providing the rat with the tone but no shock. As we saw in the previous chapter, behavioral extinction entails new activity in the infralimbic cortex that projects down to the amygdala and inhibits the learned fear response.[35]

This matches the Yadin Dudai study on courage that was mentioned in the previous chapter—Dudai and his colleagues studied humans overcoming their fear of snakes.[36] The sight of the snake triggered the emotional (Pavlovian) system that had an innate reaction to the snake ("Run away!") while the Deliberative system had to overcome that prepotent action. As is said in many a movie and many a novel, courage is not the lack of fear, but the ability to overcome that fear.[F] The fact that we now know the neural mechanisms underlying courage does not diminish what courage is.

Summary

In this first part of the book, we've defined the question of decision-making in terms of action-selection, identified that we cannot simply say that we are evaluating choices, and identified that there are multiple systems that drive action-selection within the mammal. In the next part, I want to turn to the question of what these multiple decision-making systems are and how they interact with each other. Afterwards (in the third part of the book), we'll turn to their vulnerabilities and what those vulnerabilities mean for decision-making problems such as addiction and post-traumatic stress disorder.

Books and papers for further reading

- George Ainslie (2001). *Breakdown of Will*. Cambridge, UK: Cambridge University Press.
- Robert Kurzban (2010). *Why Everyone (Else) is a Hypocrite*. Princeton, NJ: Princeton University Press.
- Uri Nili, Hagar Goldberg, Abraham Weizman, and Yadin Dudai (2010). Fear Thou Not: Activity of frontal and temporal circuits in moments of real-life courage. *Neuron*, *66*, 949–962.

[E] I had a similar experience with my fish tank a few months ago, where one of the underwater pumps was giving me a shock whenever I put my hand in the water. It became a very definite effort of will to put my hand in the water to retrieve the damaged pump.

[F] In his epic novel *Dune*, Frank Herbert defines humanity as the ability to hold your hand in a pain-box, refusing the Reflexive and Pavlovian action-selection systems that want to pull the hand away, because the Deliberative system knows that the woman testing you will kill you with her poison pin at your neck if you do.[37]

PART TWO

THE DECISION-MAKING SYSTEM

Multiple Decision-Making Systems

> Miles' trumpet
> syncopates the drumbeat,
> rises like bubbling voices
> out of a turbid pool,
> floats like soap bubbles lost in air,
> fading into the morning mists.

There are multiple neural systems that drive decision-making, each of which has different computational properties that make it better suited to drive action-selection under different conditions. We will identify four action-selection systems: Reflexes, Pavlovian, Deliberative, and Procedural. Along with motoric, perceptual, situation-categorization, and motivational support systems, these make up the decision-making system.

Imagine the first time you drive to work. You would probably look at a map, plan the best route. During the drive, you would pay particular attention to road signs and landmarks. But driving that same route each day for weeks, months, or years, the route becomes automatic. It no longer requires the same amount of attention, and you can think about other things: the test you have to write, your kids' soccer game that evening, what you're going to make for dinner. And yet, you arrive at work. In fact, it can become so automatic, you drive to work without meaning to.[A]

[A] The first time I used this analogy, I had come back to give a talk at the lab where I had done my postdoctoral work in Tucson, Arizona. I was staying with my former mentors, in their guest house. When I worked in their lab (for about three years), I lived on the east side of town, on the south side near the airbase. They also lived on the east side of town, but north, by the mountains. So the first part of driving from the lab to their house was the same as the first part of what had been my usual trip home for years. And, even fully conscious of this issue that I had just laid out in my talk that morning, I turned south when I got to the corner and didn't realize my mistake until I had turned onto the street on which I used to live.

As we will see later in this section, these two processes (the conscious, attention-demanding, map-based, planning process and the automatic, low-attention, sequence-based, routine process) actually reflect two different systems that process information about the decision in fundamentally different ways, and depend on different brain structures.[1] Scientists studying decision-making have identified at least four separate action-selection processes:

- A hardwired system that reacts quickly to immediately sensed direct dangers and events. These are your *reflexes*, genetically wired into your spinal cord, your peripheral nervous system, and your central brainstem.
- A system that predicts outcomes and reacts in a genetically prewired way to those outcomes. Computationally, what is learned in this system is a hypothesized causal relationship between the cues and the outcomes. The actions are not learned, they are "released" as appropriate responses to the expected outcome. Throughout this book, I will refer to this as the *Pavlovian* action-selection system.
- A system that deliberates over decisions, requiring a lot of resources, but also capable of complex planning and flexibility. I will refer to this as the *Deliberative* system, but it has also been described as *goal-directed learning*, as *model-based decision-making*, as the *action–outcome* system, and as the *locale* or *place* navigation system.[2]
- A system that simply learns the best action to take in a given situation. Once that association is stored, the decision process is very simple, but is inflexible. I will refer to this as the *Procedural* action-selection system as it is very involved in learned motor sequences (procedures), but it has also been referred to as the *habit*, *stimulus–response*, *stimulus–action*, *cached-action*, and *taxon* navigation system.[3]

These four systems are generally sufficient to explain action-selection in the mammalian brain;[B] however, they each have internal subtleties that we will address as we examine each system separately. In addition, their interactions produce subtleties not directly obvious from their individual computational components.

For these systems to work in the real world, we need several additional support systems. At this point, it is not clear whether these support systems are separate components that are shared among the decision-making systems, or whether there are separate versions of each, so that each decision-making system has its own copy of each support system. Alternatively, these support systems could be full-fledged systems in their own right, with their own internal components. Finally, it's possible that the support systems correspond in some way to some aspect of one or more of the decision-making systems. Nevertheless, breakdowns can occur in the support systems as well,[5] and we

---

[B] Some scientists have suggested a fifth system based on recollection of a single event in the past[4] ("It worked last time, maybe it will work again"). It is not clear, however, whether this is a different system or whether this is a special case of the Deliberative system we will see below and explore in depth in Chapter 9. The brain structures involved in this fifth system seem to be the same ones that are involved in the Deliberative system.

will need to include them in order to complete our description of the machinery of decision-making.

- First, of course, one needs a *motor control system* that produces the muscle movements, the effectors that move the body and take the actual action. As the questions being addressed in this book are primarily about the selection of the action, not the action itself, we will not spend a lot of time on the spinal motor control system, except to say that actions are generally stored as processes more complex than moving a single muscle.
- Second, one needs *perceptual systems* that receive and interpret the basic sensory signals to determine what information those signals carry. These systems need to recognize objects and their basic properties (*What is it? Where is it?*). We will discuss these in terms of the detection of features and the integration of information.
- In addition, however, one needs a system that recognizes which are the important cues on which to base one's decision, whether in terms of external cues in the world or internal body-related cues. Although many scientific decision-making literatures refer to this process as "stimulus identification," I think that term leads us to imagine that reactions are made to a single stimulus, while clearly we are recognizing multiple stimuli and integrating them into a recognition of the situation we are in. Thus, I will refer to this as the *situation-recognition* system.
- Finally, one needs a system that encodes one's goals and desires. This system is going to depend on one's internal (evolutionary) needs, but will also need to mediate conflicting goals, needs, and desires. For obvious reasons, I will refer to this as the *motivational* system.

Although I will refer to these different aspects of decision-making as "systems," I don't want you to take them as different, separate modules. A good example of what I mean by the term "system" is the electric and gas engines in the new hybrid cars (like the Toyota Prius)—the car can be driven by the electric motor or by the gas motor, but both engines still share the same drive train and the same accelerator pedal. Some parts are shared, and some parts are separate. In the end, however, the goal of both engine systems is to make the car go. And the car still requires an additional steering system to guide it on the correct course. Similarly, what matters for evolution is the behavior of the organism itself, not the separate decision-making systems. The decision-making systems are separate in that they require different information processing and involve overlapping, but also different, neural structures, even though they all interact to produce behavior. We will find it useful to separate these systems as a first step in our analysis, but we will need to come back to their interaction in order to understand behavior (and its failure modes).

Although we like to think of ourselves as a unitary decision-maker with a single set of desires, we all have experiences in which these multiple systems can come into conflict with each other. The reason that multiple systems evolved is that they each have advantages and disadvantages, and they are each better at some tasks and worse at others. If one can successfully select which system is going to be best at each time, one can gain the advantages of each and diminish the disadvantages of each. We will talk later about what is known about the mechanism by which we mediate between these systems, but there is still a lot of debate in the scientific community about exactly how that mediation happens.

The four action-selection systems

Reflexes

Our reflexes are the simplest decision-making systems we have. Scientists study-ing decision-making often dismiss the reflex as not being a decision-making sys-tem because it's too simple. But by our definition of decision-making as selecting an action, we have to include a reflex as a decision. Because reflexes interact with the other decision-making systems, we will find that it is useful to include reflexes in our taxon-omy of decision-making systems.

Let's take an example reflex. If your hand touches something hot enough to burn it (say a candle flame), you pull your hand away quickly. This is something that an animal wants to do as quickly as possible. If we took the time to think, "That's hot. Should I pull my hand away?" the flame would have done damage to our fingers. Similarly, we don't have time to learn to pull our hand away from the fire; evolution wants that to happen correctly the first time. We can think of reflexes as simple operations (actions to be selected in reaction to specific conditions) that have been learned over evolu-tionary time, but that once learned within a species, are hardwired within a given individual. These twin issues of the time it takes to compute an answer and the time it takes to learn the right answer are critical advantages and disadvantages of each of the action-selection systems.

Proof that a reflex really is a decision can be seen in its interaction with the other action-selection systems. In David Lean's *Lawrence of Arabia*, there is a famous scene where T. E. Lawrence, played by Peter O'Toole, waits for the match to burn all the way down to his fingers. His companion then tries it and complains that it hurts. "Of course," replies Lawrence, "but the trick is not minding that it hurts." It is possible to override the default Reflex action-selection with a different, more conscious system. This interaction between multiple systems as an important part of how we make decisions is something we will return to several times in this book.

The Pavlovian action-selection system

Pavlovian action-selection is also computationally simple in that it can only produce actions that have been learned over an evolutionary timescale (often called *unconditioned responses*),[6] but it differs from the Reflex action-selection system in that it learns.[C]

[C] I have struggled with finding the right terminology to use for this first learning-capable system. The computational mechanisms underlying the first system are very clear, but we need a term for it. (I was tempted at one point to call it "System X" to avoid all of the historical baggage associated with the term "Pavlovian.") Historically, learning in animals (including humans) has been assumed to arise from two different systems, one when no action was required to get the reward (Pavlovian) and a different one when action was required (Instrumental).[7]

In Pavlov's original experiments, the sound occurred (the "bell") and then the food appeared. The dog didn't have to do anything to get the food, so that was identified as the first system, which was called "Pavlovian." If, on the other hand, the dog had to push a lever with its paw after the bell rang to get food, that would be "instrumental."

(continued)

The Pavlovian system learns stimuli that predict outcomes, but it does not learn the actions to take with those outcomes.[14] Pavlovian learning is named after Ivan Pavlov (1849–1936), the great Russian neuroscientist. Supposedly, Pavlov rang a bell before feeding a dog and found that the dog learned to salivate to the bell in anticipation of the food.[D]

When describing Pavlovian learning, scientists often describe the stimuli as "releasing specific actions."[19] In classic animal learning theory, there is an *unconditioned stimulus* (the food being presented to Pavlov's dog), an *unconditioned response* (salivating), and a *conditioning stimulus* (the bell). In Pavlovian learning, the unconditioned response shifts in time from the unconditioned stimulus to the conditioning stimulus. Interpretations of Pavlovian learning tend to ignore the action-selection component of the learning, suggesting that the unconditioned response is simply a tool to identify an association between the conditioning stimulus and the unconditioned stimulus.[20]

These interpretations are based in part because the same training that makes animals take the unconditioned response after seeing the training cue (Pavlovian action-selection) also often makes animals more likely to take other, untrained actions that they know will reach the unconditioned stimulus (as if they had an increased *motivation* to reach that unconditioned stimulus).[21] This is a process called *Pavlovian-to-instrumental transfer*, which we will examine in depth when we reach our discussion of motivation, below. Recent data suggest that the two effects (release

---

We now know that these systems are more complicated—for example, the traditional term "instrumental" includes both the Deliberative and Procedural systems, which select actions using very different computational processes,[8] and Pavlovian learning is really about action-selection appropriate to cue–outcome expectations.[9] In addition, these two learning systems interact in a process called "Pavlovian-to-instrumental transfer,"[10] which we will identify with the motivational support system (later).

As we will see in our in-depth discussion of Pavlovian systems (Chapter 8), this "Pavlovian" system is related to basic survival instincts and to emotions.[11] However, neither of those terms captures all of the computational issues either, and they both have their own historical baggage associated with them—animal behavior is about genetic success, not survival,[12] and the direct relationship between what we are calling the Pavlovian action-selection system and emotion is controversial.[13] Therefore, I will use the term "Pavlovian action-selection" throughout this book as a place holder for a better term for this first learning-based action-selection system.

[D] Pavlov was the first winner of the Nobel prize in Medicine in 1904, but surprisingly to many people today, what he won it for was not the learning studies that we know him for today; rather, he won it for his work on digestion and salivation.[15] After his Nobel prize, he felt famous enough to risk working on learning, starting a tradition of Nobel prizewinners turning from unrelated medical topics to psychology and neuroscience. Other examples include Francis Crick[16] (1916–2004, Nobel prize in 1962 for DNA) and Gerry Edelman[17] (1929–, Nobel prize in 1972 for antibodies in the immune system), both of whom turned to work on consciousness after winning their prizes.

As with most popular descriptions of the process of science, the story taught in introductory science classes that Pavlov had an explicit hypothesis that he then went to test belies the actual process of discovery in science. In fact, Pavlov was working on the mechanisms of digestion.[18] As part of his animal research setup, he had to put the dog into a harness that was counterbalanced by a heavy weight. When the weight was dropped, Pavlov noticed that the dog started to salivate. Pavlov recognized that something interesting was happening and decided to chase it.

of unconditioned responses to conditioned stimuli [Pavlovian action-selection] and an increase in motivation as evidenced by increased actions taken by other systems [Pavlovian-to-instrumental transfer]) are dissociable. They are differently affected by different brain structure lesions and they are differently affected by different pharmacological manipulations.[22] The relationship between the Pavlovian action-selection and motivational systems is still an open question being actively pursued by scientists.

However, we must not forget that the animal is, in fact, taking an action. Recent interpretations suggest that Pavlovian learning plays a role in an action-selection system, in which the unconditioned responses are actions learned over an evolutionary timescale.[23] Imagine living on the savannah where there are lions that might hunt you. You can learn that the rustle in the brush predicts that a lion is stalking you and you can learn to run from the rustling grass, but you don't get a chance to learn to run from the lion—you've got to get that right the first time. The Pavlovian action-selection system can learn that the rustle in the grass is a lion stalking you, which leads to fear, and running, but it can't learn that the right response is to do jumping jacks.

A great way to understand the Pavlovian system is the phenomenon of *sign-trackers* and *goal-trackers*.[24] Imagine rats being placed in an environment with a food-release port and a light, separated by some small but significant distance. The light comes on, and a few moments later food is delivered at the food port. The connection between the light and the food is independent of what the rat does—the light simply predicts that the food will be available. The right thing for the rat to do is to go to the food port when the light comes on. (This would be "goal-tracking.") Some rats, however, go to the light during the intervening interval and gnaw on it. They still go to the food when the food is delivered, but they have wasted time and energy going out of their way to the light first. (This would be "sign-tracking.") In fact, if a sign-tracking rat has had enough experience with the light–food association, and you stop giving the food if the rat goes to the light and give it only if the rat goes directly to the food port, the rat has a devil of a time stopping going to the light.[25] The Pavlovian association is too strong.

Current thinking suggests that Pavlovian action-selection is related to what we recognize as emotional responses,[26] although the specific relationship between the Pavlovian action and the linguistically labeled emotion is controversial.[27] Some authors have suggested that emotional responses are Pavlovian actions changing internal responses (heart rate, salivation, etc.).[28] Others have suggested that the things we label emotions are a categorization process applied to these internal responses.[29] A discussion of categorization processes in mammalian brains (including humans) can be found in Appendix C. We will come back to the relationships between Pavlovian action-selection and emotion in Chapter 8.

Although flexible in the stimuli it can react to, the set of actions available to the Pavlovian action-selection system is greatly limited. Pavlovian responses can only transfer a simple "unconditioned response" to an earlier stimulus. This makes it more flexible than simple reflexes, but the Pavlovian action-selection system cannot take an arbitrary action in response to an arbitrary stimulus. For that, we need a more complex decision-making machinery, like the Deliberative or Procedural systems.

Deliberation

The Deliberative system is more flexible. It can take any action in any situation, but it is a computationally expensive system. In humans, deliberation entails planning and consists of a conscious investigation of the future. This is particularly useful for large one-time decisions, where one cannot try the individual options multiple times to determine the value of each.

For example, a friend of mine spent the last month deciding between two universities who had made him job offers. Each offer had advantages and disadvantages. This was not a decision that he could make ten times, observe what the answers are each time, and then slowly learn to make the correct choice. Obviously, it was not a decision with an action that evolved over generations.[E] Instead, he had to imagine himself in those two futures—*What would life be like at University One? What would life be like at University Two?* Through his life experience and through discussion with his colleagues,[F] he tried to work out the consequences of his decision. From that complex deliberation, he worked out what he thought was the best choice.

This is a process called *episodic future thinking*.[30] We will return to the issue of episodic future thinking in later chapters, but the concept is that when trying to plan a complex future event, one needs to draw together memories and experiences from lots of sources to imagine what the potential future might be like. By imagining ourselves in that future event, we can determine whether it is something we want to happen or something we want to avoid. As we will see, both the hippocampus and the prefrontal cortex are critically involved in episodic future thinking.[31;G]

A critical question that has plagued psychology for years is *Do animals deliberate as well?*[34] We can't ask a rat what it is thinking about, but we can decode information from neural signals. If we know what information is represented by an ensemble of cells, then we can decode that information from the activity in those cells. (See Appendix B for a discussion of current technology and methods that enable the decoding of neural

---

[E] I think it is pretty unlikely that "take the job at University One" can be encoded in one's genes. Clearly this question can't be solved by reflexes. Similarly, although this is certainly not a decision that the Pavlovian action-selection system can make (I can't imagine "sign on the dotted line" to be a genetically hard-coded response to any outcome), one could argue that the Pavlovian system influenced his decision, because he felt drawn to one place or another. I suspect that there is Pavlovian involvement when someone says, "I want to go back to that university because it's in my hometown where I grew up and I want to go home" (or "I'll never go back to that university because it's in my hometown where I grew up," which I've also heard!). In any case, the ultimate decision to go to a new job or not is one that almost certainly engages the Deliberative decision-making system.

[F] This is one of the advantages of human language—we can improve our prediction from observations and discussions with others.

[G] The hippocampus is often discussed as being critical to *episodic memory*, meaning memories of past events in one's life.[32] The role of the hippocampus in imagining the future (episodic future thinking) suggests a particularly interesting hypothesis for the role of the hippocampus in memories of the past: perhaps we don't remember the past—perhaps we actually imagine our pasts. Perhaps we are using the system evolved to imagine the future when we try to remember these past events. This may be an explanation for why our memories for past events are so fragile and so easily manipulable.[33]

signals.) The hippocampus is a critical part of episodic future thinking in humans.[35] In rats, the information represented in hippocampal cells is first the location of the animal in an environment (these are known as *place cells*).[36] From the activity in these cells, we can decode the location represented at a moment in time by the cells.[37] So, if a rat were to imagine being at another place in the environment, we should be able to decode that imagination by looking at the set of active hippocampal cells.[38]

Rats certainly look like they deliberate over choices. When rats come to a difficult or recently changed choice (say at a T-intersection in a maze), they sometimes pause, turning first one way and then the other.[39] When this behavior was first observed by Karl Muenzinger and his student Evelyn Gentry in 1931, they called it "vicarious trial and error" because they thought that the rat was vicariously trying out the possibilities. Just as my friend imagined himself at his two future jobs to try to decide between them, the rat was imagining itself taking the two choices. These ideas were further developed by Edward Tolman in the 1930s and 1940s, who showed that these vicarious trial and error processes occurred when we ourselves would deliberate over choices and argued explicitly that the animals were representing the future consciously.[H]

Unfortunately, Tolman did not have a mathematical way to explain his ideas and was attacked because he "neglected to predict what the rat will do." The psychologist Edwin Guthrie, in a 1937 review article, complained that "So far as the theory is concerned the rat is left buried in thought."[42] Tolman, however, was writing before the invention of the modern computer and had no language to say "yes, the rat is buried in thought because it is doing a complex calculation." In our modern world, we have all experienced the idea of computational complexity—algorithms take time to process. When our computers go searching for a file in a directory. When a website takes time to load. When a computer opponent in a game takes time before responding. It is not so strange to us for a computer to be "lost in thought." And, in fact, Tolman (following Muenzinger and Gentry) had directly observed rats pausing at those choice points, presumably "lost in thought."

In addition, of course, Tolman and his colleagues did not have the neurophysiological tools we have now. Just as humans with hippocampal damage cannot imagine future events,[43] so too rats with hippocampal damage no longer pause at choice points, nor do they show as much vicarious trial and error.[44] We can now decode representations of place from recorded ensembles of hippocampal neurons (Appendix B). When we did this in my laboratory, we found that during those paused "vicarious trial and error" events, the hippocampal representation swept ahead of the animal, first down one potential future choice, then down the other.[45] Just as my friend was imagining what it would be like to take one job or the other—so, too, the rat was imagining what would happen if it went running down the leftward path or down the rightward path. The most

---

[H] Whether or not animals are conscious is, of course, a big question that hinges in part on the question *What is consciousness?*[40] When I used to give talks on our vicarious trial and error data, I used to like to answer the inevitable question about whether the rats were consciously deliberating over the future by saying that I thought it was the same process as humans, but that "neither Tolman nor I would ever use the word 'consciousness.'" One day, after hearing me give one of these talks, Adam Johnson handed me Tolman's 1932 textbook and showed me the section titled "Vicarious trial and error is proof of consciousness in the rat."[41] For now, let us simply say that the question of consciousness is a difficult one we will return to at the end of the book (Chapter 24).

important observation we made was that these representations were sequential, coherent, and serial. They were sequential in that they consisted of a sequence of cells firing in the correct order down a path. They were coherent in that the sequences consisted of accurate representations of places ahead of the animal. And they were serial in that they went down one path and then the other, not both. Our rats really were imagining the future.[1]

It's one thing to imagine the future. But how did our rats escape being lost in thought? How did our rats make the actual decision? The next step in deliberation is evaluation. Our rat needs to go beyond saying "going left will get me banana-flavored food pellets" to say "and banana-flavored food pellets are good." Two structures involved in evaluation are the ventral striatum and the orbitofrontal cortex. Both of these structures are involved in motivation and are often dysfunctional in drug addiction and other motivation-problem syndromes.[47] Moreover, the ventral striatum receives direct input from the hippocampal formation.[48] Orbitofrontal cortex firing is modulated by hippocampal integrity.[49] What were these structures doing when the hippocampus represented these potential futures?

Just as we can record neural ensembles from the hippocampus and decode spatial representation, we can record neural ensembles from the ventral striatum or the orbitofrontal cortex and decode reward-related representations. We found that both ventral striatal and orbitofrontal reward-related cells (cells that normally respond when the animal gets reward) showed extra activity at the choice point where vicarious trial and error was occurring.[50] Muenzinger, Gentry, and Tolman were entirely correct—when these rats pause and look back and forth at choice points, they are vicariously trying out the potential choices, searching through the future, and evaluating those possibilities.

The deliberative decision-making system has a lot of advantages. It's extremely flexible. Knowing that going left can get you banana-flavored food pellets does not force you to go left. You can make a decision about which college to go to, which job to take, which city to move to, without having to spend years trying them. Knowing that one company has made you a job offer does not commit you to taking that offer. But deliberation is computationally expensive. It takes resources and time to calculate those potential future possibilities. If you are faced with the same situation every day and the appropriate action is the same every time, then there's no reason to waste that time re-planning and re-evaluating those options—just learn what the right choice is and take it.

Procedural action-selection

The Procedural system is, on the surface, much simpler—it simply needs to recognize the situation and then select a stored action or sequence of actions.[51] This is the classic stimulus–response theory of action-selection. The Procedural action-selection system differs from the three other systems. Unlike the hardwired reflexes, the Procedural system can learn to take any action. Like the Pavlovian system, it can learn to work from

[1] It is important to note that our rats were only representing the immediate future. If this is episodic future thinking,[46] it is future thinking of an immediate future only a few seconds ahead. Humans can imagine futures days, months, years, even centuries away.

any given situation, but unlike the Pavlovian system, it can learn to take any action in response to that recognized situation. In contrast to the Deliberative system, Procedural action-selection can work very quickly, but it doesn't include a representation of the outcome, nor is it flexible enough to change easily. In short, Procedural learning associates actions with situations. It can take the action quickly because it is just looking up which action to take, but because it is just looking things up, it doesn't have the flexibility to easily change if needed.

To see the distinction between the Deliberative and Procedural systems, we can imagine a rat trained to push a lever to receive fruit-flavored food pellets. Once the rat has learned the task (push the lever, get fruit-flavored food), when the rat is placed back in the experimental box, it will push the lever and eat the food. We can imagine two possible learning mechanisms here:[52] "If I push the lever, fruit-flavored food comes out. I like fruit-flavored food. I'll push the lever" or "Pushing the lever is a good thing to do. When the lever appears, I'll push the lever." The first logic corresponds to the Deliberative (search-based, predicting outcomes from actions) system, while the second logic corresponds to the Procedural (cached-action, automatic, habit, stimulus–response) system.

These two cognitive processes can be differentiated by changing the value of the fruit-flavored food to the rat. For example, the rat can be given fruit-flavored food pellets and then given lithium chloride, a chemical that does not hurt the rat but makes it feel ill.[53] (Lithium chloride often makes humans vomit.) When the rat is next placed into the experimental box, if it is using the Deliberative system, the logic becomes "If I push the lever, fruit-flavored food comes out. Yuck! That stuff is disgusting. Don't push the lever." If, instead, the rat is using the Procedural system, then the logic becomes "There's that lever. I should push it." When fruit-flavored food comes out, the rat ignores it and doesn't eat it—but it still pushes the lever. These two reactions depend on different brain structures, occur after different training paradigms, and require different computational calculations.[54]

Computationally, the Procedural system is very simple: learn the right action or sequence of actions, associate it with a recognized situation.[55] (Actually, most models associate a value with each available action in each situation, storing values of situation–action pairs, and then take the action with the highest value.[56]) Then the next time you face that situation, you know exactly what to do. This is very much the concept of a non-conscious habit that we are all familiar with. When a sports star learns to react quickly "without thinking," it's the Procedural system that's learning. When soldiers or police learn to respond lightning-quick to danger, it's their Procedural systems that are learning those responses.

The old-school psychology literature often talked about this system as "stimulus–response," with the idea that the specific responses (press a lever) are becoming attached to specific stimuli (the light turns on), but we know now that the responses can be pretty complex (throw the ball to the receiver) and that the stimuli are better described as full situations (he's open). Extensive experimental work on the mechanisms of motor control shows that the Procedural learning process can recognize very complex situations and can learn very complex action sequences.[57] Part of the key to being a successful sports star or making the correct police response is the ability to recognize the situation and categorize it correctly.[58] Once the situation has been categorized, the action-selection process is simple. One way to think of the difference between the Deliberative and Procedural systems is that the Procedural system shifts all of the decision-making complexity into the situation-recognition component.

One of my favorite scenes of this is in the movie *Men in Black*,[59] where the new recruit (Agent J-to-be, played by Will Smith) is faced with a simulated city scene and decides to ignore all the cutouts of scary aliens and shoot the little girl. When asked why he had shot "little Tiffany" by Chief Agent Zed, he responds by explaining how each alien looked scary but was just "trying to get home" or was "actually sneezing," but "little Tiffany was an eight-year-old girl carrying quantum mechanics textbooks through an unsafe city street at night." The point, of course, is that Agent J had excellent situation-categorization skills and noticed the subtleties (such as the scary alien's handkerchief and little Tiffany's quantum textbooks) and could react quickly to the correct situation.

Although describing Procedural action-selection as storing an action seems simple enough—recognize the situation and take the stored action—there are two important complexities in how this system works. First, one has to learn what the right action is. Unlike the Deliberative system, the Procedural system is very inflexible; which action is stored as the best choice cannot be updated on the fly. We will see later that overriding a stored action is difficult and requires additional neural circuitry (self-control systems in the prefrontal cortex, Chapter 15). Second, the circuitry in the mammalian brain (including in the human) seems to include separate "go" and "don't go" circuits—one system learns "in this situation, take this action," while another system learns "in that situation, don't."[60]

The current data strongly suggest that the Procedural system includes the basal ganglia, particularly the dorsal and lateral basal ganglia circuits, starting with the caudate nucleus and the putamen, which receive inputs from the cortex.[61] These synaptic connections between the cortical circuits (which are believed to represent information about the world) are trained up by dopamine signals.[62] If you remember our discussion of value, euphoria, and the do-it-again signal (Chapter 4), you'll remember that dopamine signaled the error in our prediction of how valuable things were[63]—if things came out better than we expected, there was an increase in dopamine and we wanted to increase our willingness to take an action; if things were worse than we expected, there was a decrease in dopamine and we wanted to decrease our willingness to take an action; and if things came out as expected, then we didn't need to learn anything about what to do in that situation. The connection between the cortex and the caudate/putamen encodes our "willingness to take an action" and is trained up by these dopamine signals.

Support systems

In addition to the four action-selection systems, we need four additional components, a **physical action** system, which can physically take the action that's been selected, a **perceptual** system, which can recognize the objects in the world around us, a **situation recognition** system that categorizes stimuli into "situations," and a **motivational system** that identifies what we need next and how desperate we are to satisfy those needs.

Taking a physical action

Most actions require that we move our muscles. This is true whether we are running down a street, turning to face an adversary, smiling or frowning, or signing on a dotted line. In the end, we move our muscles and have an effect on the world. Even speech is muscle movement. As a support system, this would often be referred to as the "motor control" system, because it is the final step in physically interacting with the world. For completeness, it is probably worth including nonmotor actions within this support system. For example, in our description of Pavlovian action-selection, Pavlov's dogs were salivating, releasing a liquid into their mouths, which is not really muscle movement. Similarly, getting overheated leads to sweating, which again is not really muscle movement. Nevertheless, most of the effects of the physical action system are motor movements.

Details of how muscles work can be found in any medical textbook. Many neuroscience textbooks have good descriptions.[64] The important issue for us is that within the motor control (physical action) system, the building blocks are not individual muscle movements, but rather components made of sets of related movements, called *muscle synergies*.[65] But even within those muscle synergies, we do not place one foot down, heel to toe, place the other down, and lift the first foot; we do not put our feet one step at a time; instead, we *walk*.[J] Human walking, like a fish or lamprey swimming, is an example of a process called a *central pattern generator*, so called because it is able to generate a sequence centrally, without external input.[67] Central pattern generators can continue to oscillate without input, but they can be modified directly from external sensory cues, and also from top-down signals (presumably from the action-selection systems themselves).

Since our target in this book is to understand the action-selection process, we are going to sidestep the question of what those actions are at the individual motor control level, but obviously these processes can be very important clinically.

Perception

Much like the thermostat that we started with at the beginning of the book (Chapter 2), to take the appropriate actions in the world, one needs to perceive the world. Of course, our perceptual systems are much more complex than simply measuring the temperature. Human perceptual systems take information about the world from sensory signals, process that information, and interpret it. Although our eyes transform light (photons) into neural activity, we don't see the photons themselves, we see objects— the tree outside my window, the chickadee hopping from branch to branch. Similarly, our ears detect vibrations in the air, but we hear sounds—the whistle of the wind, the song of the chickadee.

As with the physical action system, details of how perceptual systems work can be found in many neuroscience textbooks. Neil Carlson's *Physiology of Behavior* and Avi

---

[J] It is, of course, possible to consciously place our feet one step at a time, but this entails one of our action-selection systems taking control of a subset of motor movements. This is an example of *subsumption architecture*, in which new systems do not replace old ones, but add control loops to them.[66]

Chaudhuri's *Fundamentals of Sensory Perception* are excellent starting points. We are not going to spend much time on the transition from physical reality to neural activity (photons to sight, vibrations to sound), but we will take some time to explore how the neural systems categorize perception to identify objects and pull information out of those sensory signals (see Chapter 11).

Recognizing the situation

When psychologists classically tested animals in learning experiments, they used individually identifiable stimuli so that they could control the variables in their experiments.[68;K] But what's the important cue in the world right now? I am writing this paragraph on a black Lenovo laptop, sitting at a desk covered in a dark-brown woodgrain and glass, listening to Carlos Santana's wailing guitar, looking out the window at the darkness (it's 6 a.m. in winter). Outside, a streetlight illuminates the empty intersection, the shadow of a tree looms over my window, there's snow on the ground, and I can see the snowflakes falling. The light over my desk reflects off the window. Next to me are my notes. Which of these cues are important to the situation? If something were to happen, what would I identify as important?

Although it's controversial, my current hunch is that the neocortex is one big situation-recognition machine. Basically, each cortical system is categorizing information about the world. The visual cortex recognizes features about sights you see; the auditory cortex recognizes features about sounds you hear. There are also components of the cortex that recognize more abstract features—the parietal cortex recognizes the location of objects around you; the temporal cortex recognizes what those objects are. There is an area of the cortex that recognizes faces, and an area that recognizes the room you are in.[70] Even the motor cortex can be seen as a categorization of potential actions.[71] As one progresses from the back of the brain (where the sensory cortices tend to be) to the front of the brain, the categories get more and more abstract, but the cortical structure is remarkably conserved and the structure of the categorization process does not seem to change much.[72]

Models aimed at each of these individual cortices all seem to work through a process called *content-addressable memory*.[73] Content-addressable memory can be distinguished from the kind of *indexed memory* that we are familiar with in typical computers because content-addressable memory recalls the full memory from part of the memory, while indexed memory is recalled from an unrelated identifier. An image of your daughter's birthday party stored on your computer might be titled IMG3425.jpg (indexed memory, no relation between title and subject), but the memory would be recalled in your brain from a smile on her face, cake, candles getting blown out . . .

[K] Of course, the experiments take place in the presence of other abundant cues, such as the experimental box, room, or maze. These other cues are usually identified in a catchall description called the "context." The specific differences between context and cues are very complex and subtle and seem to have to do with differences between environmental cues (the room you're in) and small object cues (a light or tone) and with differences in stability (contexts are stable) and variability (object cues change quickly). Nevertheless, it appears clear that context and individual cues are processed by different brain systems.[69]

Content-addressable memory is a process in which partial patterns become completed. The computational processes that underlie content-addressable memories are well understood and can be thought of as a means of categorization. A thorough description of those computational processes, their neural implementation, and how they lead to categorization can be found in Appendix C.

The hypothesis that the neocortex is machinery for situation-categorization provides a potential explanation for both the extensive increase in neocortical surface area in humans and our amazing abilities that seem to be uniquely human—we are better at categorizing situations, better at learning the causal structure of the world (what leads to what), and better at abstracting this information. A more complex categorization of the world would lead to an improved ability to generalize from one situation to another and an improved ability to modify what worked in one situation for use in another. However, this also provides a potential explanation for those cognitive diseases and dysfunctions that are uniquely human, such as the paranoia and incorrect causal structure seen in schizophrenic delusions[74]—our ability to recognize the complexity of the world can lead us to find conspiracies and interactions that might not actually be present.

In a sense, the situation-recognition system is learning the structure of the world. It learns what remains constant in a given situation and what changes. It learns what leads to what. This has sometimes been referred to as *semantic* knowledge,[75] the facts about our world, our place in it, the stories we tell ourselves. Semantic knowledge in humans includes both the categorization of the features of the world (*that's a chair, but that's a table*), facts about the world (*this table is made of wood*), and the narrative structure we live in (*I have to go home so that my family can eat dinner together tonight*). This semantic knowledge forms the inputs to our action-selection systems. Changing that knowledge changes the causal structure that leads to expectations (*a rustle in the brush predicts a lion*, Pavlovian action-selection), the expected consequences of our actions (*too much alcohol will get you drunk*, Deliberative), and the set of situations in which we react (*stop at a red light*, Procedural). We'll explore this system and how changing it changes our decisions in depth in Chapter 12.

Motivation

Finally, we need a motivational system, which includes two important components: first, *What are the goals we need to achieve?* (we want to take different actions if we're hungry or if we're thirsty) and second, *How hard should we be working for those goals?* (how thirsty we are will translate into how desperate we are to find water). We will see that both of these issues are related to the concept of value that we first looked at in Chapter 3.

Historically, these issues have been addressed through the reduction of innate "drives."[76] But what creates those drives? Some motivations certainly exist to maintain our internal homeostatic balance,[L] but people often eat when they are not hungry. Why?

[L] Homeostasis is the maintenance of an internal parameter at a given level. For example, mammals are warm-blooded and try to maintain their temperature at a given level. When cold, we shiver, wrap ourselves up in warm clothes, or seek heat sources. When hot, we sweat, pant, or seek pools to swim in.

To understand this, two additional concepts need to be taken into account—first, that of *intrinsic reward functions*[77] and second, that of the role of *learning* in value calculations.[78]

Our complex decision-making system evolved because animals who made better decisions were more able to survive and to find better mates, were more likely to procreate, and were more likely to have offspring that survived themselves.[79] But there is nothing in this process that requires that the proximal reasons for decisions be related to any of these evolutionary goals. Instead, what evolution tends to do is find goals that are correlated with these factors. For example, an animal that lived in an environment where food was scarce would be less likely to starve and more likely to survive if it ate whenever food was available, whether it was hungry or not.[80] But what happens when these intrinsic processes no longer track survival? What would happen to a species that had evolved to eat whenever food was available but was now faced with an overabundance of food? It would get fat, and new diseases, such as diabetes, would appear.[81]

We can see examples of how intrinsic reward functions correlated to evolutionary success can get corrupted in many animals and many situations. Dogs love to chase large game (e.g., deer, moose, elk). They do this because that was how they got their food—that was their evolutionary niche. Domestic dogs chase cars. It is pretty clear that if a dog ever caught a car, it would not be able to eat it. But they chase cars for the sake of the chase. In humans, the classic example is pornography. Men like looking at pretty women because being attracted to a beautiful woman helped them judge who would be the best mates,[M] but reading *Playboy* or watching Internet porn is not going to help men find better mates. In fact, one could easily imagine an argument that these nonreproductive options impair the ability to find better mates.

So, yes, we have drives that are directly related to evolutionary success (hunger, thirst, sex), and we have intrinsic reward functions that are correlated to evolutionary success (chasing prey, an attraction to beauty). But there is also a learned component to motivation in mammals. This learned component can be seen both in generalized increases (or decreases) in arousal and in specific increases or decreases in the willingness to work for a given reward.

Does this learning component also occur in humans? Actually, this is one of the best-established effects in drug addicts: seeing the paraphernalia for their drug of choice leads to craving for that drug and an increase in actions leading to taking that drug.[85] Marketing symbols (Coke, McDonald's) increase our internal perceptions of thirst or hunger and make people more likely to go get a soda or a hamburger.[86] These are all examples of the motivational system driving other action systems.

[M] There's now pretty good evidence that many (but not all) standards of beauty actually correlate with health and fertility (for both men and women). Of course, this is just another example of an intrinsic reward function—certain features (such as a specific breast-to-waist-to-hip ratio, symmetry of the face) are correlated with fertility, so people are attracted to those features.[82] These features signal health and fertility and we call people with those features "beautiful." Of course, in humans, having successful children who succeed at having their own children is much more complex than simple health,[83] which may be why humans find other humans with intelligence and talent (such as musicians) particularly attractive.[84]

Motivation is a complex phenomenon related to the complexity of evaluation. It depends on intrinsic functions that we have evolved as animals.[87;N] Motivation can also be modified through an interaction between the emotional, Pavlovian systems and the other, more complex decision-making systems (Deliberative, Procedural).

Summary

Behavioral decision-making occurs as a consequence of a number of different, inter-acting systems. We have identified four action-selection systems (Reflex, Pavlovian action-selection, Deliberative, Procedural) and four support systems (taking the physi-cal action, perception, situation-recognition, motivation). One of the remarkable things that has occurred over the past several decades is the convergence of different fields on these multiple decision-making systems. A number of fields have been examining how different agents interact with each other and with the world (e.g., human psychol-ogy and psychiatry, animal learning theory, robotics and control theory, artificial intel-ligence, and neuroscience, including both computational modeling and the new fields of neuroeconomics and computational psychiatry).[91]

One of the things that motivated me to write this book has been the observa-tion that these different fields seem to be converging on a similar categorization of decision-making systems. Even the debates within the fields are similar—for example, *Is the value calculation within the search-based (Deliberative) and cached-action (Procedural) systems separate or unitary?*[92] (I have argued here and elsewhere that they are separate, but the issue is far from settled.)

For example, roboticists have come to the conclusion that one needs multiple levels of decision-making systems—fast, low-level, hardwired systems (don't bump into walls; a Reflex system), as well as slower, search processes (slow but flexible; a Deliberative system), and fast, cached-action processes (fast but inflexible; a *Procedural* system).[93]

Computer scientists studying artificial intelligence and computational neuroscien-tists trying to model animal decision-making have identified these systems in terms of their expectations—*Pavlovian* systems create an expectation of an outcome and lead to unconditioned actions related to that outcome; *Deliberative* systems search through potential futures, produce an expectation of the outcome, and evaluate it; *Procedural* systems directly evaluate actions in response to specific situations.[94]

Similarly, learning theorists working in the fields of psychology and animal-learning identify three systems.[95] First, there is a stimulus–outcome system in which uncon-ditioned reactions associated with outcomes get transferred from being done in response to the outcome to being done in response to the stimulus. (Think Pavlov's dogs salivating in response to a cue that predicts food reward.) Second, they identify an action-outcome system in which animals learn what outcomes will occur if they take a given action. These actions are taken to achieve that expected outcome. Third, they

---

[N] One of the things we will see at the very end of this book (Chapters 22 to 24) is evidence that part of human morality arises because we are social creatures who have evolved to live in large societies,[88] with intrinsic motivation functions based on enforcing cooperation.[89] As Aristotle said, "we are political animals."[90]

identify a stimulus–response or stimulus–action system in which actions are taken in response to a stimulus. The second and third systems can be differentiated by revaluation and devaluation experiments, in which the value of the outcome is changed online. (Remember our example of the rat deciding whether or not to push the lever to get food that it didn't like anymore.)

So where does that leave us? We have identified four action-selection systems and four support systems. Although these systems are separable in that different brain structures are involved in each of them, they also must interact in order to produce behavior. (The analogy brought up earlier was that of the electrical and gasoline systems in a hybrid car.) Each of these systems is a complex calculation in its own right and will require its own chapter for full treatment. In the rest of this part of the book, we will explore each of these components, the calculations they perform, and their neural substrates, and we will begin to notice potential failure points within them. Let's start with the simplest action-selection system, the reflex.

Books and papers for further reading

- Matthijs A. A. van der Meer, Zeb Kurth-Nelson, and A. David Redish (2012) Information processing in decision-making systems. *The Neuroscientist*, 18, 342–359.
- Yael Niv, Daphna Joel, and Peter Dayan (2006) A normative perspective on motivation. *Trends in Cognitive Sciences*, 10, 375–381.
- Mortimer Mishkin and Tim Appenzeller (1987) The anatomy of memory. *Scientific American*, 256 (June), 80–89.

7

Reflexes

The geography of the shell
remembers swimming,
the slow expansion and contraction of centuries,
the memory of a distant shore,
now only open sea.

A reflex is a decision-making system because it includes taking an action. A reflex entails a simple response to a stimulus based on a rule learned over long, evolutionary timescales. Although reflexes can change within a lifespan, those changes are either predetermined genetically (as animals change from children to adults) or entail only very simple learning processes (limited primarily to habituation and adaptation effects).

The reflex is the simplest decision-making system. It entails a simple rule-based reaction. In a sense, the thermostat is a reflex. When it is too hot, the thermostat turns on the air conditioning; when it is too cold, the thermostat turns on the heat. In animals, a reflex rule is prewired into the agent, presumably genetically. This means that we can imagine the rule as being learned over evolutionary timescales. Animals that had appropriate responses (pull your hand away from a burning painful stimulus) were more likely to survive and to have children that survived. But fundamentally, the key to a reflex is the simplicity of the rule and its prewired nature.[1]

The advantages of a reflex are (1) that it can respond very quickly and (2) because it has been learned over evolution, it is present from the beginning in an animal and the animal can react correctly the first time it encounters the stimulus. You don't have to learn to pull your hand away from a hot stove. (You really should learn not to touch the hot stove in the first place. But that's a different system.)

Reflexes are simple things—sensory neurons recognize the stimulus, and these neurons connect either directly or through one or more intermediate neurons to action-taking neurons that drive the muscles.[2] With vertebrates, this generally takes place in the spinal cord because the faster the system can act, the better the reflex evolutionarily. Remember, reflexes are responding to stimuli already present. That is, your hand is being burned. The longer you wait, the more damage is being done to your tissues. Having the responding neurons be as close as possible to the stimulus allows the system to react quickly. Taking the message up to the brain takes time.

Myelinated nerve fibers carry action potentials at a speed of 150 meters per second.[A] Given that the distance from your hand to your head is about a meter, the journey from your hand to your head and back could take 14 milliseconds. Given that your fingers are being burned, that's 14 milliseconds you don't have. (Imagine how long it would take a signal to go from the foot to the brain of a giraffe or from the tail to the head of a blue whale.) Reflex responses therefore tend to be located in the spinal cord, which is closer to the action.

Reflexes could be simple connections between a sensory neuron and a motor neuron, or even a sensory neuron and the muscle itself. But, in practice, most reflexes have intermediate neurons between the sensor and the motor.[4] An interesting question is why there is often an intermediate stage within the reflex, given that the time between detection and response is so precious. The presence of intermediate neurons provides additional stages at which higher, more complex decision-making systems can step in to change the responses.[5] This is how we can prevent reflexes from acting if we want. Think, for example, of that scene in *Lawrence of Arabia* we talked about in Chapter 6. Normally, Lawrence would respond by reflexively dropping the match or shaking it out when the flame reaches his fingers, but with his indomitable will, Lawrence refuses to let his reflexes react and holds the match steady. The presence of intermediate neurons allows more controls for the other systems to manipulate, but it also increases the time it takes the decision to go from sensor to action. Some reflexes do not include intermediate neurons, while other reflexes have several stages of intermediate neurons.[6]

Classic examples of reflexes are the fleeing reflexes like the wind-sensors in insects and the crossover oculomotor turning neurons (visual [oculo-] to motor) in the goldfish.[7] Insects such as crickets and cockroaches have a set of very small hairs on antennae on their tails. Each hair can be blown by the wind but can only move in a single direction, back and forth. This means that the amount that the hair moves depends on the direction of the wind—wind that is aligned with the hair will move it the most; wind that is off by 90 degrees will move it the least. These hairs (wind-sensors) project to four interneurons that represent the four cardinal directions (ahead, back, left, right). These interneurons project to the leg-muscle control structures and make the animal turn away from that wind. Why does the insect have this highly evolved wind-response reflex? Because it can flee from a stomping shoe in less than 20 milliseconds.

A similar system exists in goldfish connecting the recognition of visual signals on one side with a sudden turn to the other. A goldfish can identify that there is a looming signal (such as a goldfish-eating predator, like a diving bird) and start to turn away in less than 20 milliseconds. Goldfish can hit speeds of 22 body lengths per second within

---

[A] Neurons communicate information by sending spikes or action potentials along their output axons. A nerve fiber (such as the ones that connect your spinal cord to the brain) is just a bunch of axons all lining up in the same direction. The speed of travel of these action potentials along a nerve fiber depends on several properties, including whether or not the axons are surrounded by myelin, a form of glial "helper" cells.[3]

about 10 milliseconds of movement initiation. That's incredibly fast! Presumably, this remarkable reflex evolved because the goldfish and the diving bird are in an arms race to see who is the fastest, the hungry bird or the fleeing goldfish.

Reflexes can, and, of course, do change within a single lifetime. (Animals have life-cycles—tadpoles and frogs presumably need very different reflexes to survive in the very different environments they inhabit.) But these changes are themselves prewired into development. Human babies, for example, have a foot reflex called the Babinski reflex, where the toes curl and splay in a specific pattern in response to stroking of the bottom of the foot. The reflex is entirely normal (and is used as a check for intactness of the spinal cord) in infants. With development of the corticospinal tract (connections from the cortex in the brain to the spinal cord), the reflex disappears. In adults, a Babinski reflex indicates spinal cord damage, decoupling the cortical input from the base of the spinal cord.[8]

The problem with reflexes is their inflexibility. Reflexes are learned on an evolutionary timescale; they are prewired, genetically, into the creature. Although reflexes do change in response to repeated stimuli, the mechanisms of these changes are not particularly complex, and the potential changes are very limited. These effects have been most famously studied in detail in the aplysia gill-withdrawal reflex.[9] An aplysia is a kind of sea slug, with a broad, thin gill floating out of its back. (Imagine a snail with no shell and a pair of silk fans.) It uses this gill to breathe oxygen out of the water. But, of course, this gill is fragile and easily damaged. Imagine the aplysia in the water: the waves pick up and the aplysia pulls its gill in. But if the waves are going to be large for a long time and not get worse, then it needs to open out again. The aplysia can learn to ignore a repeated stimulus (that is, it can habituate). However, even these potential changes are prewired. For example, the gill-withdrawal reflex in the aplysia can increase its response to certain stimuli (that is, it can sensitize), but these changes are due to prewired connections between specific neurons.

Even simple prewired reactions and potential changes can produce extremely complex behavior if the changes interact with the environment appropriately. Examples of the complexity that can be built out of simple circuits without memory or explicit representation can be found in Valentino Braitenberg's delightful book *Vehicles*. Nevertheless, this inflexibility means that in the competitive game of evolution, reflexes can get an animal only so far.

While evolution can move populations pretty quickly (on the order of a couple of generations),[B] reflexes are not being learned within a single lifetime.[11] To learn to respond differently to different situations, one needs to turn to one of the other decision-making systems.

[B] A wonderful example of the speed of evolutionary change moving phenotypes within populations is the black and white moths that changed their distributions in response to smog in industrial England, where a population of peppered moths changed from being mostly white to mostly dark as coal pollution darkened the skies and trees of England in the late 1800s, and then changed from being mostly dark back to mostly white as the pollution was controlled.[10] More detailed examples of how quickly evolution can change populations can be seen in the studies by Rosemary and Peter Grant measuring the shape and length of beaks of finches in the Galapagos Islands. The Grants' finch studies are described in detail in Jonathan Wiener's *The Beak of the Finch*.

Books and papers for further reading

Because the reflex is so well understood, it is well described in many medical and neuroscience textbooks, such as

- Dale Purves et al. (2008) *Neuroscience.* Sunderland, MA: Sinauer Associates.

A thorough review of the remarkable escape reflexes can be found in

- Robert C. Eaton (1984) *Neural Mechanisms of Startle Behavior* New York: Springer-Verlag.

A delightful book showing how complex prewired reactions can be is

- Valentino Braitenberg (1986) *Vehicles: Experiments in Synthetic Psychology* Cambridge, MA: MIT Press.

Emotion and the Pavlovian Action-Selection System

see with your eyes
until they are hands
hands that feel
hands that hold other hands
hands that touch the heart

The Pavlovian action-selection system consists of response sets evolved to prepare for critical species-specific behaviors such as feeding, fighting, or mating. Learning in the Pavlovian action-selection system entails recognition that one thing likely causes another, leading to taking the response set appropriate for that expected outcome. Linguistically, we categorize these response sets and identify them as emotions. In humans, many of these response sets are important to social interactions.

Although not usually thought of in terms of action-selection, emotions are an action-selection mechanism.[1] Each emotion is a *response set* that has been learned over genetic timescales to be useful. For example, in dangerous situations, depending on emotional characterizations of the situation, one becomes afraid and one's body prepares to flee, to stand and fight, or to submit, sometimes referred to as the fight-or-flight response (or more accurately, the fight–flight–freeze response).

There is a debate going on in the scientific community as to whether the categorization process of what we consciously label as emotions is consistent between individuals.[2] These questions turn more on the issue of our conscious labels of emotions rather than the physical effect of those emotions—no one denies that anger prepares you for fighting, but other emotions (such as fear) also prepare you for fighting. Even though a given situation might make one person angry and another afraid, animals (including humans) have self-consistent response sets to consistent situations. We will return to the relationship between these response sets and emotion later in this chapter.

The advantage of having a system with these response sets is that there is a complex of body-related internal actions that need to work correctly the first time. You don't get a chance to learn to run from the lion. You can learn that a rustle in the grass likely means that a lion is stalking you. And so you can learn to run from the rustle in the grass. In fact, you can learn that a rustle in the grass means a lion is stalking you even without being stalked. You could learn it from observing a lion stalking another animal, or you could learn it from hearing a vivid story by the fire, or some other way. In any case, what you've actually learned is that lions stalking prey produce a rustle in the grass. So when you hear the rustling, you realize there's a lion, and you have the same emotional response as if a lion suddenly appeared in front of you.

What is needed is a system that can recognize the danger and implement all of the body changes quickly, all at once. That system is the Pavlovian action-selection system, in which a genetically learned action occurs in response to a given situation based on an emotional characterization of it (*I like it, I will approach it. I am afraid of it, I will run away from it. I am angry at it, I will attack it. I have nowhere to run, I will freeze in fear and hope that it won't kill me*).[3]

In classical psychology experiments, Pavlovian learning is described as what is learned when the animal does not have to take an action in order to get the outcome—famously, a bell is rung and the food is delivered, or a light is turned on and then the subject is given a small shock.[4] There is nothing the animal has to do or can do to change these events. In practice, the animal does things to prepare for the expected outcome[5]—the dog salivates, the rat freezes.

At one time it was assumed that the animal was learning that cues co-occur; however, we now know that Pavlovian conditioning entails recognition of informative contingencies—animals learn that when a cue is present, certain things are more likely to happen. An ever-present cue is not informative.[6] Animals can even learn that certain cues predict that an event will not occur. As the lion example at the start of this chapter shows, we are learning that a cue predicts an outcome. (Pavlov's bell worked this way as well—the bell was rung and then the dog was fed.) Stated in this way, the learning part of Pavlovian action-selection is that a stimulus (rustle in the grass, ringing a bell) predicts an outcome (a lion is stalking you, food is coming). From that prediction, you can take the appropriate action (run!, salivate).

When studied in classical psychology experiments, the action-selection part of the Pavlovian action-selection system is often seen as species-specific behavioral responses and approach or avoidance responses,[7] but the largest changes are in fact somatic—changes in the body itself.[8] In response to fear, for example, the heart rate increases (as does the force of each heartbeat) to move more blood to the muscles, the airways in the lungs dilate to allow more oxygen, and a host of other responses occur that prepare an animal to either fight or run. Attention increases, increasing the ability to sense stimuli.

One of the best ways to measure an animal's fear is to measure the startle responses in a given situation. A surprising sound literally makes the animal jump; under conditions of increased anticipation of danger (fear), the animal will jump higher. By measuring the force of the muscles when the animal jumps, one can quantitatively measure its preparedness for action, and its fear.[9]

One does, of course, see the same effects in humans. One time, when I was first setting up my lab, I was worried about whether I could safely plug in a very expensive computer part without turning the computer off first. (The computer was in the process of running a very long computation and I didn't want to disturb it, but I needed to access that part.) The evening before, a new Zip drive (a kind of specialized portable drive before USB flash drives were available) had caught fire and burned out at my house (with beautiful blue sparks), so I was reasonably nervous about plugging in this very expensive part. I expressed my concern to the lab, and decided that I should be the one to plug it in so that if something went wrong, it would be my fault. While I was nervously waiting to plug the part in, unbeknownst to me, one of my grad students had snuck up behind me. The instant I plugged the part in, my student whispered "bzzzzt!" in my ear. I must have jumped three feet in the air.

Another related effect in humans is that we tend to sweat when we are emotionally aroused.[10] Because sweat is basically salt water, it conducts electricity, and this is measurable by an increase in skin conductance. Even very subtle changes are detectable as a change in the conductivity of the skin. These changes are known as the *galvanic skin response* (GSR) or the *skin-conductance response* (SCR) and are a surprisingly reliable measure of emotional arousal.

Neurophysiologically, these responses are controlled by small bundles of neurons[A] in the base of the brain, called the hypothalamus,[B] and by structures at the top of the spinal cord, particularly the periaqueductal gray[C] and the amygdala.[D]

These brain structures interact with the rest of the body through a feedback loop between the hypothalamus in the brain and organs in the body via hormones circulating in the blood. The hypothalamus sends information to (and receives signals from) a structure called the pituitary gland, which is a collection of hormone-releasing and hormone-sensing cells that translate neural signals to and from hormonal signals.[12] This pathway from brain to body is actually a complete loop that includes signals from the hormones to the rest of the brain as well. Neurons in the brain are cells and thus require nutrients, which they get from blood.[E] These hormones (such as adrenaline,

---

[A] These small bundles are called "nuclei," not to be confused with the nucleus of the cell. The word *nucleus* (from the Latin word for "kernel" or "nut") just means a central concentration. In an atom, the nucleus (from which we get "nuclear bombs" and "nuclear physics") is the central concentration of particles. In a cell, a nucleus is the central repository for DNA. And in the brain, a nucleus is a concentration of cells that forms an anatomically identifiably separable object.

[B] *Hypo* (below) + *thalamus* (another part of the brain).

[C] A small structure of gray matter (neuronal cell bodies) surrounding a pocket of cerebral spinal fluid at the base of the brain (*periaqueductal*—near the aqueduct). The periaqueductal gray sits on the path of the spinothalamic tract, where cells in the spinal cord send information up to the thalamus and thalamic cells send information back down to the spinal cord.

[D] A small nucleus (kernel) of cells located between the orbitofrontal cortex and the ventral striatum, shaped like an almond. *Amygdala* is the Latin word for almond.

[E] Actually, the mammalian brain has an intermediate stage between the blood and the brain made of a kind of glial cells that filter chemicals in the blood so that only certain chemicals can transfer from the blood to the brain. The capillaries are surrounded by extra-tight walls made of these glial cells to prevent large things (like bacteria!) from getting through. This is referred to in medical textbooks as the *blood–brain barrier* and is one of the reasons that certain drugs primarily affect the body, while other drugs primarily affect the brain. Many of the hormones that we're talking about do translate across the blood–brain barrier, but others don't. The blood–brain barrier is weaker in parts of the brain where these hormone-releasing and hormone-sensing structures live (like the pituitary) and in areas where external chemical signals need to reach the brain (such as the olfactory sensors in the nose).

testosterone, estrogen, and glucocorticoids) can dramatically affect neural function, and even neural structures.[13] The brain is tightly coupled to the rest of the body through these neural–hormonal interactions.

Interestingly, one of these hormone-releasing glands that connect the brain to the body is the pineal gland, which was the specific brain structure that the philosopher René Descartes (1596–1650) identified as the connection between the body and the soul.[14] Descartes argued that animals were machines, but humans are not because humans have a soul. Descartes argued that the connection between the body and the soul lay in the pineal gland. This hypothesis (that the soul and body are different things) is called *dualism*, and is generally phrased in the modern era in terms of a hypothesis that the mind and body are different things. Of course, as everyone who has studied anatomy knows (including Descartes, who was an exceptional anatomist, well familiar with both human and nonhuman anatomy[15]), all mammals have pineal glands.[16] We will return to this discussion at the end of the book, when we directly address dualist and materialist philosophies.

An attentive reader may be wondering at this point in our discussion of "emotion" where exactly is the *emotion*? Anger, jealousy, lust, fear, happiness, sadness—these are *feelings*; they are more than a body's response to stimuli. Emotions are more than the fight-or-flight response. The answer lies in the fact that we have also developed a mechanism for monitoring these bodily responses, and we have a mechanism for categorizing them.[17]

William James[F] (1842–1910) and Carl Lange (1834–1900) first proposed that emotions were a connection between the mind and the body.[18] Everyone knows that when we get angry, our heart rate increases and our capillaries dilate to allow more blood to our muscles, which makes us flush and actually heats our skin. As pointed out by George Lakoff and Mark Johnson in their discussion of languages, the metaphors that we use for describing emotions reflect the actual bodily changes occurring during those emotions.[19]

As was mentioned when I introduced the *situation-recognition* system (Chapter 6), I suspect that the cortex is one big categorization machine. (A computational discussion of the mechanisms of categorization can be found in Appendix C. As discussed therein, the interaction between these categorization processes and reality produces categories that are often similar but can diverge between individuals. The fact that not everyone agrees on the specific boundaries of these categories does not imply that there is not a species-based set of responses that are categorized similarly between individuals.) If we applied this categorization machinery to our internal, visceral sensory system (*How fast is your heart beating?*), we would categorize these Pavlovian responses. Different parts of the cortex receive different inputs and categorize different aspects—visual cortex is processing visual input because it receives input from the retina (via the thalamus); auditory cortex is processing auditory input because it receives input from the cochlea (again via the thalamus and other structures). Is there a cortical area that receives input from the hypothalamus, that can recognize these internal states, something that receives visceral inputs?

[F] William James is the older brother of the novelist Henry James, who was, one has to say, well acquainted with emotions.

Anatomically, that part of the brain is the *ventromedial prefrontal cortex*,[G] sometimes known as the *orbitofrontal*[H] cortex, but also including the *insula*.[I] These neurons receive input from the body to both represent and control the emotional bodily states, a process referred to as *interoception*.[21] This localization of emotional processing was initially discovered by studying patients who had damaged prefrontal cortices.[22] These ventral prefrontal cortices have the necessary anatomical connectivity, are known to be active during decision-making (as evidenced by fMRI), and play an important role in decision-making (as evidenced by lesion studies).[23]

The most famous of these patients was Phineas Gage, a railroad worker who in 1848 had a tamping iron (a 13-pound, 3-foot-long, 1.25-inch-diameter cast-iron rod) blasted through his skull. His job was to tamp (pack) down the blasting powder before it was set off. Unfortunately, the process of tamping it down set it off and drove the iron stick through his skull. Remarkably, Gage survived; even more remarkably, he recovered from his injuries and lived for an additional dozen years.[24] Gage had surprisingly specific if complex deficits from his injuries—his physical and sensory abilities, his language and intellectual abilities, his ability to perceive the world, his memory, and his ability to take action were all intact. What changed, however, was his personality and his ability to make decisions. Reconstructing the path of the iron bar through a brain sized to match Phineas Gage's suggests a complete destruction of the prefrontal part of the brain, including both ventral and dorsal aspects. The dorsal prefrontal cortex seems to be involved in the ability to plan, while the ventral prefrontal cortex seems to be involved in the ability to recognize emotions.[25] If both of these were damaged, Gage's ability to make decisions, particularly intelligent ones, would have been severely compromised.

Literature has often described the difference between humans and robots as emotional—humans have emotion, robots don't. From *Star Trek*'s Data, who spends his life wishing he had the emotional interactions that his colleagues do, to the replicants in Ridley Scott's *Blade Runner* (and in Phillip K. Dick's original source book *Do Androids Dream of Electric Sheep?*, which is a much better title), who are identifiable through their lack of an emotional response, literature has identified the unemotional as "robotic." In fact, in *Blade Runner/Do Androids Dream of Electric Sheep?*, the replicants are only identifiable by the fact that when they look at emotional pictures, their eyes do not dilate. In *Descartes' Error*, Antonio Damasio follows the description of Phineas Gage with a description of a modern patient (referred to as "Elliot") with known damage to the ventral prefrontal cortex (confirmed by structural MRI),[J] who has a specific deficit in

---

[G] *Ventro* (toward the base) + *medial* (toward the middle) + *prefrontal* (in front of the front). These structures are referred to as "pre"-frontal because other anatomists had already named parts of nonhuman animal brains as "frontal," and the anatomists studying human brains wanted to identify an area that was even more frontal than the other primate brains. The extent to which nonhuman mammals, such as monkeys and rats, have "pre"-frontal cortex is a subject of much debate.[20]

[H] *Orbito* (near the eyes—from the word *orbit*, meaning the circular bone around the eyes) + *frontal*.

[I] *Insula*, from the Latin word for "island," because it sits deep in the folds of the human cortex.

[J] Structural MRI uses a similar technology to the more well-known functional MRI (fMRI) to measure the size of gray matter (neuronal bodies) and white matter (neuronal wiring—primarily axons and glial support structures [myelin]) in the brain. Because these areas are not changing, it is possible to get very accurate pictures of the structure of a brain with structural MRI.[26]

emotion. Like the replicants in *Blade Runner*, this patient was blind to emotion: unable to process feeling, to recognize it, or to show it. In situations where emotions are all but inevitable, Elliot showed no reaction. Damasio quantified this by measuring skin conductance, and found that Elliot's skin conductance was completely flat.

How does emotion relate to decision-making?

Historically, philosophers have suggested that there are two decision-making systems, an emotional (hot) decision-making system and a cognitive (cold) system. This hypothesis can be traced back to Plato, who described the human as a charioteer driving two horses, one well behaved and always doing the right thing, and the other wild and hard to control.[27;K] St. Augustine describes two souls, one living in the City of Man, connected to the animals, filled with emotion, lust, and anger, and the other in the City of God, separated from the animals, filled with reason and deliberation.[29] (The inherent dichotomy of this is embodied in the wonderful line from Augustine's *Confessions*: "Make me chaste, O Lord, but not today."[30])

Freud's theory of the unconscious follows this same dichotomy. Freud proposed that there were three components, the *id*, the *ego*, and the *super-ego*.[31] This tracks Plato's three beings in the chariot—the wild horse that needs to be held in check (the id), the angelic horse trying to lead one to reason (the super-ego), and the charioteer trapped in the middle (the ego). Much of modern psychiatry still remains within this dual-system[L] hypothesis, based in large part on Freudian concepts of the unconscious. It is, of course, as we have seen, fundamentally wrong. You are not separate from your emotional self, nor are you a charioteer driving two other decision-makers; you are the sum of all of your decision-making systems.

Modern dual-process theories argue for a separation between an unconscious, impulsive (Dionysian) system and a conscious, executive-function (Apollonian) system.[32] The typical analogy presented is that of a horse and rider, although some authors refer to this as an elephant and its rider. In this analogy, you are the rider trying to steer the horse (or the elephant), but the horse (elephant) has a mind of its own and sometimes goes its own way.

Translating these dual-process theories into our four action-selection systems suggests that the conscious being you are is the Deliberative system, while the Reflexive, Pavlovian, and Procedural systems are nonconscious. Even if we assume that there are multiple nonconscious systems, this multiple-process theory suggests that the conscious self struggles to control the other systems. This differentiation between the noncognitive

---

[K] This is a great example of the homunculus fallacy, in which the decision-maker is seen as a little person (a "homunculus") controlling a separate body or decision-making system.[28] The problem, as pointed out by Daniel Dennett in the 1980s, is that someone will then need to explain what controls that driver, leading to an infinite regress. One of the points of this book is that you are your brain—there is no separate homunculus driving; you are all of these decision-making systems, interacting with each other.

[L] The fact that this is always referred to as a "dual-system" hypothesis emphasizes the danger of the homunculus fallacy—dual-system theories forget that Plato's two horses require a driver.

(unconscious) other and the cognitive (conscious) self requires that we remove emotion from ourselves and place it in the "other" box. I don't know about you, but I have always felt (an emotional word!) that my emotions are a critical part of who I am.

Separating the cognitive "self" and the noncognitive "other" also requires that we separate out the Procedural (habit, cached-action) system as part of the "other." The Procedural system is not emotional in any sense of the word—it is a simple storage of stimulus–response pairs and response–response action chains. Instead of the two processes inherent in dual-process theory (emotional, unconscious, the horse or elephant vs. cognitive self, the rider), we would have to separate three systems (emotional, procedural, self). But, again, the procedural responses are part of us. We will see that these stimulus–response pairs and these action chains are the key to athletes hitting baseballs, making plays, throwing and catching footballs, and making other trained responses. When asked, most athletes talk about coming into themselves, not going out of themselves, when they are "in the zone."

As pointed out by Antonio Damasio in several books, people like "Elliot" with impaired emotional systems do not make normal decisions.[33] In fact, there is now some evidence that people who are psychopathic or sociopathic are calculating and unemotional, making decisions independent of any emotional sensitivity.[34]

When talking about emotions and the role of emotion in decision-making, it is important to note that our memories of the past are reconstructed, rebuilt each time anew and are not necessarily correct. (We will address this issue in depth in our discussions of episodic future thinking, episodic memory, and deliberation in Chapters 9 and 16.) This means that if we took an action based on one of our other systems—for example, because of our Procedural learning system—we may imagine that we took that action because our Deliberative system wanted to, or we may imagine that we took that action because of an emotional response. Although one may remember taking an action "because it felt right,"[35] in fact, the emotional parts of our brain that actually encode "feeling right" might not have been active at all at the time; instead, you may have back-constructed the emotion.[36] This has been explicitly seen in studies of craving and relapse to drug addiction: most addicts will report that they remember an unstoppable craving in the days before relapse, but prospective studies that look at addicts during relapse find that only a small proportion actually show craving.[37;M]

That being said, emotions do play a strong role in our decision-making. Often, situations in the world or situations with our fellow humans produce emotions, which guide our decisions. Emotions can be described as our interpretation of reactive states that have been learned over evolutionary timescales, producing changes in our bodily responses and biasing our actions.

When walking along a dark road at night, sounds begin to make us nervous, and we begin to think we may be seeing things. The developing anxiety enhances our attention to the point where we may even see things that aren't there. I have not gone into depth about perception in this book, in large part because so much is known about it that

---

[M] Prospective studies are, of course, a lot harder to do because they have to look at many more subjects to find the ones who will relapse naturally during the course of study, and because they have to be constructed very carefully so as not to prime those subjects to start craving or to relapse (which would be unethical and would be looking at cued relapse rather than natural relapse).

I would need an additional book to explain it all.[38] Two important concepts, however, are useful here. First, perception is fundamentally an interpretive action.[39] Although our retina responds to light, we do not see "light," we see objects—trees, houses, faces. Although the neurons in our cochlea in our ears respond to sound, we do not hear "sound," we hear voices and music. Illusions occur because the brain's interpretation mechanisms are being tricked and process information incorrectly. Second, perception is fundamentally about detecting signals.[40] This means that one has to make an estimate of whether the perceived set of light signals is a face or something else. When I look at a tree in broad daylight, it's pretty easy to realize that's a tree. But late at night, in the dark, is that a tree waving in the wind or something more sinister?

One time, shortly after we graduated from college, my wife and I were visiting Ireland. We were on the Aran Islands, a very rural part of the westernmost part of Ireland. We were walking back from the pub to the bed-and-breakfast where we were staying. It was pitch black except for the barest of starlight peeking through the quickly moving clouds. Well versed in Irish poetry and Irish myth, it was pretty easy to get spooked by the darkness. By the edge of the road ahead of us, we saw this orange light floating in the air, like a will-o'-the-wisp. There was this smell in the air, like a dog or a wolf. By the time we got to the light, our adrenaline was at full strength and I was ready to jump. As we passed, a young man, sitting on his front stoop, smoking a cigarette, his hand on the head of this big, furry dog, nodded to us, said "Evenin'," and asked us where we were heading. We told him and he said it was about a mile down the road. And we went on, laughing at our emotional interpretations of the floating orange light.

In signal detection, there are two types of errors one can make, false negatives and false positives. A false negative entails not recognizing something that is there, while a false positive entails recognizing something as being there when it is not. Most signal-detecting mechanisms have parameters (gains and thresholds) that can be adjusted to trade off the likelihood for making false-positive errors from false-negative errors.[41] The brain is no exception.

This means that perception, like any signal-detection machinery, has to trade off false negatives (missing something that is there) for false positives (identifying something as being there when it is not). As we become anxious, even frightened, by the dark, our hearts start to pound, our muscles become tense, ready to spring into action, and our attention looks for anything that might demand a response. At the sound of a branch cracking beneath our feet, we might literally jump in the air. (This is *fear-potentiated startle*, which we have seen before.)

Emotions are particularly important for social interactions. Love at first sight may or may not exist, but lust at first sight certainly does. A person who responds to a situation (say catching a cheating spouse) with anger and rage is going to select fundamentally different actions to take than someone who responds to the same situation with sadness and dejection. In a now-classic example, people offered unfair rewards in the ultimatum game[N] show increased activity in the anterior insula (involved in negative emotions) and reject the unfair offer with anger and disgust.[43]

[N] We will discuss the ultimatum game in detail in our discussion of morality. Briefly, the ultimatum game entails two players dividing up a sum of money, say $20. One player gets to make an offer of

(continued)

Studies of emotion have found that not only are many decisions correlated with emotional reactions to the decision itself, but also that unrelated emotional states can affect decisions.[44] Inducing a feeling of anxiety before being faced with a decision makes people less willing to take risks; inducing a feeling of anger makes people less likely to deliberate over decisions and more likely to respond quickly.[45] This observation (that being emotionally frightened, angry, or sexually aroused makes one less likely to deliberate cognitively) is almost certainly where Plato, St. Augustine, and Freud got their dichotomy between emotion and cognition pulling the person in two directions. However, as I hope I've made clear, the interaction is much more complicated than that.

Do animals show emotion?

Emotion is often seen as part of our "animal" heritage, while cognition is seen as a "higher," "more human" decision-making system.[46] As I hope I've shown throughout this book, that's a mistaken dichotomy. Rats deliberate over decisions, and emotions are fundamental to the interactions that make us human. A question that arises, however, is whether animals have emotions and feelings. All pet lovers, particularly those with a mammalian pet (a cat, a dog), will tell you that their pets have feelings, but of course, as we saw in the very beginning of the book, we are notoriously bad at judging the agency of nonhuman creatures. My father is convinced that his GPS gets annoyed when it has to recalculate a route because he missed a turn.° On the other hand, apes who have been taught limited language (such as Kanzi the chimpanzee or Koko the gorilla) are able to express emotions in words.[47] These apes use emotional words in very parallel ways to humans. In his book *The Expression of the Emotions in Man and Animals*, Charles Darwin noted that certain emotional expressions cross cultures and species. Anger, disgust, laughter, joy, sadness: these are all consistent signals across all humans and all cultures.

In fact, as we saw in Chapter 4, these facial expressions are similar across mammals. Kent Berridge and his colleagues studied facial expressions of distaste (in response to bitter liquids) and appeal (in response to sweet liquids) and found similar facial expressions across rats, monkeys, and humans (sticking one's tongue out, making a "yuck" face for bitter and licking one's lips for sweet). Berridge and colleagues were able to show that these expressions are not about taste on the tongue because they could change distaste to appeal and vice versa by manipulating the opioid system in rats.[48]

---

how to split the money, and the other gets to decide whether to take the offer (and both players get the offered split) or to reject the offer (and no one gets anything). Notice that a recipient rejecting an offer is losing money to punish the person splitting the money. This is a phenomenon called "altruistic punishment," because punishing unfair offers leads to more fair societies, but the person punishing the unfair offer has also lost money.[42] We will explore altruistic punishment and its effects on societies in our chapter on morality (Chapter 23).

° Of course, he knows that the GPS is simply using an algorithm for identifying when to recalculate and playing a voice-generation file to report it. (In fact, he could probably program the algorithm.) Nevertheless, our emotional responses to social situations (such as hearing a recorded voice of an exasperated person saying "recalculating") is evolutionarily prewired into our brains.

An interesting question, of course, is where emotion arises in the evolutionary time-line. Do bacteria have emotions? Probably not as we understand them. Do reptiles? Unlikely. Again, scientists have not been able to reliably identify them. Do mammals? Almost certainly. One intriguing proposal put forward by Michel Cabanac, Arnaud Cabanac, and André Parent is that amniotes (mammals, birds, and some reptiles) developed a categorization system that can observe the body's Pavlovian action-selection system and that this categorization system is what we now recognize as emotion.[49] This is consistent with William James' concepts of emotion as actually residing in visceral changes in the body and Antonio Damasio's concepts of emotion as the recognition and memory of bodily responses, which he refers to as the *somatic marker hypothesis*.[50]

Whenever emotions appeared evolutionarily, they are clearly an important part of human decision-making systems. Emotions need to be seen not only as feelings that drive other decision-making components to act, but as action-selection systems in their own right. Emotions interact with our categorization of feelings through visceral changes in the body, which we identify as those same emotions through memory and metaphor: the vigilance of fear, the tension of anger, the heat of lust, the warmth of comfort, the breaking-heart pain of sadness.

Books and papers for further reading

- Antonio Damasio (1994). *Descartes' Error: Emotion, Reason, and the Human Brain.* New York: Quill Press.
- Antonio Damasio (2003). *Looking for Spinoza: Joy, Sorrow, and the Feeling Brain.* New York: Harcourt.
- Joseph E. LeDoux (1996). *The Emotional Brain.* New York: Simon and Schuster.
- George Lakoff and Mark Johnson (2003). *Metaphors We Live By.* Chicago: University of Chicago Press.

9

Deliberation

Swallowing the leaf-green light,
stretching under gravity, tension across
the surface enfolds us into a moment,

until, suddenly,
disturbed by a breath,
we fall.

*Some decisions are made by explicitly imagining the potential conse-
quences of that decision. This imagination process is particularly good
for decisions that cannot be learned slowly over time, or for major
decisions that require a large upfront commitment cost. Deliberation
is a computationally expensive process that requires a number of
neural systems, including attention, imagination, and evaluation processes, and as such takes time to calculate which action to take.*

Deliberation entails the sequential, serial search through possibilities. It entails a prediction of "what would happen if," followed by an evaluation process and an action-selection
process. This means that deliberation requires a host of complex processing. This complex processing makes deliberation incredibly flexible (knowing that a path leads to an
outcome does not imply that one must take that path to that outcome) but also makes
deliberation slow (it takes time to do all that computation).

Deliberation also requires a knowledge of the structure of the world, particularly
the cause–effect structure.[1] (If you can't predict, you can't search through those predictions.) Deliberation requires imagination.[2] Deliberation requires one to be able
to construct possible futures, and a process to know that those potential futures are
imagined and not real.[A] Deliberation also requires an active memory process capable of
remembering what paths you've searched through already and what paths are still left to

---

[A] The inability to differentiate imagination from reality is, of course, a key component of several
psychological disorders (such as schizophrenia).[3]

explore.[4] When comparing options, you need to be able to keep multiple options, their evaluations, and the paths to them in your head. By attending to specific pros and cons, one can even manipulate the evaluation.[5] This requires a process called *working memory*, in which concepts are held in an active processing loop.[B]

The cognitive map and declarative memory

The concept of the cognitive map was introduced by Edward Tolman in the 1930s. Tolman suggested that both rats and humans (and presumably other mammals as well) maintained a "map of possibilities."[11] This meant that learning didn't have to be aimed at getting rewards and avoiding punishments (as suggested by his contemporaries, such as Clark Hull and B. F. Skinner[12]). Tolman's concept implied that it was worth it to an animal to learn information about the world even when that information didn't immediately lead to a reward or punishment. Information about the world could be used in future decisions, making basic information a worthwhile pursuit itself.

In modern neuroscience, the cognitive map is usually described as if it is a spatial map, but Tolman's original concept was more "cognitive" than "map," and more modern interpretations of cognitive maps are closer to the concept of a *schema* about the structure of the world.[13] Certainly, one of the most important things to know about the structure of the world is where things are and how the spatial world is connected. Knowing that there are skyways connecting the building my office is in and the mailroom will be very useful today when it is going to be 2° Fahrenheit outside.[C] But it is also part of the cognitive map to know that one can check books out of a library and therefore one doesn't need to buy them. And to remember a friend's phone number, or that one can call 911 in an emergency (in the United States). Or that Paris is in France and Tokyo in Japan, that New York is on the east coast of the United States and San Diego is on the west coast. All of this knowledge about the structure of the world forms your cognitive map. If you've already learned these facts, you can use them to search through options to find the choice you want to make.

These facts are sometimes referred to as *declarative*[14] because they are things that can be "declared"—if I tell you that Tokyo is the capital of Japan, or that I grew up near

---

[B] *Working memory* keeps ideas, concepts, and results easily accessible for immediate processing. The complexity and the mechanisms that allow working memory are a very large topic and are the subject of multiple books.[6] It is related to the concept of *rehearsal*, where one repeats the thing-to-be-remembered over and over again,[7] and *prospective memory*, where one has to remember to be ready for a future event[8] ("Don't forget the milk"). The capacity of working memory is strongly tied to IQ, mental ability, success in life, and self-control.[9] Recent experiments have suggested that it is possible to train working memory, and that this training has effects on decision-making.[10]

[C] For my metric-using readers, that's –17° Celsius! The University of Minnesota has most of its buildings connected by skyways, bridges between buildings set above the street, usually on the second or higher stories. These skyways are often beautiful, with large glass windows, but they form a complex maze. Some interbuilding connections are above the street, while others are tunnels below the street. If you know the secret passages, you can often get quite a ways across campus without ever going outside.

Washington DC but that I live in Minnesota, you know those facts. You don't need to practice them. In contrast, I can tell you how to throw a baseball or ride a bike or play the piano or clarinet, but to become any good at it, you need to practice them. In the memory literature, these other skills are called *procedural* because they require memories of the process and procedures rather than facts.

Declarative memory is often divided into two subcategories: *semantic* memory and *episodic* memory.[15] Semantic memory entails the facts and knowledge about the structure of the world. Episodic memories are the memories of your own life. The statement that at my sixth birthday party, my parents made me a cake in the shape of a rotary-dial telephone is a semantic memory. My memory that my dad said I had to wait to get the last piece because my initials were in the center (presumably trying to teach me to be polite and let my guests have cake first), and that I snuck my finger in and ate off the initials while my dad was serving a piece to someone, and then demanded a piece of cake since I had already got the letters, is an episodic memory.

The key evidence that animals (including humans) use a cognitive map in making decisions is a process called *latent learning*. Learning about the structure of the world may not show up in behavior until one needs to call upon that knowledge. Tolman's initial hypothesis came from observing rats running mazes.[16] Rats with experience on a specific maze (just exploring, with no rewards on the maze) would subsequently learn much faster than rats with no experience on that maze. The experiment that finally convinced Tolman that animals had to remember knowledge about the structure of the world was that a rat (who was neither hungry nor thirsty) who was allowed to explore a Y-shaped maze with food on the left fork and water on the right would immediately go to the left fork when made hungry and to the right fork when made thirsty. For humans, at least, this latent learning is about cause and effect. We recognize this knowledge in terms of if–then rules. If I drop this glass, it will break. If I drop this plastic bottle, it won't. Therefore, it is safer to give a plastic bottle to my three-year-old daughter since she may well drop the glass.

We can think of deliberation as having four parts: the knowledge of the world, the search process using that knowledge of the world to predict what will happen, an evaluation process measuring how good that outcome is, and, finally, an action-selection process to actually take the first step forward.

Search

The first attempts at building artificial decision-making systems were based on search processes.[17] Allen Newell and Herb Simon's *General Problem Solver* (originally proposed in 1957) searched through possibilities to find a path from a starting point to a goal. It was able to create subgoals in the plan, and then solve those subgoals. It worked by searching through potential subgoals and then solved each subgoal by searching through known actions until it was able to find a path from the starting point to the final given goal. Over the past 50 years, a tremendous amount of work has been done improving search algorithms to the point that highly efficient search algorithms can beat humans at complex games (like the now-famous *Deep Blue* that was able to beat the grandmaster Garry Kasparov at chess in 1997).[18;D]

Over the past few decades, however, it has become clear that these highly efficient, optimized search processes are not how human experts solve most of these tasks.[19] Search is something done early in learning and in response to changing situations. The more expertise people gain in a field, the smaller the set of futures they search through. Current theories suggest that this is because experts have cached (stored) the better choices ahead of them.[20] Search requires holding a lot of temporary results in memory and keeping track of a tremendous number of subparts. This means that it is effortful and requires extensive computational processing.[21]

As it became clear that human experts do not solve games like chess by deep searches through long possible paths, it became popular to say that search was uniquely human. These hypotheses suggested that search was difficult to do, that humans could do search when they needed to, but that it required complex cognitive and conscious processes. In particular, these theories suggested that search required a linguistic description of the problem (that people needed to talk to themselves as they searched through those possibilities). This implied that it is a uniquely human characteristic, and that animals wouldn't or couldn't do search.[22]

On the other hand, it had been known for many years that animals could make decisions based on expectations of the outcomes of their actions.[23] Given the simple processes that were hypothesized at the time, it was assumed that these expectations formed from simple associations between the action and the outcome. However, computational studies of decision-making that began to be developed in the past decade led to the realization that those simple associations are insufficient to solve the problem. Although one can solve a one-step decision (approach Cue One when hungry, Cue Two when thirsty) with a simple association (Cue One has food, Cue Two has water), if the recognition of expectations must cross choices (go left, then right, then left again to get to the food), then the only way to solve this is with processes that encode the entire cause-and-effect structure of the situation.[24] Thus, several authors have now suggested that animals are actually doing search-and-evaluate processes under certain conditions.[25]

In 2007, Adam Johnson and I found that neural signals in the rat hippocampus played out representations of future paths at the times when the computational theories predicted that animals would be searching through the future.[26] Hippocampal cells in the rat encode the location of the animal on a maze.[27] This means that if you record from enough cells simultaneously, you can decode that representation.[28] Adam developed a new mathematical technique[29] that allowed us to decode these representations at very fast timescales (cognition happens faster than behavior[30]), and when we looked at movies of that decoded representation over time, we found that sometimes the animal would pause at a difficult decision point and those representations would sweep down the possible paths, first one way and then the other.[E]

[D] Interestingly, although search algorithms seem to be able to reliably beat human players at chess, other games, such as the game of Go, have been much more difficult.

[E] We weren't looking for this. We were actually trying to examine hippocampal representations on a specific maze to compare them with our dorsal striatal recordings from rats running that same maze.[31] But one day, Adam came into my office and said, "Dave, my animals are showing mental time travel!"

(*continued*)

In humans, deliberation depends on the process of imagination, in which one creates a mental image of a potential future.[32] Whether these sequential sweeps of representation down the potential paths ahead of the rat that we saw are the same phenomenon as a human consciously thinking about the future is still an open question, but the neural structures involved match remarkably well. We know, for example, that humans with hippocampal lesions have difficulty imagining the future, and that episodic future thinking in humans produces hippocampal activity as measured by fMRI. In humans, consciously deliberated decisions depend on prefrontal structures coupled to hippocampal systems. In rats, similar prefrontal structures become functionally coupled to hippocampal systems during deliberative decision-making.[33] As we will see in the next section, the same structures (orbitofrontal cortex and ventral striatum [nucleus accumbens], both functionally coupled to the hippocampus) are involved in evaluation processes in both humans and animals.[34]

Evaluation

Current economic and computational neuroscience models of deliberation do not actually do much "deliberation."[F] That is, even the ones that include search processes simply look up the value of that outcome as a single number, expressed in a common currency. Obviously, if you are going to compare two choices (such as eating an apple or an orange), you have to put them onto the same scale so you can compare them. Economic models (and the computer models on which current neuroscience models are based) call this same scale a *common currency*.[37] However, this is not our conscious experience of deliberation; our conscious experience of deliberation is that we evaluate the outcomes in relation to each other.[G]

To put it politely, I didn't believe him; I was deeply incredulous. As we checked and rechecked our findings for possible alternative hypotheses, we were eventually left with the conclusion that our rats were indeed representing possible paths ahead of themselves. This is the fun of science—discovering something completely unexpected. This is captured elegantly in the famous quote usually attributed to Isaac Asimov, "The most important phrase in science is not actually 'Eureka,' but rather 'Hey, that's funny.'"

[F] One exception is the work on race-to-threshold models, which accumulate evidence for individual choices until one of the choices reaches a threshold.[35] Although there is neural evidence for these race-to-threshold models, the evidence tends to come from experiments that include perceptual ambiguity, but which have not incorporated the multiple decision-making systems known to exist. One experiment has looked at the effect of value ambiguity and found evidence for race-to-threshold integration in humans making decisions between equally valued but different foods.[36] We will examine race-to-threshold models in our discussion of the role of perception in decision-making (Chapter 11). An interesting possibility is that evaluation uses the same mechanisms as perception, applied to hypotheses about future internal states.

[G] It is worth taking a digression to talk about introspection and psychology. Introspection is the conscious internal examination of our own mental processes. It has a very long tradition in psychology, going back to the earliest philosophy—the famous dictum was "Know thyself."[38] The problem is that, as we all know (and as much of what this book is about), we are often wrong about our own decision-making processes.[39]

(*continued*)

Introspective and casual observations of the situations where we deliberate over decisions suggest that they tend to be more about difficulties in the evaluation step than the future prediction step. Much of the computational literature has spent its time working on the prediction step of decisions,[44] likely because it arose out of the robotics literature, where one needs to have the robot take each step. But, as noted in the earliest search models (such as Newell and Simon's General Problem Solver), we don't spend our time working out the path to the outcome; instead, we create *subgoals*.[45]

For example, if we imagine a person with two job offers, the action needed is simple— send an email to one job saying "yes" and another to the other job saying "sorry." This might engender a long series of subsequent actions (signing a contract, finding a house, moving), but our hypothetical applicant doesn't need to consider how to get to the job in order to evaluate the two possibilities, only to know that it is possible to move to wher- ever the job is. The complexity in determining whether subgoals matter is that traversing the subgoal can matter in some conditions, but not others. If I'm deciding whether to take the train or the airplane from Washington DC to New York, getting to either the train station or the airport is easy (they're both on the Metro). However, if I'm consid- ering whether to take the train or the airplane from Baltimore, traversing the subgoal becomes an issue because the train station is in town, while the airport is a long ways out of town. This issue of how to identify when one can skip the subgoal step and when one needs to include it is a complex issue that is the subject of much current research.

Normal psychology (the study of normal mental processing, as compared to "abnormal psychology," the study of mental disorders) arose in the 1800s with the study of perception.[40] These experimental psychologists developed a technique in which they trained themselves to respond to signals quickly, and quantitatively measured how quickly they recognized something (such as a picture of a face).

The psychologists using introspection at the end of the 19th century called themselves *Gestalt* psy- chologists, from the German word *Gestalt*, meaning form or shape, because they believed that they were learning to recognize the overall form or shape of the world. The problem was that they were mea- suring introspective responses. (*How quickly do I recognize this signal?*) With the discovery by Sigmund Freud (1856–1939) that some psychology was unconscious, the conscious-based experiments of the Gestaltists became problematic. (It is important to recognize that the Gestalt experiments were quan- titative [measuring how quickly they responded to a signal], even if they were introspective.) In the early part of the 20th century, these introspective experiments were abandoned for direct measures of behavior, under the guise of behaviorism, which led to the belief that since it was impossible to measure internal cognition, introspection was not good scientific practice.[41] The argument was that we should treat the brain as a black box, since the only thing we can measure is behavior. Of course, as we have seen throughout this book, we can now open the black box and measure things other than behav- ior (such as neural activity; see Appendix B). We can now measure those internal cognitive states.[42] Nevertheless, the problems with introspection remain.

The fundamental problem with introspection, of course, is that, as we saw in Chapter 1, we con- tradict ourselves, we each contain multitudes, and not all of our internal processes are accessible to our consciousness.[43] This doesn't mean that we can't use introspection to guide our scientific hypoth- eses, but we are going to need to check those hypotheses with careful experiments based on direct observations. In psychology, this is called *operationalizing* our hypothesis—the idea is that we can't measure introspective concepts directly, but we can measure behavior (or neural signals). If we can find something that correlates with or differentiates our introspective hypotheses, then we can scientifically study that.

In any case, once we have identified the potential outcomes, we need to evaluate them. That evaluation step is complex, depends on attention to details, and is subject to interesting framing effects.[46] Although the mechanistic process by which we evaluate these multiple noncomparable objects is currently unknown, we know that this process is affected by the other decision-making systems, particularly the emotional system.[47] It's not surprising to anyone who has observed his or her fellow human beings, but tests have shown that your emotional state at the start of a decision can influence your ultimate deliberative decision.[48] At the most trivial level, we can see this in Tolman's original rat experiment—hungry rats went to the food, thirsty rats went to the water.[49] But this also occurs at more complex levels—for example, people who are in an angry or sad mood are more likely to reject offers in trading games.[50]

We also know some of the brain structures involved in these evaluation processes, because we know what happens when these structures break down. Two structures known to be deeply involved in evaluation in general and in deliberative evaluation in particular are the *ventral striatum* and the *orbitofrontal cortex*.[51] The ventral striatum, sometimes called the *nucleus accumbens*, sits at the bottom of the striatum, which is a large, evolutionarily old, subcortical structure.[H] The orbitofrontal cortex sits at the bottom of the front of the cortex, just behind the eyes.[I] When these structures are damaged, people and animals have difficulty evaluating options.[53]

Neural firing in both of these structures relates to value judgments of outcomes. Both structures contain some cells that respond to reward consumption, as well as other cells that respond to cues that predict rewards, and other cells that seem to represent the expected value of an outcome.[54] This has been most explicitly tested in monkeys and rats making economic decisions between objects. For example, Camillo Padoa-Schioppa and John Assad gave thirsty monkeys decisions between two flavors of juices. By varying the amount of juice offered, they could determine how much each juice was worth to the monkey. (*Is one drop of grape juice worth two drops of apple juice?*) What they found is that some cells in the orbitofrontal cortex represented how valuable the apple juice was, other cells represented how valuable the grape juice was, and some cells represented how valuable the choice the monkey made was, translated into a common currency, independent of whether it chose apple or grape juice. Similar effects have been found in humans using fMRI experiments.[55]

Orbitofrontal neurons also reflect framing effects. In tasks where all of the choices are interleaved, the neurons correctly reflect the revealed preference value between the choices.[56] In tasks where the options are given in groups, the cells reflect the valuation

---

[H] *Ventral* means "toward the chest" in Latin and can be contrasted to dorsal, which means "toward the back" in Latin. In animals that run on all fours (quadrupeds, like dogs and cats), the chin of the animal is toward the chest, while the top of the head is toward the back. In humans, because we've stood up (become bipedal), the bottom of the brain is toward the ground and the dorsal part of the brain is toward the sky. Scientists stick to these terms so that they can use the same terminology for the same parts of the brain, such as the dorsal and ventral striatum, which are well conserved between other animals and humans.[52] Think of ventral as toward the bottom of the brain and dorsal as toward the top.

[I] Thus *orbito*, from the "orbit" of the eyes, referring to the circular bone that surrounds the eye, and *frontal*. We encountered the orbitofrontal cortex in our discussion of emotion and Pavlovian action-selection systems (Chapter 8).

between the available options. Leon Tremblay and Wolfram Schultz gave a monkey choices between raisins and apples or apples and cereal. From previous experiments, they knew that the monkey they were recording from preferred raisins to apples and apples to cereal. They found that value-encoding neurons fired very little to the apples in the raisin–apple comparison but a lot to apples in the apple–cereal comparison. In contrast, Camillo Padoa-Schioppa and John Assad did not find these changes to their three juice options, but the Padoa-Schioppa and Assad experiment interleaved the choices, while the Tremblay and Schultz experiment grouped the choices. This grouping is called "blocks" in the jargon of behavioral neuroscience. That is, a subject may receive a block of choices between apple and grape (say for 50 trials) and then another block of choices between orange and banana (say for 50 trials) and then another block of apple and orange... etc. In subsequent experiments, Padoa-Schioppa found that the activity of orbitofrontal cortex neurons depended on exactly this issue—*What is the available menu of choices?* Just like humans making choices between televisions determine the value of the choices relative to the other options,[J] monkeys making choices between foods or juices determine the value of the choices relative to the other options available.

Of course, these preferences can change. If you get sick after eating something, you will learn to dislike that food.[58] (This is why chemotherapy patients are given strange flavors of foods, so that the extreme nausea that chemotherapy induces does not teach them to dislike their favorite foods.[59]) Similarly, overexposure to a given food flavor can produce satiation, and preference for other foods.[60] As an animal changes its preference (say because it gets satiated because it has had enough of the apple juice, or because it has a bad experience after drinking that apple juice), the orbitofrontal cortex neurons change to reflect that changed preference.[61] One of the effects of drugs of abuse, particularly cocaine, is that they disrupt the ability of orbitofrontal cortex neurons to recognize changes in value.[62] Orbitofrontal neurons in animals with extensive cocaine experience do not successfully change valuation when the action that leads to a sweet flavor is changed to now lead to a bitter flavor. Part of the problem with drugs is that they affect the ability of the brain to correctly re-evaluate situations when they change.

In a very interesting recent experiment, Geoff Schoenbaum and his colleagues tested whether rats could recognize a change in the reward that would occur after taking an action[63] (either by increasing the number of food pellets provided, say from one food pellet to three, or by changing the flavor of the food provided, say from banana-flavored to cherry). If the change in value was numeric (that is, changing the size but not the flavor of the reward), the animal needed the ventral striatum intact, but not the orbitofrontal cortex. However, animals needed both the ventral striatum and the orbitofrontal cortex to recognize the change between flavors. This suggests the ventral striatum is key to recognizing changes in valuation, and the orbitofrontal cortex to recognizing changes in commodity.

So the data suggest that these structures are involved in evaluation, but are they active during the evaluation step in deliberation? fMRI data strongly suggest a role for both

---

[J] Remember the television example from Chapter 3. When given a choice between $100, $200, and $300 televisions, people are much more likely to pick the $200 television over the $300 one. But when given a choice between $200, $300, and $400 televisions, people are much more likely to pick the $300 television over the $200 one. This is called *framing*, because the set of choices frames your decisions.[57]

the orbitofrontal cortex and the ventral striatum during some aspect of deliberation.[64] Direct evidence for a role for these neural structures in evaluation during deliberation comes from neural recording data taken by my former postdoc Matthijs van der Meer and by my graduate student Adam Steiner.[65] As we discussed earlier, at certain difficult decisions, rats pause and look back and forth (a phenomenon known as "vicarious trial and error").[66] We have already discussed how, during this process, the hippocampus of rats represents potential choices ahead of the animal, as if the animal was searching down possible paths.[67] When he was in my lab, Matthijs van der Meer recorded from ventral striatal neurons from rats on this same task and found that at the same times that Adam Johnson had found the hippocampus sweeping through those future paths, the ventral striatal reward cells (cells that responded positively during consumption) activated again, as if the ventral striatum was covertly representing something about the fact that the animal would get reward if it went in that direction. Recording orbitofrontal cortex neurons, again, from the same task, Adam Steiner found that orbitofrontal reward cells (cells that responded positively during consumption) also activated, again, as if the orbitofrontal cortex was covertly representing something about the fact that the animal would get reward. One interesting difference we found, however, is that the ventral striatal cells reflected the expectation of reward before the animal turned toward that reward (suggesting involvement in the action-selection), while orbitofrontal cortex cells were active after the animal had already turned toward the reward (suggesting involvement in the prediction of an outcome more than the action-selection).

The evaluation step in deliberation is still an area of active research both in humans and in nonhuman animals. We know some of the structures that are involved, and something about the timing of the mechanisms, but we still don't understand how attention changes the framing of the evaluation process. For example, when comparing cars, imagine trying to decide between a sports car and a minivan or hybrid: one is snazzier, one can carry more, one gets better gas mileage. There is no direct way to compare snazz, size, and gas mileage on a "common currency." Instead, people go back and forth, deliberating between what is important to them, constructing value hypotheses for comparison. In an interesting twist, patients with orbitofrontal cortex damage do not go back and forth between options—instead, they look at one option at a time and determine if it's good enough.[68] It is not known, however, whether this change in strategy occurs because the orbitofrontal cortex actually controls the strategy used or because the orbitofrontal cortex aids in the comparison and the patients recognize that they just aren't very good at doing comparisons. In any case, it is clear that the orbitofrontal cortex is critically involved in comparing options during deliberation.

Action selection

The final step in deliberation, the taking of the action, is still a nearly completely open question. How do people and other animals converge on a decision? Is it a process of simply saying "is that good enough?" after each evaluation? Is it a process where evaluations are held in memory and directly compared? At this point, scientists don't know, but there is some evidence in favor of the comparison hypothesis (that the expected outcome and its evaluation are held in *working memory* and compared with other alternatives).

If deliberation entails predicting future options and comparing them, then you have to remember each option to be able to compare them. Working memory is the ability to hold multiple things in your head at the same time.[69] This would suggest that the effect of taxing working memory would be to make people more inconsistent in their choices—with fewer working memory resources, there is less time to get the deliberation right, and one becomes more likely to give up the search through futures early. This is what the evidence shows.[70] People with better working memory are more willing to wait for later rewards. They are also better at making choices. In fact, it is possible to train working memory and improve some people's ability to wait for delayed rewards.

The advantage of deliberation is that it provides flexibility. Knowing that going to the casino will allow me to gamble does not obligate me to go to the casino. Coupling deliberation with imagination can allow us to make decisions about very complex decisions that we can't (or shouldn't) make lots of times (like which job to take or which college to go to or whom to marry). Coupling deliberation with attention allows us to push ourselves away from choices that we are highly motivated to take (that cigarette) and toward choices that are better for us in the long run (exercising at the gym). The problem with deliberation is that we can get "lost in thought." Like Hamlet, trapped between difficult possibilities, we spend our time predicting outcomes, weighing options, listing pros and cons, and never actually taking action.[71]

Tolman and Hull

I'd like to end this chapter with a short discussion about the history of deliberation and its role in decision-making. The difference between deliberative and habit (what we have called "procedural") decision-making became one of the great scientific debates of our time.[72] In the 1930s and 1940s, two major laboratories were running rats on mazes, trying to determine how they found the goal. (Both of these labs were behaviorists in the sense that they wanted to be quantitative and to operationalize the process of decision-making in animals that they could study with appropriate controls, in response to the introspection of the Gestaltists.) On the East Coast, at Yale University, Clark Hull argued that rats learned to associate stimuli with responses, while on the West Coast, at Berkeley, Edward Tolman argued that rats were cognitive creatures that mentally planned routes to goals. As late as 1970, in a review of this still-ongoing debate, Endel Tulving and Stephen A. Madigan wrote that "Place-learning organisms, guided by cognitive maps in their heads, successfully negotiated obstacle courses to food at Berkeley, while their response-learning counterparts, propelled by habits and drives, performed similar feats at Yale."

We've already seen how latent learning led Tolman to hypothesize the presence of a cognitive map. Tolman also watched his rats learning the maze, and noticed that as they made mistakes, there seemed to be a method to those mistakes—rats would make all left turns, then all right turns, then they would alternate left and right, as if they were actually testing hypotheses.[73] The problem with these observations is that if the rats were just making random choices during learning, then sometimes rats making random choices would take all lefts. (If there are three left–right choices on the maze, then one rat in eight will go left on all three choices even if the rats were really making random choices.) Because our brain likes to find patterns, those rats making all lefts on the three left–right choices would stand out. Similarly, even a rat that knows the correct answer isn't necessarily always going to take that choice. (Maybe there's some noise in the outcome; maybe the animal is exploring to check its hypotheses.) Actually determining when the animal knows the answer is mathematically complicated.[74]

We now have the statistical methods to identify whether these sequences are random,[75] but these complex statistics were not available to Tolman. Randy Gallistel, Stephen Fairhurst, and Peter Balsam used these new statistical analyses to explicitly examine how rats learn and found that (on certain tasks) individual rats didn't learn gradually, but suddenly switched on a single trial from getting it mostly wrong to getting it mostly right.[76] They argued that the gradual learning rate seen in many studies was an artifact of averaging across different rats, each of whom reached its "Aha!" moment at different times.[K]

Because it was so hard to analyze the variability in the mistakes made early in learning, Hull decided to analyze rats who had reached a regularity in their paths and were no longer making mistakes. Hull used the analogy of a switchboard operator creating a connection between two telephones to explain his ideas, while Tolman had only the analogy to human inspiration to attempt his explanation. While Hull was able to provide a mathematical explanation for his suggestions, Tolman was not. This made it possible for Hull (and the others arguing against cognitive processes, such as B. F. Skinner) to explain specifically when phenomena would occur and made it possible for them to be quantitative about it.[78] Science is about prediction and replication. Tolman's observations were hard to quantify. Inspiration hit rats at different times. So, while any individual rat would suddenly "get it" and start running the maze correctly, the average of all the rats showed a slowly developing curve. Similarly, even though each rat would individually show vicarious trial and error on some trials, the trials on which the vicarious trial and error behavior occurred would differ from rat to rat.[79]

Mathematics is a technology. Like any other technology, it allows us to see things we could not see before. (Compare the microscope, which allowed Robert Hooke to see cells, or the telescope, which allowed Galileo Galilei to see the moons of Jupiter.[80]) It is important to realize that Tolman was before Claude Shannon, so he was lacking the mathematics of information theory. He was before the first computer (developed during World War II), before John von Neumann and Alan Turing, and before Norbert Wiener's breakthrough *Cybernetics* book (published in 1948), and thus had no access to the new conceptualization of intelligence as computation. And he was before Alan Newell and Herb Simon, so he was lacking the mathematics of algorithm.[81] Tolman's major work was in the 1930s and 1940s, summarized in his *Psychological Review* paper "Cognitive Maps in Rats and Men" published in 1948. Claude Shannon published his breakthrough paper on information theory in 1948. Alan Turing did his major work on computability in the late 1930s and through World War II in the early 1940s, but it did not have a major influence on psychology until the development of the field of artificial

---

[K] As we saw in our discussion of multiple decision-making systems (Chapter 6) and will return to in our discussion of Procedural learning (Chapter 10), there are some tasks that individuals do learn gradually and incrementally.[77] Suddenly getting the answer right (an "Aha!" moment) is a sign that a task is being solved by the Deliberative system rather than the Procedural system.

intelligence in the 1950s. Allen Newell and Herb Simon developed the first algorithmic concepts of search and intelligence with their publication of the General Problem Solver in 1959, the year Tolman died.

Information theory quantifies the ability of a signal to be pulled out of noise. Algorithm provides the concept that a sequence of computations can be linked together through control mechanisms to come to a conclusion that is hidden within data. One of the most important ideas, however, was that of computational complexity, which originated with Turing. We are now familiar with computers running long algorithms—we have all seen computers thrashing, the hard drive spinning, computing a complex calculation. Before the concepts of information theory, algorithm, and computation, the idea that results hidden within data could be found only after calculations that inherently take time to calculate was unappreciated.

We now know that both Tolman and Hull were right. When faced with complex decisions between similar choices or between changing choices, one needs a flexible system even though it may be computationally complex, but when faced with a regular decision in which the right answer does not change, animals develop response-chain habits (sequences of actions).[82] In practice, early performance on mazes is often accomplished by Tolman-like deliberative search processes, while later performance is often accomplished by Hull-like stimulus–response habit processes.[83] In fact, if we go back and look at their data, Tolman studied how the mazes were learned and concentrated his analysis on the early-learning time, while Hull studied "asymptotic performance" once behavior had settled down to a regular routine. Both systems (Tolman's computationally expensive search process and Hull's computationally simple stimulus–response process) are capable of solving tasks and making decisions. Each system, however, has advantages and disadvantages and is accomplished by a different set of interacting brain structures. In the next chapter, we'll turn to what is known about that habit system.

Books and papers for further reading

- Randy L. Buckner and Daniel C. Carroll (2007). Self-projection and the brain. *Trends in Cognitive Sciences, 11,* 49–57.
- Adam Johnson and David A. Crowe (2009). Revisiting Tolman, his theories and cognitive maps. *Cognitive Critique, 1,* 43–72.
- Yael Niv, Daphna Joel, and Peter Dayan (2006). A normative perspective on motivation. *Trends in Cognitive Sciences, 10,* 375–381.
- John O'Keefe and Lynn Nadel (1978). *The Hippocampus as a Cognitive Map.* Oxford: Oxford University Press.

10

The Habits of Our Lives

> Jogging a mountain path,
> one step after another...
>
> empty the mind
> except for the blue sky above and
> the red rocks beneath our feet

With enough experience, action-selection becomes "cached" or stored in stimulus–response pairs and response–action chains. The advantage of this system is that it can respond quickly and reliably, with the same action-sequence every time. The disadvantage of this system is that it is inflexible and is slow to change in response to changing conditions.

Poets often refer to us as "creatures of habit." In the morning, we get up at the same time, we drink the same coffee every morning, eat the same cereal. In the evening, we want our book or our television before bed. We have all developed our own habits over the course of our lives. These habits are not instincts; they are not genetically programmed into us. Instead, habits develop out of regularity, reliability. We'd like to think habits develop out of what we've individually found to be most useful to our lives, but of course, we all have habits we'd like to break. Why do we develop bad habits? Where do habits come from? What are habits? Why does the route we drive to work become a habit, but the route we drive to the airport not?[A]

Fundamentally, habits are sequences of actions that we've learned to take. The simplest example of a habit is the drive to work. The first time you drive to work, you need to use a map, follow a GPS, pay attention to the route you want to take. But if you drive the route every day for weeks, months, or years, you eventually stop paying attention to it. You drive yourself to work, even as you are thinking of something else.

[A] The obvious answer here is that you drive to work a lot more than to the airport (unless you work at the airport). As many a business traveler knows, with enough trips to the airport, the route to the airport will become a habit too.

This suggests the usual trajectory of learning—flexible, deliberative mechanisms predominate early in learning, while the inflexible, habit-based mechanisms develop with experience.[1] But, of course, control can also shift back from habit to deliberative systems.[2] When the 35W bridge that was the primary conduit across the Mississippi River through Minneapolis collapsed in 2007, traffic had to be rerouted throughout the city. This changed the flow of traffic along my route to work, and I found that the route I normally took to work was much slower than it had been. So I found a new route, which actually turned out to be faster, even once the new bridge was built and reopened. This new route requires turning left at a certain intersection. Yet, even years afterwards, if I'm not paying attention, I continue straight at that intersection. Particularly, if I'm thinking about something else, like a test I have to write, or a scientific problem, or even just trying to remember that I have to pick up milk on my way home after work, I go straight through. What's interesting about this is that no matter how distracted I am with my thoughts, I have never run the red light. I have never failed to brake in time and I have never hit another car at this intersection, even though it's a very crowded intersection. My brain is driving reliably, but I'm not paying attention to it.

This does not mean that it's safe to drive distracted! Driving while talking on a cell phone, even a hands-free phone, has been proven to increase the likelihood of crashing fourfold.[3] In particular, sensory distractions (such as talking or, worse, texting, on a cell phone) interfere with the sensory processing needed to respond appropriately while driving. As we will see, there is a big difference between allowing your mind to wander to think of additional things and taking your attention off the road.

This difference can be easily seen in learning to play a musical instrument. No musician would attempt to play a complex piece while watching television or reading a book: the sensory cues would interfere with the music. However, with experience, musicians become adept at thinking less and less about details and more and more about the artistic aspects of the music. When learning to play a musical instrument, at first you need to think what keys are where, what key combinations produce what notes. Playing a musical piece through without playing a wrong note often means pausing before each note to find the right fingering (which, of course, completely ruins the rhythm). But as one becomes experienced with the instrument, one begins to associate the notes with the keys, until at some point you no longer think about the fingering for a given note; instead, you think "play a G," and your hands just do the right thing. This allows you to concentrate on the notes. Eventually, as you learn a piece of music, you attend less and less to what the next note is, allowing you to spend your mental computation on more and more complex aspects of the music. Expert musicians with lots of experience with different pieces and different genres can even create complex musical melodies on the spot (see jazz, improvisation).

Computationally, habit learning arises from two important processes: *situation–action*[B] (S-A) associations and *chunking* (*action–action*, A-A) processes. S-A associations

---

[B] In the psychology literatures, "situation–action" learning is more often referred to as *stimulus–response* (S-R) learning,[4] but, as we've seen (Chapter 6), animals are reacting to situations, categorizations of stimuli, not to specific stimuli.[5] (We'll discuss this issue in more depth in Chapter 12.) Certainly some stimuli are more important than others in determining the situation at hand, but rarely is a situation defined entirely by a single stimulus (outside of a psychology animal-testing box where

(*continued*)

are just what they sound like, memories that have learned that in this situation, you should take this action.[6] Chunking is the chaining of A-A sequences, as if a sequence of actions was represented as a single "super-action."[7] (The habit system is sometimes called the "cached-action" system, because it has *cached* or stored the action to take.[8] In Chapter 6, we called this system "Procedural," because it learns and stores procedures.[9])

It is interesting to note that most of the examples of the "stimulus–reaction" type of behaviors typically identified as "habits" are actually voluntary initiations rather than responses—when the light turns on, the rat pushes the lever; when given the cigarette, the addict smokes it. Although the drive to work becomes an automatic "habit" and no longer requires attention through the journey, it's still a voluntary action initiated and monitored throughout. The system is retrieving a voluntary sequence of motor actions and *releasing* it in response to a cue.[10]

This is exactly how athletes play sports. A quarterback throwing a pass to a receiver is recognizing the situation, evaluating it, and retrieving an action sequence. No matter what some fans will say, no one "made" the quarterback make the throw that led to the interception; he placed "throwing the ball" on the set of actions he was ready to do and then misread the coverage. Procedural decision-making is best understood in terms of *preparation* and *possibilities*—at each moment, the agent is matching situations until one appears that is matched with a releasable action.[11;C]

Chunking is a process where subgoals are stored as completed parts so that the cognitive planning process can work at a more abstract level.[13] Thus, the expert musician does not think "to play a G on this clarinet, I need to put my fingers in this position and blow this hard on the reed"; instead, the musician just "plays G." In fact, expert musicians often chunk sequences of notes in chords and arpeggios. Similarly, a baseball pitcher doesn't think "to throw the fastball, I place two fingers on the seams of the baseball and pull my arm back, don't forget to turn the hips. . . ." Instead, the expert pitcher just throws the baseball. As the catcher Crash Davis (Kevin Costner) says to the pitcher Ebby LaLoosh (Tim Robbins) in the movie *Bull Durham*, "Don't think, meat, just throw."[14] This advice is key because thinking too much about the process disrupts both the S-A component (because it forces the deliberation component to take over) and the chunking component (because it is working at too low a level). As we saw in Chapter 9, deliberation takes a variable amount of time to get to the next action. A reliable, smooth, action sequence needs the Procedural system.

In the laboratory, these issues are studied with tasks like the sequential serial reaction time (SSRT) task. In this task, the subject's hand is placed on a keyboard and the subject is simply told to push each key as soon as the letter appears on the screen.[15] The subject is told that the letters will appear randomly; however, unbeknownst to the subject, the letters actually come up in a sequence. The sequence can be simple or complicated,

---

only a couple of very discrete stimuli are available). Therefore, I prefer the term "situation" to "stimulus" (conveniently, both start with S). I don't have any problem with the term "response" per se, but I keep getting the R in S-R confused with "reward," so I prefer the less ambiguous "action," allowing us to call this S-A learning.

[C] In the psychological literature, this has historically been known as *affordances*, because each situation "affords" (provides for, encourages) certain responses more than others.[12]

deterministic or probabilistic. The key is that the sequence is never explicitly told to the subject. As people learn to recognize the sequence, they begin to make anticipatory movements and their reaction time speeds up. This can be explicitly tested by putting in a random sequence probe session in which the sequence of letters reverts back to being random. The anticipatory movements are no longer useful; in fact, one has to undo the preparation, and one's reaction time slows down dramatically.

What's particularly interesting about the SSRT task is that there are two potential things one can learn about the sequence: one can learn that there was a sequence and one can learn how to respond to the sequence. To test whether the subject recognized that there was a sequence, we simply ask. Afterwards, when asked, some people will say, "Yes, there was a sequence" and others will say, "No, it was random." To test whether the subject learned to respond to the sequence, we measure the reaction times. If the subject shows anticipatory movements and speeds up for repeated sequences (and slows down in response to the probe session), then the subject's actions in some sense "know" the sequence (because the actions are predicting it).

We might think that these two tests should always match—if you recognize the sequence, your reaction time will speed up and if your reaction time speeds up, then you must have recognized the sequence. But this is not what is seen. Although many people do, in fact, both report the sequence afterwards and show reaction time speed-up during the task, many subjects do not recognize the sequence explicitly but still show strong reaction-time effects.[16] There are even subjects who recognize the sequence but do not show reaction-time effects.[17] In particular, patients with Parkinson's disease and Huntington's disease, both of which affect the basal ganglia, often recognize the sequence without showing reaction time changes. In contrast, patients with Alzheimer's disease, which affects learning abilities in the hippocampus and its related areas, often show normal reaction time speed-up but an inability to report recognition of the sequence. This distinction is often referred to as *implicit* versus *explicit* learning, which corresponds closely to the distinctions between procedural and declarative, between habit and goal-oriented decision-making, and the terms used in this book (between *procedural* and *deliberative* decision-making), all of which seem to be capturing this fundamental distinction between an unconscious revealed learning and a conscious, explicit learning process.[18]

The two brain structures most involved in both chunking and S-A associations are the *basal ganglia*,[19] sitting at the center of the mammalian brain (beneath the cortex, thus "subcortical"), and the *cerebellum*,[20] at the base of the brain, both of which are evolutionarily very old structures, with similar components being found in all vertebrates.[21]

The basal ganglia

The circuitry in the basal ganglia is very complex. We will spend some time exploring it in this chapter, but briefly, there are two pathways through the basal ganglia: one encourages actions and the other inhibits actions (Figure 10.1).[22] (Actually, there are three pathways through the basal ganglia; the third one stops a learned action.[23] We will return to this third pathway in Chapter 15 in our discussion of self-control and the overriding of learned actions.) The two primary pathways can be identified by their influences

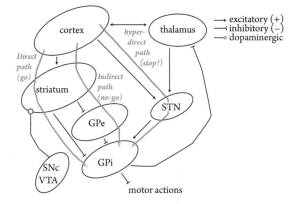

Figure 10.1 PATHWAYS THROUGH THE BASAL GANGLIA. The basal ganglia are a subcortical circuit that learns to control motor actions. There are three pathways through it. (1) The first is a "direct path" in which the cortex excites the striatum, which inhibits the internal globus pallidus (GPi). Because GPi neurons are tonically firing, inhibiting them releases thalamocortical and subcortical motor action circuits. (2) An "indirect path" adds an intervening inhibitory step (external globus pallidus, GPe), which creates a triple negative. (3) The third is a "hyperdirect pathway," in which the excitatory subthalamic nucleus (STN) increases firing in the GPi, which stops actions. Learning occurs in the striatum through dopamine inputs coming from the ventral tegmental area (VTA) and the substantia nigra pars compacta (SNc).

on thalamic and cortical action-selection systems. The "go" pathway, which encourages actions, inhibits cells that inhibit thalamic and cortical action-selection systems (a double negative, which encourages actions), while the "no-go" pathway, which discourages actions, adds a third inhibition step (a triple negative, which discourages actions). The third pathway steps in at the last stage, directly exciting those cells that inhibit the thalamic and cortical action-selection systems (a single negative, discouraging actions).

The first pathway, which encourages actions, recognizes increases in dopamine, while the second pathway, which discourages actions, recognizes decreases in dopamine.[24] (Remember that dopamine is a signal where increases mean "that was better than I expected" and should lead to an increase in the willingness to take an action, and decreases mean "that was worse than I expected" and should lead to a decrease in the willingness to take an action. See Chapter 4.) These changes in dopamine are recognized by different receptors (prosaically called D1 and D2 receptors). This means that slight differences in genetics can make one person learn more easily from positive rewards (carrots) and another learn more easily from negative punishments (sticks).[25]

This difference suggests that genetic changes in these receptors might change the ability to learn from positive or negative information. In a remarkable experiment, Michael Frank and his colleagues found exactly that.[26] They developed a task in which people learned to recognize which arbitrary characters[D] were likely to lead to reward and which

---

[D] Actually, they used Japanese *hiragana* characters. Presumably, their American experimental subjects didn't recognize them.

were not likely to. Through an elegant combination of training and test procedures, they were able to separate learning from positive information (more likely to lead to reward) than from negative (less likely to lead to reward). They did genetic testing on their subjects and examined one common genetic polymorphism[E] in the D1 receptors and another in the D2 receptors. The polymorphism in the D1 receptor pathway affected how well people learned from positive signals, while the polymorphism in the D2 receptor pathway affected how well people learned from the negative signals.[F]

As we also talked about in Chapter 4, dopamine is primarily about positive rewards (reinforcement), not negative punishments (aversion). We argued in that chapter that there should be a negative counterpart to dopamine that signals when punishments are worse than expected (learn not to go), and when punishments are not as bad as expected (relief, learn to go). As we noted in that chapter, it is not currently known what that signal is. In the past few decades, people have suggested two possible candidates for this negative anti-dopamine: serotonin and norepinephrine (also called noradrenalin).[28] Both of these neurotransmitters are chemically related to dopamine (and thus are good candidates from the perspective that evolution tends to work by modifying existing systems) and are definitely involved in decision-making.

Dopamine, serotonin, norepinephrine (noradrenaline), and another related neurotransmitter, octopamine, are all related chemicals from a family called the catecholamines.[29] Catecholamines play interesting roles in learning and decision-making in a number of very distantly related species. In insects, the positive (reinforcement) component is octopamine, while the negative (aversion) signal is dopamine.[30] Dopamine, serotonin, and octopamine also control the activation and stopping of movement (swimming, crawling) in simple animals such as leeches, worms, and lampreys.[31] This suggests that the role of these catecholamines in encouraging and discouraging actions has a long evolutionary history. How the roles that these catecholamines play in these other animals relates to their role in human decision-making is, however, still unknown.

Recent experiments have found that serotonin relates to the ability to hold memories across delays and to one's long-term perspective, but that serotonin does not reflect negative value-prediction error signals.[32] In contrast, norepinephrine is involved in negative affect, particularly in drug addiction, such as during opiate withdrawal.[33] Norepinephrine bursts drive pauses in the firing of dopamine neurons, which we've seen reflect disappointment and recognition of undelivered rewards.[34] However, other researchers have proposed that norepinephrine plays roles in attention and in representations of uncertainty.[35] (Dopamine also plays a role in vigilance and attention.[36])

[E] Any given species has a distribution of subtle genetic changes between its members—that's why we're not all identical. It's these small differences that are the key to evolution, which changes the distributions of these small differences over time.[27] These differences are called polymorphisms—poly (multiple) + morphisms (forms).

[F] They also tested a third polymorphism in a dopamine receptor that affects prefrontal cortex. This third polymorphism affected people's ability to respond to changes in the reward contingency. As we will see later in Chapter 12, the prefrontal cortex is important for the situation-recognition box, particularly in the face of changes, and these dopamine signals are used to determine when one needs to change one's mind about the situation one is in.

As with dopamine, it is likely that both serotonin and norepinephrine carry general signals that can be used in many ways.[G]

Whether the basal ganglia are actually driving movement itself or whether the basal ganglia are merely influencing decisions being made in the cortex is a subject of controversy in neuroscience today. What is most likely, of course, is that both theories are correct and that the action suggestions made by the basal ganglia are being sent to both deep brain motor structures (and then on to the spinal cord) and to cortical circuits (which then project back to those same deep brain motor structures and spinal cord).[40]

Motor cortex

How can cortical circuits make decisions? Motor control cortical structures are categorizing inputs from sensory structures.[41] Sensory structures are categorizing aspects of the world, with those aspects becoming more and more complex as they move away from the primary sensory areas.[42] (In the primary visual cortex, the "categories" are really "features of the world," dots, lines, blobs of color, corners, etc. In secondary and tertiary visual cortices, other "features" are found until they become categories, such as faces, houses, objects, etc. Similarly, the primary auditory cortex recognizes features of sound, and secondary and tertiary auditory areas recognize speech, words, music, genres of music, etc.) The output of a category of situations can be treated as an action signal.[43] In a sense, this can be thought of as *releasing* actions—the quarterback cocks his arm back to throw, and starts checking receivers. If he finds one that is open (that his categorization process identifies as a good throw to make), the motor cortex sends a signal to other structures (including the basal ganglia, cerebellum, and deep motor structures) to initiate the action of throwing the ball. Notice how this mechanism maintains the decision of whether to initiate the voluntary action within the cortical categorization system, but the action sequence itself is not part of that system. The quarterback has *chunked* the decision—the motor cortex determines "throw or not?" but does not identify the individual motor motions to take.

Computational models of the cortex suggest that the categorization process depends on a network of cells "settling" on an answer.[44;H] Initiating a decision too quickly in these models will pull up the wrong answer.[45] Studies of cortical responses to motor selection

---

[G] This issue is further complicated by the fact that these neurotransmitters have effects in the brain beyond value-prediction error,[37] and that all of these neurotransmitters also have effects outside the brain.[38] Serotonin has effects on the gut and intestines. Norepinephrine has effects on heart rate and blood pressure. Dopamine and norepinephrine affect the peripheral sympathetic and parasympathetic systems of the body (unrelated to the emotion of sympathy, of course). The sympathetic and parasympathetic systems run counter to each other: the sympathetic system prepares the body for stressful activity (fight, flight, and the act of reproduction), while the parasympathetic system maintains the body at unstressful activity (safety, rest, and postcoital relaxation).[39] The complex diverse effects of a given chemical on different structures mean that drugs often have unintended side effects and make pharmacology complicated.

[H] The computational mechanisms of this settling process (*basins of attraction* in *content-addressable memories*) are well understood. A detailed discussion of this mechanism can be found in Appendix C.

find that there are two responses to sensory cues in motor cortex, a very fast (less than 50 milliseconds) response and then a slower (greater than 100 milliseconds) response.[46] The first response occurs through direct connections between sensory cortices and the motor cortices; the second response occurs through a longer path through more frontal circuits. For example, when asked to turn away from a cue, motor cortical neurons initially represent the direction to the cue, but then, influenced by information processed in premotor frontal circuits, change their firing to reflect the direction of action.[47]

This issue can be best seen in terms of reaction to a skid on ice. The first reaction most people have is to brake and turn against the skid, but this only makes things worse. In fact, the correct thing to do in a skid is to slow down by releasing the accelerator, and then to turn *into* the skid until you get traction back.[48]

This poses an interesting problem with brain–machine interfaces. Many people have argued that brain–machine interfaces could speed up reaction times. But part of the slowness of reaction time is that your brain has to develop the correct response. Decoding the information from the motor cortex too quickly can produce the wrong answer. As with driving during a skid, you don't want the first reaction, you want the right reaction, which sometimes appears second, only after the brain has had a chance to do some additional processing to find the right categorization of the complex situation.

It is important also to remember that these categories are actually dynamic— although it is easier to build computational models of categories as a static value, the cortex is actually finding a path through these categories.[49] This path is actually a sequence of categories—my drive to work is to first go down Roselawn, then left on Hamline, and right on Larpenteur...At each point, I need to correctly execute behavior at two different levels—at one level, I need to execute the actions correctly, stop at the traffic light when red, go when green, don't hit that car in front of me, etc. And at the other (usually termed "higher" level because it's more abstract), I need to decide on the next step in our journey—which way do I turn at this intersection? The point of this chapter is that sometimes even those higher-level decisions can be unconscious. However, even when we are consciously deciding which way to turn at an intersection, we are not usually consciously thinking "red light means stop" or "green light means go." This is chunking[50]—we have stored the behavior in a chunk so that we can think "turn left," not "take your foot off the brake, put your foot on the accelerator, turn the wheel," etc. A computer programmer might say that we have compiled the process into a subroutine that we can access easily. Of course, the cognitive brain can still break into these chunks and control the components—as when we are trying to teach someone to drive and say, "It's a red light! Stop!" as we slam our foot into the imaginary pedal on the passenger's side of the car.

In general, driving is a great example of this chunking process. I remember my first experiences behind a wheel of a car, trying to figure out how much pressure I dared put on the accelerator, as the car suddenly lurched forward. Or the nervous way I clutched the steering wheel the first time I got on a highway with cars whizzing by at 70 miles per hour. Other great examples of this sort of chunking are playing a musical instrument and walking.

Walking on two legs is actually a complex interaction of balance, forward motion, and catching yourself. As Laurie Anderson sang in her 1982 song *Walking and Falling*, "You're walking. And you don't always realize it, but you're always falling. With each step you fall forward slightly. And then catch yourself from falling. Over and over, you're falling. And then catching yourself from falling. And this is how you can be walking and falling at the same time..." Anyone watching a toddler take its first steps can see how complex a process it is.

Cerebellum

The key to these compiled behaviors is the cerebellum, a fascinating brain structure that sits at the back of the brain, hanging out over the spinal cord. In a human brain, the cerebellum looks like an addendum, an extra appendix bulging out from the back of the brain, but in fact the cerebellum is an evolutionarily much older structure than the cortex. The cerebellum first appears evolutionarily with vertebrates, and it has not changed in basic structure from early fish to mammals.[51] (Because the cerebellum is a distinctive bulbous structure, the skulls of many animals have pockets to accommodate it. Thus, the location of the cerebellum can be seen in the fossils of ancient animal skulls, including fish, and even dinosaurs.[52])

The structure of the cerebellum is fascinatingly simple and regular.[53] The main component are the Purkinje cells,[1] which have dendritic trees that are remarkably two-dimensional, spread out in sheets like pieces of paper. They stack against each other like pages in a book. Two inputs converge on the Purkinje cells: the parallel fibers and the climbing fibers. Interestingly, like the basal ganglia outputs, the Purkinje cells are inhibitory. Purkinje cell firing holds down its outputs until releasing that output by a sudden decrease in firing.

The cerebellum looks like a great big spreadsheet, with the parallel fibers and the Purkinje cells lined up perpendicularly. The other major input to the Purkinje cells are the climbing fibers, which climb the Purkinje cells like ivy on a tree, and provide a teaching signal.[54] Errors in the smoothness of the actions are transmitted to the Purkinje cells and the connections between the parallel fibers and the Purkinje cells are adjusted until the error is diminished.[55]

A classic example of this learning signal is the prism experiment,[56] shown to many a high school student as part of neuroscience outreach programs. In this experiment, the subject is given a set of prisms that shift the visual world to one side (say 20 degrees to the left). The person tries to throw a beanbag into a basket a few feet in front of him or her. Because there is a mismatch between the visual world and the motor actions the person is used to, the person throws the beanbag 20 degrees to the opposite side (to the right). Over the course of a dozen throws or so, the subject adjusts his or her behavior to correctly toss the beanbag into the bucket. Then, when the prisms are removed, there is again a mismatch and the person throws the beanbag 20 degrees to the original side (to the left). Again, over the course of a few throws (fewer than before), the subject recaptures the old association and is able to hit the basket again. These changes occur due to connectivity changes in the cerebellum.

At a neuroscience outreach fair to a local high school, we once encountered a person who showed no effect of the prisms on throwing the beanbag (although he had never

---

[1] Pronounced "PURR-kin-jay" after Jan Purkinje (1787–1869), a Czech anatomist from the 1800s, who first noticed the beautiful fan-like structure of the Purkinje cells.

worn prisms before); he hit the basket on the first try, every try. At first we were very surprised, but we later learned that he was a local basketball star. Presumably, he had taught his motor system to throw straight independently of what his vision told him. He had already identified the distance to the basket before he put the prisms on. He knew he was facing forward and didn't have to use the visual signals to correct it. He had already chunked how to throw a certain distance and angle. Through extensive practice, he had developed a compiled motor action that reliably hit the basket.

The cerebellum seems to be involved in these compiled or chunked motor actions—walking, driving, playing a musical instrument. The cerebellum is the key to timing reliable motor actions and sequences.[57] There is some evidence that the cerebellum can also compile cognitive sequences as well, but this is still controversial.[58] (It's much harder to measure a cognitive sequence than a motor sequence.) However, that the cerebellum has a role in cognitive sequences shouldn't surprise us. People can certainly chunk mental cognitive sequences just like they do physical motor sequences.[59] (*What's your cell phone number?*)

Summary

In this chapter, we've seen two forms of arbitrary action decisions—the caching of stored decisions at a high (abstract) level and the compiling of stored motor sequences at a low (concrete) level. The former uses the basal ganglia to identify the correct next step and the latter uses the cerebellum to time the motor action sequences. But both of these motor control/decision-making systems can be contrasted to the three other systems we've been discussing—reflexes are hardwired (evolutionarily) into our system, they cannot change either what sensory stimuli trigger them or what actions they take; Pavlovian/emotional systems cannot change the actions triggered but can learn to associate new stimuli with them; Deliberative systems can decide to take arbitrary actions in response to arbitrary situations but require extensive attention and computational time to process. Compiling action sequences allows us to make decisions about chunks of behavior rather than worrying about every little detail. And caching situation–action pairs allows us to attend to other plans while taking even complex arbitrary actions in response to complex stimuli. In the next few chapters, we will discuss the additional systems needed to understand the human decision-making machine (perceptual, situation-recognition, and motivation systems), and then we will move on to discuss issues of interaction between the systems (the tradeoff between exploration and exploitation, and the process of self-control), before discussing the consequences of the physical brain and its potential vulnerabilities and failure modes.

Books and papers for further reading

- Rudolpho Llinas (2002). *I of the Vortex*. Cambridge, MA: MIT Press.
- Paul Cisek and John F. Kalaska (2010). Neural mechanisms for interacting with a world full of action choices. *Annual Review of Neuroscience, 33*, 269–298.
- Kenji Doya (1999). What are the computations of the cerebellum, the basal ganglia, and the cerebral cortex? *Neural Networks, 12*, 961–974.

11

Integrating Information

Leaves in the wind
or a leopard in the forest?
Don't take too long to decide!

Although our senses receive physical information from the world,
we interpret those senses in terms of the objects in the world—we
see a tree, we feel the wind, we hear a bird. Interpreting that infor-
mation requires an integration process that takes time. We can
trade off time for accuracy if need be.

When you look at a picture (say of a face), your eyes dart from one important feature to the next.[1] In part, you need to do this because the photoreceptors in the human eye are more concentrated in the center of your retina than in the periphery, which means that your vision is more accurate (has higher resolution[A]) when you are looking directly at something. Every few hundred milliseconds, your eyes make another journey (they *saccade*[B]) to another location. Over the course of a few seconds or minutes, you have integrated the important information about the picture to answer whatever question you had. Where you look, how long you look, and how long your eyes stop at each point depend on the questions you are trying to answer about the picture.[C]

Experimental studies of decision-making often make the perceptual recognition of the information difficult, which means that one has to integrate information over time.[2] Old studies did this because it allowed them to use the reaction time to differentiate between conditions. New studies do this because it allows them to study how the neural firing

---

[A] We are all familiar now with issues of visual resolution thanks to the digital camera industry.

[B] We are rarely aware of these saccades, although, like most motor systems, they can be taken under conscious control.

[C] It is possible to identify information about the world without looking directly at it. (As you might if you were trying not to let someone know you were looking at them. Because human eyes have white sclera, we can tell where someone else is looking, an important issue for social creatures.) Not looking at something takes more effort because one has to build up the information from the sensors at the periphery with lower resolution, and because one has to inhibit the natural tendency to saccade to it.

changes as the subject figures out what to do. Interestingly, because of this, much of the neuroscience literature on "decision-making" is about situation recognition rather than deliberation or the other action-selection processes we have been discussing. In these perceptually difficult tasks (which we discuss in detail later), the hard part is recognizing which situation the cues imply you are in not deciding what to do. Each situation has a single correct outcome. (Compare this to the examples we discussed in Chapter 9 when we talked about people deliberating over job options or over large purchases like cars or houses.) Nevertheless, perceptual categorization is a key part of the decision-making process, and these perceptually difficult tasks have taught us how we integrate information over time.

Race-to-threshold models

Computationally, integrating information is most easily understood in terms of the *race-to-threshold* models.[3] In these algorithms, originally used by Alan Turing and the Allies to break the German Enigma code in World War II,[D] the weight of evidence for each possibility is measured, and when the weight of evidence becomes overwhelming for one possibility over the others (when the weight of evidence for one possibility reaches a threshold), that choice wins and the decision is made.

Let us first look at this in the case of a two-choice forced decision. A two-choice forced decision is one where you must make a decision between two options. There is no third option; not choosing the first option is equivalent to choosing the second. We can measure how much better one option is than the other by measuring the ratio of the weight of evidence for one option over the weight of evidence for the other option. The ratio of the probabilities is convenient to use because any advantage to one side is equivalent to a disadvantage to the other side.

Some readers may recognize this as an *odds ratio*,[4] which is usually written as 1:X, where X measures how much better the second choice is than the first. However, these odds ratios require a lot of division and require that we represent our number from 0 (1:infinity) to infinity (infinity:1). A better option is to take the logarithm of this ratio. The advantage of logarithms is that multiplying two numbers is equivalent to adding

---

[D] Alan Turing (1912–1954) could arguably be said to have saved the world. Turing led the code-breaking team in Bletchley Park in England that broke the Nazi codes. The Germans had developed a code that was so complex they thought it was unbreakable. It was based on a machine, called *Enigma*, which consisted of three dials. The person typed a message into the machine and the machine encoded the message on a character-by-character basis as a function of the dials. The dials were set in a specific way each day and so the code-breaking team had to break each day's code anew. But a captured machine gave the Allies the set of possible dials. Even if they didn't know the settings for that day, they knew the parameters and could calculate the likelihood that a given message came from a given dial setting. Because thousands of messages were sent each day, Turing and his team could integrate the information between these messages. They measured the weight of evidence for each setting and stopped when they reached a threshold. Although they didn't crack the code every day, they cracked it often enough that they could read the German orders and they knew what the Germans were going to do. The Germans thought the Enigma was impenetrable and continued to send messages by it until the end of the war. Both David Kahn's nonfiction history book *The Code-Breakers* and Neal Stephenson's fictional novel *Cryptonomicon* tell this story in wonderfully exciting and readable detail.

their logarithms; similarly, dividing two numbers is equivalent to subtracting their logarithms. The logarithm is a function that translates this ratio into a number from minus infinity to plus infinity. (This turns out to be how much information there is to support one hypothesis over the other.) When the two choices are equal, this difference between the logarithms is zero, and the difference moves away from zero as we gather information. This allows us to define the weight of evidence of choosing left or right as a single number (greater than zero will mean go left, less than zero will mean go right). We simply start at zero and integrate our information over time by moving up with evidence for the first choice and down with evidence for the alternate choice.

This leaves us with three important parameters. First, we have the *slope*, which is how much to change our ratio with each piece of information supporting one hypothesis over the other. Second, the *bias* determines where we start our decision from.[E] Finally, third, there is the *stopping condition*, which can either be taking the best option after a certain time or (more commonly used in the experimental literature) the odds ratio where we decide that we have enough information—that is, when we have deviated from zero (the two choices being equal) to some threshold (one choice is so much better, we'll go with that one).

I find the race-to-threshold model extremely intuitive in that it entails weighing the pros and cons of two options and stopping when we're convinced that one choice is better than the other one. The primary parameters are ones that make sense intuitively—*bias* is our preference for one choice over the other, *slope* is how quickly we learn about the options, and the *threshold* is how sure we want to be before we commit to a choice.

The integration-to-threshold model produces a unique distribution of reaction times because of the way the integration occurs (Figure 11.1).[5] It works out to be related to what is known in the engineering fields as a *hazard* function—*How long will it take before something happens?*, given that we stop counting the first time it happens. This is used, for example, in measuring the first time something breaks down and has to be repaired (like an airplane).[6] It also tracks the physics of a noisy signal crossing an energy barrier.[7] Imagine popcorn in a hot-air popcorn popper. We have two cases of a "hazard" function here. First, the popcorn is bouncing around, and some of the popcorn will have enough bounce to get out and over the threshold of the popper on its own. The more the air blows, the more the popcorn bounces (more air = faster slope; getting out of the popper = crossing the threshold). Second, the heat in the popper is making the water inside each kernel of popcorn expand; at some point the water expands enough and blows the kernel open (more heat = faster slope; exploding kernel = crossing the threshold). If the first hazard function occurs before the second, you get unpopped kernels in your bowl.

These theories have been explicitly tested in a number of experimental paradigms. The simplest is the "visual noise" or "television snow" paradigm.[F] In this paradigm, the subject stares at a black screen on which bright dots are plotted. Some of those dots

---

[E] Interestingly, the English word "bias" has two related meanings. It can mean the initial expectation, an assumption made before gathering information. Second, it can mean a preference for one thing over another, particularly when one responds without appropriately integrating the information. As pointed out in *The Anatomy of Bias* by Jan Lauwereyns, these are really the same thing—a stereotype is an initial expectation (often wrong) that is unwilling to change in the face of further information.

[F] Most televisions (and all computer monitors that show television signals) are digital now, but older televisions received analog signals. Analog televisions that were not tuned to a signal would

(continued)

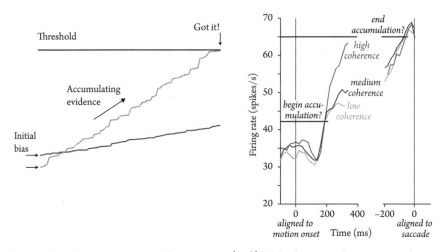

Figure 11.1 INTEGRATION TO THRESHOLD. (Left) Multiple accumulators start with an initial bias, and each races toward threshold by integrating the accumulating evidence at a different rate. The first one to reach threshold wins, and the perception collapses to decision. (Right) Individual neurons in LIP integrate information. All trials start at similar firing rates (there is no initial bias) and end at the same firing rates (on reaching threshold) but integrate at different rates depending on the coherence of the incoming sensory signal. Right panel from Gold and Shadlen (2002), redrawn from Roitman and Shadlen (2002). Reprinted with permission of author and publisher.

vanish in the next instant. Other dots move in a random direction. But some of the dots move together in a given direction (say left). The goal is to figure out which direction the subset of coherent dots is going. By varying the proportion of dots moving in the same direction, the experimenter can quantitatively control the speed at which information is provided to the subject. Both humans and monkeys are remarkably sensitive to even very small proportions, being able to easily recognize as few as 10% of the dots moving in the same direction.[8]

This task depends on the primate ability to detect motion. Your brain wants to detect things that move for two reasons. First, if you are moving, then the whole world you see moves in sync. (This is the secret to the illusions of motion that IMAX movies can produce.) But, second, your brain wants to detect other things that move in the world. The ability to detect things that move depends on a brain structure called MT,[G] which has cells that detect things that move in the visual world, and a structure called LIP,[H] which has cells that have tuning curves to a given direction and increase their firing rate

---

show a random mixture of black and white dots that was called "snow." The visual motion signals being shown in the visual noise paradigm look a lot like this analog television noise.

[G] The structure is now known solely by its acronym "MT," but at one time this acronym stood for *medial temporal cortex* (meaning "in the middle" [medial] of the temporal cortex). The temporal cortex is located underneath the rest of the brain. In the early literature, MT was also known as V5, since it was the fifth visual cortical area discovered.[9]

[H] Again, now known by its acronym (LIP), but referring to *lateral intraparietal cortex,* because it sits on the internal wall of one of the grooves in the parietal cortex.[10]

over time as the monkey watches the screen. (There is a nearby structure called MST,[1] which detects the first case, where the whole visual world is moving, usually because you are moving within it.) The features of the world detected by cells in MT are good for detecting moving animals and objects. Imagine, for example, a camouflaged animal (like a leopard) moving through a forest. Most of the dots you see would flicker on and off with the wind, but a few of them (the leopard!) would reliably move in the same direction together.

The MT cells provide information about the direction of those moving dots—each cell's firing rate has a preferred direction and the firing of that cell reflects the proportion of dots moving in that direction against a static background.[11] (MST cells also have a preferred firing rate and reflect motion of the entire screen.[12])

The LIP cells seem to be integrating the information. (MT projects directly to LIP.) The starting firing rate of an LIP cell reflects the monkey's initial predictions about whether the dots are going to be moving in that cell's favorite direction or not (the bias), the speed at which the firing increases reflects the information coming from MT (the slope), and when the LIP cells reach a certain firing rate, the animal reacts (reaching the threshold).[13] We can think of this decision as being controlled by two neurons, one which is looking for leftward motion and one which is looking for rightward motion— the first to reach threshold wins, and that's the decision made.

Now that we've seen how this integration-to-threshold idea can work with two choices, it is straightforward to imagine how it would work with more choices.[14] For example, I doubt that monkeys evolved to make a choice between whether dots were going left or right. More likely, these experiments are tapping into a system that evolved to detect the direction (any direction) that a camouflaged object was moving. Instead of two neurons, we have hundreds or thousands of neurons, representing a range of possibilities, each integrating the information, each racing to threshold.

This is something called a winner-take-all network and arises from a simple model combining excitatory and inhibitory cells (cells that increase the firing of the cells they send axons to and cells that decrease the firing of the cells they send axons to). The excitatory cells are assumed to be connected up such that cells that represent similar things (say similar directions) support each other, while cells that represent different things (say directions 180 degrees apart) don't.[15] The inhibitory cells work as simple negative feedback, so that the total activity in the excitatory cells must remain a constant. This network was first examined in the 1970s as a model of cortex, and it turns out to be a very reasonable model of many aspects of the cortex. Mathematical work in the 1980s showed that the stable final state of this network is an agreement between the excitatory cells, with a subset of cells that agree on a certain result all having high firing rates and cells that disagree with that result having low firing rates. This network was used in the 1990s as a model of the rat's sense of direction and the rat's sense of location (place cells in the hippocampus) and as a model of cortex. Functionally, these models are a special case of the *content-addressable memories* discussed in Appendix C.

---

[1] Again, now known entirely by its acronym (MST), but once meaning *medial superior temporal cortex*, "superior" meaning "above."

Parallel and serial perception

A radar sweeping around the sky, looking for incoming airplanes, is a *serial* perception—it can only see one direction at a time; each direction is checked sequentially. An analog camera perceives light in *parallel*, with each light-detecting chemical on the photographic plate reacting at the same instant. (Digital cameras use a combination of parallel and serial processing. Each charge-coupled device on each pixel of the camera detects light at the same time [integrating the photons over the time the shutter is open], but then the pixels are usually read into the memory serially.) Our perceptual systems use a combination of parallel and serial processing, but the parallel step generally goes much farther than simple light detectors.[16]

It's useful to examine this parallel and serial processing in vision. Light is detected by the retina, which works in a massively parallel manner, like the pixels on our digital camera, integrating the photons that reach our eyes. From there, signals are sent on to the thalamus, and then to the primary visual cortex, which contains feature detectors, particularly for dots, lines, and edges. Each of these feature detectors is repeated for each part of the visual field, as if for the pixels of our eyes. From there, signals are sent to many different visual systems, which attempt to pull information out of the signal in parallel. One system, for example, tries to identify objects, another tries to identify faces,[J] another recognizes objects moving through the visual field (MT).

The classic experiment examining the difference between parallel and serial perception is the pop-out experiment (Figure 11.2).[20] Your goal in this task is to identify a certain object (the target) in a field of distractors. When the target is really different from the distractors (**O** in a field of **X**s), the target seems to pop out, and the speed at

```
X X X X X X X X X X      X X X X X X X X X X
X X X X X X X X X X      X X X X X X X X X O X
X X X Y X X X X X X      X X X X X X X X X X
X X X X X X X X X X      X X X X X X X X X X
X X X X X X X X X X      X X X X X X X X X X
X X X X X X X X X X      X X X X X X X X X X
X X X X X X X X X X      X X X X X X X X X X
```

Figure 11.2 POP-OUT IN VISION. Try to find the **Y** in the left panel and the **O** in the right panel. It is much easier to find the **O** because it "pops out" in our vision, whereas the **Y** requires a serial search through the display. Of course, once you know where to look, both the **Y** and the **O** are easy to find.

[J] Humans have evolved specialized areas of cortex to recognize faces.[17] This is why we see faces everywhere (like in the shades of light and dark on the moon as seen from the Earth). Some people have a particular difficulty with this, which is a disorder called *prosopagnosia*[18] (from *prosopon* [πρόσωπον, Greek for face] and *agnosia* [αγνωσία; *a*, α not + *gnosis*, γνωσις, knowing]). People with prosopagnosia have to rely on identifying features (a distinctive hairstyle or mode of dress) to identify people. Markos Moulitsas described his prosopagnosia on his blogsite "Daily Kos," and noted his inability to watch war movies (like *Saving Private Ryan*) or Mafia movies (like *The Godfather*) because everyone has the same haircut and is dressed the same.[19] Although it is not known what causes prosopagnosia, Doris Tsao recently found that one of the monkeys she was studying had no face-selective activity in its cortex and showed an inability to recognize faces, much like people with prosopagnosia, so we know that this can occur naturally in other primates as well.

which you recognize the target does not depend on the number of distractors (because you have different feature detectors for the target and the distractors and you can just have the feature detector tuned to the target shout out when it finds it). When the target is really similar to the distractors (**Y** in a field of **X**s), you have to check each one individually. This means that the time it takes you to find the target depends on the number of distractors. For parallel recognition (pop-out), your accuracy is independent of the time it takes you to respond. However, for serial recognition (searching through candidates), the longer you take to respond, the more accurate you will be (up to some point when you have gathered all the information available). This means that there is a clear tradeoff between speed and accuracy for serial recognition.

Experts and the speed–accuracy tradeoff

The race-to-threshold model provides a good explanation for the speed–accuracy tradeoff of serial search.[21] If the agent using a race-to-threshold algorithm wants to respond faster, it just lowers the threshold. A lower threshold means that the race ends faster (so the agent responds more quickly) but with the lower threshold, the agent has had less time to analyze the information, and is thus going to be more susceptible to noise. Equivalently, the agent can increase the slope. In either case—lowering the threshold or increasing the slope—with each small piece of information you gather, you approach the threshold more quickly. Increasing slope and decreasing threshold are mathematically equivalent. On the other hand, moving your starting point closer to threshold is different—that's moving your bias—guessing before the information arrives. If you move your bias above the threshold, you don't even have to wait for information, you could just make the decision without information! (I suspect this is more common than it should be.)

Certainly, it is possible in some tasks that you have gathered all the information you can, that at some point there is no new information available, and you have reached what is mathematically called an *asymptote*. In those cases, waiting longer isn't going to make your decision worse, it's just not going to make your decision better either. At some point, you have to act. However, in psychology experiments with noisy and ambiguous data (such as the television snow experiment described above), waiting is always better and there is a tradeoff between speed and accuracy.

So why can experts act quickly? How did Ted Williams or Tony Gwynn hit close to 40% of the pitches thrown at them?[K] It takes a baseball about 400 milliseconds to get from the pitcher's mound to home plate.[L] Given that human reaction time (even for the fastest athletes) is about 200 milliseconds,[23] one has only a couple of hundred milliseconds (a couple of tenths of a second) to integrate the information about how the ball is spinning, where it's going to cross the plate, and when it's going to be there. Players with better reaction times have better batting averages.

[K] Ted Williams and Tony Gwynn were two of the greatest hitters of all time, getting on base an average of 48.4% and 38.8% of the time, with lifetime batting averages of 0.344 (34.4%) and 0.338 (33.8%) respectively.[22]

[L] A 100-mile-per-hour pitch traveling 60 feet 6 inches takes about 400 milliseconds.

Experts have two advantages over nonexperts—they have trained up their perceptual system to recognize better features about the task and they have trained up their habit system to cache the most reliable choices of what to do. Perceptual training is like the chunking that we saw in Chapter 10. Experts have learned how to represent the task in such a way that it is easier to determine the correct responses from the available inputs; they have identified good categories for the task. The classic examples of this are chess and videogames. We have already seen how a computationally expensive search algorithm can beat a grandmaster at chess (Deep Blue vs. Gary Kasparov), but that chess grandmasters don't actually do that same computationally expensive search.[24] Instead, chess grandmasters have learned to represent the board in ways that limit the search they have to do. The experiment that proved this was that chess masters are better at remembering the positions of pieces on boards when those positions can arise from legal moves than when they can't. Just as an expert musician no longer thinks about the fingering for a chord on a guitar, a chess master no longer looks at each piece on the board as an individual thing. Playing videogames produces a similar specific expertise— faster recognition of the events in the game (training perceptual recognition systems, this chapter) and faster recognition of what to do in response to those events (training procedural systems, Chapter 10).[25]

It is important to recognize that this is not saying that "intuition" is better than "analysis," even for experts. Real experts shift from intuitive decisions to analytical decisions (from procedural to deliberative) as necessary. Similarly, it is important to recognize that raw intuition is not reliable in these situations—experts have spent years (often decades!) training their perceptual and procedural systems. In a sense, what the procedural decision-making system we examined in Chapter 10 does is trade perceptual and deliberative time during the decision for time during training, so that, while it takes longer to learn to do the task, once trained, the task can be done more quickly, if less flexibly. Typical estimates of training time for most human expert-level tasks is about 10,000 hours.[26] (That's five years at 40 hours per week at 50 weeks per year, or four years at 50 hours per week for 50 weeks per year.) This is why most apprenticeships, such as graduate school, medical school, time in the minor leagues, etc., are about four to six years.[M]

It is important to recognize that the opposite of "analytical" is not "intuitive." Both analytical (deliberative) decision-making and intuitive (procedural) decision-making arise from systems that have evolved to make accurate decisions in the face of integrating information. The opposite of "analytical" is "glib," moving the threshold down so far that no information is gathered (or moving the bias above the threshold), both of which are disastrous. In fact, both analytical and intuitive responses show speed–accuracy tradeoffs. One key to Tony Gwynn's success is that he used a very light bat and waited until the last moment to hit the ball.[27] One of the big differences between Ted Williams, Tony Gwynn, and the rest of us is that Williams and Gwynn had much better eyesight. When Tony Gwynn retired, he commented to a reporter that his eyes were going and he couldn't pick up the ball as early as he used to be able to. When the reporter asked what his eyesight was now, Gwynn responded that it was now about 20/15, but at one

---

[M] This of course reminds us of the old joke—our well-dressed protagonist stops a passerby on a New York City street and asks, "How do I get to Carnegie Hall?" The inevitable answer: "Practice, lots of practice!"

time had been 20/10. With better eyesight, he could pick up the rotation of the ball earlier, giving himself more time to react, more time to integrate information, and a better chance of hitting the ball.

Books and papers for further reading

- Jan Lauwereyns (2010). *The Anatomy of Bias*. Cambridge, MA: MIT Press.
- Joshua I. Gold and Michael N. Shadlen (2002). Banburismus and the brain: Decoding the relationship between sensory stimuli, decisions, and reward. *Neuron, 36*, 299–308.
- Joshua I. Gold and Michael N. Shadlen (2007). The neural basis of decision making. *Annual Review of Neuroscience, 30*, 535–574.

12

The Stories We Tell

> the stone above weighs on you
> the tension in your voice
> betrays you
>
> human arms are weak
> but our legs are strong
> they will raise us up

Both deliberative and procedural decision-making require recognition of the "situation" we are in. Situation recognition is a categorization process in which we recognize that this moment shares similarities with previous situations we have experienced and differs from others. Although models exist of static situation-recognition processes, in actuality, situation recognition must be about recognizing sequences of events (narratives). The neural mechanisms underlying narrative remain unknown.

Animal psychology experiments tend to be run in cue-poor environments. A rat in a small box with nothing but a hole to poke its nose into and maybe a few levers to push, or a monkey in a small chair facing a blank screen, has few choices to decide between. When the tone sounds and food is delivered into the food port, there's not a lot of ambiguity about what the new cue was. When it happens a few more times, the animal quickly recognizes that the tone precedes food delivery. When a dot appears on the screen, the monkey looks at it—it's the only thing that has changed in the environment.

Even so, animal behavior has to be shaped to an environment.[1] One of the most famous experiments used in neuroscience today is the Morris Water Maze,[2] which consists of a large (several meters wide) pool of water made opaque with a small amount of water-soluble nontoxic white paint. In this task, rats or mice are trained to find a platform hidden under the water. This task is popular because it is particularly sensitive to damage to certain brain structures, such as the hippocampus.[A] From a decision-making

---

[A] As with any clinical experiment, interpretation of lesion studies needs to be tempered by an understanding of logical implications. Damage to the hippocampus leads to problems in the Morris Water Maze, but it is not true that problems in the Morris Water Maze imply damage to the hippocampus.

perspective, the Morris Water Maze is very interesting because the task can be solved by either the deliberative or procedural (habit) systems, depending on the training sequence.[3] But what is the first thing that rats do on this task? They swim around the edge of the pool, looking for a way out. Only after first thoroughly exploring this possibility do they start heading for the platform.

With humans, the important cues in psychology and neuroscience experiments are often explicitly identified to the subject: "You will see a set of faces. Try to identify which faces you have seen before . . ." Even when they are not explicitly identified, although the environments for human psychology experiments are often cue-rich, the important cue is often obvious to the subject. An fMRI machine is a claustrophobic space with tight walls around you, a metal cage around your head, and extremely loud pounding thumping noises.[4] And, yet, when the visual cue is turned on, we know to attend to it. In part, we know to attend to it because we have a storyline for what we expect to happen in one of these experiments.

But, as I've pointed out before, life outside of psychology experiments is made up of a plethora of cues impinging on our senses at all times. We are not often sitting, staring at a screen, trying to figure out if a small subset of a set of randomly moving dots tend to be moving more in one direction than another. Certainly, there are times that we see people peering into the distance or the darkness (think of a sailor standing on the crow's nest on a ship, keeping a lookout for land, or of a hunter stalking a deer); however, most of the time, the issue is too many cues, not too few.

Situation recognition

I first got interested in the question of situation recognition when talking to one of my colleagues (Steve Jensen) over lunch. Steve was fascinated by a phenomenon of one-trial learning in ICD patients.[5] These patients have a risk of sudden heart arrhythmias (where the beating of the heart changes to the wrong rhythm) and have had an implantable cardioverter-defibrillator (ICD) attached to their heart. These devices detect the rhythm of the heart and, if that rhythm goes wrong, provide an electrical shock to restart the heart. (Just as an external defibrillator can shock the heart back into rhythm, so can an internal one.) Unlike a pacemaker, which provides a slow, steady rhythm to the heart, the ICD kicks in only when the rhythm is stopped or wrong. Also, unlike a pacemaker, the ICD hurts like hell when it kicks in. Unlike an external defibrillator, which is used only on unconscious patients, the ICD usually kicks in while the patient is conscious. In such situations, the patient is suddenly provided with an extremely negative experience (even if it potentially may have saved the patient's life). These ICD patients have the strangest negative associations with things in their lives. Steve wanted to know what made the patient decide that the fork was the culprit and not the spoon, or that it was the act of sitting in a chair and not laughing with one's friends. Clearly, it has something to do with what these subjects were attending to at the time, but it got us thinking about the question of how we decide what cues are important.

In the robotics, computer science, and psychology literatures that study reinforcement learning, this is called the *credit assignment problem*.[6] Generally, the assumption in these models and experiments is that there is a small subset of potential cues that could be important, and the agent (the animal or the computer simulation) has to figure out which one is the key to making the right decision. But we know from other experiments (such as the Morris Water Maze and other spatial navigation experiments) that it is often a constellation of cues that informs the animal.[7] A subset of the cues can be removed and the animal will still find its way correctly, as long as enough of the cues are available. No one cue is key.

We realized that most of the computer models of decision-making assumed that the agent knew which possible situations were available (technically known as the *state space*) and often knew how they changed from one to another (technically known as the *transition matrix*), but that in reality, animals created situations out of cues. Real animals (including humans) categorized cues into *situations*.[8] Simple categorization in neural systems is well understood and can be modeled with *content-addressable memories*.[9] In fact, there are very well-studied learning systems that automatically categorize inputs, even without supervision.[10] These systems are called *unsupervised learning algorithms* and work by identifying regularities in the inputs.

Using a standard unsupervised learning algorithm, we built a model that incorporated a situation-categorization component into a standard reinforcement learning agent (an agent that learned what to do in what situation, essentially a procedural-learning agent in the terminology used in this book).[11] We found that this situation-recognition component turned out to change the observed psychology of our agent in a number of important ways. Most importantly, disappointment (lack of delivered reward) became different from punishment (delivery of a negative stimulus). In our model, disappointment led to the recognition of a change in the situation, while punishment led to a new association. (We've talked about the differences between reward, reinforcement, and disappointment, and their negative counterparts [punishment, aversion, and relief] in Chapter 4.)

This model suggests that there is a significant context effect to recognizing changes in our expectations of reward or punishment. This can explain why, for example, addicts who become clean in hospitals relapse on being released back into their normal lives, or why students who learn the correct answers to give about electricity in physics class are still unable to correctly build circuits when given a set of real batteries and other electrical components to build with.[12]

We were also able to manipulate parameters in our model to produce simulations of problem gambling due to incorrect situation recognition, either because the agent thought it could control a random situation (the *illusion of control*, believing that two outcomes were due to two situations when they really occurred due to random chance within a single situation) or because the agent was unable to recognize a change in a situation (which led to the phenomenon of *chasing losses*, continued playing even in the face of devastating loss because the agent thinks the difference is just random chance).[13]

Although our model was able to explain a number of psychological phenomena (such as why behavioral extinction is not the same as forgetting or why animals are slower to extinguish variably delivered rewards) and a number of clinical phenomena (such as context-related relapse in addiction or the illusion of control in gambling),[14] the unsupervised learning algorithm we used was a static cue-categorization mechanism. The algorithm took the currently available set of cues and determined whether it was part of a known situation or whether it had to be declared a new situation.[15] The real world is, of course, much more complex.

Situation recognition is complex, dynamic, and hierarchical

Of course, situation recognition is not all or none: situations are both similar and dissimilar to other situations. Making correct decisions requires that we be able to recognize both the similarities and differences between situations. The usual statement attributed to the Greek philosopher Heraclitus is that "You never step into the same river twice," but the fragments we have from the actual Greek suggest that a better interpretation is that some things stay constant through change.[16] If you are going to learn, you have to have some constancy between your past and your future. You need to recognize the similarities between your past and your present in order to translate past successes and failures into present plans. To solve this paradox, we need a system that can categorize situations, recognizing both the similarities and differences between your past and present.

I give a lot of scientific presentations to lots of different audiences. When I build my slides for a presentation, I try to make sure I have the right slides for the given audience. I remember the first time I went to give a talk in Japan. My wife pointed out that most Japanese scientists could read written English much better than they could understand spoken English. So I added a section to each of my slides describing the basic results on that slide. (I have since found that this helps native English speakers as well.) But even though the situation was slightly different, I didn't think of giving-a-talk-in-Japan to be a new situation, I defined it as a special case of my giving-a-talk category. This hierarchical nature is a key to human categorization.[17] A penguin is a bird, but it is also a water-swimmer, and it doesn't fly. Just as we categorize our concepts in a complex hierarchy with special cases that do not quite fit the categories, we also must categorize situations in complex ways.

Situations are also dynamic. We do not simply see a set of cues, categorize them as a situation, and respond to it. Instead, we recognize a sequence of situations and travel through it. I travel through the Minneapolis-St. Paul airport (MSP) approximately once per month (sometimes more, but I try to restrict myself to traveling less than once a month). Sometimes I have my laptop, sometimes I don't. Sometimes I have my family with me, sometimes I don't. Sometimes I have checked a bag, sometimes I take only carry-on. Going through security with my laptop is different from not. Similarly, security is different if it's just me or if I have my kids, and it's different if my toiletries are in my carry-on bag or checked through. And yet, I didn't need to relearn how to go through security from scratch the first time that they told me I had to take my toiletries out of my carry-on and pass them through the X-ray machine separately. I was able to take what I knew about going through airport security and modify it to include taking my toiletries out of my carry-on suitcase.

Going through airport security is a good example of a dynamic situation, what might be called a *script*.[18] The actions at each stage are very different, and yet they all go together in a recognizable sequence. First, you need your ID and boarding pass. Once those are checked, you then need to wait in line for the plastic tubs to put your stuff into. In American airports, you need to take off your shoes. (I once started to take off my shoes in a European airport and the security agent looked at me with quizzical surprise and asked, "What are you doing?") Going through airport security is a sequence of substitutions and actions.

A script is a storyline, a categorization of a sequence that can be modified at its sub-stages. The important points here are threefold. First, we categorize the situations of the world in order to act within it (*What are the important cues here?*). Second, those categories are complex and hierarchical (*Giving a talk in Japan is a special case of my giving-a-talk category*). Third, these scripts are dynamic (*Going through airport security is a complex, dynamic sequence of situations and actions*). These scripts are narratives, stories we tell ourselves about our lives.

Narrative and literature

The success of great literature is usually due to the recognizability of the characters. We ask ourselves, "Is that what this character would do in this situation?" Playwrights often talk of "keeping things in character." When a person does something that is "out of character," everyone notices. As Fergus (played by Stephen Rea) explains to Dil (played by Jaye Davidson) in Neil Jordan's *The Crying Game*, "It's in my nature." And then, to fully explain his actions to her, he tells her the fable of the frog and the scorpion. We recognize the self-consistency of his actions as a definition of his nature. This is true whether the stories be realistic or fantastical. Even explicitly unrealistic plays are based, fundamentally, on recognizable characters. I remember the first time I saw Samuel Beckett's *Krapp's Last Tape* and realized it was really about an old, alcoholic writer reminiscing over a long-past love affair. For all of its existentialist implications, Jean-Paul Sartre's *No Exit* is a simple dramatic interaction between three very real people. Even the absurdist plays like Eugene Ionesco's *Rhinoceros* have recognizable human interactions throughout.

In fact, throughout literature, the stories that survive are the ones in which we recognize human characteristics. Whether this be the remarkably human characteristics of the Greek or Norse gods, or the foibles of Biblical characters, the stories that survive are the ones that capture something "true" about human nature.

In large part the success of literature arises from the fact that human nature hasn't changed in thousands of years. We recognize ourselves in the squabbling Greeks of Homer's *Iliad* and the recovering soldier working his slow way home in Homer's *Odyssey*. We recognize ourselves in *Hamlet*'s indecision, in the rashness of *King Lear*. The soap opera of Shakespeare's *A Midsummer Night's Dream* is recognizable in any high school clique. The fables of Africa, North America, and medieval Italy all speak to us reliably.[19] We can even find ourselves in the imagined worlds of fantasy and science fiction, whether it be the hobbits learning to stand tall in J. R. R. Tolkien's *Lord of the Rings* or the political machinations in Frank Herbert's *Dune*.

It is important to recognize that this doesn't mean that literature is a morality play; true morality plays tend to be boring and quickly forgotten. Successful literature is more like an experiment, a way of testing "what would happen if." Literature is a form of fictive learning, a way to see what would happen if someone with a certain character were faced with a specific situation. It allows us to ask ourselves, "Would I do that?" Whether we ask ourselves if we would make the same mistakes or if we would have the strength to take the right action, literature is a way of trying out hypotheses about consequences, much like the *Gedanken* experiments (thought experiments) in science.

Writing instructors tell nascent writers to find the character, and then to put him or her into the most difficult situation one can.[20] What makes a situation difficult depends on the character one is writing about. At each stage of a story, we ask ourselves, "What would this character do in this situation?" We are very good at recognizing forced fiction, where the characters do something that is out of character to further the plot.

Fundamentally, humans are narrative creatures.[21] We tell ourselves stories of our lives and we define our lives in terms of those stories. We use narrative to explain our past, to recognize our present, and to predict the future. We plan the future by telling stories of what we think will happen (see Chapter 9). We recognize our present through the scripts we are passing through, and we try to understand our past actions and the things that have happened to us in terms of a narrative structure, by telling stories. Of course, as we saw in Chapter 9, that past is constructed—reconstructed, one might say. By changing the stories we tell ourselves, we reinterpret why we did what we did and we change who we are.

For example, the simple sentence "There is no such thing as one drink for an alcoholic" implies that the decision options you have in the future are not between going to the bar and having a single drink or staying home and being bored, but rather between going to the bar and getting really drunk (and thus regretting it) or staying home and not. This is a process called "bundling" in the neuroeconomics literature.[22] By bundling future decisions together, one sees both the immediate and long-term consequences. Computational models of this show that these bundling effects can change decisions in ways that nonbundled decisions cannot.

At this point, we don't know very much about the neurophysiology of how stories are represented within the brain. Clearly it must involve representations of categories and content-addressable memories. We know from the psychological literature that they must exist, and we know something of how static categories are represented within the brain, but the complexity of situation-recognition systems (such as the hierarchical nature) and the dynamics of those representations (such as the narrative structure and the effect of that narrative structure on decision-making) are still very open questions in the scientific literature today.

Books and papers for further reading

Rather than point you to scientific papers about the role of narrative, I'm just going to suggest reading fiction. Great authors are keen observers of the human condition.[B]

[B] Great fiction can be tremendously informative. But, as with any scientific paper, one has to engage the work in a dialogue and face the observations with a critical mind.

13

Motivation

> Tropical mountains
> through the netting of a blue hammock,
> snuggled together,
> reading,
> waking up

The specific goals that the decision-making systems are trying to satisfy arise from intrinsic goal functions evolutionarily prewired into our brains. However, we can also learn to identify new goals that we have learned lead to those intrinsic rewards or avoid those intrinsic punishments. The vigor with which we attempt to attain those goals depends on the level of intrinsic need and the opportunity cost of chasing those goals at the expense of others.

So far, we've talked about decisions as arising from evolutionarily learned reflexes, and from Pavlovian, Deliberative, and Procedural systems that learn from rewards and punishments. We've talked about how animals integrate information about the world and categorize situations to make their decisions. Throughout our discussion, however, we have sidestepped a fundamental question: *What defines the goal?* We identified opioid signaling as measuring the positive and negative reward and punishment components, and dopamine signaling as measuring the differences between predicted and expected (see Chapters 3 and 4). But neither of these defines what those positive rewards or negative punishments *are*.

The first explicit models of decision-making assumed that the goal was to maximize value or "utility."[1] Adam Smith (1723–1790) argued that everyone is trying to maximize his or her own utility.[2;A] From the very beginning of the economic literature, it was immediately clear that it was impossible to define utility in a general way that would be the

---

[A] Although Adam Smith is usually cited for the concept of each individual maximizing his or her own utility, it is important to note that he recognized that this was not stable in its simplest form. Smith's conceptualization was actually quite complex, and he suggested that national economic success depended on what we now recognize as empathy, sympathy, and altruistic punishment. For example, he recognized the importance of governmental assurances of market fairness, as well as the dangers of monopolies, and other complexities beyond the simplicity of maximization of individual profit.[3]

same for all people, and so the mathematicians Nicolaus Bernoulli (1695–1726) and his younger brother Daniel Bernoulli (1700–1782) proposed the idea of subjective utility, which suggests that each of us has an internal measure of that utility.[B] But it still doesn't define how our interaction with the world is translated into rewards and punishments.

Similarly, the original computer models of decision-making defined the goal to maximize as a reward function of time or situation, but never defined what the reward was.[7] These computer models did this to explicitly avoid the question that we are trying to address here. The authors of those computer models were trying to understand the decision-making algorithms in an imaginary (disembodied) computer world. When these algorithms were translated into robotics, the authors had to hard-code the goals into the robots.[8]

[B] The history of why the Bernoulli brothers came up with subjective utility is interesting, particularly because it gives an insight into the problems that arise from trying to derive microeconomics from first principles.[4] The brothers were trying to understand how to incorporate probability into utility— *How much should you like a 10% chance of getting $50?* They assumed, for simplicity, that one should like it 10% as much. Thus, 10% of $50 should be equivalent to $5. The problem with this is that you can create paradoxes from this assumption that are clearly wrong.

The case that the Bernoulli brothers came up with is called "the St. Petersburg paradox" because it was first presented to the Imperial Academy at the court of Peter the Great in St. Petersburg. Imagine a game with the following rules: You pay a fee to get in and then a coin is flipped. The game stops when the coin comes up tails. The game pays out $1 for each coin flip. Thus, if tails appears on the first flip, you get $1, but if you get 99 heads followed by a tails, you get $100. The question is *How much would you pay to play this game?* Because of the way the game is constructed, the mathematically expected payout is infinite, and a logical (which economists call "rational") person should be willing to pay anything to play this game.

Of course, people will only pay a small amount to play this. (Compare the St. Petersburg paradox, which feels wrong even though it is logical, to the distortions that were seen by Kahneman and Tversky,[5] which feel right even though we know they're illogical, such as the Asian flu example, where describing the problem in terms of people saved or people lost changes the choice [see Chapter 3].)

The Bernoulli brothers proposed that the reason people wouldn't pay large sums to play this game was because they were actually maximizing "subjective utility" in which higher and higher payouts had less and less value. Thus, $200 was not twice as valuable as $100. Bernoulli specifically suggested a square root function—that is, subjective value is the square root of the actual value offered.

However, it is not difficult to modify the St. Petersburg paradox to wreck any unbounded value function. One possible explanation is that our subjective value functions are not unbounded. Eventually, it doesn't matter how much money is paid out, it's just a "big win." The problem with this hypothesis is that it is very clear (at least for money) that this is not true. Billionaires who have long had every possible desire sated continue to fight for more money. (We will see why later in this chapter.) Current explanations for the St. Petersburg paradox are based on differences in how much we like gains and losses (people hate losses more than they like gains), and the recognition that you can never be offered an infinite amount of money because eventually you'll break the bank.

My hunch is that part of the answer may be that valuation is done online, and that the valuation system in our brains can't do the infinite sum needed to make it worth paying into the St. Petersburg paradox. If the person adds up only the first few cases and then says the chance of 10 heads in a row is so unlikely it's not worth thinking about, then the maximum payout is not infinite. (Of course, people play the lottery, which has a much lower probability of payout.) Even though the Bernoulli brothers' explanation of the St. Petersburg paradox as a transformation of utility is no longer the accepted story, the concept of an internal modification of subjective utility remains.[6]

Intrinsic reward functions

Theorists studying how animals forage for food in the wild have argued that animals (including humans) are maximizing their energy gains and minimizing their energy costs.[9] For example, imagine a hummingbird gathering nectar from a flower. To get the nectar, the hummingbird hovers in front of the flower, pulling nectar out. As the bird drinks the nectar it becomes harder and harder to pull nectar out. At some point, the energy being spent to flap its wings fast enough to hover is more than the energy it is pulling out of the flower, and it should go to another flower. Going to another flower is risky because the bird doesn't know how much nectar is available at that other flower. Maybe it has already been tapped out. Maybe the bird will search for a long time. It is possible to calculate the optimal time that the bird should spend at a patch of food and when it should leave. This optimal time depends on the size of the patch, the expectation of how much food is left in the patch, what the expected travel time is to the next patch, and the likely amount of food the bird would expect to find at the next patch. These equations correctly predict stay and leave times for foraging and hunting birds, mammals, and insects, transitions in monkey decision-making experiments, even for human hunters and gatherers deciding when and where to look for food, and for people foraging for information on the Web and in the world.[10]

But these foraging theories are based on the assumption that the only purpose of these animals is survival. Darwin's natural selection theory tells us that what really drives success is not survival but the procreation of genes into future generations, in particular successful procreation of future successful procreators.[11] There are numerous examples where animals sacrifice themselves for their genetic future. Even something as simple as a parent feeding its children is proof that there is more to the picture than individual survival.[C] We all know examples of parents sacrificing for their children, whether it be penguins starving themselves to keep eggs warm, starlings bringing food back to a nest, a polar bear protecting her cubs, or human immigrants sacrificing their dreams so their children can succeed in a new land.

Of course, there are also the classic studies of the social insects (bees, ants), who live in large colonies where drones sacrifice for a queen and her children.[12] The reason for this is now well understood, and is due to the fact that because of the way the insect genetics works, a drone is more genetically similar to her sisters than to her own children, so she evolutionarily prefers to make more sisters than to make more children.

These descriptions assume that animals are actually calculating how to maximize their genetic success. I don't know about you, but I don't generally spend each morning thinking, "How can I increase my genetic success today?" I'm pretty sure that no other animal does either. In large part, this is because determining what is going to lead to genetic success is very hard to predict. Such a calculation would take a tremendous amount of brain power—an individual spending too much time worrying about it is unlikely to actually succeed at it, and would quickly become genetically outcompeted.

So what *does* define the goals we want? One suggestion is that we have intrinsic goal functions evolutionarily prewired into our brains,[13] but that doesn't say what those goals

---

[C] I bet you never thought cooking for your kids was so fraught with meaning.

are. We are back to the hard-coded goals that the roboticists put into their robots. These authors argue that our evolutionary history has hard-coded goals into our brains that we then seek out irrespective of their actual evolutionary use. For example, dogs like to chase things, presumably because in the evolutionary past, the primary things that they got to chase were big game like deer, moose, and elk. For many dogs, the primary things they get to chase now are cars. These concepts were pushed forward in the 1970s under the guise of *sociobiology*—usually stated too simply and too unwilling to address the complexity of primate interactions.[14;D]

The origins of sociobiology were in animal ethology studies, particularly insect studies.[18] While insects are often interpretable as little robots,[19] with simple routines that are often recognizable (moths fly in a spiral toward lights), and often with simple failure modes (as anyone watching a moth fly toward a flame can see), birds and mammals are more complex, and humans particularly so. Human failure modes are also particularly complex, but that doesn't mean they're not identifiable. (We will address many of the ways that the decision-making systems break down [their *failure modes*] in the next section of the book.)

Human social interactions are incredibly complex. This does not, however, imply that they are random, unobservable, or unidentifiable. As discussed in Chapter 12, novelists and playwrights have been observing humans for millennia. As an audience, we recognize that individual humans have a consistent character. In a novel or a play or a movie, if someone does something that is "out of character," it shows up like a sore thumb. We have a very large portion of our brains devoted to recognizing social interactions. Does this mean we know which way an individual will jump? Not perfectly, but we can predict what an individual is likely to do, and we make our plans based on those predictions.

So what are those intrinsic goal functions? Obviously, when we are hungry, we want food; when we are thirsty, we want water. And obviously, we desire sex. Notice that a desire for sex is different than a desire for children. The evolutionary development of the desire for sex as the means of driving procreation rather than the desire for children as the means for procreation is a classic example of an intrinsic reward function. Of course, some couples do have sex because they are trying to have a baby. But, often, sex is for its own pleasures, and couples are surprised at the unexpected pregnancy.

[D] Sociobiology has gotten a bad rap over the past several decades because the conclusions were taken as *prescriptive* rather than *descriptive*, and because they often created broad generalizations from limited observations.[15] We will discuss the issue of differences between prescription and description later (in Chapter 23). Briefly, the goal of science is to understand causality in the world—if the world is in this configuration, then that will happen. For example, the Galilean/Newtonian theory of gravity implies that if I drop a hammer and a feather at the same time in a vacuum, they will hit the ground at the same time. (This was of course tested by Apollo 15 astronauts and found to be completely true.[16]) We call this *descriptive* because it describes the world. On the other hand, what we should do with this knowledge is *prescriptive*. To say that the double standard of loose sexuality (women lose rank for sexual promiscuity, while men gain it) arises from differences in how much effort women and men have to put into childrearing (it is easier for men to leave than for women to)[17] does not imply that one should encourage that double standard, or that a society that accepts that double standard will be better than one that doesn't. We will come back to questions of "better" and society in our discussion of morality in Chapter 23. As this issue of sociobiology is not the subject of this book, I'm going to leave it here, with the simple statement that the fact that biology is not destiny does not mean that it isn't true.

What's interesting, of course, is that humans (like all animals) are actually very picky about sex—partners who are more likely to produce strong, healthy, and intelligent children are more attractive sexually.[20] In addition, because humans require long commitments to raise successful children, humans, particularly women, often demand some sort of commitment before sex.[21] There have been a tremendous number of studies examining the complex interaction that arises in the human mating game, showing, for example, that beauty is not in the eye of the beholder, but that there are standards of beauty that are consistent across cultures and individuals that signal information about health, fecundity, and intelligence.[22]

Certainly some components of beauty do seem to vary from culture to culture, but these components tend to entail elaborate preparations that show that we have friends and the time to maintain our appearances. Because humans live in communities (it really does take a village to raise a child in normal human societies[23]), many of the variable components of definitions of beauty require a complex interaction with others of the community to maintain. (Think how difficult it is to cut one's own hair.) The specifics of these preparations may change culturally, but they consistently indicate time and effort put into appearance.

But food, water, and sex are not enough for us: we also want to be respected, and we seek out music, excitement, family, and friends. Babies seek out their mothers; mothers and fathers seek out their children. As a specific case, let's take maternal interactions. In one of the classic histories of the sequence of science, early studies of interaction suggested that animals did things only for food reward.[24] This suggested to researchers that children were "attached" to their mothers because they were fed by them.[E] In particular, the behaviorist John Watson (who we have met before as one of the major players in the development of the concept of stimulus–response "habits") argued that touching infants could only transmit disease and thus kids shouldn't be touched any more than necessary.[25] A third of a century later, a young psychologist named Harry Harlow, setting up a new laboratory at the University of Wisconsin, came across a description of how children being separated from their mothers as they entered a hospital would scream and cry. A few weeks later, his rat laboratory still not ready for experiments, he watched monkeys playing at the Madison zoo and realized he could directly test whether this anxiety was due to the separation from their mothers or whether it was some generalized stress, like going to the hospital. Harlow began a very famous series of experiments about motherhood and found that infants needed the warmth of a mother (or a mother-analog) as much as they needed food.[26]

Although these experiments galvanized the animal rights movement[27] and are still held up as terrible, nightmarish experiments (and would be very difficult to get approved under today's animal-care regulations[F]), they were a key to understanding

---

[E] This seems silly to us now, but it was due to an inability to quantify the non–food-related attachment component. Remember that psychology moved from the Gestalt theorists (in the late 19th century), who used introspection, to the Behaviorists (early 20th century), who would only examine quantifiable behaviors.

[F] The issue of animal rights is a very complex one that is far outside the scope of this book. However, for those who are interested in this issue, I recommend starting from two books by Deborah Blum, *The Monkey Wars*, which describes the interactions between the animal rights movements and scientists, and *Love at Goon Park*, which describes the life of Harry Harlow and the influence of his work on the world.

maternal interactions. As a consequence of these experiments, hospital procedures were changed. For example, infants in the neonatal intensive care unit (NICU) are now touched regularly by a parent or nurse, which has a dramatic effect on infant survival. These procedures were changed due to John Bowlby and his work on attachment theory.[28] Although Bowlby's initial hypotheses were arrived at simultaneously with Harlow's first experiments (1958/1959), throughout the subsequent decades, Harlow's careful experimental work formed the basis for Bowlby's successful campaign to change hospital procedures, as evidenced by the prominent place Harlow's experiments had in Bowlby's influential book on attachment theory. Every child that has survived the NICU owes his or her life in part to Harry Harlow and those terrible experiments.[G]

We now know that maternal interactions between children and their parents (in humans both mothers and fathers) are driven in part by the neurotransmitter *oxytocin*, a chemical released in the hypothalamus in both mothers and infants shortly after birth. Oxytocin seems to be a key component of the social glue that holds couples and families together.[32] Externally delivered oxytocin makes people more likely to trust a partner in economic decision games. In mothers and infants, oxytocin is released in response to holding children. (This was one of the points of Harlow's work—part of the maternal bond is due to the social contact.[33] In fact, oxytocin both induces mutual grooming and is released during mutual grooming in a number of mammalian species, including humans.) Merely holding and playing with a child releases oxytocin, even in men. I still remember vividly the first time I held each of my children and fed them and the absolutely overwhelming emotion associated with it. Even today, I really like cooking for my kids and seeing them like the food I've made.

Like eating, drinking, and sex, parental care is an intrinsic goal function. We don't eat or drink because it's necessary for survival, we eat and drink because we enjoy it, because it satisfies a need we feel in our bodies. Similarly, we don't have sex because we are trying to procreate (usually). Proof that parental care is an intrinsic goal function can be seen in the way people treat their pets (and, perhaps, even in the fact that people keep pets in the first place). At one time, it might have been true that dogs were hunting companions, and that cats kept granaries clean of rodents, but most households in

---

[G] Some readers may complain about the sequence that I've presented here. In 1900, John Watson is a leading psychologist and argues that children should not be hugged or cuddled, which leads, actually, to high death rates in orphanages and hospitals.[29] It takes an interaction between John Bowlby observing what we now identify as separation anxiety in children in hospitals and Harry Harlow doing terrible experiments on monkeys to overturn this view and recommend that children need (as the now-popular saying goes) "eight hugs a day." It took a half-century for science to correct this mistake. What errors are we facing today? What scientific mistakes are hidden in this book? Should we trust current science at all? This topic is too long and complex to address in this book, but the short answer is that science is a self-correcting system. One could argue that self-correction is the key to science—it may take years or even decades, but science checks itself and corrects itself.[30] That's what has allowed all of the breakthroughs we've seen today, from flight to computers. Newton corrected Aristotle, and Einstein corrected Newton. Instead of saying "science is sometimes wrong, we should ignore it," we need to identify where we think current theories are mistaken and propose experiments that will directly test them—and then trust the answers those experiments give us. (Compare this to alternative description-of-the-world paradigms that claim to have known the answer for hundreds or thousands of years, but have no means of changing hypotheses in response to their relation to facts.[31])

urban and suburban settings aren't hunting for survival, nor do they have granaries to be kept rodent free.[H] Nevertheless, more than half of U.S. households have pets of one sort or another. People with pets live longer and are more happy than people without.[34] Pets, particularly dogs and cats, capture some of that intrinsic parental care goal function. Just as dogs chase cars because they love to chase things, we have pets because we need that social interaction. Dogs have been shown to be therapeutic stress relievers for both traumatized children and for college students studying for finals. In college, during finals week, local groups would come around with their therapy dogs. I can say from personal experience that there is something remarkably relaxing about taking a break from studying to play with a big St. Bernard.

So what are the intrinsic goal functions of humans? The list would probably be very long and may be difficult to pin down directly, in part because some of these intrinsic goal functions develop at different times. It is well known that interest in the opposite sex fluctuates from not even noticing differences in the very young (say younger than seven years old), to not wanting to talk to the other sex (the famous "cootie" stage, say seven to eleven), to intrigue (twelve, thirteen), and eventually to full-blown obsession (say seventeen). Maternal and paternal interests also famously switch on at certain ages. But all of these intrinsic goal functions contain some learning as well. Although teenage girls are often obsessed with babies, teenage boys are often disdainful. However, teenagers, particularly teenage boys, with much younger siblings are often more parental (in the sense of having positive reactions to very young kids) than teenagers without younger siblings.

Many of the intrinsic goal functions in humans are cognitive. One of the most interesting that I find is the satisfaction in completion of a job well done. There is an inherent feeling of success in not just the completion, but the knowledge that the job specifically was well done.[35] The act of discovery is itself a remarkably strong driving force. Although there have been those who have argued that curiosity is really due to issues of information gathering needed for proper behavior within an environment, several recent computational studies have found that an inherent drive to explore produces better learning than simple reward-maximization algorithms and that humans and other animals seem to have an over-optimism producing exploration.[36] Even other primates will work harder for curiosity than for food rewards.[37] Many scientists (including myself!) have a strong emotional feeling of accomplishment when they identify a new discovery—we now know something that was not known before, and that emotion of accomplishment is a strongly motivating force.[38]

Similarly, many of the clear intrinsic goal functions of humans are social, the respect of one's peers (as, for example, sports stars who want to be "the highest paid wide receiver" or celebrities who can't give up the limelight). This respect is often incorrectly called social "rank," but primate societies are very complex and differ from species to species.[39] For example, baboon societies include parallel hierarchies of females and males,[40] and a remarkable reverse hierarchy in the males, where the most successful males (the ones who make decisions that everyone follows and the ones who have

---

[H] Although, when my wife and I were in college, we had an apartment kept mouse-free by our excellent hunting cat Koshka. When we moved in, there were mice living in the furnace room, but they didn't last very long.

the most matings and the most children) are the ones who lose the fights (because they walk away).[41;I]

Human societies are particularly complex and leadership roles vary with situation and context.[42] In small bands and tribes, social rank can be very dynamic. Individual expertise provides transient leadership roles and corresponding rank increases. In one of my favorite examples of this, for her Master's thesis, my wife watched children in the Carnegie Museum in Pittsburgh.[43] Some children are dinosaur experts, while other children are not. In the dinosaur section of the museum, dinosaur-expert children were treated with more respect and deference than their peers. As a control, she also watched those same children in the geology section, where their expertise no longer gave them that rank boost. Of course, rank can bleed over from one's expertise to other aspects of life. The dinosaur-expert children were more likely to be asked to make unrelated decisions (such as where to go for lunch) than the nonexpert children. We see this, for example, in celebrities (such as actors or TV pundits) asked to comment on decisions as if they were scientific experts.

Neurophysiologically, many studies have found that these intrinsic goal functions increase activity in the dopamine systems (remember, dopamine signals value-prediction error and serves as a training signal) and increase activity in a specific set of ventral structures known to be involved in pleasure, displeasure, and drive. Generally, these studies have asked what turns on these ventral decision-making structures, including both the ventral striatum, which sits underneath the rest of the striatum, and the insula (which also sits at the ventral side of the brain, but more anterior, forward, than the ventral striatum).[44] Although these studies can't answer whether these functions are intrinsic or learned because they have to be studied in adults, the studies find an intriguing list of signals that drive this activity, including food, money, drugs, attractive faces, successfully playing videogames, music, social emotions such as love and grief, even altruism (e.g., giving to charity) and justice (e.g., punishing unfairness).[45]

In particular, humans seem to have hard-coded goals that encourage positive social interactions, particularly within defined groups.[46] Humans seem to have an intrinsic goal of a sense of fairness, or at least of punishing unfair players. In one of the more interesting studies, people interacted with two opponents, one of whom played fairly and one of whom didn't.[47] The people and the two opponents were then given small (but unpleasant[J]) electric shocks. The key question in the experiment was the activation of the ventral reward-related structures of the subject watching the two opponents get electronic shocks. In both men and women, there was more activation in the insula (signaling a negative affect) when the fair opponent got shocked than when the unfair opponent got shocked. In men, there was even activity in the ventral striatum (signaling a positive affect) when the unfair opponent got shocked. Part of the intrinsic goal function in humans is a sense of fairness in our interactions with others. We will see this appear again in our discussion of morality and human behavior (Chapter 23).

[I] For those who are interested in this, there are a lot of great books on the topic of primate hierarchies and their complexity. See, for example, *A Primate's Memoir* (Robert Sapolsky), *Sex and Friendship in Baboons* (Barbara Smuts), *Almost Human* (Shirley Strum), *Chimpanzee Politics* (Frans de Waal), and of course, the entire series of Jane Goodall's popularizations of her studies of the chimpanzees of Gombe (*In the Shadow of Man*, *Through a Window*, and many others).

[J] It is remarkable how unpleasant even a small electric shock can be.[48]

In the earlier chapters on decision-making, we discussed how we make decisions based on our goals, but didn't identify what those goals were. We have mentioned some of the goals here, but the goals vary in large part from species to species and from individual to individual within a single species. Identifying the goals that generalize across human behavior and the distributions of goals that vary between humans are both areas of active research today.[49] Some of those goals are learned over evolutionary timescales and are hardwired into an individual, while others are sociological in nature, depend on inherent processes in our cultural interactions, and must be learned within the lifespan, and some are due to an interaction between genetics and culture.[50] The key point here, however, is that although goals are evolved over generations and learned over time in such a way that they have helped procreate our genetics, the goals that are learned are only indirectly aimed at successful procreation. Whether it be dogs chasing cars or college boys surfing the Internet for porn, it is the intrinsic goals that we are trying to satisfy. The decision-making systems that we have explored have evolved to satisfy these goals. In later sections, we will see how these indirect intrinsic goals can lead us astray.

Learning what's important

Hunger informs us when we need sustenance, thirst when we are dehydrated, but people also eat when they are not hungry and drink when they are not thirsty. Actually, that's not the full story—a more careful statement would be that we can become thirsty even when we are not dehydrated, and hungry even when we don't need food. This occurs because certain cues (visual cues, odor cues) can drive us to become hungry and to desire food or to become thirsty and to desire water.

The smell of baking bread, an image of pizza flashed on the screen, cues that remind us of food can make us hungry. Animals that encounter a cue predictive of food are often driven to eat.[51] Similarly, cues that appear before something bad make us afraid.[52] We've already seen how these cues can lead us to Pavlovian action-selection, which we saw in Chapter 8 primarily involved emotions and somatic actions. In addition, these cues can create motivation that drives the other action-selection systems.[53;K]

These effects are known as *Pavlovian-to-instrumental transfer* (PIT) because they involve training similar to the learning we saw in Pavlovian action-selection systems (Chapter 8) and an influence on the other two action-selection systems (Deliberative and Procedural, which were historically known as "instrumental" learning; see Footnote 6C).[55] In PIT, as in Pavlovian action-selection, two cues are presented such that one is informative about whether the other is coming (Pavlov ringing a bell means food will be delivered soon). However, here, instead of driving action-selection (salivate), the learned contingency changes your motivation, your desire for that outcome. In a sense, the bell makes the dog think of food, which makes it hungry.

Scientists studying the effects of marketing have suggested that restaurant icons (such as the "golden arches" of McDonald's or the instantly recognizable Coke or Pepsi symbols) have a similar effect on people, making them hungry (or thirsty) even when

---

[K] Several authors have suggested that this is what *craving* is—the motivation for a thing predicted by cues.[54] We will return to the question of craving in our discussion of addiction (Chapter 18).

they are not. Presumably, this only works on people with positive associations with these symbols. It might be very interesting to measure the emotional associations with certain fast-food restaurants (which tend to produce strongly positive emotions in some people and strongly negative emotions in others) and then to measure the effects of their symbols on choices, but, to my knowledge, this has not yet been done. However, Sam McClure, Read Montague, and their colleagues found that individual preferences for Coke or Pepsi were reflected in preferences for identical cups of soda labeled with different labels.[56] They found that the label changed what people liked—Pepsi-liking people preferred the Pepsi-labeled cup, even though the two cups had been poured from the same bottle. Similarly, Hilke Plassmann and her colleagues studied effects of pricing on the perception of wine and found that people thought higher-priced wines tasted better, even when they were given identical wines in expensive and inexpensive bottles.[57]

The influence of this Pavlovian learning of contingencies (cue implies outcome) on instrumental action-selection (Deliberative, Procedural) can be either *general*, leading to increased arousal and an increase in speed and likelihood of taking actions overall, or *specific*, leading to increased likelihood of taking a specific action. In generalized PIT, a cue with positive associations produces a general increase in all actions, while in specific PIT, the cue produces an increase in actions leading to the reminded outcome but not to other outcomes.[58] We will address generalized PIT in the next section, when we talk about vigor and opportunity costs; in this section, I want to look at the effects of specific PIT.

Imagine, for example, training an animal to push one lever for grapes and another lever for raspberries. (Simply, we make the animal hungry, provide it levers, and reward it appropriately for pushing each lever. Of course, in real experiments, these are done with flavored food pellets, which are matched for nutrition, size, etc. so that the only difference is the flavor.) Then, imagine training the animal (in another environment) that when it hears a tone, it gets a grape. (Simply, we play the tone and then quickly thereafter give the animal the grape. Do this enough, and the animal will expect that getting a grape will follow the tone.) Putting the animal back in the lever environment, when we play the tone, the animal will be more likely to push the lever for grapes. We can test for generalized versus specific PIT by examining whether the animal presses both levers (a generalized increase in activity) or only the grape lever (a specific increase in the action leading to getting grapes). What's happening here is that the animal is reminded of the possibility of getting grapes by the tone, which leads to an increase in the likelihood of taking an action leading to getting grapes. In a sense, the tone made the animal hungry for grapes.

Of course, this also happens in humans. Seeing the paraphernalia for a drug that an addict tends to take leads to craving for the drug.[59] Some cigarette smokers prefer to self-administer a nicotine-free cigarette rather than an intravenous injection of nicotine,[60] suggesting that the conditioned motivational cue can be even stronger than the addictive substance. And, in the examples we keep coming back to in this section, marketing symbols increase our internal perceptions of hunger and thirst.[61] I took my kids to a movie theater last week, and, while sitting waiting for the movie, my son complained that all of the food ads[L] were making him hungry, even though he had just eaten a large lunch. He said, "I wish they wouldn't show those ads, so I wouldn't get hungry because I'm already so full."

[L] Some of the ads were for pizza! Who eats pizza at the movies?

Vigor—Need and opportunity costs

Most of the choices in our lives entail doing one thing at the expense of another: if we are working at our desk, we are not exercising; if we are sleeping, we are not working.... There are dozens if not hundreds of self-help books aimed at time management. The losses that come from not doing something can be defined as an *opportunity cost*[62]—what opportunities are you losing by choosing Option A over Option B?

Yael Niv and her colleagues Nathaniel Daw and Peter Dayan recently suggested that the average (tonic) level of dopamine is a good measure of the total reward available in the environment.[63;M] This suggests that tonic dopamine is related to the opportunity cost in the environment. An animal being smart about its energy use should change the vigor with which it works as a function of this opportunity cost. (If there are lots of other rewards in the environment, one should work faster, so one can get to those other rewards quicker. On the other hand, if there are not a lot of other rewards, then don't waste the energy doing this job quickly.)

Interestingly, this tonic-dopamine-as-vigor hypothesis unifies the role of dopamine in learning (phasic bursts drive learning), incentive salience (dopamine implies a cue that leads to reward), and the motoric effects of dopamine in Parkinson's disease, Huntington's disease, and other dysfunctions of the basal ganglia.[66]

Parkinson's disease occurs when the dopamine cells die, leaving the person with a severe deficiency in dopamine available to the basal ganglia.[67] (Remember from Chapter 10 that the basal ganglia use dopamine to learn and drive Procedural learning.) For years, dopamine was thought to drive movement because excesses in dopamine to the basal ganglia produced inappropriate movements (called *dyskinesias*, from the Greek δυσ- [*dys-*, bad] + κινησία [*kinesia*, movement]), while deficiencies in dopamine to the basal ganglia produced a difficulty initiating movements and a general slowing of reaction time (called *akinesia* or *bradykinesia*, from the Greek α [*a-*, without] and the Greek βραδύ- [*brady-*, slow]).[68]

The other thing that drives motivation and the willingness to work is, of course, need. As we discussed earlier in this chapter (*Intrinsic goal functions*, above), a major role of motivation is to identify your needs—a state of dehydration means you need water. This is almost too obvious to say, but it is important to remember that these are not binary choices—it is not "Am I hungry?" but "How hungry am I?" The hungrier you are, the more willing you are to try new foods, the more willing you are to work for food, and the better that food tastes. Vigor also depends on how badly you need that outcome.[69]

Several authors have suggested that dopamine levels drive invigoration, from both the opportunity cost and need perspectives.[70] Basically, these authors suggest that tonic dopamine levels enable an animal to overcome effort—the more dopamine available, the more the animal is willing to work for a result. Intriguingly, this has evolutionary similarities to the role of dopamine in very simple vertebrates, where dopamine invigorates movement.[71]

[M] Remember that phasic bursts of dopamine signal transitions in value being better than expected, while pauses of dopamine signal transitions in value being worse than expected.[64] These phasic bursts are like taking a derivative of the expected value signal. Tonic dopamine would then be taking the integral of this value signal, which is the average reward in the environment.[65]

Manipulations of dopamine can drive an animal to work more for a specific reward cued by the presence of visual or auditory signals when that dopamine is increased.[72] The specific interactions between dopamine, learning, invigoration, and reward is an area of active research in many laboratories around the world, and a source of much controversy in the scientific literature.[73] Most likely, dopamine is playing multiple roles, depending on its source, timing, and neural targets.

In any case, how willing an animal is to work for reward or to avoid a punishment is an important motivational issue.[74] Vigor is very closely related to the issue of general PIT discussed earlier in this chapter. The presence of cues that signal the presence of rewards likely implies that the world around you is richer than you thought. If there are more rewards around to get, working slowly means spending more of that opportunity cost, and a smart agent should get the job done quicker so that it can get back to those other rewards.

Summary

In previous chapters we talked about action-selection, but not about what motivated those actions. Motivation can be seen as the force that drives actions. Motivation for specific rewards depends on the specific needs of the animal (intrinsic goal functions), which can vary from species to species. Intriguingly, humans seem to have intrinsic goal functions for social rewards. In addition to the intrinsic goal functions, cues can also be learned that can drive motivation, either to specific outcomes (specific Pavlovian-to-Instrumental Transfer) or to invigorate the animal in general (general Pavlovian-to-Instrumental Transfer). These motivational components are an important part of the decision-making system, because they define the goals and how hard you are willing to work for those goals, even if they don't directly select the actions to take to achieve those goals.

Books and papers for further reading

- David W. Stephens and John R. Krebs (1987). *Foraging Theory*. Princeton, NJ: Princeton University Press.
- Robert Wright (1995). *The Moral Animal: Why We Are the Way We Are: The New Science of Evolutionary Psychology*. New York: Vintage.
- Kent C. Berridge (2012). From prediction error to incentive salience: Mesolimbic computation of reward motivation. *European Journal of Neuroscience, 35*, 1124–1143.
- Yael Niv, Nathaniel D. Daw, Daphna Joel, and Peter Dayan (2006). Tonic dopamine: Opportunity costs and the control of response vigor. *Psychopharmacology, 191*, 507–520.

The Tradeoff Between Exploration and Exploitation

> Waterfall at the edge of the mountains
>
> beyond the swirling chaos,
> the river vanishes into the dark forest,
> racing to the sea....

To take the correct actions within an environment, one has to know the structure of the environment, the consequences of those actions. Exploration is the process through which a novel environment becomes familiar. Exploitation is the process of using that knowledge to get the most out of a familiar environment. There is a tradeoff between these two processes—exploration can be dangerous, but not knowing if there are better options available can be costly.

An issue that often comes up in theoretical discussions of decision-making is that there is a tradeoff between learning more about the world and using what you've learned to make the best decisions. Imagine that you're in a casino with a lot of different slot machines available to play. You don't know what the payout probabilities are for any of them; to find out, you have to play them. As you play a machine, you learn about its parameters (how likely it is to pay how much given its costs). But you don't know if one of the other machines would be a better choice. One can imagine where one would fall on this continuum of *exploring* to see what the payoffs of the various machines are and *exploiting* the knowledge you already have to choose the best option that you know of.[A] This is a task called the *n-armed bandit* task[1] (as an extension of the original slot machine, known as the "one-armed bandit" because it stole all your money).

In a stable world, it is best to do some exploring early and to diminish your exploration with time as you learn about the world.[2] A good system often used in the robotics

---

[A] The use of "exploit" here has unfortunate overtones in terms of "exploiting others." What is meant here by "exploit" is simply using the knowledge one has learned from exploring to make the best choices.

and machine-learning[B] literature is to give yourself a chance of trying a random machine each round. This random level is called ε (epsilon) and the strategy is called an "epsilon strategy." The question, then, is what should epsilon be on each round? Simple strategies with a constant, low epsilon are called "epsilon-greedy." For example, you might try a random action one round in a hundred and use your knowledge to pick the best choice on the other ninety-nine tries out of the hundred.[C] In a stable world, you should explore early and then settle down to the best choice later. In the machine-learning literature, a common strategy for a stable world is to use an exponentially decreasing chance of trying a random action. This explores early and exploits after you have learned the structure of the world you are living in, but never completely stops exploring.

Of course, the real world is not generally stable, and it would not generally be safe to have a pure exploration phase followed by a pure exploitation phase. More recent machine-learning algorithms have been based on explicitly tracking the uncertainty in each option.[6] When the uncertainty becomes too large relative to how much you expect to win from the option you are currently playing, it's time to try exploring again. This requires keeping track of both the *uncertainty* and the *expected value* of an option. As we will see below, there is now behavioral evidence that people keep track of uncertainty, that uncertainty is represented within the brain, and that genetic differences affect how sensitive individuals are to uncertainty (how willing they are to switch from exploitation to exploration modes).[7]

The *expected value* of an option is how much you expect to win on average if you keep playing the option; *uncertainty* is how unsure you are about that expected value. This is often called the "risk" in financial markets.[8] Imagine that you know that one time in twenty when you put a dollar into the game you get twenty-one dollars out. That game then has a positive payout of $21/$20 or 1.05, meaning you make 5% playing that game.[D] On the other hand, another machine might pay $105 one time in 100, which

---

[B] Machine learning is a branch of computer science in which algorithms are developed to learn from the world.[3] Although machine learning often lives in the artificial intelligence divisions of computer science departments, machine learning is actually distinct from artificial intelligence. "Artificial intelligence" is about trying to match (either mechanistically or computationally) human skills. "Machine learning" is about trying to build the best algorithm that will be able to solve the problem. Scientists working on machine learning believe that a machine that can learn from the world can be more efficient and perform better than a preprogrammed machine. (For example, imagine if your thermostat could learn when you typically came home or when you typically woke up in the morning. It could learn to set itself to warm the house before you arrived or just before you woke up. Of course, it could be programmed to do that, but then it would have to be programmed separately for each person. A single learning algorithm could be programmed once to learn the right timing for each person.[4])

[C] This can be most easily implemented by selecting a random number from 1 to 100 each try. If the random number is 100, then you take a random action. If it's anything else, you pick the best choice you can. One could also simply pick the random action every 100th try, but the danger is that if the winning probabilities have some oscillation to it, then your every 100th try might match the oscillation and you wouldn't know. Randomness is better. Of course, humans are terrible at being random.[5]

[D] Yes, I know slot machines always have a less than 100% payout because the goal of casinos is to make a profit. If you like, you can think of these games as putting money into savings accounts. A savings account in a bank may be FDIC insured and thus very safe (because the only way to lose money is for the United States itself to go under), but you'd make only 1% interest each year. On the other hand, a mutual

(continued)

also has a positive payout of $105/$100 or 1.05 or 5%, but is much more variable. If you played either game for a very long time, the expected value of playing would be the same. But if you play each game only a few times, you could lose more (or gain more) in the second game. The second one is riskier.

Uncertainty

It is useful to think of three different kinds of uncertainty: *expected uncertainty, unexpected uncertainty*, and *ambiguity*.[10]

In the first type (expected uncertainty), one recognizes that there is a known unpredictability in the world. We see this when a meteorologist says that there is a "60% chance of rain." If the meteorologist is correct, then 6 times out of 10 that the meteorologist says "60%," there should be rain and 4 times out of 10, it should be dry.

The second type (unexpected uncertainty) entails a recognition that the probabilities have changed. This is what is tested in *reversal learning* tasks, in which reward-delivery probabilities are changed suddenly without an explicit cue telling the subject that the probabilities have changed. Rats, monkeys, and humans can all reliably track such changes.[11] Since the reversal is uncued, recognition of the change in probabilities becomes an information-theory problem.[12] Humans and other animals can switch as quickly as information theory says anything could. When faced with a sudden change in reward-delivery probability (such as in extinction, when rewards are suddenly no longer delivered, see Chapter 4), animals show frustration, increasing their exploration of alternative options.[13]

The difference between expected and unexpected uncertainty was most famously (infamously) laid out by Secretary of Defense Donald Rumsfeld in his press conference defending the failures of the American invasion of Iraq, in which he claimed that there were "known unknowns" (expected uncertainty) and "unknown unknowns" (unexpected uncertainty) and that he should not be blamed for misjudging the "unknown unknowns."[14] Of course, the complaint was not that there was unexpected uncertainty, but that Rumsfeld and his team had not planned for unexpected uncertainty (which any military planner should do[15]) and that Rumsfeld and his team should have expected that there would be unexpected uncertainty.

The third type of uncertainty is *ambiguity*, sometimes called *estimation uncertainty*,[16] uncertainty due to a known lack of exploration. This is what is often referred to in the animal-learning literature as the transformation from novel to familiar and is the main purpose of exploration.[17] Here, the uncertainty is due to having only a limited number of samples. The more samples you take, the better an estimate you can get. Exploration entails taking more samples, thus getting a better estimate of the expected uncertainty.

Humans find ambiguity very aversive. The classic example of ambiguity is to imagine two jars containing marbles and having to decide which jar to pick from.[18] Each jar contains a mix of red and blue marbles. You will win $5 if you pick a red marble and

---

fund account might not be FDIC insured (and thus you can lose money on it), but you might make an average of 5% interest each year. Buying a stock might be very variable, making 10% one year and losing 10% the next. This is why good financial planning requires a diverse portfolio to balance out risk.[9]

$1 if you pick a blue marble. Imagine that you see the first jar being filled, so that you know that half of the marbles are red and half are blue. (You will still have to pick with your eyes closed and the jar above your head so which marble you pick will be random, but you know the distribution of marbles in the first jar.) Imagine, however, that the second jar was filled while you were not there and all you know is that there is a mix of red and blue marbles. Which jar will you pick from? In the first one, you know that you have a 50:50 chance of getting red or blue. In the second one, you might have a 90:10 chance or a 10:90 chance. Adding up all the possible chances, it turns out that you also have a 50:50 chance of getting red or blue. (The likelihood of seeing a 90:10 mix of red and blue marbles is the same likelihood of seeing a 10:90 mix. Since 90:10 is the opposite of 10:90, they average out to being equivalent to a 50:50 mix in both the first-order average [expected value] and the second-order variability [risk].) However, people reliably prefer the first jar, even when the fact that the second jar adds up to the same chance is pointed out to them. The first jar contains risk (expected uncertainty; you could get red or blue). The second jar, however, also contains ambiguity (*What's the mix?*) as well as risk (*What's the variability?*). This is known as *ambiguity aversion* and is technically an example of the Ellsberg paradox.[E]

There are a number of explanations that have been suggested for the Ellsberg paradox, including that humans[F] are averse to ambiguity due to a consequence of being more sensitive to losses than to gains or to an inability to do the full calculation of probabilities needed for the ambiguity case. Alternatively, the Ellsberg paradox could arise because humans have inherent heuristics aimed at avoiding deceit.[21] Since the subject doesn't know the mix of the second jar, it might have been chosen to be particularly bad, just so the experimenter wouldn't have to pay much out to the subject. (Rules on human-subjects studies generally do not allow an experimenter to lie to a subject, so when the experimenter tells the subject that there is a 50:50 mix, it has to be true, but when the experimenter tells the subject that there is just a "mix," it could have been chosen to be particularly poor.[G] But, of course, it is not clear that the subjects of these experiments believe that.)

Animals will reliably expend effort to reduce uncertainty. (This means that knowledge really is rewarding for its own sake.) People often say that figuring something out gives them a strong positive feeling, both of accomplishment and of knowing how things work.[23] (Certainly, I can say personally that there is no feeling like the moment when a complex problem suddenly comes clear with a solution, or the moment when I realize how a complex set of experiments that seem to be incompatible with each other can be unified in a single theory.) Not only humans, but also other animals will expend energy simply to reduce ambiguity. Ethan Bromberg-Martin and Okehide Hikosaka tested this

---

[E] The paradox was introduced by Daniel Ellsberg (of the famous Pentagon Papers[19]) in his 1962 Ph.D. dissertation in economics.[20] It is called a paradox because the simple equations of economists are unable to explain why humans are ambiguity averse.

[F] To my knowledge, although the paradox is robustly shown by humans, the paradox has not been tested on nonlinguistic animals, probably because it depends on the experimenter telling the subject the two probabilities.

[G] These rules were put in place due to egregious experiments such as the Tuskegee syphilis experiment, where subjects were lied to about the goals and consequences of experiments.[22] These rules are now followed very strictly, and it is exceptionally difficult to get approval to lie to an experimental subject.

in monkeys and found that information that reduces uncertainty, even if it has no effect on the final amount of reward the animal gets, has gotten, or expects to get, produces firing in dopamine neurons[24] (which, if you remember, we saw represent things being "better than expected," Chapter 4).

Gathering information

Computational theories have proposed that a good way to encourage a computational agent or robot to explore is to provide "exploration bonuses," where the system provides a "better than expected" signal when the agent enters a new part of the world.[25] Computationally, if this is matched by a "worse than expected" signal when the agent returns to its familiar zone, then the total value function will still be learned correctly. But it is not clear if the counteracting "worse than expected" signal appears on return. People and animals returning to a safe and familiar zone tend to show relief more than an "oh, well, that's done" disappointment signal.[26] Although it is possible to prove stability only if an agent is allowed an infinite time to live in a stable world (obviously not a useful description of a real animal in a real world), simulations have shown that for many simple simulated worlds, not having a "worse than expected" signal on return does not disrupt the value function too much. These simulations have found that an agent with only a positive "better than expected" novelty signal does as well or better than agents with no novelty signals.[27] Such an agent would be overly optimistic about future possibilities. This idea that the agent should receive a bonus for exploration is reflected in the human belief that things could always be better elsewhere. As Tali Sharot discusses in her book *The Optimism Bias*, the data are pretty strong that humans are optimistic in just such a manner—"the grass is always greener on the other side." Humans tend to overestimate the expectation of positive rewards in novel choices, which leads to exploration.[28]

Several studies have found these sorts of "novelty bonuses" in dopamine signals in monkeys and in fMRI activity from dopamine-projecting areas in humans.[29] Animals do find novelty rewarding, and will naturally go to explore a novel item placed in their environment.[30] This is so natural that it doesn't require any training at all. Harry Harlow, in his early monkey experiments, found that fully fed monkeys would work harder to see novel objects than hungry monkeys would work for food. Hungry rats will explore a new environment before eating. This suggests that exploration (the search for knowledge or information) is an intrinsic goal of the sort discussed in Chapter 13.

Learning from others

In the real world (outside of the laboratory), such exploration can, of course, also be dangerous. An advantage humans have is that they can imagine futures (*episodic future thinking*, Chapter 9) and can explore possibilities by imagining those potential future choices, even without necessarily trying them. One way this can occur is with *fictive learning*, in which one learns from watching others. One can observe another person's successes and failures and learn about what happens to him or her without directly experiencing it oneself.[31]

Of course, this is one of the most powerful aspects of human language, because language can be used to inform and to teach. A number of authors have observed that human culture is fundamentally Lamarckian; parents really do pass the lessons they learn in their lives on to their children.[32] (Although those lessons don't always stick...) Nevertheless, this Lamarckian nature of culture is one of the reasons that humans have spread so quickly to all of the corners of the globe, from the hottest jungles to the coldest tundras, even sending men to the moon and robots to the other planets in the solar system.

We now know that when a monkey observes another monkey doing a task that it is familiar with, the set of cortical neurons that normally fire when the observer is doing a task also fire when the observer is just watching the other monkey do the task.[33] These neurons are called "mirror neurons" because they *mirror* the behavior that the other monkey is doing. A similar set of human cortical circuits is active (as determined by fMRI) whether one is doing the action oneself or watching it.[34] Although the conclusions of some of these results are controversial (*Are the mirror neurons actually critical to imitation, or are they only recognizing related cues? Are they simply reflecting social interactions?*), certainly, we all know that we learn a lot by observing others.[35]

Similarly, we also know that we learn vicariously about reward and failure by watching others. A similar mirror system seems to exist for emotions, where we recognize and interpret the emotions of others.[36;H] This recognition is related to the emotions of empathy, envy, and regret.[39] These emotions are dependent on an interaction between hippocampal-based abilities to imagine oneself in another situation and orbitofrontal-based abilities to connect emotion to those situations.[40] In empathy, we recognize another's success or loss and feel a similar emotion. In envy, we recognize another's gain and wish we had achieved it. There is an interesting counter-side to envy, *gloating* or *schadenfreude*, meaning taking joy in another's adversity (from the German words *schaden*, harm, and *freude*, joy), which also depends on the same emotion-mirroring brain structures that envy does. And, in regret, we recognize a path we could have chosen but did not.

In large part, this is the key to the power of narrative and literature. We identify great stories as those that place realistic characters in situations, watching how they react. Great literature allows us to vicariously experience choices and situations that we might never experience. If one looks at the great works of literature, whether classic or popular,[I] one finds that they consistently describe human decision-making from remarkably realistic and complex perspectives. This is true whether one is talking about

---

[H] There is some evidence that part of the problem with psychopaths may be due to dysfunction in this mirror system and its ability to recognize the emotions of others,[37] but others have argued that this dysfunction is due primarily to an inability to correctly represent socially derived internal emotions.[38]

[I] One probably should not make a distinction between "classic" and "popular." Most literature that we call "classic" now was immensely popular in its time. Shakespeare, for example, was by far the most popular playwright of his day, and his plays are full of rough jokes for the popular crowds. (See, for example, Mercutio's death scene in *Romeo and Juliet*, most of *A Midsummer Night's Dream*, and the porter in *Macbeth*, to name but three.) I've often thought Shakespeare at his time was probably closest to Steven Spielberg in our day, with both blockbuster adventures like *Indiana Jones* and critically

(continued)

realistic dramas, magical worlds, or science fiction; even science fiction and magical realism depend on characters behaving realistically in strange situations. Although readers are generally willing to accept strange situations in other galaxies, or characters with magical powers, readers are generally unwilling to work through unrealistic characters.[J] Reading or watching these narratives, we place ourselves in those worlds and imagine what we would do in those situations, and we empathize with the characters and feel envy and regret about the decisions they make.

Exploration and exploitation over the life cycle

Computational work from the machine-learning literature has shown that in an unchanging world, the optimal solution to the exploration/exploitation tradeoff is to explore early and exploit late.[42] Of course, "early" and "late" have to be defined by the agent's expected lifetime. This would predict that one would see juveniles exploring and adults exploiting. While this is, in general, true, there are other important differences that change how the exploration/exploitation balance changes over the lifetime.

First, as we've discussed elsewhere, we don't live in an unchanging world. Thus, one cannot explore early and be done. Instead, one needs to titrate one's exploration based on how well one is doing overall.[43] When the rewards one is receiving start to decrease, one should increase one's exploration. When faced with a decrease in delivered rewards, animals get stressed and frustrated and show an increase in a number of behaviors, both the behavior that used to drive rewards, as well as other exploratory behaviors, starting with behaviors similar to the one that used to drive reward delivery. We've all seen ourselves do this, starting with trying the behavior again (*This used to work!*), moving to minor changes (*Why doesn't this work?*), and then on to new behaviors (*Maybe this will work instead.*).

Second, exploration is dangerous. This means that evolution will prefer creatures that develop basic abilities before going exploring. In humans, young children explore within very strict confines set by parents, and those confines expand as they age. As every parent knows, kids want to know that there are limits. They want to test those limits, but they also want those limits to exist. This suggests that the primary exploratory time in humans should occur after the person develops sufficient talents to allow handling the dangers of exploring the world.

The teen, adolescent, and early college years are notorious for high levels of drug use, exploratory sex, and risk-taking in general.[44] These are the exploratory years, where humans are determining what the shape of the world is outside the confines of their

---

acclaimed movies like *Schindler's List*. Similarly, the entire city of Athens turned out for the annual shows by Aeschylus, Sophocles, and Euripides, each of whom regularly won the best-play awards. Aristophanes' comedies contain what we now refer to as "frat-boy" humor, with lots of sex (*Lysistrata*), over-the-top characters (*The Clouds*), and fart jokes (*The Frogs*).

[J] An interesting question arises when the characters are explicitly nonhuman, whether they be aliens, magical creatures, or robots. In these stories, the nonhuman creatures tend either to be based on specific human cultures or to have exaggerated but still remarkably human, traits.[41] Writing science fiction about aliens can be said to be about finding the balance between making the aliens too human and making them too alien.

family structure. In general, most humans age out of these vices and settle down as they shift from an exploration to exploitation strategy.

In the next chapter, we will see how the prefrontal cortex plays a role in measuring risk and controlling dangerous exploration. One of the most interesting results discovered over the past few decades is that the prefrontal cortex in humans doesn't fully develop until the mid-twenties.[45] This means that adolescents do not have the same prefrontal assessment of risk and behavioral inhibition of doing stupid things as adults. As we've seen throughout the rest of this book, behaviors are generated by the physical brain, and changes in behavior are often caused by physical changes in the brain.[K]

Books and papers for further reading

- Tali Sharot (2011). *The Optimism Bias: A Tour of the Irrationally Positive Brain.* New York: Pantheon.
- Abram Amsel (1992). *Frustration Theory.* Cambridge, UK: Cambridge University Press.
- B. J. Casey, Sarah Getz, and Adriana Galvan (2008). The adolescent brain. *Developmental Review, 28,* 62–77.

[K] As I've said elsewhere in this book (see Chapter 24 for a detailed discussion), the recognition that there are physical and evolutionary causes for increased risk-taking in adolescents does not excuse the adolescent from the responsibility for his or her actions. It is important to recognize that sociobiological trends are not destiny and do not relieve one of responsibility. Although most drug users start using drugs in their adolescent years and many drug users age out of drug use and settle down to normal (non–drug-based) lives, the vast majority of adolescents do not succumb to peer pressure and drug use.[46] One hopes that before being sent off to college or out into the world for their exploration, adolescents have been taught what their limits are and have an accurate sense of the risks and dangers.

15

Self-Control

a stone is a mirror
without concentration
light reflects in all directions

We have the conscious experience that we can sometimes "override" emotional or habitual responses. This means that some process must mediate between the multiple decision-making systems. The mechanisms of that "override" process are still being studied, but some neural components, such as the prefrontal cortex, are known to be involved.

As we've seen in the past several chapters, the human decision-making system contains multiple action-selection components. Reflexes are largely driven by spinal control, but reflexes can be overridden by other systems in the brain (as we saw with Lawrence of Arabia holding the match). Emotional (Pavlovian) response systems release behaviors learned over evolutionary timescales, but, again, they can be overridden by other systems (controlling your fear). Procedural learning systems are habits that develop in response to consistent reward contingencies, but again, these can be overridden by other systems (as in the case of remembering to take the alternate route to work). And finally, there is the Deliberative system, which searches through future possibilities but does not (in general) have to pick the most desired choice. (Take, for example, the ability to select a small token of reward over a highly craved drug; the craving for a high-value option can be overridden to take what seems on the surface to be a lesser-value option.)

The word "override" comes from the ability of the nobility to dominate decisions (since the nobility served as cavalry and could literally *override* the opposition if it came to that) and echoes the Platonic concept of two horses leading a chariot—a wild uncontrollable (Dionysian) horse and an intellectual, rational, reasoned (Apollonian) horse, as well as the Augustinian and Freudian concepts of human reason controlling a wild animal past.[1] These concepts echo the popularized concept of a horse and rider, with the horse driving the emotional responses and the rider the reasoned responses.[2]

As anyone who has ridden a horse knows, riding a horse is very different from driving a car. The horse has internal sensors and will do some of the basic chores for you (like not bump into walls), while a car will do whatever you tell it to. Of course, this means that sometimes you have to fight the horse (for example, if you need to drive it into battle) in a way that you don't have to convince a car. (However, I am reminded of the scene in John Carpenter's darkly comic movie *Dark Star* where Lt. Doolittle has to convince "smart" Bomb #20 that it really "wants" to launch and blow up the planet.) It will be interesting to see how driving a car changes as we introduce more and more self-reliant decision systems into them (such as sensory-driven speed control, automatic steering, and GPS navigation systems).[3] Jonathan Haidt has popularized this analogy as an elephant and a rider rather than the traditional horse and rider, because the elephant is a more powerful creature, and no rider is ever completely in control of the elephant.[4] (Of course, this misses the possibility that the rider and the horse can understand each other so well and be in such sync as to be an even more capable team than either one individually.)

In all of these analogies, there is the belief that the "self" has to work to exert control over the "other." As we noted at the very beginning of the book (Chapter 1), you are both the horse and the rider (or the elephant and the rider). Robert Kurzban, in his new book, rejects the concept of the individual self and suggests that "self-control" is better understood as conflict between multiple modules.[5] In the language of this book, the decision-making system that is you includes the reflexes you inherited, the Pavlovian learning that drives you, the habits you have learned, the stories you tell, and the deliberation you do. Nevertheless, self-control is something that feels very real to us as humans. Consciously, we know when we successfully exert our self-control, and (afterwards) we know when we don't. Therefore, it is important to understand what this process is.

Studying self-control in the laboratory

Before we can take the mechanisms of self-control apart, we need to find a way to make a subject show self-control in the laboratory and to measure it. First, we want to be quantitative about when people are showing self-control and when they aren't. This will allow us to examine the mechanisms of failures of self-control. Second, we'd like to be able to access self-control directly and not have to wait for a person to fall off the wagon. Third, we'd like to be able to examine failures of self-control in nondangerous situations. Fourth, we'd like to be able to use our big measuring machines (fMRI, EEG, neural recordings) to see the physical correlates of self-control. And fifth, we'd like to be able to examine self-control in nonhuman animals.

Self-control has been a topic of study since the inception of modern psychology. (Freud's concept of the id, ego, and superego is a multistage theory of self-control.[6]) Several particularly sensitive measures of self-control have been introduced over the years, including the *Stroop task* and the *stop-signal task,* as well as tasks that put subjects in more realistic situations, such as the *marshmallow task* and its animal analogs that compare abstract and concrete representations (the chimpanzee and the jellybeans).[7] Finally, there is the *candy-rejection task,* which will lead us into issues of cognitive load and how self-control can tire out.[8]

Perhaps the simplest experiment to address the question of self-control is the *Stroop* task, a remarkably simple yet subtle task in which a person is shown a word in a color and is supposed to name the color of the text. This is normally very easy. But if the word is itself a color (such as the word "red" written in blue), then an interference appears between reading the word itself and recognizing the color that it is printed in. This interference produces a slowing of the time it takes to say the word (the reaction time) and increases the likelihood of making an error. Both of these measures produce quantitative measures of *cognitive dissonance* and track other measures of self-control.[9] The increase and decrease in reaction times in the Stroop task is so reliable that it is now used to test for cognitive dissonance and attention to other concepts—for example, for food-related words in obese individuals and drug-related words in addicts.[10]

The Stroop task can't be used with animals (who can't read), and here the *stop-signal task* has been very useful. In the stop-signal task, the subject is trained to react as quickly as possible to a *go* signal (such as "when the light comes on, push the button"), but sometimes a different signal (a *Stop!* signal) appears between the *go* signal and the subject's reaction. If the subject sees the stop signal, he or she is rewarded for not reacting and is punished for reacting—the subject has to stop the already started motor-action sequence. The stop-signal task has successfully been used in rats, monkeys, and humans, and performance is similar across the different species.[11]

Generally, the most successful description of the task is that there are separate processes each racing to a threshold (a *go* process and a *Stop!* process). The *Stop!* signal is assumed to run faster than the *go* signal, but also to start later. If the *Stop!* signal reaches threshold before the *go* signal, the subject is able to cancel the action and stop himself or herself.[12] Neural recordings have found increasing activity in certain areas (cortical motor control structures, and the subthalamic nucleus [a part of the basal ganglia]) that track the two racing components and their interaction.[13]

Both the Stroop and stop-signal tasks are computer-driven, timed tasks. The other tasks listed above depend on physically real objects being offered to subjects; this produces different results than symbols or images of objects.[14] In the first few chapters of the book, we encountered an experiment (the Parable of the Jellybeans, Chapter 1) in which chimpanzees had to choose between two sets of jellybeans. The key to this task was that the subject got the tray he didn't pick—to get the tray with more jellybeans, he had to reach for the other one.[15] Sarah Boysen and Gary Berntson found that their subjects were much better at picking the "humble portion" if they were using symbols rather than actual jellybeans. Humans also show a preference for real objects, particularly sensory-positive objects, when faced with experimental decision tasks.[16]

This preference for real objects leaves us with an important (and interesting) inconsistency in decision-making systems and underlies some of the problems with valuation that we saw in our initial discussion of "value" (Chapter 3). The idea of a thing and the physical thing may have very different values. This occurs because there are multiple decision-making systems competing for that valuation. If the Pavlovian system (Chapter 8) is engaged (when the object is physically in front of us), we make one valuation, but if it is not (if we are using the Deliberative system, Chapter 9), we make another.

This creates an interesting inconsistency in decision-making.[17] Even though an alcoholic might deny the urge to drink when sitting at home, that same alcoholic sitting in the bar an hour later will take that drink. Some authors have argued that the way to think about this is that there are two selves: that your present self is in conflict with your future self. Other authors have suggested that there are two modules, one that thinks long term and one that responds more immediately. I think it's simpler to recognize that we are inconsistent and irrational and to figure out how to work our lives around that inconsistency and irrationality. One way to exert self-control is to recognize this inconsistency and to *precommit* to a condition that does not allow you to reach that future difficult choice.[18] For example, the alcoholic might realize that it will be very difficult to not drink in the bar and might decide not to go to the bar in the first place. A gambler with a known problem might take a different route home so as not to drive by the casino.[19]

This suggests the importance of attention and distraction in self-control[20]—if we can keep our attention on the other option, we may be better able to avoid the Pavlovian choice. Similarly, if we can attend to specific aspects of an alternative, we may be able to change the valuation of that alternative against the temptation. This may be one of the reasons that personal religion is often a source of strength in the face of severe danger or temptation. Religion may enable people to maintain their attention on an alternative option that precludes committing the "sin" that they are trying to control.[21]

But what if you are faced with that immediate choice? Is it a lost cause? What are the mechanisms of self-control? Even the alcoholic facing a drink in a bar can sometimes deny that driving urge to drink.

In the classic *marshmallow task*, introduced by Walter Mischel in the 1960s,[22] a child is brought into a room, a marshmallow (or equivalent high-value candy or toy) is placed in front of the child, and the child is told, "If you can wait fifteen minutes without eating the marshmallow, I'll give you two marshmallows." Then the adult leaves the room. Videos from the original experiments are now famous in the psychological literature because the children show classic self-control behaviors. They try to distract themselves from the marshmallow. They cover their eyes so they don't have to look at the marshmallow. They turn away. They do other actions like kicking the desk. The problem is that keeping attention off the marshmallow is hard. Follow-up experiments have shown that the ability to wait is surprisingly well correlated to later success, including staying out of jail, avoiding drug addiction, getting good grades in high school, SAT scores, and job success.

Adults are generally able to reject a single marshmallow in this situation, but rejecting that marshmallow takes cognitive effort. This leads us to the *candy-rejection task*.[23] In this task, young women who have expressed an interest in dieting are asked to watch a movie with a bowl of high-sugar snacks placed next to them. By quantitatively measuring how many of the snacks are eaten, one can quantitatively measure their lack of self-control. Some of the women are asked to not respond to the movie, while others are told to just watch it. The more they have to control their emotions while watching the movie, the more they eat. A host of similar self-control and fatigue tests can be used as the quantitative test, including willingness to drink a bitter-tasting medicine, willingness to hold one's hand in a cold ice-bath, and physical stamina on a lever-pulling or handle-squeezing task. All of these require some aspect of self-control, and they are impaired (decreased) by preceding them with tasks that engage excess emotional and/or cognitive components.

This leads us to the concept of *cognitive load*. Many of these tasks, such as the candy-rejection task, and even the Stroop task, depend on the ability to allocate some sort of limited cognitive resource to the self-control component.[24] We can see this most clearly in the candy-rejection task—spending your self-control attention and effort on keeping your emotions in check reduces your ability to reject temptation and increases the amount of candy that you eat. Putting your override abilities elsewhere allows your Pavlovian system free rein. (Ask anyone nibbling on chips and pretzels in a sports bar.) In fact, we see this sort of effect all the time—when one is distracted, one tends to forget to override prepotent actions, whether they are driven by the emotional (Pavlovian) system or by the overlearned (Procedural) system, or whether they are highly motivated targets in the Deliberative system.[25] This is a specific instantiation of the general process of having limited resources. Complex processing, including memory, navigation, and self-control, all require a similar set of limited resources. If these resources are taken up by one task, they cannot be used in another.[26]

In one of my favorite examples of limited cognitive resources, following on an experiment introduced by Ken Cheng and Randy Gallistel for rats,[27] Linda Hermer and Elizabeth Spelke tested how well children (two-year-olds) could find a favorite hidden toy.[28] The toy was placed in one of two boxes in the corners of a rectangular room. The key is that a rectangular room has a 180-degree rotational symmetry. The children watched the toy being placed in the box and were then spun around until they were dizzy. Although the children had watched the toy being placed in the box only a few minutes earlier, they were unable to remember where it was; they were able to use the geometry of the room to identify two of the four corners, but they were unable to remember which of the two opposite corners had the box.[A] Even with colored boxes and salient wall cues (one wall painted white, one painted black), the children were unable to break that 180-degree symmetry. (Children who were not spun had no trouble at all finding the favorite toy.) Adults were of course able to remember even through being spun. (Of course, what the adults were doing was saying, "It's left of the black wall" or "It's in the blue box.") If the adults were given a linguistic blocking task at the same time (to stop them from repeating the location over and over again, linguistically), they ended up just like the children—unable to remember where they left the toy. Classic cognitive load tasks used in experiments include saying the alphabet backwards, and counting down from 1000 by sevens. (Counting down from 1000 by sevens is really hard to do and really distracting.)

Distracted people revert to the other systems. I recently changed the route I drive to work. If I get distracted (say by thinking about how I'm going to deal with a problem at work or at home or even just by thinking about writing this book instead of driving), then I miss my turn and go straight through to the old route. I'm sure if I was counting down from 1000 by sevens as I drove through that corner, I would miss it every time.

[A] Rats were trained to find food. Even with highly salient cues in each corner (different smells, numbers of colored lights, etc.), rats who were disoriented each time before being placed in the box were unable to break that 180-degree rotational symmetry.[29] Rats who were not disoriented were easily able to break the symmetry. See my earlier book *Beyond the Cognitive Map* for a detailed discussion of the rat experiment and what is known about its neurophysiological correlates and mechanisms.

The neurophysiology of willpower

Using these limited resources takes energy. One of the most interesting things about self-control is that not only does it depend on paying attention, and not only does it diminish when one is tired, but accomplishing self-control takes energy.[30] (Humans are aware of this. We talk of "willpower" as if it is a limited resource that we need to conserve for when we need it. In fact, if subjects are told that they will need to use their self-control later, they can conserve it, showing less self-control in earlier tasks but then being more able to express self-control in later tasks.) Even something as simple as resisting tempta-tion (such as not eating offered chocolate) can have an effect on one's ability to perform some physical task requiring stamina.[31]

Many scientists argue that this is one of the reasons that stress often leads to fall-ing back into habits that have been stopped, such as smoking or drug use. Coping with stress depletes one's self-control and leaves one vulnerable to tasks that depend on that self-control resource, such as preventing relapse. In fact, it has been argued that one of the reasons that regular meetings (such as in Contingency Management or 12-step pro-grams such as Alcoholics Anonymous and its more-regulated cousins) work so well is that they provide daily rewards for accomplishing self-control, which helps strengthen those self-control "muscles."[32] In a similar vein, Walter Mischel has argued that much of what we call good parenting entails an explicit training of self-control[33] (such as telling kids that "it's ok to wait for two marshmallows").

These self-control resources can be replenished through sleep, rest, or relaxation.[34] Roy Baumeister and his colleagues have suggested that this limited resource depends on glucose levels in the bloodstream;[35] however, this suggestion is extremely contro-versial.[36] Glucose (sugar) is a resource required by neurons to power neural function.[37] Blood-glucose levels in subjects performing a self-control task were much lower than in subjects performing a similar control task that did not require self-control, and subjects who drank a sugar drink showed improved self-control relative to those who drank a similarly sweet but artificially flavored drink.[38] Apparently, eating sugar really does help with self-control, which may be why stressed people crave sweets.[B] If this glucose theory is correct, then self-control may really be like a muscle, in that it gets tired because it runs out of resources. However, other scientists have suggested that the taste of glucose may be priming expectations of goals and changing the distribution of which systems are driving decision-making. Merely tasting (but not swallowing) a sweet solution can increase exercise performance.[39] Perhaps the glucose solutions are changing one's motivation, invigorating the subject (Chapter 13).

It is also not clear why self-control requires additional glucose compared to other brain-intensive phenomena, such as increased attention (listening for a very small sound), increased perception (finding a hidden image in a picture), fine motor control (playing piano or violin), or even doing a cognitively difficult problem (a math test). To my knowledge, the glucose theory has not been tested in these other brain-intensive

---

[B] I know that when I'm writing a grant application or working really hard on a paper, I often find that I need a regular infusion of severe sugar to keep my writing stamina up. You can tell I'm working hard when I've got a donut for my midmorning snack.

phenomena.[c] It may be that self-control simply engages more neural systems than just going with the flow does, and those neural systems require resources.

There is also evidence that self-control can be trained,[42] but whether this is more akin to a practice effect (through which neural systems learn to perform tasks better) or to a homeostatic change (such as muscles increasing their resource buffers from exercise) is still unclear.

So why does self-control engage additional parts of the brain and require more neuronal resources?

Self-control and the prefrontal cortex

Two structures in the human brain appear again and again in self-control tasks: the dorsolateral prefrontal cortex (dlPFC) and the anterior cingulate cortex (ACC).[43] These structures are often talked about as being involved in "top-down control" because they are involved in abilities to recognize and change goals and tasks.[44] These two structures seem to be involved in the monitoring of conflicting information and desires, task-setting, and the overriding of plans.[45] Both of these structures are located in the front of the human brain, and they are often referred to as part of the "prefrontal" cortex.[D]

---

[c] As discussed in Appendix B, fMRI measurements depend on increased blood flow because "highly active" neurons require additional resources (but not additional oxygen) from the blood. Although it is not known what all of those additional resources are, a likely candidate is glucose.[40] So, when a neural structure increases its activity (whatever that actually means[41]), the brain accommodates those needs by increasing blood flow. However, the increased flow is much larger than the increased oxygen needs, so with increased blood flow and the same oxygen needs, more oxygen is left in the bloodstream, which is what is detected by fMRI and similar imaging systems. Increased activity can also be tracked by using a radioactive glucose molecule, 2-deoxyglucose. The radioactive 2-deoxyglucose is injected into an animal's bloodstream and is then taken up by particularly active neurons. The presence of the marked 2-deoxyglucose can be detected postmortem in certain tissues, which have been "highly active." 2-deoxyglucose tends to mark the same structures that fMRI does. The fact that fMRI identifies certain structures as "involved" in certain tasks suggests that different abilities draw on different parts of the brain and that the glucose hypothesis may affect more systems than just the self-control systems.

[D] The term "prefrontal" comes from the idea that it is in the "front of the frontal cortex." Because this part of the cortex is one of the most differentiated between primates and other mammals and between humans and other primates,[46] it was historically identified as the locus of the abilities deemed to be uniquely human (such as the "superego"[47]). However, as anatomical studies have become more detailed and more developed, it has become possible to identify homologous areas in the frontal brain regions of other animals as well.[48] (A homologous structure is one that serves the same purpose between two species and shares an evolutionary history. For example, no one would deny that the rat heart, the monkey heart, and the human heart are all homologous structures. As we have seen throughout this book, many brain structures are conserved between these species as well.) Similarly, as we have begun to develop self-control tasks that can be used in animals (such as the stop-signal task), we have begun to identify specific pathways, structures, and information-processing mechanisms through which self-control works.[49] The exact details of the homology between species and the exact details of their respective roles in decision-making are an area of active research.[50]

The implication that the prefrontal cortex is involved in self-control originally came from inadvertent lesion studies, including soldiers returning from the wars of the late 19th and early 20th centuries.[51] But the first and most important indication that the prefrontal cortex played a role in self-control, particularly the Augustinian nature of it, came from Phineas Gage,[52] whom we met in our discussion of emotion (Chapter 8). To remind you, Phineas Gage was a railway worker who had an iron spike shot through his head, obliterating his frontal cortices. One of the key descriptions of Phineas Gage after his accident was his lack of self-control, particularly in emotional situations. More modern results, including both fMRI data from humans and neural recordings in monkeys, have found dorsolateral prefrontal cortical activity to be related to working memory, to self-control, and to the construction and maintenance of alternate plans (such as one might take in the face of an error-related contingency), particularly complex alternate plans.[53]

Because the stop-signal task is trainable in animals, particularly monkeys, the anatomical pathways through which the "stop" behavior is achieved are well known. In a pair of remarkable recent papers, Masaki Isoda and Okehide Hikosaka found that an area to the front of the motor cortex (the "supplementary motor area" [SMA]) stops unwanted behaviors through its strong projection to the subthalamic nucleus in the basal ganglia.[54] In our discussion of the Procedural action-selection system (Chapter 10), we talked of go/no-go pathways in the basal ganglia—cortical input enters the striatum in the basal ganglia and is then passed through two pathways (a "go" pathway, often called the "direct" pathway, in which the striatum inhibits an area that inhibits actions, making a double negative that learns to encourage actions, and a "no-go" pathway, often called the "indirect" pathway, in which there is a triple negative that learns to discourage actions). There is also a third pathway through the basal ganglia in which the frontal areas of the cortex project directly to the subthalamic nucleus, which projects directly to the final negative stage of the two pathways. (See Figure 10.1.) The subthalamic nucleus is excitatory (positive) and excites the final inhibitory stage, making a single negative— a *Stop!* pathway. To differentiate it from the direct "go" pathway and the indirect "no-go" pathway, it is sometimes called the "hyper-direct" pathway.[55]

This can be seen as a general phenomenon—the frontal cortices provide signals that allow other structures to change previously learned responses.[56] Historically, this has been called the *behavioral inhibition* system because it is usually tested in experiments in which behaviors are stopped rather than changed,[57] but I've always suspected that the prefrontal cortex is better understood as a biasing system that allows complex plans to control behavior through the manipulation of simpler systems. This architecture reflects the *subsumption architecture* proposed by Rodney Brooks[58] in which more complex systems are overlaid on top of simpler systems. The more complex systems listen to the inputs and step in if needed by either modulating the simpler systems (by providing them with additional inputs) or by directly driving the output themselves.

In the rodent, the anterior cingulate cortex (ACC) and the medial frontal cortex (particularly the infralimbic and prelimbic cortices) provide signals to the amygdala to override learned fear-related responses.[59] In the monkey, the prefrontal cortex overrides habitual responses to allow more controlled responses. In general, this can be seen as a form of what is sometimes called top-down processing,[60] in which frontal cortical systems modulate the "lower" systems to change expectations, attention, and behaviors. Reflexes may be driven by the spinal cord, but there is a loop through which the brain examines the inputs to the reflexes and can modulate them if needed. The ACC modulates emotional action-selection systems.[61] The frontal motor areas (like the SMA) modulate Procedural learning.[62] And dorsolateral prefrontal cortex modulates evaluation systems to select longer-term options in Deliberative systems.[63]

To see how this works, we can take a specific example. In a recent fMRI study, Yadin Dudai and his colleagues in Israel studied humans overcoming their fear of snakes.[64] They found people who had specific phobias of snakes and gave them the chance to pull a rope that brought a snake closer to them. The sight of the snake produced activity in the amygdala and limbic emotional areas, which have long been associated with fear in both animals and humans. (We can recognize these as Pavlovian [emotional] action-selection circuits, Chapter 8.) People who were able to overcome their fear (pulling the rope) had decreased activity in the amygdala, but increased activity in the subgenual anterior cingulate cortex (sgACC), an area of prefrontal cortex that projects to the amygdala. Somehow, activity in the sgACC has inhibited activity in the amygdala and allowed these people to overcome their fear and pull the rope toward them.

Books and papers for further reading

- Roy F. Baumeister, Todd F. Heatherton, and Dianne M. Tice (1994). *Losing Control: How and Why People Fail at Self-Regulation.* San Diego, CA: Academic Press.
- George Ainslie (2001). *Breakdown of Will.* Cambridge, UK: Cambridge University Press.
- Robert Kurzban (2010). *Why Everyone (Else) is a Hypocrite.* Princeton, NJ: Princeton University Press.
- Uri Nili, Hagar Goldberg, Abraham Weizman, and Yadin Dudai (2010). Fear Thou Not: Activity of frontal and temporal circuits in moments of real-life courage. *Neuron, 66,* 949–962.

PART THREE

THE BRAIN WITH A MIND
OF ITS OWN

16

The Physical Mind

Between two mirrors,
light reaches to infinity,
seeing
requires an embodied interruption.

The mind is physically instantiated by the brain, but the mind is not simply software running on the hardware of the brain. The physical structure of the brain changes the computations that are available. We saw earlier that there are multiple action-selection systems, each with different advantages and disadvantages. Although it is possible to learn new tasks after brain lesions, it is not that the same software is running on another part of the brain; instead, other action-selection systems are doing their best to accomplish tasks.

Historically, debates about the relationship between mind and brain have been between those who argued that they were fundamentally different things (*dualism*) and those who argued that the mind was instantiated in the brain.[1] There is strong evidence against dualism because manipulations of the brain affect the mind. There is no evidence for a nonphysical entity, and few scientists still consider it a possibility. However, more recently, dualism debates have been between whether the mind depends on the physical brain, or whether it is a software that just happens to run on neural hardware.[2]

We now have examples of things that can be physically translated from one instantiation to another without any loss. When we download a song from the Internet, the music has been translated from sound waves in the air through a microphone into a digital representation on a computer hard drive, translated from that onto a series of electrical pulses over a wire, often through an intermediate step of light pulses over a fiber-optic cable, then back into electrical pulses, back into a digital representation on your local hard drive, and then back into sound waves in the air through speakers attached to your computer. Although there is some change from the sound waves to the digital representation and back, there is no change at all from one digital representation to another. The physical nature of the mind is not like that. To understand how the material nature of how the brain processes information is different from the immaterial nature of digital information, let us take a moment to understand just what digital information is.

What's wrong with the software/hardware analogy?

Within a computer, information can be transferred from one place in memory to another (as when you copy a file from disk to memory) or, within a network, from one computer to another. The information may be stored in physically different mechanisms, but the information itself is the same. For example, digital information stored in the form of magnetic orientations on a hard drive can be written to a compact disc (CD) in the form of dark spots on an optical disk.[A] This has led computer scientists to separate the concept of hardware (the physical entity) from the concept of software (the digital information).

There are cases in biology where information is stored digitally. For example, DNA stores the genetic sequence as a series of four amino acids (guanine, cytosine, thymine, and adenine, usually labeled GCTA). One can make a case that the information in DNA is software and the cell's complex mechanisms that turn that information into proteins and other physical changes in the cell are the hardware that reads and operates on the software.[B]

In the 1970s and 1980s, the hardware/software analogy became popular, both among scientists and the public, as an explanation for the mind/brain problem, with the idea that the brain was the hardware and the mind was the software.[4] This software/hardware dualism was particularly appealing because it meant that the mind occurred at a different level than the brain and could be studied separately. It also held out the hope

---

[A] A hard drive (HD) stores information as a series of small pieces of magnetizable materials called ferromagnetics. Under the influence of a magnetic field, these small spots (called domains) can be oriented in one of two directions (up or down). The hard drive stores a series of zeros and ones as a sequence of up and down domains. A compact disc (CD) stores information as a series of small pits in a colored plastic, making a series of dark and light spots. Hard drives and CDs can store the exact same series of zeros and ones. Although instantiated in the physical realm (magnetic domains, dark/light pits), the actual information is the sequence of zeros and ones.

[B] The actual mechanism by which a cell reads the information stored in DNA is extremely complex, with new mechanisms discovered over the past several decades where the physical environment within and around the cell changes which components of the DNA are read.[3] For example, specialized proteins called *histones* can block part of the DNA from being read, while other proteins called *transcription factors* can encourage part of the DNA to be read. At this point, geneticists have created entire logic control structures (if this protein is present but that protein is not, then read this part of the DNA to create a third protein). The physical environment of the cell can change which part of the program is read. But this is not that different from current computer programs, which have mechanisms to check physical aspects of the computer to decide what parts of the program need to be run. For example, when your computer starts up, it checks to see if you have a DVD reader installed or a network card. (These days, programs don't tend to tell users what they are doing, so it may just show you a little blue bar cycling around or a corporate logo to look at, but what it's really doing is checking for hardware.) If it finds that hardware, it installs appropriate drivers (small pieces of software) for it.

that a computer program could be built using a completely different hardware and still create an artificial intelligence.

At the time, the software being studied was generally symbolic—sets of arbitrary symbols that were being manipulated through specific algorithms.[5] In 1956, Allen Newell and Herb Simon showed that a search algorithm that looked through possibilities of mathematical steps could find basic mathematical proofs, showing that they could replicate many of the proofs from Bertrand Russell's *Principia Mathematica*.[6] In fact, their program found a more elegant proof to one of the theorems in Russell's *Principia* than Russell had.[7]

With faster and larger computers, the search process that was developed by these early artificial intelligence researchers has been able to do remarkable things[8]—it is as good as or better than human doctors at identifying diseases,[C] it is used by oil-exploration industries to find oil pockets deep in the ground, and, famously, it beat the best chess player in the world. Recently, the combination of search processes with a deep knowledge base of semantic relationships beat the best human players at the TV game show *Jeopardy*. However, it is important to remember that this search-through-possibilities theory is a hypothesis as to how humans make decisions. Extensive psychological tests have shown that humans do not search as many steps into the future as these programs do.[10] Better chess players do not look farther ahead than weaker chess players. Doctors have to be explicitly trained to use *differential diagnosis* paradigms, and even well-trained doctors tend to use experience-based pattern recognition rather than explicit reasoning in practice.

The search-through-possibilities theory requires a manipulation of symbols. The reason artificial intelligence researchers started with symbol manipulation (as told by Allen Newell in one of his last public lectures given at Carnegie Mellon[11]) was that scientists thought that "perception was going to be easy," so they would start with the hard part of cognition. At the end of his career, Allen Newell came to the conclusion that in fact they had been going at it backwards, that perception was far from easy and that cognition was actually perceptions applied to the perception mechanisms. But at the time (from the 1950s through the 1980s), artificial intelligence entailed manipulations of symbols and led to what Newell and Simon called "the physical symbol systems hypothesis," which proposed that cognition consisted entirely of the manipulation of abstract symbols.[12]

Even in the 1980s, the concept that the mind entailed the manipulation of symbols was attacked, primarily by John Searle, a philosopher at the University of California, Berkeley. Searle attacked the symbol-manipulation hypothesis with a thought experiment that he called the *Chinese room*.[13] To understand Searle's thought experiment, we need to first start with the famous *Turing test*, proposed by Alan Turing in 1950.[14]

How do I know that you are conscious? Turing rephrased this question in terms of thinking, as in *Can a machine think*? As we have seen throughout this book, in order to be scientific about this, we need to operationalize this question. Turing suggested that

---

[C] Even though early (1979) artificial intelligence programs outperformed typical medical faculty in controlled comparisons, these programs were abandoned due to concerns about legal issues—*Who would be responsible for errors in diagnosis*? A similar concern may be limiting successful automatic driving programs.[9]

we can operationalize the concept of thinking by trying to determine if the person you are having a conversation with is a computer or a human. Unfortunately, humans are actually very bad at this and often attribute human characteristics to nonhuman objects (such as naming a GPS).

Searle's Chinese room thought experiment is a direct attack on the concept of the Turing test. In Searle's thought experiment, imagine that a Chinese speaker is having an email chat with someone in Chinese.[D] Our speaker types Chinese ideograms into the computer and reads Chinese ideograms on the computer. Somewhere else, a non-Chinese speaker sits in an enclosed room with a set of index cards. Chinese characters appear on the screen in front of him, and he matches the ideograms (which he does not recognize, but we assume he can match them pictorially) to index cards that have complex if-then statements on them. Some of those cards tell him to draw specific ideograms on a tablet, which is then translated to the outside.[E] Searle correctly points out that even if the outside Chinese speaker (our user) cannot tell the difference between the enclosed room and another Chinese speaker (that is, the room passes the Turing test), we cannot say that our inside man speaks Chinese. This is completely correct. However, it also completely misses the point of the Turing test. While our inside man does not speak Chinese, the room (the man manipulating the index cards, the rules on the index cards themselves, and the input–output system) *does*.

This is a common mistake made by people trying to understand brain functionality. We keep looking for mechanisms where consciousness resides (in a specific neuron subtype or in the quantum fluctuations of microtubules[16]), but this is not how the brain works. The brain is an interactive, computational machine that takes information in from the world, processes that information, and then takes actions to respond to it. There are many modules in the brain (we explored some of them in the previous section of this book), but, in the end, it is the person as a whole that takes an action. When you hold your sleeping baby daughter for the first time, that uncontrollable, overwhelming emotion created by your Pavlovian action-selection system is you, not someone else; when your Procedural system slams on the brakes of your car and avoids the accident, that was you making the right choice. Conscious or not, it's still you.

There are two important hypotheses underlying the hardware/software distinction. The first hypothesis is that there are different levels of description of an object.[17] One can describe the digital information stored on a hard disk or DVD in terms of the physical object that it is stored on (for example, as changes in orientation of the ferromagnetic domains on the hard disk) or in terms of the information that is stored (as the sequence

---

[D] At the time that Turing proposed his test, getting input and output from computers was very complicated, and Turing spent a large part of his original proposal ensuring that the test can't be fooled by seeing or hearing the person or computer. We are now very familiar with the concept of communicating with invisible entities over computer networks, and, in fact, the Turing test regularly occurs in the context of videogame interactions, where some of the characters are computer-controlled and some are human-controlled.

[E] Apparently, this was, in fact, how the first version of Newell and Simon's General Problem Solver was implemented. Computers were too difficult to program at the time (in 1956), so they encoded it on 3×5 index cards and had their families manipulate the cards symbolically by specific rules, thus producing, literally, the Chinese room.[15]

of zeros and ones). The second hypothesis is that the information level is independent of the physical description[18] (that is, the sequence of zeros and ones stored on the hard disk is the same as the sequence of zeros and ones stored on the DVD). Both of these statements are incorrect when applied to the physical brain. While we will find both the physical and computational or informational levels useful in understanding brain function, experimental evidence suggests that the hypotheses that these are distinct and separable descriptions does not apply to the brain.[F]

The hardware/software analogy arose from two scientific literatures (an inability to explain consciousness from physical effects[20] and observations of patients recovering from lesion studies[21]) and gained traction as artificial intelligence researchers tried to show that symbol manipulation could explain intelligence.[22] Psychology experiments have found that symbol manipulation is particularly hard for humans, and that the more expertise one has with a subject, the *less* symbol manipulation one seems to do.[23] This suggests that there is something else going on beyond symbol manipulation.

It is tempting to throw up our hands and say that because we can't yet explain how consciousness arises from the brain, it can't be a physical object. However, physical manipulations affect conscious thought,[24] and operationalizing consciousness has been elusive.[25] Every time scientists operationalize a part of consciousness so that it can be studied experimentally (for example, by concentrating on one aspect such as attention, perception, emotion, or voluntary motor control), these studies have produced detailed physical (and computational) explanations for how the process works in brain tissue.[26] Similarly, when we actually test the timing of consciousness, much of it seems to occur after rather than before behavior.[27] Not having an explanation for consciousness seems to be a rather weak starting point for the major theory that consciousness is the software running on the brain's hardware.

Historically, however, what really seemed to drive the software analogy was the observations that animals and patients could sometimes recover from brain injury.[28] Patients with aphasia (language impairments) due to damage to part of their brain would sometimes (with sufficient training) recover some language abilities.[29] Animals with brain lesions would sometimes be able to learn to do tasks that they couldn't do shortly after the lesion.[30] And, most importantly, long-term memories seemed to be stored in a different part of the brain from recently stored memories.[31]

Learning new tasks with different brain structures

The idea that the brain is an amorphous container and that all parts of the brain are equivalent goes back to a famous experiment by Karl Lashley in the 1920s in which he observed rats running mazes with large swaths of brain tissue removed.[32] Lashley certainly recognized that there was a difference between parts of cortex (for example, visual cortex was obviously specialized for vision, even in the rat[33]), but Lashley found that the ability of rats to solve a maze depended on the amount of brain tissue removed—the

---

[F] The symbol-manipulation hypothesis is a hypothesis about how we process information.[19] It is wrong—not because it cannot be true, but because it doesn't seem to be how the brain processes information.

more tissue he removed, the worse the animal did. Generally, Lashley didn't see much difference between lesions that were of similar size but that involved different parts of the cortex—but he also wasn't watching the rats do much in the first place. When we actually observe not just whether an animal accomplishes a task, but *how* the animal accomplishes the task, what we find is that animals (including humans) bypass brain lesions not by moving information but by solving tasks using other systems.

We have already seen a difference between Deliberative decision-making (Chapter 9) and Procedural decision-making (Chapter 10). This distinction matches very closely a distinction seen in the human psychological literature between *declarative* and *procedural* memory.[34] Although the idea that there were multiple, dissociable memory systems dates back to the 1970s, the specific distinction between declarative and procedural memory in human learning, and the specific idea that they were dissociable, goes back to a 1980 paper by Neal Cohen and Larry Squire and the famous patient H.M.[35]

H.M. (now known to be Henry Molaison[G]) was a young man who suffered terribly from intractable, debilitating epileptic seizures that made it impossible for him to work.[37] Epilepsy is a breakdown in the negative feedback systems in the brain that normally prevent the highly interconnected positive (excitatory) connections between neurons from running amok. Like an avalanche or a wildfire, one over-excited event can spread throughout the brain.[H]

In 1953, at the age of 27, H.M. agreed to a highly experimental (and presumably desperate) procedure being done by William Scoville at Hartford Hospital in Connecticut: they would remove the part of the brain that contained the epileptic focus, the starting point of the epileptic avalanche.[42] In the subsequent procedure, Scoville removed both of H.M.'s hippocampi and much of the surrounding tissue (called the "medial temporal lobe").

[G] Traditionally, patients are referred to by their initials to preserve their privacy. When H.M. died in 2008, his full name was revealed.[36] But even before, known only as H.M., he was arguably the best-known brain lesion patient in neuroscience, rivaled only by Phineas Gage, whom we met in our discussion of frontal cortex and emotion (Chapter 8).

[H] In highly interconnected tissue (such as the hippocampus and neocortex), excitatory recurrent connections (which encourage neurons to fire) are balanced by local negative recurrent connections (which discourage neurons from firing). If the excitation and inhibition are out of balance for a transient moment, you can get runaway excitation leading to massive firing of neurons.[38] Interestingly, seizures can arise from too much transient excitation or too much transient inhibition. Brain function generally sits in dynamic balance, which makes it easier to respond quickly and makes the brain more flexible in its responses, but it also means that a transient event takes time to return to normal. The epileptic event is a phenomenon known in the physics and electrical engineering fields as "ringing"—the system gets pushed too far to one side, and as it returns to its base point, it bounces too far to the other side, much like a spring that oscillates when pulled or pushed.

Thus epilepsy is incorrect, extraneous firing of neurons. Since the firing of neurons *is* memory, perception, and cognition, this extra firing of neurons will be perceived by other parts of the brain as real. Epileptic seizures in the auditory cortex are often preceded by patients hearing music, events in temporal-lobe structures can trigger memory, and seizures in emotional parts of the brain (such as the ventral frontal cortex) can trigger feelings.[39] Dostoevsky (a noted epileptic) described seizures in his novel *The Idiot* as being preceded by an emotional moment of exceptional clarity of joy, hope, and vitality.[40] This emotional feeling of deep religious connection has been seen in some modern patients with temporal-lobe epilepsy as well.[41]

This procedure was introduced by Wilder Penfield and Herbert Jasper at the Montreal Neurological Institute in the early 1940s.[43] It is still done today as a last resort for intractable epilepsy.[44] But today, before any tissue is removed, doctors spend time locating the focal site (the starting point) of the epilepsy by recording for long periods of time (even up to weeks) to make sure that they localize the focus as tightly as possible, and then they spend time determining, as best they can, what that part of the brain does. In 1957, none of these techniques were available; all Scoville and his colleagues had available was the electroencephalogram (EEG), which doesn't have enough resolution to break down the information being processed, and which was only good enough to show him that the epileptic focus was somewhere in the medial temporal region. So, desperate to stop the epileptic seizures, H.M. agreed to let the surgeon remove a large portion of his hippocampi and his medial temporal lobe bilaterally.

The brain (and the mind) are physical things—removing a part of the brain removes a part of the computation. (Sometimes other parts can step in to accomplish a task in a different way, but sometimes not. This is the fundamental error in the software/hardware analogy.) At the time, in 1957, the computational role of hippocampus was still unknown.

In terms of its immediate effect, the surgery improved H.M.'s epilepsy dramatically and made it possible to control the epilepsy with medications. His general intelligence did not seem to be affected and his linguistic abilities remained normal, but the surgery left H.M. with a devastating memory impairment—he couldn't remember anything new. While he could remember his past, new information could be remembered only as long as he attended to it.[45] If he was distracted, it was gone. This strange memory disability had been seen before and was known as *anterograde amnesia*.[46] It was often seen in patients with Korsakoff's syndrome, a disease caused by chronic alcoholism combined with a vitamin B (thiamine) deficiency.[47] Case studies of anterograde amnesia are described beautifully in Oliver Sacks' *The Man who Mistook his Wife for a Hat* (see "The Lost Mariner" and "A Matter of Identity"), in A. R. Luria's *The Man with a Shattered World*, and (fictionalized into a complex mystery story) in Christopher Nolan's *Memento*.

H.M. was a patient who was normal (except for his epilepsy), of above-average intelligence, with a sudden loss of this very specific ability to learn new things. Here was a chance, in this terrible tragedy, to learn what went wrong and to understand how not to make this same mistake in the future.[48] Scoville called in Brenda Milner, a neuropsychologist who had studied with Donald Hebb and Wilder Penfield at McGill University. While Milner found that H.M.'s inability to learn new memories was pervasive and crossed all subjects and domains (visual, auditory, linguistic, etc.), she also found that H.M. could learn a mirror-tracing task that took both H.M. and control subjects several days to learn.[49] Along with her student Suzanne Corkin, they found that H.M. could, in fact, learn new tasks, but wouldn't remember doing them. These tasks were all the kind that take lots of practice and are learned slowly, like mirror-writing or tracing intricate paths. Corkin and Milner described how H.M. would be incredulous that he could do a task because he could not remember that he had ever tried it before, yet the rate at which he learned these slowly learning, practice-requiring tasks was approximately normal.

This led to the suggestion that there were two memory systems—one that learned stateable facts ("My car is parked at the airport.") and another that learned skills (riding a bicycle, throwing a baseball). Facts could be declared—I can tell you where my car is ("at the airport") and you know it immediately. But skills are procedures that can only be learned through practice. No matter how much I tell you how to throw a baseball, you won't be able to do it until you try it for a while. The first kind of memory was termed *declarative*, the second kind *procedural*.[50]

Subsequent work has suggested that declarative memory has two components, an episodic component including memories of specific places and times (the time I forgot my wife's birthday) and a semantic component consisting of facts (the actual date of my wife's birthday).[51] We now know that episodic memory is a constructed imagination of the past—it likely corresponds to the same system used to imagine the future.[52] This is the Deliberative system that we described earlier (Chapter 9). Semantic memory does not yet have an accepted correspondence in our decision-making taxonomy but may be similar to the situation-recognition and narrative components (Chapter 12).

What is important here, and what dooms the hardware/software analogy, is that patients such as H.M. are not shifting the software from one part of the computer to another. Rather, each component is able to perform certain calculations on the incoming information. When the lost mariner in Oliver Sacks' case study learns to become familiar with his life among the nuns and finds peace in his garden, he has not found a way to regain his ability to learn new memories. Instead, he has found peace in the way he uses other systems to accomplish his tasks. When H.M. learned to accomplish mirror-writing, he learned it using the procedural memory system.

Cortical structures—Can visual cortex take over for auditory cortex?

H.M. lost his hippocampi and other specialized subcortical structures.[53] Subcortical and cortical processing are quite different: while subcortical structures tend to be specialized, the cortex is a large two-dimensional sheet of repeated processing units, arranged in small, repeated columns.[54]

Current theories suggest that each repeated part of the cortex performs a similar computation on a unique set of inputs. (Exactly what that computation is remains controversial, but it seems to be some form of categorization process occurring via a content-addressable memory mechanism.[55] See Appendix C for a discussion of what is known about the computations occurring in the cortex.) However, that computation is fundamentally dependent on the inputs, and, unlike digital computers, those inputs are incomplete.[56] That is, you can't send any input anywhere you want in the cortex. Each cortical column receives a limited set of inputs, and the information carried by those inputs is all that it has available.

We can see the limitations of this by looking at how cortical representations can shift with changes in sensory inputs. This has been studied in the most detail in the context of primary sensory systems (particularly somatosensory [touch] systems).[57] Cells in these sensory areas receive inputs from a broad range of input cells, with stronger inputs usually at the center and input strength falling off as the input changes.[58] We talk of "tuning curves," which generally have a peak sensitivity but a broad range (see Appendix B). The cells compete with each other to determine which signals will form the peak of each tuning curve. Take your palm, for example: at each point on your palm, a host of mechanoreceptors have molecular mechanisms that detect touch. These detectors lead the cell to fire spikes, which are transmitted to the spinal cord and then through multiple steps to your sensory cortices, where they are interpreted as touch sensations. Even though these individual mechanoreceptors cover very large areas of your palm, you can localize a pinprick touch to a small point because your somatosensory cortex implements a sort of winner-take-all process using a mechanism called *lateral inhibition*, in which cortical cells inhibit their neighbors. This means that although lots of cells received input, only the ones representing the touched location remain active. This system integrates information from a very large area but provides a very accurate interpretation of the sensation.

More areas of your somatosensory cortex are sensitive to your palm and fingertips than to your arm, which makes your palm and fingers a more sensitive sensor than your arm. A classic high school experiment is to close your eyes and have a lab partner touch two pencils to your hand or arm or back. Can you tell that they are two points, or do you feel it as one? (As a control, the experiment is usually done with the lab partner sometimes using one pencil and sometimes using two and then asking the subject "one or two?") The sensitivity of your palm is much more accurate than your arm or back. This nonuniform distribution occurs in all sensory systems. Your auditory cortex spends more cortical area interpreting the frequencies at which human speech occurs than other frequencies, while your visual cortex spends more cortical area interpreting the center of your vision (called the fovea) than the periphery.[59]

But what happens when one loses part of the input? Because the cells are actually receiving input from large areas of the sensory field, but the far inputs are usually competed out, if the central part of the input is lost, the far inputs will now win the competition, and the cell will shift the area it listens to and show responses to the areas that remain.[60] Notice that although the compensation is a change in what information is processed by the cortex, the compensation is not due to a shift in software to the no-longer-used cortex; rather, it is due to a shift in which already-wired-up inputs are being listened to.

This effect produces interesting consequences, particularly in the sensations in phantom limbs. Patients who have lost a limb often feel sensations in that vanished limb. V. S. Ramachandran has shown that these sensations are due to sensory stimuli arriving at structures represented nearby on the somatosensory cortex.[61] The layout of the primate somatosensory cortex has been known since the late 1800s.[62] It has some strange discontinuities—for example, the fingertips are represented near the face. Patients missing a hand will sometimes feel sensation on their hand when their faces are touched. Patients with amputations often complain of pain or itching in their phantom limb; these sensations are extremely uncomfortable because they cannot scratch a limb that isn't there. But scratching the adjacently represented area can sometimes relieve the phantom limb pain.

If the inhibition between areas is incomplete or disinhibited or the connections are incompletely pruned or overconnected during development, these connections can cross between sensory systems and lead to experiences of relationships between sensations—one can hear colors or see sounds.[63] This process, called *synesthesia* (from *syn*, meaning "with" or "together," and *asthesia*, meaning "feel" or "perceive" [as in *anesthesia* or *aesthetics*]), is a fascinating interaction between sensory systems. Intriguingly, these relationships are not random; they tend to be constant within a given person. Flavors taste like shapes. Numbers have associated colors.[64]

There is some evidence that during development, cortical representations can shift more than during adulthood.[65] In part, this seems to be because cortical connectivity in juveniles and children is broader and gets pared down as cortical systems develop. This has been studied most quantitatively by Eric Knudsen, looking at how representations in the colliculi of owls change in response to sensory changes. The superior and inferior colliculi are subcortical brain structures in birds and mammals that perform an attention or targeting function—the cells are organized in a topographic manner representing position around the head of the animal, horizontally and vertically.[66] Stimulation leads to the animal attending to that horizontal and vertical position. The cells in the inferior colliculus respond primarily to auditory (but also more weakly to visual) input, using auditory cues (volume and time difference between the two ears) to localize a target in space, while cells in the superior colliculus respond primarily to visual (but also more weakly to auditory and tactile) input. When you hear a footfall behind you and whirl around to see what it is, that's your colliculi at work. The inferior colliculus derives from the auditory tectum of reptiles, while the superior colliculus derives from the optic tectum in reptiles, which are their primary sensory systems. In birds and mammals, both the inferior and superior colliculi sit underneath evolutionarily newer structures, the auditory and visual cortices.[67] Because these colliculi are organized topographically in terms of an output, the multiple sensory systems have to be co-aligned. Likely because it is easier to calculate an orientation from visual cues than from auditory ones, the alignment of both (even the inferior colliculus) turns out to be based on visual signals.[68]

Eric Knudsen and his students used this phenomenon to study how the inferior colliculus of barn owls changes when the visual inputs are changed.[69] Owls are particularly good at localizing sounds in three-dimensional space (since they usually hunt at night). An owl can track the footfalls of a mouse from meters away, target in on it, and hit it accurately.[70] As the owl is developing, it needs to learn to align the spatial information it derives from auditory cues with the spatial information it derives from visual cues. Knudsen and colleagues fitted owls with prism glasses that shifted the visual signals to the left or the right by a certain angle.[1] In the owl, the auditory system shifts to align to the visual, so the auditory inputs to the inferior colliculus had to arrive at slightly different locations.

What Knudsen and colleagues found was that, initially, the auditory inputs to the inferior colliculus were very broad, but that they were pruned away as animals progressed

---

[1] These prism glasses may be familiar to some people visiting science museums. A typical neuroscience game shown at science museums and during presentations to school students is to have a volunteer toss a beanbag into a basket with prism glasses on . Because the prism shifts the visual world to the left by some angle (say 20 degrees), the person typically misses the basket by 20 degrees in the opposite direction. With continued tries, the person can learn to compensate over the course of a few minutes. And then, when the prisms are removed, there is an after-effect where the person misses the basket by 20 degrees in the shifted direction, which takes a few minutes to correct. With more experience with and without prisms, the time it takes to shift decreases.[71]

through development. In particular, the owls passed through a specific age, called a *sensitive period*, after which the auditory inputs crystallized into place and became no longer malleable.[72] Manipulations of the prisms before the crystallization were much more effective than manipulations afterwards.

This sort of sensitive period is seen in many systems, including the visual system, the auditory system, and others. Similar sensitive periods are seen in cats and monkeys learning to see, birds learning to sing, and human children learning language.[73] This is why children are much better at learning foreign languages than adults. The timing of the sensitive periods is due to a physiological change in the brain, ending when plasticity crystallizes in different brain structures at different ages.[74]

But, again, just as was seen in the phantom limb results, above, the shifts that the owls could accommodate behaviorally completely matched the extent of the physical changes.[75] The shifts available depended on the connectivity changes. Similar dependences have been seen in somatosensory systems and in auditory systems.[76] Sensory changes reflect actual changes in physical connectivity within the brain. But what about memories? Can't information be translated from short-term to long-term memory?

Transferring memories from one part of the brain to another

On recovery from his surgery, H.M. showed a new and profound deficit in his ability to learn new memories. However, H.M.'s earlier memories seemed to be intact. Older memories were better represented than more recent memories.[77] At the time, this was taken to imply that memories were transferred from a short-term memory store to a long-term memory store (like information being written from your computer memory to a hard disk or to a CD). But further studies have shown that these older memories are different from the more recent memories.[78] Something is changed in the transfer.

Long-term memories tend to be very semantic, stored as facts, as narratives, as scripts and stories, while short-term memories tend to be episodic, with a personal "I was there" emotion to them.[79] This does not mean that we don't have long-term memories with strong "I was there" emotions, but in H.M. and other similar amnesic patients, those older episodic memories vanished along with the short-term memories.[80] What seems to happen to memories is that, in the short term, they are stored as episodic events, but with time, they become relegated to a semantic storage that is fundamentally different. All of H.M.'s long-term memories, for example, were semantic descriptions and did not contain the episodic descriptions that we normally associate with important long-term memories.

How might this difference between semantic and episodic memory arise? Throughout this book, I've tried to explain mechanism with theories that can actually explain how the information level arises from the physical. In this case, we require the answers to four questions: (1) *How are episodic memories stored?* (2) *How are semantic memories stored?* (3) *How is information transferred from one to the other?* In addition, it would be nice to understand (4) *Why is such a mechanism evolutionarily useful?*

We have encountered episodic memories elsewhere in this book (in Chapter 9). We noted that they were not stored flawlessly, but rebuilt from components stored in different cortical areas.[81] The structure tying those components together seems to be the hippocampus, which receives input (through the entorhinal cortex) from pretty much the entire neocortex, and which sends output (again through the entorhinal cortex) to pretty much the entire neocortex.[82] We have also encountered semantic memories elsewhere in this book (in Chapter 12).

Why would we need these two different systems? Presumably, as with the other examples of multiple decision-making systems that we've encountered so far, each mechanism has advantages and disadvantages. By using the right one at the right time, we can access the advantages of each and reduce the disadvantages. One theory, proposed by Jay McClelland, Randy O'Reilly, and Bruce McNaughton in the 1990s, was that we need two learning systems—one system that could store a few memories quickly by making sure the representations were really separable, and another system that could store lots of memories, but took the time to store them slowly so that they wouldn't interfere with each other.[83] The theory arose from work in the computational aspects of content-addressable memories (see Appendix C), in which it was observed that storing memories sequentially in a neural system where memories were distributed across many neurons produced *catastrophic interference*—as one memory was stored, older memories were lost.[84]

Because these systems stored information in a distributed manner, through small changes in individual connections, each connection between neurons (each synapse) participated in many memories. This meant that if you stored a memory, the changes in synapses needed to store the new memory could undo some of the changes needed for the previous memories. This is a process called *interference*—new memories *interfere* with the old ones.[85] On the other hand, if you interleaved the storage of the memories, changing the synapses a little bit toward what they would need to be to store the first memory, and then a little bit toward what they would need to be to store the second, the synapses could find a way to store both memories simultaneously.

Effectively, there is a tradeoff between being malleable enough to learn new things quickly and stable enough to hold memories for a long time. McClelland, O'Reilly, and McNaughton proposed that if you had a system that could store memories quickly, without interference, then you could use that fast-storing system to interleave the memories into the slower, longer-term storage. They proposed that the hippocampus, which contains mechanisms to reduce interference between stored memories (and thus can store memories quickly), served as the fast storage and the cortex (which learned more slowly and contained many more synapses) served as the slow storage.[86] Although this theory does seem to be primarily correct, as we've discussed in this chapter, the transfer is a transfer, not just of information but also of kind, from an episodic representation to a semantic representation.[87]

This means that the brain needs to transfer a memory from a quickly learned system which reconstructs it from parts into a slowly learned storage system in which it is stored in the strength of connections between neural structures.[88] Before we look at how this transfer occurs, it is important to note that the evidence is very strong that these are two separate systems, each of which can learn memories separately. Although learning generally proceeds from quickly learned episodic memories to more slowly learned semantic memories, if structures critical for the episodic memory systems are damaged, the semantic memory system can still learn.[89] For example, patients with hippocampal damage are impaired at episodic future thinking but are still able to learn to recognize familiar scenes that they experience multiple times and are still able to construct narratives.[90] Just such an example can be found in Oliver Sacks' lost mariner, who found a way to become comfortable with his new garden but remained unable to ever learn explicit (episodic) memories.[91] Suzanne Corkin says that through her long interaction with him, H.M. began to recognize her and thought he knew her from high school.[92] This construction of an explanation is sometimes called *confabulation*[93] and is a consequence of the construction of narratives (Chapter 12) through content-addressable-memory processes (Appendix C).

Although it is possible for semantic memories to be constructed through extended experience, it is also possible to take a single experience (encoded in episodic memory) and, through internal repetition, transfer it to a semantic memory. This transfer seems to occur primarily during sleep.[94] Scientists have known for a long time that sleep is a critical part of the learning process. Not only do animals and humans deprived of sleep not learn well, but they also do not easily remember the tasks that were learned before they were deprived of sleep.[95]

One of the most interesting phenomena discovered over the past couple of decades is a phenomenon called "replay," in which neural firing patterns seen during behavior replay themselves during sleep afterwards.[96] The phenomenon was originally seen in neural recordings of the hippocampus but is now known to occur throughout the hippocampus, neocortex, and some subcortical structures. Because it is so hard to record neural signals from humans, the replay phenomenon has generally been studied in rats and monkeys, but the timing of the replay events corresponds nicely to when sleep-deprivation studies have found that sleep is critical to consolidating memories.[97]

Reactivation of behavioral neural patterns during sleep was first seen in 1989 by Constantine Pavlides and Jonathan Winson, who recorded from pairs of hippocampal cells from rats.[98] Hippocampal cells in rats (place cells) have the very convenient tuning function that they respond only when the rat is in a specific position in an environment (the place field of the cell). Each cell has a different place field.[99] Pavlides and Winson chose place cells with nonoverlapping place fields; thus, they were able to expose the rat to the place field of one cell while not exposing it to the place field of the other. They then found that during sleep after the behavior, the cell with the place field the animal had been exposed to fired much more than the cell with the other place field—even though the animal was not in either place field when allowed to sleep.

Our ability to observe reactivation and replay took a giant step forward with the development in 1993 of multi-tetrode recording technology by Matthew Wilson and Bruce McNaughton, who brought together several technologies and were able to record from almost 150 cells simultaneously from their behaving rats.[100] Because each place cell has a different place field, from the activity across the set of cells, Wilson and McNaughton were able to decode the position of the rat during behavior from its neural ensemble. (See Appendix B for a description of how this decoding process works.) From a large neural ensemble, one can also determine whether patterns observed during behavior repeat (reactivate) afterwards during sleep.[101] From a large neural ensemble, one can even determine whether *sequences* observed during behavior repeat (replay) afterwards during sleep. A host of studies over the subsequent years, starting from Wilson and McNaughton's follow-up paper in 1994 and culminating in dozens of papers in the past decade, have shown that what is reactivated is actually the full neural pattern—cells that were coactive during behavior remain coactive during reactivation, while cells that were not coactive are not, and that what is replayed is the actual sequences observed by the rat: cells reactivate in the same order during sleep as during behavior.[102] Control studies have shown that this reactivation is a consequence of the behavior—it does not occur during sleep before the behavior, only afterwards. Reactivation and replay are also seen in neocortical systems during sleep as well. As with the hippocampal reactivation and replay, the same neural patterns observed during behavior appear afterwards during sleep. Reactivation and replay have been seen in a host of cortical systems, including the prefrontal, parietal, and even primary visual cortex.[103;J]

At this point the computational and neurophysiological function of replay is unknown.[106] Is it to aid storage of information within the structure itself (hippocampus or cortex)?[107] Is it to transfer information from the hippocampally based episodic system to the cortically based semantic system?[108] Is it to erase old memories from the hippocampus while enhancing new ones?[109] While these questions are still being addressed by researchers today, we have intriguing hints that all of these functions may be important. What is known is that blocking replay, either pharmacologically (through chemical means) or electrically (by stimulating the hippocampus whenever a replay event is about to happen[K]), disrupts memory retention.[111] It is also known that replay events in hippocampus tend to correspond to reactivation events in cortical structures, and that after replay events, neural patterns in cortical structures become more tightly coupled, even between cortical structures, exactly as would be predicted by the transfer and integration hypothesis.[112]

Throughout this discussion, I have avoided calling these replay events "dreams," because we don't know if these replay events seen in animals correspond to what we experience as dreams. (We can't ask the animal if it is dreaming, and it is very difficult to record from humans during dreams.) But, of course, it is very likely that this reactivation/replay phenomenon being studied in animals is the physical instantiation of the phenomenon we refer to as dreams. Dreams are often jumbled sequences of past experiences.[113] Although the animal experiments report actual replay of direct

---

J Replay in nonhippocampal subcortical structures, such as the dorsal system in the basal ganglia (Chapter 10), has not yet been reported, but there has not been the same level of extensive study done on these structures during sleep. The one exception is that the ventral striatum (the nucleus accumbens, which we saw was involved in representing potential outcomes during deliberation; see Chapter 9), replays reward-related activity in conjunction with the hippocampal replay of experienced sequences.[104] Sleep is also critical for procedural learning, but whether this is due to replay events in dorsal basal ganglia systems remains, as yet, unknown.[105]

K Replay events in the hippocampus tend to occur during an identifiable local field potential (LFP) event called a ripple or a sharp wave (sometimes called a "sharp-wave-ripple-complex") that is observable in the hippocampus. Because these LFP events can be detected quickly, they can be disrupted as soon as they start through a short electrical stimulation of the hippocampus.[110]

events, in part this may be because those sequences are the easiest to recognize. Some experiments have found interleaved representations of old and new experiences in rats during REM sleep.[114] During awake, resting behavior, recent experiments have found "replays" of sequences that the animal has never actually experienced, such as the sequence experienced by the animal but backwards, or chains of experienced sequences that share commonalities but have not actually been experienced together.[115]

In a very intriguing experiment, Robert Stickgold and colleagues trained a population of patients with hippocampal amnesia (like H.M.) to play the videogame Tetris.[116] These patients can learn tasks using their nonhippocampal memory but do not remember that they have played the game before. When Stickgold and his colleagues woke these people up from sleep and asked them about their dreams, they reported seeing strange shapes falling from the sky but were terrified because they had no idea where these shapes were coming from. It seems likely that the cortex was replaying the sensory stimuli it had seen (falling shapes) but that, without a hippocampus, these patients could not integrate these events into their episodic memories or remember where these images came from.

Summary

So even after lesions, animals (including humans) can learn new tasks, but these new tasks are learned in different ways, using different decision-making systems. Similarly, intact cortical structures can take over for damaged cortical structures, but only to the extent that input connections are available. And memories can be transferred from hippocampal-dependent episodic structures to cortical-dependent semantic processes, but they are modified in that transition. The brain is a physical machine. The mind is not software that happens to be implemented on the brain's hardware, but is directly dependent on the processes of the physical brain.

The mind used to be thought of as a hiker through a forest, or a surfer on a wave, or perhaps as the wave itself flowing through a physical ocean, or as something affected by but separate from the brain itself.[117] Historically, this separation was based on Descartes' dualism between the physical and cognitive entities.[118] In the modern cognitive science of the past century, this separation was based on the new theories of digital information.[119]

However, as we have seen in this chapter, the theory that mind and brain are separable is untenable, and the available data suggest instead that they are the same thing. The evidence for mentation as the processing of information is overwhelming, but the different components of the brain process that information differently. It is not a wave flowing through an open ocean, capable of traveling in any direction, but rather a wave traveling through a series of highly restrictive canyons. This has implications for every aspect of our mental lives, from mental processes like imagination to diseases and mental disorders like Parkinson's disease, Alzheimer's disease, post-traumatic stress disorder, and addiction, to mental constructs of behavior like craving, impulsivity, free will, and morality.

Books and papers for further reading

- V. S. Ramachandran and Sandra Blakeslee (1999). *Phantoms in the Brain: Probing the Mysteries of the Human Mind.* New York: Harper Perennial.
- Patricia S. Churchland and Terrence J. Sejnowski (1994). *The Computational Brain.* Cambridge, MA: MIT Press.
- Suzanne Corkin (2002). What's new with the amnesic patient H.M.? *Nature Reviews Neuroscience, 3,* 153–160.
- Douglas R. Hofstadter (1979). *Gödel, Escher, Bach: An Eternal Golden Braid.* New York: Basic Books.
- Douglas R. Hofstadter (1985). *Metamagical Themas: Questing for the Essence of Mind and Pattern.* New York: Basic Books.

17

Imagination

I want to walk on the beach with you,
feel the cool ocean pull at our feet,
memory like water
filling our footprints in the wet sand.

*If the brain is the physical instantiation of the mind, then every
mental event must be reflected in the physical realm, from imagination to hallucination to mental imagery. The current theory in
neuroscience is that this physical realm is the firing of neurons—
that is, just as we know that the firing of sensory neurons responds
to sensory cues, and the firing of motor neurons controls muscles,
this theory predicts that nonsensory mental (cognitive) events are
not just reflected in but actually are the firing of neurons.*

The fact that the cortex can be better understood as a two-dimensional sheet of repeating columns rather than as a three-dimensional structure suggests that we can think of
the cortex as a series of interconnected maps. Visual structures map the visual field in
front of you, auditory structures map tones and sounds, and both sensory and motor
structures map your body.[1]

In the mammal (including the human), the primary visual cortex happens to be at
the back of the brain. The axons connecting your eyes to your visual cortex have to run
all the way across the brain (they run underneath), which is why a concussion (in which
your brain slams against your skull like an unconstrained object in a suddenly stopping
car) often leads to visual problems.[2] Recordings of neurons from primary visual cortex
find that for the most part, the cells in each visual cortical column are tuned to the
same point on the retina. Some of these cells are tuned to spots on the retina, while
others are tuned to oriented lines, and others are tuned to moving oriented lines. Some
are excited by light at the location, while others are inhibited. But each column in the
primary visual cortex is tuned to light arriving at one spot on the retina.[3]

Connectivity in the cortex is based on a center-surround architecture, in which cells
representing similar locations on the retina are more tightly coupled than cells representing distal locations, with a larger-scale inhibitory connectivity. There are also some

longer-spaced connections that have subtle effects (they will be particularly important when we discuss migraines and the fortification hallucination), but the primary connectivity seems to be between adjacent columns representing similar information.[4] At the simplest level, cortex can be thought of as a sheet of local excitation and broader inhibition. This connectivity produces what is known mathematically as a *local coupling kernel*, a connectivity repeated at every location.[5] Such coupling kernels are seen in physical objects as well, such as the relationship between the coils of a spring or the physical connectivity of a guitar string (in one dimension), the physical connectivity of a bed sheet (in two dimensions), or the relationship between molecules of water (in three dimensions).

Those are three particularly interesting examples, because they all show wave effects. We have all seen waves on water, and we have all snapped a bed sheet flat, sending a wave across it; a classic junior high school physics experiment is to take a spring and send a traveling wave through it. And, of course, the sound generated by a guitar string is based on a standing wave, as it vibrates under the restricted conditions (mathematically termed the *boundary conditions*) that the two ends are held fixed and cannot move. Just as waves can travel across physical objects, so too can waves of neural activity travel across the cortical sheet.[6]

What would it feel like to have a wave of activity travel across your visual cortex? If neural activity in visual cortex *is* visual perception, then you would perceive a wave across your visual cortex as a wave of light traveling across your vision. In other words, you would hallucinate a wave of light. But people have been reporting their hallucinations for thousands of years, and random hallucinations don't appear as a wave of light across your vision.[7]

The reason for this is that the primary visual cortex in the primate (including the human) does not represent the retinal input with a one-to-one transformation. Instead, there is more representation of the center of your retina (an area called the fovea) and less representation of the periphery.[8] The specific mathematical description for this transformation is called a *log-polar transformation*. Think of your visual cortex as two rectangles pasted onto the back of your brain, lying next to each other. Each side of your visual cortex represents half your visual field. Cells in the fovea project (through an intermediate thalamic structure that does additional processing[A] called the lateral geniculate nucleus) to cells in the visual cortex near the midline, while cells in the periphery project (again through intermediate structures) to cells in the visual cortex more laterally. Moving along the horizontal axis of the visual cortex is equivalent to moving out from the fovea. Just as there are more cells in the fovea than the periphery, there is more visual cortex dedicated to the fovea than the periphery. Similarly, moving along the vertical axis is equivalent to moving in a circle around the fovea, with the top of your visual cortex corresponding to the top of your visual field.

This means that a wave that was perfectly aligned to the vertical axis of your visual cortex, one that started at the midline and progressed away from the midline, would appear as an expanding ring. Because more and more visual field is represented by the

---

[A] A lot of processing is done in the retina as well. This book, however, is not about how the brain processes sensory information, and so I won't go into those details, but a good resource for anyone who is interested is the recent textbook by Chaudhuri.

same-size area of cortex as one moves out to the periphery, a traveling wave moving at a constant speed on the cortical surface would appear to speed up as it travels to the periphery.

Simple visual hallucinations are often seen when falling asleep and waking up, under certain flickering lights, and in sealed dark rooms. They are also seen under the influence of certain recreational chemicals (drugs). These simple visual hallucinations are very similar to those painted on and carved into sacred stones and cave walls. People have been reporting their chemically-induced hallucinations for thousands of years. They are also the same patterns often seen in "near-death" experiences.[9]

These images tend to be made of radial lines, spirals, and spider-web shapes. They often appear as spiral checkerboards, honeycombs, or dots. And sometimes they are as simple as a white light in the center of the vision. Sometimes the images are stable and sometimes they move in a spiral inward or outward pattern. The images move with the retina (and are thus seen in "retinal space," which is particularly strange to experience because we are used to seeing things in "allocentric" or real-world space, which moves on our retina when we move our eyes). These images are the visual interpretation of waves in the cortex.

A vertical wave flowing from top to bottom along the visual cortex will appear as rotating radial lines. A collapsing wave flowing from the lateral to medial aspects will appear as a collapsing light, and may easily be interpreted as a tunnel. A wave that is diagonally oriented along the visual cortex will appear as a spiral. As the wave moves, the spiral can appear to spiral inward or outward. See Figure 17.1.

The primary visual cortex in the primate is actually connected up in a more complex manner than a simple center-surround kernel.[10] The cortical columns are arranged into local hypercolumns, which represent a single location on the visual field, but contain orientation-selective cells, which respond to lines oriented in different ways. A hypercolumn contains columns of cells representing each potential orientation. Each column is coupled to cells within its own hypercolumn (because they represent the same location in the visual field) and to nearby columns in other hypercolumns that share its preferred orientation (because they represent lines of the same orientation). The cross-hypercolumn connections seem to be laid out in an approximately hexagonal grid. It is the hexagonal grid across hypercolumns that produces the checkerboard or honeycomb components of some visual hallucinations.

The visual system in the primate (including the human) is very complex, including a host of separate cortical areas, each of which is dedicated to a different useful feature, such as colors, spatial locations in the visual world, even faces, rooms, and other dedicated objects.[11] Current theories suggest that this complex network of visual fields is a set of separate, dedicated feature detectors, tuned to the set of natural images we experience in our lives.

Hallucinations of more complex events and objects are likely to depend on the firing of other cortices, such as those representing objects, faces, locations, and other sensations. However, because we don't know how these higher-order representations are encoded, we don't know how waves would appear on them. Random firing in the visual cortex is also seen under hallucination conditions, which appear as small colored spots on the visual field (again, that follow your retina as it moves).[12] Just as the firing of the primary visual cortex is perceived as vision, the random firing of neurons in the

Pattern in   Visual
visual cortex   perception

Figure 17.1 The log-polar transformation in the primate visual cortex. Patterns on the visual cortex (horizontal lines, vertical lines, diagonal lines) are transformed into retinal perceptions (radial lines, concentric circles, a spiral) because of the log-polar transformation from the retina to the visual cortex. Similar patterns are seen during sensory deprivation, drug-induced hallucinations, and near-death experiences. Similar patterns also appear drawn on ancient petroglyphs.

face-representation area (a small, dedicated piece of the cortex called the superior temporal sulcus or STS)[13] would be perceived as seeing a specific person.

Migraine and the fortification illusion

One of the best-described visual hallucinations occurs during migraines and is described as the "fortification" hallucination or "visual aura."[14] Generally, these are experienced as extremely bright jagged edges, progressing slowly across the visual field, followed behind by a visual scotoma or blackness, obscuring one's vision. Interestingly, the line of jagged edges speeds up as it progresses from the center of one's vision to the edge, over the course of 10 to 20 minutes. At this point, you may be able to guess why the jagged edge speeds up as it progresses out from the center to the periphery of vision.

These "fortification" auras are directly explainable as the firing of cells in the visual cortex.[15] As noted above, cells in the visual cortex represent visual information by being tuned to short, oriented lines. Different orientations within a hypercolumn are connected to each other. Thus, if much of a hypercolumn was active, it would appear as a set of angular lines, at sharp orientations to each other. Because the columns are connected across hypercolumns, one sees a continuous hexagonal wall. As the wave progresses from the medial edge (the center of one's vision) to the lateral edge (the periphery of one's vision), the wall seems to move. It is exceptionally bright because all of the cells are firing as the wave progresses through them. Firing uses up cellular resources, and cells become unable to fire (become *refractory*) afterwards.[16] The inability of cells to fire behind the wave appears as a blank darkness or a scotoma. The wave appears to speed up because our cortex represents the center of our visual field with more cortical area than the periphery. Thus a constant-speed wave in the visual cortex covers more and more of our visual field as it progresses laterally and appears to speed up as it moves.

The term "fortification" is an allusion to St. Hildegard von Bingen, a 12th-century nun, living in Germany, who left descriptions of visions of lights more brilliant than the sun progressing through her vision, which turn into black coals, of visions of a spreading fire of God, followed by gloomy darkness, leaving ethereal stars behind, and of visions of a head of fire scourging the darkness.[17] Several authors in the 20th century have suggested that St. Hildegard's visions were migraine auras.[18] The jagged edges of the fortification illusion do, in fact, look like crenellations and battlements that might be seen atop a medieval castle. They are often brilliantly bright (being the firing of many cells simultaneously) and followed by a darkness (as the cells shut off and become refractory, tiring out and becoming unable to fire), which obscures vision (because vision is the firing of specific cells; which subset of cells fires is the information about what you see—if all the cells are silent, one sees only darkness). Figure 17.2 shows a modern depiction of the fortification illusion. Hildegard explicitly described that the visions occurred during normal wakefulness, not during sleep or trances, and that she could not see the length or breadth of these visions (presumably because the images were on her visual cortex, so they moved with her vision when she moved her eyes). One can easily imagine the

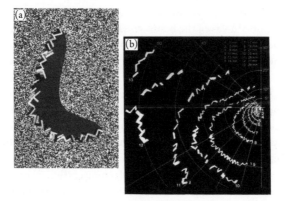

Figure 17.2 Fortification illusions in migraines. (a) Migraine sufferers see scintillating zigzags followed by darkness. A migraine sufferer watched a flickering display and drew what was seen. (b) The subject was asked to focus at a single point and draw the edges of these fortifications on a piece of paper at 2-minute intervals. The results reveal that the fortifications expand outward at accelerating speeds. From Grüsser (1995), reprinted with permission from the publisher.

effect on a young woman in the 12th century of an inexplicable jagged bright line lead-ing an area of darkness expanding through her vision, especially one that continued whether her eyes were open or closed, that she could not look away from, and that was accompanied by a blazing, inescapable headache.

Imagination

If waves in the cortex and the random firing of cells produce hallucinations and the illu-sion of seeing things that are not there, what about the other direction? When we imag-ine something, is that also a physical process? This has been most thoroughly studied through visual imagery, in which people are asked to imagine a visual image.[19]

The first study to directly address this question was an examination of the abil-ity to mentally rotate images in one's mind. In a now-classic experiment, Roger Shepherd and Jacqueline Metzler asked subjects to determine whether two pictures of three-dimensional objects were pictures of the same object rotated through space, or whether they were different objects.[20] What they found was that the time it took a per-son to determine if the two objects were related was a linear function of the rotational angle between the two objects. They concluded from this that people were mentally rotating the objects (at a rate of about 60 degrees per second). Of course, when we look at the two objects and try to compare them, we have the subjective feeling that we are mentally rotating them (at least I do!). These rotations appear to activate visual and motor structures, as if people were imagining rotating the objects manually.

Following up on this work, Stephen Kosslyn and his colleagues began testing the psy-chophysics[B] of mental imagery.[21] If I ask you to imagine a pirate boat and then to talk about the prow of the boat (What is the figurehead on the prow of the boat?), you are faster to answer questions about the prow than about the stern (How many guns are pointing aft?). Somehow distances matter in the mental imagery. These visual representa-tions have been validated by fMRI results that have shown that mental imagery activates the appropriate sensory areas of the brain: visual mental imagery entails activity in the visual cortices and auditory mental imagery entails activity in auditory cortices, etc.

Of course, there is more to the brain than the primary sensory cortices. Normal people know the difference between imagining a boat and seeing one. This means that somewhere in the brain (likely the frontal cortices), other neurons are firing that differ-entiate them. One theory about hallucinations is that hallucinations entail mental imag-ery without those other neurons saying, "this is just your imagination—it's not real."[22]

A particularly interesting example of this sort of mental imagery has captured the imagination of neuroscience and psychology recently—motor control neurons in the monkey premotor cortices (the motor-related planning cortices[23]) show similar activity whether the animal is performing the movement itself or whether it is watching another primate perform the movement.[24] These neurons have been called "mirror" neurons; however, it is not clear at this point whether they are a special type of representation in the primate cortex or whether they are simply reflecting the animal's imagination of the other's actions in its own motor-control neurons.[25] We have encountered these mirror

---

[B] Psychophysics is the study of the timing of perceptual responses.

neurons previously in Chapter 14, where we discussed them in terms of our ability to empathize and sympathize with others.

Measuring mental imagery

Mental imagery is the firing of neurons in the brain. This means that we might be able to identify a covert cognitive process if we recorded enough neurons and identified manipulations of a covert variable.[26]

The first study to do this was done in the 1980s by Apostolos Georgopoulos and his colleagues, who trained a monkey to reach toward a target.[27] Initially, the monkeys were trained to touch a center light and hold it until the light went off, at which time one of eight surrounding lights would turn on. The monkey was simply to reach to one of the surrounding lights for a juice reward. What Georgopoulos and his colleagues found was that neurons in the primary motor cortex were tuned to the direction the animal was reaching and that from a large set of neurons (thousands[C]), they could decode the direction the animal was reaching (or was about to reach).[29] They then trained the monkey to reach not to the lit-up light on the outer circle, but rather 90 degrees counterclockwise to it. When they decoded the neurons, they found that the ensemble originally decoded to represent the direction of the lit-up light and rotated (through the intermediate directions) to the direction the animal was going to reach before the animal actually began its movement.[30] The animal was mentally rotating the reaching direction from the target to the cue.[D] In fact, the speed of that mental rotation in the monkey motor cortex matched the speed of mental rotation found by the classic Shepherd and Metzler study in humans from two decades earlier in which humans matched images of three-dimensional blocks.

If it is possible to decode covert cognitive and imagined information from neural ensembles, then it should be possible to record the neural activity from the brain, to ask subjects to imagine moving their arms, to decode the neural activity of how they want their arms to move, and to move robotic arms to match. This is the promise of *brain–machine interfaces* and sounds like science fiction, but it is already a reality in limited conditions.[32]

Using the same motor-tuned areas that Apostolos Georgopoulos recorded from two decades earlier, Andy Schwartz (then at Arizona State University, now at the University of Pittsburgh) trained a monkey to track a ball in a virtual-reality three-dimensional space.[33] Wearing specially designed goggles, the monkey saw two balls—a yellow ball

---

[C] At the time, only one neuron could be recorded at a time. Georgopoulos and his colleagues trained the monkey so well that each reach from center out was almost exactly the same motion. Recording one or two neurons per day, they then combined all of the reaches the monkey made over the course of several years to create a "pseudo-ensemble" of thousands of neurons. Their experiments have more recently been replicated using smaller sets (dozens) of simultaneously recorded neurons, but the conclusions have not changed.[28]

[D] This mental rotation by the monkey between the immediate reaction of reaching to the cue and the later correction to reach 90 degrees off from it is a special case of the issue we discussed in Chapter 10 that the brain first plans the quick and obvious reaction but can correct it if given time.[31]

that appeared at a random point in three-dimensional space, and a blue ball that it controlled. If it could get the blue ball to catch the yellow one, it would get a juice reward. The secret (for which the monkey was never explicitly trained) was that the movement of the blue ball was not based on the movement of the monkey's hand but instead on the decoded information from the monkey's brain. When he presented his data, Andy Schwartz used to show a video in which the monkey initially tracked the virtual ball with its hands, but then as it realized that the tracking was moving faster than its hands, it dropped its hands to its sides and continued tracking the ball using only its mind. For obvious reasons, this video was affectionately referred to in the neuroscience community as the "Jedi Monkey video."

More recently, it has become possible to decode this imagined information to move robotic arms, not just in monkeys but now also in humans.[34] The work on this has been slow because it required two separate breakthroughs to work—from neuroscience, it required decoding algorithms that could identify what the arm was supposed to do, and from robotics, it required reliable robot arms that could be controlled with sufficient accuracy and simplicity. But both of those breakthroughs have been accomplished and several labs have now driven robotic arms from mental imagery. In 2008, a monkey in Andy Schwartz's lab was able to feed itself using a robotic arm.[35] John Donoghue's lab has shown that tetraplegic patients (who are paralyzed from the neck down) can guide robotic hands to move and to open and close.[36] In one of the videos that John Donoghue shows at his presentations, one of the patients, watching the robotic arm grasp a soda can and lift it up under the control of his own mental imagination, stares at the robotic hand, moving with his thoughts, and says, in clear amazement, "Whoa."

Brain manipulation

The concept of a separation between brain and mind (dualism) can still survive the observation that mental imagery is reflected in neuronal firing, because it could be that the brain only reflects what is going on in the mind. The real test of whether the mind truly corresponds to neuronal firing in the brain is whether manipulations of that firing change experiences. In fact, at the sensory level, this technology is so successful that we often don't realize that it exists. The cochlear implant, a technology implanted in hundreds of thousands of patients, stimulates sensory neurons in the ear to translate auditory signals from a microphone directly into the brain.[37] Retinal stimulators translating video images into sensory signals on the retina are currently in Phase II clinical trials.[38]

However, clinical stimulation of the deep brain beyond sensory cortices has been limited to simple waveforms and frequencies without information. The main clinical stimulation of nonsensory structures has been a procedure called deep-brain stimulation, which is currently a common treatment for Parkinson's disease.[39] Although the mechanism by which it works is still unknown, stimulating the basal ganglia at low frequencies (under a few hundred cycles per second) often re-enables motion in akinetic patients (patients who can't move). Some researchers think that this stimulation effectively shuts off the basal ganglia structures, producing a lesion-like effect, allowing other decision-making systems to take over. Other researchers think that the basal ganglia need to work at a certain rhythm,[E] and the stimulation enables it to get back into that rhythm. Deep-brain stimulation targeted at other areas is now being tried for other disorders[41] (such as epilepsy and depression), but most of these experiments are pretty much flying blind—no one knows why they are working when they do or why they don't when they don't.

Research-wise, however, stimulation has been shown to be able to control everything, including pleasure, pain, and memories. In Chapter 4, we encountered medial forebrain bundle stimulation, where some stimulation targets produced euphoric pleasure and other stimulation sites did not. Stimulation has been used for everything from pain management to muscular control.[42] The motor cortices themselves were defined in the 1800s when scientists passed small amounts of current and stimulated the cortex, producing motion in anesthetized animals.[43] Stimulating one location on the motor cortex led to arm motion, while stimulation of another led to leg motion.

In the 1940s, Wilder Penfield and Herbert Jasper were trying to help epilepsy patients avoid just the sort of disaster that led to H.M.'s memory loss, and examined the effect of cortical stimulation in these epilepsy patients. Using local anesthesia to open up a small piece of the skull,[F] Penfield and Jasper stimulated areas of the cortex of awake, resting patients,[44] and found that stimulations could trigger memories, hints of songs, even smells, and visions.

The most impressive manipulation of brain signals is still the work by Bill Newsome and colleagues from the 1990s, in which they were able to change a monkey's perception enough to change its ultimate decision.[45] Newsome and colleagues trained monkeys to observe the flow of random dots on a screen. Some of the dots moved truly randomly and some moved in a given direction (say left or right). The monkey's goal was to determine which direction the (very small) proportion of dots was moving. We encountered this task earlier in our discussion of integrating perceptual signals (Chapter 11). If you remember that discussion, one of the visual areas (MST) determines whether the whole field is moving together. Because cortical representations in MST are arranged in columns, with each column representing a different direction, Newsome and his students were able to stimulate single columns in MST and change the perceived direction of motion, and the monkey's responses. Similar experiments have been able to change the direction of visual saccades (by stimulating other areas, as well as in subcortical structures such as the superior colliculus, which drives orientation of attention).[46]

[E] There is some evidence, for example, that giving some of these patients a rhythm to work with (e.g., through music) can renormalize motion. Sometimes the presence of visual cues is enough to re-enable motion. For example, placing a stick across a patient's path can force the patient to step over the stick and get started walking again. This is shown very nicely in the movie *Awakenings*, in which the doctor has the floor painted with black and white squares, which allows the patient, "Rose," to walk to the window.[40]

[F] The brain does not have any local, internal pain sensors, so it is possible to use local anesthesia to silence the sensors in the skin and then manipulate the brain of the patient, while the patient is awake and on the table. I have seen this done during a deep-brain-stimulation surgery in which deep-brain stimulation electrodes were being implanted. The patient was calm and comfortable and chatted with the doctors as they implanted the electrodes in his brain. Most lesion surgeries (e.g., for epilepsy) are done on awake patients, so that surgeons can determine the role of the structures they are removing to make sure they do not remove anything critical (to avoid the tragedy of H.M.).

The brain is the physical instantiation of the mind. Interfering with brain function changes mental function. One of the reasons people are worried about learning how the brain works and learning how the physical brain instantiates the mind is that they are worried that we will develop a form of mental control, where machines manipulating your brain control your thoughts, desires, and actions. But just as changing the brain changes the mind, changing the mind changes the brain. Whenever you learn something new, your brain is physically changed. When you realize that you really do have two choices—to drink or not to drink—that is a physical change in your brain as well as a change in your mental state. Humans are already very adept at controlling each other—a tremendous amount of our brain power is dedicated to predicting what our neighbors, colleagues, friends, and enemies will do. It is said that charm is the ability to get people to do something that you want them to do without them realizing that you got them to do it. Just because the manipulation is not physical does not mean it is not manipulation. The brain is the physical instantiation of the mind. Every mental event is reflected in the physical realm, from imagination to hallucination to mental imagery.

Books and papers for further reading

- Paul C. Bressloff, Jack D. Cowan, Martin Golubitsky, Peter J. Thomas, and Matthew C. Wiener (2002). What geometric visual hallucinations tell us about the visual cortex. *Neural Computation*, 14, 473–491.
- Stephen M. Kosslyn.(1994). *Image and Brain*. Cambridge, MA: MIT Press.
- Adam Johnson, André A. Fenton, Cliff Kentros, and A. David Redish (2009). Looking for cognition in the structure in the noise. *Trends in Cognitive Sciences*, 13, 55–64.
- Andrew B. Schwartz (2007). Useful signals from motor cortex. *Journal of Physiology*, 579, 581–601.

18

Addiction

> a falling leaf
> interrupted
> yellow flower petal in my hand

Addiction is a disorder of decision-making. Defined this way, the question of addiction becomes one of identifying the different vulnerabilities or failure modes that have arisen within an individual's decision-making systems. This hypothesis suggests that addiction treatments need to be tailored to the individual, based on the identification of those failure modes. Treatment processes are beginning to be tailored in just such a way.

Addiction is the classic disorder of decision-making—an addict continues taking drugs even in the face of massive negative consequences, and sometimes even in the case of a stated desire to stop.[1] How can an addict both state that he or she wants to stop taking drugs and yet continue taking them? As we've seen, human decision-making arises from a complex interaction of components. What we will see in this chapter is that this complex interacting set of decision-making systems, this decision-making machinery, can break down in many different ways. While each of these different vulnerabilities may produce subtle differences in how the addict acts (*Does the addict crave the drug before taking it? Does the addict take only the one drug, or is any drug good enough? Is the addict chasing pleasure or avoiding dysphoria?*), they all come down to the same problem—the addict continues the behavior, even though he or she should stop.

What is addiction?

Most modern definitions of addiction are based on the concept of maladaptive decisions—continuing to take drugs even in the face of severe negative consequences, whether they be illness, dysphoria, or longer-term negatives, such as loss of friends, family, job, etc.[2] But this concept can be taken to ludicrous extremes—do we really want to say that we are all addicted to breathing? If you take the oxygen away, we die; it's hard to imagine a more negative consequence than that. More problematically, there are many cases where we celebrate an individual making a decision with severe negative consequences, such as a soldier defending his or her country, or a firefighter risking his or her life in a burning building. We celebrate Martin Luther King, who fought for civil rights, knowing full well that it was likely to end in his death. Sometimes, however, this view leads to interesting perspectives. The Russian poet Osip Mandelstam continued to write poetry even after he had been sent to the Soviet Gulag for it.[3] The future Hall of Fame football quarterback Brett Favre continued to play football long after many suggested he stop, despite severe injuries and an aging body that was far less resilient to punishment than it had been.[4] Should we say that Mandelstam was addicted to writing poetry or that Favre was addicted to football?

Other definitions of addiction have been based on the presence of a disconnect between stated desires and actions[5] ("I want to stop, but I can't"). Of course, this definition implies that animals (who cannot state such a desire even if they feel it) cannot be defined as addicts. Given that animals reliably self-administer the same pharmacological substances that humans do, even in the face of negative consequences,[6] this definition seems problematic. Another problem with defining addiction as a verbal disconnect is that many of us know addicts who do not state a desire to stop their addiction, who refuse to admit their "problem." Many a high school clique has needed to intervene for a friend with a drug or alcohol problem, and there are many people alive today because their friends stepped in with just such an intervention.

Some economists have suggested that addiction should be defined by the *elasticity* of the decision. As discussed in Chapter 3, elasticity is defined by how much your decision to buy something changes in response to changes in price. As the economy worsens, people tend to go out to the movies or to dinner less often. These luxury items are highly elastic. On the other hand, people continue to buy food, even at high prices, so food purchases are highly inelastic. Addiction can then be defined as "irrational" inelasticity.[7] As noted in Chapter 3, this allows economists to say that Americans are "addicted to oil"[8]—we continue to use it and to use it unwisely (driving individual cars rather than taking more efficient mass transit; depending on it for electricity and heating rather than using non–fossil-fuel systems or taking the time to ensure that our houses are energy-efficient), even in the face of severe negative consequences (major oil spills, high prices, and unnecessary wars).

It is important to note that drugs (like oil) are, in fact, economic objects;[A] as the cost of drugs goes up, their use goes down, even among the most dedicated and physiologically dependent addicts.[10] The number of people quitting smoking, for example, is directly proportional to the cost of cigarettes. Similarly, studies of changes in heroin or cocaine pricing (remember, the black market is still a market) find that increases in pricing lead to direct changes in the number of users and the amount of use. This elasticity is why one of the best ways to decrease the use of legal drugs (nicotine, alcohol, and, in the near future, marijuana) is to have "sin taxes," which increase the price of the drug.

This elasticity is also one of the best arguments against the legalization of harder drugs (heroin, cocaine, methamphetamine). The argument for or against legalization is

---

[A] The technical term is "economic good"[9] because one buys "goods and services," but that would lead to the unfortunate sentence "Drugs are, in fact, an economic good...."

very complicated. On the one hand, the negative consequences of getting caught with drugs is a cost that decreases use. For example, studies of the amount of opium use in Taiwan during the Chinese crackdowns in the 1920s find a direct elastic relationship between the severity of punishment and initial use.[11] On the other hand, jailing users can interfere with treatment because it can reduce the positive options and positive interactions that are often closely related to recovery.[12] Jail time without treatment can throw users who have not yet committed violent criminal acts in with dangerous criminals who are, in fact, dangers to society. The other problem with criminalizing drug use is that it shifts drugs from an open market to a criminal market and tends to lead to violent business interactions, which have strong negative consequences for bystanders not actually involved in the criminal market.[13] (See Prohibition, US 1920–1933; Columbia and the Medellin Cartel 1976–1993; and drug and gang violence in some American cities today.)

In part because of this complexity of defining addiction (and in an attempt to remove the stigma that had become attached to the word "addict"), psychiatrists in the DSM-IV and ICD-10 (regularly released books detailing the currently agreed-upon definitions in psychiatry) abandoned the word "addiction" and referred to drug users as "dependent" and overuse of drugs as "dependency."[14] I believe that this definition overemphasizes the pharmacological effects of drugs more than the interactions with decision-making. It also makes it hard to ask questions about "addiction" to nonpharmacological substances. I will continue to use the terms "addict" and "addiction" to refer to people making these maladaptive decisions to continue using drugs, while recognizing that the question of when one is an addict is more of a policy question than a scientific one. The scientific question is *Why is the person continuing to pursue this drug? How can we change that?* Whether we want to interfere, and how much we should be willing to push to interfere, is a personal question for affected individuals and family members and a policy question for society.

Addiction as a failure of decision-making

If we look at the decision-making system that we have explored so far in this book, what we have is a machinery of decision-making. Like any machine, there are multiple places it can break down. Looking at the system in detail, there are several dozen different ways that this machinery can make the wrong choice[15]—the Pavlovian system can assign increased emotional motivation to a drug,[16] the Deliberative system can misjudge the expected outcomes of a choice,[17] the Procedural (habit) system can overvalue[18] or automate too quickly,[19] the situation-recognition system can overseparate or overgeneralize situations,[20] etc. Each of these different failure modes or vulnerabilities could have an effect of driving the addict to continue making the addictive choice.[21] Differences between these *failure modes* or *vulnerabilities* imply differences in how the addict makes those choices, and each one will likely require different treatments.

I do not mean to suggest that each addict's behavior will be due to only one failure mode in his or her decision-making system. Biology tends to have lots of backup mechanisms. It may well be that full-blown addiction arises only when multiple systems break down. Drugs themselves also tend to create additional failure modes. For example, a massively pleasurable effect (the high of cocaine[22]) leads to increased motivation for cocaine (a "desire" for it[23]), as well as tolerance (requiring more cocaine to produce that high[24]), and an increased likelihood of taking actions leading to cocaine (the Procedural system, driving unthinking decision-making[25]). Alcohol leads to a reduction in anxiety (thus driving a learned need[26]), tolerance (thus requiring more and more alcohol to produce the same effect[27]), and reductions in the effectiveness of self-control and Deliberative systems.[28] Addressing only one vulnerability may not be enough to stop the addiction. On the other hand, sometimes one can find a key to allow the patient to find another path to prevent relapse.[29]

To understand the concept of a *failure mode* or a *vulnerability in the system*, the simplest example is to look at opiate agonists. As we saw, there is good evidence that euphoria (pleasure) and dysphoria (displeasure) are instantiated in the brain by the flow of endogenous opioids (endorphin and dynorphin, see Chapter 4). This means that the feeling of pleasure *is* the flow of endorphins onto μ-opioid receptors. (This is a direct consequence of the rejection of the mind/brain duality that we have been discussing in the last few chapters.) Just as stimulating auditory nerves produces hearing sounds,[30] and waves of random activity across the visual cortex produce images,[31] changing the flow of endorphins onto μ-opioid receptors changes euphoria signals. This means that a pharmacological chemical that tricked the μ-opioid receptors into thinking that they had seen endorphins would be experienced as euphoric pleasure. What are some chemicals that activate the μ-opioid receptors? They are the ones that gave us the words *opioid* and *opiate*, derived from the opium poppy (including such mainstays of addiction as morphine and heroin).[32]

Addiction researchers will often talk of the drug as "hijacking" the neural system, but I think what is going on is something more subtle. We are taking an engineer's view of the brain—there is a physical system and that physical system has ways it can break down. We evolved a machinery that includes a "pleasure" component as part of how it processes decisions (Chapter 4). This pleasure component is signaled by a chemical pathway. A foreign pharmacological substance is changing that chemical pathway. This takes us back to the "Car Talk" perspective that we started with in Chapter 2. To return to our original example at the start of the book, just as the thermostat in your house would react incorrectly if you held a match underneath it (it would think the house was hotter than it is), your thermostat would also react incorrectly if you passed a current over the wire that signals "I'm hot" to the thermostat. Heroin is changing that internal wire.

When Steve Jensen, Adam Johnson, and I looked at the decision-making machinery in this way in 2008,[33] we found many examples of these sorts of vulnerability points in the machinery; in fact, most of those failure points had already been found by other researchers. Many researchers had proposed theories of why addicts continue to take their drugs (for example, that their system gets out of balance and they need the drugs to return to balance;[34] that they are chasing euphoric properties;[35] that they learn to overvalue the drugs;[36] that the drugs become secondary reinforcers and draw attention away from other things;[37] that the drugs shift the balance between deliberative and habit systems;[38] etc.). What we found is that these theories were all stated in the form of "if you have this problem, you might be an addict." What was interesting was that these theories were generally attacked by a researcher finding an addict without that problem. Logically, what the theories were saying was that a given problem would lead to addiction, not that all addicts had a given problem. Viewed in this way, addiction is a symptom that can arise from multiple underlying "diseases." Our multiple-vulnerabilities hypothesis said that everyone was right—all of these problems could lead to addiction, because all of these problems were potential failure modes of the decision-making system. Figure 18.1 shows a list of some of the current known failure modes of the decision-making machinery.

It is important to note that addiction, by definition, is an interaction between nature and nurture. If one never takes cocaine, one never becomes addicted to cocaine and cocaine never takes over one's life. Similarly, there are many different reactions to taking cocaine; there are many different reactions to smoking cigarettes.[39] Some people remain able to control their use, while others are lost to it after one experience with it, and others become lost to it only after extended experience. We do not yet know whether this is a function of the situations in which these users find themselves, or a function of the specific formulation of the drug itself, or the genetics of the user, or the learned background and life experiences of the user. (Most likely it is a complex combination of all of these.) What we do know is that drug addiction presents in many different ways, even among the population of people who are unable to control their drug use.

Craving: The difference between desire, withdrawal, and habit

One example of this difference is the now-clear clinical dissociation between craving and relapse.[40] For years, clinicians and research scientists have studied craving in addicts as a substitute for measuring what's really important—relapse. In large part, they do this because craving is something that can be studied in the laboratory, in terms of a controlled, experimental paradigm. For example, in cue-induced craving, pictures of drug paraphernalia are shown to admitted drug addicts and to nonaddicts, and the addicts show more signs of craving (stress, sweats, nervous behaviors) and rate their feeling of craving higher on survey scales.[41] However, it has been known for decades now that craving does not imply relapse. While craving and relapse are related (people who show a lot of craving are more likely to relapse, and people who relapse are more likely to show craving), they do not always co-occur. The problem is that while craving is a phenomenon of a moment, relapse is a long-term event that happens only (as an ethologist would say) "in the field." Before we can actually measure this, we need to address what craving is, neurobiologically.

Craving is the inexorable desire for a thing—we've all felt it at one time or another. To quote the Rolling Stones, "you can't always get what you want, but sometimes you get what you need."[42] The mechanism of craving has been studied extensively, particularly in terms of drug addicts being reminded of their addiction, for example by being shown pictures of drug paraphernalia. But craving is not such a simple thing. For example, it turns out to be dissociable from relapse in drug addiction. Even though someone might crave a cigarette or a drug hit, it is possible to resist that craving, and not relapse back into the addiction. Others may take the drug-taking action without ever craving it. As one patient with a gambling problem told a colleague of mine, "I don't know what happened. I just found myself at the casino." (Were they lying? Were they lying to themselves?) As we've seen, there are multiple decision-making systems driving our actions,

Failure-point	key systems	clinical consequence
Moving away from homeostasis (Koob and Le Moal, 2006; Koob and Volkow, 2010)	*motivation*	withdrawal
Changing allostatic set-points (Koob and Le Moal, 2006; Koob and Volkow, 2010)	*motivation*	physiological needs, craving
Sensitization of motivation (Robinson and Berridge, 2001, 2003)	*motivation*	incorrect action-selection, craving
Cue-outcome associations elicit pre-wired visceral actions (Damasio, 1994; Bechara and Damasio, 2002; Bechara, 2005)	*emotions and motivation*	incorrect action-selection, craving
Escape from negative emotions (Koob, 2009)	*emotion*	incorrect action-selection
Mimicking reward (Volkow et al., 2002; Wise, 2005)	*multiple systems*	incorrect action-selection, craving
Errors in expected outcomes (Goldman et al., 1999; Jones et al., 2001; Redish and Johnson, 2007)	*deliberation*	incorrect action-selection
Increased likelihood of retrieving a specific expected action-outcome path (Redish and Johnson, 2007)	*deliberation*	obsession
Over-valuation of expected outcomes (Redish et al., 2008)	*deliberative*	incorrect action-selection
Over-valuation of learned actions (Di Chiara, 1999; Redish, 2004)	*habit*	automated, robotic drug-use
Timing errors (Ross, 2008)	*habit*	preferences for unpredictable events
Over-fast discounting processes (Bickel and Marsch, 2001; Bickel and Mueller, 2009)	*deliberative, habit*	impulsivity
Changes in learning rates (Franken et al., 2005; Gutkin et al., 2006; Piray et al., 2010; Redish et al., 2008)	*deliberative, habit*	excess drug-related cue-associations
Selective inhibition of the deliberative system (Bernheim and Rangel, 2004; Bechara, 2005; Bickel and Yi, 2008; Baumeister and Tierney, 2011; Bickel et al., 2012)	*system-selection*	fast development of habit learning
Selective excitation of the habit system (Everitt and Robbins, 2005; Bickel and Yi, 2008)	*system-selection*	fast development of habit learning
Misclassification of situations: overcategorization (Redish et al., 2007)	*situation-recognition*	illusion of control, hindsight bias
Misclassification of situations: overgeneralization (Redish et al., 2007)	*situation-recognition*	perseveration in the face of losses

Figure 18.1 Some failure modes of the decision-making system that can lead to addiction. Obviously incomplete.

only some of which are conscious. It is likely that if a person were to relapse through the Procedural system (Chapter 10), this relapse would not entail any craving beforehand (or perhaps even any prior recognition beforehand). They might well just find themselves "at the casino."

An important aspect of craving is that we crave *things*.[43] We do not simply crave pleasure; we do not simply crave. The word *craving* is transitive; it must include an object. We crave sex, we crave a cigarette, we crave a drink. Perhaps we can even crave love— but even then, what we are craving is a feeling, a moment, a romantic dinner, a walk on the beach. While that craving might be satisfied by something different from your original goal, there is no question that craving includes an identifiable target or goal. When someone craves something, there are extensive effects on the body itself.[44] Part of craving is that it increases arousal—the heart beats faster and harder, one's attention increases, one gets jittery. These are Pavlovian actions that we saw in Chapter 8— untrained actions that occur in response to the delivery of the desired object that are now occurring in response to delivery of the expectation of that object.

Some people have explicitly identified craving with the Pavlovian system—something reminds us of the existence of an outcome (through a stimulus–outcome association), and we remember that the outcome was very desirable.[45] Just as we discussed when we introduced the multiple decision-making systems (Chapter 6), Pavlovian training has both action-selection effects (Chapter 8) and motivational effects (Chapter 13). It is not clear at this point whether the motivational effects of craving are identical to the physiological changes of craving or whether they just tend to co-occur.[46]

Other people have identified craving with the Deliberative system, in that a Deliberative system entails a search for an outcome, finding paths that can reach to it.[47] This means that part of the Deliberative system must maintain a representation of the target so that it can be recognized when one finds it. Early studies of craving found that craving does not tend to occur for easily achieved goals; instead, it tends to occur for blocked goals. Consider an alcoholic who goes to the bar every day at a certain time and does not show craving until one day arriving to find the bar closed. Then the craving sets in.[48] This blocked path forces the alcoholic from a well-trained, regular habit-based (Procedural) decision-making system to the more flexible, more conscious planning (Deliberative) system.[49]

When we discussed the motivation system (Chapter 13), we discussed a particular phenomenon called *Pavlovian-to-instrumental transfer* (PIT), in which Pavlovian associations reminded one of an outcome, which led to increased actions taken to achieve a specific goal. This suggests that craving may be an interaction between the motivational and Deliberative systems. Experiments directly aimed at PIT suggest a strong role for the nucleus accumbens shell, which is strongly involved in craving.[50] A relationship between PIT and craving would imply that craving is an interaction between the Pavlovian motivation (Chapter 13) and Deliberative (Chapter 9) decision-making components.

It is important to dissociate craving from the negative feelings associated with ceasing drug-taking. As quoted from a patient to Anna Rose Childress and her colleagues, "No, doc, craving is when you want it—want it so bad you can almost taste it…but you ain't sick…sick is, well, sick."[51] Ceasing drug-taking produces dramatic withdrawal symptoms, both physical and mental. Physical withdrawal symptoms come because the drug affects more than just the central nervous system. Biological systems are fundamentally chemical systems, and the chemistry of the drug is going to have profound effects on the body. Of course, one of the points this book is about is that the mental changes are physical as well, and those chemical changes are going to have profound effects on both brain and mind.

Generally, withdrawal symptoms come from homeostatic shifts. The term "homeostasis" means maintenance of something at a given level, from the Greek words ομοιο (*homeo-*, meaning "same") and στάσις (*stasis*, meaning "standing still"). Much of biology is about maintaining the system at some point that will enable continued survival.[52] These homeostatic levels are related to the intrinsic goals discussed in Chapter 13—when you need food, you are hungry; when you are too cold, you want to warm yourself up. The classic case of homeostasis is body temperature. Just like the thermostat that we saw at the very beginning of the book, your body contains temperature sensors (in the biological case, neurons throughout that project to a small nucleus of cells in the hypothalamus). If these sensors determine that the body is too hot, processes are initiated to cool the body down—capillaries near the skin surface open wider to provide more blood flow to the skin, allowing a faster transfer of heat from the internal core to the surface; pores open up, producing sweat, providing evaporative cooling. In extreme cases, humans will even open their mouths and pant. Similarly, if these sensors determine that the body is too cold, opposite processes are initiated to heat the body up, constricting capillaries, pulling the skin tighter (producing goose bumps), exercising muscles, etc.[53]

These days, however, a number of scientists have recommended replacing the term with "allostasis," from the Greek word αλλο- ("allo-," meaning "other").[54] In part, this redefinition is due to the implication that in homeostasis one maintains the parameter at a single target, while, in actuality, the target changes with one's needs. (We used to hear that a normal human body temperature is 98.6 degrees Fahrenheit, but body temperature actually changes throughout the day and, of course, changes in fever.[55]) In addition, biological systems learn to plan—if you are in a world where food is scarce, it's better to overeat when food is available than to eat just until you're full, because you don't know if you'll be starving later.[56] Part of the role of the Pavlovian motivation system (Chapter 13) is to guide that plan.

So what does this have to do with withdrawal symptoms? The key is that homeostatic systems react slowly. Imagine that your body is trying to maintain a certain oxygen flow through the bloodstream. If you move to a high altitude (say Katmandu in the Nepalese Himalayas), then getting enough oxygen to your tissues requires your body to put more resources into hemoglobin and oxygen transfer. This happens over the course of days or longer. Similarly, if you then move back to a lower altitude, the extra oxygen flow remains for a couple of weeks while your system readjusts. Athletes who require high oxygen flow (such as Olympic long-distance runners) often live or train at high altitudes so that their body will adjust and be better at delivering oxygen to their tissues when they run the actual race (although the efficacy of this is still controversial).[57]

A cigarette smoker has been flooding his or her tissues with nicotine, which is an analog of a very common brain chemical called acetylcholine.[58] The music that I am listening to right now on my computer has three volume knobs in sequence. The media player has a volume, which changes how loud the music is that is sent to the computer, which has a system volume, which changes how loud the music is that is sent to the speakers, which have their own volume. If the media player volume increases, then I can get the same level of music out by decreasing the volume on the speakers (which is easier to reach than the internal system volume). But then if the media player volume suddenly decreases, the music will be too soft, and I won't be able to hear it.

In response to the chemical flooding of nicotine, the brain has learned to turn the volume down on acetylcholine receptors. So when a person stops smoking, the body and brain react as if they weren't getting enough acetylcholine—because the ex-smoker isn't getting enough acetylcholine, because the volume on the acetylcholine receptors has been turned down too low. Such changes occur throughout the brain and peripheral systems. Withdrawal symptoms typically occur for a time after stopping drug use (days, weeks, months). These withdrawal symptoms are due to the body's adjustment being out of alignment with the drug expectation.[59] Of course, as we discussed above, it is possible to change the body's homeostatic (allostatic) target based on cues and situations. This means that cues can remind an addict of an expectation of drug, leading to a shift in the allostatic target, leading to what is effectively cue-induced withdrawal symptoms.[60]

But craving can also occur in the absence of any explicit withdrawal symptoms.[61] Craving is a mental process due to more permanent changes in learning and memory systems and can arise long after the withdrawal symptoms have gone away. Even though craving occurs through a physical process (everything in the brain is a physical process), understanding what craving is physically has been much more elusive and will likely depend on understanding how craving interacts with the multiple decision-making systems.

The key experiment would be to measure craving continuously as people live their lives, and then to compare those who report high craving levels and those who don't and to compare those who relapsed and those who didn't. This is, of course, a very hard experiment to do. There have been some attempts using cell-phones and PDAs to ask people to report craving at regular intervals.[62] These experiments generally find that craving does often occur before relapse, but that sometimes craving occurs without relapse and sometimes relapse occurs without craving. Many readers may be asking why we don't use retrospective experiments that find people who relapsed and ask them whether they showed craving beforehand. The problem comes back to the reconstruction of memory that we saw in the last few chapters. We don't actually remember the episodes of our past; instead we reconstruct them from our memories of what was, what should have been, and what probably happened. In fact, careful experiments have found that people who relapse without craving often remember (incorrectly) that they showed craving before the relapse.[63]

Craving can occur in an attempt to alleviate withdrawal symptoms.[64] Craving can occur because the emotional (Pavlovian, Chapter 8) system is expecting a strong reward (or needs to avoid a strong punishment),[65] or because the planning (Deliberative, Chapter 9) system recognizes a path to a strong reward.[66] It is not yet known whether these different drives will be dissociable experimentally or not, but they all entail mechanisms by which a person would express a strong desire for the drug.

Interestingly, all three of these mechanisms may lead to craving, but they don't necessarily lead to relapse. The separation between craving and relapse comes back to the multiple decision-making systems that we have seen throughout this book. Craving is a function of the expectation of the outcome; you can't crave something you don't know you're going to get. This means that craving won't occur when actions are selected by the Procedural system (Chapter 10), which doesn't include a representation of the outcome. Since the Deliberative system implies recognition of a path to a goal, but knowing that path does not mean one takes it (remember, the Deliberative system is flexible), one can have craving without relapse. Since both reflexes and the Pavlovian system can be overridden by self-control systems (Chapter 15), they don't necessarily lead to relapse either. While craving and relapse are related, they are not identical.

Paths out of drug use

Although drug users, scientists, and society would very much like to have a single magic bullet that would "cure" a drug user of the predilection for drugs, the multiple-vulnerabilities theory of drug addiction suggests that there isn't going to be a single path out of addiction.[67] That being said, current practice is to try multiple options, and some subset of these options often works for specific individuals.[68] My suspicion is that we need to see drug addiction not as the problem in itself, but rather as a symptom of an underlying problem or set of problems.[B]

Although this book is explicitly not a self-help book, and I am not going to attempt to tell a drug user how to escape from his or her predicament,[C] the multiple decision-making story that we have been telling throughout this book has some interesting implications for identifying potential paths out of the cycle of drug use.

The implication of this engineer's view on addiction and the concept that there are multiple decision-making systems with multiple vulnerabilities provide two important perspectives on treatment that can be addressed. First, the effect of treatments should be to normalize vulnerabilities. It should be possible to predict treatment success from identification of outcomes of successful and unsuccessful treatment attempts. Second, different vulnerabilities will likely require different treatments. If we could identify which vulnerabilities an addict has fallen victim to, we could potentially provide the right treatment for those vulnerabilities.[73]

[B] This view, that psychiatric categorizations (drug dependence, schizophrenia, depression, etc.) are actually categories of symptoms rather than reflections of an underlying disease, is related to the concept of *endophenotypes*. The term "endophenotype" comes from the idea that different genes can have the same effects (phenotypes), but the concept here goes beyond simple statements of genetic variation. The concept is closer to that of *hypothetical constructs* or *trans-disease processes*.[69] Hypothetical constructs are intervening variables that allow one to look for underlying concepts in neural activity (such as subjective value,[70] which we discussed in Chapter 3), while trans-disease processes are treatable vulnerabilities that produce different dysfunctions in different contexts (such as impulsivity,[71] Chapter 5).

It is true that psychiatric categories have become reliable over the past decades such that they can be consistently applied—multiple psychiatrists will generally assign the same people to the same categories. However, successful treatment has lagged behind. Unfortunately, category reliability does not necessarily imply a unified mechanistic validity.[72] There is a current movement afoot called *computational psychiatry* that attempts to redefine psychiatric illnesses in terms of their underlying mechanisms, connecting psychiatric symptoms with underlying dysfunction based on computational models of decision-making. We will return to this concept in Chapter 21.

[C] As noted in the preface, treatment needs to be tailored to the individual. Thus, one should check with one's own medical professionals before embarking on any treatment regimen.

Some evidence exists suggesting that these perspectives are correct—different addicts are better served by different treatments. For example, behavioral impulsivity measures predict success in smoking cessation. Neural structures and cognitive tests can be identified that predict treatment outcome success in cocaine addiction.[74]

Some vulnerabilities will be simple to treat. A homeostatic imbalance can be alleviated by replacement with reduced-harm alternatives, such as nicotine replacement therapy for smoking or methadone replacement for heroin.[75] However, long-term relapse rates after ceasing these treatments are notoriously high.[76] This is likely a consequence of the fact that these therapies do not address the other vulnerabilities that an addict may have fallen victim to.[77]

For example, it is important not to underestimate the negative component of drug addiction on emotion and affect. Because of the way that biological systems have limited internal resources, and because biological properties are always trying to balance themselves, a biological high (euphoria) will be followed by a crash (dysphoria).[78] If euphoria, for example, is the release of endorphins onto μ-opioid receptors, then heroin flooding the system will produce an overcompensating reaction like "ringing" in an oscillator. These negative effects can occur after even a single dose of morphine.[79] And, as we saw above in our discussion of homeostatic (allostatic) systems, these systems will learn to compensate for that overabundance of signal, leading to a negative assessment in contrast, when everything else just feels terrible. This is shown clearly in the movies *Sid and Nancy* and *Trainspotting*: the addicts' senses have become so dulled to everything that drugs are the only thing left that can hold their interest for even a moment. Finding healthier activities that can substitute for drugs or alternative emotional factors that can capture one's desires can be difficult but potentially useful. Sometimes the key is recognizing just how bad off one is and that alternatives do exist.[80]

Some users have been able to break their addiction through attention to concrete alternatives, whether those alternatives are social (such as attending regular social interactions where one is praised for rejecting the addiction) or physical (such as earning money or points toward a new television set).[81] There is good evidence now that concrete targets are easier to aim toward than abstract ones and that concrete targets draw more of one's attention.[82] When those concrete targets are immediately-available things one wants to reject, they are more difficult to reject. When those concrete targets are positive goals in the future, they are easier to attend to and easier to assign value to (thus making them easier to use as alternatives). I know a person who broke his smoking addiction by putting the money he usually spent on cigarettes in a jar every day. He was a jazz fan and set himself a goal of buying a new saxophone. When enough money had accumulated in the jar, he had quit his smoking habit and celebrated by buying himself the saxophone.

Some vulnerabilities can be exceptionally difficult to treat. As we saw in Chapter 10, stimulus–response decisions can be made without conscious attention or thought, and such habits can be very hard to break. We examined one potential solution in self-control, in that one can override those actions with frontal cortical self-control mechanisms (Chapter 15). However, those mechanisms require constant attention and are very tiring. Distraction, exhaustion, and stress can all make maintaining self-control very difficult.[83] Another alternative is to identify what cues lead to relapse and to avoid those cues. For example, an alcoholic might drive a different path home to avoid driving by the bar where he usually stops in for a drink.

This leads us to the concept of *precommitment* and *bundling*.[84] Imagine an alcoholic who knows that he will drink if he goes to a party that evening, but would prefer to stay sober when asked in the light of day. This alcoholic is, in a sense, two people—in the light of the day, sober and sane, and in the Pavlovian context of the party, a wild alcoholic. (This dichotomy of choice is, of course, the central theme of Robert Louis Stevenson's *Dr. Jekyll and Mr. Hyde*.) These two temporally separated people are in conflict with each other.[85] If the sober and sane person in the light of the day (let us call him Dr. Jekyll) wishes to stay sober through the night, he only has to avoid the party. The problem is that in the evening, Dr. Jekyll will have changed his mind and will want to go to the party. One option is to find a way to commit himself to the nondrug option during the light of the day (for example, by making other plans for that evening). This is called *precommitment* because Dr. Jekyll has precommitted himself to an option so that the later option is not available.

Bundling is a similar process through which one changes the set of available outcomes by rethinking what the potential outcomes are.[86] For example, the concept "there is no such thing as one drink for an alcoholic" implies that one does not have the option to go to the bar and have "just one drink."[87] Instead, the options are to not drink and be the boring Dr. Jekyll or to drink and become the devil Mr. Hyde. Being the cool Mr. Suave drinking one drink and charming the ladies is not an option for our protagonist Dr. Jekyll. Recognizing that there are only the two options (boring Dr. Jekyll and dangerous Mr. Hyde) leads our protagonist to a very different decision process (between the two options of Jekyll and Hyde rather than between the three options of Jekyll, Hyde, and trying to be Mr. Suave). Bundling and precommitment are two examples of ways that changing one's perspective can change decision-making.

One interesting issue is that many (though unfortunately not all[D]) addicts *age out* of their addiction.[88] Whether this is due to changes in brain function with age (addiction often starts in adolescence, when prefrontal self-control functions are impaired[89]) or whether this is due to changes in life (such as gaining a family) is still unknown (and probably differs from person to person). Nevertheless, it is interesting that case studies of addicts who do age out usually talk of changes in perspective that lead to a rejection of the addictive choices.[90]

There are too many treatment options available and their successes and failures are too complex to list here or to identify how each one interacts with the multiple decision-making systems. As noted above, different treatment options seem to work for different patients.[91] Current treatments are now suggesting that patients go through a flowchart of options—if the patient has impulsivity problems, this can be treated with executive function therapy (which decreases impulsivity); if the patient has a homeostatic problem, this can be treated with pharmacological replacement.[92] Other problems require other treatments.

Although there are some examples where treatments aimed at specific dysfunctions are identifiably successful,[93] a vulnerability-by-vulnerability treatment regimen is as yet unavailable. How to identify which failure mode is active (or which failure modes are active) in a given addict and how to treat those failure modes are a focus of active research throughout the neuroscientific and medical communities today.[94]

[D] Some addicts die before getting a chance to age out and others never stop their addiction.

Books and papers for further reading

- Gene Heyman (2009). *Addiction: A Disorder of Choice*. Cambridge, MA: Harvard.
- George F. Koob and Michel Le Moal (2006). *Neurobiology of Addiction*. Amsterdam: Elsevier Academic Press.
- A. David Redish, Steve Jensen, and Adam Johnson (2008). A unified framework for addiction: Vulnerabilities in the decision process. *Behavioral and Brain Sciences, 31,* 415–487, including discussion (pp. 437–461) and author's reply (pp. 461–470).

‖ 19 ‖

Gambling and Behavioral Addictions

Driving to the city of illusions,
the cars ahead disappear
into the mirage at the point of
perspective.
In the shimmering desert,
pyramids and towers scrape the sky.

From the perspective of addiction as dysfunctional decision-making, gambling and other behaviors can also be seen as "addictions." These nonpharmacological addictions tend to depend on vulnerabilities in the support systems (e.g., motivational systems, situation-recognition systems) more than in the action-selection systems themselves, but they do also depend, of course, on how action-selection systems use those support systems.

An interesting question that has arisen over the past few years is whether addiction is fundamentally related to drug use or whether one can be addicted to something that is not drug-related.[1] From the old "dependence" theory of addiction—that drugs change your internal balance of some chemical[2]—it is very hard to describe nondrugs as an addiction. But from the "maladaptive" theory (that you put up with high costs to get your hit) or the similar economic "inelastic" theory (that use doesn't decrease as much as one expects when costs increase),[3] there are lots of things that one can get addicted to. But there are also lots of things that are inelastic that we don't want to say are bad (like breathing!). However, working from the "malfunctioning decision-making machinery" theory described in this book, we can see that behaviors too can become overselected given the underlying correct valuation they should have.

In the clinical world, the most common non–drug-related addiction is problem gambling, which affects between 1% and 4% of the U.S. population, depending on the specific criteria used to define it.[4] Problem gambling is usually identified because the maladaptive consequences (losing money, family, stability of life) are often so clear. From the decision-making perspective, problem gambling is definitely an addiction. Our decision-making system is not optimal; it can be fooled into making poor decisions under the wrong conditions.[5] As with our description of multiple potential ways that pharmacological substances (drugs) can access the decision-making system and can drive incorrect decisions, there are multiple ways that sequences of wins and losses (gambling) can drive incorrect decision-making. We discussed some of these potential vulnerabilities in the last chapter, which concentrated on the pharmacological addictions.

In addition to these motivational effects, humans are very poor at recognizing random sequences as random and are always looking for underlying causes.[6] This means that we can be fooled by limited experience with a probabilistic event. Because we do not see the correct distribution of possibilities, or the correct distribution of the likelihood of those possibilities happening, we think we have more control over the system than we actually do. (This is most likely a failure in the situation-recognition system[7]—we are unwilling to accept coincidence and are always constructing narratives to explain why things turned out the way they did.[8])

In particular, humans are very susceptible to the "near-miss,"[9] where we are told that we "almost got it," which leads us to think that we are making progress on figuring out the complex system that is the world in which we live. This is something that slot-machine makers have learned to exploit.[10] Over the past several decades, slot machines have gotten more and more complex until they are almost like videogames these days. Of course, casinos have also learned how to reduce one's ability to recognize these complexities by providing an abundance of lights and cues all around the casino to draw your attention away, and by providing alcohol to diminish your ability to plan and think.

The illusion of control

Imagine taking the 10 digits (0 through 9) and ordering them. Which sequence of numbers seems more random to you: 4037981562 or 0123456789? I'll bet it's the former (unless that's your Social Security Number). Actually, they are each equally likely. If you are selecting a random sequence of 10 digits (without replacement), the probability of seeing any specific sequence is 1 in 3.5 million.[A]

Several researchers have argued that the reason animals evolved brains is prediction: the better you can predict what's going to happen, the better you can prepare for it, the better you can react to it, the better you are going to be at surviving and procreating your genes into the next generation.[11] We are evolved to recognize patterns, even if they arise from true randomness. This has several effects on our decision-making abilities. First, it means that we are terrible at generating random sequences.[12] Second, it means that we find patterns even in randomness.[13]

Generating randomness—you just can't do it

Ask a hundred people to generate a string of five random digits and I'll bet none of them will say "00000" or "99999." (Unless they're neuroscientists or psychologists

---

[A] With 10 digits to choose from there are 10 possibilities for the first digit, 9 for the second (all but the one you already chose), 8 for the third, etc. This works out to be $10 \times 9 \times 8 \times 7 \times 6 \times 5 \times 4 \times 3 \times 2 \times 1 = 10! = 3{,}628{,}800$. All possibilities, including 9876543210, are equally likely.

who study this stuff and will come up with those numbers just to screw with your experiment—but of course, then those numbers aren't random either.) In general, people will start off with a number (say 7) and then try to find a number that is different from that, and then come back to another number. This is a process called the "inhibition of return" and is suggested to be a means of improving foraging.[14] In a sense, one is "foraging" for numbers,[15] and, having found 7, one wants to find the next number elsewhere.

My favorite demonstration that randomness is hard to do is that computer programs can learn to beat us at rock-paper-scissors.[16] This is the game where you and your opponent count to three and, on three, place your hand as a fist (rock), as a flat palm (paper), or with two fingers making a cutting motion (scissors). In this game, each choice beats one of the other choices and each loses to one choice in a ring: rock beats scissors, which beats paper, which beats rock. If you can predict what your opponent is going to do, then you can always win. But if you can't predict, then the optimal strategy is to play randomly. Unfortunately, humans are terrible at playing randomly. As part of his graduate thesis work, Steve Jensen at the University of Minnesota developed an algorithm that basically remembers sequences that it has observed. It uses these sequences to predict future outcomes. Because it has a very large memory, this program will eventually beat a human opponent. If it plays only one game against you, then who wins will be random. But if you play a hundred games against it, it will win more than half the time (a lot more than half!). It's a remarkably frustrating experience, because even if you know you have to play randomly and you try to play randomly, the computer keeps guessing correctly what you're going to do!

Predicting what your opponent is going to do is a key factor in most competitive sports, whether it be a baseball batter predicting which pitch the pitcher is going to throw (and where he is going to throw it), a football coach predicting whether a pass play or a running play will be coming up next, or a tennis player predicting where her opponent will serve the ball next. Even a small improvement in knowing the next option will play out big over the course of a match or a season. And, of course, the ability to generate randomness (or its converse, the ability to predict what an opponent is going to do) has important implications for other pursuits as well, including business, politics, and war.[B]

Recognizing patterns

The other implication of our predilection for prediction is that we recognize patterns that are not there.[17] From the man in the moon to religious icons on moldy bread to

---

[B] This doesn't mean that being random is the best strategy to win in any of these pursuits, whether it be football, business, politics, or war. Because some options are actually better than others and because interactions between people are rarely zero–sum, true randomness is rarely an optimal strategy. (Rock-paper-scissors is one of the few cases where random is the optimal strategy.) Because we are social creatures, two cooperating players are going to be much stronger than two random players. Randomness rarely wins you the game, but it often takes down your nearby opponents as well. We'll come back to the issue of cooperation in our discussion of morality (Chapter 23). Suffice to say for now that cooperation also depends on the ability to predict what your colleagues are going to do.

patterns in marble tiles, our brains look for patterns in the world. Some of these patterns are real. Mushrooms and flowers tend to appear after a big rainstorm. A fist coming at your face is likely to hit you if you don't block it and likely to hurt if it hits you. Other patterns are not real. The man in the moon is an illusion caused by an interaction between the specific pattern of dark lowlands and bright highlands on the moon's surface with the facial-recognition systems genetically hardwired into our brains.

The recognition of patterns that don't exist becomes a real problem when it leads to the *illusion of control*.[18] In a casino, playing a game, sometimes you win and sometimes you lose. Let us assume, for now, that these games are truly random. But imagine that you notice that you broke a long losing streak just after you touched your hat and wiped your brow. Maybe that's worth trying again. Of course, it probably won't work the second time, but now we're in a probabilistic world—trying to figure out whether winning is just a little bit more likely in one condition or another.

Of course, logically, it doesn't make sense why wiping your brow would change a slot machine's outcome, but what if, instead, we think of how you push the button, or when you push the button in the course of a spin of some video effect on the machine? Now, we have a potential logical cause that could affect the machine's outcome. Imagine a slot machine with a simple switch. The switch could even have a sign on it that says "this switch does nothing." Yet someone playing the machine will likely try the switch, and will be more likely to win with the switch in one position or the other. (Although flipping a coin will come up tails half the time on average, the chance is very low that any specific sequence of coin flips will be half heads and half tails. Similarly, the number of wins you observe with the switch in each position is very unlikely to be exactly the same.) So, the player will believe (incorrectly) that the switch has an effect. This is the illusion of control.

This is effectively a form of superstition.[19] B. F. Skinner (whom we met as a prominent behaviorist in our discussion of reinforcement in Chapter 4) showed that pigeons would eventually do interesting, individual random behaviors if they had done them a couple of times before getting a reward, even if the reward was actually being delivered randomly.

A large part of our intelligence is dedicated to trying to predict the world. Several researchers have argued that learning is about recognizing *contingencies*—whether an event is more (or less) likely to occur in the context of another event.[20] As we saw in our discussion of situation-recognition and the construction of narratives (Chapter 12), much of our cognitive effort is spent on recognizing causal structure within the world. This has been a hypothesis for the origin of mythologizing[21] since Giambatista Vico.[C]

So what happens when your causal hypotheses make mistakes—when you recognize differences between two situations that are not really different? This leads to the illusion of control—if you think that there are two situations (one in which you win and one in which you lose) and you can find a way to get yourself into the winning situation, then gambling makes sense. Of course, this is where cognitive errors can lead to problem gambling.[23] Think of the stereotypical gambler in the movies—"I know what's

---

[C] Giambatista Vico was an Italian scientist and philosopher who lived from 1668 to 1744 (just after Newton and Descartes). Vico is best known for his *Scienza Nuovo* (*New Science*), which is one of the main sources for the structure of James Joyce's *Finnegans Wake*.[22]

different. Loan me the money; it's a sure thing this time. I'll pay you back when I win." That gambler isn't hooked on randomness. That gambler isn't looking to play the game. That gambler thinks he understands the causal structure of the world well enough to control it. That gambler has succumbed to the illusion of control.

We can also see that incorrectly recognizing when a situation has changed can lead to gambling problems. If a situation has changed, but you do not recognize the change, then you will be performing the wrong actions in the wrong situations. Again, cognitive errors lead to incorrect decision-making. Here, again, we can see this effect best in classic literature of tragic inabilities to recognize when the world has changed—an athlete who no longer has the abilities of his youth but can't quit, the businessman unable to recognize that the new competitors are using different tactics, the generals fighting the last war.[24]

This is something that casino operators and slot-machine makers understand. Over the past several decades, slot machines have become more complicated, not less.[25] In her book *Addiction by Design*, Natasha Dow Schüll describes slot and video machine gamblers as succumbing to a particularly procedural deficit, getting drawn in to the "flow" of a Procedural system, and describes how slot and video game designers have focused the machines to access that procedural (non-Deliberative) learning system. Video gambling machines include more and more complex decisions and controls, providing more of a "game-like" experience, and are less and less about simply putting money in and pulling the lever. More complex options provide more potential options for the illusion of control to grab hold of.[26]

In a classic study from 1975, Ellen Langer and Jane Roth trained 90 Stanford undergraduate students to play a coin-flip game.[27] Students who guessed correctly early were much more likely to decide that they were correctly predicting the outcomes than students who guessed incorrectly early. That is, a sequence of wins followed by losses led the students to imagine they understood the task and needed to try to figure out what was going wrong, while a series of losses intermixed with wins led the students to think it was random. A sequence of four correct early guesses was enough to lead people to believe they could correctly guess the sequence "even for sophisticated subjects." This is how the casinos hook people—a quick series of wins leads you to think that you can beat the game, even though (as we've seen) WWWWWLLLLL is just as random as WLWLLLWWLW.[28]

Wins and losses

Another potential breakdown is that wins and losses are represented differently in the decision-making system. We've already seen how people value wins and losses differently.[D] We've already seen how the differences between punishment and disappointment imply that there must be different signals for wins (gains, rewards) and losses

---

[D] You may remember the framing examples that we saw in Chapter 3, where phrasing the exact same problem in terms of gains or losses changed which option someone preferred. In the Asian flu example, being certain to save 200 lives (out of 600, thus losing 400) was preferred against the gamble of saving or losing everyone, but the gamble was preferred over being certain to lose 400 lives.[29]

(punishments), because disappointment (lack of delivery of an expected gain) is not a simple punishment, and relief (lack of a delivery of an expected or potential punishment) is not a simple win (see Chapter 4).

An interesting example of this can be found in Parkinson's disease, which occurs when a subject has lost his or her dopamine cells, particularly those in the dorsal aspects of the dopamine areas of the midbrain called the substantia nigra.[30] These are, in fact, the dopamine cells that we've seen train up the Procedural system (Chapters 4 and 10). One of the primary treatments for Parkinson's disease is to increase the amount of dopamine in the system, to allow the surviving dopamine cells to work harder (usually by providing a dopamine precursor such as levodopa).[31] This can cause a problem because Parkinson's patients still have some of their dopamine cells intact, particularly those in more ventral aspects, which seem to be involved in the more cognitive, deliberative, and impulsive (particularly the emotional and evaluative) decision-making systems, leading to impulsivity and manic, emotional problems.[32] This is what happens to Leonard in the movie *Awakenings*.[33] Leonard's Parkinsonianism is cured by levodopa, but over time, the dopamine builds up and Leonard becomes psychotic and his treatment has to be stopped.

If these dopamine cells are involved in learning, then Parkinson's patients should have trouble learning new things from rewards. Both Michael Frank and Mark Gluck have run separate experiments training patients to learn from rewarding or punishing signals.[34] They both find that normal subjects can learn from positive examples (get rewards if they choose the correct thing, get nothing if they choose wrong) and from negative examples (lose nothing if they choose the correct thing, lose something [usually money] if they choose wrong), but Parkinson's patients have difficulty learning from the positive examples (rewards). They can, however, learn from the negative examples (punishments). If the key to learning is actually dopamine, then one might expect this to reverse under levodopa treatment—with levodopa boosting the overall dopamine levels, one might predict that it would be possible for Parkinson's patients to learn from positive rewards, but no longer from negative punishments. That is, in fact, exactly what happens.

As noted above, slot machines and other casino games have increased the number of near-misses (*I almost won!*) that turn a true loss into a sensed win.[35] If part of the effect of these drugs is to increase a patient's sensitivity to rewards while decreasing the sensitivity to losses, one would expect Parkinson's patients on levodopa and other similar drugs that increase dopamine's efficacy to become highly susceptible to impulse disorders such as problem gambling, where they learn from the positive examples (*I won!*) and not from the negative (*I lost*). That is exactly what happens.[36]

Other behavioral addictions

There have also been descriptions of people "addicted" to a number of behaviors, such as food, sex, porn, shopping, video games, and even surfing the Internet.[37;E] A number

---

[E] What people tend to get addicted to when surfing the Internet are things like gambling, porn, videogames, and shopping, so it is not clear whether the problem is the Internet per se or if the Internet is just a new medium enabling other behavioral addictions.

of these behaviors have been shown to release dopamine, which is often referred to (unfortunately in the scientific literature as well as the popular news media) as the key to addiction. (Remember that dopamine is one access point, but not the only one, to addiction.[38] See Chapter 18.) Even video games lead to the release of dopamine in player's brains.[39] But, as we've seen, this is exactly what should happen in the normal learning system (Chapter 4), which uses dopamine to learn appropriate behavior. The question (the answer to which is not known) is whether that dopamine signal becomes correctly compensated as you learn the game.

For example, is obesity an addiction? There are some data showing that obese people have some of the homeostatic compensation and other dysfunctional dopamine mechanisms seen in long-term drug addicts.[40] Some of the data suggest that the problem with obesity is related to the high fat and sugar content of junk food. Remember that sugar may well have some of the misattribution problems we've seen in addictive drugs.[41] So it is not completely out of the realm of possibilities that obesity is a sign of a form of food addiction, but it is still an open question being discussed in the neuroscientific and medical literatures.

Many of these behaviors are internally driven needs and desires that get out of control. As we saw in our discussion of intrinsic reward functions (Chapter 13), evolution only requires that the behaviors have the correct outcome, not that they be "for the right reason." There are a number of behaviors that have evolved to be pleasurable for themselves, but were evolved because they were really useful for their consequences in the environment they were evolved in. The classic example is, of course, sex. The reason that sex is necessary evolutionarily is, of course, to produce the next generation. But the reason that our brains want to have sex is because it feels good and it satisfies an internally driven need, not because it produces children. Dogs love to chase things (cars, sticks, squirrels). In the wild, dogs were pack hunters that chased down big game. So dogs evolved to like to chase things. The chase itself became pleasurable. The human male's propensity for porn is presumably a similar effect. It can be easily seen how this can lead to overselection of these behaviors in ways that can interfere with one's life.

So do we want to say that one is "addicted" to these behaviors? What about other behaviors, such as shopping or setting fires?[42] Are these behaviors one can become addicted to? From the decision-making perspective, the term "addicted" is not the important scientific question. From the decision-making perspective, the scientific question is why the person is continuing to do the behavior, whether that behavior is taking drugs, gambling, or watching porn. Fundamentally, whether or not we should call that person "addicted" is a policy question, which determines whether we should encourage or discourage that behavior, and how much we are willing to commit to that policy. But if we understand how the decision-making process is working to drive the person to continue the behavior, we can understand better what one needs to do to strengthen or weaken, to enable or disable, to encourage or discourage it.

Books and papers for further reading

- Constance Holden (2001). "Behavioral" addictions: Do they exist? *Science, 294,* 980–982.

- Natasha Dow Schüll (2012). *Addiction by Design: Machine Gambling in Las Vegas.* Princeton, NJ: Princeton University Press.
- Mark G. Dickerson and John O'Connor (2006). *Gambling as an Addictive Behavior.* Cambridge, MA: Cambridge University Press.
- Willem Albert Wagenaar (1998). *Paradoxes of Gambling Behavior.* Hillsdale, NJ: Lawrence Erlbaum Associates.

20

Post-Traumatic Stress Disorder (PTSD)*

> water pooling on the floor
> shards of glass remember
> a bright red rose

In PTSD, devastating memories interact with vulnerable neural structures to produce an overwhelming emotional, episodic memory of an experience. The multiple decision-making system theory and its interacting support structures suggest a perspective on PTSD as interacting episodic and emotional memories.

After World War I, soldiers returning from the trenches of Europe were described as succumbing to "shell shock": jumpy, cowering at the slightest noise, often unable to function in normal society. In World War II, the term was "battle fatigue." The classic image is that of a father in 1950, sitting at the kitchen table, smoking his cigarette, staring out into his memory. This difficulty that some soldiers have is not a new phenomenon.[1] In his description of soldiers coming back from the American Civil War, Jacob Mendes Da Costa described a phenomenon of sudden-onset heart palpitations, which he called "irritable heart" and came to be known colloquially as "soldier's heart."[2] A 2006 historical study found that the best predictor of soldier's heart in Civil War veterans was the percentage of the company killed, presumably a reliable proxy for experiencing devastating emotional trauma.[3] The term used now, *post-traumatic stress disorder*, recognizes that this problem can arise from traumatic non-military experiences as well: victims of violent crime, sexual assault, terrorist attack, car crashes, and other disasters are also vulnerable to PTSD.[4]

At this point, it is not clear what the cause of PTSD is. The symptoms, however, are consistent and recognizable (as can be seen in the similarities of the descriptions of shell shock, battle fatigue, and soldier's heart).[5] These symptoms include uncontrollable re-experiences of the event. Based on our separation of episodic and semantic memories (Chapter 16), these re-experiences would be unquestionably episodic in nature. They are often vividly present and intrusive. Patients with PTSD also show a withdrawal from

* I am indebted to Larry Amsel of Columbia University for our discussions related to this topic.

society and friends, as well as hyperarousal, increased vigilance, and increased startle responses, which we can take as evidence of Pavlovian action-selection (Chapter 8) and motivational (Chapter 13) learning. These startle responses can be extremely dangerous in well-trained soldiers, who have learned to associate violent action responses with those situations (Chapter 10).

Like addiction and problem gambling, PTSD seems to be an interaction between inherent vulnerability and external cause. For example, it is not true that everyone exposed to a difficult or traumatic situation gets PTSD.[6] There is now evidence that there is a significant difference in hormonal levels and several brain structures between soldiers and other patients who end up with PTSD after an incident and those who don't.[7] Twins without PTSD (who share the same genetic code) of soldiers who got PTSD reacted more strongly to startling cues than twins of soldiers who didn't get PTSD from similar experiences.[8] Similarly, the hippocampus (a brain structure we've seen to be deeply involved in memory, see Chapter 16) is physically smaller in twins of soldiers with PTSD than twins of soldiers without.[9] As with all of these vulnerabilities (like the genetic vulnerabilities we've discussed elsewhere), these are correlations. People with smaller hippocampi may be more likely to end up with PTSD than people with larger hippocampi; however, there are lots of other factors involved. Simply having a smaller hippocampus does not mean that you will get PTSD if you are ever exposed to a trauma.

Three theories have been proposed to explain PTSD: (1) that PTSD patients have stored a "flashbulb" memory, which cannot be forgotten,[10] (2) that PTSD patients have difficulty extinguishing fear-related memories,[11] particularly through altered fear processing,[12] and (3) that PTSD patients have difficulty identifying the context of memories, allowing those memories to intrude on other contexts.[13] A fourth possibility is that PTSD patients have difficulty consolidating memories from hippocampal-dependent episodic representations into hippocampal-independent semantic representations (Chapter 16). We will address each of these theories and then try to bring them back together into a coherent picture of decision-making and PTSD.

Flashbulb memories

The first psychological theories of PTSD suggested that the traumatic event produced a flashbulb memory, a perfect photographic memory of an instance. The concept was that the stress and intensity of the memory storage overwhelmed the cortical storage systems, "burning it into the brain."[14] This theory, however, predicts that the memory will be recalled identically each time, which is not how these memories occur.

Although the original definition of flashbulb memories put forward by Roger Brown and James Kulik recognized that the flashbulb illuminated only part of the picture, the concept remained that the illuminated images remained steady. In fact, Jennifer Talarico and David Rubin found that, although they remained vivid, "flashbulb" memories (defined as memories that stayed for long periods of time) decreased in consistency over time, suggesting that they were being reconstructed each time.[15] Talarico and Rubin suggest that the primary difference between flashbulb memories and more common, everyday memories, was the internal confidence in it, rather than in the properties of the recalled memory itself.

Interestingly, this suggests that although the traumatic memories are vivid and intrusive, they are constructed, much like ordinary memories, and also suggests a relationship between episodic memory and PTSD.

PTSD and fear associations

We have already seen (in Chapter 4) how animals extinguishing responses to learned associations change their behavior because of additional components entering into the equation, not because they have forgotten the learned association.[16] The addition of a new process rather than the forgetting of the original association leads to spontaneous renewal of responses and cued recovery of those responses.

Central to this concept is the recognition that there are multiple memory (and action-selection) systems. In particular, there is a Pavlovian (emotional) action-selection system that works through direct connections from sensory thalamic systems to the amygdala.[17] As we saw in Chapter 8, our Pavlovian responses produce visceral, emotional reactions to stimuli, sometimes even without our knowledge. But Pavlovian mechanisms also affect the motivational system (Chapter 13) as well, which influences the Deliberative and Procedural systems (see Chapter 6). This means that a Pavlovian, emotional response could label a memory particularly salient and particularly likely to be retrieved.

However, we should be wary of simply saying that PTSD patients have difficulty extinguishing their behaviors. There are several key differences between the sort of associative learning that occurs in typical extinction paradigms and PTSD. Extinction paradigms usually entail multiple exposures to the cueing stimulus to create the original association, and the reaction to the association is common among all animals exposed.[18] Spontaneous reappearance of the association occurs after long time periods, not immediately after the event.[19] Cued reappearance of the association occurs with a re-exposure to the specific cues that created the original association.[20] In contrast, PTSD generally occurs in response to a single, traumatic event, the intruding memories occur quickly after the event and fade with time, and the intruding memories appear, even uncued, in situations with little or no relationship to the original association.[21]

Memories out of context

Lynn Nadel and W. Jake Jacobs have suggested that PTSD patients have specific difficulties in separating contexts, which allows the memories to reappear (to intrude) in situations where they would normally not.[22] Specifically, they propose that glucocorticoids in the hippocampus that arise during stress disable the hippocampus during memory storage, allowing the memory to become unlabeled spatiotemporally, thus allowing the memory to become, in a sense, unstuck in time. Stress affects the storage and retrieval of memories, primarily through the action of glucocorticoids (such as cortisol).[23] In particular, Nadel, Jacobs, and their colleagues have found that stressful events prior to an experience facilitate the storage of emotional memories through a hippocampal–amygdala interaction, even while they impair hippocampal processing on hippocampally-dependent memory tasks.[24] Although stress during retrieval impairs that retrieval (it's harder to remember things under stress), stress immediately following training increases storage and later retrieval (it's easier to remember things that happen to you when you are stressed).[25]

This interaction (between salient, value-marked memories and uncoupled hippocampal memory) has been suggested as a key factor in PTSD by several researchers.[26] In these theories, PTSD occurs when stress levels enhance amygdala learning and suppress hippocampal learning.[27] Nadel and Jacobs suggest that the effect of the massive stress event is to enhance learning in the amygdala, decrease learning in the hippocampus, and produce a highly value-laden but contextually-uncoupled memory.[28] These theories, however, suggest that the PTSD patient will not be able to provide a spatiotemporal image of the event, particularly the patient's location within the sequence of the event, which does not seem to fit with the descriptions of the vivid nature of the traumatic memory in PTSD.[29]

From episodic to semantic memory

We saw in Chapter 16 how the normal progress of memory is a transition from episodic (*you are there*) to semantic (*I remember that*) memories. An intriguing possibility is that PTSD occurs not when the hippocampus is unable to create an episodic memory of the event, but rather when the hippocampal–cortical system is unable to consolidate the memory into semantic storage. As we discussed in Chapter 16, although early studies of consolidation suggested that memory transferred intact from hippocampally-dependent structures to hippocampally-independent structures over time, more recent studies have suggested that certain functions of memory remain hippocampally-dependent forever.[30] Recent studies have suggested that the transferred memories have a fundamentally different character than recently stored memories—recently stored memories (dependent on the hippocampus) are stored in an *episodic* manner, while the consolidated ones are stored in a *semantic* manner extrahippocampally.

These theories are consistent with new views of the hippocampus as playing a key role in *mental time travel*, both of reconstructing the past and of imagining the future.[31] If normal recovery from trauma entails a consolidation of a memory away from an episodic (*you-are-there, return-to-the-past*) memory into a semantic (*narrative, detached*) memory, then PTSD patients may be stuck in the episodic mode. They may be unable to accomplish this transformation and continue to reconstruct their past every time they access the memory, leaving the memory with an immediacy that intrudes on normal function.

This is, in fact, consistent with the original studies on flashbulb memories,[32] which suggested that the normal "flashbulb" memory was stored, replayed and rehearsed, and decreased in its emotional impact with time. Importantly, Brown and Kulik were studying normal people remembering distant tragedies (e.g., *Where were you when you heard the World Trade Center had been hit by terrorists?*), not people with PTSD involved in the event itself (e.g., firefighters escaping from the falling buildings). Brown and Kulik hypothesized that eventual accounts of flashbulb memories were derived from continued covert and overt rehearsal of these stories, translating them into a narrative and perhaps even verbal form.

This hypothesis rests on the concept that the hippocampus in PTSD patients is weak or dysfunctional, not nonfunctional. Patients with complete hippocampal lesions do not show any episodic memory recall events at all, and when they recall past events or imagine future events, their descriptions are primarily semantic, not episodic.[33] PTSD experiences are vivid and spatially and temporally located, with strong suggestions of mental time travel, all indications of episodic memories, and a dysfunctional (but not nonfunctional) hippocampus.[A]

Summary

Attempted treatment for PTSD has included pharmacological treatments, attempts to extinguish the memory by acquiring safety cues, and attempts to recontextualize the memory, effectively transferring it from the emotionally-tagged episodic to the more detached semantic systems.[34] Although there is still a lot of work to do determining the vulnerabilities that engender PTSD, the mechanisms by which it creates dysfunction, and what might serve as potential treatments, it's clear that the mental disorder known as PTSD has a physical manifestation in brain function.

What is clear is that PTSD entails a complex and dysfunctional interaction between memory systems. Somehow, the emotional and episodic memory systems have become entangled in a way that is difficult to disentangle. Because they are reconstructed each time, PTSD memories are not "flashbulb memories," yet they are, in a very real sense, burned into the brain. PTSD includes problems with emotional memories, which affect Pavlovian motivational and action-selection systems, but PTSD also includes hippocampal interactions, particularly with episodic memory retrieval. PTSD patients seem to have a dysfunctional hippocampus, unable to transition memories from episodic to semantic representations with time.

Books and papers for further reading

- Jonathan Shay (1994) *Achilles in Vietnam: Combat Trauma and the Undoing of Character*. New York: Scribner.
- Frontline (2009). *Soldier's Heart*. PBS.
- Joseph E. LeDoux (1996). *The Emotional Brain*. New York: Simon and Schuster.
- Chris Cantor (2005). *Evolution and Posttraumatic Stress: Disorders of Vigilance and Defence*. London: Routledge.

[A] In a similar vein, Alzheimer's patients are well known for their ability to re-experience episodic memories. This suggests that both PTSD and Alzheimer's patients have a hippocampus that is acting incorrectly, rather than one that is simply inactive.

21

Computational Psychiatry*

dragonfly buzzing
every which way
Can't get out!

*Current psychiatric categorizations of patients are based on a tax-
onomy of symptoms. While this categorization seems to be reliable
(in that different practitioners tend to categorize similar patients in
similar ways), there seems to be a disconnect between the categorization and the underlying mechanisms. The detailed understanding of
decision-making systems presented in Chapters 6–15 and the engineer's view on the brain looking for failure modes, vulnerabilities, and
dysfunction (Chapters 18–20) provide a new view on psychiatry,
which is now emerging as a field called "computational psychiatry."*

Our discussions of addiction, problem gambling, and PTSD suggest that the neuroscientific view of the decision-making system has implications for psychiatric disorders.
Since the introduction of the DSM-III in 1980,[A] psychiatry has been developing a taxonomy of categories for identifying patients, presumably under the assumption that
patients who fall in the same category should require similar treatment. Although these
categories seem to be reliable in that different psychiatrists tend to categorize example
patients into similar categories (that is, they agree on what categories look like), these
categories have not been as good at identifying treatments for patients.[2]

In part, this arises because many of these categories are disjunctive; they are made
up of subcomponents linked by an "or" relationship—if you have symptom A *or* symptom B then you are in category C.[3] If the two symptoms included in the disjunctive category are both reliable, then the disjunctive combination of them will also be reliable.

---

* I am indebted to Larry Amsel of Columbia University for our discussions on this topic.

[A] The *Diagnostic and Statistical Manual of Mental Disorders* is the go-to guide for identifying psychiatric illness. The current edition is the DSM-IV-TR ("TR" stands for "text revision"), and the DSM-V is
in the works. The other major manual used by clinicians for the identification of psychiatric disorders
is the *International Classification of Diseases,* known as the ICD-10.[1]

This disjunctive categorization can be seen by the predominance of DSM categories based on adding up symptoms. In the DSM-IV-TR, the diagnosis of problem gambling can be made if the patient has five or more of ten criteria. This means that two people can both be identified as problem gamblers even though they have no symptoms in common. The fact that the categories are reliable does not imply that they are *valid*, that they say anything about shared mechanism.[4]

The other problem with the categories identified in the DSM is that they are based on symptoms. As everyone knows, a given symptom could be caused by any of a number of potential underlying problems. Imagine a patient who arrives at a hospital with chest pain. Imagine if the doctor tells the patient, "Some proportion of chest-pain patients require open-heart surgery and some proportion of chest-pain patients respond well to an antacid, so we'll try both." Treatment would obviously succeed better if we reliably differentiate patients who were having heart attacks from patients who had indigestion.[B]

Sometimes the only option available is to cure the symptom. For a doctor looking down at a patient who has just lost a leg from a landmine explosion, there is nothing to do at the time but treat the wound and eventually provide a mechanical, replacement leg. Similarly, the inability to initiate movement (akinesia) and the slowness of movement initiation (bradykinesia) seen in Parkinson's disease are due to the loss of dopamine cells in the brain.[6] Just as it would be great to address the underlying causes that placed the landmine in the field[7] (*Ain't gonna study war no more*), it would be great to prevent the loss of dopamine neurons in the first place. However, the only treatment option for a patient presenting with Parkinson's disease is treating the symptoms, either by increasing the dopamine available to the surviving cells (such as through dopamine precursors like levodopa or through attempts to replace the lost cells) or by allowing the brain to sidestep whatever it was that the dopamine cells were providing (as is done in deep-brain stimulation).[8]

Similarly, sometimes the right treatment is to prevent the symptoms from doing too much damage to the body and allowing the body to heal itself. It is the symptoms caused by cholera that kill, not the disease itself. Rehydration is a reliable treatment that effectively cures the disease by treating the symptoms.[9]

At this point, there is a recognition that there is a problem in psychiatry, but practitioners are still debating how to restructure the taxonomy so as to get at the mechanisms we do know, while allowing for the fact that there are a lot of mechanisms we don't know, all while continuing to do our best to treat patients, many of whom desperately need help.[10] A new field of *computational psychiatry* seems to be emerging to make these connections.[11] The term is meant to invoke the use of theoretical constructs (like those we've been exploring in this book) to redefine the categories and proposed treatment for psychiatric disorders.

The question at hand is thus *What are the mechanisms and causes that underlie psychiatric illness?* What is depression? What drives it? What is schizophrenia? How do we define it? What is an anxiety disorder? Psychiatry has identified lots of different psychiatric

---

[B] In actuality, it can be difficult to differentiate the chest pain of a heart attack from the chest pain of indigestion without an EKG,[5] which is why one should not try to diagnose oneself at home. Of course, this just underscores the issue of understanding the causes and mechanisms, rather than just the symptoms, and having clinical tests that can reliably differentiate those causes.

illnesses: the DSM-IV-TR has over a thousand different diagnoses. How many of these are the same dysfunction manifesting itself in different ways? Is "social phobia" (fear of being out in society) the same or a different disorder than "agoraphobia" (fear of places where escape or help might be difficult)? How many of these are different dysfunctions manifesting as a single symptom? (See our discussion of addiction in Chapter 18.)

Anxiety disorders, for example, entail a pathological fear of taking actions in specific situations. In humans, anxiety manifests itself in terms of fear and worry about future outcomes. In animals, anxiety manifests itself in observable avoidance and fear behaviors.[12] The circuits and brain structures involved are similar in both animal and human anxiety experiments.[13] They involve the structures we've examined as part of the Pavlovian action-selection system (Chapter 8) and structures we've examined as part of the Deliberative action-selection system (Chapter 9). Current models suggest that there are two components that drive anxiety. First, direct negative expectations of outcomes can drive fear-related actions through the periaqueductal gray (PAG) and the amygdala, which we saw earlier to be a key part of the Pavlovian fear circuitry (*the rustle in the grass that signals the lion; the tone that came before the shock*). Second, indirect negative expectations of outcomes can be generated by hippocampal–prefrontal interactions that are then evaluated as likely leading to a negative outcome[14] (*don't go down that dark alley!*).

In fact, when rats or mice come to an open space, they tend to hesitate, leaning out and then returning back to shelter, as if they are nervous about whether to go or not.[15] This "stretch-attend posture" is very similar to the vicarious trial and error behavior that we saw in Chapter 6. Like vicarious trial and error behavior, the stretch-attend posture behavior depends on the hippocampus, the prefrontal cortex, and their interaction.[16] This suggests that this hesitation likely entails predictions of future dangers. Of course, rats and mice are prey animals and dangers really do lurk around every corner. Humans are generally at the top of the food chain and tend not to worry as much about being eaten by cats or owls.[C] Generally humans are more concerned with social dangers, but the same stress–response mechanisms seem to be involved.[18] Anxiety attacks can come from a variety of sources, including social interactions (such as public speaking), financial futures, personal danger, danger to one's friends or family, availability of escape and rescue (in claustrophobia and agoraphobia), and even rare circumstances (such as earthquakes or buildings collapsing). The DSM-IV-TR considers PTSD a form of anxiety disorder; certainly, the description of soldier's heart sounds like a panic attack.[19] As another example, anxiety is now considered to play an important role in obsessive-compulsive disorder (OCD). Interestingly, OCD seems to be a combination of an anxiety disorder about future dangers combined with an uncertainty about the memory of completed actions.[20]

Computational models are beginning to be built to explain fear and anxiety. While they haven't yet led to changes in treatment, there is consensus building as to the underlying mechanisms. We've already discussed addiction, gambling, and PTSD in the previous chapters. Similarly, other psychiatric diseases are beginning to be addressed by computational models—for example, depression, schizophrenia, and other disorders.[21]

There are a number of major psychiatric disorders that are related not to individual action-selection systems, but rather to social interaction systems—for example, *borderline personality disorder* and *sociopathy* or *psychopathy*.[22] These interactive dysfunctions

---

[C] Except perhaps in *Twin Peaks*, where the owls are not what they seem.[17]

entail people who do not show normal social interactions. We will leave these interactive issues aside until we can address *neuroeconomics, game theory*, the propensity for humans to organize into groups, and the mechanisms through which cooperation within those groups is maintained (in Chapters 22 and 23).

With all of these examples (as with all psychiatric disorders), there is an important issue that it is extremely difficult to define the line between normality and dysfunction.[23] There has been a lot of discussion in recent years about the overdiagnosis of attention-deficit/hyperactive disorder (ADHD).[24] Where is the line between a rambunctious boy who is not getting time to run every day and ADHD? How much is ADHD being used as a diagnosis to control overcrowded classrooms? Similarly, is it really true that one American in ten is depressed? (In 2008, 10% of Americans were taking antidepression medication, presumably mostly selective serotonin reuptake inhibitors [SSRIs].[25]) How often are these SSRIs being used to increase confidence, and how much are they being used to treat normal grief?[26]

On the other hand, it is important to recognize that there are people with severe psychiatric dysfunction who desperately do need help. True depression and normal grief are very different things.[27] Suicide is the tenth leading cause of death in the United States.[28] Similarly, while some rambunctious children may be incorrectly diagnosed with ADHD and treated with Ritalin, there are others who really do have a problem and for whom Ritalin is the difference between getting an education or not. Trichotillomania (hair pulling) is not about the 10-year-old who twirls her hair nervously while shuffling her feet and smiling cutely up at you, nor is it about pulling that first gray hair. Trichotillomania is about people who have pulled their head bald and their scalp bloody.[29] There are people with severe dysfunction who do need help.

At this point, we don't have clear answers. Although this is not a new problem and has been recognized as an issue within psychiatry for many years,[30] there does seem to be a change coming where the connections are being identified between neuroscientific mechanisms and psychiatric dysfunction.[31] What these mechanisms are, where the severe dysfunctions are, and how to treat them are all open questions being actively explored within the neuroscience, psychological, and psychiatric communities.

Books and papers for further reading

- Paul R. McHugh and Phillip R. Slavney (1998). *The Perspectives of Psychiatry.* Baltimore, MD: Johns Hopkins.
- P. Read Montague, Raymond J. Dolan, Karl J. Friston, and Peter Dayan (2012). Computational psychiatry. *Trends in Cognitive Sciences, 16,* 72–80.
- Steven E. Hyman (2007). Can neuroscience be integrated into the DSM-V? *Nature Reviews Neuroscience, 8,* 725–732.
- Thomas Insel et al. (2010). Research Domain Criteria (RDoC): Toward a new classification framework for research on mental disorders. *American Journal of Psychiatry, 167,* 748–751.
- Matthijs A. A. van der Meer, Zeb Kurth-Nelson, and A. David Redish (2012). Information processing in decision-making systems. *The Neuroscientist, 18,* 342–359.

PART FOUR

THE HUMAN CONDITION

22

What Makes Us Human?

> This stadium once held twenty thousand,
> but the river moved, and now only
> tourists stand on its crumbling walls.

Humans are animals with unique abilities, particularly in the realms of language, imagination, and culture. However, like our physical bodies, our mental abilities contain echoes of our related mammalian cousins. Like our decision-making systems, our tremendous abilities have precursors in other animal behaviors.

I am fascinated by history and love to travel and see the old ruins of great civilizations. I have stood on the walls of Troy and looked out over the plains of Hisarlik where Achilles and Odysseus once stood. I have stood on the stage of the ancient Greek city of Miletus and sat in the stands of the Roman stadium of Ephesus. I am always fascinated by how much remains constant. The defensive fortifications of a medieval castle in Japan (such as Himeji Castle) are similar to those of a medieval European fortress (such as Harlech Castle, in Wales). The components of an ancient Roman stadium are instantly recognizable to anyone who has attended a modern sports stadium, the rows of benches (numbered and labeled by row), even the concession stands. Similarly, we can appreciate narratives from the world over. The modern reader recognizes Achilles' petulance at Agamemnon's demands in Homer's *Iliad* and Odysseus' war-driven exhaustion in the *Odyssey*. The trickster Anansi continues to capture children's imaginations,[1] and the adventures of d'Artagnan and the Three Musketeers[2] still spark the interest of young boys and girls everywhere. Whether it be the graffiti on the wall of the boys' dormitory in Priene (a ruined city in Turkey) or the shape of the council seats in Wupatki (in northern Arizona), we recognize familiar human interactions in our ancient ancestors. Something is constant through the ages, something that makes it possible for us to look at a set of drawings on the cave walls of Lascaux and know that some person painted them.

Certainly, there is a qualitative difference between humans and the other animals that have been mentioned in this book. Beavers may create dams of wood that modify their local environment, but they have never put a man (a beaver?) on the moon. Outside of literature, no rats have ever built cities or written novels.[3] But as we have seen throughout this book, our decision-making system, much like our physical bodies, contain echoes of our related mammalian cousins. If we evolved from animals, then how are we different from them? Even the phrase "evolved from animals" implies a trajectory from animals to humans, with humans placed above and beyond. A better statement would be that we are part of the evolutionary history, a moment in evolutionary time. We are not evolved from animals—we too are animals.

There is much about humans that seems unique among animals. No other animal has language skills like ours. (Although it has been possible to teach some animals the rudiments of language, none of them has ever achieved language skills beyond that of a young child.[4]) The complexity of the cities we build and our individual specializations within those cities are unparalleled. (Although termites and other social insects also build large hives, these hives are made of a limited number of specific individual castes and do not resemble the flexible complexity of human cities.[5]) And we seem to be destroying our ecosystem at an unprecedented speed.[6] However, as is nicely pointed out by Matt Ridley in *The Agile Gene*, lots of species are unique. Termites build in mud, squids squirt ink, and cobras spit venom. Simply being unique is not enough. The question is *What makes us unique?*

Jane Goodall, who has studied a tribe of chimpanzees in Gombe for the past 50 years, complained that every time she found her chimpanzees showing signs of what makes us human, the philosophers would move the goalposts.[7] At first, humans were tool users. But as early as the 1920s, the psychologist Wolfgang Köhler found that apes could learn to stack boxes purposefully to find reward.[8] In the field, Jane Goodall observed chimpanzees using twigs to pull ants and termites from tree stumps.[9]

Then humans were the only ones to make tools. But then Goodall observed that the chimpanzees were actually making their tools, finding the right stick, cleaning it off, and preparing it.[10] (It is now known that otters and crows and many other species also use tools. Otters will use rocks to break open sea urchins, and crows have been found to make tools out of twigs and leaves to fish for insects.[11])

Then it was suggested that humans are the only ones to have developed separate cultures. But chimpanzee tribes use different tools to attain food. In the Tai Forest in the Ivory Coast, a chimpanzee tribe uses rocks to crack kola nuts (which have a very hard shell). Chimpanzees from the Gombe tribe do not know how to use rocks to crack kola nuts, and chimpanzees from the Tai Forest tribe do not know how to fish for termites.[12] These different abilities are spread from chimpanzee to chimpanzee culturally.

Cultural abilities have even been observed as they were discovered. In the 1960s, Japanese macaque monkeys began to wash sweet potatoes in the ocean to remove dirt and to add salt.[13] The ability spread first from the discoverer (a young female) to others she knew, and then to the others in the tribe. It followed trails of kin, parenting, and training. Subsequent observations of cultural behaviors have found that they generally spread through celebrity and dominance such that higher-rank primates (who are closely observed by lower-rank ones) spread the meme faster than lower-rank primates.[14]

So other animals show tool use, and other primates have the presence of culture (or at least a precursor to culture). What makes humans different?

One suggestion has been that humans are the only ones to think about other places and other times, to (as it were) "mentally time-travel."[15] But, as we've seen, rats show search behaviors when making choices and seem to represent expectations of the outcomes of their actions.[16] Nikki Clayton at Cambridge has seen that scrub jays recognize when and where they cached food, can take into account how long that food will remain edible, and can take into account the likelihood that another jay is aware of the hiding location of the food cache.[17] Both monkeys and rats can represent alternative options that might have been when they make errors (as in "I could have got reward if I had made the other choice").[18]

That being said, it is not clear that scrub jays can maintain episodic memory beyond food caches,[19] that monkeys or rats can imagine far-distant futures or pasts, or that chimpanzee culture extends to the kind of narrative stories that we tell ourselves. I suspect that the difference is going to be one of quantitative differences becoming a qualitative one. Nevertheless, the things that make us human have their roots in our evolutionary history.[20]

Careful observations have shown that other animals play, laugh, fight, even mount what, for lack of any other terminology, can only be called wars.[21] And yet, there are differences. We have a flexibility in our decision-making systems that is far beyond what other animals can do. We communicate with language that is infinitely flexible and capable of depth of meaning. We can work together in groups larger and more complex than other species. In particular, our groups come and go. We are capable of shifting groups with context more easily than other species.[22] As Aristotle defined us, we are the "political" animal.[23]

Our social identity can be remarkably dynamic and flexible. We have extended families, tribes, and nations, but also groups based on the places where we work, our churches, mosques, and temples, and our sports teams and political parties.[A] People who work together as part of the same group in one context (at a job or cheering for a sports team) can dissolve into anger and intractable argument in another context (such as politics).

Some philosophers attribute the difference to language,[25] which has several important properties that may explain our differences. First, language can communicate very detailed information (such as plans or instructions) quickly.[26] Second, it can store knowledge outside of an individual (as in books or webpages).[27] Third, language provides an interactive social network and marks our place within it.[28]

We often use language as actions in themselves.[29] A person saying "I do" at his or her wedding is committing to a specific contractual deal. As pointed out by Orson Scott Card in his novel *Speaker for the Dead*, a marriage is a contract between three parties—the two people being married and the community that agrees to treat them as married.[30]

Language can also be used to build on itself—one person can provide part of the answer, and another can build on it.[31] This is the misnamed "wisdom" of the group, which is not so much wisdom (groups can be very unwise) but rather a positive feedback process of knowledge.[32] One of the major breakthroughs that led to the scientific revolution and our modern world was the development of the scientific journal

---

[A] In one of the strangest disasters I have witnessed, politics has become a sports question of who is winning rather than a policy question of what is the right thing to do. This has led to political tribalism, in which the leader of a party can say publicly that he is more interested in the other party's leader losing the presidency than in fixing the problems that are facing his country.[24]

in the 1600s.[B] A scientific article reports a single result or finding, and, although it is generally a complete story, it does not have to completely answer all the questions that might arise. Before the journals, science was reported in books and monographs, which required decades to write. This meant that other scientists could not follow up on one's work until it was complete. By providing a means of reporting a partial answer, scientific journals allowed scientists to point other scientists in the right direction, to put a single brick in the edifice of science rather than having to construct an entire building by oneself.

The other thing that language can do is point. Language allows us to coordinate our goals and to coordinate our attention.[33] It can point a direction, identify a danger, a target, or an outcome. The level to which other animals can track referents is still being debated, but they do not seem to track them as easily as humans do. For example, humans are the only ape with white sclera, which enables others to know where we are looking.[34] Much of our social interaction is based on knowing where the other person is looking. Take, for example, the importance of eye contact in conversation.[35] (Of course, knowing where someone is looking is not always a good thing, as any intercepted NFL quarterback knows.)

Fundamentally, however, one of the largest differences between humans and other animals is in what has traditionally been called *morality*.[36] Jane Goodall observed sociopathy in her chimpanzees—a mother and daughter (named Passion and Pom) developed a cannibalistic procedure attacking new mothers and their infants where one of them would distract a new mother and the other would attack and kill the infant.[37] If one of the large males was in the area, he would defend the new mother and infant, but the males did not attack Passion and Pom outside of the context of their crime. Humans do not tolerate such sociopaths.[38]

Whether the difference is a qualitative leap (a change in kind that can be clearly separated) or merely the repeated effect of small quantitative changes (changes in level or depth) is still unknown. Yet, something is different. Termites may build mounds, and other animals may build nests of incredible complexity, but those mounds are not cities on the scale of New York or Tokyo or Alexandria. Chimpanzees may fight wars, but those wars do not include machine guns, tanks, or nuclear bombs.[C] Bower birds may create art, but that art is not disseminated to and discussed by millions of bower birds all over the world. Baboons may live in groups, but those groups do not "friend" each other on Facebook.

There have been fascinating discussions of just how intelligent some species are. Elephants have highly complex societies, calculate expectations for the availability of fruit and water as a function of recent weather patterns, and remember their dead for years.[39] Vervet monkeys lie about attacking predators to escape bullies.[40] And whales

---

[B] The first scientific journal was the *Philosophical Transactions of the Royal Society*, which has been publishing scientific papers since 1665, including the first scientific reports from Newton, Darwin, and others.

[C] Whether this is a good thing or not is, of course, debatable. As pointed out by Douglas Adams in his classic *The Hitchhiker's Guide to the Galaxy*, "man had always assumed that he was more intelligent than dolphins because he had achieved so much—the wheel, New York, wars and so on—whilst all the dolphins had ever done was muck about in the water having a good time. But conversely, the dolphins had always believed that they were far more intelligent than man—for precisely the same reasons."

and dolphins sing amazingly complex songs that depend on their cultural and societal interactions.[41] Although something may be different about humans, the things that fundamentally make us human, our language, our minds, and our decision-making systems, like our physical bodies, share commonalities with and derive from our animal nature.

In the next two chapters, we will explore two of those uniquenesses: morality and consciousness.

Books and papers for further reading

- Jane Goodall and Hugo van Lawick (1971/1988/2000). *In the Shadow of Man.* Boston: Houghton Mifflin.
- Jane Goodall (1990). *Through a Window.* Boston: Houghton Mifflin.
- Frans de Waal (1982/2000). *Chimpanzee Politics: Power and Sex among Apes.* Baltimore, MD: Johns Hopkins Press.
- Frans de Waal (2001). *The Ape and the Sushi Master: Cultural Reflections of a Primatologist.* New York: Basic Books.
- Robert M. Sapolsky (2001). *A Primate's Memoir.* New York: Touchstone.
- Michael Tomassello (2005). *Constructing a Language: A Usage-Based Theory of Language Acquisition.* Cambridge, MA: Harvard.

23

The Science of Morality

Fear grips a nation.
The destruction of barbarians at the gates
are no match for the destruction
of the barbarians within.

In much of current discussion, morality is said to be outside of the pur-
view of science because science is descriptive, not prescriptive. Simply
said, this means that science cannot tell you what to do. Although
there is certainly a clear and important difference between description
and prescription, the implications of the science of decision-making
for morality are more complex than they would seem at first glance.

Description and prescription

Everyone agrees that there is a fundamental philosophical difference between *descrip-*
tion and *prescription*. In the famous words of David Hume, there is a difference between
"is" and "ought to be."[1] Description is about what will happen. (If you drop that heavy
rock, it will fall. If you drop it on your foot, it will hurt.) Prescription is about what you
should do. (Don't drop that rock on your foot!)

This distinction is very clear in modern medicine. Description is the effect of the
treatment. (Antibiotics are ineffective against viruses. Bacteria evolve in response to
antibiotics.) Prescription is what we should do to treat the disease. (If you have a bacte-
rial infection, antibiotics are a good idea. If you have a viral infection, don't use antibiotics because you are only helping the bacteria in the world evolve resistance to them.)

Science is fundamentally descriptive. Science is a method to determine the causal
structure of the world through prediction and replication.[A] We need a different term

---

[A] The complex issues of the sociology of science and whether science works by explicit falsification
or through integrated framework construction[2] are not important for the debate here. For those interested, there are lots of books on this issue. My favorite is *Just a Theory* by Moti Ben-Ari. In any case, let
us simply say here that, over the long term, our control of the world has improved because scientific
theories have become more accurate descriptions of reality over the centuries.

for how to make prescriptive decisions between individuals and groups who disagree. These are *policy* questions, and the best term, I think, is *politics*.[B] Saying that prescriptive decisions are fundamentally political questions is not meant to imply that they depend on one's party allegiance (capital-P Politics) or the specifics of what gets written into laws (morality is not legality)—we are talking small-p politics here: *How do humans interact with other humans and their societies?* As we will see below, humans spontaneously organize into small-p political structures to handle their social interactions, and much of that small-p politics is unwritten social constructions.[3]

As we will see, the role of small-p politics becomes clear when we disagree about goals. If one kid wants to play basketball with dad outside and the other kid wants to play a computer game with dad inside, some negotiation has to occur to settle a fair distribution of dad's time. Similarly, a company may decry regulations that are preventing it from opening new stores and new markets, while others demand those regulations to ensure a locally desired principle. Or one may need to make a decision about whether to risk prospecting for oil in fragile shrimp-farming grounds. Notice that I have been very careful in these examples not to make any claims about right and wrong; I have only shown examples where goals differ and negotiation is required. Right and wrong in each of these examples will likely depend on the details of the situation. For example, it makes a big difference if those regulations are preventing the company from dumping toxic waste into a neighboring city's drinking water or if those regulations state that only white people are allowed to own companies.

The statement that goals differ does not imply that both sides are morally equivalent (the members of one side may say that their goal is to exterminate all people of a certain ethnicity, while the other side may say that they want to both live in peace). Similarly, the statement that negotiation is required does not mean that an accommodation has to be made—in the American Civil War and World War II, the "negotiation" between two opposing moral codes (slavery or not, fascism and genocide or not) entailed the two sides fighting a war.

There are three literatures that have tried to claim control of the prescriptive magisteria of morality: religion, philosophy, and economics.

Religion

In the separation of "is" from "ought to be," morality is often seen as the purview of religion and philosophy.[4] Stephen Jay Gould famously argued for what he called "NOMA," or *non-overlapping magisteria,* and tried to define the difference between science and religion as being of different "magisteria" (different realms of thought)— religion could remain about what we should do, while science could remain about what happens when we do something. Religion could be about meaning, while science could be about the physical world. Religion could be about *why,* while science could be about *how.*

[B] I am indebted to Peter Collins of Salford University, whose presentation at a small conference organized by Don Ross in 2007 clarified this distinction with the simple, startling sentence: "Science is about what happens when we do something. Politics is about what we should do, given that we disagree about our goals."

Although many people have argued that morality is the purview of religion, I will argue here that this is incorrect.[C] In fact, religion is also descriptive, not prescriptive. The prescription of religion is based on creating a descriptive theory in which the prescription becomes obvious—God says this is what you must do. If you do this, you will be rewarded. The reward is usually some sort of heaven, while punishment is hell.[6] (Even religions without gods describe reward and punishment for correct behavior, such as the ideas that appropriate behavior will allow one to reach nirvana, or that good deeds will lead to reincarnation into a better life in the next cycle.) But reward can also be suggested to occur in this life, such as the prosperity theology movement arising recently in the United States.

Notice that this is fundamentally a descriptive statement: If you do the right thing, then you will be rewarded. The fact that this is descriptive can be seen in Pascal's famous wager in which he has to decide whether or not to believe in God, and decides to do so because the cost of belief if God does not exist is small, while the cost of disbelief if God does exist is large.[7] The bet is laid down on the accuracy of the description. The prescription comes from the goal of attaining reward (Heaven) and avoiding punishment (Hell).

The separation of prescription from religion can be seen in George Bernard Shaw's play *Man and Superman*, where several of the characters reject the goal (rejecting prescription but not description) and decide they would rather go to Hell than suffer in Heaven. Similarly, in Milton's *Paradise Lost*, Lucifer famously says, "It is better to rule in Hell than to serve in Heaven." We can say that these people are misguided, that they have made the wrong choices (in Milton that's clear, in Shaw not so much), but the fact that a change in goals changes the morality implied by religious belief makes clear the inadequacy of religion as the prescriptive magisteria.

Some nonsupernatural moral codes are often referred to under the rubric of religion, such as Confucianism, Taoism, and Utilitarianism.[8] However, these are really examples of optimization functions—Confucianism's stated goal is to maximize stability within a society, while Taoism aims for "inner peace" and harmony with one's environment, and Utilitarianism attempts to maximize total happiness. These are prescriptive statements—they define a goal to optimize and say that we "ought" to do things that maximize that goal. The discussion of optimization functions leads us first into philosophy and then to economics.

Philosophy

Historically, philosophers have been searching for a categorical imperative, a simple statement that can be used to define morality from first principles.[9] The classic example is of course the Golden Rule, "Do unto others as you would have them do unto you," with versions in the Torah, the New Testament, and the Analects of Confucius.[10]

[C] These statements are not meant to imply that religion is not a useful human construct. Religion could serve many useful purposes, including as comfort, or as a means of organizing human groups for the purposes of enforcing within-group altruism. Religion may also serve as a psychological construct to enforce morality and encourage self-control, but the content of that morality and the goals of that self-control derive from nonreligious mechanisms.[5]

The complexity of this is interesting in that versions differ in terms of whether phrased in positive (*Do unto others what you would have them do unto you*) or negative (*Do not do unto others what you would not have them do unto you*) terms.

Many such categorical imperatives have been proposed, but, as pointed out by Patricia Churchland in her book *BrainTrust*, it has always been possible to find extreme situations that undercut these imperatives. Applying the rule to real situations demands exceptions, and we end up with a hodgepodge of rules and regulations. For example, the statement that we should increase the total happiness in the world suggests that one would have to sacrifice food for one's children to feed starving children elsewhere. While we might celebrate someone who works tirelessly for starving children, there aren't many people who would be willing to let their own child starve to death for another's, even for two others. Similarly, the statement that we should do unto others what we would like to have done to us if we were that other person leads to problematic situations in the face of fanatical prejudices. Imagine someone who says they would rather die than live as a paraplegic. Obviously, we would not want that person to carry out their imagined wishes on someone else who is paralyzed. In fact, paraplegic (and even tetraplegic) patients who become paralyzed from an accident tend to return to the same happiness levels they had before their accident.[11] (Happiness readjusts allostatically to the new situation.)

Again, we come back to the political question of *How do we negotiate different goals?* John Rawls put forward an elegant proposal based on his theory of *the ignorance of original position*.[12] Rawls suggests that laws and justice should be defined in such a way that these are the laws one would like to see given that one does not know where one will be in the society before one writes the laws. So, you would not want to make a law endorsing slavery because you would not know beforehand whether you were going to be born a slave or free. Rawls' proposal is a philosophical description of a political solution. He explicitly states that his goal is that he starts from the assumption of a constitutional democracy, from the assumption that all men (all people) are created equally.

The problem with this theory is, of course, that people are not always willing to assume that they could have started anywhere in society. Aristocracies, religious selectionism, and differences in individual talent can lead to an unwillingness to accept Rawls' premise. People are not equally talented. Some people are smarter than others. Some people are stronger. Some people are more deliberative and others more emotional. Although these differences are influenced by genetics, they are clearly an interaction between those genetics and societal influences.[13]

As pointed out by Stephen Jay Gould in *A Mismeasure of Man*, these genetic effects are notoriously difficult to measure accurately, are dangerously susceptible to cultural influences, and tend to get swamped by variability in those cultural influences. Nevertheless, it is easy for a successful individual (who is usually the one writing the law) to look at an unsuccessful individual and say that the reason for the difference in success is a moral failing. Rawls' proposal is fundamentally dependent on empathy, the ability to put oneself in another's place (a critical component of both religious and philosophical moral codes[14]).

It can be difficult to say, "There but for the grace of God, go I." Amoral individuals have explicit difficulties with empathy.[15] One of the things we will see later, when we directly examine what people do, is that people tend to be less willing to share if they think they've worked for their reward.[16] Even if we believe in Rawls' premise, we will still need to understand how to negotiate with individuals who do not.

Economics—The hazards of optimization functions

One field that has, in fact, made "scientific" claims about morality is economics. These claims have been implicit rather than explicit, but by our separation between descriptive and prescriptive, a remarkable number of economic results are prescriptive rather than descriptive. This is because they are defined under an optimization function.

The most common optimization function used in economics is that of *efficiency*, which is defined as an economy with no missed opportunities.[17] Imagine that country A can grow carrots for $10 a bushel and celery for $20 a bushel, while it costs country B $20 to grow a bushel of carrots but only $10 a bushel to grow celery. This means that if each country grows all of its own vegetables, the two countries are wasting money— they are *inefficient*. It would be more efficient for country A to grow only carrots and country B to grow only celery and for country A to trade some of its carrots to country B for some of the celery grown in country B. This would be more efficient even if there was a small cost to transporting carrots and celery across the border. If transportation cost $1 a bushel, then country A could effectively grow carrots for $10 and celery for $11. Similarly, country B could effectively grow celery for $10 and carrots for $11. Economists usually discuss this in terms of monetary costs, but we get the same results if we think of this in terms of person-power, how many hours it takes how many people to accomplish something. Country A grows carrots with less work than country B, while country B grows celery with less work than country A. Together, they can grow more food with less work. This is the advantage of specialization.

This all sounds well and good, but it assumes that the goal of an economy is to mini- mize the "missed opportunities." The effect of this free-trade agreement between coun- tries A and B is that the celery growers in country A are now out of work, as are the carrot growers in country B. If your goal is to maximize jobs, then this deal is a bad one. The problem is that economists use words laden with morality like *efficiency* or *rationality*.[18;D] An inefficient car that gets poor gas mileage is obviously a bad thing. Is an inefficient economy also a bad thing?

The assumption that efficiency is the only goal is a strange one.[20;E] Sometimes inef- ficiency is an obvious problem, such as when the costs and purchasing prices are too far out of balance and the economy grinds to a halt, or with corruption that pulls eco- nomic production out of an economy;[22] but, as with a car that gets poor gas mileage, efficiency is really only one element of a more complex optimization function.[23] Lots of

---

[D] We've discussed the dangerous use of the terminology of "rationality" and "irrationality" through- out this book, in particular the idea that there is a rational self trying to control an irrational other. Many philosophers and psychiatrists and even many cognitive scientists still share this view.[19] (See the discussion in Chapters 8 and 15.) As I hope I've made clear, I am uncomfortable with this rejection of the nonconscious decision-making systems as irrational.

[E] Why have economists latched onto "efficiency" as the goal? Some have argued that it is because this creates mathematically solvable problems. I find this conclusion strange because it would seem to me that one could just as easily define other optimization functions. Some have argued that this is due to an inherent feedback loop of students being taught early that efficiency is the only optimization function that matters. I wonder how much it depends on the self-interest of certain individuals, as this efficiency argument creates winners and losers in an economy.[21]

people buy inefficient cars because they like the safety features or the ability to carry large objects (like lots of kids) or for their style and their look.

In fact, these economic descriptions of maximizing efficiency are poor descriptors of what humans actually do, particularly at the microeconomic (individual) level, and require extensive additional components to properly describe behavior.[24]

At a microeconomic level, these questions of interpersonal interactions can be captured in the context of *game theory*,[25] which assumes that two people are playing a game. This game is assumed to be specified as a sequence of choices (actions and their consequences) leading to a final set of payoffs. Each situation is a node in a tree, and each action takes the two players from one node to another. (Notice how this concept of situation and action mirrors the decision-making definitions we've been using throughout this book.) A classic example would be the game tic-tac-toe (Figure 23.1). At the start, the situation has an empty board. Player **X** has nine options. When player **X** puts an **X** in one of the squares, player **O** now has eight options. At the end of the game, there are three possible payoffs: Player **X** wins and **O** loses, Player **O** wins and **X** loses, or there is a tie. (It can be shown that if both players play optimally, tic-tac-toe will always end in a tie.) Strategy is defined as the set of choices that a player would make at each point in the sequence. (What should Player **X** do at the start of the game? [The center is optimal.] What should Player **O** do when Player **X** has two in a row? [Block it.])

If neither player can improve his or her strategy by changing something, then the players are in a *Nash equilibrium*.[26;F] The problem with this is that this breaks down in cooperative games. (Nash's proof of optimality was technically only for zero–sum noncooperative games.[28]) As we will see later, in cooperative games (such as the *prisoner's*

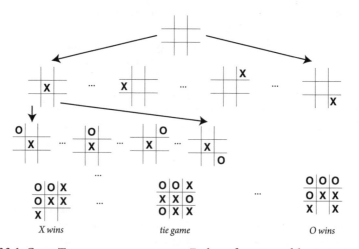

Figure 23.1 GAME THEORY AND TIC-TAC-TOE. Each configuration of the tic-tac-toe board is a *state*. The action of each player changes the state. Tic-tac-toe is a zero–sum game: if player **X** wins, then player **O** loses, and vice versa. Compare the prisoner's dilemma game (Figures 23.2 and 23.3).

[F] The Nash equilibrium is named after John Nash, the famous mathematician who discovered this as part of his Ph.D. thesis in 1950. Both Nash's mathematics and his trials with schizophrenia were described eloquently in the book and movie *A Beautiful Mind*.[27]

dilemma, below), a player can improve his or her gain by not cooperating, but if both players don't cooperate, then they both do worse. In fact, as we will see below, people are remarkably cooperative, even when it is explicitly stated that games will only be played once and when no one knows who you are, so that there is no opportunity for reciprocity to affect decision-making.[29]

So what do humans really do?

The rest of this chapter will ask the question *What do humans do in their interactions?* Rather than address the prescriptive question, I'm going to spend the rest of this chapter addressing what we know about human behavior (descriptively). Just as knowing the correct description improves prescription in medicine (see the antibiotic example earlier), we can hope that a better description of human behavior may help us know what prescriptions are possible.[G] Just as we sidestepped the question of whether taking drugs is right or wrong in Chapter 18, and instead asked *Why do people take drugs?* and *How do we change that (if we want to)?*, I am going to sidestep the question of *what* is moral and instead ask *What do people do when faced with moral (social, personal interaction) questions?*

Fundamentally, the things that we call "morality" are about our interactions with other people (and other things, such as our environment). Our daily interactions rest on an underlying societal trust (civilization).[32] As noted in the previous chapter (where we discussed what makes us human), these groups spontaneously organize, whether it be for mutual protection, for societal stability, or because well-organized groups outcompete poorly organized groups. Simply stated, if two armies face each other and one works together, but the other is made up of individually selfish members, it is pretty clear which group will most likely win the battle.[33]

So what does that mean for morality? How can science address morality? What does it mean to study morality? We know humans can be gloriously moral (Martin Luther King, the Freedom Riders, soldiers sacrificing their lives for their country, firefighters running into a burning building, donations to charity). We know humans can be gloriously immoral (Nazis, the KKK, genocide in Rwanda, Serbia, and Darfur). The first question we will need to ask is *What do humans do when faced with a moral situation? What do humans do, and what are the parameters that drive their action choices?* If we understand how humans think about morality, then we will be able to decide whether we want to change it, and if so, how to change it.

Early studies: The identification of evil

Fundamentally, morality is about our interaction with each other. As with the other questions we've been addressing in this book, in order to study morality, we need a

---

[G] It is very important not to fall into the sociobiology flaw.[30] The fact that something is descriptively true should not be taken as implying that it is prescriptively good. As noted in footnote *D* in Chapter 13, although it is true that how much effort is required to put into reproduction changes the dynamics of risk and investment and therefore explains both many observed human dynamics between men and women and the (inverted) dynamics of seahorses (where the male broods the eggs in a pouch),[31] we should not take this fact as a prescription for appropriate male and female roles in modern society.

way to take those interactions and bring them into the laboratory, where we can use controlled experiments to study them. Early attempts at morality studies were based on role-playing games, where confederates would pretend to structure the world in such a way as to drive certain behaviors. Two very famous early experiments on morality were the Milgram obedience experiment and the Zimbardo prison experiment.[34]

In the Milgram experiment, a subject was told that he or she was to play the role of "teacher" while another played the role of "learner." (The subject thought the learner was another subject also participating in the experiment and did not know that the learner was an actor.) The two were separated by a wall, so they could not see each other. The teacher provided questions to the learner (arbitrary word-pairs that the learner had to memorize). The "learners" gave wrong answers to many of the pairs. Whenever the learner got it wrong, the teacher was to push a button that would shock the learner. As the learner made more errors, the voltage was increased to the point that the learner would scream, bang on the wall, beg to stop, and finally, go silent. In reality, there were no shocks. The "learner" was an actor playing a part. But the descriptions from the subjects (playing the role of "teacher") make it very clear that they believed the shocks were real.

The Milgram experiment is usually taken as demonstrating the human unwillingness to question authority; however, although many subjects continued to deliver shocks to the maximal levels, many of those subjects asked to stop and continued only after being assured that it was OK, even necessary, to go on. Other subjects refused to deliver shocks beyond certain levels. Over the subsequent years, Milgram ran dozens of variations of the experiment trying to identify what would make people more or less likely to continue. The numbers varied dramatically based on the physical and emotional connection between the teacher and the learner and on the authority inherent in the experimenter assuring the subject that the experiments were necessary. Recent re-examinations of the original data suggest that the assurance that the experiments were "necessary" was a critical component driving the subjects' willingness to continue.[35] Most likely, a combination of both is needed—an authority figure who can convince one that the crimes are necessary for an important cause. This is a good description of many of the worst evils perpetrated by humans on each other (genocide to "purify the race," torture to "extract information," etc.). The key to the Milgram experiment may have been an authority figure stating that the "experiment requires that you continue" and implying that not continuing would ruin an important scientific endeavor.

In the Zimbardo experiment, two groups of college students were arbitrarily assigned roles of guards and prisoners in a mock jail in the basement of a Stanford University psychology building. Over the course of less than a week, the guards became arbitrarily violent, abusive, and even sadistic. It was so bad that the experiment was stopped after only six days—more than a week before it was supposed to. The Zimbardo experiment is usually taken as demonstrating how power structures drive dehumanization and mistreatment.

The problem with both of these experiments is that they address extremes and they are one-off experiments. They are very hard to replicate, and they are very hard to use to get at the underlying mechanisms of human behavior. Nevertheless, both of these effects clearly occur in real life. For example, the recent cases of torture in Abu Ghraib prison are examples of both the Milgram and Zimbardo effects. (What limited investigations have been done suggest that the soldiers were pushed to create negative-impact situations by interrogator authority figures and then went beyond and reveled in the torture they were doing as the moral authority deteriorated.[36])

Although extremely important, the Milgram and Zimbardo studies tell us what we fear we already knew—humans are often susceptible to authority (particularly an authority cloaked in a cause), and humans given power will often misuse it. But most people don't live their lives in these extremes. These studies, and the horrors of Rwanda or Abu Ghraib, are extremes. Certainly, these situations do occur, but the question with situations like the Milgram and Zimbardo experiments (or Rwanda, the Holocaust, Nanking, Abu Ghraib) is never *Are they wrong?* They are obviously wrong; the question is how to prevent reaching them in the first place. The contributions of the Milgram and Zimbardo studies have been *When are humans susceptible to authority figures? What makes them able to question that authority?* (Remember that some subjects in the Milgram experiment did question the experimenter and stop the experiment and that other subjects were clearly uncomfortable and asked if the other person was OK and continued only after assurance from the authority figure that the experiment was necessary. One soldier was uncomfortable enough with the situation at Abu Ghraib to leak the photos to the media.)

The revulsion that we feel at what is clearly evil (abuse of children by trusted authority figures in the Catholic church or the abuse of prisoners [including innocent children] by soldiers at Abu Ghraib or the murder of millions of innocents in genocide) identifies that evil exists in the world and that humans can do evil, but it doesn't really help us get at the mechanism of that evil. In fact, our institutions have a demonstrated inability to deal with evil of that magnitude (e.g., the Catholic church's inability to come to terms with pedophile priests, or the U.S. government's inability to bring the originators of the Abu Ghraib incidents to justice, or the inability of the United Nations to stop genocides in Rwanda, Bosnia, or Darfur). The problem isn't *Can we identify evil?* We reliably identify true evil. The problem with true evil is dealing with it.

Instead, the more difficult question is that of morality in our everyday lives.[H] In our daily lives, we are given opportunities to do good and bad—whether or not to give a dollar to the homeless person on the street, whether or not to cheat on a test or on our taxes. For most people in the world, our normal lives do not resemble either Milgram's or Zimbardo's horrors. In her chapter in the book *Moral Markets*, Lynn Stout points out that most of our lives are spent in "passive altruism"—we don't randomly beat people up on the street and steal their money.[38]

Some have suggested that this is due to having laws and that people would devolve into violent "savages"[I] without them, for example as depicted in the famous (and deeply flawed) book *Lord of the Flies* by William Golding. But actually, small communities

---

[H] We would also like to get at human questions of fairness and decency without requiring that our laboratories devolve into evil Hell-scapes. One of the consequences of the Zimbardo experiment is that studying evil is a slippery slope. Part of the reason the experiment was stopped after only six days was because of the psychological effect on the guards as much as on the prisoners.[37]

[I] I put the word "savages" in quotes because the term was originally used to refer to non-Western, non-highly technological cultures, essentially "barbarians." The word "barbarian" comes from the Greek word describing the unintelligible speech of foreigners (which sounded like "bar bar" to them).[39] The important point, however, is that "savages" were not particularly savage, any more than the "barbarians" were barbarous (certainly no more than "civilized" people), and they lived in communities with (often unwritten) rules that dictated fairness and morality.[40]

generally do not look anything like *Lord of the Flies*. They contain neighbors helping each other, sharing food, with extensive examples of both passive and active altruism.[41]

When we see our neighbors' car stuck in the snow (or even a stranger's car, as happened outside my house in the big snowstorm we had last winter), we don't stand laughing, we don't shoot the person and take their car, we all bring out our shovels and snowblowers and clear out the car and get the person safely back on their way. Firefighters, police officers, and ordinary citizens rush toward danger to help those in need. When the 35W bridge in Minneapolis fell during rush hour in August 2007, throwing cars into the Mississippi River near the university, our first responders were on the scene within minutes, and college students, faculty, and medical personnel from the local hospital ran to help. Even from a bridge carrying rush-hour traffic, only 13 people died that day, due in large part to the remarkable work by the first responders and the help they got.[42] Even ruthless pirate ships operated under (written and often very detailed) community rules. *The Invisible Hook* by Peter Leeson gives a vivid description of how the "lawless" pirates used carefully constructed internal rules to ensure a viable community. We don't live in a *Lord of the Flies* situation. So, then, what makes communities work? If it's not the laws, what is it?

Fairness and the creation of communities

Throughout this book, we've seen the importance of breaking the mechanism of decision-making into its component parts. We'd like to be able to understand the mechanisms of morality in a way that is repeatable and can be studied reliably in the context of a laboratory. It would be really useful to be able to study moral questions in such a way that we can ask how the brain represents these issues, perhaps by studying them while observing brain activity using fMRI. To get at these questions in a more controlled, more scientific (and less disturbing) setting, we will turn back to game theory. However, instead of trying to determine what the optimal choice is under some *normative* (prescriptive) assumption, we will examine what choices humans actually make. These choices become particularly interesting when we make the games non-zero–sum.

A zero–sum game is one in which the total wins and losses cancel out. That is, if one player wins, then another must lose. In physics, the total amount of energy within a closed system cannot be created or destroyed. If two billiard balls hit each other, and one speeds up, then the other must slow down. Life, however, is not zero–sum. Many human jobs take a tremendous amount of training and practice. I would prefer to pay an expert to rebuild my roof so that it will be done right rather than try to learn how to do it myself and probably do a mediocre job of it. This is the advantage of specialization. Each person becomes better at his or her task, able to produce both more and better products, which we can trade between each other, thus increasing the total amount of goods and services we have in the system. Our economy has become more *efficient*.[J]

[J] Although I complained earlier that using efficiency as a sole optimizing criterion is a problem, this does not mean that efficiency is a bad thing in and of itself. Specialization can let people concentrate on the jobs they prefer while also improving efficiency. There are many things in our modern world (such as the laptop computer on which I am writing this book) that would never exist if everyone had to farm all their own food and build all their own tools.

Thus, we need laboratory experiments in which we have non-zero–sum games. Several such games have been developed for studying moral questions.[43] The simplest one is the *prisoner's dilemma,* which introduces the issue of *cooperation* and *defection* into our discussion. In the prisoner's dilemma, a pair of thieves have been caught robbing a store, but the police can't find the hidden loot. Without the loot, the police have only enough evidence to get them on breaking and entering. But if the police can get one prisoner to confess, they can convict the other one. The police tell each one that if he confesses and the other doesn't, they'll throw the book at the other one and let the confessing prisoner off free. If they both confess, then the prisoners will both get light sentences (presumably because the police won't need to go to trial). Basically, we can write this as a table with four conditions: if player 1 confesses but player 2 doesn't, then player 1 gets 0 years but player 2 gets 10 years. Similarly, if player 2 confesses and player 1 doesn't, player 2 gets 0 years but player 1 gets 10 years. If neither confesses, they get 1 year. If they both confess, they get 5 years (Figure 23.2).

The key to the structure of this game is that cooperating[K] when the other player defects against you plays you for a sucker and you lose big. However, if both players defect, then both players lose. We can write this in a positive form as well as in a negative one.[L] Simply put, imagine two players; each one can either "cooperate" or "defect." If both cooperate, both win $50. If one cooperates and the other defects, that defecting player gets $80 and the other player gets nothing. If both defect, neither gets anything (Figure 23.3). As with the negative version, the key is that if player 1 cooperates, then it is better for player 2 to defect than to cooperate, but both players defecting is worse than both players cooperating.

Of course, the key to a community is that we don't tend to play these games only once; we play what is more generally called the repeated (or "iterated") prisoner's dilemma.[46] In this version, the two players keep playing again and again. Imagine two communities trading goods between them. Your community grows wheat and the other grows fruit. In year one, you bring wheat to the other community and they give you fruit for it. In year two, they bring you fruit and you give them wheat for it. Every other year, you put yourself at risk, bringing lots of wheat to their community where they have all their

	Prisoner 1 "cooperates" (stays silent)	Prisoner 1 defects (confesses)
Prisoner 2 "cooperates" (stays silent)	Prisoner 1 gets 1 year Prisoner 2 gets 1 year	Prisoner 1 gets 0 years Prisoner 2 gets 10 years
Prisoner 2 defects (confesses)	Prisoner 1 gets 10 years Prisoner 2 gets 0 years	Prisoner 1 gets 5 years Prisoner 2 gets 5 years

Figure 23.2 The prisoner's dilemma: negative version.

[K] The terminology of this traditional example is unfortunate. The prisoners are cooperating with each other, not with the police.

[L] I started with this in a negative form because it would be kind of weird to talk about the "prisoner's dilemma" with shared money. In any case, throughout the rest of this chapter, I will base these games on transfers of money, because that's how most of the experiments have been done.[44] It is true that there are differences in how humans treat positively and negatively framed decisions[45] (see Chapter 3), but it is not yet known how these issues interact.

people and they could steal it from you and send you home without fruit. Of course, if they did that, you wouldn't come back. This leads to the simple concept of "tit-for-tat."

In the early 1980s, Robert Axelrod, a scientist interested in game theory and cooperation, ran a series of computer tournaments in which players submitted strategies for cooperation and defection.[47] Each player would play a sequence of 200 prisoner's dilemma games with each other player. (That is, each player would play an iterated prisoner's dilemma with 200 repetitions against each other player.) What this meant was that a player could punish or trick another player. Although lots of very complicated strategies were submitted, the consistent winner was a very simple strategy called "tit-for-tat" submitted by Anatol Rapoport, a mathematician studying game theory himself. The strategy was to cooperate on the first play, and from then on to do whatever the other player did. If the other player started defecting, tit-for-tat would defect, but as long as the other player cooperated, tit-for-tat would cooperate.

One of the things that Axelrod discovered in his series of tournaments is that a community of tit-for-tat players was remarkably stable. If one simulated evolution among the players (that is, the players with the largest wins replicated a larger proportion of that strategy into the next generation, while players with the smallest wins died off), then tit-for-tat generally filled out the population and became an evolutionarily stable population—other strategies could not break in to the community. Remember that tit-for-tat playing against tit-for-tat would both cooperate. Anyone defecting against it would win big once, but would then be punished by tit-for-tat and would start losing. Although the tit-for-tat player would lose against that one defector, it would still do well cooperating with the other tit-for-tat players, but the defector would lose against everybody.

The problem with tit-for-tat, particularly when playing against another tit-for-tat player, is that if there are any errors, then defections begin to propagate through the future. Imagine if one time on your way to take your wheat to the other community, you are set upon by bandits and all your wheat is stolen. The other community thinks you defected and, ignoring all your pleas and explanations, refuses to trade with you again. Axelrod found that when errors are included in the game, the optimal strategy was "tit-for-tat with forgiveness." Even among a series of defects, occasionally the player would try a cooperation. It might be just enough to reinstate both players cooperating again.

The key to all of these issues is that two players cooperating produces more advantage than alternating defections (see Figure 23.3). Strategies in a game world in which this is true evolve to produce communities that cooperate.

Fundamentally, we are social creatures. We live in just such communities. Several studies have shown that if you have two groups (think of this as two tribes or two villages), one of which contains a lot of altruistic cooperators (think of this one as the high-tax, high-collaboration village, where people volunteer to help each other out) and one of which contains a lot of selfish defectors (think of this as the "I got mine" village,

	Player 1 cooperates	Player 1 defects
Player 2 cooperates	Player 1 gets $50	Player 1 gets $80
	Player 2 gets $50	Player 2 gets $0
Player 2 defects	Player 1 gets $0	Player 1 gets $0
	Player 2 gets $80	Player 2 gets $0

Figure 23.3 The prisoner's dilemma: positive version.

where people do their best to get their own from the community), then the altruistic village will succeed as a group better than the selfish village.[48] The people in the altruistic village will spend more time in the cooperate–cooperate entry of the interaction table, while people in the selfish village will spend more time in the defect–defect entry of the interaction table.

This is a form of group selection, in that even though the determination of selective success is completely based on the individual, certain groups do better than other groups. Groups that are successful may grow large enough to split into two groups, while groups that are not successful may destroy themselves from the inside. The evolutionary implications of this group-selection process is laid out most clearly in the book *Unto Others*, by Elliot Sober and David Sloan Wilson.

This theory, however, does predict that one is likely to be more cooperative with members of one's own village or group rather than between villages or groups. This difference is called *in-group altruism* and *out-group xenophobia*. In his book *Darwin's Cathedral*, David Sloan Wilson argues that one of the keys to humanity is the flexibility and complexity with which we define our groups. He argues that many of our societal constructs (religion, nationalism, culture, even sports franchises) are ways of defining who is in the in-group and who is not. In *Darwin's Cathedral*, Wilson explicitly examines the development of Calvinism in the 1530s, where exile and ostracism were the main tools of ensuring in-group cooperative behavior.

In his book *Historical Dynamics*, Peter Turchin defines a term *asabiya*, which means "cohesion" or "group unity." Turchin argues that the success of dynasties, tribes, nation-states, and groups depends on the willingness of individuals to sacrifice for the group. Turchin argues that groups, nation-states, tribes, and dynasties all have a cycle, where groups arise with a lot of *asabiya* (in-group cooperation), take over (because they are stronger together than other groups that cannot work together), but then lose that *asabiya* over a couple of generations (defectors spread within the group), which makes them vulnerable to the next group with *asabiya*.

This effect that Turchin is describing occurs because although everyone in the altruistic village will do better on average, a selfish person in the altruistic village is going to do even better than the altruists in that village.[49] (That person will spend more time in the I-defect-you-cooperate entry in the interaction table. Think of the person who rides the government-built subway system to protest paying taxes.[50]) This sets up a conflict between levels: at the level of the villages, altruistic villages do better than other villages, but at the individual level, selfish defectors within that village do better than the altruists in that (mostly altruistic) village. There are two ways to deal with this problem (called the *free-rider* problem[51]): exile and altruistic punishment.

Exile entails identifying those defectors and explicitly pushing them out of the community. One of the major purposes of gossip seems to be the identification of such defectors.[52] Exile forces the person out of the community, thus removing the person from the cooperate–cooperate entry in the table. Many groups use ostracism or exile as a devastating punishment, one that is clearly strong enough to keep communities in line.[53]

A great example of the development of in-group altruism as critical for success on a group-by-group basis can be seen in the development of shipboard rules on pirate ships.[54] It would be hard to imagine more selfish individuals than pirates, but being trapped on a ship together in the middle of the open ocean, facing battle together, certainly defines a very specific in-group. The key factor described by Leeson in *The Invisible Hook* is that of punishment for stealing from the crew or for not pulling one's weight. Not cooperating with the rest of the crew led to the rest of the crew punishing the selfish pirate, who would then change his ways or else.

Altruistic punishment entails the community identifying and explicitly punishing defectors. In a sense, a group of cooperators come together and each sacrifices a small amount to ensure that the advantage a defector gains is minimal.

The simplest game that gets at this question of altruistic punishment is the *ultimatum game*, a laboratory experiment that directly tests a person's willingness to sacrifice for fairness.[55] In the ultimatum game, one player (the donor) gets $20 to split with another player (the recipient). The recipient then gets to decide whether to "take it or leave it." If the recipient accepts the distribution, both players get the money, as divided by the donor. If the recipient rejects the distribution, neither player gets anything. In a perfectly "rational" world, the recipient should take whatever he or she gets. The donor should thus give the recipient the minimum amount (say $1 or 1¢) and the recipient should take it. But if you look at your own reaction to this, you will probably have a visceral, emotional reaction to being given only $1 or 1¢ and throw it back in the donor's face. In practice, recipients reject anything below about a third of the money, and donors (knowing this) divide the money in about a 60/40 split.[M]

Interestingly, other animals, even highly intelligent animals like chimpanzees, do not seem to show this propensity for altruistic punishment; they take whatever is given to them.[58] There are some differences in how the chimpanzees have been run through the experiments (they have to run multiple cases because one can't tell the chimpanzee how to play the game). And chimpanzees *are* sensitive to inequality and unfairness, particularly among compatriots.[59] Nevertheless, there seem to be clear differences between humans and our closest genetic relative. Although chimpanzees are our closest genetic relative, they have very different social interactions and do not live in the same village-based, close-knit communities that humans do.[60] Other animals that do live in such communities (such as wolves) do seem to show altruistic punishment.[61] This suggests that the difference may be less an issue of humanity than an issue of community.

The point here is that part of our brains demand fairness. Cooperation, trust, and the lack of it produce changes in activation of emotional reward circuitry.[62] fMRI results have identified that altruistic punishment (rejecting an unfair offer) is associated with increases in blood flow in the amygdala and the insula, two structures involved in emotional (Pavlovian) reactions to negative results. In fact, rejection of unfair offers is correlated to the emotion of anger and disgust, and punishment of unfair players is associated with the emotion of satisfaction. Punishment of unfair players produces increases in blood flow in positive emotional structures such as the ventral medial prefrontal cortex and the ventral striatum. The satisfaction of punishing unfair players occurs even when

[M] Economists tell us that this is "irrational" in that one loses money by not taking the smaller offer.[56] Two groups that play more "rationally" than expected (both accept and offer smaller-than-normal amounts) are sociopaths, who do not seem able to recognize the other player's emotional reaction, and business-school graduates, who have been trained to act based on their "rational" optimization equations.[57] Business-school graduates look normal before entering business school but abnormal leaving it. I will leave you to draw your own conclusions.

the punisher is a third party—that is, player A defects against player B, who cooperated (and thus got played for a sucker), and player C spends some of his or her own money to punish player A. Players observing an unfair player receiving painful shocks expressed satisfaction, an achieved desire for revenge, and showed activity in reward-related areas such as the ventral striatum. When we evaluate goals, some of those goals are complex and social.

Variations of the ultimatum game have been examined as well. If the recipient thinks the other person is actually a computer program offering choices randomly, that recipient is more likely to take unfair offers[63] (implying that the rejection of an unfair offer is about punishing other players). Donors who think they "earned" the money (through some effort, say by performing a task prior to playing the game) offer less than if the money is just given to them. The harder the donor worked for the money (the harder the task was), the less they will offer.[64;N]

As noted above, altruistic punishment may be the reason for gossip, shame, and reputation. One of the human interactions that I have always found particularly interesting is the success of Amnesty International. One of the main things Amnesty International does is to write letters to dictators, governments, and human-rights abusers to free dissidents and stop those human-rights abuses. They don't threaten. They don't have an army. They don't even threaten with religious "burn-in-Hell" threats. They merely write letters—and the remarkable thing is that this often works.

A similar issue relates to that of forgiveness. As we saw in the tit-for-tat experiments, the most resistant strategy to errors and noise is tit-for-tat with forgiveness. Although some crimes may be unforgivable, forgiving (possibly after completing an appropriate punishment) is a tool to rehabilitate a defector. If the person cooperates from then on, he or she can again become part of the community. In one of the most remarkable stories of our time, after the end of apartheid in South Africa, Archbishop Desmond Tutu led the *Truth and Reconciliation Commission*, where the criminals were asked to provide a full description, disclosure, and apology.

The science of morality is still in its infancy. At this point, it is concentrating on the descriptive question of *What do humans actually do?* The evidence seems to be that we have evolved a host of "moral" judgments that allow us to live in (mostly) peaceful communities. These interactions are not always simple and depend on a complex interaction that encourages cooperation and reduces the advantages of defection.

What is particularly interesting is that humanity agrees in large part on morality, particularly that of social interactions. The Golden Rule is recognized the world over, as part of most religions and as part of most nonreligious moral tracts. Specific prohibitions (gay marriage, abortion, eating pork) vary from religion to religion and from

---

N This is why the "it's your money" anti-tax meme is so effective and insidious:[65] it encourages selfish defection from the community. (As Supreme Court Justice Oliver Wendell Holmes famously stated, "Taxes are what we pay for civilized society." This is often restated as "Taxes are the price we pay to live in a civilized society.") Similarly, this is why anti-tax groups are trying to get rid of the "withholding" that occurs in most paid jobs (but not for the self-employed). The more that the anti-tax groups can get citizens to see the money as earned and then given away, the less those citizens are willing to pay taxes. (Of course, like most selfish defectors in a community, the anti-tax groups want all of the services from the community—they just don't want to pay for them.[66])

culture to culture, but the primary social and moral interactions (be fair in your dealings with others, treat others as you would like to be treated, help when you can) do not.

When a nonbeliever pressed Rabbi Hillel (110 BCE–10 BCE) to describe his entire religion while standing on one foot, promising to convert if Hillel could do so, Rabbi Hillel replied, "That which is hateful to you, do not do to others. All the rest is just commentary. Go and learn."[67] The Golden Rule is a first step toward cooperation, but it alone is not enough. The commentary is long and complicated, and still being discovered.

Books and papers for further reading

- Elliot Sober and David Sloan Wilson (1998). *Unto Others: The Evolution and Psychology of Unselfish Behavior*. Cambridge, MA: Harvard.
- David Sloan Wilson (2002). *Darwin's Cathedral: Evolution, Religion, and the Nature of Society*. Chicago: University of Chicago Press.
- Robert Axelrod (1984/2006). *The Evolution of Cooperation*. New York: Basic Books.
- Patricia S. Churchland (2011). *BrainTrust*. Princeton, NJ: Princeton University Press.
- Sam Harris (2010). *The Moral Landscape*. New York: Free Press.
- Paul J. Zak [Editor] (2008). *Moral Markets: The Critical Role of Values in the Economy*. Princeton, NJ: Princeton University Press.

24

The Conundrum of Robotics

> More often than not,
> we are only trying to know
> that we are not the only ones
> who risk everything for love.

Free will includes three different issues wrapped up in one philosophical term: (1) the outside perspective (Why do some other beings appear as agents with free will to us?), (2) the societal perspective (Whom should we blame for criminal actions?), and (3) the internal perspective (What is the internal sensation that we identify as "consciousness"?). By separating free will into these three perspectives, I will show that the first two are not truly issues of "free will," and that there is no reason to think that physical machines cannot experience an internal sensation of consciousness.

Free will is a funny term. A pairing of such simple words, it carries with it all that makes us feel human. What does it mean to be *free*? What does it mean to *will* something? One of the great terrors in modern life is that the concept of free will is an illusion.[A] For, if free will is an illusion, then we are just riding a roller coaster, taken to great heights, thrown down to great depths, with no control over our journey. But this terror assumes that there are only two choices—that either we have complete freedom to choose whatever we want or that our feeling of self is an illusion, that we are not in control, that we are merely machines, completely predictable in what we do. This dichotomy is the illusion.

The truth is that we are never completely *free*. We are constrained by the laws of physics, by our immediate interactions with society, by our physical and monetary resources. I can want to fly like a bird all that I want, but no matter how high I jump, I will never

---

[A] The irreverent comic strip *Jesus and Mo* captured this entanglement elegantly—"Did you know that free will is an illusion?" "What about personal responsibility?" "That's exactly it! Once you accept that there's no such thing as free will, you can do whatever the hell you want!"[1]

take off and soar into the sky.[B] I can want to pitch in the major leagues, but I don't have a 100-mile-per-hour fastball. We all accept these limitations, and yet we hold on to the term *free will*.

Will is an old word, meaning wish or desire. Will is the agency that defines us. Fundamentally, it is the fact that the concept of will implies a dualism that lies at the heart of the problem of the term *free will*. If we can explain the reason for an action from a source not of our "will," then we deny our own agency in the taking of that action.[3] We will see that this is not a new concept, and that whether or not we are machines is really unrelated to whether or not we have free will.

We need to address free will from three perspectives. From an *outside perspective*, free will is about whether we treat another being as an agent or as a machine. From a *societal perspective*, free will is about whether we can blame individuals for their actions. And from an *inside perspective*, free will is about whether we are truly slaves to our own machinery.

The outside perspective: The agency of others

From an outside perspective, we have already seen that we assign agency to many things that are not agents. (Remember the discussion of the GPS in Chapter 2?) The assumption of agency is a way for the human brain to handle unpredictability. In particular, the assumption of agency allows us to address the complex interaction of predictability based on probabilities of action-selection.

Individuals have personality, character; they are predictable. It is not true that humans act randomly. Think for a moment what kind of a world that would be: every person you meet could suddenly break into song or could suddenly break into a killing spree. Such a world is unimaginable to us. Instead, we talk reliably about propensities, about a person's *nature*. "It's in my nature," says Fergus to Dil at the end of *The Crying Game*,[4] owning his actions, explaining why he took the fall for her. Fergus explains his agency by saying that this is within the bounds of what you would expect if you really knew him. Agency requires predictability, but only a limited predictability—we identify a character, a nature, a range of possibilities, and expect that the agent will act somewhere within that range.

The problem of mechanics and free will goes back to the time of Galileo, Newton, and Descartes, all of whom recognized that physical systems did not have agency in the manner we are talking about here—they are completely predictable. (Of course, we know now that this only occurs for objects at the macro scale that Galileo and Newton were studying. At small enough (quantum) scales, predictability breaks down.[5] Whether quantum objects are deterministic or not is still unknown, but our best understanding today suggests that they are not; instead, they seem to be probabilistic. As we will see later in this chapter, it is possible for quantum effects to expand into the macro world, making them fundamentally probabilistic as well.[6]) Before Galileo, objects themselves had agency—Aristotle explained gravity because things wanted to fall to the earth, and proposed that objects had both a driving cause, which pushed them into their actions, and a teleological cause, which pulled them based on their agency and goals.[7]

Descartes, through his own medical studies, and following directly on Galileo's observations of mechanics, realized that the body itself was a machine. Descartes was

---

[B] Never having been willing to test *The Hitchhiker's Guide to the Galaxy*'s suggestion to aim at the ground and miss.[2]

an accomplished anatomist and recognized that animals were machines; however, he denied that he himself was a machine and explicitly separated the mind from the body.[8] Descartes' concerns lay in predictability—Newtonian mechanics implies that if you know enough details about the state of the universe at any moment, it is completely predictable from then on. Sometimes called the "clockwork universe" theory, the remarkable success of Newtonian mechanics in predicting motion in the physical world led to the hypothesis of determinism.[9] Philosophers at the time believed that there were only two choices—an extra-universe decision-making agent with free will, or that everything is predetermined, and all free will is an illusion.

Some philosophers have tried to rescue the randomness needed for free will from quantum mechanics.[10] The best current physics theories suggest that the universal determinism implied by Newton is wrong—we cannot predict the actions of a quantum particle, it is truly random (within the constraints of probabilities[C]).[11] Neuroscientists have tended to be dismissive of theories that base free will on quantum mechanics because quantum randomness does not generally reach to the macro level that we experience in our everyday world. In large part, this occurs because quantum randomness is constrained by probabilities. With enough elements, the probability distributions fill out and things become extremely predictable. Even products that depend on quantum properties (the laser, the transistor) provide predictable results that we depend on daily.[12] However, nonlinear mathematics provides a mechanism through which small (micro) fluctuations can drive large (macro) events.[13] In these equations, small changes percolate through the system, producing a large divergence in final outcomes.[D] Individual neurons are highly nonlinear, containing many positive feedback functions that could carry these micro-level effects into the macro-level world of neuronal function.[E]

[C] One of my favorite quotes is one I first heard from my father (who is a theoretical physicist): "Electrons have free will." We can predict very accurately what electrons will do in the aggregate. We can provide a probabilistic prediction about what a single electron will do, but it is impossible to say with certainty what a single electron will do.

[D] This growth from micro-level manipulations to macro-level effects is sometimes called the "butterfly effect," from the concept that how a butterfly flaps its wings in China (a small change) can change the path of a hurricane in the Caribbean (a large effect). It was first described by Henri Poincaré (1854–1912) in the late 1800s but was hard to really see until the development of the computer allowed reliable computation of complex equations. The first computer demonstration that small changes led to large divergences under certain conditions was from a meteorologist named Edward Lorenz (1917–2008), who was trying to simulate weather patterns in the 1950s. His simulations cycled through a series of simple differential equations. Each cycle, the simulation printed out what should have been a complete description of the system at a given time. When his computation would stop (due to electrical problems with the old computers of the time), he would retype in the printed numbers. This was a completely deterministic system, but what he found was that differences in the least significant digits would percolate up into the most significant digits and produce highly divergent effects. For those interested in this effect, James Gleick's 1987 popular science book *Chaos* remains one of the best introductions to the field.

[E] Cells have many individual components that work at quantum levels. One of the most straightforward examples is that of ion channels. These ion channels are a key component of cellular function, including neuronal function. Ion channels are made up of intricately shaped proteins that form mechanical devices that allow certain ions to pass through the cellular membrane while restricting the flow of other ions. The distribution of ions—which are inside the cell and which are outside the

(continued)

Identifying agency in others comes down to predictability in the aggregate but unpredictability in the specific. Thus, one has an identifiability of personality and character ("It's in my nature") and yet an inability to know exactly what an agent will do in a specific case. Quantum randomness (particularly when combined with nonlinear chaotic systems) can provide the necessary constrained randomness to give us what we observe as agency in others. But all that is really required for us to find agency in another is a predictable randomness. Whether that comes from quantum randomness or simply from an inability to know enough details to predict accurately, we reliably use the concept of agency to describe randomness occurring within a shape of possibilities.

It is important to differentiate these points I have made here from popular books on quantum theories of mind such as Roger Penrose's *The Emperor's New Mind*. Penrose argues that machines without quantum mechanics cannot be intelligent because quantum mechanics provides a special component to our brain function. Penrose's proposal is just a new version of Descartes' error—identifying a conduit from a nonphysical self to the physical. Descartes identified that connectivity with the pineal gland, fully aware that all mammals have a pineal gland; Penrose identifies the quantum components as the special key. The problem is that *all* matter is quantum and that *all* animals have quantum components in their neurons.[F] What I am saying here is that there is probabilistic randomness in the other creatures we interact with (whether it be from quantum

---

cell—controls the cell's function, including firing a spike (carrying information) and releasing neurotransmitter (communicating to another cell). Each ion channel has a number of different configurations; each configuration has different propensities to be open or closed, to allow ions to flow through or not. Whether an ion channel is open or closed at any moment is a random occurrence.[14]

Measures of each individual ion channel show that while the likelihood of an open channel closing or a closed channel opening has a characterizable probability, the actual timing of each is random. Because a cell typically has thousands of ion channels of a given type, performing a specific function, the individual randomness averages out and the macro level of the cellular function is extremely consistent from event to event.

But there are some cases where the number of channels is actually very small, where feedback processes can translate quantum micro changes into macro changes. One of those situations is in the firing of action potentials. Neurons integrate information and then send that information on by firing action potentials or spikes. (See Appendix A.) The spike itself is a positive feedback from voltage-sensitive sodium channels.[15] This means that the threshold between spiking and not can depend on a very small number of extra sodium channels opening up.

Computational studies and experiments that have replaced quantum-random channels with persistent channels have found that there are macro-level network properties that vanish without that quantum randomness. (For example, cells in the entorhinal cortex show an inherent oscillation at the theta rhythm of 5–7 Hz. This oscillation depends on channel noise and vanishes without the randomness inherent in these channels.[16]) Other examples in which stochastic randomness at the micro (quantum) level can be reflected in macro-level effects include whether or not a synapse releases neurotransmitter, and how a neuron's axon reaches out to find other neurons during development (which relates to how the network is wired up).[17] But, as with transistors, lasers, and other phenomena dependent on quantum properties, macro-level effects in cells (such as spiking) are highly reliable phenomena.[18] How much quantum randomness affects subtle properties in neuroscience (through the butterfly effect) is still unknown.

[F] In fact, the quantum components (microtubules) that Penrose and his colleague Stuart Hameroff reach for[19] are in every cell in every multicelled creature from the smallest worm to the largest whale.

randomness or chaotic indeterminacy) and that randomness leads us to assign agency to others. As we have already seen, humans assign agency to anything they interact with that is unpredictable within a limited range (such as fire or weather); I am making no claims about the consciousness of those other agents.

So we can identify why *other* people appear to be agents to us—they are predictably random. But I suspect that readers are unlikely to be satisfied with this story, because I have sidestepped the two real problems with free will. First, *How can we hold people responsible for their actions if they don't have free will?* and second, *Do you, dear reader, have free will?*

The societal perspective: The question of blame

Ethicists and legal scholars have come to the conclusion that someone forced to do something is not at fault.[20] Originally, this came from the concept that if someone holds a gun to our head and says, "commit this crime," then we are not at fault for the crime, because we are not the agent that initiated the action.[G]

The problem, however, arises when we start to have explanations for why someone committed a crime. If we find that someone has a brain tumor that impairs the processing of his prefrontal cortex, do we blame the person for the action? What if the person has an addiction? What if we come to the point that we can explain the neuroscience of decision well enough that we can say that anyone with a brain like this would have made that choice? Do we forgive the criminal the crime then?

It is important to note that this concept predates neuroscience by millennia. In every era, there have been explanations for why someone does something that does not imply their responsibility. Before science, there were witches and devils.[21] Before neuroscience, there were societal and developmental explanations.[22]

This question of our ability to predict criminal behavior also opens up an entirely different set of problems—if we can absolutely predict that someone will commit a crime, aren't we obligated to stop him?[23] What if we can only predict that he will commit the crime with a high probability? What is the balance between that probability and the person's rights to freedom? Most modern legal systems have decided to side on the balance of freedom, that one has to give the person the opportunity to not commit the crime, that it is unfair to judge a person for his or her thoughts and only fair to judge a person for his or her actions, and thus that one has to wait for the crime to be committed before acting.[H]

In large part, the problem of the ethics of choice lies in the distinction that has been drawn between the goal of punishing the responsible agent and the goal of ensuring that dangers to society are successfully removed from that society. As we saw in the last two chapters, one of the key factors that makes us human and has allowed us to live in stable

---

[G] This is not entirely true. For many of these situations, there is a choice, but the other option is so heinous that the crime becomes the best choice. Perhaps instead of saying that the person committing the crime is "not at fault," we should say that we are merciful, and forgive the action, because we understand the limitations of the options available.

[H] Of course, there's no reason one can't prepare defenses beforehand. Locking your door is a very different response to preventing theft than locking up the potential thief.

and complex societies is our willingness to take part in *altruistic punishment*, in which we sacrifice some of our own resources to punish a wrongdoer. The effect of this is to make it less worthwhile for wrongdoers to do wrong, which helps enforce cooperation.

In small groups, where everyone knows everyone else, where an individual is highly dependent on the willingness of the rest of the tribe to work with that individual, cooperation is reliably enforced by altruistic punishment (see Chapter 23). However, as societies get larger, it becomes more and more difficult for altruistic punishment at an individual level to produce sufficient incentive to enforce cooperation. It becomes too easy for an individual to cheat and then walk away and vanish into the city. In situations where there are two rival groups, it becomes too easy for altruistic punishment to devolve into a fight between groups and to escalate into what is effectively a tit-for-tat gang war. (The unfortunate flip side of in-group altruism is out-group xenophobia.) The legal system shifts the inflictor of the punishment from the individual to the society itself.

The real goal of a modern legal system is to ensure the ability of a society to function. However, although the medical community has spent the past several decades fighting to ensure that only scientifically-tested therapies get used, a process called "evidence-based medicine," no such constraint yet exists in the legal system.[24] This means that laws are sometimes based on simple conclusions from prescriptive moral principles rather than descriptive measures of reality. Two clear examples of this are the surprising decisions to implement austerity measures in response to shrinking economies, and the legal decisions to criminalize rather than to treat drug use.[25]

Much of the ethical argument is based on whether or not it is "fair" to punish someone, rather than how best to maintain societal function. One of the best examples of this is the "war on drugs."[1] No one denies that drug use is a problem. As we saw in the addiction chapter (Chapter 18), drug use leads to clear diminishments of well-being, both within the individual and within society. However, drug use, even highly addictive drug use, particularly early on an individual's path, is often a nonviolent individual problem rather than a societal problem.[27] Extensive data have shown that sending nonviolent addicts to treatment reduces the addiction, reduces the likelihood that they will turn violent, and has good success rates bringing them back to society. In contrast, sending addicts to prison increases the likelihood that they will turn violent, has poor success rates bringing them back to society, and is more likely to lead to relapse, often with worse drugs, on return to society. And yet, the discussion within American society today has clearly settled on criminal punishment and prison for individual drug use.

I will never forget an example of just such a disconnection, which I heard at my college graduation. The speaker was the novelist Tom Clancy, who was trying to pander to engineers in a speech at the engineering school graduation ceremony. Early in the speech, he talked about how important it was to look at the scientific data, and how sometimes the scientific data were different from common sense, so engineers had to learn to look at the data itself. Not ten minutes later, in the same speech, Clancy denounced drug addiction treatment centers, saying that he didn't care if the data said that treatment worked better than prison, the addicts knew they would go to jail and decided to take the drugs

---

[1] As has been pointed out by many commentators and philosophers, the terminology "war on drugs" enhances certain perspectives on handling the problem and likely limits our political options in handling the problem of addictive drug use.[26]

anyway, and had to be sent to prison. These logical disconnects lie in the limited view of free will ensconced within our legal system as an all-or-none phenomenon: either someone is free to choose and should be punished, or someone is a slave and the actual agent of the decision needs to be found instead. As we've seen throughout this book, the story isn't so simple.

The legal system has had problems with the question of blame and punishment long before the problem that understanding the mechanism of decision-making can lead to explanations independent of free will.[28] However, if we move away from the question of "blame" and toward goals of *mercy* and *forgiveness* at the individual level, while maintaining the goal of keeping a working society at the societal level, we find that the question of free will again becomes moot.

Of course, as we discussed in the first part of this chapter, free will means we can predict in the aggregate but not in the individual.[29] This means that the prediction of future action is only that: a prediction. As shown in the movie *Minority Report*, it is inherently dangerous to assume that a prediction is reality.[30] There is a big difference between locking your door to prevent theft and locking up the thief before he breaks into your apartment (Footnote H, above).

We can understand the reasons why someone has done something and rather than worrying about whether to blame them for their actions or not, we can worry about how to ensure that it does not happen again. Punishment is only one tool in that toolbox; there are many others. Knowing which ones will work when and how to implement them are scientific questions that depend on our understanding of the human decision-making machine.

Two great examples of using other tools are the successful uses of shame by Mahatma Gandhi and Martin Luther King.[31] They were able to achieve their aims by showing the world what others were doing. (Do not underestimate the importance of television and movie newsreels in their successes.) By using the human intersocial mechanism that recognizes strength not just in terms of physical ability but also in terms of "heart," of an ability to remain standing even in the face of greater physical power,[J] Gandhi and King were able to accomplish great things.

So a random process combined with a mechanism to ensure that the randomness falls within a probability distribution is sufficient to explain what we observe as agency in others. And recognizing that altruistic punishment is only one tool in society's toolbox to ensure cooperation rather than defection leaves moot the ethical question of whether someone actually has free will or not. However, we have so far avoided the hard question of consciousness—*Do you, dear reader, have free will?*

The inside perspective: Consciousness

We all have the experience of making decisions but not knowing why we made them. We all have the experience of not paying attention and looking up to recognize that we've done something we would have preferred not to, whether it be letting our addiction, our

---

[J] Rocky is the hero of his movie because he remains standing at the end, even as he loses the fight.[32]

anger, or our lust get the better of us, or whether it be that we stopped paying attention and found ourselves having driven our friend to our office instead of the airport. This led to the rider-and-horse theory—that there is a conscious rider and an unconscious horse. The rider can steer the horse, but the rider can also release control, allowing the horse to take its own path.[33] Sometimes the horse takes a sudden action that the rider then has to compensate for.[K]

Similarly, we have all had the experience of rationalizing an action that was clearly taken in haste: "I meant to do that." Following the famous Libet experiments, which showed that conscious decisions to act are preceded by brain signals long before the time we believe that we made the decision, many philosophers have retreated to the hypothesis that consciousness is wholly an illusion and that the rider is but a passenger, watching the movie unfold. Others have suggested that consciousness is more like a press secretary than an executive, and that consciousness entails rationalizing the actions that we take. Daniel Wegner differentiates actions that we identify as voluntary and those that we do not, and notes that there are both cases of (1) actions we do not have control of but believe we do and (2) actions we do have control of but believe we do not. Wegner explicitly identifies "free will" with the illusion of agency. However, Libet's experiments are based on the idea that the conscious decision to act occurs when we recognize (linguistically) the decision to act. Libet and others have suggested that consciousness is monitoring the actions we take so that it can stop, modify, or veto the action.[34]

The problem, as I see it, is that philosophers have the concept that consciousness must be an external thing, external to the physical world, or an emergent property of physical things that is (somehow) fundamentally different from the underlying physical things.[35] This issue first came to the fore with Descartian determinism, following on the implications of Galileo and Newton and Johannes Kepler that one could accurately predict the motion of objects, and that they did not need agency to move.[L] If the planets did not need agency to act, then neither did the machinery of the body.[38] Clearly desperate not to abandon human free will, Descartes concluded that although animals were machines, he himself was not.

[K] The multiple decision-making system theory suggests why we have multiple (sometimes conflicting) desires. Sometimes the Pavlovian system wants one thing, while the Deliberative wants another...all while the Procedural system is taking actions on its own.

[L] Compare Thomas Aquinas (1225–1274), who hypothesized that angels pushed the planets in their orbits.[36] Although angels are not taken seriously as an explanation for planetary motion anymore, it was a serious theory at the time. Aquinas believed that things could not move without agency. With the breakthroughs by Galileo, Descartes, Newton, Brahe, and Kepler, agents were no longer needed to move the planets, and the angel-pushing theory was abandoned.

The timeline is actually that Galileo (1564–1642) precedes Descartes (1596–1650) who precedes Newton (1643–1727). Galileo showed that one could measure physical reality experimentally. Descartes showed that space could be represented mathematically. And Newton derived accurate mathematical descriptions of deterministic motion. The two other key important figures in this timeline are Tycho Brahe (1553–1601) and his student Johannes Kepler (1571–1630), who showed that the planets moved in regular orbits, which could be described as ellipses. As with modern science, these men all knew each other's work well, read each treatise as it came out, and built on them. None of them worked in isolation.[37]

Descartes' famous line is, of course, *cogito ergo sum* (*I think, therefore, I am*), which is fine but says nothing about whether his fellow humans think or whether the language they spoke to him merely gave him the illusion that they thought, and says nothing about whether his fellow animals think, even though they cannot tell him their introspections. Descartes concluded that the pineal gland is the connection from an external conscious soul to a physical being. While the pineal gland does connect the brain to the body,[M] all mammals have pineal glands.[40] An accomplished anatomist, Descartes was well aware of this yet concluded that only the human pineal gland "worked" to connect souls to bodies.[41]

A more modern version of this desperate hypothesis can be found in the quantum theories of Roger Penrose and Stuart Hameroff, who have argued that consciousness cannot arise from a deterministic system and thus that it must depend on quantum fluctuations.[42] In particular, they have argued that the mind interacts with the brain by manipulating quantum probabilities—free will occurs because our separate souls can manipulate the quantum probabilities to give us free will. Notice that Penrose and Hameroff's theory that an external soul controls quantum probabilities is very different from the earlier discussion of quantum probabilities as a potential source of randomness in others. I suspect that if we were actually able to control quantum probabilities, we would, as shown in Neal Stephenson's *Anathem*, actually be much better at certain problems (like code-breaking) than we are. This quantum theory is often stated as a statement along the lines of *Machines cannot be conscious. Since I am conscious, I am not a machine*,[43] which is a thinly veiled restating of Descartes' *cogito ergo sum*.

My take on this is that the problem is, when we imagine it, we believe that there are only two choices—either we are conscious beings who can take any action or we are slaves who have no choices. But like Fergus and Dil in *The Crying Game*, we have personalities, and we are true to our "nature."

The word *robot* comes from a play by Karel Čapek (titled *R.U.R.* [*Rossum's Universal Robots*]), which was really about the effect of industrialization on individuality. Similarly, our more modern concept of robots comes from observations of highly complex machines, many of which are used in industrialized factories. It speaks to our fear that robotics leads to slavery, but as we've seen, the issue isn't slavery. Even if consciousness were to be an illusion, it wouldn't change our perception of our consciousness. It's not that we are suddenly going to become slaves—either we are already or we aren't.[N]

The world is more complex than that. Certainly there are decisions that are made without conscious intent, but there are also very long conscious deliberations that take minutes, hours, days, weeks, or even months. Even in the case of specific decisions that occur too quickly to be conscious, we can decide to train ourselves to make the right decisions at the right time. It takes time to learn to ride a bicycle. Both sports stars and soldiers know that doing the right thing at the right time quickly (without thinking) takes lots of practice. Although the action at the moment may be reactive, the decision to practice is

---

[M] The pineal gland releases hormones into the bloodstream based on the firing of neurons and detects hormone levels in the bloodstream, translating neural representations into hormone levels and hormone levels into neural representations.[39]

[N] I have a friend who likes to say that it doesn't really matter whether you have free will or not. If you do, then you better believe you do. If you don't, then you're predetermined to believe that you do.

often a conscious one. In cases where we decide to actually get up and go to the anger management seminar or the addiction treatment center, the conscious decision isn't to not be angry or to not take drugs; the conscious decision is to retrain ourselves.

A more nuanced discussion has appeared in the science fiction literature of the past several decades—with *Star Trek: The Next Generation*, as the android Data tried to become human; with *Blade Runner* and its "replicants"; and recently with the newly reinterpreted *Battlestar Galactica*, in which the humans have to decide whether the Cylons have sufficient free will to be treated as human.

In many of these examples, the journey for the robot to become human is based on the belief that the robots need to feel emotions. A recurring theme in *Star Trek: The Next Generation* is Data's search for emotions. Yet, throughout, he is clearly as human as the rest, with foibles, errors, and decision-making abilities. In *Blade Runner*, the replicants are identifiable only because they do not have the correct emotional reactions to shocking images. But a theme in the movie is the question of whether Rick Deckard, the hard-bitten human detective hunting the replicants, would pass the emotional test for humanity if he were to take it. (This theme is only implicit in the movie but is something Deckard worries about explicitly in the Philip K. Dick novel *Do Androids Dream of Electric Sheep?*, from which *Blade Runner* derives.) In the end, the movie hinges on a decision made by the lead replicant Roy Batty, who decides not to throw Deckard off the building ledge and instead to lift him back up. Deckard wonders at the reasons for the decision but never doubts that the replicant made a decision of his own free will that saved Deckard's life. Similarly, throughout the new *Battlestar Galactica* series, the Cylons make clear decisions, and while the humans debate whether to treat the Cylons as humans or machines, they never doubt for a second that Cylons are dangerous decision-makers.

The problem with all of these discussions is that we haven't (yet) built machines that have free will, and we don't know what it would be like to build such a machine. Obviously, there are many machines that do not have free will. But that doesn't preclude the possibility of a machine with free will. It doesn't preclude the possibility that we are living machines with free will, that we are machines who fall in love, robots who write poetry, that we are physical brains capable of making our own decisions.

Books and papers for further reading

- Antonio Damasio (2010). *Self Comes to Mind: Constructing the Conscious Brain*. New York: Pantheon.
- Jeffrey Gray (2004). *Consciousness: Creeping up on the Hard Problem*. New York: Oxford University Press.
- Robert Kurzban (2010). *Why Everyone (Else) is a Hypocrite*. Princeton, NJ: Princeton University Press.
- Neil Levy (2007). *Neuroethics*. Cambridge, UK: Cambridge University Press.
- Daniel M. Wegner (2002). *The Illusion of Conscious Will*. Cambridge, MA: MIT Press.

EPILOGUE

We've taken quite a long journey in this book, from our first discussions of decision-making and the sense–evaluate–act cycle of the thermostat to imagination, morality, and how we are machines with free will. In this book, we've explored the science of decision-making, and how humans (and other animals) make decisions, sometimes consciously, sometimes less so. We like to think we are rational creatures, but we often make irrational decisions. This irrationality comes from the separation between the Deliberative "self" and the Pavlovian and habit-driven (Procedural) "other," but those other decision-making systems, the Pavlovian action-selection and motivation systems, the situation-recognition (memory) components, the habits learned over years, all make up the person you are. To paraphrase Jonathan Haidt's horse-and-rider analogy,[1] you are *both* the horse and the rider. These are the stories we tell ourselves, the memories that define for us who we are.

Although this is not a self-help book, the theory that the decisions you make arise from multiple, interacting decision-making systems has implications for how we can change our lives if we desire to. The reason that some decisions are made by emotional (Pavlovian) systems, while others are reactive action-chains (Procedural), and others are taken only after extensive consideration of the options (Deliberative) is that each of these systems has advantages and each has disadvantages. The Deliberative system is slow to execute (it takes time to consider those options) but flexible (considering leaving your job doesn't mean you will). The Procedural system is really good for actions that need to happen the same way every time quickly (like playing a musical instrument). Emotional systems are critical for social interactions.

If you could steer yourself from one system to another at the right time, you could improve your decision-making. For example, engaging the Deliberative system makes it easier to reject impulsive, emotional desires. Contingency Management is a technique where one concentrates on a concrete alternative reward as a means of behavioral modification. This seems to have the effect of engaging Deliberative over emotional or reactive systems.[2]

As another example, disengaging the Deliberative system and allowing the Procedural system to run is critical for appropriate performance in sports and other behaviors that require repetitive behaviors. My favorite example of this is how Annie Savoy (Susan Sarandon) distracts the pitcher Ebby LaLoosh's (Tim Robbins') Deliberative system by providing him women's lingerie to wear in the baseball movie *Bull Durham*.[3] Once his (well-trained) Procedural system is given free rein, he discovers that he can pitch strikes reliably. Of course, this only works if the Procedural system has been properly trained. Although we do not generally have conscious control of Procedural behaviors during execution of that behavior, the decision to practice is often a conscious one.[4] As every musician knows, the key to playing a piece well is practicing it.[A]

Similarly, the emotional, Pavlovian systems are critical to making appropriate decisions.[5] Courage is not the absence of fear, but the overcoming of fear.[6] One *should* be afraid of a burning building. And, as we saw in Chapter 23, these emotional reactions are critical to appropriately navigating the social milieu we live in. Altruistic punishment (the willingness to sacrifice some of one's own gain to punish a cheater) occurs because we feel emotional responses to unfairness.[7]

Not only is it possible to train each of the systems individually, it is possible to learn how to steer oneself between systems, learning when to deliberate and when to allow the Procedural system to run.[8] In addition, changes in the support structures (such as the situation-recognition system, Chapter 12) can change one's decisions.[9] For example, realizing that there is "no such thing as one drink" for an alcoholic means that the choices are not between the boring Dr. Jekyll and a suave man-about-town, but rather between Dr. Jekyll and Mr. Hyde. This changes one's decisions.

Our understanding of how we make decisions has enormous implications for how we understand ourselves, how we interact with others, how we see the world around us, and how we define and treat mental dysfunction. Although a lot is known about the decision-making system and how the brain creates the mind, there is a lot that is still unknown. Most of the concepts that we've discussed in this book are still areas of very active research within the scientific community. There are a slew of open questions still unanswered. How do these multiple systems interact? What controls which system drives behavior when the multiple decision systems are in conflict? How does the transition from Deliberative to Procedural (habit) occur? What is self-control, really? How does changing our conceptual narrative change us? How does the Pavlovian motivation system affect the Deliberative and Procedural (habit) action-selection systems? What is the role of attention in evaluation, particularly during deliberation? What does treatment do in addiction or the other psychiatric ailments? What is going wrong in these psychiatric ailments? How do we ascertain the underlying causes? Can we learn to guide each individual patient to the right treatment? There's a lot of work still to do here. What are we going to find next? I don't know. But I'm sure it's going to be a great ride.

A. David Redish
Minneapolis, Minnesota, 2010–2013

[A] Often the push to practice is driven from the outside, as every parent cajoling a child to practice a musical instrument, every drill sergeant driving new recruits, and every advisor pushing graduate students knows.

APPENDIX

In these three appendices, I turn to issues of neuronal function (A), representation (B), and memory (C). Within each of these, there are interesting computational issues that bear indirectly on decision-making processes, but the complexity of which is tangential to the main theme of the book (how we make decisions).

Appendix A

INFORMATION PROCESSING IN NEURONS

dancing sunlight on the path
reveals flashes of information
leaves dancing in the morning breeze

It is often said that the brain is an "information-processing device," that it takes information in from the world, transforms it into an internal representation, and takes actions that change the world around it. Even if the brain does process information, the brain is not a computer like the computer on your desk anymore than the swan we saw in Chapter 2 is an airplane. In this chapter, I will provide a starting discussion of cells, neurons, and information processing therein.

First of all, the brain is made of cells. Each neuron has all of the biological material needed for normal cellular function. Each individual neuron in the brain has a nucleus and shares the same DNA blueprint with every other cell in your body. Each neuron has all of the machinery to translate that DNA blueprint into RNA and then into proteins. Second, a neuron is an information-processing device. It has a tremendous amount of intracellular (and extracellular) machinery that reacts to changes in such a way as to calculate information.

Information

What is *information*? In the modern world, we encounter information processing every day.[A] The mathematics of information that enabled the computer revolution (sometimes called the information revolution) was worked out in the 1940s by Claude

---

[A] In *The Amazing Story of Quantum Mechanics*, Jim Kakalios argues that the technologies that changed our world in the 20th century are all breakthroughs in information processing.

Shannon,[1] an engineer working for Bell Labs,[B] building on work he did in cryptography,[C] both on his own and in collaboration with Alan Turing during World War II.[2]

Mathematically, Shannon realized that "information" was about separating possible codes into groups.[D] Shannon characterized this as answering yes/no questions. Each answer to a yes/no question equaled *one bit* of information. In the modern world, we encounter this definition of information every day. Computer memory and hard drive capacity are generally measured in eight-bit units called "bytes" (as in megabytes [one million bytes] and gigabytes [one billion bytes]). A byte consists of eight small physical things that can each be in one of two states (on/off, yes/no). In the memory of your computer or in a USB flashstick, that small physical thing is usually a tiny magnet that can be flipped back and forth. On a CD, that small physical thing is a miniscule pit dug into the plastic that reflects light of different colors depending how deep it's been dug.

Shannon realized how to use probability theory to mathematically define less than one bit of information. The game *Twenty Questions* is based on this concept. If birds fly and mammals walk, then answering the question *Does it fly?* provides information about whether the person is thinking of a bird or a mammal. Of course, some birds don't fly (think penguins) and some mammals do (think bats). Since *Does it fly?* mostly, but not completely, separates birds and mammals, the answer to *Does it fly?* provides less than one bit of information about whether the person is thinking of a bird or a mammal. Decision-making is about changing our actions based on the information available to us in the world.

Neurons

Neurons (like all cells) maintain a voltage difference between the intracellular and extracellular space. There are more negatively charged ions inside the cell than outside, which creates a voltage difference between the inside and the outside of the cell. In effect, a neuron is like a battery, maintaining a voltage across the cellular membrane. This battery is maintained through small holes in the membrane called *ion channels*.[E] These ion

---

[B] Bell Labs was the research department for the telephone monopoly AT&T. For those too young to remember, the landline telephone system in the United States was originally controlled by a monopoly company AT&T. It was broken up into many little companies in 1984.

[C] The best description of information theory and its role in cryptography that I've ever seen is in Neal Stephenson's *Cryptonomicon*, in which the Allies are trying to determine how to use the German and Japanese codes that they've broken (which they broke using the nascent information theory) in such a way that the Germans and Japanese do not realize that the codes have been broken.

[D] The concept of "information" turns out to be identical to the thermodynamic concept of entropy, and thus the amount of information needed to describe a system is termed the "entropy" of the system. The physics of entropy, information theory, and thermodynamics is beyond the scope of this book, but there are many good books on the subject. I recommend Charles Seife's *Decoding the Universe*, Murray Gell-Mann's *The Quark and the Jaguar*, or Heinz Pagels' *The Cosmic Code* or his *Perfect Symmetry*. James Gleick's new *The Information, A Theory, A History, A Flood* is an excellent discussion of the history and meaning of information theory.

[E] Actually, ion channels are not really holes so much as they are specialized pumps. Each channel will only permit certain ions through. Thus, there are potassium channels, which only allow potassium

(*continued*)

channels are made up of intricately shaped proteins that form mechanical devices that allow certain ions to flow through, while restricting the flow of other ions. Proteins are made up of long chains of amino acids following the blueprint in the DNA, translated through the mechanisms of RNA.

These ion channels are little tiny mechanical machines. While some of them are constituently open, always allowing their specific ions to flow through, others can open and close. For example, one channel type, the voltage-gated potassium channel, literally has a ball of amino acids on a chain of amino acids attached to the base of it. When the voltage in the cell changes, the chain changes shape and the ball pops into the channel, blocking it. As another example, the voltage-gated sodium channel twists like an iris so as to open or close depending on the membrane voltage. There are actually many subtypes of voltage-gated potassium and voltage-gated sodium channels, each with slightly different properties. These properties change the dynamics of the neuron to make it do the information processing it does. This step from which ion channels are expressed where on the neuron to how that neuron processes information is a very active area of research in neuroscience today. Some of these steps are known, some are still being investigated.

Information processing in neurons

The key to information processing in the brain is a phenomenon called the *action potential* or (more colloquially) the "spike." A spike is a short event in which specific channels open up allowing positive ions to rush in, which changes the cross-membrane voltage; then the first set of channels starts to close, and a second set of channels opens up, which brings the voltage back down. This entire process takes a few thousandths of a second (a few milliseconds). A cell integrates changes in its cross-membrane voltage and fires a spike when that voltage gets large enough (crosses a threshold).[3]

Following Shannon's definitions, information can be measured by comparing the group of situations in which a cell (or a set of cells) spikes to the group of situations in which the cell (or set of cells) is silent.[4] Remember that Shannon defined information as separations between groups: spiking or not spiking is a yes/no question about something and carries information about that something, whatever it is. To answer how neuroscientists learn what that something is, we will have to wait until Appendix B, where we will turn to issues of measuring what cells are *tuned* to.

How do cells get information to the next cell? This brings us to the concept of a *synapse*, which connects one cell to another. A spike in one cell releases a chemical (called a *neurotransmitter*) across the very small (20 nanometers or 20 billionths of a meter) gap between the cells and changes the voltage of the other cell. Some synapses are *excitatory* and make the second cell more likely to fire spikes, while other synapses are *inhibitory* and make the second cell less likely to fire spikes.

---

ions through, sodium channels, which only allow sodium through, calcium channels, chloride channels, etc. How ion channels work and how the membrane voltage is generated is well understood, and descriptions can be found in many neuroscience textbooks. For those interested, *Neuroscience*, edited by Dale Purves and colleagues, is an excellent starting point. For those who want a more in-depth understanding of the channels themselves, Bertil Hille's *Ion Channels of Excitable Membranes* remains the classic text and is readable by an advanced undergraduate.

Of course, whenever we're talking about biological systems, things are never so simple. Actually, there are lots of different neurotransmitters and lots of different synaptic receptors to detect them. There are synaptic receptors on the presynaptic neuron. There are also synaptic receptors, called *G-protein-coupled receptors*, that, instead of allowing ions to flow in, release an attached protein complex, which then interacts with other proteins inside the cell. This engenders an extremely complex interflow of intracellular information processing. In general, we won't need to go into detail about protein cascades for this book, but they are an important part of cellular processing, particularly in how cells change during learning.

To a first approximation, neurons take information in through their dendrites, perform computation on it in the dendrites and the soma, and then send information out through the axon, primarily by deciding when and whether to fire an action potential (spike), which travels down the axon and releases a chemical across a synapse connecting to other neurons in the brain. As with all first approximations, this description is often wrong in detail, even if correct in general. Some neurons are also performing calculations in their dendrites; some neurons connect through dendrite-to-dendrite synapses; some neurons do not fire action potentials; some neurons connect up to other neurons with electrical connections rather than chemical synapses; etc. But the starting description of a neuron with a dendrite, a soma, and an axon, connected to other neurons via synapses, is good enough for now.

You can imagine each neuron poised between excitatory inputs encouraging it to fire and inhibitory inputs suppressing it. The brain spends its time poised in a dynamic balance between choices, like a baseball player up on the balls of his feet, ready to jump forward to steal second base or ready to dive back to first. It does this for exactly the same reason that the base runner does: so it can react quickly.

Current theories suggest that many brain dysfunctions are conditions in which something has fallen out of balance. Epilepsy, for example, is almost certainly a consequence of an instability in excitation (encouraging neurons to fire spikes) and inhibition (holding them back).[5] What is interesting about the nature of dynamic balance (particularly because of its dependence on feedback) is that you can get the wildfire spiking of epilepsy with either an instability in excitation or an instability in inhibition. Other diseases as well, such as schizophrenia, are also now being investigated as dynamic balances gone unstable.[6]

This balance exists at all levels, from the systems level, where multiple decision-making systems compete for a decision, down to the neural level, where both excitatory and inhibitory inputs balance to keep neurons firing at just the right rate, to the subcellular level, where learning and memory reside.

Memory

Memory can be defined as changes that reflect a history so that future responses differ because of it. Just as anything that allowed us to differentiate two signals is information, anything that reliably changes in response to a past can be thought of as a memory of that past. The dent in the car fender "remembers" that it was hit. The fender will be weaker and may respond differently the next time. One of the tenets of this book is that all of the psychological and mental observations that we observe have physical instantiations.

The physical instantiation of memory resides in changes in the synapses that connect neurons one to the other and in the internal protein cascades within each neuron. The primary changes in the nervous system during learning occur in the synapses—how much of an effect the presynaptic cell has on the postsynaptic cell when the presynaptic cell fires its spike. These changes are now known to exist throughout the brain, in the hippocampus, cortex, cerebellum, basal ganglia, and even the spinal cord.[7] We now know that these connection strengths depend on the internal milieu of the protein cascades within the cell and the timing of the presynaptic and postsynaptic spikes.[8]

A journey from sensory to motor

It might be useful to take a journey from a sensory receptor into the brain. As we saw in our thermostat example at the beginning of the book, a decision process requires measuring the world, processing the information hidden within those measurements, and then acting upon that information. How does the neural system perceive the world? The first step is that there must be sensory neurons—neurons that fire action potentials in response to sensory stimuli.[F] Some cells, like the rods and cones in the retina, react through protein cascades. Rods and cones contain a light-sensitive protein called an *opsin*; in response to photons hitting the retina, these molecules change their shape, which causes a cascade of other protein changes, the last of which is to open up an ion channel and change the voltage in the cell. In other cells, the translation protein is a direct ion channel itself. For example, hair cells in the ear contain ion channels with little springs made of protein in them. As the sound wave moves the hairs on the cell, the hairs pull on the protein springs, stretching the ion channel open and allowing ions to flow in, changing the voltage of the cell. So, literally, these cells have sensors that translate or transduce the physical reality of the world into the inner information-world of our brains.

On the other end, motor neurons send axons to muscles. Muscles are excitable cells just like neurons and can also fire action potentials (spikes). Because the muscles all line up in arranged structures, the firing of many action potentials in muscle tissue can be detected electrically quite easily. These muscle-based action potentials are what is being detecting in an electrocardiogram (EKG [the K comes from the German *Kardio*, meaning "heart"]). In other muscle groups, these same signals are generally detected with electromyography (EMG [*myo* comes from the Greek word for muscle]). As you move any muscle in your body, the muscles are firing action potentials. The action potentials open up calcium channels in the muscle cell, which are then translated back into physical force by a calcium-sensitive protein (*myosin*) that contracts in the presence of calcium.

[F] Actually, most direct sensory cells in the mammal do not fire action potentials. They release synaptic chemicals at a rate proportional to their voltage. The next cells downstream (e.g., the visual ganglion cells in the retina or the neurons in the auditory nerve) do, however, generally fire action potentials.

The neural network that is the brain can take information in from the world through its sensory systems and can act on the world through its motor systems. This book is about the steps in the middle, how a network of cells, in constant dynamic flux, processes the information therein to take the right actions in the right situations.

Books and papers for further reading

- Eric Kandel (2006). *In Search of Memory: The Emergence of a New Science of Mind.* New York: Norton.
- Joseph E. LeDoux (2002). *The Synaptic Self.* London, UK: Penguin.
- Peter Dayan and Larry F. Abbott (2001). *Theoretical Neuroscience.* Cambridge, MA: MIT Press.

The details of how neurons themselves work are given in the first few chapters of many neuroscience textbooks, many of which are actually easy to read for those who are not scared to dive in.

- Dale Purves et al. (2008). *Neuroscience.* Sunderland, MA: Sinauer Associates.
- Neil R. Carlson (2010). *Physiology of Behavior.* Boston: Pearson.
- Eric Kandel, James H. Schwartz, and Thomas M. Jessell (2000). *Principles of Neural Science.* New York: Elsevier.

Appendix B

GLEANING INFORMATION FROM THE BRAIN

Clouds hide the summit,
but I create it in my mind.
Seeing the mountain,
I create it in my mind.

Neurons transmit information by firing action potentials and connect to other neurons via synapses. As we have just seen, an action potential is a short change in the membrane voltage of the cell (usually a millisecond or so in duration). If we had a wire or other conducting medium near that neuron when it fired its action potential, it would be detectable on the wire as a quick spike. If we had a sensitive enough instrument, we could detect that spike. There are many technologies that allow us to see signals that reflect this activity. These technologies allow us to (in effect) read the animal's mind, to ask what it is thinking about, to see what it sees, and to hear what it hears. We will also see technologies that allow us to manipulate (at a limited level) those physical signals and change what is in the animal's mind, what it sees and what it hears.

Representing information with spiking cells: Tuning curves

Each neuron fires its spikes carrying information about some aspect of the world, some sensory signal, some motor action to be taken, some internal process, or some combination of all three. One of the key questions in behavioral neuroscience is *What information does a neuron's spiking pattern encode?*

We generally answer this question by relating the neural firing of a cell to some behavioral variable through a *tuning curve*. Classically, a tuning curve defines the likelihood that you will see spikes from a given neuron when an event occurs. For example, an auditory cell in the primary auditory cortex may be tuned to a specific frequency of sound. If you hear a tone at that frequency, that cell will fire spikes. Other cells will be tuned to aspects of that sound, the timbre, even the specific song if you recognize it. A visual cell in the primary visual cortex may be tuned to a spot of light, but other cells in deeper visual cortices (sometimes called "higher-order cortices" because their representations require more processing) are tuned to faces, trees, or other objects.

It is important to note that a cell's tuning curve does not explain why the cell is tuned to that information in the world, only that the cell's firing is *correlated with it*. Visual cells are tuned to visual signals because light impacts the retina, which fires the retinal ganglion cells, which transmits information to the thalamus, which then sends signals to the visual cortex, making the spikes fired by the neuron in visual cortex correlated to the visual input. Primary motor cortex cells are tuned to specific muscle movements because they send their output to motor-controlling neurons in the spinal cord, so their firing influences the muscle and their spikes are correlated with its movements.

Many neuroscientists will say that tuning curves can only be applied to behavioral variables that directly relate to the immediate world of the animal, sensory signals (following a flash of light, a specific sound) or motor actions (preceding the movement of a specific muscle), but the brain is a physical object. When you think of your grandmother, some cells are firing that represent the information about your grandmother. If you think about what she looked like the last time you saw her, cells are firing that represent information about her face. If you think about her voice, cells are firing that represent information about what she sounded like.

Much of the older popular neuroscience literature talked about the "grandmother cell," implying that there was a single cell in the brain that fired to thoughts of your grandmother and only to your grandmother. As we will see later, this hypothesis is incorrect. Representations in the brain are *distributed*. Some cells will fire more to women than to men, other cells to old people more than young, and still other cells to specific aspects of your grandmother such as her voice or her face, and it is that *set* of cells that represents the concept of your grandmother, not any one of those cells.

To understand the concept of a distributed representation, imagine turning on the television to find it showing a football game. You want to know which teams are playing because you want to decide if it's a game you want to watch, but the camera is just passing over the audience. (To make this thought-experiment work, you'll need to ignore the fact that modern television sports programs have little text-boxes in the corner of the screen that tell you who's playing and what the score is.) From the clothes of the fans, you could probably make a very good guess about the two teams. Looking at any one fan won't tell you. Maybe that person just happens to like that team. Fans might not be wearing the team jersey, but they'll likely be wearing clothes with the team colors. If you notice that most of the fans are wearing a specific team's colors, that's a pretty good indication of which teams are playing. You'll probably notice that there are two teams' jerseys and colors that are much more commonly represented. The fans are representing information about which teams are playing. In fact, you can probably determine which team is doing well at a given moment by the expressions on the faces of one team's fans versus another. The fans are a distributed representation of the two teams—you can learn a lot about the game just by watching the fans.

Mathematically, a cell can represent any variable as long as its spiking is reliably related to that variable. For example, cells in the rodent hippocampus are tuned to the location of the animal.[1] As the animal runs around an environment, a given *place cell* will fire spikes in a preferred location (the *place field* of the cell). This is not a sensory response, nor is it a motor initiation signal; it is actually a representation of location.[A]

Tuning curves often entail firing strongly to a single preferred stimulus, which then falls off as the stimulus differs from that preferred stimulus. For example, auditory neurons in the primary auditory cortex have a preferred frequency at which they fire the most spikes; as the supplied sound frequency drops off in each direction, the number of spikes that the cell fires decreases.[2] Each auditory neuron has a different preferred frequency. When you hear a note, each cell will fire spikes reflecting the harmonics of that note. Place cells in the hippocampus have a preferred location. At the center of that place field, the cell fires the most spikes the most reliably; at distances from that place field, the cell fires fewer and fewer spikes, until it becomes quiet. Each place cell is tuned to a different location in space in a different environment. The representation of a position in the environment entails a *distribution* of cells firing, some (with preferred locations near the position) firing a lot and some (with preferred locations far from the position) firing only a little.

However, tuning curves don't have to have a single preferred stimulus.[3] All that matters is that the spiking of the cell be reliably informative about the behavioral variable. Because information is about defining groups, this is equivalent to saying that the behavioral variable must be reliably informative about the spiking times of the cell.[4]

This means that we can determine information about the animal's representation of the world from the firing of cells. Let's go back to place cells. Each place cell is tuned to a different location in space. This means that we can invert the tuning curve—if we know what location is represented by that place cell, then when that place cell fires spikes, we can infer that the animal is representing information about that location. Even so, a typical place field is pretty large. (In rats, place fields can range in size from 20 centimeters to meters in length.[5]) Even more importantly, the relationship between firing spikes and the location of the animal is not 100%. Sometimes a cell fires spikes when the animal is outside the cell's place field; sometimes the cell doesn't fire when the animal is in the place field. But if we have two cells with overlapping place fields, we can be more accurate because we can determine if the first cell is firing but not the second, if the second cell is firing but not the first, or if both are firing. Current technologies allow us to record as many as several hundred cells, simultaneously, from awake, behaving animals. By integrating information from hundreds of cells, we can decode location quite accurately.[6] From several hundred cells, we can typically decode location to an accuracy of better than 1 centimeter! We can even determine when the cells are representing a location different from the animal's current location;[7] we can determine where the animal is imagining or thinking about. We can read the rat's mind.

[A] How these place cells determine the location of the animal in order to decide when to fire spikes is a complex issue—the rat does not have a built-in GPS to determine its location. What actually happens is that it keeps track of its position by dead reckoning—if I know where I am and I take a step forward, I still know where I am, I'm one step forward of where I was—and learns to associate spatial cues (like landmarks) with those location representations, allowing the animal to reset its representation when lost. For those interested, my earlier book *Beyond the Cognitive Map* describes this process in great detail.

Other signals

Local field potentials (LFP)

Since we've already talked about recording electrical signals and identifying neural firing patterns from them, a good next signal to discuss is the *local field potential* (LFP). If one takes the same electrical signal appearing on the electrodes and listens to the low-frequency components instead of the high-frequency components, one can record LFPs.[B] Currently, no one is completely sure how LFPs are generated, but they seem to be related to the slow electrical currents arising from synapses.[8]

In many brain structures like the hippocampus and the basal ganglia, nearby cells do not tend to be processing the same information, and LFP signals do not carry information about the task at hand, but they carry information about how the brain is processing those tasks.[9] These LFPs tend to indicate the state of the system and most likely reflect different processing regimes. For example, when you are attentive, actively listening to someone talking to you or actively trying to understand new information you are reading about, the LFP in your hippocampus shows a 7 to 10 Hz, almost sinusoidal rhythm, called "rhythmic slow activity" (RSA) or *theta* (for the frequency band it covers). In contrast, if you are fading out, not really listening, losing your attention, nodding off, the LFP in your hippocampus shows a more broad-spectrum arrhythmic activity called "large amplitude irregular activity" (LIA).[10]

In contrast, in the mammalian neocortex, nearby cells do process similar information.[11] (One of the most remarkable things about the mammalian cortex is that although the brain itself is unquestionably three-dimensional in its connectivity and its structure, the cortex itself is more of a sheet than a three-dimensional structure. The six layers of cortex form a thin sheet that changes tremendously in area but not much in depth between mammals. Evolution seems to be taking a specific template and copying it in two dimensions to make larger and larger cortices.[12]) Because the processing units in cortex are arranged in small 0.3-millimeter-wide columns, where all the cells in a column are processing similar things, there is evidence that LFPs in the cortex can carry signals about the information in that column.[13]

Imagine you are trying to understand the game of American football but you can't see the game. All you have is a microphone, which you could lower to listen to a single person. Perhaps you get to listen to the quarterback or the coach and learn a lot about the game. This is like single-cell recording, where you find that the signal on your microphone tells you a lot about the behavioral variable (the game). On the other hand, you might end up listening to the drunk fan in the third row, or the businessman discussing stock sales, and not find much relationship to what is going on in the game. If, however, you pull your microphone up and listen to the roar of the crowd, you can also learn about the game. If you hear

---

[B] Remember that spikes are 1-millisecond blips, so they are best seen with frequency filters set around 1 kilohertz (changes happening on the order of 1 millisecond). Spikes are usually recorded using filters set from 600 Hz to 10 kHz, which pick up things happening on the order of a millisecond or faster. LFPs are usually recorded using filters set from 0.1 to 400 Hz, which pick up things happening on the order of tenths or hundredths of a second.

the crowd chanting "Defense! Defense!" or the crowd being really quiet, you can determine pretty accurately which team is on offense when. You can learn when a really good (or really bad) play happens just by listening to the volume of the crowd. That's like LFP in the hippocampus or the basal ganglia. If all the fans from one team are sitting together and all the fans from the other team are sitting together, you might even be able to tell which team is winning by the volume of the shouts of each group. That's like LFP in the cortex.

The electroencephalogram (EEG)

Many people are familiar with a form of LFP recorded outside the skull: the electroencephalogram (EEG).[14] EEG electrodes are placed around the scalp and record the same sorts of waves as LFPs. Just as with LFPs, EEGs are primarily used to categorize brain states. Many people, for example, are familiar with slow-wave and REM sleep, which can be identified by EEG oscillations. Different moods and attention states can also be measured by EEG changes. For example, calm, relaxed states are often identified with EEG rhythms (arising from the cortex) in the 8 to 12 Hz range (confusingly called "alpha waves" in the EEG literature and "theta waves" in the LFP literature).

People can learn to control their EEG rhythms.[15] There are now games available that use EEG signals to control balls or lights. Touted as allowing one to "control the ball with your mind," these games are measuring EEG signals from a headset and using the ratio of the power in different frequency regimes (usually alpha [8–12 Hz] to beta [12–30 Hz]) to change the speed of a fan that blows a ball up or down.[16]

When EEG signals are measured in response to impulse events rather than looking at the ongoing frequencies in the oscillation, these signals are sometimes referred to as *event-related potentials* (ERPs).[17] They occur when a single event drives enough activity in the brain to be detected as a sharp change in the EEG.

One of the most common ERP signals studied is the *error-related negativity* (ERN), in which EEG recorded from the frontal part of the scalp changes in response to making an error.[18] Interestingly, this activity occurs approximately 100 milliseconds after one starts the movement, which can be long before the movement is complete. (The ERN seems to reflect that "oops, that's wrong" signal we sometimes feel when we react too quickly.) We now know that the ERN arises from signals in the anterior cingulate cortex, which is involved in monitoring actions and allowing one to take a different action than one usually might. (See, for example, the discussion of overcoming a phobia and facing one's fears in our discussion of self-control in Chapter 15.)

Recording spikes from human patients

The primary information-measuring experiments in this book come from animal experiments because we have the technology to record from single neurons and neuronal ensembles in animals.[c] Such technology works in humans as well but requires

---

[c] It is important to note the great care taken by neuroscientists, particularly behavioral neuroscientists, in the treatment of their animals. A distressed animal does not perform tasks well, particularly complicated tasks like those required for decision-making experiments. All animal experiments

(continued)

implantation of wire electrodes into the subject; therefore, this is done only for clinical treatment.

Sometimes scientists are allowed to piggyback onto the clinical implantation and (with the permission of the subject and the oversight of a review board) record from electrodes implanted for other reasons. Two examples where such electrodes are routinely implanted are for the determination of the initiation sites of epileptic seizures and for deep-brain stimulation for the treatment of Parkinson's disease.

Briefly, epilepsy entails neurons going haywire. The first treatment attempted is generally antiseizure drugs, but that works for only a limited portion of the epileptic population.[19] If pharmacological treatments don't work, an alternate option is to literally burn away the part of the brain going haywire. Of course, damaging the wrong part of the brain is extremely problematic (we have seen some tragic examples in this book), and physicians are very careful to do their best to ensure that they get only the right starting point for the epilepsy and that the part they are going to remove is not involved in critical intellectual faculties. To do this, they implant electrodes and record single neurons and LFPs as the subject does tasks.[20] Since having the electrodes in one's brain is not a painful process and recording from neurons does not damage the brain, many patients are happy to do a few extra cognitive tasks and to allow scientists to record from their brain during the procedure.

These recordings, however, can be taken in only very limited situations (during the rare times when a patient has a clinical reason for having electrodes implanted) and in patients with dysfunctional brains (that's why they're getting the clinical treatment). To study normal function in nonpatients, we need a technology capable of recording neural signals from awake subjects. We've already discussed EEG. There is a related measurement technology called MEG that works like EEG but uses the magnetic component of the electromagnetic wave. Although MEG is less distorted by the skull than EEG, both MEG and EEG suffer from an inability to localize the signal. These technologies can target "frontal cortex" versus "visual cortex" (which is in the far back of the brain), but they can't tell you what is going on in the shape-recognition component of the visual cortex, or the striatum of the basal ganglia, or the hippocampus.

Functional magnetic resonance imaging (fMRI)

If you've been following neuroscience over the past few decades in the popular press, you are probably wondering why I haven't brought in functional magnetic resonance imaging (fMRI) until now. fMRI has become beloved by the popular press because it allows insight into the brains of normal human subjects. It creates beautiful pictures. It can be run on normal people performing complex, human tasks, such as language and cognition. But what's really important to understand about fMRI (and its cousins, such as positron emission tomography [PET]) is that it measures blood flow, not neural activity.[21]

---

done in any modern university are required to be approved by an animal-care committee that includes both veterinarians and community activists as well as scientists. This committee is tasked not only with checking the treatment of the animals but also with determining if the experiment being done is "important enough" to justify the use of the animals.

fMRI measures the magnetic spin of hemoglobin molecules in the blood. Mammalian blood carries oxygen to the tissues by binding it to the hemoglobin molecule. Hemoglobin with bound oxygen is redder than unbound hemoglobin; it also has a different resonance to magnetic changes. An fMRI machine is a very big, very strong set of magnets. By changing the magnetic field in specific ways, it can detect the level of oxygen in the blood.

Modern high-field magnet fMRI machines can measure the oxygenation level in approximately a one-millimeter cube of tissue. While a 1 mm×1 mm×1 mm voxel (volume-pixel) sounds small, individual neurons are typically 50 micrometers in diameter (8000 times smaller). For computational reasons, fMRI experiments often use much larger voxels, even as large as 3 or 4 mm on a side. (PET requires an even larger voxel size.) That means that each voxel could contain a hundred thousand neurons. Even allowing that neurons are only a small portion of the brain tissue (most of which contains support structures, like capillaries, glial support cells, and the axons and dendrites of the neurons), that voxel still contains tens of thousands of neurons.

So what does blood oxygenation have to do with neural activity? At this point, we know they are related, but not exactly how. This is still an area of active investigation in neuroscience.[22] We know that when an area is "neurally active" (for example, your primary visual cortex is more active when you are looking at a flashing visual scene, like a movie, than when you are closing your eyes and listening to an auditory scene, say listening to music), the cells are using glucose, drawing extra energy from the body.[23;D] The overworked neurons send a signal to the capillaries to allow more blood to flow. The neurons don't actually need more oxygen, so there's more blood flowing, but the same amount of oxygen is pulled out, so what's flowing by becomes less deoxygenated, which is detectable with fMRI. These changes in blood flow are called the hemodynamic response, which occurs over the course of about 4 to 5 seconds. (Remember that a single neural spike is 1 millisecond—that is, 1/1000th of a second!) Typical human reaction time to a surprising stimulus is only a few hundred milliseconds.[E] fMRI researchers have developed ways to infer the "neural activity" from the hemodynamic response to identify the timing, by essentially relating the blood flow to events that occurred 4 to 5 seconds before the signal was detected, but even that can't get to what single neurons are doing or the specific timing of their spikes.

It's not clear at this point what is causing the neurons to spend all that energy.[25] This means that fMRI can tell you which parts of the brain are working hard, but it can't tell you how the neurons in that part of the brain are processing information.

[D] The brain is a very energy-costly component of your body. Even though your brain is only a couple of percent of your body weight (a typical brain weighs a little less than 1.5 kg [3 lbs]), it consumes about 20% of your typical energy reserves.[24]

[E] This is the key to baseball—a 100-mph pitch takes 400 milliseconds to reach the plate. This means that a batter has about less than half the distance between the mound and the plate to decide whether or not to hit the ball and to determine where the ball will be and when it will cross the plate. Of course, if a batter can predict what pitch is going to come before the pitcher throws the pitch, the batter can be better prepared to recognize the pitch. This is the essence of intelligence—using information and expectation to help make better decisions quickly.

Correlation and causation

All of the technologies described above are *correlational*. They ask to what extent two signals change together: a neural signal (firing of neurons, LFPs, EEG, blood flow in the brain) and a behavioral variable (the location of the animal, a sensory signal, a motor action). Logically, correlation is not causation. Just because two things co-occur does not mean that one has caused the other. Correlation is necessary (though not sufficient) for causation, and, in practice, it's a pretty good indicator of causation. Nevertheless, scientists in general, and medical scientists in particular, are particularly concerned with causation because they do not want to make the mistake of thinking that two things that co-occur are causing one another. They have, thus, developed several technologies that allow control of the system.

Lesions

The oldest method of manipulating the system was to damage it physically, to lesion part of it. If that part is critical for accomplishing some task, then the animal (human or otherwise) will be impaired at that task. Obviously, one cannot go in and lesion human tissues for experimental purposes. However, the brain is a particularly sensitive biological organ, requiring constant blood flow. Cutting off the blood (or even just the oxygen) supply for even a few minutes can lead to neuronal death, leaving the person with an unfortunate brain lesion.[26] This is what happens during a stroke, for example.[F]

Because of the way that the blood vessels in the brain branch, a common stroke occurs above the right parietal cortex (just above and behind your right ear).[28] When this part of the brain is damaged, people have trouble recognizing the left side of visual objects.[G] This inability to recognize objects on one side of the visual field is called *hemispatial neglect* because it entails the inability to process (it neglects) half of (hemi) the spatial visual field. Patients with hemispatial neglect will draw only the right side of a clock, and will see the clock at all only if it is on the right side of their visual field.

Hemispatial neglect even occurs in imagined spaces. In a classic experiment, Eduardo Bisiach and Claudio Luzatti asked hemispatial neglect patients to imagine the Piazza Del Duomo in Milan (the patients' native city).[30] They asked the patients to imagine standing on the south end of the Piazza and to name the buildings in the square. The patients each listed only the buildings on the east side (their right). When they were asked to imagine standing on the north end and to name the buildings, they named only those on the west side (their right). When pressed, they said that was all they could

---

[F] Actually, in a stroke, several damaging processes occur over the course of minutes to hours to days. One of those processes is that the decreased blood flow can mean that cells fall out of balance and start to fire at high rates, which drives the cells to death. Treatment that can reach the cells before they die can help reduce or even prevent brain damage due to stroke.[27]

[G] Sensory and motor systems cross in the brain. Thus, the left visual field and the left hand are both processed by the right side of the brain. What, in the evolution of the systems, drove them to cross is still being debated, but there is some evidence that early prey animals have direct connections from sensory systems to the opposite-side muscles.[29] If something is coming at you on the left side, you want to go right fast!

imagine, even though they had named the other buildings only a few minutes earlier! Visual imagination uses the same perceptual systems that we use in seeing.[31]

Other common strokes notoriously affect certain motor and language areas, leading to inabilities to process language. Because different strokes affect the ability to recognize or to produce language, even as early as the 1870s, Paul Broca (1824–1880) and Carl Wernicke (1848–1905) were able to separately identify the locations of the human brain that controlled speech production (now called *Broca's area*) or speech recognition (now called *Wernicke's area*).[32]

Brain lesions can also arise from medical procedures, some intentional, others not. For example, epilepsy that cannot be controlled by pharmacological means (with drugs) can still sometimes be controlled by taking out the focus or starting site.[33] Epilepsy is like an avalanche or a wildfire: it has a starting point, from which it spreads. If that starting point is consistent from seizure to seizure within a patient and can be found, it can be removed. Of course, removing a part of the brain damages its ability to process information, but sometimes a balance has to be found between living with epilepsy and living with a damaged brain. Hippocampal resection (removal) in epileptic patients (such as H.M.) was critical to the discovery that there are at least two separate decision-making systems (Deliberative, dependent on hippocampal function, and Procedural, independent of hippocampal function).[34]

The problem with inferring function from lesion studies is that solving tasks requires lots of components. Let's go back to the thermostat analogy in Chapter 2—there are lots of lesions that could be made to the thermostat that would make your house cold. The furnace could be broken. If it's a gas furnace, the pilot light could be out or the gas turned off. The temperature sensor could be broken. All of these would cause the furnace not to be on and the house to be cold, but we wouldn't want to conclude that the temperature sensor and the pilot light were doing the same thing.

The other problem with lesions is that of *compensation*. As biological organisms, we have backup systems. (During most of evolution, there was no repair shop to take ourselves to if something broke down, so animals that evolved backup systems were more likely to survive and procreate than those without.) If an animal has had enough time to recover from the lesion, it may have found new ways to do something and may be able to solve the same tasks in different ways from how an intact animal would solve them.

Temporary inactivation of parts of the brain

To prevent compensation, and since one cannot morally control the lesions one sees in humans (the only human lesions one is going to see are caused by natural phenomena), scientists have developed several complex techniques to inactivate parts of the brain reliably. The most common technique used in animals is pharmacological, in which a very small amount of chemical that temporarily affects the neurons is infused into an area of the brain. For example, lidocaine blocks a certain kind of sodium ion channel, which prevents neurons from firing. When the dentist injects lidocaine under the gum, it prevents the nerves in the skin from communicating with the brain, leaving your mouth numb to any pain that would be caused by the subsequent procedure.

In humans, one does not want to inject chemicals into the brains of experimental subjects, but a new technology has been recently developed called *transcranial magnetic stimulation* (TMS).[35] TMS creates a quickly changing magnetic field that can stimulate and then disrupt neural firing in a targeted area of cortex. The effect is disruptive but transient, wearing off after a few minutes.[H]

Genetic manipulations

Because the neuronal processes (such as the synaptic channels that listen to specific neurotransmitters) depend on the genetic structure of the cell on an ongoing basis, changing that genetic structure changes how the cell processes information. New technologies are now available that allow direct manipulation of that genetic structure.[37];[I] If the DNA is changed (say to include the information to build a new, different kind of ion channel), then the cell will follow that DNA.

We now know that DNA is more like a programming language, with "if–then" statements and other sorts of local control (as in, "if protein X is present, then also generate protein Y"). This means that modern genetic manipulations can express new proteins (new ion channels, new processes) so that they appear only in a limited subset of cells, such as only in the CA3 neurons of the hippocampus; or so that they appear only in the presence of an extrinsic chemical, such as the antibiotic doxycycline; or so that they only appear after a certain time, such as only in cells that are active (firing a lot of spikes) during the task.[39] These manipulations produce changes in the abilities of animals to solve tasks, which informs us how the system works, physically.

In the past few years, researchers have developed a new technology where a light-sensitive ion channel is genetically implanted into an animal.[40] These channels produce voltage changes in response to certain frequencies of light. This means that if a light is shined on cells with these channels in them, the cells can be induced to fire spikes or prevented from firing spikes. Because these ion channels can be placed in specific cells in specific brain areas, it can give remarkable control of the neural mechanism. This is a burgeoning field called *optogenetics* and has the potential to revolutionize our understanding of the actual mechanisms of brain function.

Stimulation—electrical manipulations

Of course, cellular systems are also electrical, and one can also pass current into the system to manipulate it. For example, a common treatment for Parkinson's disease is deep-brain stimulation, in which an electrode is placed into a structure (commonly the subthalamic nucleus, a part of the basal ganglia). Regular stimulation from this electrode (at between 50 and 200 Hz, depending on what works for the patient) somehow resets the subthalamic nucleus, allowing it to process information correctly again.[41] Although deep-brain stimulation works wonders in some patients, we don't know why, we don't

---

[H] The safety of TMS is still being debated.[36] For most people, it seems that the short-term effects wear off pretty quickly, but the long-term effects are still unknown.

[I] It should be noted that we have been able to manipulate genes for thousands of years through selective breeding.[38] Humans bred dogs to be more friendly, cows to give more milk, and corn to be edible long before modern genetic manipulations. Modern technologies just make the manipulation more direct.

know what the mechanism is. There are lots of theories, including that it prevents neural firing, thus shutting down a dysfunctional structure; that it resets neural oscillations that have become pathological; and that it is making it easier (or harder) for axons that pass by the structure to transmit information.[42]

Stimulation can also be used to manipulate information being represented within the brain.[J] In the mid-1990s, William Newsome and his colleagues were able to change decisions made by a monkey watching a visual stimulus by stimulating certain parts of the visual cortex. The monkey had to decide if a set of dots on a screen was moving in one direction or another. By stimulating the part of the brain that represented visual motion, they could change the monkey's decision, presumably by changing its perception.[43]

Actually, stimulation to write information into the brain has been used in humans for over 40 years. Cochlear implants work by laying electrical contacts along the inner ear.[44] An external microphone translates the sound into the appropriate electrical signal that the ear cells expect. The electrical contacts stimulate the cells, allowing the brain to hear sounds.

Several laboratories have attempted to use retinal implants to restore vision in blind patients.[45] Similar to the cochlear implants, external images are translated by a camera to electrical signals that are sent to stimulation electrodes in the retina. Early clinical trials are now under way. One of the major complications of both the cochlear and visual implants is that the stimulation has to match the neural representations that the brain expects. By understanding the principles of representation, we've been able to begin the process of cybernetics, actually recovering lost function.

Books and papers for further reading

- Andrea M. Green and John F. Kalaska (2011). Learning to move machines with the mind. *Trends in Neurosciences, 34,* 61–75.
- Adam Johnson, André A. Fenton, Cliff Kentros, and A. David Redish (2009). Looking for cognition in the structure in the noise. *Trends in Cognitive Sciences, 13,* 55–64.
- Frederick Rieke, David Warland, Rob de Ruyter van Steveninck, and William Bialek (1996). *Spikes.* Cambridge, MA: MIT Press.

[J] If you still need convincing at this point that the mind exists within the brain, this is the final proof. Manipulating the spiking of cells within the brain changes the perception, the decision, and the action taken. We truly are physical beings.

Appendix C

CONTENT-ADDRESSABLE MEMORY

> Cacti glisten in the sun.
> Then clouds hid the mountain,
> the streets like canyons rushed with water...
>
> I smell sweet
> prickly pear in bloom.

Memories in the brain are stored as patterns of firing across cells and are retrieved by the content they contain. This process is called "pattern completion" because a memory is retrieved by completing a partial pattern of cellular firing. The neural mechanisms of this are well understood and have important implications for how we recognize and remember, which has important implications for decision-making systems.

When a digital camera takes a picture of your kid's birthday party and writes it onto its flash memory card, it translates that picture into a set of on-and-off signals ("bits"[A]), which it writes onto the card. It then writes the location into the "file allocation table," which is basically an index of locations on the memory card. When you want to recall the picture, the camera checks the index, follows it, and reads the file. When the camera first stored the picture on its memory card, it gave it a name like `img_3541.jpg`, which tells you nothing about the content of that image. Your brain can also store information like the memory of your kid's birthday party in small changes across many neurons, in this case through changes in the connection strength between neurons. But there's no central index. Instead, the full memory is retrieved from the partial content—the smell of the birthday cake, the sound of kids' laughter, the sight of a specific toy.

[A] Remember that one bit is the answer to one yes/no question (Appendix A). Eight bits = one byte. When your computer has 4 GB of memory, that's 4 gigabytes, or 4 billion bytes. Of course, it wasn't that long ago that computers only had 1 MB (one megabyte = 1 million bytes) or even 640 KB (one kilobyte = 1 thousand bytes). Now, the flash card in my digital camera has 32 GB, and even larger ones are available.

Retrieval   Image   Content-addresable memory
by index

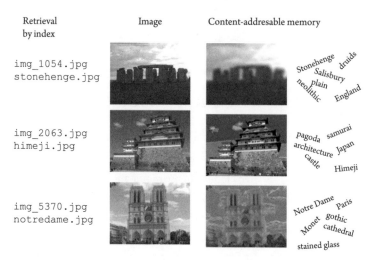

img_1054.jpg   *Stonehenge druids Salisbury plain neolithic England*

stonehenge.jpg

img_2063.jpg   *Pagoda samurai architecture Japan castle Himeji*

himeji.jpg

img_5370.jpg   *Notre Dame Paris Monet gothic cathedral stained glass*

notredame.jpg

Figure C.1 CONTENT-ADDRESSABLE MEMORY. Information can be addressed by indexes (whether by related names [such as stonehenge.jpg] or by unrelated names [such as img_1054.jpg]) or by content-addressable memory. Content-addressable memories are stored so that similar pictures and similar concepts are linked. Thus, a blurry image of Stonehenge, a paper-cutout image of Himeji, and a pencil drawing of Notre Dame retrieve their respective pictures. Similarly, memories can be retrieved by conceptual content.

The term *content-addressable memory* comes from the computer science and psychology literatures of the 1980s. In computer science, the term was used to contrast with index-addressable memory, which is how your laptop, desktop, or smartphone stores information.[1] In psychology, the term was used because human memory is triggered by content, like the sights, sounds, or smells of the birthday party.[2] (Compare Figure C.1.) The concept, though, comes from Donald Hebb's famous 1949 book.[3]

Cell assemblies

One of the most famous sentences in neuroscience is "cells that fire together wire together," which is supposedly from a 1949 book on neuropsychology by the psychologist Donald Hebb. However, that sentence isn't actually in Hebb's book; instead, the citation is to a paragraph that concludes, "When an axon of cell A is near enough to excite a cell B and repeatedly or persistently takes part in firing it, some growth process or metabolic change takes place in one or both cells such that A's efficiency, as one of the cells firing B, is increased" (Hebb, 1949/2002, p. 62). From this paragraph, we get the terms *Hebbian synapse* and *Hebbian learning*.

The concept that co-firing leads to an increase in connectivity almost certainly predates Hebb. In a sense, it is the obvious translation of the theories that mentation is associative, which goes back to David Hume in the 1700s, if not earlier.[4] Hebb himself says that the general idea is an old one (Hebb, 1949/2002, p. 70). In his historical perspective on LTP, Bruce McNaughton tells that Hebb was surprised at the excitement about the "Hebbian synapse," that it dates at least to Lorento de No, and that it is the only obvious mechanism of association.[5] In fact, the famous paragraph in Hebb's book is the assumption step in his theory, not the prediction step: the full paragraph starts with "Let us assume that…" What Hebb was really proposing was that if we see this mechanism in a cortical system, then we would get *cell assemblies* and *content-addressable memory*.

Hebb defined a *cell assembly* as a set of cells that worked together to represent a specific set of information. Sometimes the term "cell assembly" is used to identify a single thing—thus, the set of cells active when you think of the dog you had growing up forms a cell assembly. Sometimes the term is used to identify a set of things—thus, the set of cells active whenever you see or think about dogs would form a cell assembly.

The important concept in both cases is that it's not a single cell that forms these sets.[6] In both cases, we're talking about groups of cells that work together. A single cell may participate in multiple cell assemblies, but some cells will differ between them. This means that it will only be in the aggregate that an observer can differentiate representations in this population of cells. We can ask what the tuning curve is from a single cell, but we cannot decode the representation from it. For that we need a population of cells, an ensemble of cells. This kind of a representation is called *distributed* because the representation is distributed across the population.

Hebb's concept was that cells that represent, say, the sound of that dog barking, the color of its fur, and how you felt when you hugged it would all be linked together because these experiences tended to co-occur.[7] Thus, the taste of ratatouille made the way your mom made it could bring back a flood of memory—of your hometown, your youth, and that family emotion that can melt your heart.[8] The Hebbian synapses would complete a part of the cell assembly into the whole memory. The memory could be addressed by its content alone.

Hebb's conceptual derivation occurred before the necessary mathematical basis that was needed to study it, and the concepts of cell assembly and content-addressable memory were not tested or explored until the 1980s and 1990s, after the development of the needed computational and neurophysiological technologies.[9]

Memory as pattern completion

Computationally, content-addressable memory is equivalent to completing a partial pattern.[10] Imagine a degraded picture, where some of the pixels have been replaced with noise. With enough noise, so much of the picture will be changed that you won't be able to recognize it anymore, but for a long time before that, you will still be able to recognize the picture, even through the noise.

Computer models of this have shown that a very good system for completing partial patterns is to store connections between each pixel representing the similarities and differences between the pixels. For simplicity, let's imagine a black and white picture, where each pixel is either *on* or *off*. If two pixels are both on, then they can support each other, but when the pair of pixels are opposite to each other (one on, the other off), they counteract each other. This is a network originally studied by John Hopfield, who showed in a very famous 1982 paper that such a network will complete a degraded picture to an original stored picture.[11] Hopfield was a physicist at CalTech at the time.

Using mathematics originally derived in physics to describe how iron becomes magnetic when it cools down (the magnetic poles of the individual atoms slowly align), he showed how you can define an *error* or *energy* surface to understand how the system settled from the noisy, degraded picture into the remembered picture.

Imagine that we represent the activity across all of our neurons as a point in a very high-dimensional space.[12] Each neuron provides a dimension and the position along that dimension is the firing rate of the neuron. This is easiest to think of with only two neurons, so we have only two dimensions, but the mathematics works with any number of dimensions. At any moment in time, our firing pattern across the population of neurons is a point in this n-dimensional space. We can describe the error (energy) function as height in a third dimension ($(n + 1)$th dimension). This gives us a surface with hills and valleys. What Hopfield was able to show was that his network would always roll downhill and that the synaptic weights in his network could be constructed so that the bottom of the valleys correctly corresponded to the stored (remembered) patterns. The connection strength between the cells of the pattern determine the depth of the basin representing that pattern, and the likelihood that one will roll down into it.[13]

So imagine that we store some pattern (say a picture of Rodin's *The Thinker*) in our network (Figure C.2). This means that the pattern of activity across the network that corresponds to our picture of that iconic image is going to be at the bottom of one of these valleys. We then degrade that pattern by adding noise. When we put that degraded pattern into our network, it starts at some point different from our stored memory. But then the activity of our network starts to change—neurons that are off, but have lots of other connected neurons that say they should be on, start to turn on; neurons that are on, but don't have a lot of support to stay on, turn off. As the activity pattern changes, we are moving along that energy/error surface. We are a ball rolling downhill. Eventually, we will arrive at the bottom of the valley of *The Thinker*.

Of course, as we saw in our discussion of actual neurons (Appendix A), neurons are not *off* or *on*. Instead, they fire spikes, but these spikes are in response to signals arriving in the neuron's dendrites, which depend on the firing of other neurons and the synaptic weight between those other neurons and the neuron in question. This produces a network of neurons working together.

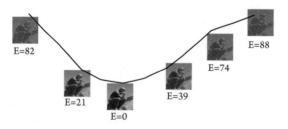

Figure C.2 Degraded Patterns. We can measure the difference between patterns as the *mean squared error E*. As the pattern changes from the remembered pattern, the error increases. We can use this error as an energy function. If a means can be found to move down in this "error" function, we will find ourselves completing the pattern, "remembering" our image. Content-addressable memories work this way—by moving downhill of the error or energy function.

The concept of this network of neurons working together to recall a memory is sometimes called *connectionism*, because it is the connections (synapses) between the neurons where the memory is stored.[B] Hopfield's contribution was to simplify the model to the point where he could define the energy or error function and prove that his system would recall the stored memory through pattern completion. In fact, these sorts of models work well, even if we only change the excitatory connections and use inhibition only to maintain an overall level of activity, or if we have graded neurons, which are trying to recall *firing rates*, or if we have detailed models of spiking neurons.[15;C] These models have been able to explain how changes in neuromodulators (like dopamine, acetylcholine, or serotonin) can change the ability of a network to store memories, as well as very specific (and often surprising) firing rate patterns observed in neural recordings from behaving animals.[22] What these models give us is an explanation for memory as *categorization*, which has a number of interesting consequences.

Memory as categorization

What if you have two memories stored in this network? Then you would have two valleys. This would mean that there was a set of patterns that would roll down into the first valley and a different set of locations that would roll down into the second valley. We call each of these sets the *basin of attraction* for a given valley. Just as water to the east of the Continental Divide in the Rocky Mountains in the United States flows east to the Atlantic, while water to the west of the Continental Divide flows west to the Pacific, starting points in one basin of attraction flow to one memory, while starting points in the other basin flow to the other (Figure C.3).

What is really going on here is that the pattern of hills and valleys depends on the connections between cells. By changing those connections, we change the hills and valleys and change how our memory completes patterns. Storing a memory entails changing

---

[B] The term "connectionism" is often limited to highly abstract models like the Hopfield model, which is obviously a very poor description of actual neurons. However, the original concept of connectionism was the general idea that it is the connections that matter and that information processing can occur by information flow across those connections.[14]

[C] One of the great ongoing debates in neuroscience is whether information is represented by the specific timing of spikes or by the average firing rate.[16] My suspicion is that both spiking and average firing rates contain information that is used by the brain.

In some cases, it is clear that specific timing is critical. For example, in the bat echolocation system, spikes are timed to an accuracy of a microsecond (one millionth of a second), because the speed of sound means the bat has to recognize microsecond time differences.[17] In other cases, it is less clear. Depolarizations in cortical neurons, particularly in their inputs along their dendrites, do not reliably produce spikes, suggesting that spiking is more rate-based in the cortex.[18]

My take on this is that there is a continuum that depends on the neural structure involved. A useful thought experiment is that we can rephrase this question as "By how much time could you shift the spike randomly before the information was lost?"[19] Obviously, even cortical spikes could not shift by seconds.[20] Similarly, the bat echolocation system needs spike accuracy to the microsecond.[21] But would the cortical information be lost if you shifted the cortical spikes by a microsecond? By a millisecond? By a centisecond?

Figure C.3 WATERSHEDS OF NORTH AMERICA AS BASINS OF ATTRACTION. The simplest example of a basin of attraction is that of a watershed. Water to the west of the Continental Divide ends in the Pacific Ocean, while water east of it ends in the Atlantic. Most of the Canadian water flows to the Arctic, but some flows to the St. Lawrence Seaway, and some flows to the Pacific. Water in the Great Basin flows into the Great Salt Lake and does not end up in an ocean. (Map modified from the U.S. Geological Survey.)

those connections so that the memory is at the bottom of a valley.[23] Recalling a memory entails rolling down that surface to the bottom of the valley (Figure C.4). Changing connection weights changes the basins of attraction for each valley and changes what memories are recalled from what cues. It turns out that (as originally predicted by Hebb) the Hebbian synapse (or modifications of it that include both increases and decreases[24]) changes the connection weights in the right ways to change the basins of attraction. In fact, many memories, with many valleys and many basins of attraction, can be stored in these networks. There's good evidence now that several brain structures that store and recall memory work this way, including both the hippocampus and frontal cortex.[25]

Examples of the effects of these basins can be seen in how they affect categorization— for example, in speech, in the ability to recognize differences between sounds, or, in perception, in the ability to differentiate colors.

Although human speech is capable of making many sounds reliably, each language selects a subset of those sounds to use to communicate information.[26] Thus, the Xhosian languages in southern Africa include different kinds of clicks (e.g., a slap of the tongue vs. a sounded swallowing), something not included in any Indo-European language. Some languages differentiate sounds that others don't. For example, in Japanese, the sounds /l/ and /r/ (as in "glossary") are both categorized as the same sound. Japanese words do include both /l/ and /r/ sounds, but native Japanese speakers don't hear the difference. Every language has sounds it categorizes together. English, for example, doesn't differentiate aspirated and unaspirated /t/ sounds—although English uses both

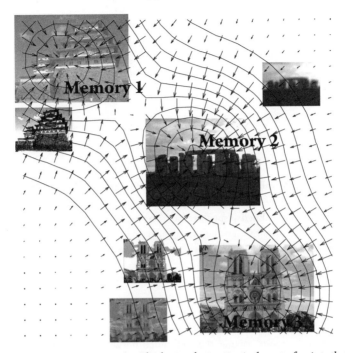

Figure C.4 BASINS OF ATTRACTION. The *basin of attraction* is the set of points that, when allowed to change through a dynamic system, converge on the same place. If we think of the state of a neural system as a point in a high-dimensional space, then we can describe the flow of points in this space as a space of hills and valleys. Similar patterns will change to recall a stored pattern.

aspirated and unaspirated consonants (for example, between the sound of the /t/ in the English words "ton" and "stun"), English speakers generally don't hear the difference.[D] In Hindi, the aspiration of certain consonants differentiates words (just as /l/ and /r/ differentiate "light" and "right"). We can explain this categorization ability in terms of basins of attraction[27] (Figure C.5).

In actuality, the two sounds (/l/ and /r/) form a continuum in the shape of the mouth and the position of the tongue. /l/ is the tongue touching the front top of the palate, while /r/ is the tongue against the side teeth. (The rolled /r/ of French or Spanish includes a glottal purring with the tongue against the side teeth.) In Japanese, all of the sounds in this continuum between /l/ and /r/ fall into the same basin of attraction; they activate the same cell assembly, and they are categorized as a single sound. In English, we draw a line between the extremes of this continuum, separating them. More /l/-like sounds fall into the /l/ basin, while more /r/-like sounds fall into the /r/ basin; they activate different cell assemblies, and they are categorized differently. This understanding of categorization has led to new techniques for teaching Japanese speakers to

---

[D] To prove to yourself that the /t/ is different in "ton" and "stun," hold your hand a couple of inches in front of your mouth and say the two words. You'll feel your breath when saying the /t/ in "ton" but not in "stun."

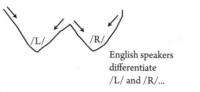

Figure C.5 PHONEME-RECOGNITION DEPENDS ON LEARNED BASINS OF ATTRACTION.
The difference between being able to distinguish two categories depends on them being
in different basins. Native English speakers have learned that the sounds /l/ and /r/ are
in different basins, while native Japanese speakers have learned that they are in the same
basin. This makes it very difficult for native Japanese speakers to recognize the differences
between the /l/ and /r/ sounds.

recognize the English differentiation between /l/ and /r/ by starting with the largest
separation, thus overemphasizing the difference between them, and then explicitly
training the categorization skills.[28] This enables Japanese speakers to create new basins
of attraction, to learn to separate these categories, and to improve their ability to differentiate the sounds.[29] Similarly, parents talking to young children overemphasize the
difference between individual vowels, which may help demonstrate the clear category
differences to the children.[30]

Another classic example of learned categorization is color differentiation, which
turns out to be helped by being able to name the colors.[31] Although there are universals in some of the color labels between languages, likely due to the neurophysiology
of color vision, every language differentiates colors a little differently.[32] (The nice
thing about color is that one can use pure colors, which means that one can quantitatively measure the difference between the two colors in terms of the wavelength
of light.) English speakers are more easily able to distinguish colors at the boundary
between blue and green than two colors that are both blue or that are both green,
even when faced with color pairs that are separated by the same wavelength difference.[33] This is a general property across languages. For example, while English has a
single color term for blue ("blue"), Russian has two (синий "seenee," dark blue, and
голубой "goloboi," light blue). This doesn't mean that English speakers can't separate
light and dark blue; we often talk about sky blue and navy blue. These are small and
subtle effects; certainly, we recognize the differences between the many blues in a
big box of crayons. These effects should not be confused with the idea that some
concepts do not exist in some languages, and that one cannot think about things one
cannot name.

For example, some people have argued that some languages do not represent time
or number, and that those people live ever in the present.[34] This hypothesis is known as
the "Sapir-Whorf" hypothesis (named after the linguists Edward Sapir and Benjamin

Whorf, not to be confused with the Klingon Worf) and is best known through the use of Newspeak in George Orwell's *1984*, where concepts are manipulated by changing the language itself. While it is clear that political discourse is changed by the framing of concepts and issues, it is still possible to think about things, even without terminology for them.[35] Similarly, the myth that the Inuit have twenty words for snow[36] should not be taken as so different from English.[37] English can also identify twenty different kinds of snow: *sleet, ice, rain, snow, fluffy snow, heavy snow,* etc. We certainly recognize the differences between these forms of snow (I know I do when I'm trying to shovel my driveway!). The difference is that the Inuit tend to use more accurate words for snow because it is an important part of their lives. Similarly, while a casual observer may label a bird as "a bird," a birdwatcher or a hunter would be more accurate, labeling it as a "hawk" or even a "red-tailed hawk."[38]

Russian speakers have learned to categorize dark blue (синий, seenee) and light blue (голубой, goloboi) rather than to categorize blue together. Native Russian speakers are faster to identify differences in blue colors that cross the синий (seenee)–голубой (goloboi) boundary than native English speakers. These abilities depend on language—if one is given a linguistic blocking task (like repeating random strings of numbers silently while doing the task[E]), then the differences between color pairs crossing categories and color pairs within categories disappears.[39]

Presumably, the difference between native English and native Russian speakers is that the native Russian speakers have developed two basins of attraction to separate light and dark blue while the native English speakers have only one. What is particularly interesting about these categories is that they are not arbitrary; they relate to universal perceptual experiences and an interaction between our sensory perceptions and the world.[40] The cell assemblies in the color-recognition structures in our cortex are working from the specific color signals in the world (the blue of the sky, the blue of the ocean, the red of a sunset, the green of a leaf, the yellow of a sunflower) and the specific color signals that the photoreceptors in the retina of our eyes can detect.[F]

[E] We've seen several cases throughout the book where a decision-making ability depends on using resources that are also used by linguistic or executive-function (conscious, requiring mental effort) tasks. If those resources are used by another task, then the ability disappears. The second task *interferes* with the first task. Good examples of linguistic and executive-function blocker tasks include being asked to remember a long random string of letters or numbers, saying the alphabet backwards, or counting back from 1000 by sevens. Try doing the last two tasks at the same time. It's really hard!

[F] Normal humans have three color-detecting photoreceptors called cones, each of which has a broad sensitivity to color (making this a distributed representation of color!). Subsequent calculations occurring in our retina and visual cortex compare the activity in contrasting pairs of color-detecting photoreceptors. This is why if you stare at a red picture long enough, when you look at a white screen, you'll see a green afterimage. (The red cones have gotten tired and don't fire as strongly as they should when you look away at the white screen.) Colorblind people are usually missing one or more of the cones, which is why people with red–green color blindness (missing the red photoreceptor) can differentiate blue and yellow but not red and green. The specifics of color perception would take up an entire book in itself, but for those interested, most neuroscience textbooks have a good description of the mechanisms of color perception.[41]

The neurophysiology of cell assemblies

Neurophysiologically, studying cell assemblies, content-addressable memory, and pattern completion requires the ability to record the activity of large numbers of neurons simultaneously, yet separately. It is not enough to see the broad activity of a network, as, for example, from EEG, LFP, or fMRI; one needs to see the actual pattern of neuronal firing. Additionally, it is not enough to see the activity of a single neuron because what matters is not whether a single neuron fires when a stimulus is presented or an action is taken; what is needed is to see how the activity of a single neuron reflects the activity of its neighbors.

The first major steps toward the identification of cell assemblies in real nervous systems were due to work by Bruce McNaughton and his colleagues in the 1990s, where they developed techniques capable of recording large ensembles of neurons simultaneously. In a famous paper published in 1993, Matt Wilson and Bruce McNaughton[42] recorded from over a hundred hippocampal *place cells* simultaneously. The hippocampus has been a particularly useful place to examine cell assemblies because hippocampal cells in the rat have a very identifiable representation—they encode the location of the animal in space.[43] This has enabled neuroscientists to use mathematics originally derived for spatial reasoning to examine hippocampal cell assemblies.[44]

More recently, it has been possible to examine patterns of cortical cells during action selection by examining the trajectory of the ensemble neural firing pattern through the high-dimensional space. As discussed above, we can imagine the population as a point in a very high-dimensional space, one dimension for each neuron. The activity of the cells at a moment in time can be described as a point in that space. Several labs studying action-taking have found that just before the animal takes the action, the firing pattern of the population of cells in motor cortex moves to a consistent point in that space and then takes a consistent trajectory to another point in that space.[45] Similar analyses have been done for ensembles of prefrontal neurons in rats—the firing pattern of the population of cells clusters into subspaces at important times, say when the animal changes between tasks.[46]

Just as Hebb predicted, the mental representation of decisions requires pattern completion of cell assemblies and entails trajectories through cell-assembly space.

Books and papers for further reading

- George Lakoff (1990/1997). *Women, Fire, and Dangerous Things*. Chicago: University of Chicago Press.
- Donald O. Hebb (1949/2002). *The Organization of Behavior*. New York: Wiley/Lawrence Erlbaum.
- John Hertz, Anders Krogh, and Richard G. Palmer (1991). *Introduction to the Theory of Neural Computation*. Reading, MA: Addison-Wesley.

BIBLIOGRAPHY

BIBLIOGRAPHIC NOTES

Preface

1. Firestein, 2012.
2. Redish, 2013.

Chapter 1. What is a Decision?

1. Freud, 1923/1990; Augustine of Hippo (Saint Augustine), 398/1961; *distributed computing*, Minsky, 1985; *evolutionary psychology*, Kurzban, 2010; *behavioral economics*, Kahneman, 2011.
2. Haidt, 2006.
3. Ramachandran and Blakeslee, 1999; Ramachandran, 2011; Sharot, 2011; Levy, 2007; Wegner, 2002; Kurzban, 2010.
4. Libet, Wright, Feinstein, and Pearl, 1979; Libet, 1985, 1993.
5. Vinogradova, 2001; Cabanac, Cabanac, and Parent, 2009; Gray, 2004.
6. The human eye is built backwards, see any neuroscience textbook, e.g., Kandel, Schwartz, and Jessell, 2000; Carlson, 2010; Chaudhuri, 2011. *Octopi*: Wells, 1962.
7. Akins, 1996; Chaudhuri, 2011.
8. Ramachandran and Blakeslee, 1999.
9. Chiu, Lohrenz, and Montague, 2008.
10. *Rats*, Steiner and Redish, 2012; *monkeys*, Abe and Lee, 2011; *humans*, Coricelli, Critchley, Joffily, O'Doherty, Sirigu, and Dolan, 2005; Chiu, Lohrenz, and Montague, 2008.
11. Kurzban, 2010.
12. Patterson and Linden, 1981; Savage-Rumbaugh and Lewin, 1996; Fouts, 1997; Pepperberg, 2009.
13. Glimcher, 2004; Glimcher, Camerer, Poldrack, and Fehr, 2008; Glimcher, 2010.
14. Smith, 2009; Glimcher, 2010; Kurzban, 2010.
15. Libet, 1985; Akins, 1996; Ramachandran and Blakeslee, 1999.
16. Kurzban, 2010.
17. Johnson and Bickel, 2002; Kang, Rangel, Camus, and Camerer, 2011.
18. Bushong, King, Camerer, and Rangel, 2010.
19. Boysen and Berntson, 1995.
20. Beran, Savage-Rumbaugh, Pate, and Rumbaugh, 1999.
21. Metcalfe and Mischel, 1999; Mischel and Underwood, 1974.
22. Cisek and Kalaska, 2010.

Chapter 2. The Tale of the Thermostat

1. Searle, 1980; Newell, 1990; McCorduck, 2004.
2. Snodgrass, 1989.
3. Pearl, 1988; Rich and Knight, 1991.
4. Groopman, 2007.
5. McCorduck, 2004.
6. Wegner, 2002.

Chapter 3. The Definition of Value

1. Hull, 1943.
2. Glimcher, Camerer, Poldrack, and Fehr, 2008.
3. Sutton and Barto, 1998.
4. Krugman and Wells, 2006; Glass, 2011.
5. Festinger, 1954.
6. Samuelson, 1937; Krugman and Wells, 2006; Glimcher, Camerer, Poldrack, and Fehr, 2008; Smith, 2009.
7. Kahneman, Knetsch, and Thaler, 1990, 1991; Kahneman, 2011; Plous, 1993; Ariely, 2008.
8. Kahneman and Tversky, 1979; Kahneman, Slovic, and Tversky, 1982; Kahneman and Tversky, 2000; Kahneman, 2011; Plous, 1993; Ariely, 2008.
9. Tversky and Kahneman, 1981.
10. Simonson and Tversky, 1992; Shapiro and Varian, 1999; Plous, 1993; Kahneman and Tversky, 2000; Hui, Yoo, and Tam, 2007; Ariely, 2008.
11. Plous, 1993; Ariely, 2008; Kahneman, 2011.
12. Gigerenzer and Goldstein, 1996; Gilovich, Griffin, and Kahneman, 2002; Kahneman, 2011.
13. Simon, 1955; Gigerenzer and Goldstein, 1996.
14. Ahmed, 2010; Hernandez, Breton, Conover, and Shizgal, 2010.
15. Ahmed, 2010; Padoa-Schioppa and Assad, 2006.
16. Deroche-Gamonet, Belin, and Piazza, 2004.
17. Madden and Bickel, 2010.
18. Bickel and Marsch, 2001.
19. Kahneman, Knetsch, and Thaler, 1991.
20. Politser, 2008; Kurniawan, Seymour, Vlaev, Trommershäuser, Dolan, and Chater, 2010.
21. Ainslie, 1992; Bickel and Marsch, 2001; McClure, Ericson, Laibson, Loewenstein, and Cohen, 2007.
22. Berns, Chappelow, Cekic, Zink, Pagnoni, and Martin-Skurski, 2006.
23. Boysen and Berntson, 1995.
24. Cai, Kim, and Lee, 2011.
25. Mackintosh, 1974.
26. Vanderschuren and Everitt, 2004; Deroche-Gamonet, Belin, and Piazza, 2004.
27. Carroll, Lac, and Nygaard, 1989; Nader and Woolverton, 1991; Hatsukami, Thompson, Pentel, Flygare, and Carroll, 1994; Grossman and Chaloupka, 1998; Liu, Liu, Hammit, and Chou, 1999; Bickel and Marsch, 2001; Chaloupka, Emery, and Liang, 2003; Rachlin, 2004.
28. Rutledge, 2006; Krauss, 2008.
29. Lenoir, Serre, Cantin, and Ahmed, 2007; Ahmed, 2010.
30. Lenoir and Ahmed, 2007.
31. Higgins, Alessi, and Dantona, 2002; Higgins, Heil, and Lussier, 2004; Stitzer and Petry, 2006; Petry, 2011.
32. Moos and Moos, 2004, 2006.
33. Daw, Niv, and Dayan, 2005; Redish, Jensen, and Johnson, 2008; van der Meer, Kurth-Nelson, and Redish, 2012; Montague, Dolan, Friston, and Dayan, 2012.
34. Hill, 2008.

35. Simon, 1955; Kahneman, Slovic, and Tversky, 1982; Plous, 1993; Baumeister, Heatherton, and Tice, 1994; Gigerenzer and Goldstein, 1996; Kahneman and Tversky, 2000; Ariely, 2008; Andrade and Ariely, 2009; Peters and Büchel, 2010; Kahneman, 2011; van der Meer, Kurth-Nelson, and Redish, 2012.
36. Plous, 1993; Ariely, 2008; Kahneman, 2011.
37. Glimcher, Camerer, Poldrack, and Fehr, 2008.
38. Simon, 1955; Gigerenzer and Goldstein, 1996; Bettman, Luce, and Payne, 1998.
39. Gigerenzer and Goldstein, 1996.
40. Dhar, Nowlis, and Sherman, 2000; Plous, 1993; Ariely, 2008.
41. Plous, 1993.
42. Ballard, Houde, Silver-Balbus, and McClure, 2009.
43. Ariely, 2008; Kahneman, 2011.

Chapter 4. *Value, Euphoria, and the Do-It-Again Signal*

1. Fields, 1987; Coghill, McHaffie, and Yen, 2003; Purves, Augustine, Fitzpatrick, Hall, LaMantia, McNamara, and White, 2008; Carlson, 2010.
2. Olds and Milner, 1954; Olds and Fobes, 1981; Bielajew and Harris, 1991; Arvanitogiannis and Shizgal, 2008.
3. Niven, 1969.
4. Heath, 1963.
5. Olds and Fobes, 1981; Shizgal, 1997; Wise, 2005.
6. Cooper, Bloom, and Roth, 1986.
7. Kopin, 1993; Dauer and Przedborski, 2003.
8. Arendt and Skene, 2005; Arendt, 2009; Touitou and Bogdan, 2007.
9. Zisapel, 2002; Arendt, 2009; Gerstner, Lyons, Wright, Loh, Rawashdeh, Eckel-Mahan, and Roman, 2009.
10. Wise, 2004; Berridge, 2007.
11. Bielajew and Harris, 1991; Olds and Fobes, 1981; Shizgal, 1997.
12. Wise, 2005; Berridge, 2007, 2012.
13. See Koob and Le Moal, 2006, for a thorough review.
14. Heishman and Henningfield, 2000; Koob and Le Moal, 2006; Perkins, Gerlach, Broge, Fonte, and Wilson, 2001; Russell, 1990.
15. Berridge and Robinson, 2003; Berridge, 2007, 2012.
16. Herz, 1998; De Vries and Shippenberg, 2002; Meyer and Mirin, 1979; Chavkin, James, and Goldstein, 1982; Mucha and Herz, 1985; Bals-Kubik, Herz, and Shippenberg, 1989; Kieffer, 1999; Broom, Jutkiewicz, Folk, Traynor, Rice, and Woods, 2002; Laurent, Leung, Maidment, and Balleine, 2012.
17. Arbisi, Billington, and Levine, 1999; Levine and Billington, 2004.
18. Munn, 1950; Mackintosh, 1974; Gallistel, 1990; Domjan, 1998; Watson, 1907; Pavlov, 1927; Thorndike, 1932; Hull, 1943, 1952; Ferster and Skinner, 1957.
19. Kamin, 1969.
20. Rescorla and Wagner, 1972.
21. Mackintosh, 1974; McNally, Pigg, and Weidemann, 2004; Burke, Franz, Miller, and Schoenbaum, 2007; McDannald, Lucantonio, Burke, Niv, and Schoenbaum, 2011.
22. Sutton and Barto, 1998; Bellman, 1958; Daw, 2003.
23. Sutton and Barto, 1998; Daw, 2003; Redish, Jensen, Johnson, and Kurth-Nelson, 2007.
24. Sutton and Barto, 1998; Montague, 2006.
25. Ljungberg, Apicella, and Schultz, 1992; Schultz, 1998; Schultz and Dickinson, 2000; Montague, Dayan, and Sejnowski, 1996; Schultz, Dayan, and Montague, 1997.
26. Duvoisin and Sage, 2001; Parkinson, 1817/2002; Manyam, 1990.
27. Denny-Brown, 1962; Purdon-Martin, 1967; Koller, 1992; Jankovic and Tolosa, 2007.

28. Purdon-Martin, 1967; Sacks, 1973/1990; Siegert, Harper, Cameron, and Abernethy, 2002; Mazzoni, Hristova, and Krakauer, 2007.
29. Glickstein and Stein, 1991; Niv and Rivlin-Etzion, 2007.
30. Dauer and Przedborski, 2003.
31. Floresco, West, Ash, Moore, and Grace, 2003.
32. Frank, Moustafa, Haughey, Curran, and Hutchison, 2007a; Shohamy, Myers, Grossman, Sage, and Gluck, 2005; Rutledge, Lazzaro, Lau, Myers, Gluck, and Glimcher, 2009.
33. Niv, Daw, Joel, and Dayan, 2006b; Niv and Rivlin-Etzion, 2007; Moustafa and Gluck, 2011; Frank, Samanta, Moustafa, and Sherman, 2007b.
34. Redish, Jensen, Johnson, and Kurth-Nelson, 2007.
35. Niv, Daw, Joel, and Dayan, 2006b; Salamone, Correa, Farrar, Nunes, and Pardo, 2009; Berridge and Robinson, 2003; Berridge, 2012.
36. Ljungberg, Apicella, and Schultz, 1992.
37. Montague, Dayan, Person, and Sejnowski, 1995; Montague, Dayan, and Sejnowski, 1996; Schultz, Dayan, and Montague, 1997.
38. Tobler, Fiorillo, and Schultz, 2005; Hollerman and Schultz, 1998; Bayer and Glimcher, 2005.
39. Waelti, Dickinson, and Schultz, 2001.
40. *Rats:* Pan, Schmidt, Wickens, and Hyland, 2005; Roesch, Calu, and Schoenbaum, 2007; *Monkeys:* Bayer and Glimcher, 2005; Bromberg-Martin and Hikosaka, 2009; Matsumoto and Hikosaka, 2007; *fMRI of dopamine-projecting areas in humans:* O'Doherty, Dayan, Friston, Critchley, and Dolan, 2003; O'Doherty, 2004; Pagnoni, Zink, Montague, and Berns, 2002; D'Ardenne, McClure, Nystrom, and Cohen, 2008; Schonberg, O'Doherty, Joel, Inzelberg, Segev, and Daw, 2010.
41. Loomes and Sugden, 1982; Bell, 1982, 1985; Redish, Jensen, Johnson, and Kurth-Nelson, 2007; Steiner and Redish, 2012.
42. Brischoux, Chakraborty, Brierley, and Ungless, 2009; Ungless, Magill, and Bolam, 2004; Ungless, 2004; Matsumoto and Hikosaka, 2007, 2009; Bromberg-Martin, Matsumoto, Nakahara, and Hikosaka, 2010; Ungless, Argilli, and Bonci, 2010.
43. Kakade and Dayan, 2002; see Schultz, 1998, for the original description of the generalization effect.
44. Laurent, 2008.
45. Schultz, 1998.
46. Redgrave, Prescott, and Gurney, 1999.
47. Daw, Kakade, and Dayan, 2002; Redish, Jensen, Johnson, and Kurth-Nelson, 2007; McNally, Johansen, and Blair, 2011.
48. Daw, Kakade, and Dayan, 2002.
49. Miyazaki, Miyazaki, and Doya, 2010.
50. Cooper, Bloom, and Roth, 1986.
51. Schwaerzel, Monastirioti, Scholz, Friggi-Grelin, Birman, and Heisenberg, 2003; Unoki, Matsumoto, and Mizunami, 2005.
52. Cooper, Bloom, and Roth, 1986.
53. Matsumoto and Hikosaka, 2007; Bromberg-Martin, Matsumoto, Nakahara, and Hikosaka, 2010.
54. McNally, Johansen, and Blair, 2011.
55. Albin, Young, and Penney, 1989; Robinson, Frank, Sahakian, and Cools, 2010; Cohen and Frank, 2009; Kravitz, Tye, and Kreitzer, 2012.
56. Pavlov, 1927; Myers and Davis, 2002; Bouton, 2004; Rescorla, 2004; Redish, Jensen, Johnson, and Kurth-Nelson, 2007.
57. Milad and Quirk, 2002; Myers and Davis, 2002; Quirk, 2006; McNally, Johansen, and Blair, 2011.
58. Nili, Goldberg, Weizman, and Dudai, 2010.
59. Redish, Jensen, Johnson, and Kurth-Nelson, 2007.
60. Redish, Jensen, Johnson, and Kurth-Nelson, 2007.

61. Tolman, 1932; Buzsáki, 1982.
62. Capaldi, 1957, 1958; Ferster and Skinner, 1957; Capaldi and Lynch, 1968; Domjan, 1998.

Chapter 5. Risk and Reward

1. Markowitz, 1952; Payzan-LeNestour and Bossaerts, 2011.
2. Preuschoff, Bossaerts, and Quartz, 2006; Yu and Dayan, 2005.
3. Archer and Birke, 1983; Bromberg-Martin and Hikosaka, 2009.
4. O'Keefe and Nadel, 1978; Whishaw and Brooks, 1999; Redish, 1999.
5. Tversky and Kahneman, 1981; Kahneman and Tversky, 1979; Kahneman, 2011.
6. Steinberg, 2005; Casey, Getz, and Galvan, 2008a; Casey, Jones, and Hare, 2008b; Heyman, 2009.
7. Sharot, Riccardi, Raio, and Phelps, 2007; Sharot, 2011.
8. Golani, Benjamini, and Eilam, 1993; Redish, 1999; Drai and Golani, 2001.
9. Zuckerman and Kuhlman, 2000.
10. Samuelson, 1937; Ainslie, 2001; Frederick, Loewenstein, and O'Donoghue, 2002; Rachlin, 2004; Madden and Bickel, 2010.
11. Stephens and Krebs, 1987; Sozou, 1998; Rachlin, 2004; Andersen, Harrison, Lau, and Rutström, 2008; Redish and Kurth-Nelson, 2010.
12. Samuelson, 1937.
13. Stephens and Krebs, 1987.
14. Madden and Bickel, 2010.
15. Mazur, 2001; Madden and Bickel, 2010.
16. Mazur, 2001.
17. Papale, Stott, Powell, Regier, and Redish, 2012.
18. Samuelson, 1937; Frederick, Loewenstein, and O'Donoghue, 2002; Andersen, Harrison, Lau, and Rutström, 2008.
19. Ainslie, 2001; Mazur, 2001; Frederick, Loewenstein, and O'Donoghue, 2002; Madden and Bickel, 2010; *Humans answering questionaires:* e.g., Johnson and Bickel, 2002; *Animals pressing levers for food:* e.g., Mazur, 2001; *Humans pressing levers for food:* e.g., McClure, Ericson, Laibson, Loewenstein, and Cohen, 2007.
20. Ainslie, 2001; Frederick, Loewenstein, and O'Donoghue, 2002.
21. Mintz, 1986; Barrett, 2010; Sapolsky, 2001.
22. Kang, Rangel, Camus, and Camerer, 2011.
23. Kurth-Nelson and Redish, 2012c; *For additional discussion of the role of concreteness in slowing discouting rates:* Baumeister, Heatherton, and Tice, 1994; Peters and Büchel, 2010; Baumeister and Tierney, 2011; *For descriptions of Contingency Management:* Higgins, Alessi, and Dantona, 2002; Stitzer and Petry, 2006; Petry, 2011.
24. Ainslie, 2001; Kurzban, 2010; Kurth-Nelson and Redish, 2010, 2012a.
25. Ainslie, 1992; Rachlin, 2004; Kurzban, 2010.
26. Baumeister, Heatherton, and Tice, 1994; Vohs and Baumeister, 2010; Baumeister and Tierney, 2011; Kurth-Nelson and Redish, 2010, 2012c.
27. Ainslie, 2001.
28. Baumeister, Heatherton, and Tice, 1994; Grewal, Shepherd, Bill, Fletcher, and Dourish, 1997; Rodgers, Cao, Dalvi, and Holmes, 1997; Gray and McNaughton, 2000.
29. LeDoux, 1996; Paré, Quirk, and Ledoux, 2004; Phelps and LeDoux, 2005.
30. Mishkin and Appenzeller, 1987; Graybiel, 1995; Schmitzer-Torbert and Redish, 2004; Barnes, Kubota, Hu, Jin, and Graybiel, 2005; Barnes, Mao, Hu, Kubota, Dreyer, Stamoulis, Brown, and Graybiel, 2011; Frank, 2011.
31. Baumeister, Heatherton, and Tice, 1994; Gray, 2004; Buckner and Carroll, 2007; Hassabis, Kumaran, Vann, and Maguire, 2007; Schacter, Addis, and Buckner, 2007; Johnson, van der Meer, and Redish, 2007; Peters and Büchel, 2010; Hassabis and Maguire, 2011; Schacter and Addis, 2011; van der Meer, Kurth-Nelson, and Redish, 2012.

32. Myers and Davis, 2002, 2007; Quirk, 2002, 2006.
33. Phelps, O'Connor, and Chi, 2001; Berns, Chappelow, Cekic, Zink, Pagnoni, and Martin-Skurski, 2006; Delgado, Olsson, and Phelps, 2006.
34. Berns, Chappelow, Cekic, Zink, Pagnoni, and Martin-Skurski, 2006.
35. Milad and Quirk, 2002; Quirk, 2006.
36. Nili, Goldberg, Weizman, and Dudai, 2010.
37. Herbert, 1965.

Chapter 6. Multiple Decision-Making Systems

1. O'Keefe and Nadel, 1978; Redish, 1999; Daw, Niv, and Dayan, 2005; van der Meer, Kurth-Nelson, and Redish, 2012.
2. *Goal-directed learning:* Dayan and Balleine, 2002; Coutureau and Killcross, 2003; Botvinick and An, 2009; Rangel and Hare, 2010; *Model-based decision-making:* Daw, Niv, and Dayan, 2005; Niv, Joel, and Dayan, 2006c; Simon and Daw, 2011; Doll, Simon, and Daw, 2012; *Action–outcome:* Balleine and Dickinson, 1998; Balleine, 2004; *Locale/place:* O'Keefe and Nadel, 1978; Redish, 1999.
3. *Procedural:* Cohen and Squire, 1980; Mishkin and Appenzeller, 1987; Squire, 1987; *Habit:* Graybiel, 1995; Redish, 1999; Killcross and Coutureau, 2003; Yin, Knowlton, and Balleine, 2004; Duhigg, 2012; van der Meer, Kurth-Nelson, and Redish, 2012; *Stimulus–response:* Hull, 1943; Balleine, 2004; *Stimulus–action:* Redish, Jensen, and Johnson, 2008; *Cached action:* Daw, Niv, and Dayan, 2005; *Taxon:* O'Keefe and Nadel, 1978; Schöne, 1984.
4. Lengyel and Dayan, 2007.
5. Redish, Jensen, Johnson, and Kurth-Nelson, 2007; Redish, Jensen, and Johnson, 2008; Robinson and Flagel, 2009.
6. Pavlov, 1927; Mackintosh, 1974; Domjan, 1998; Bouton, 2007.
7. Pavlov, 1927; Ferster and Skinner, 1957; Skinner, 1971; Gray, 1975; Mackintosh, 1974; Domjan, 1998; Bouton, 2007.
8. Squire, 1987; Balleine and Dickinson, 1998; Daw, Niv, and Dayan, 2005; Niv, Joel, and Dayan, 2006c.
9. Rescorla, 1988; Huys, 2007; van der Meer, Kurth-Nelson, and Redish, 2012.
10. Kruse, Overmier, Konz, and Rokke, 1983; Corbit and Janak, 2007; Talmi, Seymour, Dayan, and Dolan, 2008; Bray, Rangel, Shimojo, Balleine, and O'Doherty, 2008.
11. Damasio, 1994; LeDoux, 1996, 2012.
12. Darwin, 1859; Dawkins, 1976.
13. Barrett, 2006; LeDoux, 2012.
14. Mackintosh, 1974; Rescorla, 1988; Bouton, 2007.
15. Gray, 1979; Kandel, 2006.
16. Crick, 1995.
17. Edelman, 1992.
18. Gray, 1979; Kandel, 2006.
19. Mackintosh, 1974; Domjan, 1998; Bouton, 2007.
20. Mackintosh, 1974; Rescorla, 1988; Balleine, 2004.
21. Kruse, Overmier, Konz, and Rokke, 1983; Corbit and Janak, 2007; Talmi, Seymour, Dayan, and Dolan, 2008; Bray, Rangel, Shimojo, Balleine, and O'Doherty, 2008.
22. Corbit, Muir, and Balleine, 2001; Corbit and Balleine, 2005; Wassum, Cely, Balleine, and Maidment, 2011a; Wassum, Ostlund, Balleine, and Maidment, 2011b.
23. Breland and Breland, 1961; Dayan, Niv, Seymour, and Daw, 2006; Huys, 2007; Redish, Jensen, and Johnson, 2008; LeDoux, 2012.
24. Breland and Breland, 1961; Robinson and Flagel, 2009; Flagel, Akil, and Robinson, 2009.
25. Breland and Breland, 1961.
26. Damasio, 1994, 2003; LeDoux, 1996.
27. Barrett, 2006; LeDoux, 2012.

28. Damasio, 1994; LeDoux, 1996; Huys, 2007.
29. James, 1890; Barrett, 2006; Lakoff and Johnson, 2003.
30. Buckner and Carroll, 2007; Schacter, Addis, and Buckner, 2007, 2008.
31. Hassabis, Kumaran, Vann, and Maguire, 2007; Hassabis and Maguire, 2011; Johnson and Redish, 2007; Peters and Büchel, 2010; Schacter and Addis, 2011.
32. Squire, 1987; Cohen and Eichenbaum, 1993.
33. Loftus and Palmer, 1974; Schacter, 2001; Schacter, Addis, and Buckner, 2007.
34. Tolman, 1932, 1948; Guthrie, 1937; Schacter, 2001.
35. Hassabis, Kumaran, Vann, and Maguire, 2007; Hassabis and Maguire, 2011; Peters and Büchel, 2010; Schacter and Addis, 2011.
36. O'Keefe and Nadel, 1978; Redish, 1999.
37. Wilson and McNaughton, 1993; Brown, Frank, Tang, Quirk, and Wilson, 1998; Zhang, Ginzburg, McNaughton, and Sejnowski, 1998.
38. Johnson, Fenton, Kentros, and Redish, 2009.
39. Muenzinger and Gentry, 1931; Muenzinger, 1938; Tolman, 1932, 1939, 1948; Johnson and Redish, 2007; Johnson, van der Meer, and Redish, 2007; Papale, Stott, Powell, Regier, and Redish, 2012; Steiner and Redish, 2012.
40. Griffin, 1985, 2001; Dennet, 1992; Gray, 2004; Cabanac, Cabanac, and Parent, 2009; Damasio, 2010; Kurzban, 2010.
41. Tolman, 1932.
42. Guthrie, 1937.
43. Hassabis, Kumaran, Vann, and Maguire, 2007; Hassabis and Maguire, 2011; Schacter, Addis, and Buckner, 2007, 2008; Schacter and Addis, 2011.
44. Grewal, Shepherd, Bill, Fletcher, and Dourish, 1997; Hu and Amsel, 1995.
45. Johnson and Redish, 2007; van der Meer, Johnson, Schmitzer-Torbert, and Redish, 2010; Gupta, van der Meer, Touretzky, and Redish, 2012.
46. Buckner and Carroll, 2007.
47. *Ventral striatum:* Mogenson, Jones, and Yim, 1980; Roesch, Singh, Brown, Mullins, and Schoenbaum, 2009; van der Meer and Redish, 2011b; McDannald, Lucantonio, Burke, Niv, and Schoenbaum, 2011; *Orbitofrontal cortex:* Zald and Rauch, 2008; Tremblay and Schultz, 1999; Schoenbaum and Roesch, 2005; Padoa-Schioppa and Assad, 2006; Padoa-Schioppa, 2009; Wallis, 2007; Bray, Shimojo, and O'Doherty, 2010; McDannald, Lucantonio, Burke, Niv, and Schoenbaum, 2011; *For discussions of dysfunction:* Redish, Jensen, and Johnson, 2008; Schoenbaum, Roesch, and Stalnaker, 2006; Robbins, Ersche, and Everitt, 2008; Flagel, Akil, and Robinson, 2009; Koob and Volkow, 2010.
48. Groenewegen, Vermeulen-Van der Zee, te Kortschot, and Witter, 1987; Voorn, Vanderschuren, Groenewegen, Robbins, and Pennartz, 2004; Martin, 2001; Lansink, Goltstein, Lankelma, Joosten, McNaughton, and Pennartz, 2008; Lansink, Goltstein, Lankelma, McNaughton, and Pennartz, 2009; van der Meer and Redish, 2011a.
49. Ramus, Davis, Donahue, Discenza, and Waite, 2007.
50. *Ventral striatum:* van der Meer and Redish, 2009; *Orbitofrontal cortex:* Steiner and Redish, 2012.
51. Hull, 1943; Ferster and Skinner, 1957; O'Keefe and Nadel, 1978; Redish, 1999; Daw, Niv, and Dayan, 2005; Redish, Jensen, and Johnson, 2008; Dezfouli and Balleine, 2012.
52. Schoenbaum, Roesch, and Stalnaker, 2006.
53. Nachman and Ashe, 1973; Schoenbaum, Roesch, and Stalnaker, 2006.
54. Dickinson, 1980; Balleine and Dickinson, 1998; Coutureau and Killcross, 2003; Killcross and Coutureau, 2003; Yin, Knowlton, and Balleine, 2004; Myers, Shohamy, Gluck, Grossman, Onlaor, and Kapur, 2003; Schoenbaum, Roesch, and Stalnaker, 2006; Daw, Niv, and Dayan, 2005; Niv, Joel, and Dayan, 2006c; Johnson, van der Meer, and Redish, 2007; van der Meer, Kurth-Nelson, and Redish, 2012.
55. Hull, 1943, 1952; O'Keefe and Nadel, 1978; Shohamy, Myers, Grossman, Sage, Gluck, and Poldrack, 2004; Knowlton, Mangels, and Squire, 1996; Redish, 1999; Daw, Niv, and Dayan,

2005; Redish, Jensen, and Johnson, 2008; Cohen and Frank, 2009; Cisek and Kalaska, 2010; Dezfouli and Balleine, 2012.

56. Watkins and Dayan, 1992; Sutton and Barto, 1998; Doya, 1999; Daw, 2003; Daw, Niv, and Dayan, 2005; Morris, Nevet, Arkadir, Vaadia, and Bergman, 2006; Niv, Daw, and Dayan, 2006a; Niv and Schoenbaum, 2008.

57. Cisek and Kalaska, 2010; Rand, Hikosaka, Miyachi, Lu, and Miyashita, 1998; Alexander and Crutcher, 1990.

58. Redish, Jensen, Johnson, and Kurth-Nelson, 2007.

59. Sonnenfield, 1997.

60. Albin, Young, and Penney, 1989; Frank, Moustafa, Haughey, Curran, and Hutchison, 2007a; Cohen and Frank, 2009; Kravitz, Tye, and Kreitzer, 2012.

61. Mishkin and Appenzeller, 1987; Graybiel, 1995; Shohamy, Myers, Grossman, Sage, Gluck, and Poldrack, 2004; Frank, 2011.

62. Houk, Davis, and Beiser, 1995; Aosaki, Graybiel, and Kimura, 1994; Wickens, Reynolds, and Hyland, 2003; Calabresi, Picconi, Tozzi, and Di Fillipo, 2007.

63. Schultz, Dayan, and Montague, 1997; Schultz, 1998; Montague, 2006.

64. Purves, Augustine, Fitzpatrick, Hall, LaMantia, McNamara, and White, 2008; Kandel, Schwartz, and Jessell, 2000; Carlson, 2010.

65. Grillner, 1981; Bizzi, Mussa-Ivaldi, and Giszter, 1991; Bizzi, Cheung, d'Avella, Satiel, and Tresch, 2008.

66. Brooks, 1991.

67. Grillner, 1985, 2003; Llinas, 2002; Dominici, Ivanenko, Cappellini, d'Avella, Mondí, Cicchese, Fabiano, Silei, Di Paolo, Giannini, Poppele, and Lacquaniti, 2011.

68. Pavlov, 1927; Ferster and Skinner, 1957.

69. O'Keefe and Nadel, 1978; Nadel and Willner, 1980; Good and Honey, 1991; Cassaday and Rawlins, 1997; Redish, 1999; Delamater and Oakeshott, 2007; Fuhs and Touretzky, 2007; Bouton, 2007; Redish, Jensen, Johnson, and Kurth-Nelson, 2007; Rudy, 2009.

70. *Visual cortex as feature detectors:* Zeki, 1993; *Objects:* e.g., Ungerleider and Pessoa, 2008; *Faces:* e.g., Tsao, Moeller, and Freiwald, 2008; Liu, Harris, and Kanwisher, 2010; *Space:* e.g., Epstein and Kanwisher, 1998.

71. Cisek and Kalaska, 2010.

72. *Cortical structure:* White, 1989; Abeles, 1991; Fuster, 1997/2008; Purves, Augustine, Fitzpatrick, Hall, LaMantia, McNamara, and White, 2008; *Process:* Wilson and Cowan, 1973; Grossberg, 1976; Hertz, Krogh, and Palmer, 1991; Redish, Jensen, Johnson, and Kurth-Nelson, 2007.

73. Hebb, 1949/2002; Hertz, Krogh, and Palmer, 1991; Wilson and Cowan, 1973; Grossberg, 1976; Tanaka, 2006; Redish, Jensen, Johnson, and Kurth-Nelson, 2007; Durstewitz, Vittoz, Floresco, and Seamans, 2010.

74. Frith, 1996; Frith and Dolan, 1996; Frith, 2007; Tanaka, 2006; Durstewitz and Seamans, 2008.

75. Tulving, 1983; Schacter and Tulving, 1994; Squire, 1987; Schacter, 2001.

76. Hull, 1943.

77. Edelman, 1992; Uchibe and Doya, 2008.

78. Balleine, 2001, 2004.

79. Darwin, 1871.

80. Stephens and Krebs, 1987; Giraldeau and Caraco, 2000; Stephens, 2008.

81. Sapolsky, 2001.

82. Johnston and Franklin, 1993; Rhodes, 2006; Jasieńska, Ziomkiewicz, Ellison, Lipson, and Thune, 2004; Singh, 1993.

83. Wright, 1995; de Waal, 2001; Wilson, 2002.

84. Goodman, 2000.

85. O'Brien, Childress, Ehrman, and Robbins, 1998; Childress, Mozley, McElgin, Fitzgerald, Reivich, and O'Brien, 1999.

86. McClure, Li, Tomlin, Cypert, Montague, and Montague, 2004b; Montague, 2006.

87. Edelman, 1992; Haidt, 2006.
88. de Waal, 1982; Wright, 1995; Sapolsky, 2001.
89. Wilson, 2002; Harris, 2010; Zak, 2008.
90. Aristotle, 350 BCE/2004.
91. A very partial list of converging ideas. *Human psychology:* Squire, 1987; Schacter and Tulving, 1994; *Psychiatry:* Robbins, Gillan, Smith, de Wit, and Ersche, 2012; *Animal learning theory:* Balleine and Dickinson, 1998; Balleine, 2004; Dayan and Balleine, 2002; *Robotics and control theory:* Sutton and Barto, 1998; Thrun, Burgard, and Fox, 2005; *Artificial intelligence:* Newell, 1990; Rich and Knight, 1991; *Neuroscience:* O'Keefe and Nadel, 1978; Squire, 1987; Schacter and Tulving, 1994; Doya, 1999, including both *computational modeling* (Redish, 1999; Daw, Niv, and Dayan, 2005; Niv, Joel, and Dayan, 2006c) and the new fields of *neuroeconomics* (Bernheim and Rangel, 2004; Montague, 2006; Glimcher, Camerer, Poldrack, and Fehr, 2008) and *computational psychiatry* (Redish, Jensen, and Johnson, 2008; Huys, Moutoussis, and Williams, 2011; Montague, Dolan, Friston, and Dayan, 2012).
92. *Evidence in favor of a separation:* McClure, Ericson, Laibson, Loewenstein, and Cohen, 2007; van der Meer and Redish, 2011b; *Evidence in favor of a unified value-function:* Kable and Glimcher, 2009; Wunderlich, Dayan, and Dolan, 2012.
93. Wikman, Branicky, and Newman, 1994.
94. Daw, Niv, and Dayan, 2005; Niv, Joel, and Dayan, 2006c; van der Meer, Kurth-Nelson, and Redish, 2012.
95. Balleine and Dickinson, 1998; Dayan and Balleine, 2002; Balleine, 2004; see also Dickinson, 1980; Flagel, Akil, and Robinson, 2009; Schoenbaum, Roesch, and Stalnaker, 2006.

Chapter 7. Reflexes

1. Brooks, 1991; Wikman, Branicky, and Newman, 1994.
2. Sherrington, 1906.
3. Kandel, Schwartz, and Jessell, 2000; Purves, Augustine, Fitzpatrick, Hall, LaMantia, McNamara, and White, 2008.
4. Sherrington, 1906; Kandel, Schwartz, and Jessell, 2000; Purves, Augustine, Fitzpatrick, Hall, LaMantia, McNamara, and White, 2008; Kandel, 2006.
5. Brooks, 1991; Braitenberg, 1986.
6. Eaton, 1984.
7. Eaton and Hackett, 1984; Ritzmann, 1984; Miller, Jacobs, and Theunissen, 1991; Liebenthal, Uhlmann, and Camhi, 1994; Levi and Camhi, 2000.
8. Kandel, Schwartz, and Jessell, 2000; Purves, Augustine, Fitzpatrick, Hall, LaMantia, McNamara, and White, 2008.
9. Kandel, 2006; Carew, 2004.
10. Majerus, 1998, 2002.
11. Tinbergen, 1951; Lorenz, 1952/1962.

Chapter 8. Emotion and the Pavlovian Action-Selection System

1. Damasio, 2003; Seymour and Dolan, 2008; LeDoux, 2012.
2. Barrett, 2006; LeDoux, 2012.
3. Seymour and Dolan, 2008.
4. Pavlov, 1927; Mackintosh, 1974; Dickinson, 1980; Domjan, 1998; LeDoux, 2002; Phelps and LeDoux, 2005; Bouton, 2007.
5. Rescorla, 1988.
6. Gallistel, 1990; Durlach and Shane, 1993; Delamater, 1995; Balleine and Dickinson, 1998; Corbit and Balleine, 2000; Corbit, Ostlund, and Balleine, 2002; Ostlund and Balleine, 2007.
7. Breland and Breland, 1961; Hershberger, 1986; Konorski, 1967; Dayan, Niv, Seymour, and Daw, 2006.

8. Damasio, 1994, 2003; LeDoux, 1996; Sapolsky, 1998b.
9. Davis, 1986.
10. Damasio, 1994; Delgado, Olsson, and Phelps, 2006; Phelps, 2008.
11. LeDoux, 1996; McNally, Pigg, and Weidemann, 2004; Phelps, 2008; Phelps and LeDoux, 2005.
12. Sapolsky, 1998b; Purves, Augustine, Fitzpatrick, Hall, LaMantia, McNamara, and White, 2008.
13. Sapolsky, 1998b; McEwan, 1991; Kandel, Schwartz, and Jessell, 2000; Carlson, 2010.
14. Descartes, 1647/1989; Damasio, 1994.
15. Damasio, 1994; Lokhorst, 2011.
16. Striedter, 2005.
17. Damasio, 2003, 2010; Cabanac, Cabanac, and Parent, 2009; Barrett, 2006; LeDoux, 2012.
18. James, 1890; Gleitman, 1991.
19. Lakoff and Johnson, 2003.
20. Preuss, 1995; Uylings, Groenewegen, and Kolb, 2003; Koechlin, 2011; Tsujimoto, Genovesio, and Wise, 2011.
21. Craig, 2003.
22. Damasio, 1992, 1994, 2003.
23. Damasio, 1994; Bechara, Tranel, and Damasio, 2000; Sanfey, Rilling, Aronson, Nystrom, and Cohen, 2003; Bechara, 2005; Bechara and van der Linden, 2005; Fellows, 2006; Zald and Rauch, 2008.
24. Harlow, 1848; Damasio, 1994, 2003; LeDoux, 1996.
25. Fuster, 1997/2008; Damasio, 2003; Tanji and Hoshi, 2007; Fellows, 2006; Wallis, 2007; Seamans, Lapish, and Durstewitz, 2008; Clark, Bechara, Damasio, Aitken, Sahakian, and Robbins, 2008; Gläscher, Adolphs, Damasio, Bechara, Rudrauf, Calamia, Paul, and Tranel, 2012.
26. Symms, Jäger, Schmierer, and Yousry, 2004.
27. Lehrer, 2009b; Plato, 4th century BCE/2008b.
28. Hofstadter, 1979; Dennet, 1981, 1992.
29. Augustine of Hippo (Saint Augustine), 427/1972.
30. Augustine of Hippo (Saint Augustine), 398/1961.
31. Freud, 1923/1990.
32. Baumeister, Heatherton, and Tice, 1994; Bechara, 2005; Haidt, 2006; Lehrer, 2009b.
33. Damasio, 1994, 2003.
34. Hare, 1999; Damasio, 2003; Singer, 2008; Kishida, King-Casas, and Montague, 2010; Ronson, 2011.
35. Lehrer, 2009b.
36. Sharot, 2011.
37. Sayette, Shiffman, Tiffany, Niaura, Martin, and Shadel, 2000; Robbins and Everitt, 1999; Everitt and Robbins, 2005.
38. Chaudhuri, 2011.
39. Marr, 1982; Akins, 1996.
40. Chaudhuri, 2011.
41. Green and Swets, 1966; Swets, 1996; Duda, Hart, and Storyk, 2001.
42. Güth, Schmittberger, and Schwarze, 1982; Wilson, 2002; Fehr and Fishbacher, 2003; Sanfey, Rilling, Aronson, Nystrom, and Cohen, 2003; Glimcher, Camerer, Poldrack, and Fehr, 2008; Zak, 2008; Fehr and Fishbacher, 2004; Kishida, King-Casas, and Montague, 2010.
43. Pillutla and Murnighan, 1996; Sanfey, Rilling, Aronson, Nystrom, and Cohen, 2003.
44. Harlé and Sanfey, 2007; Ariely, 2008; Andrade and Ariely, 2009.
45. Raghunathan, 1999; Haidt, 2006; Andrade and Ariely, 2009.
46. Augustine of Hippo (Saint Augustine), 398/1961; MacLean, 1973; Haidt, 2006.
47. Savage-Rumbaugh and Lewin, 1996; Patterson and Linden, 1981.
48. Berridge and Robinson, 2003.
49. Cabanac, Cabanac, and Parent, 2009; see also Damasio, 2003; Barrett, 2006; LeDoux, 2012.
50. James, 1890; Gleitman, 1991; Damasio, 1994, 2003, 2010.

Chapter 9. Deliberation

1. Niv, Joel, and Dayan, 2006c; van der Meer, Kurth-Nelson, and Redish, 2012.
2. Buckner and Carroll, 2007; Schacter, Addis, and Buckner, 2007.
3. Frith, 1996.
4. Rich and Knight, 1991; Nilsson, 1998; Johnson, van der Meer, and Redish, 2007.
5. Hill, 2008.
6. Baddeley, 2007; Fuster, 1997/2008.
7. Luria, 1976; Milner, 1998; Shrager, Levy, Hopkins, and Squire, 2008.
8. McDaniel and Einstein, 2007; Kliegel, McDaniel, and Einstein, 2008.
9. Baddeley, 2007; Burks, Carpenter, Goette, and Rustichini, 2009; Eigsti, Zayas, Mischel, Shoda, Ayduk, Dadlani, Davidson, Aber, and Casey, 2006.
10. Bickel, Yi, Landes, Hill, and Baxter, 2011.
11. Tolman, 1948.
12. Hull, 1943; Ferster and Skinner, 1957.
13. O'Keefe and Nadel, 1978; Redish, 1999; Johnson and Crowe, 2009; Tse, Langston, Kakeyama, Bethus, Spooner, Wood, Witter, and Morris, 2007; Tse, Takeuchi, Kakeyama, Kajii, Okuno, Tohyama, Bito, and Morris, 2011.
14. Cohen and Squire, 1980; Squire, 1987; Cohen and Eichenbaum, 1993.
15. Tulving, 1983, 1984; Squire, 1987.
16. Tolman, 1948.
17. Newell, Shaw, and Simon, 1959; McCorduck, 2004; Rich and Knight, 1991; Nilsson, 1998.
18. IBM, 1997; Saletan, 2007.
19. Chase and Simon, 1973; Ericsson, 2006.
20. Ericsson, 2006.
21. Baddeley, 2007.
22. Dreyfus, 1992; McCorduck, 2004.
23. Tolman, 1932; Balleine and Dickinson, 1998; van der Meer and Redish, 2010.
24. Niv, Joel, and Dayan, 2006c; Sutton and Barto, 1998; Daw, Niv, and Dayan, 2005; Ainge, Tamosiunaite, Woergoetter, and Dudchenko, 2007; Botvinick and An, 2009; van der Meer and Redish, 2010.
25. Niv, Joel, and Dayan, 2006c; Johnson and Redish, 2007; Johnson, van der Meer, and Redish, 2007; Pezzulo and Castelfranchi, 2009; Kurth-Nelson and Redish, 2012c.
26. Johnson and Redish, 2007.
27. O'Keefe and Nadel, 1978; Redish, 1999.
28. Wilson and McNaughton, 1993; Brown, Frank, Tang, Quirk, and Wilson, 1998; Zhang, Ginzburg, McNaughton, and Sejnowski, 1998.
29. Johnson, Jackson, and Redish, 2008.
30. Johnson, Fenton, Kentros, and Redish, 2009.
31. Schmitzer-Torbert and Redish, 2002, 2004; van der Meer, Johnson, Schmitzer-Torbert, and Redish, 2010.
32. Buckner and Carroll, 2007; Schacter, Addis, and Buckner, 2007, 2008.
33. *Humans:* Frith, 1996; Buckner and Carroll, 2007; Hassabis, Kumaran, Vann, and Maguire, 2007; Peters and Büchel, 2010; Hassabis and Maguire, 2011; Schacter, Addis, and Buckner, 2008; Schacter and Addis, 2011; *Rats:* Jones and Wilson, 2005; Johnson and Redish, 2007; Benchenane, Peyrache, Khamassi, Tierney, Gioanni, Battaglia, and Wiener, 2010; Hyman, Zilli, Paley, and Hasselmo, 2010.
34. *Humans:* Damasio, 1994; O'Doherty, 2004; Coricelli, Critchley, Joffily, O'Doherty, Sirigu, and Dolan, 2005; Bray, Shimojo, and O'Doherty, 2010; *Monkeys:* Tremblay and Schultz, 1999; Padoa-Schioppa and Assad, 2006; Padoa-Schioppa, 2009; *Rats:* Mogenson, Jones, and Yim, 1980; Martin, 2001; Schoenbaum, Roesch, and Stalnaker, 2006; Ramus, Davis, Donahue, Discenza, and Waite, 2007; McDannald, Lucantonio, Burke, Niv, and Schoenbaum, 2011; Steiner and Redish, 2012; van der Meer and Redish, 2011a,b.

35. Ratcliff and McKoon, 2008; Gold and Shadlen, 2002; Britten, Shadlen, Newsome, and Movshon, 1992; Platt and Glimcher, 1999; Hayden, Pearson, and Platt, 2011; Rangel and Hare, 2010.
36. Krajbich and Rangel, 2011.
37. Kable and Glimcher, 2009; Glimcher, 2010; Wunderlich, Dayan, and Dolan, 2012.
38. Plato, 4th century BCE/2008b.
39. Kurzban, 2010; Kahneman, 2011.
40. Wade, 2005.
41. Watson, 1913; MacCorquodale and Meehl, 1948; Skinner, 1971.
42. Johnson, Fenton, Kentros, and Redish, 2009.
43. Whitman, 1900; Minsky, 1985; Libet, 1985; Kurzban, 2010.
44. Sutton and Barto, 1998; Botvinick and An, 2009.
45. Newell, 1990; Botvinick, Niv, and Barto, 2009.
46. Hill, 2008; Kahneman, 2011; Tversky and Kahneman, 1981.
47. Phelps, 2008; Damasio, 2003; Fellows, 2006.
48. Andrade and Ariely, 2009.
49. Tolman, 1948.
50. Pillutla and Murnighan, 1996; Harlé and Sanfey, 2007.
51. Mogenson, Jones, and Yim, 1980; Damasio, 1994; Zald and Rauch, 2008; Fellows, 2006; Schoenbaum, Roesch, and Stalnaker, 2006.
52. Parent, 1986; Striedter, 2005.
53. Damasio, 1994, 2003; Bechara, Tranel, and Damasio, 2000; Fellows, 2006; Zald and Rauch, 2008; McDannald, Lucantonio, Burke, Niv, and Schoenbaum, 2011.
54. Tremblay, Hollerman, and Schultz, 1998; Tremblay and Schultz, 1999; Padoa-Schioppa and Assad, 2006; Padoa-Schioppa, 2009; van Duuren, Escámez, Joosten, Visser, Mulder, and Pennartz, 2007; van Duuren, van der Plasse, Lankelma, Joosten, Feenstra, and Pennartz, 2009; van der Meer and Redish, 2011a; Schoenbaum and Roesch, 2005; Roesch, Singh, Brown, Mullins, and Schoenbaum, 2009; Steiner and Redish, 2012.
55. Chib, Rangel, Shimojo, and O'Doherty, 2009.
56. Tremblay and Schultz, 1999; Padoa-Schioppa and Assad, 2006; Padoa-Schioppa, 2009.
57. Simonson and Tversky, 1992; Plous, 1993; Shapiro and Varian, 1999; Ariely, 2008; Kahneman, 2011.
58. Garcia, Hankins, and Rusiniak, 1974.
59. Bernstein, 1978, 1999.
60. Balleine and Dickinson, 1998.
61. Tremblay and Schultz, 1999; Schoenbaum, Roesch, and Stalnaker, 2006; Pritchard, Nedderman, Edwards, Petticoffer, Schwartz, and Scott, 2008; Kobayashi, de Carvalho, and Schultz, 2010.
62. Stalnaker, Roesch, Franz, Burke, and Schoenbaum, 2006; Schoenbaum, Roesch, and Stalnaker, 2006; Koob and Volkow, 2010.
63. McDannald, Lucantonio, Burke, Niv, and Schoenbaum, 2011.
64. Hare, O'Doherty, Camerer, Schultz, and Rangel, 2008; Plassmann, O'Doherty, and Rangel, 2010; Hare, Camerer, and Rangel, 2009; Hare, Malmaud, and Rangel, 2011.
65. van der Meer and Redish, 2009, 2010; Steiner and Redish, 2012.
66. Muenzinger and Gentry, 1931; Tolman, 1932; Johnson, van der Meer, and Redish, 2007; van der Meer, Johnson, Schmitzer-Torbert, and Redish, 2010.
67. Johnson and Redish, 2007.
68. Fellows, 2006.
69. Baddeley, 2007.
70. *Increased consistency and better options chosen with improved working memory:* Franco-Watkins, Rickard, and Pashler, 2010; Hinson, Jameson, and Whitney, 2003; Shamosh, DeYoung, Green, Reis, Johnson, Conway, Engle, Braver, and Gray, 2008; Burks, Carpenter, Goette, and Rustichini, 2009; *Training:* Bickel, Yi, Landes, Hill, and Baxter, 2011; see Kurth-Nelson and Redish, 2012c, for a computational discussion.
71. Guthrie, 1937; Shakespeare, 1601.

72. Tolman, 1932, 1948; Hull, 1943, 1952; Tulving and Madigan, 1970; Cohen and Squire, 1980; O'Keefe and Nadel, 1978; Squire, 1987; Cohen and Eichenbaum, 1993; Redish, 1999.

73. Tolman, 1932; Munn, 1950; O'Keefe and Nadel, 1978; Gallistel, 1990; Gallistel, Fairhurst, and Balsam, 2004.

74. Smith, Frank, Wirth, Yanike, Hu, Kubota, Graybiel, Suzuki, and Brown, 2004.

75. Gallistel, Mark, King, and Latham, 2001; Smith, Frank, Wirth, Yanike, Hu, Kubota, Graybiel, Suzuki, and Brown, 2004.

76. Gallistel, Fairhurst, and Balsam, 2004.

77. Cohen and Squire, 1980; Squire, 1987; Mishkin and Appenzeller, 1987; Graybiel, 1995; van der Meer, Johnson, Schmitzer-Torbert, and Redish, 2010.

78. Hull, 1943, 1952; Ferster and Skinner, 1957.

79. Tolman, 1939; Papale, Stott, Powell, Regier, and Redish, 2012.

80. Hooke, 1665; Galileo, 1610.

81. *Information theory:* Shannon, 1948; Gleick, 2011; *Computers and computation:* Goldstine, 1980; von Neumann, 1958/2000; Turing, 1937; Kahn, 1967/1996; Wiener, 1948; *Algorithm:* Newell, Shaw, and Simon, 1959; McCorduck, 2004.

82. O'Keefe and Nadel, 1978; Packard and McGaugh, 1996; Balleine and Dickinson, 1998; Redish, 1999; Daw, Niv, and Dayan, 2005; Niv, Joel, and Dayan, 2006c; Johnson, van der Meer, and Redish, 2007; van der Meer, Johnson, Schmitzer-Torbert, and Redish, 2010; Dezfouli and Balleine, 2012; van der Meer, Kurth-Nelson, and Redish, 2012.

83. Restle, 1957; O'Keefe and Nadel, 1978; Packard and McGaugh, 1996; Redish, 1999; Redish, Jensen, and Johnson, 2008; van der Meer, Johnson, Schmitzer-Torbert, and Redish, 2010.

Chapter 10. The Habits of our Lives

1. Mishkin and Appenzeller, 1987; Rand, Hikosaka, Miyachi, Lu, and Miyashita, 1998; Rand, Hikosaka, Miyachi, Lu, Nakamura, Kitaguchi, and Shimo, 2000; Killcross and Coutureau, 2003; Redish, Jensen, and Johnson, 2008; van der Meer, Johnson, Schmitzer-Torbert, and Redish, 2010.

2. Iversen and Mishkin, 1970; Isoda and Hikosaka, 2007; Redish, Jensen, and Johnson, 2008.

3. McCartt, Hellinga, and Bratiman, 2006; Collet, Guillot, and Petit, 2010a,b.

4. Mackintosh, 1974; Domjan, 1998.

5. Redish, Jensen, Johnson, and Kurth-Nelson, 2007.

6. Hull, 1943; Daw, Niv, and Dayan, 2005; Redish, Jensen, and Johnson, 2008.

7. Miller, 1956; Graybiel, 1995; Newell, 1990; Botvinick, Niv, and Barto, 2009; Dezfouli and Balleine, 2012.

8. Daw, Niv, and Dayan, 2005; Johnson, van der Meer, and Redish, 2007.

9. Cohen and Squire, 1980; Squire, 1987; Mishkin and Appenzeller, 1987.

10. Hull, 1943; Tinbergen, 1951.

11. Cisek and Kalaska, 2010.

12. Gibson, 1977, 1979; Norman, 1988.

13. Miller, 1956; Newell, 1990; Botvinick, Niv, and Barto, 2009.

14. Shelton, 1988.

15. Nissen and Bullemer, 1987; Willingham, Nissen, and Bullemer, 1989.

16. Nissen and Bullemer, 1987; Willingham, Nissen, and Bullemer, 1989; Knopman and Nissen, 1991; Knowlton, Mangels, and Squire, 1996; Werheid, Zysset, Müller, Reuter, and von Cramon, 2003; Shohamy, Myers, Grossman, Sage, Gluck, and Poldrack, 2004; Myers, Shohamy, Gluck, Grossman, Onlaor, and Kapur, 2003.

17. Knopman and Nissen, 1987; Reber, 1989; Knowlton, Squire, and Gluck, 1994; Werheid, Zysset, Müller, Reuter, and von Cramon, 2003; Myers, Shohamy, Gluck, Grossman, Onlaor, and Kapur, 2003.

18. *Implicit vs. explicit:* Pascual-Leone, Grafman, and Hallett, 1994; Willingham, 1999; Boyd and Winstein, 2004; *Procedural vs. Declarative:* Cohen and Squire, 1980; Mishkin and Appenzeller,

1987; Squire, 1987; *Habit vs. goal-oriented:* Balleine and Dickinson, 1998; Yin, Knowlton, and Balleine, 2004; Daw, Niv, and Dayan, 2005; Redish, Jensen, and Johnson, 2008.

19. Mishkin and Appenzeller, 1987; Graybiel, 1995; Frank, 2011.

20. Doya, 1999; Hikosaka, Nakahara, Rand, Sakai, Lu, Nakamura, Miyachi, and Doya, 1999; Diener and Dichgans, 1992.

21. Jerison, 1973; Grillner, 1981; Parent, 1986; Rogers, 1998; Striedter, 2005; Llinas, 2002.

22. Albin, Young, and Penney, 1989; Frank, 2011.

23. Nambu, Tokuno, and Takada, 2002; Frank, Samanta, Moustafa, and Sherman, 2007b; Isoda and Hikosaka, 2008.

24. Frank, Moustafa, Haughey, Curran, and Hutchison, 2007a; Kravitz, Tye, and Kreitzer, 2012.

25. Cools, Altamirano, and D'Esposito, 2006; Frank, Seeberger, and O'Reilly, 2004; Frank, Moustafa, Haughey, Curran, and Hutchison, 2007a; Kéri, Moustafa, Myers, Benedek, and Gluck, 2010.

26. Frank, Seeberger, and O'Reilly, 2004; Frank, Moustafa, Haughey, Curran, and Hutchison, 2007a.

27. Darwin, 1859; Wiener, 1995.

28. *Serotonin:* Daw, Kakade, and Dayan, 2002; Boureau and Dayan, 2011; *Norepinephrine/ Noradrenaline:* Redish, Jensen, Johnson, and Kurth-Nelson, 2007; Koob, 2009.

29. Cooper, Bloom, and Roth, 1986.

30. Unoki, Matsumoto, and Mizunami, 2005; Mizunami, Unoki, Mori, Hirashima, Hatano, and Matsumoto, 2009; Busto, Cervantes-Sandoval, and Davis, 2010.

31. Crisp and Mesce, 2004; Friesen and Kristan, 2007; Puhl and Mesce, 2008; Mesce and Pierce-Shimomura, 2010.

32. Miyazaki, Miyazaki, and Doya, 2010; *Delays and perspective:* Mobini, Chiang, Al-Ruwaitea, Ho, Bradshaw, and Szabadi, 2000; Doya, 2008; Tanaka, Shishida, Schweighofer, Okamoto, Yamawaki, and Doya, 2009; Miyazaki, Miyazaki, and Doya, 2012a,b.

33. Aston-Jones, Delfs, Druhan, and Zhu, 1999; Harris and Gewirtz, 2005; Aston-Jones and Kalivas, 2008; Koob, 2009.

34. Paladini and Williams, 2004; *Dopamine and disappointment:* Ljungberg, Apicella, and Schultz, 1992; Schultz, Dayan, and Montague, 1997; Bayer and Glimcher, 2005.

35. *Attention:* Aston-Jones, Chiang, and Alexinsky, 1991; Aston-Jones and Cohen, 2005; *Uncertainty:* Yu and Dayan, 2005; Doya, 2008.

36. Niv, Daw, Joel, and Dayan, 2006b; Redish, Jensen, Johnson, and Kurth-Nelson, 2007.

37. Yu and Dayan, 2005; Niv, Daw, Joel, and Dayan, 2006b; Redish, Jensen, Johnson, and Kurth-Nelson, 2007; Servan-Schreiber, Printz, and Cohen, 1990; Dalley, Cardinal, and Robbins, 2004; Arnsten, 2011.

38. Iversen, Iversen, Bloom, and Roth, 2008; Purves, Augustine, Fitzpatrick, Hall, LaMantia, McNamara, and White, 2008; Carlson, 2010.

39. Sapolsky, 1998b; Carlson, 2010.

40. Swanson, 2000; Strick, Dum, and Picard, 1995; Middleton and Strick, 2000.

41. Alexander and Crutcher, 1990; Cisek and Kalaska, 2010.

42. Chaudhuri, 2011; *e.g., Visual cortices:* Van Essen, Anderson, and Felleman, 1992; Zeki, 1993; Epstein and Kanwisher, 1998; Op de Beeck, Haushofer, and Kanwisher, 2008; Tsao, Moeller, and Freiwald, 2008; Liu, Harris, and Kanwisher, 2010; *e.g., Auditory cortices:* Nourski and Brugge, 2011; Carlson, 2010.

43. Cisek and Kalaska, 2010.

44. Hebb, 1949/2002; Rumelhart and McClelland, 1986; McClelland and Rumelhart, 1986; Kohonen, 1980, 1984; Hertz, Krogh, and Palmer, 1991.

45. Jackson and Redish, 2003; Johnson, Jackson, and Redish, 2008; Cisek and Kalaska, 2010.

46. Cisek and Kalaska, 2010.

47. Georgopoulos, Lurito, Petrides, Schwartz, and Massey, 1989; Alexander and Crutcher, 1990.

48. Dunlop, 2009.

49. Afshar, Santhanam, Yu, Ryu, Sahani, and Shenoy, 2011; Hebb, 1949/2002; Hertz, Krogh, and Palmer, 1991; Redish, Jensen, Johnson, and Kurth-Nelson, 2007.

50. Miller, 1956; Newell, 1990.

51. Barlow, 2002; Llinas, 2002; Striedter, 2005.
52. Jerison, 1973; Rogers, 1998.
53. Eccles, Itō, and Szentágothai, 1967; Barlow, 2002.
54. Itō, 1984; Barlow, 2002; Rokni, Llinas, and Yarom, 2008.
55. Marr, 1969; Itō, 1984; Barlow, 2002.
56. Martin, Keating, Goodkin, Bastian, and Thach, 1996a,b.
57. Bares, Lungu, Liu, Waechter, Gomez, and Ashe, 2007; Llinas, 2002.
58. Molinari, Chiricozzi, Clausi, Tedesco, Lisa, and Leggio, 2008.
59. Miller, 1956.

Chapter 11. Integrating Information

1. Gleitman, 1991; Chaudhuri, 2011.
2. Britten, Shadlen, Newsome, and Movshon, 1992; Platt and Glimcher, 1999; Gold and Shadlen, 2002; Wade, 2005; Churchland, Kiani, and Shadlen, 2008; Ratcliff and McKoon, 2008; Lauwereyns, 2010; Krajbich and Rangel, 2011.
3. Gold and Shadlen, 2002; Ratcliff and McKoon, 2008; Lauwereyns, 2010.
4. Jaynes, 2003; Gold and Shadlen, 2002; Ratcliff and McKoon, 2008; Lauwereyns, 2010; Gleick, 2011.
5. Ratcliff and McKoon, 2008.
6. Kalbfleisch and Prentice, 2002.
7. Ratcliff and McKoon, 2008; Gell-Mann, 1995.
8. Britten, Shadlen, Newsome, and Movshon, 1992.
9. Van Essen, Anderson, and Felleman, 1992.
10. Van Essen, Anderson, and Felleman, 1992.
11. Britten, Shadlen, Newsome, and Movshon, 1992.
12. Sato, Kishore, Page, and Duffy, 2010; Wurtz and Duffy, 1992.
13. Gold and Shadlen, 2002, 2007.
14. Churchland, Kiani, and Shadlen, 2008.
15. Amari, 1977; Wilson and Cowan, 1973; Kohonen, 1980, 1984; Hertz, Krogh, and Palmer, 1991; Redish, Elga, and Touretzky, 1996; Zhang, 1996; Deneve, Latham, and Pouget, 1999; Laing and Chow, 2001; Redish, 1999.
16. Treisman and Gelade, 1980; Treisman and Gormican, 1988; Chaudhuri, 2011.
17. Tsao, Moeller, and Freiwald, 2008; Liu, Harris, and Kanwisher, 2010.
18. Behrmann and Avidan, 2005; Yin, 1970; Sacks, 1985/1998.
19. Moulitsas, 2010.
20. Treisman and Gelade, 1980; Treisman and Gormican, 1988; Julesz, 1991; Koch, 2004; Gilden, Thornton, and Marusich, 2010.
21. Ratcliff and McKoon, 2008.
22. *The Baseball Encyclopedia*, www.baseball-reference.com.
23. Classé, Semes, Daum, Nowakowski, Alexander, Wisniewski, Beisel, Mann, Rutstein, Smith, and Bartolucci, 1997.
24. *Deep Blue vs. Kasparov:* IBM, 1997; Saletan, 2007; *but chess masters do less search:* Chase and Simon, 1973; de Groot, 1978; Charness, 1991.
25. Green and Bavalier, 2003.
26. Ericsson, Krampe, and Tesch-Römer, 1993; Ericsson, 2006.
27. Kurkjian, 2006.

Chapter 12. The Stories We Tell

1. Whishaw and Kolb, 2004; Domjan, 1998.
2. Morris, 1981; Redish, 1999.
3. Morris, Garrud, Rawlins, and O'Keefe, 1982; Whishaw, 1985; Eichenbaum, Stewart, and Morris, 1990; Day, Weisend, Sutherland, and Schallert, 1999; Redish, 1999.

4. Huettel, Song, and McCarthy, 2009.

5. Bourke, Turkington, Thomas, McComb, and Tynan, 1997; Hamner, Hunt, Gee, Garrell, and Monroe, 1999; Godemann, Ahrens, Behrens, Berthold, Gandor, Lampe, and Linden, 2001.

6. Sutton and Barto, 1998.

7. Watson, 1907; Gallistel, 1990; Eichenbaum, Stewart, and Morris, 1990; Nakazawa, Quirk, Chitwood, Watanabe, Yeckel, Sun, Kato, Carr, Johnston, Wilson, and Tonegawa, 2002; Redish, 1999.

8. Redish, Jensen, Johnson, and Kurth-Nelson, 2007.

9. Hebb, 1949/2002; Kohonen, 1984; Lakoff, 1990/1997; Hertz, Krogh, and Palmer, 1991; see Appendix C for a discussion of the mechanism of content-addressable memory.

10. Grossberg, 1976; Hertz, Krogh, and Palmer, 1991.

11. Redish, Jensen, Johnson, and Kurth-Nelson, 2007.

12. *Animals:* Bouton, 2004; *Addicts:* O'Brien, Childress, Ehrman, and Robbins, 1998; *Students:* McDermott, 1991.

13. Redish, Jensen, Johnson, and Kurth-Nelson, 2007; *Illusion of control:* Langer and Roth, 1975; Custer, 1984; *Chasing losses:* Lesieur, 1977; Wagenaar, 1988.

14. *Extinction is not forgetting:* Pavlov, 1927; Bouton, 2004; Myers and Davis, 2007; *Changes in speed of extinction:* Capaldi, 1957, 1958; Capaldi and Lynch, 1968; *Context-related relapse:* O'Brien, Childress, Ehrman, and Robbins, 1998; *Gambling and the illusion of control:* Custer, 1984; Wagenaar, 1988.

15. Redish, Jensen, Johnson, and Kurth-Nelson, 2007; *Original algorithm:* Grossberg, 1976; Hertz, Krogh, and Palmer, 1991.

16. Plato, 4th century BCE/2008a; Graham, 2011.

17. Lakoff, 1990/1997.

18. Schank and Abelson, 1977; Schank, 1980.

19. Abrahams, 1983; Erdoes and Ortiz, 1985; Calvino, 1956.

20. Bova, 1981; Gardner, 1983.

21. Mateas and Sengers, 2003.

22. Ainslie, 1992; Kurth-Nelson and Redish, 2010.

Chapter 13. Motivation

1. Glimcher, Camerer, Poldrack, and Fehr, 2008.

2. Smith, 1776/1904.

3. Smith, 1759/1790, 1776/1904; Glimcher, Camerer, Poldrack, and Fehr, 2008; Zak, 2008.

4. Plous, 1993; Glimcher, Camerer, Poldrack, and Fehr, 2008; Kahneman, 2011.

5. Tversky and Kahneman, 1981; Plous, 1993; Kahneman, 2011.

6. Plous, 1993; Glimcher, Camerer, Poldrack, and Fehr, 2008; Glimcher, 2010.

7. Sutton and Barto, 1998.

8. Uchibe and Doya, 2008.

9. Stephens and Krebs, 1987.

10. Stephens and Krebs, 1987; Giraldeau and Caraco, 2000; *Monkeys:* Hayden, Pearson, and Platt, 2011; *Hunter-gatherers:* Kennett and Winterhalder, 2006; *Information foraging:* Pirolli, 2007.

11. Darwin, 1859; Dawkins, 1976; Ridley, 1995; Wright, 1995.

12. Wilson, 1980.

13. Edelman, 1987; Ridley, 1995.

14. Wilson, 1980; Wright, 1995; Ridley, 2000, 2003; see Goodall and van Lawick, 1971/1988/2000; Sapolsky, 2001; Strum, 1987; Goodall, 1990, for some examples of the complexity of primate interactions.

15. Wilson, 1980; Brown, 1991; Wright, 1995; Churchland, 2011.

16. NASA, 2011.

17. Wright, 1995; Hill and Halliday, 1998; Brown, 1991.

18. Wilson, 1980.

19. Braitenberg, 1986; Schöne, 1984.
20. Brown, 1991; Ridley, 1995; Wright, 1995.
21. Wilson, 1980; Brown, 1991; Wright, 1995.
22. Johnston and Franklin, 1993; Rhodes, 2006.
23. Brown, 1991; Wright, 1995; Wilson, 2002.
24. Watson, 1913; Skinner, 1971.
25. Blum, 2002.
26. Harlow, 1958; Harlow and Zimmermann, 1959.
27. Blum, 1995.
28. Bowlby, 1969/1982, 1977; Blum, 2002; van der Horst, LeRoy, and van der Veer, 2008.
29. Blum, 2002.
30. Popper, 1935/1959/1992; Kuhn, 1962/1996; Ben-Ari, 2005.
31. Ben-Ari, 2005.
32. Insel and Young, 2001; Kosfeld, Heinrichs, Zak, Fischbacher, and Fehr, 2005; Zak, Stanton, and Ahmadi, 2007; White-Traut, Watanabe, Pournajafi-Nazarloo, Schwertz, Bell, and Carter, 2009; Feldman, Gordon, and Zagoory-Sharon, 2010.
33. Harlow, 1958; Harlow and Zimmermann, 1959; Feldman, Gordon, and Zagoory-Sharon, 2010.
34. Beck and Katcher, 1996.
35. Haidt, 2006.
36. Sutton and Barto, 1998; Kakade and Dayan, 2002; Laurent, 2008; *Information gathering:* Glanzer, 1958; Loewenstein, 1994; *Over-optimism:* Daw, O'Doherty, Dayan, Seymour, and Dolan, 2006; Sharot, Riccardi, Raio, and Phelps, 2007; Sharot, 2011.
37. Harlow, 1953.
38. Feynman, 1997.
39. Kummer, 1971; Southwick, 1963; Fossey, 1983/2000; Goodall and van Lawick, 1971/1988/2000; Goodall, 1990; Sapolsky, 1998b; de Waal and Lanting, 1997.
40. Smuts, 1985; Strum, 1987.
41. Sapolsky, 2001.
42. Brown, 1991; Diamond, 1999; de Waal, 2001; Sapolsky, 2001; de Waal, 2009.
43. Redish, 1997.
44. Elliot, Friston, and Dolan, 2000; O'Doherty, Dayan, Friston, Critchley, and Dolan, 2003; Tobler, O'Doherty, Dolan, and Schultz, 2007; Singer, Seymour, O'Doherty, Stephan, Dolan, and Frith, 2006.
45. *Food:* O'Doherty, Buchanan, Seymour, and Dolan, 2006; Kang, Rangel, Camus, and Camerer, 2011; Hare, Malmaud, and Rangel, 2011; *Money:* Elliot, Friston, and Dolan, 2000; Breiter, Aharon, Kahneman, Dale, and Shizgal, 2001; Pagnoni, Zink, Montague, and Berns, 2002; Tobler, O'Doherty, Dolan, and Schultz, 2007; *Drugs:* Volkow, Fowler, and Wang, 2002; *Attractive faces:* Aharon, Etcoff, Ariely, Chabris, O'Connor, and Breiter, 2001; Bray and O'Doherty, 2007; *Video games:* Mathiak, Klasen, Weber, Ackermann, Shergill, and Mathiak, 2011; *Music:* Menon and Levitin, 2005; *Love and grief:* Najib, Lorberbaum, Kose, Bohning, and George, 2004; Fischer, Aron, and Brown, 2006; Fischer, Brown, Aron, Strong, and Mashek, 2010; *Altruism:* Moll, Krueger, Zahn, Pardini, de Oliveira-Souza, and Grafman, 2006; Harbaugh, Mayr, and Burghart, 2007; *Justice:* de Quervain, Fischbacher, Treyer, Schellhammer, Schnyder, Buck, and Fehr, 2004; Singer, Seymour, O'Doherty, Stephan, Dolan, and Frith, 2006; Sanfey and Dorris, 2009.
46. Boyer, 2002; Wilson, 2002; Zak, 2008.
47. Singer, Seymour, O'Doherty, Stephan, Dolan, and Frith, 2006.
48. Berns, Chappelow, Cekic, Zink, Pagnoni, and Martin-Skurski, 2006.
49. Brown, 1991; Boyer, 2002.
50. Tinbergen, 1951; Levi-Strauss, 1970; LeVay, 1993; Wright, 1995; Ridley, 1995, 2003; Zak, 2008.
51. Berridge, 2012.
52. Phelps and LeDoux, 2005.

53. Wassum, Cely, Balleine, and Maidment, 2011a; Wassum, Ostlund, Balleine, and Maidment, 2011b; LeDoux, 2012.
54. Ludwig, 1989; Childress, Mozley, McElgin, Fitzgerald, Reivich, and O'Brien, 1999; Robinson and Berridge, 2003; Skinner and Aubin, 2010; Berridge, 2012.
55. Kruse, Overmier, Konz, and Rokke, 1983; Corbit and Janak, 2007; Talmi, Seymour, Dayan, and Dolan, 2008; van der Meer and Redish, 2010; Wassum, Cely, Balleine, and Maidment, 2011a.
56. McClure, Li, Tomlin, Cypert, Montague, and Montague, 2004b.
57. Plassmann, O'Doherty, Shiv, and Rangel, 2008.
58. Kruse, Overmier, Konz, and Rokke, 1983; Corbit and Janak, 2007; Talmi, Seymour, Dayan, and Dolan, 2008; van der Meer and Redish, 2010.
59. O'Brien, Childress, Ehrman, and Robbins, 1998; Childress, Mozley, McElgin, Fitzgerald, Reivich, and O'Brien, 1999.
60. Rose, Salley, Behm, Bates, and Westman, 2010.
61. McClure, Li, Tomlin, Cypert, Montague, and Montague, 2004b; Montague, 2006.
62. Shaw, 1992; Niv, Daw, Joel, and Dayan, 2006b.
63. Niv, Daw, Joel, and Dayan, 2006b.
64. Schultz, Dayan, and Montague, 1997; Bayer and Glimcher, 2005.
65. Daw, 2003; Niv, Daw, Joel, and Dayan, 2006b.
66. Schultz, Dayan, and Montague, 1997; Berridge, 2012; Denny-Brown, 1962; Jankovic and Tolosa, 2007.
67. Koller, 1992.
68. Jankovic and Tolosa, 2007.
69. Jagger and Richards, 1969; Berridge, 2007.
70. Berridge and Robinson, 2003; Wise, 2004; Salamone, Correa, Farrar, Nunes, and Pardo, 2009; Kurniawan, Guitart-Masip, and Dolan, 2011; Walton, Kennerley, Bannerman, Phillips, and Rushworth, 2006; Salamone, Correa, Farrar, and Mingote, 2007; Niv, Daw, Joel, and Dayan, 2006b; Tindell, Smith, Berridge, and Aldridge, 2009.
71. Crisp and Mesce, 2004; Puhl and Mesce, 2008.
72. Tindell, Smith, Berridge, and Aldridge, 2009.
73. Schultz, 1998; Berridge, 2007, 2012.
74. Maier and Seligman, 1976; Niv, Daw, Joel, and Dayan, 2006b.

Chapter 14. The Tradeoff Between Exploration and Exploitation

1. Whittle, 1988; Sutton and Barto, 1998; Daw, O'Doherty, Dayan, Seymour, and Dolan, 2006.
2. Sutton and Barto, 1998.
3. Mitchell, 1997; Newell, 1993.
4. Mozer, 2004.
5. Mlodinow, 2009.
6. Gittins, 1989.
7. Bossaerts and Plott, 2004; Preuschoff, Bossaerts, and Quartz, 2006; Behrens, Woolrich, Walton, and Rushworth, 2007; Frank, Doll, Oas-Terpstra, and Moreno, 2009.
8. Bernstein, 1998.
9. Markowitz, 1952.
10. Winstanley, Balleine, Brown, Büchel, Cools, Durstewitz, O'Doherty, Pennartz, Redish, Seamans, and Robbins, 2012.
11. *Rats:* Gallistel, 1990; Gallistel, Fairhurst, and Balsam, 2004; *Monkeys:* Corrado, Sugrue, Seung, and Newsome, 2005; Sugrue, Corrado, and Newsome, 2004; Lau and Glimcher, 2005; *Humans:* Behrens, Woolrich, Walton, and Rushworth, 2007.
12. Shannon, 1948; Jensen, 2010; Gleick, 2011.
13. Amsel, 1992; Domjan, 1998; Rick, Horvitz, and Balsam, 2006; Bouton, 2007.
14. Donald Rumsfeld, U.S. Secretary of Defense speech to NATO HQ, June 7, 2002.
15. Sun Tzu, 5th century BCE/1910/1994; Bujold, 2002.

16. Winstanley, Balleine, Brown, Büchel, Cools, Durstewitz, O'Doherty, Pennartz, Redish, Seamans, and Robbins, 2012; Payzan-LeNestour and Bossaerts, 2011.
17. O'Keefe and Nadel, 1978; Archer and Birke, 1983; Redish, 1999.
18. Ellsberg, 1961; Camerer and Weber, 1992; Plous, 1993; Glimcher, Camerer, Poldrack, and Fehr, 2008.
19. *New York Times*, 2011.
20. Ellsberg, 1961; Camerer and Weber, 1992; Epstein, 1999; Glimcher, Camerer, Poldrack, and Fehr, 2008.
21. *Losses and gains:* Plous, 1993; Kahneman, 2011; *Inability to do the full calculation:* Epstein, 1999; *Avoiding deceit:* Frisch and Baron, 1988; Camerer and Weber, 1992.
22. Centers for Disease Control and Prevention, 2011.
23. Feynman, 1997; Haidt, 2006.
24. Bromberg-Martin and Hikosaka, 2009.
25. Kakade and Dayan, 2002.
26. Chance and Mead, 1955; Gray and McNaughton, 2000; Haidt, 2006.
27. Kakade and Dayan, 2002; Laurent, 2008.
28. Sharot, Riccardi, Raio, and Phelps, 2007; Sharot, 2011.
29. *Monkeys:* Bromberg-Martin and Hikosaka, 2009; *Humans:* Daw, O'Doherty, Dayan, Seymour, and Dolan, 2006; Bunzeck, Doeller, Dolan, and Duzel, 2012; Krebs, Schott, Schütze, and Düze, 2009; Sharot, Riccardi, Raio, and Phelps, 2007; Sharot, 2011.
30. Harlow, 1953; O'Keefe and Nadel, 1978; Archer and Birke, 1983; Thinus-Blanc, 1996.
31. de Waal, 2001; Malfait, Valyear, Culham, Anton, Brown, and Gribble, 2010; Rizzolatti and Sinigaglia, 2010; Nicolle, Symmonds, and Dolan, 2011.
32. Dawkins, 1976; Richerson and Boyd, 2005; Aunger, 2001; de Waal, 2001; Sterelny, 2006.
33. Rizzolatti, Fadiga, Gallese, and Fogassi, 1996; Rizzolatti and Craighero, 2004.
34. Malfait, Valyear, Culham, Anton, Brown, and Gribble, 2010; Rizzolatti and Craighero, 2004.
35. de Waal, 2001; Malfait, Valyear, Culham, Anton, Brown, and Gribble, 2010; Nicolle, Symmonds, and Dolan, 2011; see Rizzolatti and Sinigaglia, 2010, and Schilbach, 2010, for a discussion of the controversy of mirror neurons.
36. Keysers and Gazzola, 2006; Shamay-Tsoory, Tibi-Elhanany, and Aharon-Peretz, 2007; Singer, 2008; Bastiaansen, Thioux, and Keysers, 2009.
37. Singer, 2008.
38. Damasio, 2003; Krajbich, Adolphs, Trane, Denburg, and Camerer, 2009.
39. *Empathy:* Damasio, 2003; Singer, 2008; Hein, Lamm, Brodbeck, and Singer, 2011; *Envy:* Shamay-Tsoory, Tibi-Elhanany, and Aharon-Peretz, 2007; Takahashi, Kato, Matsuura, Mobbs, Suhara, and Okubo, 2009; *Regret:* Bell, 1982, 1985; Loomes and Sugden, 1982; Coricelli, Critchley, Joffily, O'Doherty, Sirigu, and Dolan, 2005.
40. Coricelli, Critchley, Joffily, O'Doherty, Sirigu, and Dolan, 2005; Hassabis, Kumaran, Vann, and Maguire, 2007; Schacter, Addis, and Buckner, 2008.
41. Tolkien, 1965; Lucas, 1977; Cherryh, 1989.
42. Sutton and Barto, 1998.
43. Amsel, 1992; Domjan, 1998; Rick, Horvitz, and Balsam, 2006; Redish, Jensen, Johnson, and Kurth-Nelson, 2007.
44. Spear, 2000; Somerville, Jones, and Casey, 2010.
45. Casey, Getz, and Galvan, 2008a; Somerville, Jones, and Casey, 2010; Somerville and Casey, 2010; Luna, Padmanabhan, and O'Hearn, 2010.
46. Anthony, Warner, and Kessler, 1994; Heyman, 2009; Lowinson, Ruiz, Millman, and Langrod, 1997; Koob and Le Moal, 2006; Wagner and Anthony, 2002.

Chapter 15. Self-Control

1. Plato, 4th century BCE/2008b; Augustine of Hippo (Saint Augustine), 398/1961; Freud, 1923/1990.
2. Haidt, 2006; Lehrer, 2009b.

3. Hayes, 2011.
4. Haidt, 2006.
5. Kurzban, 2010, see also Minsky, 1985, for a very early description of agency as conflict between multiple modules.
6. Freud, 1923/1990.
7. *Stroop task*: Stroop, 1935; Gleitman, 1991; MacLeod, 1991; *Stop-signal task*: Logan and Cowan, 1984; Frank, Samanta, Moustafa, and Sherman, 2007b; Isoda and Hikosaka, 2007; Boucher, Palmeri, Logan, and Schall, 2007; Eagle, Bari, and Robbins, 2008; *Marshmallow task*: Mischel and Underwood, 1974; Mischel, Shoda, and Rodriguez, 1989; Metcalfe and Mischel, 1999; Boysen and Berntson, 1995.
8. Vohs and Heatherton, 2000; Baumeister, Heatherton, and Tice, 1994.
9. Stroop, 1935; Festinger, 1954; Read, Vanman, and Miller, 1997; McCusker, 2001; Gailliot, Baumeister, DeWall, Maner, Plant, Tice, Brewer, and Schmeichel, 2007.
10. Nijslow, Franken, and Muris, 2010; Waters, Marhe, and Franken, 2012.
11. *Rats*: Eagle, Bari, and Robbins, 2008; *Monkeys*: Hanes and Schall, 1995; Isoda and Hikosaka, 2007; Boucher, Palmeri, Logan, and Schall, 2007; *Humans*: Logan and Cowan, 1984; Frank, Samanta, Moustafa, and Sherman, 2007b; Eagle, Bari, and Robbins, 2008.
12. Boucher, Palmeri, Logan, and Schall, 2007; Verbruggen and Logan, 2009.
13. Isoda and Hikosaka, 2007; Frank, Samanta, Moustafa, and Sherman, 2007b; Isoda and Hikosaka, 2008; Schall, Stuphorn, and Brown, 2002.
14. Mischel and Underwood, 1974; Boysen and Berntson, 1995; Bushong, King, Camerer, and Rangel, 2010.
15. Boysen and Berntson, 1995.
16. Bushong, King, Camerer, and Rangel, 2010.
17. Ainslie, 1992, 2001; Rachlin, 2004; McClure, Laibson, Loewenstein, and Cohen, 2004a; McClure, Ericson, Laibson, Loewenstein, and Cohen, 2007; Bechara, 2005; Kurzban, 2010.
18. Ainslie, 2001; Kurth-Nelson and Redish, 2010.
19. Dickerson and O'Connor, 2006.
20. Mischel, Shoda, and Rodriguez, 1989; Baumeister, Heatherton, and Tice, 1994; Hill, 2008.
21. Ludwig, 1989; Boyer, 2002; Heyman, 2009.
22. Mischel and Underwood, 1974; Mischel, Shoda, and Rodriguez, 1989; Metcalfe and Mischel, 1999; Baumeister, Heatherton, and Tice, 1994; Lehrer, 2009a,b; Eigsti, Zayas, Mischel, Shoda, Ayduk, Dadlani, Davidson, Aber, and Casey, 2006.
23. Baumeister, Heatherton, and Tice, 1994; Vohs and Heatherton, 2000.
24. Baumeister, Heatherton, and Tice, 1994; Vohs and Faber, 2007; Vohs and Baumeister, 2010; Gailliot, Baumeister, DeWall, Maner, Plant, Tice, Brewer, and Schmeichel, 2007.
25. Baumeister, Heatherton, and Tice, 1994.
26. Baddeley, 2007; Gleitman, 1991; Baumeister, Heatherton, and Tice, 1994; Redish, 1999; Hofmann, Schmeichel, and Baddeley, 2012.
27. Cheng, 1986; Gallistel, 1990; Redish, 1999.
28. Hermer and Spelke, 1994; Gallistel, 1990; Redish, 1999.
29. Cheng, 1986; Margules and Gallistel, 1988; Gallistel, 1990.
30. Baumeister, Heatherton, and Tice, 1994; Baumeister, Vohs, and Tice, 2007.
31. Muraven, Shmueli, and Burkley, 2006; Baumeister, Heatherton, and Tice, 1994; Vohs and Baumeister, 2010.
32. Baumeister, Heatherton, and Tice, 1994; *Contingency Management*: Higgins, Heil, and Lussier, 2004; Petry, 2011; *12-step programs*: Moos and Moos, 2004, 2006.
33. Mischel, Shoda, and Rodriguez, 1989; Lehrer, 2009a.
34. Baumeister, Heatherton, and Tice, 1994; Vohs and Baumeister, 2010.
35. Gailliot, Baumeister, DeWall, Maner, Plant, Tice, Brewer, and Schmeichel, 2007.
36. Kurzban, 2010.
37. Purves, Augustine, Fitzpatrick, Hall, LaMantia, McNamara, and White, 2008; Carlson, 2010; Kandel, Schwartz, and Jessell, 2000.

38. Gailliot, Baumeister, DeWall, Maner, Plant, Tice, Brewer, and Schmeichel, 2007.
39. Chambers, Bridge, and Jones, 2009; Kurzban, 2010.
40. Huettel, Song, and McCarthy, 2009; Maandag, Coman, Sanganahalli, Herman, Smith, Blumenfeld, Shulman, and Hyder, 2007; Sokolof, 1978.
41. Logothetis, 2002; Nair, 2005; D'Ardenne, McClure, Nystrom, and Cohen, 2008; Huettel, Song, and McCarthy, 2009.
42. Metcalfe and Mischel, 1999; Baumeister, Vohs, and Tice, 2007.
43. *Dorsolateral prefrontal cortex (dlPFC):* Fuster, 1997/2008; Damasio, 1994; Knoch and Fehr, 2007; Lee, Rushworth, Walton, Watanabe, and Sakagami, 2007; Somerville and Casey, 2010; Heatherton and Wagner, 2011; *Anterior cingulate cortex (ACC):* van Veen and Carter, 2002; Lee, Rushworth, Walton, Watanabe, and Sakagami, 2007; Nili, Goldberg, Weizman, and Dudai, 2010; Heatherton and Wagner, 2011; Winstanley, Balleine, Brown, Büchel, Cools, Durstewitz, O'Doherty, Pennartz, Redish, Seamans, and Robbins, 2012.
44. Fuster, 1997/2008; Miller and Cohen, 2001; Dalley, Cardinal, and Robbins, 2004.
45. *Monitoring:* van Veen and Carter, 2002; Schall, Stuphorn, and Brown, 2002; Rushworth, Walton, Kennerly, and Bannerman, 2004; Botvinick, 2007, *Task-setting:* Dalley, Cardinal, and Robbins, 2004; Rich and Shapiro, 2009; Wallis, Anderson, and Miller, 2001; Durstewitz, Vittoz, Floresco, and Seamans, 2010, *Overriding plans:* Gray and McNaughton, 2000; Gray, 2004; Knoch and Fehr, 2007; Nili, Goldberg, Weizman, and Dudai, 2010; Heatherton and Wagner, 2011.
46. Fuster, 1997/2008; Seamans, Lapish, and Durstewitz, 2008; Koechlin, 2011; Tsujimoto, Genovesio, and Wise, 2011.
47. Freud, 1923/1990; MacLean, 1973.
48. Seamans, Lapish, and Durstewitz, 2008; Rushworth, Noonan, Boorman, Walton, and Behrens, 2011.
49. Isoda and Hikosaka, 2007, 2008.
50. Seamans, Lapish, and Durstewitz, 2008; Rushworth, Noonan, Boorman, Walton, and Behrens, 2011; Koechlin, 2011; Tsujimoto, Genovesio, and Wise, 2011; Kesner and Churchwell, 2011.
51. Luria, 1976.
52. Damasio, 1994, 2003.
53. Frith, 1996; Isoda and Hikosaka, 2007; Fuster, 1997/2008; Miller and Cohen, 2001; Holroyd and Coles, 2002; Dalley, Cardinal, and Robbins, 2004.
54. Isoda and Hikosaka, 2007, 2008; see also Frank, Samanta, Moustafa, and Sherman, 2007b, for an excellent review.
55. Nambu, Tokuno, and Takada, 2002; Albin, Young, and Penney, 1989; Frank, 2011.
56. Frith, 1996; Miller and Cohen, 2001; Redish, Jensen, Johnson, and Kurth-Nelson, 2007.
57. Gray and McNaughton, 2000.
58. Brooks, 1991.
59. LeDoux, 1996; Milad and Quirk, 2002.
60. Isoda and Hikosaka, 2007; Frith, 1996; Miller and Cohen, 2001.
61. LeDoux, 2002; Damasio, 2003.
62. Iversen and Mishkin, 1970; Isoda and Hikosaka, 2007.
63. McClure, Laibson, Loewenstein, and Cohen, 2004a; McClure, Ericson, Laibson, Loewenstein, and Cohen, 2007; Peters and Büchel, 2010; Kesner and Churchwell, 2011; Luo, Ainslie, Pollini, Giragosian, and Monterosso, 2012.
64. Nili, Goldberg, Weizman, and Dudai, 2010.

Chapter 16. The Physical Mind

1. *Dualism:* Descartes, 1647/1989; Sherrington, 1940/2009; Eccles et al., 1965; *Mind instantiated in the brain:* Dennet, 1992; Damasio, 1994, 2010; Churchland and Sejnowski, 1994; Levy, 2007.
2. *Mind as software:* McCorduck, 2004; Eccles et al., 1965; McHugh and Slavney, 1998; Levy, 2007.

3. Anholt and Mackay, 2010; Ridley, 2000, 2003.
4. Hofstadter, 1979, 1985; Marr, 1982; Newell, 1990; McHugh and Slavney, 1998; Nilsson, 1998; McCorduck, 2004.
5. Newell, 1990; Nilsson, 1998; McCorduck, 2004.
6. Newell, Shaw, and Simon, 1959.
7. McCorduck, 2004.
8. *Medical diagnosis:* Yu, Fagan, Wraith, Clancey, Scott, Hannigan, Blum, Buchanan, and Cohen, 1979; Buchanan and Shortliffe, 1984; *Oil exploration:* Pearl, 1988; *Chess:* IBM, 1997; *Jeopardy:* IBM, 2011.
9. *Medical diagnosis:* Lipscombe, 1989; *Cars:* Hayes, 2011.
10. Miller, 1956; Baddeley, 2007; *Chess:* Chase and Simon, 1973; de Groot, 1978; *Doctors:* Groopman, 2007.
11. Newell, 1993.
12. Newell, 1990; McCorduck, 2004.
13. Searle, 1980.
14. Turing, 1950.
15. McCorduck, 2004.
16. *Von Economo neurons:* Allman, Hakeem, and Watson, 2002; Allman, Watson, Tetreault, and Hakeem, 2005; *Microtubules:* Penrose, 1980/1989; Hameroff, 1994.
17. Marr, 1982.
18. Newell, 1990; McCorduck, 2004; Gleick, 2011.
19. McCorduck, 2004; Newell, 1990.
20. McHugh and Slavney, 1998.
21. Squire, 1987; Milner, 1998.
22. Hofstadter, 1985; McCorduck, 2004.
23. Miller, 1956; Baddeley, 2007; Chase and Simon, 1973; Charness, 1991; Ericsson, 2006.
24. Penfield, 1946; Wassermann, Walsh, Epstein, Paus, Ziemann, and Lisanby, 2008.
25. Hofstadter, 1979, 1985; Dennet, 1992; Gray, 2004; Damasio, 2010.
26. *Attention:* Crick, 1995; *Perception:* Ramachandran and Blakeslee, 1999; *Emotion:* Damasio, 2010; *Voluntary motor control:* Libet, 1993; Ramachandran and Blakeslee, 1999.
27. Libet, Wright, Feinstein, and Pearl, 1979; Libet, 1985, 1993; Gray, 2004; Soon, Brass, Heinze, and Haynes, 2008.
28. Levy, 2007.
29. Marsh and Hillis, 2006.
30. Kim and Fanselow, 1992; Anagnostaras, Maren, and Fanselow, 1999; Tse, Langston, Kakeyama, Bethus, Spooner, Wood, Witter, and Morris, 2007.
31. Squire, 1987; Milner, 1998.
32. Lashley, 1929.
33. Lashley, 1931.
34. O'Keefe and Nadel, 1978; Mishkin and Appenzeller, 1987; Squire, 1987; Redish, 1999.
35. Cohen and Squire, 1980; Milner, 1998; Squire, 2004.
36. Corkin, 2008; Squire, 2009.
37. Scoville, 1968.
38. Engel and Pedley, 2008; Hertz, Krogh, and Palmer, 1991; Soltesz and Staley, 2008.
39. Penfield, 1946; Sacks, 1985/1998; Devinsky and Lai, 2008.
40. Dostoevsky, 1869; Morgan, 1990.
41. Devinsky and Lai, 2008.
42. Scoville and Milner, 1957; Scoville, 1968.
43. Penfield and Steelman, 1947.
44. Wyler and Herman, 1994; Duncan, 2007; Harkness, 2006.
45. Scoville and Milner, 1957; Scoville, 1968; Milner, Corkin, and Teuber, 1968.
46. Luria, 1987; Squire, 1987.
47. Kopelman, Thomson, Guerrini, and Marshall, 2009.

48. Corkin, 2008.
49. Milner, Corkin, and Teuber, 1968; Milner, 1998; Corkin, 2002; Squire, 2004.
50. Cohen and Squire, 1980; Cohen and Eichenbaum, 1993; Squire, 2004.
51. Squire, 2004.
52. Schacter, 2001; Schacter, Addis, and Buckner, 2007; Buckner and Carroll, 2007.
53. Salat, van der Kouwe, Tuch, Quinn, Fischl, Dale, and Corkin, 2006.
54. Hubel and Wiesel, 1977; Jerison, 1973; Hofman, 1985; White, 1989; Abeles, 1991; Mountcastle, 1997; Striedter, 2005.
55. Hebb, 1949/2002; Kohonen, 1980, 1984; Doya, 1999; Miikulainen, Bednar, Choe, and Sirosh, 2005.
56. Kaas, Merzenich, and Killackey, 1983; Merzenich and Sameshima, 1993; Buonomano and Merzenich, 1998.
57. Kaas, Merzenich, and Killackey, 1983; Merzenich and Sameshima, 1993; Buonomano and Merzenich, 1998.
58. Wilson and Cowan, 1973; Kohonen, 1980, 1984; White, 1989; Miikulainen, Bednar, Choe, and Sirosh, 2005.
59. Chaudhuri, 2011; Purves, Augustine, Fitzpatrick, Hall, LaMantia, McNamara, and White, 2008.
60. Knudsen, du Lac, and Esterly, 1987; Buonomano and Merzenich, 1998.
61. Ramachandran and Blakeslee, 1999.
62. Ferrier, 1876; Penfield and Rasmussen, 1950; Kandel, Schwartz, and Jessell, 2000.
63. Bargary and Mitchell, 2008; Grossenbacher and Lovelace, 2001; Edelman, 1987; Purves, White, and Riddle, 1996.
64. Cytowic, 1998; Grossenbacher and Lovelace, 2001.
65. Knudsen, Zheng, and DeBello, 2000; Knudsen, 2004; White and Fitzpatrick, 2007; Feldman and Knudsen, 1998; Linkenhoker, von der Ohe, and Knudsen, 2004; Hensch, 2005.
66. Stein and Meredith, 1993.
67. Knudsen, 1991; Stein and Meredith, 1993.
68. Knudsen, 1991; Knudsen and Brainard, 1995.
69. Knudsen and Brainard, 1995; Knudsen, Zheng, and DeBello, 2000; Knudsen, 2004; Linkenhoker, von der Ohe, and Knudsen, 2004.
70. Carew, 2004.
71. Martin, Keating, Goodkin, Bastian, and Thach, 1996a,b.
72. Knudsen, 2004; Linkenhoker, von der Ohe, and Knudsen, 2004.
73. Hensch, 2005; *Vision:* Beradi, Pizzorusso, and Maffei, 2000; *Birdsong:* Balmer, Carels, Frisch, and Nick, 2009; *Language:* Tomasello and Bates, 2001.
74. Hensch, 2005; Balmer, Carels, Frisch, and Nick, 2009; Somerville, Jones, and Casey, 2010.
75. Knudsen, Zheng, and DeBello, 2000; Linkenhoker, von der Ohe, and Knudsen, 2004.
76. *Somatosensory systems:* Kaas, Merzenich, and Killackey, 1983; Merzenich and Sameshima, 1993; Buonomano and Merzenich, 1998; *Auditory systems:* Merzenich and Sameshima, 1993; Zhou, Panizzutti, de Villers-Sidani, Madeira, and Merzenich, 2011; de Villers-Sidani and Merzenich, 2011.
77. Milner, Corkin, and Teuber, 1968; Squire, 2009.
78. Nadel and Moscovitch, 1997; Corkin, 2002; Tse, Langston, Kakeyama, Bethus, Spooner, Wood, Witter, and Morris, 2007; Squire, 2009; Sutherland, Sparks, and Lehmann, 2010.
79. Cohen and Eichenbaum, 1993; Nadel and Moscovitch, 1997; Squire, 2004; Tulving, 1983.
80. Corkin, 2002; Squire, 2009; Sutherland, Sparks, and Lehmann, 2010.
81. Loftus and Palmer, 1974; Schacter, 2001; Schacter, Addis, and Buckner, 2007.
82. Alvarez and Squire, 1994; Andersen, Morris, Amaral, Bliss, and O'Keefe, 2007.
83. O'Reilly and McClelland, 1994; McClelland, McNaughton, and O'Reilly, 1995.
84. Hopfield, 1982; Hertz, Krogh, and Palmer, 1991; Rumelhart and McClelland, 1986; McClelland and Rumelhart, 1986; McClelland, McNaughton, and O'Reilly, 1995.
85. Hasselmo and Bower, 1993.

86. McClelland, McNaughton, and O'Reilly, 1995; *For discussions of how the hippocampus reduces interference between inputs:* Marr, 1971; McNaughton and Morris, 1987; McNaughton and Nadel, 1990; Hasselmo and Bower, 1993; Redish, 1999; Kesner, 2007; Leutgeb, Leutgeb, Moser, and Moser, 2007.

87. Nadel and Moscovitch, 1997; Redish and Touretzky, 1998; Squire, 2009; Tse, Takeuchi, Kakeyama, Kajii, Okuno, Tohyama, Bito, and Morris, 2011.

88. Hebb, 1949/2002; Alvarez and Squire, 1994.

89. Nadel and Moscovitch, 1997; Day, Weisend, Sutherland, and Schallert, 1999; Tse, Langston, Kakeyama, Bethus, Spooner, Wood, Witter, and Morris, 2007.

90. Hassabis, Kumaran, Vann, and Maguire, 2007; Verfaellie and Cermak, 1994; Race, Keane, and Verfaellie, 2011.

91. Sacks, 1985/1998.

92. Corkin, 2008.

93. Sacks, 1985/1998; Luria, 1987; Ramachandran and Blakeslee, 1999.

94. Marr, 1971; Buzsáki, 1989; Sutherland and McNaughton, 2000.

95. Diekelmann and Born, 2010; Poe, Walsh, and Bjorness, 2010; Smith, 1995, 2001; Hobson and Pace-Schott, 2002.

96. Pavlides and Winson, 1989; Wilson and McNaughton, 1994; Sutherland and McNaughton, 2000; Hoffman and McNaughton, 2002; Euston, Tatsuno, and McNaughton, 2007; Ji and Wilson, 2007; Lansink, Goltstein, Lankelma, McNaughton, and Pennartz, 2009.

97. Smith, 1995; Gais and Born, 2004.

98. Pavlides and Winson, 1989.

99. O'Keefe and Nadel, 1978; Redish, 1999.

100. Wilson and McNaughton, 1993.

101. Johnson, Fenton, Kentros, and Redish, 2009.

102. Wilson and McNaughton, 1994; Skaggs and McNaughton, 1996; Kudrimoti, Barnes, and McNaughton, 1999; Nádasdy, Hirase, Czurkó, Csicsvari, and Buzsáki, 1999; Jackson, Johnson, and Redish, 2006; Euston, Tatsuno, and McNaughton, 2007; Wikenheiser and Redish, 2013.

103. *Prefrontal:* Euston, Tatsuno, and McNaughton, 2007; *Parietal:* Qin, McNaughton, Skaggs, and Barnes, 1997; *Visual cortex:* Ji and Wilson, 2007.

104. Pennartz, Lee, Verheul, Lipa, Barnes, and McNaughton, 2004; Lansink, Goltstein, Lankelma, Joosten, McNaughton, and Pennartz, 2008; Lansink, Goltstein, Lankelma, McNaughton, and Pennartz, 2009.

105. Doyon, 2008.

106. Sutherland and McNaughton, 2000.

107. Buzsáki, 1989.

108. Marr, 1971; Seifert, 1983; Alvarez and Squire, 1994; Redish and Touretzky, 1998.

109. Poe, Nitz, McNaughton, and Barnes, 2000; Poe, Walsh, and Bjorness, 2010.

110. Ego-Stengel and Wilson, 2010; Girardeau, Benchenane, Wiener, Buzsáki, and Zugaro, 2009; Jadhav, Kemere, German, and Frank, 2012.

111. O'Keefe and Nadel, 1978; Redish, 1999; Ego-Stengel and Wilson, 2010; Girardeau, Benchenane, Wiener, Buzsáki, and Zugaro, 2009; Jadhav, Kemere, German, and Frank, 2012.

112. Battaglia, Sutherland, and McNaughton, 2004; Hoffman and McNaughton, 2002; Hoffman, Battaglia, Harris, MacLean, Marshall, and Mehta, 2007; see Marr, 1971; Alvarez and Squire, 1994, for early theoretical work.

113. Hobson, 2005.

114. Poe, Nitz, McNaughton, and Barnes, 2000.

115. Foster and Wilson, 2006; Davidson, Kloosterman, and Wilson, 2009; Gupta, van der Meer, Touretzky, and Redish, 2010; Wikenheiser and Redish, 2013.

116. Stickgold, Malia, Maguire, Roddenberry, and O'Connor, 2000.

117. Haidt, 2006; Freeman, 1975, 2000; McHugh and Slavney, 1998; Levy, 2007; Frith, 2007.

118. Descartes, 1647/1989; Levy, 2007.

119. McCorduck, 2004.

Chapter 17. Imagination

1. Ferrier, 1876; Hubel and Wiesel, 1977; Penfield and Rasmussen, 1950; Abeles, 1991; Miikulainen, Bednar, Choe, and Sirosh, 2005; Kandel, Schwartz, and Jessell, 2000; Chaudhuri, 2011.
2. Jay, 2000; Shaw, 2002.
3. Hubel and Wiesel, 1977; Chaudhuri, 2011.
4. Wilson and Cowan, 1973; White, 1989; Abeles, 1991; Miikulainen, Bednar, Choe, and Sirosh, 2005; see Dahlem and Chronicle, 2004, and Bressloff, Cowan, Golubitsky, Thomas, and Wiener, 2001, 2002, for discussion of the effects of longer-spaced connections.
5. Wilson and Cowan, 1973; Miikulainen, Bednar, Choe, and Sirosh, 2005; Murray, 2003.
6. Ermentrout and Kleinfeld, 2001; Murray, 2003.
7. Kosslyn, 1994; Bressloff, Cowan, Golubitsky, Thomas, and Wiener, 2001, 2002.
8. Tootell, Silverman, Switkes, and Valois, 1982; Schwartz, Tootell, Silverman, Switkes, and Valois, 1985; Bressloff, Cowan, Golubitsky, Thomas, and Wiener, 2001, 2002; Duncan and Boynton, 2003; Chaudhuri, 2011.
9. Ermentrout and Cowan, 1979; Bressloff, Cowan, Golubitsky, Thomas, and Wiener, 2001, 2002; Gutkin, Pinto, and Ermentrout, 2003; Golubitsky, Shiau, and Török, 2004; Bloom, 2009.
10. Hubel and Wiesel, 1977; White, 1989; Abeles, 1991; White and Fitzpatrick, 2007.
11. Van Essen, Anderson, and Felleman, 1992; Grill-Spector and Malach, 2004; Zeki, 1993; Milner and Goodale, 1995; Kandel, Schwartz, and Jessell, 2000; Chaudhuri, 2011; *Faces:* Tsao, Moeller, and Freiwald, 2008; *Rooms:* Epstein and Kanwisher, 1998.
12. Tyler, 1978.
13. Tsao, Moeller, and Freiwald, 2008; Liu, Harris, and Kanwisher, 2010.
14. Sacks, 1973/1999; Grüsser, 1995; Dahlem and Chronicle, 2004.
15. Grüsser, 1995; Reggia and Montgomery, 1996; Dahlem and Chronicle, 2004.
16. Sokolof, 1981.
17. Fürkötter, 1977.
18. Sacks, 1973/1999; Podoll and Robinson, 2002, 2009.
19. Kosslyn, 1994.
20. Shepherd and Metzler, 1971.
21. Kosslyn, 1994; Kosslyn, Thompson, and Ganis, 2006.
22. Frith, 1996.
23. Mushiake, Inase, and Tanji, 1991; Passingham, 1993.
24. Rizzolatti, Fadiga, Gallese, and Fogassi, 1996; Rizzolatti and Craighero, 2004.
25. Schilbach, 2010; Rizzolatti and Sinigaglia, 2010.
26. Johnson, Fenton, Kentros, and Redish, 2009.
27. Georgopoulos, Lurito, Petrides, Schwartz, and Massey, 1989.
28. Georgopoulos, Schwartz, and Kettner, 1986; Schwartz, 2007.
29. Georgopoulos, Schwartz, and Kettner, 1986.
30. Georgopoulos, Lurito, Petrides, Schwartz, and Massey, 1989.
31. Alexander and Crutcher, 1990; Cisek and Kalaska, 2010.
32. Friehs, Zerris, Ojakangas, Fellows, and Donoghue, 2004; Donoghue, Nurmikko, Black, and Hochberg, 2007; Schwartz, 2007; Reger, Fleming, Sanguineti, Alford, and Mussa-Ivaldi, 2000; Mussa-Ivaldi, 2000; Karniel, Kositsky, Fleming, Chiappalone, Sanguineti, Alford, and Mussa-Ivaldi, 2005; Mussa-Ivaldi, Alford, Chiappalone, Fadiga, Karniel, Kositsky, Maggiolini, Panzeri, Sanguineti, Semprini, and Vato, 2009.
33. Helms-Tillery, Taylor, and Schwartz, 2003; Schwartz, 2007.
34. *Monkeys:* Velliste, Perel, Spalding, Whitford, and Schwartz, 2008; Nicolelis and Lebedev, 2009; *Humans:* Hochberg, Serruya, Friehs, Mukand, Saleh, Caplan, Branner, Chen, Penn, and Donoghue, 2006; Donoghue, Nurmikko, Black, and Hochberg, 2007.
35. Velliste, Perel, Spalding, Whitford, and Schwartz, 2008.
36. Hochberg, Serruya, Friehs, Mukand, Saleh, Caplan, Branner, Chen, Penn, and Donoghue, 2006.
37. *Cochlear implants:* Zeng, 2004; Zeng, Rebscher, Harrison, Sun, and Feng, 2009.

38. *Retinal stimulators:* Weiland, Liu, and Humayun, 2005; Dowling, 2009.
39. *Deep-brain stimulation:* Dostrovsky, Hutchinson, and Lozano, 2002; Benabid, Chabardes, Mitrofanis, and Pollak, 2009, see McIntyre, Savast, Goff, and Vitek, 2004; Frank, Samanta, Moustafa, and Sherman, 2007b; Birdno and Grill, 2008; Deniau, Degos, Bosch, and Maurice, 2010, for discussions of mechanism.
40. Sacks, 1973/1990; Marshall, 1990.
41. *Deep-brain stimulation for epilepsy:* Rahman, Abd-El-Barr, Vedam-Mai, Foote, Murad, Okun, and Roper, 2010; *for depression:* Blomstedt, Sjöberg, Hansson, Bodlund, and Hariz, 2010; Hamani and Nóbrega, 2010.
42. Gater, Dolbow, Tsui, and Gorgey, 2011.
43. Ferrier, 1876.
44. Penfield, 1946; Penfield and Steelman, 1947; Penfield, 1975.
45. Salzman, Murasugi, Britten, and Newsome, 1992.
46. Robinson, 1972; Sparks and Mays, 1983; Sparks and Nelson, 1987.

Chapter 18. Addiction

1. Goldstein, 2000; Heyman, 2009; Koob and Le Moal, 2006.
2. DSM-IV-TR, 2000; ICD-10, 1992; Altman, Everitt, Robbins, Glautier, Markou, Nutt, Oretti, and Phillips, 1996; Lowinson, Ruiz, Millman, and Langrod, 1997; Goldstein, 2000; Koob and Le Moal, 2006; Heyman, 2009.
3. Mandelstam, 1991.
4. ESPN, 2010.
5. Ainslie, 2001; Heyman, 2009.
6. Koob and Le Moal, 2006; Vanderschuren and Everitt, 2004; Deroche-Gamonet, Belin, and Piazza, 2004.
7. Redish, 2004.
8. Rutledge, 2006.
9. Krugman and Wells, 2006.
10. Liu, Liu, Hammit, and Chou, 1999; Bickel and Marsch, 2001; Grossman and Chaloupka, 1998; Manski, Pepper, and Petrie, 2001; Chaloupka, Emery, and Liang, 2003.
11. Liu, Liu, Hammit, and Chou, 1999.
12. Manski, Pepper, and Petrie, 2001; Heyman, 2009; Leukefeld, Gullotta, and Gregrich, 2011.
13. Haller, 1989; Goldstein, 2000; Manski, Pepper, and Petrie, 2001; Leukefeld, Gullotta, and Gregrich, 2011; U.S. Department of Justice, 1992.
14. O'Brien, 2011; ICD-10, 1992; DSM-IV-TR, 2000.
15. Redish, Jensen, and Johnson, 2008.
16. Flagel, Akil, and Robinson, 2009.
17. Bobo and Husten, 2001; Goldman, Boca, and Darkes, 1999; Redish and Johnson, 2007.
18. Redish, 2004.
19. Tiffany, 1990; Robbins and Everitt, 1999; Everitt and Robbins, 2005; Piray, Keramati, Dezfouli, Lucas, and Mokri, 2010.
20. Redish, Jensen, Johnson, and Kurth-Nelson, 2007.
21. Redish, Jensen, and Johnson, 2008.
22. Koob and Le Moal, 2006.
23. Flagel, Akil, and Robinson, 2009.
24. Koob and Le Moal, 2006.
25. Redish, 2004.
26. Greeley and Oei, 1999.
27. Koob and Le Moal, 2006.
28. Hunt, 1998; White, 2003; Oscar-Berman and Marinkovic, 2003.
29. Ainslie, 1992; Baumeister, Heatherton, and Tice, 1994; Heyman, 2009; Petry, 2011.
30. Zeng, 2004.

31. Bressloff, Cowan, Golubitsky, Thomas, and Wiener, 2002; Grüsser, 1995.

32. Meyer and Mirin, 1979; De Vries and Shippenberg, 2002; Koob and Le Moal, 2006.

33. Redish, Jensen, and Johnson, 2008.

34. Solomon and Corbit, 1973, 1974; Koob and Le Moal, 2006.

35. Koob and Le Moal, 2006; Koob, 2009.

36. Redish and Johnson, 2007; Redish, 2004.

37. Robinson and Berridge, 2001, 2003; Flagel, Akil, and Robinson, 2009.

38. Tiffany, 1990; Bechara, 2005.

39. Anthony, Warner, and Kessler, 1994; Heyman, 2009.

40. Sayette, Shiffman, Tiffany, Niaura, Martin, and Shadel, 2000; Perkins, 2009; Tiffany and Wray, 2009; Redish, 2009.

41. O'Brien, Childress, Ehrman, and Robbins, 1998; Childress, Mozley, McElgin, Fitzgerald, Reivich, and O'Brien, 1999.

42. Jagger and Richards, 1969.

43. Kozlowski and Wilkinson, 2006; Skinner and Aubin, 2010.

44. Koob and Le Moal, 2006.

45. Flagel, Akil, and Robinson, 2009.

46. Skinner and Aubin, 2010.

47. Redish and Johnson, 2007.

48. Tiffany and Conklin, 2000.

49. Redish, Jensen, and Johnson, 2008; Redish, Jensen, Johnson, and Kurth-Nelson, 2007.

50. Corbit, Muir, and Balleine, 2001; Laurent, Leung, Maidment, and Balleine, 2012.

51. Childress, McLellan, Ehrman, and O'Brien, 1988.

52. Mayr, 1998.

53. Kandel, Schwartz, and Jessell, 2000; Carlson, 2010; Sherwood, 2010.

54. Schulkin, 2003; Koob and Le Moal, 2006.

55. Mackowiak, Wasserman, and Levine, 1992; Sherwood, 2010.

56. Stephens and Krebs, 1987; Schulkin, 2003.

57. Lenfant and Sullivan, 1971; Stray-Gundersen and Levine, 2008; Chapman, Stickford, and Levine, 2009, see also de Paula and Niebauer, 2012.

58. Cooper, Bloom, and Roth, 1986; Koob and Le Moal, 2006.

59. Altman, Everitt, Robbins, Glautier, Markou, Nutt, Oretti, and Phillips, 1996; Lowinson, Ruiz, Millman, and Langrod, 1997; Saitz, 1998; Harris and Gewirtz, 2005; Koob and Le Moal, 2006; Redish, Jensen, and Johnson, 2008.

60. O'Brien, Testa, O'Brien, Brady, and Wells, 1977; Meyer and Mirin, 1979; Koob, 2009; Koob and Volkow, 2010.

61. Skinner and Aubin, 2010.

62. Carter, Lam, Robinson, Paris, Waters, Wetter, and Cinciripini, 2008; Epstein, Marrone, Heishman, Schmittner, and Preston, 2010.

63. Sayette, Shiffman, Tiffany, Niaura, Martin, and Shadel, 2000.

64. Koob and Le Moal, 2006.

65. Flagel, Akil, and Robinson, 2009.

66. Redish and Johnson, 2007.

67. Redish, Jensen, and Johnson, 2008.

68. Hardcastle, 2008; Heyman, 2009; Potenza, Sofuoglu, Carroll, and Rounsaville, 2011.

69. *Psychiatric categorizations as needing endophenotypes:* Insel, Cuthbert, Garvey, Heinssen, Pine, Quinn, Sanislow, and Wang, 2010; *Genetic endophenotypes:* Gottesman and Gould, 2003; *Hypothetical constructs:* MacCorquodale and Meehl, 1948; *Trans-disease processes:* Bickel and Mueller, 2009.

70. Kable and Glimcher, 2009; Glimcher, 2010.

71. Bickel and Mueller, 2009.

72. McHugh and Slavney, 1998; Hyman, 2007; Insel, Cuthbert, Garvey, Heinssen, Pine, Quinn, Sanislow, and Wang, 2010.

73. Redish, Jensen, and Johnson, 2008.
74. Krishnan-Sarin, Reynolds, Duhig, Smith, Liss, McFetridge, Cavallo, Carroll, and Potenza, 2007; Xu, DeVito, Worhunsky, Carroll, Rounsaville, and Potenza, 2010; Brewer, Worhunsky, Carroll, Rounsaville, and Potenza, 2008.
75. *Nicotine replacement therapy:* Rose, Herskovic, Trilling, and Jarvik, 1985; Benowitz, 1996; Balfour and Fagerström, 1996; Hanson, Allen, Jensen, and Hatsukami, 2003; *Methadone therapy:* Meyer and Mirin, 1979; Kreek, LaForge, and Butelman, 2002; Potenza, Sofuoglu, Carroll, and Rounsaville, 2011.
76. Meyer and Mirin, 1979; Balfour and Fagerström, 1996; Hanson, Allen, Jensen, and Hatsukami, 2003; Monti and MacKillop, 2007.
77. Kreek, LaForge, and Butelman, 2002; Redish, Jensen, and Johnson, 2008.
78. Solomon and Corbit, 1974; Koob and Le Moal, 2006.
79. Azolosa, Stitzer, and Greenwald, 1994; Harris and Gewirtz, 2005; Koob and Le Moal, 2006.
80. Heyman, 2009, see Burroughs, 1959/1984; Bukowski, 1996.
81. Moos and Moos, 2004, 2006; Petry, 2011.
82. Peters and Büchel, 2010; Kurth-Nelson and Redish, 2012c; Guisewite, 1996; Bushong, King, Camerer, and Rangel, 2010; Kang, Rangel, Camus, and Camerer, 2011.
83. Baumeister, Heatherton, and Tice, 1994; Ainslie, 2001; Baumeister, Vohs, and Tice, 2007.
84. Ainslie, 1992, 2001; Dickerson and O'Connor, 2006; Kurth-Nelson and Redish, 2010, 2012b.
85. Ainslie, 1992, 2001; Rachlin, 2004; Kurzban, 2010.
86. Ainslie, 2001; Kurth-Nelson and Redish, 2012b.
87. Ludwig, 1989.
88. Heyman, 2009.
89. Koob and Le Moal, 2006; Heyman, 2009; Casey, Getz, and Galvan, 2008a; Casey, Jones, and Hare, 2008b; Luna, Padmanabhan, and O'Hearn, 2010.
90. Heyman, 2009.
91. Hardcastle, 2008; Potenza, Sofuoglu, Carroll, and Rounsaville, 2011; Bullock and Potenza, 2012.
92. *Executive function therapy:* Bickel, Yi, Landes, Hill, and Baxter, 2011; *Nicotine replacement therapy*: Koob and Le Moal, 2006; Rose, Herskovic, Trilling, and Jarvik, 1985; Benowitz, 1996; Balfour and Fagerström, 1996; Hanson, Allen, Jensen, and Hatsukami, 2003; *Methadone therapy:* Meyer and Mirin, 1979; Kreek, LaForge, and Butelman, 2002; Potenza, Sofuoglu, Carroll, and Rounsaville, 2011.
93. Bickel, Yi, Landes, Hill, and Baxter, 2011; Potenza, Sofuoglu, Carroll, and Rounsaville, 2011; Petry, 2011.
94. Redish, Jensen, and Johnson, 2008; Insel, Cuthbert, Garvey, Heinssen, Pine, Quinn, Sanislow, and Wang, 2010; Robbins, Gillan, Smith, de Wit, and Ersche, 2012; Potenza, Sofuoglu, Carroll, and Rounsaville, 2011.

Chapter 19. Gambling and Behavioral Addictions

1. Holden, 2001; Potenza, Kosten, and Rounsaville, 2001.
2. Koob and Le Moal, 2006.
3. Vanderschuren and Everitt, 2004; Deroche-Gamonet, Belin, and Piazza, 2004; Rutledge, 2006.
4. Potenza, Kosten, and Rounsaville, 2001; Grant and Potenza, 2012; Schüll, 2012.
5. Montague, 2006; Redish, Jensen, Johnson, and Kurth-Nelson, 2007; Redish, Jensen, and Johnson, 2008.
6. Mlodinow, 2009; Langer and Roth, 1975; Redish, Jensen, Johnson, and Kurth-Nelson, 2007.
7. Redish, Jensen, Johnson, and Kurth-Nelson, 2007, see also Chapter 12.
8. Langer and Roth, 1975; Sagan, 1997; Boyer, 2002; Ramachandran and Blakeslee, 1999; Kurzban, 2010; Ramachandran, 2011.
9. Reid, 1986; Griffiths, 1991; Chase and Clark, 2010; Winstanley, Cocker, and Rogers, 2011; Qi, Ding, Song, and Yan, 2011; Clark, Crooks, Clarke, Aitken, and Dunn, 2012.

10. Lesieur, 1977; Wagenaar, 1988; Dickerson and O'Connor, 2006; Green, 2004; Rivlin, 2004; Schüll, 2012.
11. Mayr, 1998; Llinas, 2002; Frith, 2007.
12. Jensen, Boley, Gini, and Schrater, 2005; Mlodinow, 2009.
13. Vulkan, 2000; Mlodinow, 2009.
14. Klein, 2000.
15. Winstanley, Balleine, Brown, Büchel, Cools, Durstewitz, O'Doherty, Pennartz, Redish, Seamans, and Robbins, 2012.
16. Jensen, Boley, Gini, and Schrater, 2005; Jensen, 2010.
17. Sagan, 1997; Boyer, 2002.
18. Langer and Roth, 1975; Wagenaar, 1988; Redish, Jensen, Johnson, and Kurth-Nelson, 2007.
19. Skinner, 1948; Sagan, 1997; Mlodinow, 2009.
20. Gallistel, 1990.
21. Sagan, 1997; Boyer, 2002.
22. Joyce, 1939, see McHugh, 1980; Campbell, 1944; Vico, 1725/1984.
23. Wagenaar, 1988; Joukhador, Maccallum, and Blaszczynski, 2003; Dickerson and O'Connor, 2006; Redish, Jensen, Johnson, and Kurth-Nelson, 2007.
24. ESPN, 2010; Scorsese, 1995; Coppola, 1972/1974/1990; Tuchman, 1962; Manchester, 1978.
25. Green, 2004; Rivlin, 2004; Dickerson and O'Connor, 2006; Schüll, 2012.
26. Griffiths, 1991.
27. Langer and Roth, 1975.
28. Wagenaar, 1988; Cummins, Nadorff, and Kelly, 2009.
29. Tversky and Kahneman, 1981; Kahneman and Tversky, 2000; Kahneman, 2011.
30. Jankovic and Tolosa, 2007.
31. Jankovic and Tolosa, 2007.
32. Sacks, 1973/1990; Voon, Potenza, and Thomsen, 2007; Classen, van den Wildenberg, Ridderinkhof, Jessup, Harrison, Wooten, and Wylie, 2011.
33. Marshall, 1990.
34. Frank, Seeberger, and O'Reilly, 2004; Frank, Samanta, Moustafa, and Sherman, 2007b; Shohamy, Myers, Geghman, Sage, and Gluck, 2006; Rutledge, Lazzaro, Lau, Myers, Gluck, and Glimcher, 2009; Kéri, Moustafa, Myers, Benedek, and Gluck, 2010.
35. Reid, 1986; Griffiths, 1991; Schüll, 2012.
36. Classen, van den Wildenberg, Ridderinkhof, Jessup, Harrison, Wooten, and Wylie, 2011; Voon, Potenza, and Thomsen, 2007; Voon, Mehta, and Hallett, 2011.
37. Holden, 2001.
38. Redish, Jensen, and Johnson, 2008.
39. Koepp, Gunn, Lawrence, Cunningham, Dagher, Jones, Brooks, Bench, and Grasby, 1998.
40. Wang, Volkow, Logan, Pappas, Wong, Zhu, Netusll, and Fowler, 2001; Volkow, Wang, and Baler, 2011.
41. Mintz, 1986; Johnson and Kenny, 2010; Lenoir, Serre, Cantin, and Ahmed, 2007.
42. See Grant and Potenza, 2012, particularly the chapters by Black and by Lejoyeaux and Germain.

Chapter 20. Post-Traumatic Stress Disorder

1. FrontLine, 2009; Jones and Wessely, 2005.
2. Da Costa, 1884; Paul, 1987; Frontline, 2009.
3. Pizarro, Silver, and Prause, 2006.
4. Shiromani, Keane, and Ledoux, 2009; Kessler, Sonnega, Bonnet, Hughes, and Nelson, 1995.
5. Yehuda and Ledoux, 2007; Shiromani, Keane, and Ledoux, 2009.
6. Kessler, Sonnega, Bonnet, Hughes, and Nelson, 1995.
7. Yehuda and Ledoux, 2007.
8. Pitman, Gilbertson, Gurvits, May, Lasko, Metzger, Shenton, Yehuda, and Orr, 2006.

9. Gilbertson, Shenton, Ciszewski, Kasai, Lasko, Orr, and Pitman, 2002.
10. Brown and Kulik, 1977.
11. Ressler, Rothbaum, Tannenbaum, Anderson, Graap, Zimand, Hodges, and Davis, 2004; LeDoux, 1996; Dębiec and LeDoux, 2006; Redish, Jensen, Johnson, and Kurth-Nelson, 2007; Yehuda and Ledoux, 2007.
12. LeDoux, 1996; Protopoescu, Pan, Tuescher, Clotre, Goldtein, Engelien, Epstein, Yang, Gorman, LeDoux, Silbersweig, and Stern, 2005; Yehuda and Ledoux, 2007.
13. Nadel and Jacobs, 1996; Jacobs and Nadel, 1998; Layton and Krikorian, 2002; Moscowitz, Nadel, Watts, and Jacobs, 2008; Verfaellie and Vasterling, 2009.
14. Brown and Kulik, 1977.
15. Talarico and Rubin, 2003.
16. Pavlov, 1927; Bouton, 2004, 2007; Rescorla, 2004; Quirk, 2006; Redish, Jensen, Johnson, and Kurth-Nelson, 2007.
17. Dębiec and LeDoux, 2006, 2009.
18. Bouton, 2007; Myers and Davis, 2007.
19. Rescorla, 2004; Myers and Davis, 2007.
20. Bouton, 2007.
21. Nadel and Jacobs, 1996; Yehuda and Ledoux, 2007; Shiromani, Keane, and Ledoux, 2009.
22. Nadel and Jacobs, 1996; Jacobs and Nadel, 1998; Moscowitz, Nadel, Watts, and Jacobs, 2008.
23. Shors, 2004.
24. Payne, Jackson, Hoscheidt, Ryan, Jacobs, and Nadel, 2007.
25. Cahill, McGaugh, and Weinberger, 2001; Cahill, Gorski, and Le, 2003; Kuhlmann, Piel, and Wolf, 2005.
26. Layton and Krikorian, 2002; LeDoux, 1996; Shiromani, Keane, and Ledoux, 2009.
27. Elzinga and Bremner, 2002; Verfaellie and Vasterling, 2009.
28. Nadel and Jacobs, 1996.
29. Brown and Kulik, 1977.
30. Nadel and Moscovitch, 1997; Sutherland, Sparks, and Lehmann, 2010, compare Squire, 1987, 2004; Teng and Squire, 1999.
31. Nadel and Moscovitch, 1997; Jacobs and Nadel, 1998; Buckner and Carroll, 2007; Hassabis, Kumaran, Vann, and Maguire, 2007; Schacter, Addis, and Buckner, 2007, 2008; Schacter and Addis, 2011.
32. Brown and Kulik, 1977.
33. Squire, 1987; Nadel and Moscovitch, 1997; Vargha-Khadem, Gadian, Watkins, Connelly, Van Paesschen, and Mishkin, 1997; Nadel and Land, 2000; Hassabis, Kumaran, Vann, and Maguire, 2007; St.-Laurent, Moscovitch, Tau, and McAndrews, 2011.
34. *Pharmacological treatments:* Raskind, 2009; Choi, Rothbaum, Gerardi, and Ressler, 2009; Schneier, Neria, Pavlicova, Hembree, Suh, Amsel, and Marshall, 2012; Gibson, Hamblen, Zvolensky, and Vujanovic, 2006; *Extinction:* Cammarota, Bevilaqua, Vianna, Medina, and Izquierdo, 2006; Choi, Rothbaum, Gerardi, and Ressler, 2009; *Recontextualization:* Rizzo, Reger, Gahm, Difede, and Rothbaum, 2009; Harvey, Bryant, and Tarrier, 2003; Strauss, Calhoun, and Marx, 2009; Gibson, Hamblen, Zvolensky, and Vujanovic, 2006; Marshall, Amsel, Neria, and Suh, 2006; Schneier, Neria, Pavlicova, Hembree, Suh, Amsel, and Marshall, 2012.

Chapter 21. Computational Psychiatry

1. DSM-III, 1980; DSM-IV-TR, 2000; ICD-10, 1992; see Hyman, 2007, for a discussion of the new DSM-V.
2. McHugh and Slavney, 1998; Insel, Cuthbert, Garvey, Heinssen, Pine, Quinn, Sanislow, and Wang, 2010.
3. McHugh and Slavney, 1998.
4. McHugh and Slavney, 1998; Hyman, 2007; Redish, Jensen, and Johnson, 2008; Insel et al., 2011.

5. Simpson, Kay, and Aber, 1984; Mayo Clinic, 2011.

6. Dauer and Przedborski, 2003; Jankovic and Tolosa, 2007.

7. International Campaign to Ban Landmines, 2011.

8. *Levodopa:* Kopin, 1993; *Cell replacement:* Björklund, Dunnett, Brundin, Stoessl, Freed, Breeze, Levivier, Peschanski, Studer, and Barker, 2003; *Deep-brain stimulation:* Dostrovsky, Hutchinson, and Lozano, 2002; McIntyre, Savast, Goff, and Vitek, 2004; Benabid, Chabardes, Mitrofanis, and Pollak, 2009.

9. World Health Organization, 2011.

10. Hyman, 2007; Insel, Cuthbert, Garvey, Heinssen, Pine, Quinn, Sanislow, and Wang, 2010; Insel et al., 2011.

11. Redish, Jensen, and Johnson, 2008; Kishida, King-Casas, and Montague, 2010; Maia and Frank, 2011; Huys, Moutoussis, and Williams, 2011; Hasler, 2012; van der Meer, Kurth-Nelson, and Redish, 2012.

12. LeDoux, 1996; Simpson, Neria, Lewis-Fernández, and Schneier, 2010; Gordon and Adhikari, 2010.

13. Gordon and Adhikari, 2010; Etkin and Wagner, 2010; McNally, Johansen, and Blair, 2011.

14. Gray and McNaughton, 2000; Adhikari, Topiwala, and Gordon, 2010.

15. *The stretch-attend posture,* Grewal, Shepherd, Bill, Fletcher, and Dourish, 1997; Molewijk, van der Poel, and Oliver, 1995.

16. Gray and McNaughton, 2000; Gordon and Adhikari, 2010; Adhikari, Topiwala, and Gordon, 2010.

17. Lynch and Frost, 1990–1991.

18. Simpson, Neria, Lewis-Fernández, and Schneier, 2010; Sapolsky, 1998a,b.

19. Da Costa, 1884.

20. DSM-IV-TR, 2000; Goodman, Rudorfer, and Maser, 2000; McNally, 2000.

21. *Anxiety:* Armony, Servan-Schreiber, Cohen, and LeDoux, 1997, see also LeDoux, 1996, and Simpson, Neria, Lewis-Fernández, and Schneier, 2010; *Depression:* Huys, 2007; *Schizophrenia:* Tanaka, 2006; Durstewitz and Seamans, 2008.

22. Hare, 1999; King-Casas, Sharp, Lomax-Bream, Lohrenz, Fonagy, and Montague, 2008; Singer, 2008; Kishida, King-Casas, and Montague, 2010.

23. McHugh and Slavney, 1998.

24. LeFever, Dawson, and Morrow, 1999; Levy, 2007.

25. Olfson and Marcus, 2009.

26. Haidt, 2006; Levy, 2007.

27. Haidt, 2006; Levy, 2007.

28. NIMH, 2011.

29. Chamberlain, Odlaug, Boulougouris, Fineberg, and Grant, 2009.

30. Mirowsky and Ross, 1989; McHugh and Slavney, 1998.

31. Hyman, 2007, 2010; Insel, Cuthbert, Garvey, Heinssen, Pine, Quinn, Sanislow, and Wang, 2010.

Chapter 22. What Makes us Human?

1. Krensky and Reeves, 2007; McDermott, 1972; Abrahams, 1983.

2. Dumas, 1844/1984.

3. O'Brien, 1971; Titus, 1958/1989.

4. Patterson and Linden, 1981; Savage-Rumbaugh and Lewin, 1996; Fouts, 1997; Pepperberg, 2009.

5. *Termites and social insects:* Wilson, 1980; *Humans:* Diamond, 1999; Wilson, 2002.

6. U.S. National Academy, 2001; Intergovernmental Panel on Climate Change, 2011; Diamond, 2005.

7. Peterson and Goodall, 2000.

8. Köhler, 1925/1959.

9. Goodall, 1986; Tomassello and Call, 1997.
10. Goodall, 1986.
11. Hall and Schaller, 1964; von Frisch, 1974; Hunt, 1996; Clayton, 2007.
12. Matsuzawa, 2008; Goodall, 1986; Tomassello and Call, 1997.
13. Kawai, 1965; Tomassello, 1999; Hirata, Watanabe, and Kawai, 2008.
14. Strum, 1987; Sapolsky, 2001; de Waal, 2001; Horner, Proctor, Bonnie, Whiten, and De Waal, 2010; see Dawkins, 1976, and Boyer, 2002, for discussions of *memes.*
15. Suddendorf and Corballis, 2007, 2008; Corballis, 2012.
16. Tolman, 1939; Johnson, van der Meer, and Redish, 2007; van der Meer and Redish, 2010; van der Meer, Johnson, Schmitzer-Torbert, and Redish, 2010.
17. Clayton, Griffiths, Emery, and Dickinson, 2001.
18. Abe and Lee, 2011; Steiner and Redish, 2012.
19. Raby and Clayton, 2009.
20. Dawkins, 2004.
21. Hinde, 1966; Wilson, 1980; Goodall, 1986; Bekoff and Byers, 1998; Peterson and Goodall, 2000; Fothergill and Linfield, 2012.
22. Sober and Wilson, 1998; Diamond, 1999; Wilson, 2002.
23. Aristotle, 350 BCE/2004.
24. Garrett, 2010.
25. Tomassello, 1999, 2005; Pinker, 2007.
26. Tomassello, 2005; Pinker, 2007.
27. Norman, 1988; Tomassello, 1999.
28. Levi-Strauss, 1970; Giglioli, 1972/1990; Tomassello, 1999.
29. Searle, 1965.
30. Card, 1986; see Boyer, 2002, for an anthropological discussion of the marriage contract as between individuals and the group.
31. Dawkins, 1976; Richerson and Boyd, 2005; Aunger, 2001; Sterelny, 2006.
32. Surowiecki, 2005.
33. Tomassello, 2005, 2008.
34. Matsuzawa, 2008; Tomassello, 2005; Call and Tomassello, 2008.
35. Argyle and Dean, 1965; Senju and Johnson, 2009.
36. Wright, 1995; Zak, 2008.
37. Goodall, 1986.
38. Sober and Wilson, 1998; Zak, 2008; Ronson, 2011.
39. Moss, 2000; McComb, Baker, and Moss, 2005; Byrne, Bates, and Moss, 2009.
40. Cheney and Seyfarth, 1990.
41. Noad, Cato, Bryden, Jenner, and Jenner, 2000; Fripp, Owen, Quintana-Rizzo, Shapiro, Buckstaff, Jankowski, Wells, and Tyack, 2005; Janak, 2009.

Chapter 23. The Science of Morality

1. Hume, 1740/2000; Churchland, 2011.
2. Kuhn, 1962/1996; Popper, 1935/1959/1992; Mayr, 1998; Ben-Ari, 2005.
3. LeGuin, 1974; Boyer, 2002; Wilson, 2002; Leeson, 2009; Churchland, 2011.
4. Gould, 2000; Churchland, 2011.
5. *As comfort:* Boyer, 2002; Haidt, 2006; *As an organization principle:* Wilson, 2002; *As an enforcement of morality and self-control:* Wright, 1995; Boyer, 2002; Zak, 2008; de Waal, 2009; Baumeister and Tierney, 2011.
6. e.g., Alligheri, 1321/1961/2003.
7. Pascal, 1669.
8. *Confucianism:* Confucius, 3rd century BCE/1979, see also Riegel, 2011; *Taoism:* Lao Tsu, 6th century BCE/1997; *Utilitarianism:* Mill, 1863, see also Harris, 2010.
9. Kant, 1797/1998.

10. *Leviticus*, 19:18; *Mark*, 12:31; Confucius, 3rd century BCE/1979. See Churchland, 2011, for a discussion of the complexity of the Golden Rule and modern neuroscience.
11. *Happiness readjusts:* Haidt, 2006.
12. Rawls, 1971, 1985.
13. Wright, 1995; Ridley, 2000, 2003.
14. Johnson, 1994.
15. Damasio, 1994; Hare, 1999; Singer, 2008; Kishida, King-Casas, and Montague, 2010.
16. Hoffman, McCabe, Shachat, and Smith, 1994; Kimbrough, Smith, and Wilson, 2008; Smith, 2009.
17. Krugman and Wells, 2006; Reinhardt, 2010a.
18. Reinhardt, 2010b; Krugman and Wells, 2006; Smith, 2009.
19. Augustine of Hippo (Saint Augustine), 427/1972, 398/1961; Plato, 4th century BCE/2008b; Freud, 1923/1990; McHugh and Slavney, 1998; Bechara, 2005; Haidt, 2006; Lehrer, 2009b.
20. Reinhardt, 2010a,b.
21. *Mathematical tractability:* Krugman, 2009b; *Feedback loop in training:* Gintis and Khurana, 2008; *Winners and losers:* Krugman, 2009a; Reinhardt, 2010a.
22. Sweeney and Sweeney, 1977; Krugman and Wells, 2006; Krugman, 2009b; Smith, 2009.
23. Hill, 2008.
24. Kahneman and Tversky, 1979; Ainslie, 1992; Plous, 1993; Ariely, 2008; Fehr, 2008; Kahneman, 2011.
25. von Neumann and Morganstern, 1944/2004; Camerer, 2003; Osborne, 2004; Houser and McCabe, 2008.
26. Nash, 1951; Osborne, 2004; Houser and McCabe, 2008.
27. Nash, 1951; Osborne, 2004; fictionalized in *A Beautiful Mind*, Nassar, 2001; Howard, 2001.
28. Houser and McCabe, 2008.
29. Fehr, Fishbacher, and Kosfeld, 2005.
30. Hume, 1740/2000; Wilson, 1980; Wright, 1995; Churchland, 2011.
31. Vincent, Ahnesjö, Berglund, and Rosenqvist, 1992; Wright, 1995; Hill and Halliday, 1998.
32. Sober and Wilson, 1998; Boyer, 2002; Wilson, 2002; Turchin, 2003; Zak, Stanton, and Ahmadi, 2007; Leeson, 2009; Churchland, 2011.
33. Rushdie, 1990; Sober and Wilson, 1998; Turchin, 2003; Leeson, 2009.
34. Milgram, 1974/2009; Zimbardo, 2007.
35. Walters, 2012; Reicher and Haslam, 2011.
36. Hersh, 2004, 2007; Zimbardo, 2007.
37. Zimbardo, 2007.
38. Stout, 2008.
39. *Oxford English Dictionary*, www.oed.com.
40. Diamond, 1999; Levi-Strauss, 1970; Turchin, 2003.
41. Sober and Wilson, 1998; Wilson, 2002.
42. Brown, 2008.
43. Axelrod, 1984/2006; Camerer, 2003; Sanfey, 2007.
44. Camerer, 2003; Sanfey, 2007; Smith, 2009.
45. Kahneman and Tversky, 1979; Tversky and Kahneman, 1981; Plous, 1993.
46. Axelrod, 1984/2006; Kimbrough, Smith, and Wilson, 2008; Smith, 2009.
47. Axelrod, 1984/2006.
48. Sober and Wilson, 1998.
49. Sober and Wilson, 1998.
50. Taibbi, 2010.
51. Sober and Wilson, 1998; Wilson, 2002; Smith, 2009.
52. Wilson, Wilczynski, Wells, and Weiser, 2000; Wilson, 2002; King-Casas, Tomlin, Anen, Camerer, Quartz, and Montague, 2005.
53. Wilson, 2002.
54. Leeson, 2009.

55. Sanfey, Rilling, Aronson, Nystrom, and Cohen, 2003; Sanfey, 2007; Houser and McCabe, 2008.
56. Dawes and Thaler, 1988; Sanfey, Rilling, Aronson, Nystrom, and Cohen, 2003.
57. *Sociopaths and the ultimatum game:* Smith, 2009; Kishida, King-Casas, and Montague, 2010; *Sociopaths and empathy:* Singer, 2008; *Business school graduates and the ultimatum game:* Gintis and Khurana, 2008.
58. Jensen, Call, and Tomasello, 2007.
59. de Waal, 1982; Goodall, 1986; Brosnan, 2008, 2009.
60. Diamond, 2006; Goodall, 1986.
61. Sober and Wilson, 1998.
62. Pillutla and Murnighan, 1996; Rilling, Gutman, Zeh, Pagnoni, Berns, and Kilts, 2002; Sanfey, Rilling, Aronson, Nystrom, and Cohen, 2003; de Quervain, Fischbacher, Treyer, Schellhammer, Schnyder, Buck, and Fehr, 2004; Rilling, Sanfey, Aronson, Nystrom, and Cohen, 2004; Singer, Seymour, O'Doherty, Stephan, Dolan, and Frith, 2006; Seymour, Singer, and Dolan, 2007; Sanfey and Dorris, 2009; Cooper, Kreps, Wiebe, Pirkl, and Knutson, 2010; Gospic, Mohlin, Fransson, Petrovic, Johannesson, and Ingvar, 2011.
63. Sanfey, 2007; Sanfey and Dorris, 2009.
64. Hoffman, McCabe, Shachat, and Smith, 1994; Smith, 2009.
65. Frank, 2007; Warren, 2011; *Wikipedia*, "Tax freedom day."
66. Taibbi, 2010.
67. *Talmud, Shabbat* 31a; Telushkin, 2010a,b.

Chapter 24. The Conundrum of Robotics

1. Anonymous (Mohammed Jones), 2011.
2. Adams, 1979/1997.
3. Wegner, 2002.
4. Jordan, 1992.
5. Feynman, 1965; Pagels, 1984; Greene, 1999.
6. Gleick, 1987; Lorenz, 1993; Kakalios, 2010.
7. Aristotle, 350 BCE/1930.
8. Descartes, 1637/2008, 1647/1989; Watson, 2002; Galileo, 1638.
9. Newton, 1687/1726; Laplace, 1814/1902; Earman, 1986.
10. Penrose, 1980/1989; Hameroff, 1994.
11. Feynman, 1965; Greene, 1999.
12. Gell-Mann, 1995; Kakalios, 2010.
13. Lorenz, 1993; Gleick, 1987; Galison, 2003.
14. Hille, 2001.
15. Hodgkin and Huxley, 1952.
16. White, Klink, Alonso, and Kay, 1998; Dorval and White, 2005.
17. Katz, 1966; Lin and Holt, 2007; Guirland and Zheng, 2007; Pak, Flynn, and Bamburg, 2008.
18. Mainen and Sejnowski, 1995.
19. Penrose, 1980/1989; Hameroff, 1994.
20. Levy, 2007.
21. Sagan, 1997; Boyer, 2002.
22. Darrow, 1932.
23. Spielberg, 2002.
24. *Evidence-based medicine:* Evidence-Based Medicine Working Group (Gordon Guyatt et al.), 1992; Groopman, 2007; *Legal system:* Rosenberg, 2011.
25. *Austerity in response to shrinking economies:* Krugman, 2011, 2012; *Criminalization of drug use:* Manski, Pepper, and Petrie, 2001; Leukefeld, Gullotta, and Gregrich, 2011; Haller, 1989; U.S. Department of Justice, 1992.
26. Lakoff, 2001.

27. *Effect on individuals:* Goldstein, 2000; Heyman, 2009; *Incarceration versus treatment:* Manski, Pepper, and Petrie, 2001; Leukefeld, Gullotta, and Gregrich, 2011; Haller, 1989.
28. Darrow, 1932; Levy, 2007.
29. Asimov, 1951–1953.
30. Spielberg, 2002.
31. Hampton, 1987/1990.
32. Alvidson and Stallone, 1976.
33. Plato, 4th century BCE/2008b; Freud, 1923/1990; Haidt, 2006; Lehrer, 2009b.
34. *Original Libet experiments:* Libet, Wright, Feinstein, and Pearl, 1979; Libet, 1985, 1993; *Consciousness as illusion:* Wegner, 2002; Fischer, 2006; *Consciousness as rationalization:* Ramachandran and Blakeslee, 1999; Ramachandran, 2011; Kurzban, 2010; *Consciousness as monitor:* Eccles et al., 1965; Levy, 2007; Gray, 2004; Damasio, 2010.
35. Descartes, 1637/2008, 1647/1989; Searle, 2006; Hofstadter, 1985, 2008.
36. Aquinas, 1274/1947.
37. Galileo, 1610, 1638; Descartes, 1637/1886/2008; Newton, 1687/1726; Kepler, 1609.
38. Descartes, 1647/1989; Laplace, 1814/1902; Earman, 1986.
39. Carlson, 2010.
40. Striedter, 2005.
41. Descartes, 1647/1989; Watson, 2002; Lokhorst, 2011.
42. Penrose, 1980/1989; Hameroff, 1994.
43. Penrose, 1980/1989; McCorduck, 2004.

Epilogue

1. Haidt, 2006; Lehrer, 2009b.
2. Higgins, Alessi, and Dantona, 2002; Petry, 2011; Metcalfe and Mischel, 1999; McClure, Laibson, Loewenstein, and Cohen, 2004a; Peters and Büchel, 2010; Kang, Rangel, Camus, and Camerer, 2011; Kurth-Nelson and Redish, 2012c.
3. Shelton, 1988.
4. Gray, 2004; Kurzban, 2010.
5. Damasio, 1994.
6. Nili, Goldberg, Weizman, and Dudai, 2010.
7. Sanfey, 2007; Zak, 2008.
8. Shelton, 1988; Baumeister, Heatherton, and Tice, 1994; Stitzer and Petry, 2006; Baumeister and Tierney, 2011.
9. Ainslie, 1992; Redish, Jensen, Johnson, and Kurth-Nelson, 2007; Kurth-Nelson and Redish, 2012b.

Appendix A. Information Processing in Neurons

1. Shannon, 1948; Gleick, 2011.
2. Kahn, 1967/1996.
3. Hodgkin and Huxley, 1952.
4. Rieke, Warland, de Ruyter van Steveninck, and Bialek, 1997.
5. Soltesz and Staley, 2008.
6. Tanaka, 2006; Durstewitz and Seamans, 2008; Grace, 2000.
7. Hebb, 1949/2002; Bliss, Collingridge, and Morris, 2004; Kandel, 2006; *Hippocampus:* Bliss and Lømo, 1973; Andersen, Morris, Amaral, Bliss, and O'Keefe, 2007; *Cortex:* Bear and Kirkwood, 1993; *Cerebellum:* Hartell, 2002; *Basal ganglia:* Lovinger, 2010; *Spinal cord:* Wills, 2002; Ikeda, Kiritoshi, and Murase, 2009.
8. McNaughton, Douglas, and Goddard, 1978; Kandel, Schwartz, and Jessell, 2000; Dan and Poo, 2006; Kandel, 2006; Sacktor, 2008; Lisman, Yasuda, and Raghavachari, 2012.

Appendix B. Gleaning Information from the Brain

1. O'Keefe and Nadel, 1978; Redish, 1999.
2. Wu, Arbuckle, Liu, Tao, and Zhang, 2008.
3. Fyhn, Molden, Witter, Moser, and Moser, 2004; Hafting, Fyhn, Molden, Moser, and Moser, 2005.
4. Rieke, Warland, de Ruyter van Steveninck, and Bialek, 1997.
5. Jung, Wiener, and McNaughton, 1994; Kjelstrup, Solstad, Brun, Hafting, Leutgeb, Witter, Moser, and Moser, 2008.
6. Wilson and McNaughton, 1993.
7. Johnson, Fenton, Kentros, and Redish, 2009.
8. Buzsáki, 2006; Katzner, Nauhaus, Benucci, Bonin, Ringach, and Carandini, 2009.
9. O'Keefe and Nadel, 1978; Buzsáki, 2006; van der Meer, Kalensher, Lansink, Pennartz, Berke, and Redish, 2010.
10. Vanderwolf, 1971; O'Keefe and Nadel, 1978.
11. Hubel and Wiesel, 1977; Mountcastle, 1997.
12. Abeles, 1991; Krubitzer and Kaas, 2005; Krubitzer, 2009; Jerison, 1973; Hofman, 1985; Abeles, 1991; Striedter, 2005.
13. Katzner, Nauhaus, Benucci, Bonin, Ringach, and Carandini, 2009; Ince, Gupta, Arica, Tewfik, Ashe, and Pellizzer, 2010.
14. Niedermeyer and Lopes da Silva, 1999.
15. Nowlis and Kamiya, 1970; Ros, Munneke, Ruge, Gruzelier, and Rothwell, 2010.
16. Silver, 2009.
17. Niedermeyer and Lopes da Silva, 1999.
18. Holroyd and Coles, 2002; Gehring, Goss, Coles, Meyer, and Donachin, 1993; Falkenstein, Hoormann, Christ, and Hohnsbein, 2000.
19. Wyler and Herman, 1994; Duncan, 2007.
20. e.g., Jacobs, Kahana, Ekstrom, and Fried, 2007.
21. See Huettel, Song, and McCarthy, 2009, for a thorough review of fMRI and the related neuroimaging technologies.
22. Logothetis, 2002; Heeger and Ress, 2002; Lippert, Steudel, Ohl, Logothetis, and Kayser, 2010; Cardoso, Sirotin, Lima, Glushenkova, and Das, 2012.
23. Nair, 2005; Huettel, Song, and McCarthy, 2009.
24. Ahmed, Hu, Paczynski, and Hsu, 2001.
25. Ames, 2000; Nair, 2005; Huettel, Song, and McCarthy, 2009.
26. Ahmed, Hu, Paczynski, and Hsu, 2001.
27. Ahmed, Hu, Paczynski, and Hsu, 2001.
28. Bisiach, Perani, Vallar, and Berti, 1986; Mohr, Lazar, Marshall, and Hier, 2004.
29. Foreman and Eaton, 1993.
30. Bisiach and Luzatti, 1978.
31. Kosslyn, 1994.
32. Damasio, 1992; Purves, Augustine, Fitzpatrick, Hall, LaMantia, McNamara, and White, 2008.
33. Wyler and Herman, 1994; Duncan, 2007.
34. Cohen and Squire, 1980; Squire, 1987; Corkin, 2008; Squire, 2009.
35. Wassermann, Walsh, Epstein, Paus, Ziemann, and Lisanby, 2008.
36. Wassermann, 1998; Anand and Hotson, 2002.
37. Anholt and Mackay, 2010.
38. Darwin, 1859.
39. Anholt and Mackay, 2010; Joyner, 2000; Pei, Rogan, Yan, and Roth, 2008, e.g., Nakazawa, Quirk, Chitwood, Watanabe, Yeckel, Sun, Kato, Carr, Johnston, Wilson, and Tonegawa, 2002, and Garner, Rowland, Hwang, Baumgaertel, Roth, Kentros, and Mayford, 2012.
40. Boyden, Zhang, Bamberg, Nagel, and Deisseroth, 2006; Deisseroth, 2011; Scanziani and Häusser, 2009.

41. Benabid, Chabardes, Mitrofanis, and Pollak, 2009; Frank, Samanta, Moustafa, and Sherman, 2007b; Dostrovsky, Hutchinson, and Lozano, 2002.
42. *Shutting down structures:* McIntyre, Savast, Goff, and Vitek, 2004; *Resetting oscillations:* Birdno and Grill, 2008; Brown and Eusebio, 2008; *Axons:* Deniau, Degos, Bosch, and Maurice, 2010.
43. Salzman, Murasugi, Britten, and Newsome, 1992.
44. Zeng, 2004; Zeng, Rebscher, Harrison, Sun, and Feng, 2009.
45. Weiland, Liu, and Humayun, 2005; Dowling, 2009.

Appendix C. Content-Addressable Memory

1. Rumelhart and McClelland, 1986; Hertz, Krogh, and Palmer, 1991; Churchland and Sejnowski, 1994.
2. McClelland and Rumelhart, 1986; Lakoff, 1990/1997.
3. Hebb, 1949/2002.
4. Hume, 1748/2003.
5. McNaughton, 2003.
6. Rumelhart and McClelland, 1986; Churchland and Sejnowski, 1994; Harris, 2005.
7. Hopfield, 1982; Mitchell, 1993; Churchland and Sejnowski, 1994; Schacter, 2001.
8. Bird, 2007.
9. Hebb, 1949/2002; Hopfield, 1982; McClelland and Rumelhart, 1986; Rumelhart and McClelland, 1986; Wilson and McNaughton, 1993.
10. Kohonen, 1980; Hopfield, 1982; Hertz, Krogh, and Palmer, 1991.
11. Hopfield, 1982.
12. Churchland and Sejnowski, 1994.
13. Hopfield, 1982; Kohonen, 1980, 1984; Hertz, Krogh, and Palmer, 1991; Kurth-Nelson and Redish, 2012c.
14. Rumelhart and McClelland, 1986; Churchland and Sejnowski, 1994.
15. *Changing excitatory connections only:* Wilson and Cowan, 1973; Kohonen, 1980, 1984; Eliasmith and Anderson, 2003; *Graded neurons:* Wilson and Cowan, 1973; Redish, 1999; Eliasmith and Anderson, 2003; *Spiking neurons:* Laing and Chow, 2001.
16. Mainen and Sejnowski, 1995; Fenton and Muller, 1998; Shadlen and Newsome, 1998; Chichilnisky and Kalmar, 2003; VanRullen, Guyonneau, and Thorpe, 2005.
17. Carr and MacLeod, 2010.
18. Mainen and Sejnowski, 1995; Shadlen and Newsome, 1998.
19. Amarasingham, Harrison, Hatsopoulos, and Geman, 2011.
20. Chichilnisky and Kalmar, 2003.
21. Carr and MacLeod, 2010.
22. Hasselmo and Bower, 1993; Hasselmo and Wyble, 1997; Durstewitz, Kelc, and Gunturkun, 1999; Redish, 1999; Durstewitz, Seamans, and Sejnowski, 2000; Tanaka, 2006.
23. Hopfield, 1982; Hertz, Krogh, and Palmer, 1991.
24. Abbott and Nelson, 2000; Dayan and Abbott, 2001.
25. Redish, 1999; Durstewitz, Seamans, and Sejnowski, 2000; Tanaka, 2006.
26. Miyawaki, Jenkins, Strange, Liberman, Verbrugge, and Fujimura, 1975; Kenstowicz and Kisseberth, 1979; Akmajian, Demers, and Harnish, 1984; Kuhl, 1994.
27. Guenther and Bohland, 2002; Vallabha and McClelland, 2007.
28. Logan, Lively, and Pisoni, 1991; McClelland, Fiez, and McCandliss, 2002; Vallabha and McClelland, 2007.
29. Vallabha and McClelland, 2007.
30. Kuhl, Williams, Lacerda, Stevens, and Lindblom, 1992; Kuhl, Andruski, Chistovich, Chistovich, Kozhevnikova, Ryskina, Stolyarova, Sundberg, and Lacerda, 1997.
31. Lakoff, 1990/1997; Roberson and Davidoff, 2000.
32. Berlin and Kay, 1969; Rosch, 1973.
33. Roberson and Davidoff, 2000; Winawer, Witthoft, Frank, Wu, Wade, and Boroditsky, 2007.

34. Sapir, 1929; Whorf, 1956.
35. Lakoff and Johnson, 2003; Lakoff, Dean, and Hazen, 2004.
36. Whorf, 1956.
37. Martin, 1986; Kaplan, 2003.
38. Lakoff, 1990/1997.
39. Winawer, Witthoft, Frank, Wu, Wade, and Boroditsky, 2007.
40. Rosch, 1973.
41. Purves, Augustine, Fitzpatrick, Hall, LaMantia, McNamara, and White, 2008; Chaudhuri, 2011.
42. Wilson and McNaughton, 1993.
43. Redish, 1999.
44. Harris, 2005; Jackson and Redish, 2007; Johnson, Fenton, Kentros, and Redish, 2009; Kelemen and Fenton, 2010.
45. Hatsopoulos, Ojakangas, Paninski, and Donoghue, 1998; Hatsopoulos, Paninski, and Donoghue, 2003; Churchland, Yu, Ryu, Santhanam, and Shenoy, 2006.
46. Benchenane, Peyrache, Khamassi, Tierney, Gioanni, Battaglia, and Wiener, 2010; Durstewitz, Vittoz, Floresco, and Seamans, 2010.

CITATIONS

Abbott LF and Nelson SB (2000). Synaptic plasticity: Taming the beast. *Nature Neuroscience* 3:1178–1183.

Abe H and Lee D (2011). Distributed coding of actual and hypothetical outcomes in the orbital and dorsolateral prefrontal cortex. *Neuron* 70(4):731–741.

Abeles M (1991). *Corticonics: Neural Circuits of the Cerebral Cortex*. Cambridge, UK: Cambridge University Press.

Abrahams RD (1983). *African Folktales*. New York: Pantheon.

Adams D (1979/1997). *The Hitchhiker's Guide to the Galaxy*. New York: Random House.

Adhikari A, Topiwala MA, and Gordon JA (2010). Synchronized activity between the ventral hippocampus and the medial prefrontal cortex during anxiety. *Neuron* 65(2):257–269.

Aeschylus (458 BCE/1969). *The Oresteia*. Translated by David Grene. Chicago: University of Chicago Press.

Afshar A, Santhanam G, Yu BM, Ryu SI, Sahani M, and Shenoy KV (2011). Single-trial neural correlates of arm movement preparation. *Neuron* 71(3):555–564.

Aharon I, Etcoff N, Ariely D, Chabris CF, O'Connor E, and Breiter HC (2001). Beautiful faces have variable reward value: fMRI and behavioral evidence. *Neuron* 32(3):537–551.

Ahmed SH (2010). Validation crisis in animal models of drug addiction: Beyond non-disordered drug use toward drug addiction. *Neuroscience and Biobehavioral Reviews* 35(2):172–184.

Ahmed SH, Hu CJ, Paczynski R, and Hsu CY (2001). Pathophysiology of ischemic injury. In Fisher M (ed.), *Stroke Therapy*. Boston: Butterworth-Heinemann, Chapter 2, pp. 25–59.

Ainge JA, Tamosiunaite M, Woergoetter F, and Dudchenko PA (2007). Hippocampal CA1 place cells encode intended destination on a maze with multiple choice points. *Journal of Neuroscience* 27(36):9769–9779.

Ainslie G (1992). *Picoeconomics*. Cambridge, UK: Cambridge University Press.

Ainslie G (2001). *Breakdown of Will*. Cambridge, UK: Cambridge University Press.

Akins K (ed.) (1996). *perception*. New York: Oxford University Press.

Akmajian A, Demers RA, and Harnish RM (1984). *Linguistics: An Introduction to Language and Communication*. Cambridge, MA: MIT Press.

Albin RL, Young AB, and Penney JB (1989). The functional anatomy of basal ganglia disorders. *Trends in Neurosciences* 12(10):366–374.

Alexander GE and Crutcher MD (1990). Preparation for movement: Neural representations of intended direction in three motor areas of the monkey. *Journal of Neurophysiology* 64(1):133–150.

Alligheri D (1321/1961/2003). *The Divine Comedy: Inferno, Purgitorio, Paradiso*. Translated by John Ciardi. New York: Penguin Classics.

Allman J, Hakeem A, and Watson K (2002). Two phylogenetic specializations in the human brain. *Neuroscientist* 8(4):335–346.

Allman J, Watson K, Tetreault N, and Hakeem A (2005). Intuition and autism: A possible role for Von Economo neurons. *Trends in Cognitive Sciences* 9(8):367–373.

Altman J, Everitt BJ, Robbins TW, Glautier S, Markou A, Nutt DJ, Oretti R, and Phillips GD (1996). The biological, social and clinical bases of drug addiction: commentary and debate. *Psychopharmacology* 125(4):285–345.

Alvarez P and Squire LR (1994). Memory consolidation and the medial temporal lobe: A simple network model. *Proceedings of the National Academy of Sciences, USA* 91:7041–7045.

Alvidson JG and Stallone S (1976). *Rocky*. United Artists.

Amarasingham A, Harrison MT, Hatsopoulos NG, and Geman S (2011). Conditional modeling and the jitter method of spike resampling. *Journal of Neurophysiology* 107(2):517–531.

Amari SI (1977). Dynamics of pattern formation in lateral-inhibition type neural fields. *Biological Cybernetics* 27:77–87.

Ames A (2000). CNS energy metabolism as related to function. *Brain Research Reviews* 34(1–2):42–68.

Amsel A (1992). *Frustration Theory*. Cambridge, UK: Cambridge University Press.

Anagnostaras SG, Maren S, and Fanselow MS (1999). Temporally graded retrograde amnesia of contextual fear after hippocampal damage in rats: Within-subjects examination. *Journal of Neuroscience* 19(3):1106–1114.

Anand S and Hotson J (2002). Transcranial magnetic stimulation: Neurophysiological applications and safety. *Brain and Cognition* 50(3):366–386.

Andersen P, Morris RGM, Amaral D, Bliss T, and O'Keefe J (eds.) (2007). *The Hippocampus Book*. New York: Oxford University Press.

Andersen S, Harrison GW, Lau MI, and Rutström EE (2008). Eliciting risk and time preferences. *Econometrica* 76(3):583–618.

Anderson L (1982). Walking and falling. On *Big Science*, Warner Bros. records.

Andrade EB and Ariely D (2009). The enduring impact of transient emotions on decision making. *Organizational Behavior and Human Decision Processes* 109(1):1–8.

Anholt RRH and Mackay TFC (2010). *Principles of Behavioral Genetics*. New York: Academic Press.

Anonymous (Mohammed Jones) (2011). Jesus and mo: Roof. www.jesusandmo.net/ October 12, 2011.

Anthony JC, Warner LA, and Kessler RC (1994). Comparative epidemiology of dependence on tobacco, alcohol, controlled substances, and inhalants: Basic findings from the National Comorbidity Survey. *Experimental and Clinical Psychopharmacology* 2(3):244–268.

Aosaki T, Graybiel AM, and Kimura M (1994). Effect of the nigrostriatal dopamine system on acquired neural responses in the striatum of behaving monkeys. *Science* 265:412–415.

Aquinas T (1274/1947). *Summa Theologica*. Translated by the Fathers of the English Dominican Province. Sacred-Texts.com.

Arbisi PA, Billington CJ, and Levine AS (1999). The effect of naltrexone on taste detection and recognition threshold. *Appetite* 32(2):241–249.

Archer J and Birke L (eds.) (1983). *Exploration in Animals and Humans*. Cambridge, UK: Cambridge University Press.

Arendt J (2009). Managing jet lag: Some of the problems and possible new solutions. *Sleep Medicine Reviews* 13(4):249–256.

Arendt J and Skene DJ (2005). Melatonin as a chronobiotic. *Sleep Medicine Reviews* 9(1):25–39.

Argyle M and Dean J (1965). Eye-contact, distance, and affiliation. *Sociometry* 28(3):289–304.

Ariely D (2008). *Predictably Irrational: The Hidden Forces that Shape Our Decisions*. New York: Harper-Collins.

Aristophanes (405 BCE/1964). *The Frogs*. Translated by Richmond Lattimore. New York: Penguin.

Aristophanes (411 BCE/1964). *Lysistrata*. Translated by Douglass Parker. New York: Penguin.

Aristophanes (423 BCE/1962). *The Clouds*. Translated by William Arrowsmith. New York: Penguin.

Aristotle (350 BCE/1930). *Physics*. Translated by R. P. Hardie and R. K. Gaye. New York: Oxford University Press.

Aristotle (350 BCE/2004). *Politics: A Treatise on Government*. Translated by William Ellis, 1912. Project Gutenberg. www.gutenberg.org.

Armony JL, Servan-Schreiber D, Cohen JD, and LeDoux JE (1997). Computational modeling of emotion: Explorations through the anatomy and physiology of fear conditioning. *Trends in Cognitive Sciences* 1(1):28–34.

Arnsten AF (2011). Catecholamine influences on dorsolateral prefrontal cortical networks. *Biological Psychiatry* 69(12):e89–e99.

Arvanitogiannis A and Shizgal P (2008). The reinforcement mountain: Allocation of behavior as a function of the rate and intensity of rewarding brain stimulation. *Behavioral Neuroscience* 122(5):1126–1138.

Asimov I (1951–1953). *The Foundation Trilogy (Foundation, Foundation and Empire, Second Foundation)*. New York: Doubleday.

Aston-Jones G, Chiang C, and Alexinsky T (1991). Discharge of noradrenergic locus coeruleus neurons in behaving rats and monkeys suggests a role in vigilance. *Progress in Brain Research* 88:501–520.

Aston-Jones G and Cohen JD (2005). An integrative theory of locus coeruleus-norepinephrine function: Adaptive gain and optimal performance. *Annual Review of Neuroscience* 28(1):403–450.

Aston-Jones G, Delfs JM, Druhan J, and Zhu Y (1999). The bed nucleus of the stria terminalis: A target site for noradrenergic actions in opiate withdrawal. *Annals of the New York Academy of Sciences* 877:486–498.

Aston-Jones G and Kalivas PW (2008). Brain norepinephrine rediscovered in addiction research. *Biological Psychiatry* 63(11):1005–1006.

Augustine of Hippo (Saint Augustine) (398/1961). *Confessions*. Translated by R. S. Pine-Coffin. New York: Penguin Classics.

Augustine of Hippo (Saint Augustine) (427/1972). *The City of God*. Translated by Henry Bettenson. New York: Penguin Classics.

Aunger R (ed.) (2001). *Darwinizing Culture: The Status of Memetics as a Science*. New York: Oxford University Press.

Axelrod R (1984/2006). *The Evolution of Cooperation*. New York: Basic Books.

Azolosa JL, Stitzer ML, and Greenwald MK (1994). Opioid physical dependence development: Effects of single versus repeated morphine pretreatments and of subjects' opioid exposure history. *Psychopharmacology* 114(1):71–80.

Baddeley A (2007). *Working Memory, Thought and Action*. New York: Oxford University Press.

Balfour DJK and Fagerström KO (1996). Pharmacology of nicotine and its therapeutic use in smoking cessation and neurodegenerative disorders. *Pharmacology and Therapeutics* 72(1):51–81.

Ballard KA, Houde S, Silver-Balbus S, and McClure SM (2009). The decimal effect: Nucleus accumbens activity correlates with within-subject increases in delay discounting rates. *Society for Neuroeconomics Annual Meeting*, p. 66.

Balleine BW (2001). Incentive processes in instrumental conditioning. In: Klein SB and Mowrer RR (eds.), *Handbook of Contemporary Learning Theories*. Hillsdale, NJ: Lawrence Erlbaum, pp. 307–366.

Balleine BW (2004). Incentive behavior. In: Whishaw IQ and Kolb B (eds.), *The Behavior of the Laboratory Rat: A Handbook with Tests*. New York: Oxford University Press, pp. 436–446.

Balleine BW and Dickinson A (1998). Goal-directed instrumental action: Contingency and incentive learning and their cortical substrates. *Neuropharmacology* 37(4–5):407–419.

Balmer TS, Carels VM, Frisch JL, and Nick TA (2009). Modulation of perineuronal nets and parvalbumin with developmental song learning. *Journal of Neuroscience* 29(41):12878–12885.

Bals-Kubik R, Herz A, and Shippenberg T (1989). Evidence that the aversive effects of opioid antagonists and κ-agonists are centrally mediated. *Psychopharmacology* 98:203–206.

Bares M, Lungu O, Liu T, Waechter T, Gomez CM, and Ashe J (2007). Impaired predictive motor timing in patients with cerebellar disorders. *Experimental Brain Research* 180(2):355–365.

Bargary G and Mitchell KJ (2008). Synaesthesia and cortical connectivity. *Trends in Neurosciences* 31(7):335–342.

Barlow JS (2002). *The Cerebellum and Adaptive Control*. Cambridge, UK: Cambridge University Press.

Barnes TD, Kubota Y, Hu D, Jin DZ, and Graybiel AM (2005). Activity of striatal neurons reflects dynamic encoding and recoding of procedural memories. *Nature* 437:1158–1161.

Barnes TD, Mao JB, Hu D, Kubota Y, Dreyer AA, Stamoulis C, Brown EN, and Graybiel AM (2011). Advance-cueing produces enhanced action-boundary patterns of spike activity in the sensorimotor striatum. *Journal of Neurophysiology* 105(4):1861–1878.

Barrett D (2010). *Supernormal Stimuli: How Primal Urges Overran Their Evolutionary Purpose*. New York: W. W. Norton.

Barrett LF (2006). Are emotions natural kinds? *Perspectives on Psychological Science* 1(1):28–58.

Bastiaansen JACJ, Thioux M, and Keysers C (2009). Evidence for mirror systems in emotions. *Philosophical Transactions of the Royal Society B* 364(1528):2391–2404.

Battaglia FP, Sutherland GR, and McNaughton BL (2004). Hippocampal sharp wave bursts coincide with neocortical "up-state" transitions. *Learning and Memory* 11(6):697–704.

Baumeister RF, Heatherton TF, and Tice DM (1994). *Losing Control: How and Why People Fail at Self-Regulation*. New York: Academic Press.

Baumeister RF and Tierney J (2011). *Willpower: Rediscovering the Greatest Human Strength*. New York: Penguin Press.

Baumeister RF, Vohs KD, and Tice DM (2007). The strength model of self-control. *Psychological Science* 16(6):351–355.

Bayer HM and Glimcher P (2005). Midbrain dopamine neurons encode a quantitative reward prediction error signal. *Neuron* 47:129–141.

Bear MF and Kirkwood A (1993). Neocortical long-term potentiation. *Current Opinion in Neurobiology* 3(2):197–202.

Bechara A (2005). Decision making, impulse control and loss of willpower to resist drugs: A neurocognitive perspective. *Nature Neuroscience* 8(11):1458–1463.

Bechara A and Damasio H (2002). Decision-making and addiction (part I): Impaired activation of somatic states in substance dependent individuals when pondering decisions with negative future consequences. *Neuropsychologia* 40(10):1675–1689.

Bechara A, Tranel D, and Damasio H (2000). Characterization of the decision-making deficit of patients with ventromedial prefrontal cortex lesions. *Brain* 123(11):2189–2202.

Bechara A and van der Linden M (2005). Decision-making and impulse control after frontal lobe injuries. *Current Opinion in Neurology* 18:734–739.

Beck AM and Katcher AH (1996). *Between Pets and People: The Importance of Animal Companionship*. West Lafayette, IN: Purdue University Press.

Beckett S (2010). *The Collected Shorter Plays*. New York: Grove Press.

Beethoven LV (1824). *Symphony No. 9 in D minor*, Opus 125.

Behrens TE, Woolrich MW, Walton ME, and Rushworth MFS (2007). Learning the value of information in an uncertain world. *Nature Neuroscience* 10:1214–1221.

Behrmann M and Avidan G (2005). Congenital prosopagnosia: Face-blind from birth. *Trends in Cognitive Sciences* 9(4):180–187.

Bekoff M and Byers JA (eds.) (1998). *Animal Play: Evolutionary, Comparative, and Ecological Perspectives*. Cambridge, UK: Cambridge University Press.

Bell DE (1982). Regret in decision making under uncertainty. *Operations Research* 30(5):961–981.

Bell DE (1985). Disappointment in decision making under uncertainty. *Operations Research* 33(1):1–27.

Bellman R (1958). On a routing problem. *Quarterly Journal of Applied Mathematics* 16(1):87–90.

Ben-Ari M (2005). *Just a Theory: Exploring the Nature of Science*. New York: Prometheus.

Benabid AL, Chabardes S, Mitrofanis J, and Pollak P (2009). Deep brain stimulation of the subthalamic nucleus for the treatment of Parkinson's disease. *Lancet Neurology* 8(1):67–81.

Benchenane K, Peyrache A, Khamassi M, Tierney PL, Gioanni Y, Battaglia FP, and Wiener SI (2010). Coherent theta oscillations and reorganization of spike timing in the hippocampal-prefrontal network upon learning. *Neuron* 66(6):921–936.

Benowitz NL (1996). Pharmacology of nicotine: Addiction and therapeutics. *Annual Review of Pharmacology and Toxicology* 36:597–613.

Beradi N, Pizzorusso T, and Maffei L (2000). Critical periods during sensory development. *Current Opinion in Neurobiology* 10:138–145.

Beran MJ, Savage-Rumbaugh ES, Pate JL, and Rumbaugh DM (1999). Delay of gratification in chimpanzees (*Pan troglodytes*). *Developmental Psychobiology* 34(2):119–127.

Berlin B and Kay P (1969). *Basic Color Terms: Their Universality and Evolution*. Berkeley, CA: University of California Press.

Bernheim BD and Rangel A (2004). Addiction and cue-triggered decision processes. *American Economic Review* 94(5):1558–1590.

Berns GS, Chappelow J, Cekic M, Zink CF, Pagnoni G, and Martin-Skurski ME (2006). Neurobiological substrates of dread. *Science* 312(5774):754–758.

Bernstein IL (1978). Learned taste aversions in children receiving chemotherapy. *Science* 200(4347):1302–1303.

Bernstein IL (1999). Taste aversion learning: A contemporary perspective. *Nutrition* 15(3):229–234.

Bernstein PL (1998). *Against the Gods: The Remarkable Story of Risk*. New York: Wiley.

Berridge KC (2007). The debate over dopamine's role in reward: The case for incentive salience. *Psychopharmacology* 191(3):391–431.

Berridge KC (2012). From prediction error to incentive salience: Mesolimbic computation of reward motivation. *European Journal of Neuroscience* 35:1124–1143.

Berridge KC and Robinson TE (2003). Parsing reward. *Trends in Neurosciences* 26(9):507–513.

Bettman JR, Luce MF, and Payne JW (1998). Constructive consumer choice processes. *Journal of Consumer Research* 25(3):187–217.

Bickel WK, Jamolowicz DP, Mueller ET, Gatchalian KM, and McClure SM (2012). Are executive function and impulsivity antipodes? A conceptual reconstruction with special reference to addiction. *Psychopharmacology* 221(3):361–387.

Bickel WK and Marsch LA (2001). Toward a behavioral economic understanding of drug dependence: Delay discounting processes. *Addiction* 96:73–86.

Bickel WK and Mueller ET (2009). Toward the study of trans-disease processes: A novel approach with special reference to the study of co-morbidity. *Journal of Dual Diagnosis* 5(2):131–138.

Bickel WK and Yi R (2008). Temporal discounting as a measure of executive function: Insights from the competing neuro-behavioral decision system hypothesis of addiction. *Advances in Health Economics and Health Services Research* 20:289–309.

Bickel WK, Yi R, Landes RD, Hill PF, and Baxter C (2011). Remember the future: Working memory training decreases delay discounting among stimulant addicts. *Biological Psychiatry* 69(3):260–265.

Bielajew CH and Harris T (1991). Self-stimulation: A rewarding decade. *Journal of Psychiatry* 16(3):109–114.

Bird B (2007). *Ratatouille*. Disney/Pixar.

Birdno MJ and Grill WM (2008). Mechanisms of deep brain stimulation in movement disorders as revealed by changes in stimulus frequency. *Neurotherapeutics* 5(1):14–25.

Bisiach E and Luzatti C (1978). Unilateral neglect of representational space. *Cortex* 14:129–133.

Bisiach E, Perani D, Vallar G, and Berti A (1986). Unilateral neglect: Personal and extra-personal. *Neuropsychologia* 24(6):759–767.

Bizzi E, Cheung VCK, d'Avella A, Satiel P, and Tresch M (2008). Combining modules for movement. *Brain Research Reviews* 57:125–133.

Bizzi E, Mussa-Ivaldi FA, and Giszter S (1991). Computations underlying the execution of movement: A biological perspective. *Science* 253:287–291.

Björklund A, Dunnett SB, Brundin P, Stoessl AJ, Freed CR, Breeze RE, Levivier M, Peschanski M, Studer L, and Barker R (2003). Neural transplantation for the treatment of Parkinson's disease. *Lancet* 2:437–445.

Black DW (2012). Epidemiology and phenomenology of compulsive buying disorder. In: Grant JE and Potenza MN (eds.), *The Oxford Handbook of Impulse Control Disorders*. New York: Oxford University Press, pp. 196–206.

Bliss TVP, Collingridge GL, and Morris RGM (eds.) (2004). *Long-Term Potentiation: Enhancing Neuroscience for 30 Years*. New York: Oxford University Press.

Bliss TVP and Lømo T (1973). Long-lasting potentiation of synaptic transmission in the dentate area of the anaesthetized rabbit following stimulation of the perforant path. *Journal of Physiology* 232:331–356.

Blomstedt P, Sjöberg RL, Hansson M, Bodlund O, and Hariz MI (2010). Deep brain stimulation in the treatment of depression. *Acta Psychiatrica Scandanavica* 123:4–11.

Bloom JD (2009). *A Dictionary of Hallucinations*. New York: Springer.

Blum D (1995). *The Monkey Wars*. New York: Oxford University Press.

Blum D (2002). *Love at Goon Park: Harry Harlow and the Science of Affection*. Cambridge, MA: Perseus.

Bobo JK and Husten C (2001). Sociocultural influences on smoking and drinking. *Alcohol Research and Health* 24(4):225–232.

Bossaerts P and Plott C (2004). Basic principles of asset pricing theory: Evidence from large-scale experimental financial markets. *Review of Finance* 8(2):135–169.

Botvinick M (2007). Conflict monitoring and decision making: Reconciling two perspectives on anterior cingulate function. *Cognitive, Affective, and Behavioral Neuroscience* 7(4):356–366.

Botvinick M and An J (2009). Goal-directed decision making in prefrontal cortex: A computational framework. In: Koller D, Schuurmans D, Bengio Y, and Bottou L (eds.), *Advances in Neural Information Processing Systems (NIPS)*. Cambridge, MA: MIT Press, volume 21, pp. 169–176.

Botvinick M, Niv Y, and Barto AC (2009). Hierarchically organized behavior and its neural foundations: A reinforcement learning perspective. *Cognition* 113(3):262–280.

Boucher L, Palmeri TJ, Logan GD, and Schall JD (2007). Inhibitory control in mind and brain: An interactive race model of countermanding saccades. *Psychological Review* 114(2):376–397.

Boureau YL and Dayan P (2011). Opponency revisited: Competition and cooperation between dopamine and serotonin. *Neuropsychopharmacology* 36:74–97.

Bourke JP, Turkington D, Thomas G, McComb JM, and Tynan M (1997). Florid psychopathology in patients receiving shocks from implanted cardioverter-defibrillators. *Heart* 78:581–583.

Bouton ME (2004). Context and behavioral processes in extinction. *Learning and Memory* 11(5):485–494.

Bouton ME (2007). *Learning and Behavior: A Contemporary Synthesis*. Sunderland, MA: Sinauer Associates.

Bova B (1981). *Notes to a Science Fiction Writer*. Boston: Houghton Mifflin.

Bowlby J (1969/1982). *Attachment*. New York: Basic Books.

Bowlby J (1977). The making and breaking of affectional bonds. *British Journal of Psychiatry* 130:201–210.

Boyd LA and Winstein CJ (2004). Providing explicit information disrupts implicit motor learning after basal ganglia stroke. *Learning and Memory* 11(4):388–396.

Boyden ES, Zhang F, Bamberg E, Nagel G, and Deisseroth K (2006). Millisecond-timescale, genetically targeted optical control of neural activity. *Nature Neuroscience* 8(9):1263–1268.

Boyer P (2002). *Religion Explained*. New York: Basic Books.

Boyle D (1996). *Trainspotting*. Miramax.

Boysen ST and Berntson GG (1995). Responses to quantity: Perceptual versus cognitive mechanisms in chimpanzees (*Pan troglodytes*). *Journal of Experimental Psychology: Animal Behavior Processes* 21(1):82–86.

Braitenberg V (1986). *Vehicles: Experiments in Synthetic Psychology*. Cambridge, MA: MIT Press.

Bray S and O'Doherty JP (2007). Neural coding of reward-prediction error signals during classical conditioning with attractive faces. *Journal of Neurophysiology* 97(4):3036–3045.

Bray S, Rangel A, Shimojo S, Balleine B, and O'Doherty JP (2008). The neural mechanisms underlying the influence of Pavlovian cues on human decision making. *Journal of Neuroscience* 28(22):5861–5866.

Bray S, Shimojo S, and O'Doherty JP (2010). Human medial orbitofrontal cortex is recruited during experience of imagined and real rewards. *Journal of Neurophysiology* 103(5):2506–2512.

Breiter HC, Aharon I, Kahneman D, Dale A, and Shizgal P (2001). Functional imaging of neural responses to expectancy and experience of monetary gains and losses. *Neuron* 30(2):619–639.

Breland K and Breland M (1961). The misbehavior of organisms. *American Psychologist* 16(11):682–684.

Bressloff PC, Cowan JD, Golubitsky M, Thomas PJ, and Wiener MC (2001). Geometric visual hallucinations, Euclidean symmetry and the functional architecture of striate cortex. *Philosophical Transactions of the Royal Society B* 40:299–330.

Bressloff PC, Cowan JD, Golubitsky M, Thomas PJ, and Wiener MC (2002). What geometric visual hallucinations tell us about the visual cortex. *Neural Computation* 14:473–491.

Brewer JA, Worhunsky PD, Carroll KM, Rounsaville BJ, and Potenza MN (2008). Pretreatment brain activation during Stroop task is associated with outcomes in cocaine-dependent patients. *Biological Psychiatry* 64:998–1004.

Brischoux F, Chakraborty S, Brierley DI, and Ungless MA (2009). Phasic excitation of dopamine neurons in ventral VTA by noxious stimuli. *Proceedings of the National Academy of Sciences, USA* 106(12):4894–4899.

Britten KH, Shadlen MN, Newsome WT, and Movshon JA (1992). The analysis of visual motion: A comparison of neuronal and psychophysical performance. *Journal of Neuroscience* 12(12):4745–4765.

Bromberg-Martin ES and Hikosaka O (2009). Midbrain dopamine neurons signal preference for advance information about upcoming rewards. *Neuron* 63(1):119–126.

Bromberg-Martin ES, Matsumoto M, Nakahara H, and Hikosaka O (2010). Multiple timescales of memory in lateral habenula and dopamine neurons. *Neuron* 67(3):499–510.

Brooks RA (1991). Intelligence without representation. *Artificial Intelligence* 47:139–159.

Broom DC, Jutkiewicz EM, Folk JE, Traynor JR, Rice KC, and Woods JH (2002). Nonpeptidic δ-opioid receptor agonists reduce immobility in the forced swim assay in rats. *Neuropsychopharmacology* 26:744–755.

Brosnan SF (2008). Fairness and other-regarding preferences in nonhuman primates. In: Zak PJ (ed.), *Moral Markets*. Princeton, NJ: Princeton University Press, pp. 77–104.

Brosnan SF (2009). Responses to inequity in non-human primates. In: Glimcher PW, Camerer CF, Fehr E, and Poldrack RA (eds.), *Neuroeconomics: Decision-making and the Brain*. London: Elsevier, pp. 285–301.

Brown C (2008). One year after: Remembering, rebuilding. *Minneapolis Star Tribune* www. startribune.com/26145649.html.

Brown D (1991). *Human Universals*. New York: McGraw Hill.

Brown EN, Frank LM, Tang D, Quirk MC, and Wilson MA (1998). A statistical paradigm for neural spike train decoding applied to position prediction from ensemble firing patterns of rat hippocampal place cells. *Journal of Neuroscience* 18(18):7411–7425.

Brown P and Eusebio A (2008). Paradoxes of functional neurosurgery: Clues from basal ganglia recordings. *Movement Disorders* 23(1):12–20.

Brown R and Kulik J (1977). Flashbulb memories. *Cognition* 5:73–99.

Buchanan BG and Shortliffe EH (eds.) (1984). *Rule-Based Expert Systems: The MYCIN Experiments of the Stanford Heuristic Programming Project*. Boston: Addison-Wesley.

Buckner RL and Carroll DC (2007). Self-projection and the brain. *Trends in Cognitive Sciences* 11(2):49–57.

Bujold LM (2002). *The Vor Game*. Riverdale, NY: Baen Books.

Bukowski C (1996). *Betting on the Muse*. New York: Harper-Collins.

Bullock SA and Potenza MN (2012). Pathological gambling: Neuropsychopharmacology and treatment. *Current Psychopharmacology* 1:67–85.

Bunzeck N, Doeller CF, Dolan RJ, and Duzel E (2012). Contextual interaction between novelty and reward processing within the mesolimbic system. *Human Brain Mapping* 33(6):1309–1324.

Buonomano DV and Merzenich MM (1998). Cortical plasticity: From synapses to maps. *Annual Review of Neuroscience* 21:149–186.

Burke KA, Franz TM, Miller DN, and Schoenbaum G (2007). Conditioned reinforcement can be mediated by either outcome-specific or general affective representations. *Frontiers in Integrative Neuroscience* 1:2 doi: 10.3389/neuro.07/002.2007.

Burks SV, Carpenter JP, Goette L, and Rustichini A (2009). Cognitive skills affect economic preferences, strategic behavior, and job attachment. *Proceedings of the National Academy of Sciences, USA* 106(19):7745–7750.

Burroughs WS (1959/1984). *Naked Lunch*. New York: Grove Press.

Bushong B, King LM, Camerer CF, and Rangel A (2010). Pavlovian processes in consumer choice: The physical presence of a good increases willingness-to-pay. *American Economic Review* 100(4):1556–1571.

Busto GU, Cervantes-Sandoval I, and Davis RL (2010). Olfactory learning in drosophila. *Journal of Physiology* 25(6):338–346.

Buzsáki G (1982). The "where is it?" reflex: Autoshaping the orienting response. *Journal of the Experimental Analysis of Behavior* 37(3):461–484.

Buzsáki G (1989). Two-stage model of memory trace formation: A role for "noisy" brain states. *Neuroscience* 31(3):551–570.

Buzsáki G (2006). *Rhythms of the Brain.* New York: Oxford University Press.

Byrne RW, Bates LA, and Moss CJ (2009). Elephant cognition in primate perspective. *Comparative Cognition and Behavior Reviews* 4:65–79.

Cabanac M, Cabanac AJ, and Parent A (2009). The emergence of consciousness in phylogeny. *Behavioural Brain Research* 198:267–272.

Cahill L, Gorski L, and Le K (2003). Enhanced human memory consolidation with post-learning stress: Interaction with the degree of arousal at encoding. *Learning and Memory* 10:270–274.

Cahill L, McGaugh JL, and Weinberger NM (2001). The neurobiology of learning and memory: Some reminders to remember. *Trends in Neurosciences* 24(10):578–581.

Cai X, Kim S, and Lee D (2011). Heterogeneous coding of temporally discounted values in the dorsal and ventral striatum during intertemporal choice. *Neuron* 69(1):170–182.

Calabresi P, Picconi B, Tozzi A, and Di Fillipo M (2007). Dopamine-mediated regulation of corti-costriatal synaptic plasticity. *Trends in Neurosciences* 30:211–219.

Call J and Tomassello M (2008). Does the chimpanzee have a theory of mind? 30 years later. *Trends in Cognitive Sciences* 12(5):187–192.

Calvino I (1956). *Italian Folktales.* Orlando, FL: Harcourt.

Camerer C (2003). *Behavioral Game Theory: Experiments in Strategic Interaction.* Princeton, NJ: Princeton University Press.

Camerer C and Weber M (1992). Recent developments in modeling preferences: Uncertainty and ambiguity. *Journal of Risk and Uncertainty* 5:325–370.

Cammarota M, Bevilaqua LRM, Vianna MRM, Medina JH, and Izquierdo I (2006). The extinction of conditioned fear: Structural and molecular basis and therapeutic use. *Revista Brasileira de Psiquiatria* 29(1):80–85.

Campbell J (1944). *A Skeleton Key to Finnegans Wake.* Novato, CA: New World Library.

Cantor C (2005). *Evolution and Posttraumatic Stress: Disorders of Vigilance and Defence.* London: Routledge.

Capaldi EJ (1957). The effect of different amounts of alternating partial reinforcement on resistance to extinction. *American Journal of Psychology* 70(3):451–452.

Capaldi EJ (1958). The effect of different amounts of training on the resistance to extinction of different patterns of partially reinforced responses. *Journal of Comparative and Physiological Psychology* 51(3):367–371.

Capaldi EJ and Lynch AD (1968). Magnitude of partial reward and resistance to extinction: Effect of N-R transitions. *Journal of Comparative and Physiological Psychology* 65(1):179–181.

Čapek K (1923/2001). *R. U. R.* New York: Doubleday.

Card OS (1986). *Speaker for the Dead.* New York: Tor Books.

Cardoso MMB, Sirotin YB, Lima B, Glushenkova E, and Das A (2012). The neuroimaging signal is a linear sum of neurally distinct stimulus- and task-related components. *Nature Neuroscience* 15:1298–1306.

Carew TJ (2004). *Behavioral Neurobiology: The Cellular Organization of Natural Behavior.* Sunderland, MA: Sinauer Associates.

Carlson NR (2010). *Physiology of Behavior.* Boston: Pearson.

Carpenter J (1974). *Dark Star.* Jack H. Harris Enterprises.

Carr CE and MacLeod KM (2010). Microseconds matter. *PLoS Biology* 8(6):e1000405.

Carroll ME, Lac ST, and Nygaard SL (1989). A concurrently available nondrug reinforcer prevents the acquisition or decreases the maintenance of cocaine-reinforced behavior. *Psychopharmacology* 97(1):23–29.

Carter BL, Lam CY, Robinson JD, Paris MM, Waters AJ, Wetter DW, and Cinciripini PM (2008). Real-time craving and mood assessments before and after smoking. *Nicotine and Tobacco Research* 10(7):1165–1169.

Casey BJ, Getz S, and Galvan A (2008a). The adolescent brain. *Developmental Review* 28(1):62–77.

Casey BJ, Jones RM, and Hare TA (2008b). The adolescent brain. *Annals of the New York Academy of Sciences* 1124:111–126.

Cassaday HJ and Rawlins JNP (1997). The hippocampus, objects, and their contexts. *Behavioral Neuroscience* 111(6):1228–1244.

Centers for Disease Control and Prevention (2011). U.S. Public Health Service Syphilis Study at Tuskegee. www.cdc.gov/tuskegee.

Chaloupka FJ, Emery S, and Liang L (2003). Evolving models of addictive behavior: From neoclassical to behavioral economics. In: Vuchinich RE and Heather N (eds.), *Choice, Behavioural Economics and Addiction*. Oxford, UK: Pergamon, pp. 71–89.

Chamberlain SR, Odlaug BL, Boulougouris V, Fineberg NA, and Grant JE (2009). Trichotillomania: Neurobiology and treatment. *Neuroscience and Biobehavioral Reviews* 33(6):831–842.

Chambers ES, Bridge MW, and Jones DA (2009). Carbohydrate sensing in the human mouth: Effects on exercise performance and brain activity. *Journal of Physiology* 587(8):1779–1794.

Chance MRA and Mead AP (1955). Competition between feeding and investigation in the rat. *Behavior* 8:174–181.

Chapman RF, Stickford JL, and Levine BD (2009). Altitude training considerations for the winter sport athlete. *Experimental Physiology* 95:411–421.

Charness N (1991). Expertise in chess: The balance between knowledge and search. In: Ericsson KA and Smith J (eds.), *Toward a General Theory of Expertise: Prospects and Limits*. Cambridge, UK: Cambridge University Press, Chapter 2, pp. 39–63.

Chase HW and Clark L (2010). Gambling severity predicts midbrain response to near-miss outcomes. *Journal of Neuroscience* 30(18):6180–6187.

Chase WG and Simon HA (1973). Perception in chess. *Cognitive Psychology* 4:55–81.

Chaudhuri A (2011). *Fundamentals of Sensory Perception*. New York: Oxford University Press.

Chavkin C, James IF, and Goldstein A (1982). Dynorphin is a specific endogenous ligand of the kappa opioid receptor. *Science* 215(4531):413–415.

Cheney DL and Seyfarth RM (1990). *How Monkeys See the World*. Chicago: University of Chicago Press.

Cheng K (1986). A purely geometric module in the rat's spatial representation. *Cognition* 23:149–178.

Cherryh CJ (1989). *The Pride of Chanur*. New York: DAW books.

Chib VS, Rangel A, Shimojo S, and O'Doherty JP (2009). Evidence for a common representation of decision values for dissimilar goods in human ventromedial prefrontal cortex. *Journal of Neuroscience* 29(39):12315–12320.

Chichilnisky EJ and Kalmar RS (2003). Temporal resolution of ensemble visual motion signals in primate retina. *Journal of Neuroscience* 23(17):6681–6689.

Childress AR, McLellan AT, Ehrman R, and O'Brien CP (1988). Classically conditioned responses in opioid and cocaine dependence: A role in relapse? *NIDA Research Monographs* 84:25–43.

Childress AR, Mozley PD, McElgin W, Fitzgerald J, Reivich M, and O'Brien CP (1999). Limbic activation during cue-induced cocaine craving. *American Journal of Psychiatry* 156:11–18.

Chiu PH, Lohrenz TM, and Montague PR (2008). Smokers' brains compute, but ignore, a fictive error signal in a sequential investment task. *Nature Neuroscience* 11:514–520.

Choi DC, Rothbaum BO, Gerardi M, and Ressler KJ (2009). Pharmacological enhancement of behavioral therapy: Focus on posttraumatic stress disorder. In: Stein MB and Steckler T (eds.), *Behavioral Neurobiology of Anxiety and Its Treatment*. New York: Springer, pp. 279–301.

Churchland AK, Kiani R, and Shadlen MN (2008). Decision-making with multiple alternatives. *Nature Neuroscience* 11(6):693–702.

Churchland MM, Yu BM, Ryu SI, Santhanam G, and Shenoy KV (2006). Neural variability in premotor cortex provides a signature of motor preparation. *Journal of Neuroscience* 26(14):3697–3712.

Churchland PS (2011). *BrainTrust*. Princeton, NJ: Princeton University Press.

Churchland PS and Sejnowski TJ (1994). *The Computational Brain*. Cambridge, MA: MIT Press.

Cisek P and Kalaska JF (2010). Neural mechanisms for interacting with a world full of action choices. *Annual Review of Neuroscience* 33:269–298.

Clark L, Bechara A, Damasio H, Aitken MRF, Sahakian BJ, and Robbins TW (2008). Differential effects of insular and ventromedial prefrontal cortex lesions on risky decision-making. *Brain* 131(5):1311–1322.

Clark L, Crooks B, Clarke R, Aitken MRF, and Dunn BD (2012). Physiological responses to near-miss outcomes and personal control during simulated gambling. *Journal of Gambling Studies* 28:123–137.

Classé JG, Semes LP, Daum KM, Nowakowski R, Alexander LJ, Wisniewski J, Beisel JA, Mann K, Rutstein R, Smith M, and Bartolucci A (1997). Association between visual reaction time and batting, fielding, and earned run averages among players of the Southern Baseball League. *Journal of the American Optometric Association* 68(1):43–49.

Classen DO, van den Wildenberg WPM, Ridderinkhof KR, Jessup CK, Harrison MB, Wooten GF, and Wylie SA (2011). The risky business of dopamine agonists in Parkinson disease and impulse control disorders. *Behavioral Neuroscience* 125(4):492–500.

Clayton NS (2007). Animal cognition: Crows spontaneously solve a metatool task. *Current Biology* 17(20):R894–R895.

Clayton NS, Griffiths DP, Emery NJ, and Dickinson A (2001). Elements of episodic-like memory in animals. *Philosophical Transactions of the Royal Society B* 356(1413):1483–1491.

Coghill RC, McHaffie JG, and Yen YF (2003). Neural correlates of interindividual differences in the subjective experience of pain. *Proceedings of the National Academy of Sciences, USA* 100(14):8538–8542.

Cohen MX and Frank MJ (2009). Neurocomputational models of basal ganglia function in learning, memory and choice. *Behavioural Brain Research* 199(1):141–156.

Cohen NJ and Eichenbaum H (1993). *Memory, Amnesia, and the Hippocampal System.* Cambridge, MA: MIT Press.

Cohen NJ and Squire LR (1980). Preserved learning and retention of pattern-analyzing skill in amnesia: Dissociation of knowing how and knowing that. *Science* 210:207–210.

Collet C, Guillot A, and Petit C (2010a). Phoning while driving I: A review of epidemiological, psychological, behavioural and physiological studies. *Ergonomics* 53(5):589–601.

Collet C, Guillot A, and Petit C (2010b). Phoning while driving II: A review of driving conditions influence. *Ergonomics* 53(5):602–616.

Confucius (3rd century BCE/1979). *The Analects.* Translated by Dim Cheuk Lau. New York: Penguin.

Cools R, Altamirano L, and D'Esposito M (2006). Reversal learning in Parkinson's disease depends on medication status and outcome valence. *Neuropsychologia* 44(10):1663–1673.

Cooper JC, Kreps TA, Wiebe T, Pirkl T, and Knutson B (2010). When giving is good: Ventromedial prefrontal cortex activation for others' intentions. *Neuron* 67(3):511–521.

Cooper JR, Bloom FE, and Roth RH (1986). *The Biochemical Basis of Neuropharmacology*, 5th ed. New York: Oxford University Press.

Coppola FF (1972/1974/1990). *The Godfather I, II, III.* Paramount Pictures.

Corballis M (2012). Mind wandering. *American Scientist* 100(3):210–217.

Corbit LH and Balleine BW (2000). The role of the hippocampus in instrumental conditioning. *Journal of Neuroscience* 20(11):4233–4239.

Corbit LH and Balleine BW (2005). Double dissociation of basolateral and central amygdala lesions on the general and outcome-specific forms of Pavlovian-instrumental transfer. *Journal of Neuroscience* 25(4):962–970.

Corbit LH and Janak PH (2007). Inactivation of the lateral but not medial dorsal striatum eliminates the excitatory impact of Pavlovian stimuli on instrumental responding. *Journal of Neuroscience* 27(51):13977–13981.

Corbit LH, Muir JL, and Balleine BW (2001). The role of the nucleus accumbens in instrumental conditioning: Evidence of a functional dissociation between accumbens core and shell. *Journal of Neuroscience* 21(9):3251–3260.

Corbit LH, Ostlund SB, and Balleine BW (2002). Sensitivity to instrumental contingency degradation is mediated by the entorhinal cortex and its efferents via the dorsal hippocampus. *Journal of Neuroscience* 22(24):10976–10984.

Coricelli G, Critchley HD, Joffily M, O'Doherty JP, Sirigu A, and Dolan RJ (2005). Regret and its avoidance: a neuroimaging study of choice behavior. *Nature Neuroscience* 8:1255–1262.

Corkin S (2002). What's new with the amnesic patient H.M.? *Nature Reviews Neuroscience* 3:153–160.

Corkin S (2008). Eulogy for Henry Gustave Molaison. www.memory-disorders.org/sue-corkins-eulogy-for-hm.

Corrado GS, Sugrue LP, Seung HS, and Newsome WT (2005). Linear-Nonlinear-Poisson models of primate choice dynamics. *Journal of the Experimental Analysis of Behavior* 84(3):581–617.

Coutureau E and Killcross S (2003). Inactivation of the infralimbic prefrontal cortex reinstates goal-directed responding in overtrained rats. *Behavioural Brain Research* 146:167–174.

Cox A (1986/2003). *Sid and Nancy*. Samuel Goldwyn/MGM.

Craig AD (2003). Interoception: The sense of the physiological condition of the body. *Current Opinion in Neurobiology* 13(4):500–505.

Crick F (1995). *The Astonishing Hypothesis: The Scientific Search for the Soul*. New York: Touchstone Books.

Crisp K and Mesce K (2004). A cephalic projection neuron involved in locomotion is dye coupled to the dopaminergic neural network in the medicinal leech. *Journal of Experimental Biology* 207:4535–4542.

Cummins LF, Nadorff MR, and Kelly AE (2009). Winning and positive affect can lead to reckless gambling. *Psychology of Addictive Behaviors* 23(2):287–294.

Custer RL (1984). Profile of the pathological gambler. *Journal of Clinical Psychiatry* 45(12, Sec.2):35–38.

Cytowic RE (1998). *The Man who Tasted Shapes*. Cambridge, MA: MIT Press.

Da Costa JM (1884). *Medical Diagnosis, With Special Reference to Practical Medicine*. Philadelphia: Lippincott Williams & Wilkins.

Dahlem MA and Chronicle EP (2004). A computational perspective on migraine aura. *Progress in Neurobiology* 74:351–361.

Dalley JW, Cardinal RN, and Robbins TW (2004). Prefrontal executive and cognitive functions in rodents: Neural and neurochemical substrates. *Neuroscience and Biobehavioral Reviews* 28(7):771–784.

Damasio A (1994). *Descartes' Error: Emotion, Reason, and the Human Brain*. New York: G. P. Putnam and Sons.

Damasio A (2003). *Looking for Spinoza: Joy, Sorrow, and the Feeling Brain*. Orlando, FL: Harcourt.

Damasio A (2010). *Self Comes to Mind: Constructing the Conscious Brain*. New York: Pantheon.

Damasio AR (1992). Aphasia. *New England Journal of Medicine* 326:531–539.

Dan Y and Poo MM (2006). Spike timing-dependent plasticity: From synapse to perception. *Physiological Reviews* 86(3):1033–1048.

D'Ardenne K, McClure SM, Nystrom LE, and Cohen JD (2008). BOLD responses reflecting dopaminergic signals in the human ventral tegmental area. *Science* 319(5867):1264–1267.

Darrow C (1932). *The Story of My Life*. New York: Scribner.

Darwin C (1859). *On the Origin of Species*. London: John Murray.

Darwin C (1871). *The Expression of the Emotions in Man and Animals*. London: John Murray.

Dauer W and Przedborski S (2003). Parkinson's disease: Mechanisms and models. *Neuron* 39:889–909.

Davidson TJ, Kloosterman F, and Wilson MA (2009). Hippocampal replay of extended experience. *Neuron* 63(4):497–507.

Davis M (1986). Pharmacological and anatomical analysis of fear conditioning using the fear-potentiated startle paradigm. *Behavioral Neuroscience* 100(6):814–824.

Daw ND (2003). *Reinforcement Learning Models of the Dopamine System and their Behavioral Implications*. Ph.D. thesis, Carnegie Mellon University, Pittsburgh, PA.

Daw ND, Kakade S, and Dayan P (2002). Opponent interactions between serotonin and dopamine. *Neural Networks* 15:603–616.

Daw ND, Niv Y, and Dayan P (2005). Uncertainty-based competition between prefrontal and dorsolateral striatal systems for behavioral control. *Nature Neuroscience* 8:1704–1711.

Daw ND, O'Doherty JP, Dayan P, Seymour B, and Dolan RJ (2006). Cortical substrates for exploratory decisions in humans. *Nature* 441:876–879.

Dawes RM and Thaler RH (1988). Anomalies: Cooperation. *Journal of Economic Perspectives* 2(3):187–197.

Dawkins R (1976). *The Selfish Gene*. New York: Oxford University Press.

Dawkins R (2004). *The Ancestor's Tale: A Pilgrimage to the Dawn of Evolution*. Boston: Houghton Mifflin.

Day LB, Weisend M, Sutherland RJ, and Schallert T (1999). The hippocampus is not necessary for a place response but may be necessary for pliancy. *Behavioral Neuroscience* 113(5):914–924.

Dayan P and Abbott LF (2001). *Theoretical Neuroscience*. Cambridge, MA: MIT Press.

Dayan P and Balleine BW (2002). Reward, motivation, and reinforcement learning. *Neuron* 36:285–298.

Dayan P, Niv Y, Seymour B, and Daw ND (2006). The misbehavior of value and the discipline of the will. *Neural Networks* 19:1153–1160.

Dębiec J and LeDoux JE (2006). Noradrenergic signaling in the amygdala contributes to the reconsolidation of fear memory. *Annals of the New York Academy of Sciences* 1071:521–524.

Dębiec J and LeDoux JE (2009). The amygdala and the neural pathways of fear. In: Shiromani PJ, Keane TM, and Ledoux JE (eds.), *Post-Traumatic Stress Disorder: Basic Science and Clinical Practice*. New York: Humana, pp. 23–38.

de Groot AD (1978). *Thought and Choice in Chess*. The Hague: Mouton

de Paula P and Niebauer J (2012). Effects of high altitude training on exercise capacity: Fact or myth. *Sleep and Breathing* 16:233–239.

de Quervain DJF, Fischbacher U, Treyer V, Schellhammer M, Schnyder U, Buck A, and Fehr E (2004). The neural basis of altruistic punishment. *Science* 305(5688):1254–1258.

de Villers-Sidani E and Merzenich MM (2011). Lifelong plasticity in the rat auditory cortex: Basic mechanisms and role of sensory experience. *Progress in Brain Research* 191:119–131.

De Vries TJ and Shippenberg TS (2002). Neural systems underlying opiate addiction. *Journal of Neuroscience* 22(9):3321–3325.

de Waal F (1982). *Chimpanzee Politics: Power and Sex among Apes*. Jonathan Cape. (Revised) Baltimore, MD: Johns Hopkins Press, 2000.

de Waal F (2001). *The Ape and the Sushi Master: Cultural Reflections of a Primatologist*. New York: Basic Books.

de Waal F (2009). *The Age of Empathy*. New York: Random House.

de Waal F and Lanting F (1997). *Bonobo: The Forgotten Ape*. Berkeley, CA: University of California Press.

Deisseroth K (2011). Optogenetics. *Nature Methods* 8:26–29.

Delamater AR (1995). Outcome-selective effects of intertrial reinforcement in a Pavlovian appetitive conditioning paradigm with rats. *Animal Learning and Behavior* 23:31–39.

Delamater AR and Oakeshott S (2007). Learning about multiple attributes of reward in Pavlovian conditioning. *Annals of the New York Academy of Sciences* 1104(1):1–20.

Delgado MR, Olsson A, and Phelps EA (2006). Extending animal models of fear conditioning to humans. *Biological Psychology* 73:39–48.

Deneve S, Latham PE, and Pouget A (1999). Reading population codes: A neural implementation of ideal observers. *Nature Neuroscience* 2(8):740–745.

Deniau JM, Degos B, Bosch C, and Maurice N (2010). Deep brain stimulation mechanisms: Beyond the concept of local functional inhibition. *European Journal of Neuroscience* 32(7):1080–1091.

Dennet D (1981). *Brainstorms*. Cambridge, MA: MIT Press.

Dennet D (1992). *Consciousness Explained*. New York: Back Bay Books.

Denny-Brown D (1962). *The Basal Ganglia and Their Relation to Disorders of Movement*. London: Oxford University Press.

Deroche-Gamonet V, Belin D, and Piazza PV (2004). Evidence for addiction-like behavior in the rat. *Science* 305(5686):1014–1017.

Descartes R (1637/1886/2008). *La Géométrie (The Geometry)*. A. Hermann, Project Gutenberg. www.gutenberg.org.

Descartes R (1637/2008). *Discourse on the Method of Rightly Conducting One's Reason and of Seeking Truth*. Translated by John Veitch. Project Gutenberg. www.gutenberg.org.

Descartes R (1647/1989). *The Passions of the Soul*. Translated by Stephen H. Voss. Indianapolis, IN: Hackett.

Devinsky O and Lai G (2008). Spirituality and religion in epilepsy. *Epilepsy and Behavior* 12(4):636–643.

Dezfouli A and Balleine B (2012). Habits, action sequences and reinforcement learning. *European Journal of Neuroscience* 35(7):1036–1051.

Dhar R, Nowlis SM, and Sherman SJ (2000). Trying hard or hardly trying: An analysis of context effects in choice. *Journal of Consumer Psychology* 9(4):189–200.

Di Chiara G (1999). Drug addiction as dopamine-dependent associative learning disorder. *European Journal of Pharmacology* 375:13–30.

Diamond J (2006). *The Third Chimpanzee*. New York: Harper-Collins.

Diamond JM (1999). *Guns, Germs, and Steel: The Fates of Human Societies.* New York: W. W. Norton.

Diamond JM (2005). *Collapse: How Societies Choose to Fail or Succeed.* New York: Penguin.

Dick PK (1968). *Do Androids Dream of Electric Sheep?* New York: Doubleday.

Dickerson MG and O'Connor J (2006). *Gambling as an addictive behavior.* Cambridge, UK: Cambridge University Press.

Dickinson A (1980). *Contemporary Animal Learning Theory.* Cambridge, UK: Cambridge University Press.

Diekelmann S and Born J (2010). The memory function of sleep. *Nature Reviews Neuroscience* 11:114–126.

Diener HC and Dichgans J (1992). Pathophysiology of cerebellar ataxia. *Movement Disorders* 7:95–109.

Doll BB, Simon DA, and Daw ND (2012). The ubiquity of model-based reinforcement learning. *Current Opinion in Neurobiology* 22:1075–1081.

Dominici N, Ivanenko YP, Cappellini G, d'Avella A, Mondí V, Cicchese M, Fabiano A, Silei T, Di Paolo A, Giannini C, Poppele RE, and Lacquaniti F (2011). Locomotor primitives in newborn babies and their development. *Science* 334:997–999.

Domjan M (1998). *The Principles of Learning and Behavior,* 4th ed. Pacific Grove, CA: Brooks/ Cole.

Donoghue JP, Nurmikko A, Black M, and Hochberg LR (2007). Assistive technology and robotic control using motor cortex ensemble-based neural interface systems in humans with tetraplegia. *Journal of Physiology* 579:603–611.

Dorval AD and White JA (2005). Channel noise is essential for perithreshold oscillations in entorhinal stellate neurons. *Journal of Neuroscience* 25(43):10025–10028.

Dostoevsky F (1869). *The Idiot.* Translated by Frederick Wishaw. New York: Macmillan.

Dostrovsky JO, Hutchinson WD, and Lozano AM (2002). The globus pallidus, deep brain stimulation, and Parkinson's disease. *The Neuroscientist* 8(3):284–290.

Dowling J (2009). Current and future prospects for optoelectronic retinal prostheses. *Eye* 23:1999–2005.

Doya K (1999). What are the computations of the cerebellum, the basal ganglia, and the cerebral cortex? *Neural networks* 12:961–974.

Doya K (2008). Modulators of decision making. *Nature Neuroscience* 11:410–416.

Doyon J (2008). Motor sequence learning and movement disorders. *Current Opinion in Neurology* 21(4):478–483.

Drai D and Golani I (2001). SEE: A tool for the visualization and analysis of rodent exploratory behavior. *Neuroscience and Biobehavioral Reviews* 25:409–426.

Dreyfus HL (1992). *What Computers Still Can't Do: A Critique of Artificial Reason.* Cambridge, MA: MIT Press.

DSM-III (1980). *Diagnostic and Statistical Manual of Mental Disorders,* 3rd ed. American Psychiatric Association.

DSM-IV-TR (2000). *Diagnostic and Statistical Manual of Mental Disorders,* 4th ed., text revision. American Psychiatric Association.

Duda RO, Hart PE, and Storyk DG (2001). *Pattern Classification.* New York: Wiley.

Duhigg C (2012). *The Power of Habit.* New York: Random House.

Dumas A (1844/1984). *The Three Musketeers.* Translated by Lowell Bair. New York: Bantam Books.

Duncan JS (2007). Epilepsy surgery. *Clinical Medicine, Journal of the Royal College of Physicians* 7(2):137–142.

Duncan RO and Boynton GM (2003). Cortical magnification within human primary visual cortex correlates with acuity thresholds. *Neuron* 38(4):659–671.

Dunlop N (2009). www.edmunds.com/how-to/how-to-drive-in-the-snow.html Published February 11, 2003. Updated May 05, 2009.

Durlach PJ and Shane DO (1993). The effect of intertrial food presentations on anticipatory goal-tracking in the rat. *Quarterly Journal of Experimental Psychology Section B: Comparative and Physiological Psychology* 46(3):289–319.

Durstewitz D, Kelc M, and Gunturkun O (1999). A neurocomputational theory of the dopaminergic modulation of working memory functions. *Journal of Neuroscience* 19(7):2807–2822.

Durstewitz D and Seamans JK (2008). The dual-state theory of prefrontal cortex dopamine function with relevance to catechol-o-methyltransferase genotypes and schizophrenia. *Biological Psychiatry* 64(9):739–749.

Durstewitz D, Seamans JK, and Sejnowski TJ (2000). Dopamine-mediated stabilization of delay-period activity in a network model of prefrontal cortex. *Journal of Neurophysiology* 83(3):1733–1750.

Durstewitz D, Vittoz NM, Floresco SB, and Seamans JK (2010). Abrupt transitions between prefrontal neural ensemble states accompany behavioral transitions during rule learning. *Neuron* 66(3):438–448.

Duvoisin RC and Sage J (2001). *Parkinson's Disease: A Guide for Patient and Family*. Philadelphia: Lippincott Williams & Wilkins.

Dylan B (1973). "Knockin' on Heaven's Door." Columbia Records.

Eagle DM, Bari A, and Robbins TW (2008). The neuropsychopharmacology of action inhibition: Cross-species translation of the stop-signal and go/no-go tasks. *Psychopharmacology* 199(3):439–456.

Earman J (1986). *A Primer on Determinism*. New York: Springer.

Eaton RC (ed.) (1984). *Neural Mechanisms of Startle Behavior*. New York: Springer.

Eaton RC and Hackett JT (1984). The role of the Mauthner cell in fast-starts involving escape in teleost fishes. In: Eaton RC (ed.), *Neural Mechanisms of Startle Behavior*. New York: Springer, pp. 213–266.

Eccles JC, Itō M, and Szentágothai J (1967). *The Cerebellum as a Neuronal Machine*. Berlin: Springer-Verlag.

Eccles JC et al. (1965). Final discussion, Pontifica Academia Scientiarum, 28/Sept to 4/Oct 1964. In: *Brain and Conscious Experience*. Berlin: Springer-Verlag, pp. 548–574.

Edelman G (1987). *Neural Darwinism: The Theory of Neuronal Group Selection*. New York: Basic Books.

Edelman GM (1992). *Bright Air, Brilliant Fire: On the Matter of the Mind*. New York: Basic Books.

Ego-Stengel V and Wilson MA (2010). Disruption of ripple-associated hippocampal activity during rest impairs spatial learning in the rat. *Hippocampus* 20(1):1–10.

Eichenbaum H, Stewart C, and Morris RGM (1990). Hippocampal representation in place learning. *Journal of Neuroscience* 10(11):3531–3542.

Eigsti IM, Zayas V, Mischel W, Shoda Y, Ayduk O, Dadlani MB, Davidson MC, Aber JL, and Casey BJ (2006). Predicting cognitive control from preschool to late adolescence and young adulthood. *Psychological Science* 17:478–484.

Eliasmith C and Anderson CH (2003). *Neural Engineering*. Cambridge, MA: MIT Press.

Elliot R, Friston KJ, and Dolan RJ (2000). Dissociable neural responses in human reward systems. *Journal of Neuroscience* 20(16):6159–6165.

Ellsberg D (1961). Risk, ambiguity, and the savage axioms. *Quarterly Journal of Economics* 75(4):643–669.

Elzinga BM and Bremner JD (2002). Are the neural substrates of memory the final common pathway in posttraumatic stress disorder (PTSD)? *Journal of Affective Disorders* 70(1):1–17.

Engel J and Pedley TA (eds.) (2008). *Epilepsy: A Comprehensive Textbook*. Philadelphia: Lippincott Williams & Wilkins.

Epstein DH, Marrone GF, Heishman SJ, Schmittner J, and Preston KL (2010). Tobacco, cocaine, and heroin: Craving and use during daily life. *Addictive Behavior* 35(4):318–324.

Epstein LG (1999). A definition of uncertainty aversion. *Review of Economic Studies* 66(3):579–608.

Epstein R and Kanwisher N (1998). A cortical representation of the local visual environment. *Nature* 392:598–601.

Erdoes R and Ortiz A (1985). *American Indian Myths and Legends*. New York: Pantheon.

Ericsson KA (ed.) (2006). *The Cambridge Handbook of Expertise and Expert Performance*. Cambridge, UK: Cambridge University Press.

Ericsson KA, Krampe R, and Tesch-Römer C (1993). The role of deliberate practice in the acquisition of expert performance. *Psychological Review* 100(3):363–406.

Ermentrout GB and Cowan JD (1979). A mathematical theory of visual hallucination patterns. *Biological Cybernetics* 34:137–150.

Ermentrout GB and Kleinfeld D (2001). Traveling electrical waves in cortex: Insights from phase dynamics and speculation on a computational role. *Neuron* 29:33–44.

ESPN (2010). Favre to discuss future with family. sports.espn.go.com/nfl/playoffs/2009/news/story?id=4857006.

Etkin A and Wagner TD (2010). Brain systems underlying anxiety disorders: A view from neuroimaging. In: Simpson HB, Neria Y, Lewis-Fernández R, and Schneier F (eds.), *Anxiety Disorders: Theory, Research, and Clinical Perspectives.* Cambridge, UK: Cambridge University Press, pp. 192–203.

Euripides (431 BCE/1955). *Medea.* Translated by David Grene. Chicago: University of Chicago Press.

Euston DR, Tatsuno M, and McNaughton BL (2007). Fast-forward playback of recent memory sequences in prefrontal cortex during sleep. *Science* 318(5853):1147–1150.

Everitt BJ and Robbins TW (2005). Neural systems of reinforcement for drug addiction: From actions to habits to compulsion. *Nature Neuroscience* 8:1481–1489.

Evidence-Based Medicine Working Group (Gordon Guyatt et al.) (1992). Evidence-based medicine: A new approach to teaching the practice of medicine. *Journal of the American Medical Association* 268(17):2420–2425.

Falkenstein M, Hoormann J, Christ S, and Hohnsbein J (2000). ERP components on reaction errors and their functional significance: A tutorial. *Biological Psychology* 51(2–3):87–107.

Fehr E (2008). Social preferences and the brain. In: Glimcher PW, Camerer CF, Fehr E, and Poldrack RA (eds.), *Neuroeconomics: Decision Making and the Brain.* New York: Academic Press, pp. 215–232.

Fehr E and Fishbacher U (2003). The nature of human altruism. *Nature* 425:785–791.

Fehr E and Fishbacher U (2004). Third-party punishment and social norms. *Evolution and Human Behavior* 25(2):63–87.

Fehr E, Fishbacher U, and Kosfeld M (2005). Neuroeconomic foundations of trust and social preferences: Initial evidence. *American Economic Review* 95(2):346–351.

Feldman DE and Knudsen EI (1998). Experience-dependent plasticity and the maturation of glutamatergic synapses. *Neuron* 20(6):1067–1071.

Feldman R, Gordon I, and Zagoory-Sharon O (2010). The cross-generation transmission of oxytocin in humans. *Hormones and Behavior* 58(4):669–676.

Fellows LK (2006). Deciding how to decide: Ventromedial frontal lobe damage affects information acquisition in multi-attribute decision making. *Brain* 129(4):944–952.

Fenton AA and Muller RU (1998). Place cell discharge is extremely variable during individual passes of the rat through the firing field. *Proceedings of the National Academy of Sciences, USA* 95:3182–3187.

Ferrier D (1876). *The Functions of the Brain.* New York: G. P. Putnam and Sons.

Ferster CB and Skinner BF (1957). *Schedules of Reinforcement.* New York: Appleton-Century-Crofts.

Festinger L (1954). A theory of social comparison processes. *Human Relations* 7:117–140.

Feynman RP (1965). *The Character of Physical Law.* Cambridge, MA: MIT Press.

Feynman RP (1997). *Surely You're Joking, Mr. Feynman.* New York: W. W. Norton.

Fields HL (1987). *Pain.* New York: McGraw-Hill.

Firestein S (2012). *Ignorance: How It Drives Science.* New York: Oxford University Press.

Fischer HE, Aron A, and Brown LL (2006). Romantic love: A mammalian brain system for mate choice. *Philosophical Transactions of the Royal Society B* 361(1476):2173–2186.

Fischer HE, Brown LL, Aron A, Strong G, and Mashek D (2010). Reward, addiction, and emotion regulation systems associated with rejection in love. *Journal of Neurophysiology* 104(1):51–60.

Fischer JM (2006). Free will and moral responsibility. In: Copp D (ed.), *The Oxford Handbook of Ethical Theory.* New York: Oxford University Press, pp. 321–353.

Flagel SB, Akil H, and Robinson TE (2009). Individual differences in the attribution of incentive salience to reward-related cues: Implications for addiction. *Neuropharmacology* 56(Suppl. 1):139–148.

Floresco SB, West AR, Ash B, Moore H, and Grace AA (2003). Afferent modulation of dopamine neuron firing differentially regulates tonic and phasic dopamine transmission. *Nature Neuroscience* 6(9):968–973.

Foreman MB and Eaton RC (1993). The directional change concept for reticulospinal control of goldfish escape. *Journal of Neuroscience* 13(10):4101–4113.

Fossey D (1983/2000). *Gorillas in the Mist*. Boston: Houghton Mifflin.

Foster DJ and Wilson MA (2006). Reverse replay of behavioural sequences in hippocampal place cells during the awake state. *Nature* 440(7084):680–683.

Fothergill A and Linfield M (2012). *Chimpanzee*. Great Ape Productions.

Fouts R (1997). *Next of Kin*. New York: William Morrow.

Franco-Watkins AM, Rickard TC, and Pashler H (2010). Taxing executive processes does not necessarily increase impulsive decision making. *Experimental Psychology* 57(3):193–201.

Frank MJ (2011). Computational models of motivated action selection in corticostriatal circuits. *Current Opinion in Neurobiology* 21(3):381–386.

Frank MJ, Doll BB, Oas-Terpstra J, and Moreno F (2009). Prefrontal and striatal dopaminergic genes predict individual differences in exploration and exploitation. *Nature Neuroscience* 12:1062–1068.

Frank MJ, Moustafa AA, Haughey HM, Curran T, and Hutchison KE (2007a). Genetic triple dissociation reveals multiple roles for dopamine in reinforcement learning. *Proceedings of the National Academy of Sciences, USA* 104(41):16311–16316.

Frank MJ, Samanta J, Moustafa AA, and Sherman SJ (2007b). Hold your horses: Impulsivity, deep brain stimulation, and medication in Parkinsonism. *Science* 318(5854):1309–1312.

Frank MJ, Seeberger LC, and O'Reilly RC (2004). By carrot or by stick: Cognitive reinforcement learning in Parkinsonism. *Science* 306(5703):1940–1943.

Frank RH (2007). Reshaping the debate on raising taxes. *New York Times* www.nytimes.com/2007/12/09/business/09view.html.

Franken IH, Booij J, and van den Brink W (2005). The role of dopamine in human addiction: From reward to motivated attention. *European Journal of Pharmacology* 526(1–3):199–206.

Frederick S, Loewenstein G, and O'Donoghue T (2002). Time discounting and time preference: A critical review. *Journal of Economic Literature* 40(2):351–401.

Freeman WJ (1975). *Mass Action in the Nervous System: Examination of the Neurophysiological Basis of Adaptive Behavior through the EEG*. New York: Academic Press.

Freeman WJ (2000). *How Brains Make Up Their Minds*. New York: Columbia University Press.

Freud S (1923/1990). *The Ego and the Id*. New York: W. W. Norton.

Friehs GM, Zerris VA, Ojakangas CL, Fellows MR, and Donoghue JP (2004). Brain-machine and brain-computer interfaces. *Stroke* 35:2702–2705.

Friesen WO and Kristan WB (2007). Leech locomotion: Swimming, crawling, and decisions. *Current Opinion in Neurobiology* 17(6):704–711.

Fripp D, Owen C, Quintana-Rizzo E, Shapiro A, Buckstaff K, Jankowski K, Wells R, and Tyack P (2005). Bottlenose dolphin (*Tursiops truncatus*) calves appear to model their signature whistles on the signature whistles of community members. *Animal Cognition* 8(1):17–26.

Frisch D and Baron J (1988). Ambiguity and rationality. *Journal of Behavioral Decision Making* 1:149–157.

Frith C (1996). The role of the prefrontal cortex in self-consciousness: The case of auditory hallucinations. *Philosophical Transactions of the Royal Society B* 351(1346):1505–1512.

Frith C (2007). *Making Up the Mind: How the Brain Creates our Mental World*. Malden, MA: Blackwell.

Frith C and Dolan R (1996). The role of the prefrontal cortex in higher cognitive functions. *Cognitive Brain Research* 5(1–2):175–181.

Frontline (2009). *Soldier's Heart*. PBS. http://www.pbs.org/wgbh/pages/frontline/shows/heart.

Fuhs MC and Touretzky DS (2007). Context learning in the rodent hippocampus. *Neural Computation* 19(12):3172–3215.

Fürkötter A (1977). *The Miniatures from the Book Scivias (Know the Ways) of St. Hildegard of Bingen from the Illuminated Rupertsberg Codex*. Turnhout, Belgium: Brepols Publishers.

Fuster J (1997/2008). *The Prefrontal Cortex*. New York: Academic Press.

Fyhn M, Molden S, Witter MP, Moser EI, and Moser MB (2004). Spatial representation in the entorhinal cortex. *Science* 305(5688):1258–1264.

Gailliot MT, Baumeister RF, DeWall CN, Maner JK, Plant EA, Tice DM, Brewer LE, and Schmeichel BJ (2007). Self-control relies on glucose as a limited energy source: Willpower is more than a metaphor. *Journal of Personality and Social Psychology* 92(2):325–336.

Gais S and Born J (2004). Declarative memory consolidation: Mechanisms acting during human sleep. *Learning and Memory* 11:679–685.

Galileo G (1610). *Sidereus Nuncius*. Venice: Thomas Baglioni.

Galileo G (1638). *Dialogue Concerning Two World Systems (Discorsi e Dimostrazioni Matematiche Intorno a Due Nuove Scienze)*. Leiden: Elzevir.

Galison P (2003). *Einstein's Clocks, Poincaré's Maps: Empires of Time*. New York: W. W. Norton.

Gallistel CR (1990). *The Organization of Learning*. Cambridge, MA: MIT Press.

Gallistel CR, Fairhurst S, and Balsam P (2004). The learning curve: Implications of a quantitative analysis. *Proceedings of the National Academy of Sciences, USA* 101(36):13124–13131.

Gallistel CR, Mark TA, King AP, and Latham PE (2001). The rat approximates an ideal detector of changes in rates of reward: Implications for the law of effect. *Journal of Experimental Psychology: Animal Behavior Processes* 27(4):354–372.

Garcia J, Hankins WG, and Rusiniak KW (1974). Behavioral regulation of the milieu interne in man and rat. *Science* 185(4154):824–831.

Gardner J (1983). *The Art of Fiction*. New York: Knopf.

Garner AR, Rowland DC, Hwang SY, Baumgaertel K, Roth BL, Kentros C, and Mayford M (2012). Generation of a synthetic memory trace. *Science* 335(6075):1513–1516.

Garrett M (2010). Top GOP priority: Make Obama a one-term president. *National Journal,* published October 23, 2010, updated October 29, 2010.

Gater DR, Dolbow D, Tsui B, and Gorgey AS (2011). Functional electrical stimulation therapies after spinal cord injury. *NeuroRehabilitation* 28:231–248.

Gehring WJ, Goss B, Coles MGH, Meyer DE, and Donachin E (1993). A neural system for error detection and compensation. *Psychological Science* 4(6):385–390.

Gell-Mann M (1995). *The Quark and the Jaguar*. New York: Henry Holt Publishers.

Georgopoulos AP, Lurito JT, Petrides M, Schwartz AB, and Massey JT (1989). Mental rotation of the neuronal population vector. *Science* 243:234–236.

Georgopoulos AP, Schwartz AB, and Kettner RE (1986). Neuronal population coding of movement direction. *Science* 233:1416–1419.

Gerstner JR, Lyons LC, Wright KP Jr, Loh DH, Rawashdeh O, Eckel-Mahan KL, and Roman GW (2009). Cycling behavior and memory formation. *Journal of Neuroscience* 29(41):12824–12830.

Gibson JJ (1977). The theory of affordances. In: Shaw R and Bransford J (eds.), *Perceiving, Acting, and Knowing: Toward an Ecological Psychology*. Hillsdale, NJ: Lawrence Erlbaum, pp. 67–82.

Gibson JJ (1979). *The Ecological Approach to Visual Perception*. Boston: Houghton Mifflin.

Gibson LE, Hamblen JL, Zvolensky MJ, and Vujanovic AA (2006). Evidence-based treatments for traumatic stress. In: Norris FH, Galea S, and Friedman MJ (eds.), *Methods for Disaster Mental Health Research*. New York: Guilford, pp. 208–225.

Gigerenzer G and Goldstein DG (1996). Reasoning the fast and frugal way: Models of bounded rationality. *Psychological Review* 103:650–669.

Giglioli PP (ed.) (1972/1990). *Language and Social Context*. New York: Penguin.

Gilbertson MW, Shenton ME, Ciszewski A, Kasai K, Lasko NB, Orr SP, and Pitman RK (2002). Smaller hippocampal volume predicts pathologic vulnerability to psychological trauma. *Nature Neuroscience* 5:1242–1247.

Gilden DL, Thornton TL, and Marusich LR (2010). The serial process in visual search. *Journal of Experimental Psychology: Human Perception and Performance* 36(3):533–542.

Gilovich T, Griffin DW, and Kahneman D (eds.) (2002). *Heuristics and Biases: The Psychology of Intuitive Judgement*. Cambridge, UK: Cambridge University Press.

Gintis H and Khurana R (2008). Corporate honesty and business education: A behavioral model. In: Zak PJ (ed.), *Moral Markets: The Critical Role of Values in the Economy*. Princeton, NJ: Princeton University Press, pp. 300–327.

Giraldeau LA and Caraco T (2000). *Social Foraging Theory*. Princeton, NJ: Princeton University Press.

Girardeau G, Benchenane K, Wiener SI, Buzsáki G, and Zugaro MB (2009). Selective suppression of hippocampal ripples impairs spatial memory. *Nature Neuroscience* 12:1222–1223.

Gittins JC (1989). *Multi-Armed Bandit Allocation Indices*. New York: Wiley.

Glanzer M (1958). Curiosity, exploratory drive, and stimulus satiation. *Psychological Bulletin* 55(5):302–315.

Gläscher J, Adolphs R, Damasio H, Bechara A, Rudrauf D, Calamia M, Paul LK, and Tranel D (2012). Lesion mapping of cognitive control and value-based decision making in the prefrontal cortex. *Proceedings of the National Academy of Sciences, USA* 109(36):14681–14686.

Glass I (2011). The invention of money. First broadcast January 07, 2011. *This American Life.* Episode 423. www.thisamericanlife.org/radio-archives/episode/423/the-invention-of-money.

Gleick J (1987). *Chaos.* New York: Viking.

Gleick J (2011). *The Information: A History, a Theory, a Flood.* New York: Pantheon.

Gleitman H (1991). *Psychology.* New York: W. W. Norton.

Glickstein M and Stein J (1991). Paradoxical movement in Parkinson's disease. *Trends in Neurosciences* 14(11):480–482.

Glimcher PW (2004). *Decisions, Uncertainty, and the Brain: The Science of Neuroeconomics.* Bradford Books. Cambridge, MA: MIT Press.

Glimcher PW (2010). *Foundations of Neuroeconomic Analysis.* New York: Oxford University Press.

Glimcher PW, Camerer C, Poldrack RA, and Fehr E (eds.) (2008). *Neuroeconomics: Decision Making and the Brain.* New York: Academic Press.

Godemann F, Ahrens B, Behrens S, Berthold R, Gandor C, Lampe F, and Linden M (2001). Classic conditioning and dysfunctional cognitions in patients with panic disorder and agoraphobia treated with an implantable cardioverter/defibrillator. *Psychosomatic Medicine* 63:231–238.

Golani I, Benjamini Y, and Eilam D (1993). Stopping behavior: Constraints on exploration in rats (*Rattus norvegicus*). *Behavioral Brain Research* 53(1–2):21–33.

Gold JI and Shadlen MN (2002). Banburismus and the brain: Decoding the relationship between sensory stimuli, decisions, and reward. *Neuron* 36(2):299–308.

Gold JI and Shadlen MN (2007). The neural basis of decision making. *Annual Review of Neuroscience* 30:535–574.

Golding W (1954). *Lord of the Flies.* London: Faber and Faber.

Goldman MS, Boca FKD, and Darkes J (1999). Alcohol expectancy theory: The application of cognitive neuroscience. In: Leonard KE and Blane HT (eds.), *Psychological Theories of Drinking and Alcoholism.* New York: Guilford, pp. 203–246.

Goldstein A (2000). *Addiction: From Biology to Drug Policy.* New York: Oxford University Press.

Goldstine HH (1980). *The Computer from Pascal to von Neumann.* Princeton, NJ: Princeton University Press.

Golubitsky M, Shiau L, and Török A (2004). Symmetry and pattern formation on the visual cortex. In: Dangelmayr G and Oprea I (eds.), *Dynamics and Bifurcation of Patterns in Dissipative Systems.* Singapore: World Scientific, pp. 3–19.

Good M and Honey RC (1991). Conditioning and contextual retrieval in hippocampal rats. *Behavioral Neuroscience* 105:499–509.

Goodall J (1986). *The Chimpanzees of Gombe: Patterns of Behavior.* Cambridge, MA: Harvard University Press.

Goodall J (1990). *Through a Window.* Boston: Houghton Mifflin.

Goodall J and van Lawick H (1971/1988/2000). *In the Shadow of Man.* Boston: Houghton Mifflin.

Goodman J (2000). *The Tao of Steve.* Sony Pictures.

Goodman WK, Rudorfer MV, and Maser JD (eds.) (2000). *Obsessive-Compulsive Disorder: Contemporary Issues in Treatment.* Hillsdale, NJ: Lawrence Erlbaum.

Gordon JA and Adhikari A (2010). Learned fear and innate anxiety in rodents and their relevance to human anxiety disorders. In: Simpson HB, Neria Y, Lewis-Fernández R, and Schneier F (eds.), *Anxiety Disorders: Theory, Research, and Clinical Perspectives.* Cambridge, UK: Cambridge University Press, pp. 180–191.

Gospic K, Mohlin E, Fransson P, Petrovic P, Johannesson M, and Ingvar M (2011). Limbic justice—amygdala involvement in immediate rejection in the ultimatum game. *PLoS Biology* 9(5):e1001054.

Gottesman II and Gould TD (2003). The endophenotype concept in psychiatry: Etymology and strategic intentions. *American Journal of Psychiatry* 160:636–645.

Gould SJ (1981). *The Mismeasure of Man.* New York: W. W. Norton.

Gould SJ (2000). *Rocks of Ages: Science and Religion in the Fullness of Life.* New York: Random House.

Grace AA (2000). Gating of information flow within the limbic system and the pathophysiology of schizophrenia. *Brain Research Reviews* 31:330–341.

Graham DW (2011). Heraclitus. In: Zalta EN (ed.), *The Stanford Encyclopedia of Philosophy,* summer 2011 edition. Stanford University, Center for the Study of Language and Information. plato.stanford.edu/archives/sum2011/entries/heraclitus.

Grant JE and Potenza MN (eds.) (2012). *The Oxford Handbook of Impulse Control Disorders.* New York: Oxford University Press.

Gray J (2004). *Consciousness: Creeping up on the Hard Problem.* New York: Oxford University Press.

Gray J and McNaughton N (2000). *The Neuropsychology of Anxiety.* New York: Oxford University Press.

Gray JA (1975). *Elements of a Two-Process Theory of Learning.* New York: Academic Press.

Gray JA (1979). *Pavlov.* New York: Oxford University Press.

Graybiel AM (1995). Building action repertoires: Memory and learning functions of the basal ganglia. *Current Opinion in Neurobiology* 5:733–741.

Greeley J and Oei T (1999). Alcohol and tension reduction. In: Leonard KE and Blane HT (eds.), *Psychological Theories of Drinking and Alcoholism.* New York: Guilford, pp. 14–53.

Green AM and Kalaska JF (2011). Learning to move machines with the mind. *Trends in Neurosciences* 34(2):61–75.

Green CS and Bavalier D (2003). Action video game modifies visual selective attention. *Nature* 423:534–537.

Green DM and Swets JA (1966). *Signal Detection Theory and Psychophysics.* New York: Wiley.

Green R (2004). Upping the ante. *The Hartford Courant,* published May 11, 2004. articles.courant. com/2004-05-11/news/0405110789_1_slot-machine-igt-successful-slot.

Greene B (1999). *The Elegant Universe.* New York: Vintage Books.

Grewal SS, Shepherd JK, Bill DJ, Fletcher A, and Dourish CT (1997). Behavioural and pharmacological characterisation of the canopy stretched attend posture test as a model of anxiety in mice and rats. *Psychopharmacology* 133(1):29–38.

Griffin DR (1985). *Animal Thinking.* Cambridge, MA: Harvard University Press.

Griffin DR (2001). *Animal Minds.* Chicago: University of Chicago Press.

Griffiths MD (1991). Psychobiology of the near-miss in fruit machine gambling. *Journal of Psychology* 125(3):347–357.

Grill-Spector K and Malach R (2004). The human visual cortex. *Annual Review of Neuroscience* 27:649–677.

Grillner S (1981). Control of locomotion in bipeds, tetrapods, and fish. In: *Handbook of Physiology, The Nervous System, Motor Control.* Bethesda, MD: American Physiological Society, pp. 1179–1236.

Grillner S (1985). Neurobiological bases of rhythmic motor acts in vertebrates. *Science* 228:143–149.

Grillner S (2003). The motor infrastructure: From ion channels to neuronal networks. *Nature Reviews Neuroscience* 4(7):573–586.

Groenewegen HJ, Vermeulen-Van der Zee E, te Kortschot A, and Witter MP (1987). Organization of the projections from the subiculum to the ventral striatum in the rat. A study using anterograde transport of *Phaseolus vulgaris* leucoagglutinin. *Neuroscience* 23(1):103–120.

Groopman J (2007). *How Doctors Think.* Boston: Houghton Mifflin.

Grossberg S (1976). Adaptive pattern classification and universal recoding: I. Parallel development and coding of neural feature detectors. *Biological Cybernetics* 23:121–134.

Grossenbacher PG and Lovelace CT (2001). Mechanisms of synaesthesia: Cognitive and physiological constraints. *Trends in Cognitive Sciences* 5(1):36–41.

Grossman M and Chaloupka FJ (1998). The demand for cocaine by young adults: A rational addiction approach. *Journal of Health Economics* 17:427–474.

Grüsser OJ (1995). Migraine phosphenes and the retino-cortical magnification factor. *Vision Research* 35(8):1125–1134.

Guenther FH and Bohland JW (2002). Learning sound categories: A neural model and supporting experiments. *Acoustical Science and Technology* 23(4):213–221.

Guirland C and Zheng JQ (2007). Membrane lipid rafts and their role in axon guidance. In: Bagnard D (ed.), *Axon Growth and Guidance.* New York: Springer.

Guisewite C (1996). *Cathy Twentieth Anniversary Collection*. Kansas City, MO: Andrews McMeel.

Gupta AS, van der Meer MAA, Touretzky DS, and Redish AD (2010). Hippocampal replay is not a simple function of experience. *Neuron* 65(5):695–705.

Gupta AS, van der Meer MAA, Touretzky DS, and Redish AD (2012). Segmentation of spatial experience by hippocampal theta sequences. *Nature Neuroscience* 15:1032–1039.

Güth W, Schmittberger R, and Schwarze B (1982). An experimental analysis of ultimatum bargaining. *Journal of Economic Behavior and Organization* 3(4):367–388.

Guthrie ER (1937). Tolman on associative learning. *Psychological Review* 44(6):525–528.

Gutkin B, Pinto D, and Ermentrout B (2003). Mathematical neuroscience: From neurons to circuits to systems. *Journal of Physiology Paris* 97(2–3):209–219.

Gutkin BS, Dehaene S, and Changeux JP (2006). A neurocomputational hypothesis for nicotine addiction. *Proceedings of the National Academy of Sciences, USA* 103(4):1106–1111.

Hafting T, Fyhn M, Molden S, Moser MB, and Moser EI (2005). Microstructure of a spatial map in the entorhinal cortex. *Nature* 436:801–806.

Haidt J (2006). *The Happiness Hypothesis*. New York: Basic Books.

Hall KRL and Schaller GB (1964). Tool-using behavior of the California sea otter. *Journal of Mammology* 45(2):287–298.

Haller MH (1989). Bootlegging: The business and politics of violence. In: Gurr TR (ed.), *Violence in America: The History of Crime*. Newbury Park, CA: SAGE Publications, pp. 146–162.

Hamani C and Nóbrega JN (2010). Deep brain stimulation in clinical trials and animal models of depression. *European Journal of Neuroscience* 32(7):1109–1117.

Hameroff SR (1994). Quantum coherence in microtubules: A neural basis for emergent consciousness? *Journal of Consciousness Studies* 1(1):91–118.

Hamner M, Hunt N, Gee J, Garrell R, and Monroe R (1999). PTSD and automatic implantable cardioverter defibrillators. *Psychosomatics* 40:82–85.

Hampton H (1987/1990). *Eyes on the Prize*. PBS.

Hanes DP and Schall JD (1995). Countermanding saccades in macaque. *Visual Neuroscience* 12:929–937.

Hanson K, Allen S, Jensen S, and Hatsukami D (2003). Treatment of adolescent smokers with the nicotine patch. *Nicotine and Tobacco Research* 5(4):515–526.

Harbaugh WT, Mayr U, and Burghart DR (2007). Neural responses to taxation and voluntary giving reveal motives for charitable donations. *Science* 316(5831):1622–1625.

Hardcastle VG (2008). Neither necessary nor sufficient for addiction. *Behavioral and Brain Sciences* 31(4):447–448.

Hare RD (1999). *Without Conscience: The Disturbing World of Psychopaths Among Us*. New York: Guilford Press.

Hare TA, Camerer CF, and Rangel A (2009). Self-control in decision-making involves modulation of the vmPFC valuation system. *Science* 324(5927):646–648.

Hare TA, Malmaud J, and Rangel A (2011). Focusing attention on the health aspects of foods changes value signals in vmPFC and improves dietary choice. *Journal of Neuroscience* 31(30):11077–11087.

Hare TA, O'Doherty J, Camerer CF, Schultz W, and Rangel A (2008). Dissociating the role of the orbitofrontal cortex and the striatum in the computation of goal values and prediction errors. *Journal of Neuroscience* 28(22):5623–5630.

Harkness W (2006). Temporal lobe resections. *Child's Nervous System* 22(8):936–944.

Harlé KM and Sanfey AG (2007). Incidental sadness biases social economic decisions in the ultimatum game. *Emotion* 7(4):876–881.

Harlow HF (1953). Mice, monkeys, men, and motives. *Psychological Review* 60(1):23–32.

Harlow HF (1958). The nature of love. *American Psychologist* 13(12):673–685.

Harlow HF and Zimmermann RR (1959). Affectional responses in the infant monkey. *Science* 130(3373):421–432.

Harlow JM (1848). Passage of an iron rod through the head. *Boston Medical and Surgical Journal* 39(20):389–393.

Harris AC and Gewirtz JC (2005). Acute opioid dependence: Characterizing the early adaptations underlying drug withdrawal. *Psychopharmacology* 178(4):353–366.

Harris KD (2005). Neural signatures of cell assembly organization. *Nature Reviews Neuroscience* 6:399–407.

Harris S (2010). *The Moral Landscape*. New York: Free Press.

Hartell NA (2002). Parallel fiber plasticity. *The Cerebellum* 1:3–18.

Harvey AG, Bryant RA, and Tarrier N (2003). Cognitive behavioral therapy for posttraumatic stress disorder. *Clinical Psychology Review* 23(3):501–522.

Hasler G (2012). Can the neuroeconomics revolution revolutionize psychiatry? *Neuroscience and Biobehavioral Reviews* 36(1):64–78.

Hassabis D, Kumaran D, Vann SD, and Maguire EA (2007). Patients with hippocampal amnesia cannot imagine new experiences. *Proceedings of the National Academy of Sciences, USA* 104:1726–1731.

Hassabis D and Maguire EA (2011). The construction system in the brain. In: Bar M (ed.), *Predictions in the Brain: Using our Past to Generate a Future*. New York: Oxford University Press, pp. 70–82.

Hasselmo ME and Bower JM (1993). Acetylcholine and memory. *Trends in Neurosciences* 16(6):218–222.

Hasselmo ME and Wyble BP (1997). Free recall and recognition in a network model of the hippocampus: Simulating effects of scopolamine on human memory function. *Behavioural Brain Research* 89:1–34.

Hatsopoulos NG, Ojakangas CL, Paninski L, and Donoghue JP (1998). Information about movement direction obtained from synchronous activity of motor cortical neurons. *Proceedings of the National Academy of Sciences, USA* 95(26):15706–15711.

Hatsopoulos NG, Paninski L, and Donoghue JP (2003). Sequential movement representations based on correlated neuronal activity. *Experimental Brain Research* 149(4):478–486.

Hatsukami DK, Thompson TN, Pentel PR, Flygare BK, and Carroll ME (1994). Self-administration of smoked cocaine. *Experimental and Clinical Psychopharmacology* 2(2):115–125.

Hayden BY, Pearson JM, and Platt ML (2011). Neuronal basis of sequential foraging decisions in a patchy environment. *Nature Neuroscience* 14:933–939.

Hayes B (2011). Leave the driving to it. *American Scientist* 99(5):362–367.

Heath RG (1963). Electrical self-stimulation in man. *American Journal of Psychiatry* 120:571–577.

Heatherton TF and Wagner DD (2011). Cognitive neuroscience of self-regulation failure. *Trends in Cognitive Sciences* 15(3):132–139.

Hebb DO (1949/2002). *The Organization of Behavior*. New York: Wiley / Hillsdale, NJ: Lawrence Erlbaum.

Heeger DJ and Ress D (2002). What does fMRI tell us about neuronal activity? *Nature Reviews Neuroscience* 3:142–151.

Hein G, Lamm C, Brodbeck C, and Singer T (2011). Skin conductance response to the pain of others predicts later costly helping. *PLoS ONE* 6(8):e22759.

Heishman SJ and Henningfield JE (2000). Tolerance to repeated nicotine administration on performance, subjective, and physiological responses in nonsmokers. *Psychopharmacology* 152(3):321–334.

Helms-Tillery SI, Taylor DM, and Schwartz AB (2003). Training in cortical control of neuroprosthetic devices improves signal extraction from small neuronal ensembles. *Reviews in the Neurosciences* 14:107–119.

Hensch TK (2005). Critical period plasticity in local cortical circuits. *Nature Reviews Neuroscience* 6:877–888.

Herbert F (1965). *Dune*. New York: Ace.

Hermer L and Spelke ES (1994). A geometric process for spatial reorientation in young children. *Nature* 370:57–59.

Hernandez G, Breton YA, Conover K, and Shizgal P (2010). At what stage of neural processing does cocaine act to boost pursuit of rewards? *PLoS ONE* 5(11):e15081.

Hersh SM (2004). Torture at Abu Ghraib. *New Yorker* www.newyorker.com/archive/2004/05/10/040510fa_fact.

Hersh SM (2007). The General's Report. *New Yorker* www.newyorker.com/reporting/2007/06/25/070625fa_fact_hersh.

Hershberger WA (1986). An approach through the looking glass. *Learning and Behavior* 14(4):443–451.

Hertz J, Krogh A, and Palmer RG (1991). *Introduction to the Theory of Neural Computation*. Boston: Addison-Wesley.

Herz A (1998). Opioid reward mechanisms: A key role in drug abuse? *Canadian Journal of Physiology and Pharmacology* 76(3):252–258.

Heyman G (2009). *Addiction: A Disorder of Choice*. Cambridge, MA: Harvard University Press.

Higgins ST, Alessi SM, and Dantona RL (2002). Voucher-based incentives: A substance abuse treatment innovation. *Addictive Behaviors* 27:887–910.

Higgins ST, Heil SH, and Lussier JP (2004). Clinical implications of reinforcement as a determinant of substance use disorders. *Annual Review of Psychology* 55(1):431–461.

Hikosaka O, Nakahara H, Rand MK, Sakai K, Lu X, Nakamura K, Miyachi S, and Doya K (1999). Parallel neural networks for learning sequential procedures. *Trends in Neurosciences* 22(10):464–471.

Hill C (2008). The rationality of preference construction (and the irrationality of rational choice). *Minnesota Journal of Law, Science, and Technology* 9(2):689–742.

Hill M and Halliday T (1998). *Behaviour and Evolution*. New York: Springer.

Hille B (2001). *Ion Channels of Excitable Membranes*. Sunderland, MA: Sinauer Associates.

Hinde RA (1966). *Animal Behaviour*. New York: McGraw-Hill.

Hinson JM, Jameson TL, and Whitney P (2003). Impulsive decision making and working memory. *Journal of Experimental Psychology* 29(2):298–306.

Hirata S, Watanabe K, and Kawai M (2008). "Sweet-potato washing" revisited. In: Matsuzawa T (ed.), *Primate Origins of Human Cognition and Behavior*. New York: Springer, pp. 487–508.

Hobson JA (2005). *Dreaming: A Very Short Introduction*. New York: Oxford University Press.

Hobson JA and Pace-Schott EF (2002). The cognitive neuroscience of sleep: Neuronal systems, consciousness, and learning. *Nature Reviews Neuroscience* 3:679–693.

Hochberg LR, Serruya MD, Friehs GM, Mukand JA, Saleh M, Caplan AH, Branner A, Chen D, Penn RD, and Donoghue JP (2006). Neuronal ensemble control of prosthetic devices by a human with tetraplegia. *Nature* 442:164–171.

Hodgkin AL and Huxley AF (1952). A quantitative description of membrane current and its application to conduction and excitation in nerve. *Journal of Physiology* 117:500–544.

Hoffman E, McCabe K, Shachat K, and Smith V (1994). Preferences, property rights, and anonymity in bargaining games. *Games and Economic Behavior* 7:346–380.

Hoffman KL, Battaglia FP, Harris K, MacLean JN, Marshall L, and Mehta MR (2007). The upshot of up states in the neocortex: From slow oscillations to memory formation. *Journal of Neuroscience* 27(44):11838–11841.

Hoffman KL and McNaughton BL (2002). Coordinated reactivation of distributed memory traces in primate neocortex. *Science* 297(5589):2070–2073.

Hofman MA (1985). Size and shape of the cerebral cortex in mammals: I. The cortical surface. *Brain Behavior and Evolution* 27:28–40.

Hofmann W, Schmeichel BJ, and Baddeley AD (2012). Executive functions and self-regulation. *Trends in Cognitive Sciences* 16(3):174–180.

Hofstadter DR (1979). *Gödel, Escher, Bach: An Eternal Golden Braid*. New York: Basic Books.

Hofstadter DR (1985). *Metamagical Themas: Questing for the Essence of Mind and Pattern*. New York: Basic Books.

Hofstadter DR (2008). *I Am a Strange Loop*. New York: Basic Books.

Holden C (2001). "Behavioral" addictions: Do they exist? *Science* 294:980–982.

Hollerman JR and Schultz W (1998). Dopamine neurons report an error in the temporal prediction of reward during learning. *Nature Neuroscience* 1(4):304–309.

Holmes OW (1927). *Compania General de Tabacos de Filipinas v. Collector of Internal Revenue*. U.S. Supreme Court Ruling 275 US. 87.

Holroyd CB and Coles MGH (2002). The neural basis of human error processing: Reinforcement learning, dopamine, and the error-related negativity. *Psychological Review* 109(4):679–709.

Homer (12th century BCE/1951). *The Illiad*. Translated by Richmond Lattimore. Chicago: University of Chicago Press.

Homer (12th century BCE/1965). *The Odyssey*. Translated by Richmond Lattimore. New York: Harper Torchbooks.

Hooke R (1665). *Micrographia or Some Physiological Descriptions of Minute Bodies Made By Magnefying Glasses with Observations and Inquiries Thereupon*. Royal Society, London.

Hopfield JJ (1982). Neural networks and physical systems with emergent collective computational abilities. *Proceedings of the National Academy of Sciences, USA* 79:2554–2558.

Horner V, Proctor D, Bonnie KE, Whiten A, and de Waal F (2010). Prestige affects cultural learning in chimpanzees. *PLoS ONE* 5(5):e10625.

Houk JC, Davis JL, and Beiser DG (eds.) (1995). *Models of Information Processing in the Basal Ganglia*. Cambridge, MA: MIT Press.

Houser D and McCabe K (2008). Experimental neuroeconomics and non-cooperative games. In: Glimcher PW, Camerer CF, Fehr E, and Poldrack RA (eds.), *Neuroeconomics: Decision Making in the Brain*. New York: Academic Press, pp. 47–62.

Howard R (2001). *A Beautiful Mind*. Universal Pictures.

Hu D and Amsel A (1995). A simple test of the vicarious trial-and-error hypothesis of hippocampal function. *Proceedings of the National Academy of Sciences, USA* 92:5506–5509.

Hubel DH and Wiesel TN (1977). Functional architecture of macaque monkey visual cortex. *Proceedings of the Royal Society of London Series B* 198(1130):1–59.

Huettel SA, Song AW, and McCarthy G (2009). *Functional Magnetic Resonance Imaging*. Sunderland, MA: Sinauer Associates.

Hui W, Yoo B, and Tam KY (2007). The optimal number of versions: Why does goldilocks pricing work for information goods? *Journal of Management Information Systems* 24(3):167–169.

Hull CL (1943). *Principles of Behavior*. New York: Appleton-Century-Crofts.

Hull CL (1952). *A Behavior System: An Introduction to Behavior Theory Concerning the Individual Organism*. New Haven, CT: Yale University Press.

Hume D (1740/2000). *A Treatise on Human Nature*. New York: Oxford University Press.

Hume D (1748/2003). *Enquiries concerning Human Understanding*. Project Gutenberg. www.gutenberg.org.

Hunt GR (1996). Manufacture and use of hook-tools by New Caledonian crows. *Nature* 379:249–251.

Hunt WA (1998). Pharmacology of alcohol. In: Tarter RE, Ammerman RT, and Ott PJ (eds.), *Handbook of Substance Abuse: Neurobehavioral Pharmacology*. New York: Plenum, pp. 7–22.

Huys QJM (2007). *Reinforcers and Control: Towards a Computational Ætiology of Depression*. Ph.D. thesis, Gatsby Computational Neuroscience Unit, University College London.

Huys QJM, Moutoussis M, and Williams J (2011). Are computational models of any use to psychiatry? *Neural Networks* 24(6):544–551.

Hyman JM, Zilli EA, Paley AM, and Hasselmo ME (2010). Working memory performance correlates with prefrontal-hippocampal theta interactions but not with prefrontal neuron firing rates. *Frontiers in Integrative Neuroscience* 4:2. doi: 10.3389/neuro.07.002.2010.

Hyman SE (2007). Can neuroscience be integrated into the DSM-V? *Nature Reviews Neuroscience* 8:725–732.

Hyman SE (2010). The diagnosis of mental disorders: The problem of reification. *Annual Review of Clinical Psychology* 6:155–179.

IBM (1997). Kasparov vs. Deep Blue. researchweb.watson.ibm.com/deepblue.

IBM (2011). The deep QA project. searchweb.watson.ibm.com/deepqa/deepqa.shtml.

ICD-10 (1992). *International Classification of Diseases*. World Health Organization.

Ikeda H, Kiritoshi T, and Murase K (2009). Synaptic plasticity in the spinal dorsal horn. *Neuroscience Research* 64(2):133–136.

Ince NF, Gupta R, Arica S, Tewfik AH, Ashe J, and Pellizzer G (2010). High-accuracy decoding of movement target direction in non-human primates based on common spatial patterns of local field potentials. *PLoS ONE* 5(12):e14384.

Insel T, Cuthbert B, Garvey M, Heinssen R, Pine DS, Quinn K, Sanislow C, and Wang P (2010). Research Domain Criteria (RDoC): Toward a new classification framework for research on mental disorders. *American Journal of Psychiatry* 167:748–751.

Insel T et al. (2011). NIMH Research Domain Criteria (RDoC). Draft 3.1, June 2011. www.nimh.nih.gov/research-funding/rdoc/nimh-research-domain-criteria-rdoc.shtml

Insel TR and Young LJ (2001). The neurobiology of attachment. *Nature Reviews Neuroscience* 2:129–136.

Intergovernmental Panel on Climate Change (2011). www.ipcc.ch.

International Campaign to Ban Landmines (2011). www.icbl.org/.

Ionesco E (1960). *Rhinoceros*. New York: Grove Press.

Isoda M and Hikosaka O (2007). Switching from automatic to controlled action by monkey medial frontal cortex. *Nature Neuroscience* 10:240–248.

Isoda M and Hikosaka O (2008). Role for subthalamic nucleus neurons in switching from automatic to controlled eye movement. *Journal of Neuroscience* 28(28):7209–7218.

Itō M (1984). The modifiable neuronal network of the cerebellum. *Japanese Journal of Physiology* 34(5):781–792.

Iversen L, Iversen S, Bloom FE, and Roth RH (2008). *Introduction to Neuropsychopharmacology*. New York: Oxford University Press.

Iversen SD and Mishkin M (1970). Perseverative interference in monkeys following selective lesions of the inferior prefrontal convexity. *Experimental Brain Research* 11(4):376–386.

Jackson JC and Redish AD (2007). Network dynamics of hippocampal cell-assemblies resemble multiple spatial maps within single tasks. *Hippocampus* 17:1209–1229.

Jackson JC, Johnson A, and Redish AD (2006). Hippocampal sharp waves and reactivation during awake states depend on repeated sequential experience. *Journal of Neuroscience* 26:12415–12426.

Jackson JC and Redish AD (2003). Detecting dynamical changes within a simulated neural ensemble using a measure of representational quality. *Network: Computation in Neural Systems* 14:629–645.

Jacobs J, Kahana MJ, Ekstrom AD, and Fried I (2007). Brain oscillations control timing of single-neuron activity in humans. *Journal of Neuroscience* 27(14):3839–3844.

Jacobs WJ and Nadel L (1998). Neurobiology of reconstructed memory. *Psychology, Public Policy, and Law* 4(4):1110–1134.

Jadhav SP, Kemere C, German PW, and Frank LM (2012). Awake hippocampal sharp-wave ripples support spatial memory. *Science* 336:1454–1458.

Jagger M and Richards K (1969). You can't always get what you want. On *Let it Bleed*, Decca Records.

James W (1890). *The Principles of Psychology* (Reprint). New York: Dover Press, 1960.

Janak VM (2009). Whale song. *Current Biology* 19(3):R109–R111.

Jankovic J and Tolosa E (eds.) (2007). *Parkinson's Disease and Movement Disorders*. Philadelphia: Lippincott Williams & Wilkins.

Jasieńska G, Ziomkiewicz A, Ellison PT, Lipson SF, and Thune I (2004). Large breasts and narrow waists indicate high reproductive potential in women. *Proceedings of the Royal Society London B* 271:1213–1217.

Jay GW (ed.) (2000). *Minor Traumatic Brain Injury Handbook: Diagnosis and Treatment*. Boca Raton, FL: CRC Press.

Jaynes ET (2003). *Probability Theory: The Logic of Science*. Cambridge, UK: Cambridge University Press.

Jensen K, Call J, and Tomasello M (2007). Chimpanzees are rational maximizers in an ultimatum game. *Science* 318(5847):107–109.

Jensen S (2010). *Learning in Dynamic Temporal Domains Using Contextual Prediction Entropy as a Guiding Principle*. Ph.D. thesis, University of Minnesota, Minneapolis, MN.

Jensen S, Boley D, Gini M, and Schrater P (2005). Non-stationary policy learning in 2-player zero sum games. *Proceedings of the Twentieth National Conference on Artificial Intelligence*, pp. 789–794.

Jerison HJ (1973). *Evolution of the Brain and Intelligence*. New York: Academic Press.

Ji D and Wilson MA (2007). Coordinated memory replay in the visual cortex and hippocampus during sleep. *Nature Neuroscience* 10:100–107.

Johnson A and Crowe DA (2009). Revisiting Tolman, his theories and cognitive maps. *Cognitive Critique* 1:43–72.

Johnson A, Fenton AA, Kentros C, and Redish AD (2009). Looking for cognition in the structure in the noise. *Trends in Cognitive Sciences* 13(2):55–64.

Johnson A, Jackson J, and Redish AD (2008). Measuring distributed properties of neural representations beyond the decoding of local variables—implications for cognition. In: Hölscher C and Munk MHJ (eds.), *Mechanisms of Information Processing in the Brain: Encoding of Information in Neural Populations and Networks*. Cambridge, UK: Cambridge University Press, pp. 95–119.

Johnson A and Redish AD (2007). Neural ensembles in CA3 transiently encode paths forward of the animal at a decision point. *Journal of Neuroscience* 27(45):12176–12189.

Johnson A, van der Meer MAA, and Redish AD (2007). Integrating hippocampus and striatum in decision-making. *Current Opinion in Neurobiology* 17(6):692–697.

Johnson M (1994). *Moral Imagination: Implications of Cognitive Science for Ethics.* Chicago: University of Chicago Press.

Johnson MW and Bickel WK (2002). Within-subject comparison of real and hypothetical money rewards in delay discounting. *Journal of the Experimental Analysis of Behavior* 77(2):129–146.

Johnson PM and Kenny PJ (2010). Dopamine D2 receptors in addiction-like reward dysfunction and compulsive eating in obese rats. *Nature Neuroscience* 13:635–641.

Johnston VS and Franklin M (1993). Is beauty in the eye of the beholder? *Ethology and Sociobiology* 14(3):183–199.

Jones BT, Corbin W, and Fromme K (2001). A review of expectancy theory and alcohol consumption. *Addiction* 96:57–72.

Jones E and Wessely S (2005). *Shell Shock to PTSD: Military Psychiatry from 1900 to the Gulf War.* New York: Taylor and Francis.

Jones MW and Wilson MA (2005). Theta rhythms coordinate hippocampal-prefrontal interactions in a spatial memory task. *PLOS Biology* 3(12):e402.

Jordan N (1992). *The Crying Game.* Miramax.

Joukhador J, Maccallum F, and Blaszczynski A (2003). Differences in cognitive distortions between problem and social gamblers. *Psychological Reports* 92:1203–1214.

Joyce J (1939). *Finnegans Wake.* London: Faber and Faber.

Joyner AL (ed.) (2000). *Gene Targeting: A Practical Approach.* New York: Oxford University Press.

Julesz B (1991). Early vision and focal attention. *Reviews of Modern Physics* 63(3):735–772.

Jung MW, Wiener SI, and McNaughton BL (1994). Comparison of spatial firing characteristics of the dorsal and ventral hippocampus of the rat. *Journal of Neuroscience* 14(12):7347–7356.

Kaas JH, Merzenich MM, and Killackey HP (1983). The reorganization of somatosensory cortex following peripheral nerve damage in adult and developing mammals. *Annual Review of Neuroscience* 6:325–356.

Kable JW and Glimcher PW (2009). The neurobiology of decision: Consensus and controversy. *Neuron* 63(6):733–745.

Kahn D (1967/1996). *The Code-Breakers: The Comprehensive History of Secret Communication from Ancient Times to the Internet.* New York: Scribner.

Kahneman D (2011). *Thinking, Fast, and Slow.* New York: Farrar, Straus and Giroux.

Kahneman D, Knetsch JL, and Thaler RH (1990). Experimental tests of the endowment effect and the Coase theorem. *Journal of Political Economy* 98(6):1325–1348.

Kahneman D, Knetsch JL, and Thaler RH (1991). The endowment effect, loss aversion, and status quo bias. *Journal of Economic Perspectives* 5(1):193–206.

Kahneman D, Slovic P, and Tversky A (eds.) (1982). *Judgement Under Uncertainty: Heuristics and Biases.* Cambridge, UK: Cambridge University Press.

Kahneman D and Tversky A (1979). Prospect theory: An analysis of decision under risk. *Econometrica* 47(2):263–292.

Kahneman D and Tversky A (eds.) (2000). *Choices, Values, and Frames.* Cambridge, UK: Cambridge University Press.

Kakade S and Dayan P (2002). Dopamine: Generalization and bonuses. *Neural Networks* 15:549–599.

Kakalios J (2010). *The Amazing Story of Quantum Mechanics: A Math-Free Exploration of the Science that Made Our World.* New York: Gotham.

Kalbfleisch JD and Prentice RL (2002). *The Statistical Analysis of Failure Time Data.* New York: Wiley.

Kamin LJ (1969). Predictability, surprise, attention, and conditioning. In: Campbell BA and Church RM (eds.), *Punishment and Aversive Behavior.* New York: Appleton-Century-Crofts, pp. 279–296.

Kandel E (2006). *In Search of Memory: The Emergence of a New Science of Mind.* New York: W. W. Norton.

Kandel E, Schwartz JH, and Jessell TM (eds.) (2000). *Principles of Neural Science.* New York: McGraw-Hill.

Kang MJ, Rangel A, Camus M, and Camerer CF (2011). Hypothetical and real choice differentially activate common valuation areas. *Journal of Neuroscience* 31(2):461–468.

Kant I (1797/1998). *Groundwork of the Metaphysics of Morals*. Cambridge, UK: Cambridge University Press.

Kaplan L (2003). Inuit snow terms: How many and what does it mean? In: *Building Capacity in Arctic Societies: Dynamics and Shifting Perspectives. Proceedings from the 2nd IPSSAS Seminar.* Iqaluit, Nunavut, Canada: May 26–June 6, 2003.

Karniel A, Kositsky M, Fleming KM, Chiappalone M, Sanguineti V, Alford ST, and Mussa-Ivaldi FAS (2005). Computational analysis in vitro: Dynamics and plasticity of a neuro-robotic system. *Journal of Neural Engineering* 2:S250–S265.

Katz B (1966). *Nerve, Muscle, and Synapse*. New York: McGraw-Hill.

Katzner S, Nauhaus I, Benucci A, Bonin V, Ringach DL, and Carandini M (2009). Local origin of field potentials in visual cortex. *Neuron* 61(1):35–41.

Kawai M (1965). Newly-acquired pre-cultural behavior of the natural troop of Japanese monkeys on Koshima Islet. *Primates* 6(1):1–30.

Kelemen E and Fenton AA (2010). Dynamic grouping of hippocampal neural activity during cognitive control of two spatial frames. *PLoS Biology* 8(6):e1000403.

Kennett DJ and Winterhalder B (eds.) (2006). *Behavioral Ecology and the Transition to Agriculture*. Berkeley, CA: University of California Press.

Kenstowicz M and Kisseberth C (1979). *Generative Phonology: Description and Theory*. New York: Academic Press.

Kepler J (1609). *Astronomia Nova*. Prague: Rudolphus II.

Kéri S, Moustafa AA, Myers CE, Benedek G, and Gluck MA (2010). α-synuclein and gene duplication impairs reward learning. *Proceedings of the National Academy of Sciences, USA* 107(36):15992–15994.

Kesner RP (2007). A behavioral analysis of dentate gyrus function. *Progress in Brain Research* 163:567–576.

Kesner RP and Churchwell JC (2011). An analysis of rat prefrontal cortex in mediating executive function. *Neurobiology of Learning and Memory* 96(3):417–431.

Kessler RC, Sonnega A, Bonnet E, Hughes M, and Nelson CB (1995). Posttraumatic stress disorder in the National Comorbidity Survey. *Archives of General Psychiatry* 52(12):1048–1060.

Keysers C and Gazzola V (2006). Towards a unifying neural theory of social cognition. *Progress in Brain Research* 156:379–401.

Kieffer BL (1999). Opioids: First lessons from knockout mice. *Trends in Pharmacological Sciences* 20(1):19–26.

Killcross S and Coutureau E (2003). Coordination of actions and habits in the medial prefrontal cortex of rats. *Cerebral Cortex* 13(8):400–408.

Kim JJ and Fanselow MS (1992). Modality-specific retrograde amnesia of fear. *Science* 256:675–677.

Kimbrough EO, Smith VL, and Wilson BJ (2008). Building a market. In: Zak PJ (ed.), *Moral Markets*. Princeton, NJ: Princeton University Press, pp. 280–299.

King-Casas B, Sharp C, Lomax-Bream L, Lohrenz T, Fonagy P, and Montague PR (2008). The rupture and repair of cooperation in borderline personality disorder. *Science* 321(5890):806–810.

King-Casas B, Tomlin D, Anen C, Camerer CF, Quartz SR, and Montague PR (2005). Getting to know you: Reputation and trust in a two-person economic exchange. *Science* 308(5718):78–83.

Kishida KT, King-Casas B, and Montague PR (2010). Neuroeconomic approaches to mental disorders. *Neuron* 67(4):543–554.

Kjelstrup KB, Solstad T, Brun VH, Hafting T, Leutgeb S, Witter MP, Moser EI, and Moser MB (2008). Finite scale of spatial representation in the hippocampus. *Science* 321(5885):140–143.

Klein RM (2000). Inhibition of return. *Trends in Cognitive Sciences* 4(4):138–147.

Kliegel M, McDaniel MA, and Einstein GO (eds.) (2008). *Prospective Memory*. Hillsdale, NJ: Lawrence Erlbaum.

Knoch D and Fehr E (2007). Resisting the power of temptations: The right prefrontal cortex and self-control. *Annals of the New York Academy of Sciences* 1104:123–134.

Knopman DS and Nissen MJ (1987). Implicit learning in patients with probable Alzheimer's disease. *Neurology* 37(5):784–788.

Knopman DS and Nissen MJ (1991). Procedural learning is impaired in Huntington's disease: Evidence from the serial reaction time task. *Neuropsychologia* 29(3):245–254.

Knowlton BJ, Mangels JA, and Squire LR (1996). A neostriatal habit learning system in humans. *Science* 273:1399–1402.

Knowlton BJ, Squire LR, and Gluck MA (1994). Probabilistic classification learning in amnesia. *Learning and Memory* 1(2):106–120.

Knudsen EI (1991). Dynamic space codes in the superior colliculus. *Current Opinion in Neurobiology* 1:628–632.

Knudsen EI (2004). Sensitive periods in the development of the brain and behavior. *Journal of Cognitive Neuroscience* 16(8):1412–1425.

Knudsen EI and Brainard MS (1995). Creating a unified representation of visual and auditory space in the brain. *Annual Review of Neuroscience* 18:19–43.

Knudsen EI, du Lac S, and Esterly SD (1987). Computational maps in the brain. *Annual Review of Neuroscience* 10:41–65.

Knudsen EI, Zheng W, and DeBello WM (2000). Traces of learning in the auditory localization pathway. *Proceedings of the National Academy of Sciences, USA* 97(22):11815–11820.

Kobayashi S, de Carvalho OP, and Schultz W (2010). Adaptation of reward sensitivity in orbitofrontal neurons. *Journal of Neuroscience* 30(2):534–544.

Koch C (2004). *The Quest for Consciousness.* Englewood, CO: Roberts and Company.

Koechlin E (2011). Frontal pole function: What is specifically human? *Trends in Cognitive Sciences* 15(6):241.

Koepp MJ, Gunn RN, Lawrence AD, Cunningham VJ, Dagher A, Jones T, Brooks DJ, Bench CJ, and Grasby PM (1998). Evidence for striatal dopamine release during a video game. *Nature* 393:266–268.

Köhler W (1925/1959). *The Mentality of Apes.* London: Routledge.

Kohonen T (1980). *Content-Addressable Memories.* New York: Springer.

Kohonen T (1984). *Self-Organization and Associative Memory.* New York: Springer-Verlag.

Koller WC (ed.) (1992). *Handbook of Parkinson's Diseases.* New York: Marcel Dekker.

Konorski J (1967). *Integrative Activity in the Brain: An Interdisciplinary Approach.* Chicago: University of Chicago Press.

Koob GF (2009). Neurobiological substrates for the dark side of compulsivity in addiction. *Neuropharmacology* 56(Suppl. 1):18–31.

Koob GF and Le Moal M (2006). *Neurobiology of Addiction.* London: Elsevier Academic Press.

Koob GF and Volkow ND (2010). Neurocircuitry of addiction. *Neuropsychopharmacology* 35(1):217–238.

Kopelman MD, Thomson AD, Guerrini I, and Marshall EJ (2009). The Korsakoff syndrome: Clinical aspects, psychology and treatment. *Alcohol and Alcoholism* 44(2):148–154.

Kopin IJ (1993). The pharmacology of Parkinson's disease therapy: An update. *Annual Review of Pharmacology and Toxicology* 33:467–495.

Kosfeld M, Heinrichs M, Zak PJ, Fischbacher U, and Fehr E (2005). Oxytocin increases trust in humans. *Nature* 435:673–676.

Kosslyn SM (1994). *Image and Brain.* Cambridge, MA: MIT Press.

Kosslyn SM, Thompson WL, and Ganis G (2006). *The Case for Mental Imagery.* New York: Oxford University Press.

Kozlowski LT and Wilkinson DA (2006). Use and misuse of the concept of craving by alcohol, tobacco, and drug researchers. *Addiction* 82:31–36.

Krajbich I, Adolphs R, Trane D, Denburg NL, and Camerer CF (2009). Economic games quantify diminished sense of guilt in patients with damage to the prefrontal cortex. *Journal of Neuroscience* 29(7):2188–2192.

Krajbich I and Rangel A (2011). Multialternative drift-diffusion model predicts the relationship between visual fixations and choice in value-based decisions. *Proceedings of the National Academy of Sciences, USA.* 108(33):13852–13857.

Krauss C (2008). Driving less, Americans finally react to sting of gas prices, a study says. *New York Times,* June 19, 2008. www.nytimes.com/2008/06/19/business/19gas.html.

Kravitz AV, Tye LD, and Kreitzer AC (2012). Distinct roles for direct and indirect pathway striatal neurons in reinforcement. *Nature Neuroscience* 15:816–818.

Krebs RM, Schott BH, Schütze H, and Düze E (2009). The novelty exploration bonus and its attentional modulation. *Neuropsychologia* 47(11):2272–2281.

Kreek MJ, LaForge KS, and Butelman E (2002). Pharmacotherapy of addictions. *Nature Reviews Drug Discovery* 1:710–726.

Krensky S and Reeves J (2007). *Anansi and the Box of Stories*. Minneapolis, MN: Millbrook Press.

Krishnan-Sarin S, Reynolds B, Duhig AM, Smith A, Liss T, McFetridge A, Cavallo DA, Carroll KM, and Potenza MN (2007). Behavioral impulsivity predicts treatment outcome in a smoking cessation program for adolescent smokers. *Drug and Alcohol Dependence* 88:79–82.

Krubitzer L (2009). In search of a unifying theory of complex brain evolution. *Annals of the New York Academy of Sciences* 1156:44–67.

Krubitzer L and Kaas J (2005). The evolution of the neocortex in mammals: how is phenotypic diversity generated? *Current Opinion in Neurobiology* 15(4):444–453.

Krugman P (2009a). *The Conscience of a Liberal*. New York: W. W. Norton.

Krugman P (2009b). How did economists get it so wrong? *New York Times Magazine* www.nytimes.com/2009/09/06/magazine/06Economic-t.html.

Krugman P (2011). The austerity delusion. *New York Times* www.nytimes.com/2011/03/25/opinion/25krugman.html.

Krugman P (2012). *End This Depression Now!* New York: W. W. Norton.

Krugman P and Wells R (2006). *Macroeconomics*. New York: Worth.

Kruse JM, Overmier JB, Konz WA, and Rokke E (1983). Pavlovian conditioned stimulus effects upon instrumental choice behavior are reinforcer specific. *Learning and Motivation* 14(2):165–181.

Kudrimoti HS, Barnes CA, and McNaughton BL (1999). Reactivation of hippocampal cell assemblies: Effects of behavioral state, experience, and EEG dynamics. *Journal of Neuroscience* 19(10):4090–4101.

Kuhl PK (1994). Learning and representation in speech and language. *Current Opinion in Neurobiology* 4:812–822.

Kuhl PK, Andruski JE, Chistovich IA, Chistovich LA, Kozhevnikova EV, Ryskina VL, Stolyarova EI, Sundberg U, and Lacerda F (1997). Cross-language analysis of phonetic units in language addressed to infants. *Science* 277(5326):684–686.

Kuhl PK, Williams KA, Lacerda F, Stevens KN, and Lindblom B (1992). Linguistic experience alters phonetic perception in infants by 6 months of age. *Science* 255:606–608.

Kuhlmann S, Piel M, and Wolf OT (2005). Impaired memory retrieval after psychosocial stress in healthy young men. *Journal of Neuroscience* 25(11):2977–2982.

Kuhn TS (1962/1996). *The Structure of Scientific Revolutions*. Chicago: University of Chicago Press.

Kummer H (1971). *Primate Societies*. Piscataway, NJ: AldineTransaction.

Kurkjian T (2006). Since Williams, no greater hitter than Gwynn. *ESPN* sports.espn.go.com/mlb/hof07/columns/story?columnist=kurkjian_tim&id=2708775.

Kurniawan IT, Guitart-Masip M, and Dolan RJ (2011). Dopamine and effort-based decision making. *Frontiers in Neuroscience* 5(81):1–10.

Kurniawan IT, Seymour B, Vlaev I, Trommershäuser J, Dolan RJ, and Chater N (2010). Pain relativity in motor control. *Psychological Science* 21(6):840–847.

Kurth-Nelson Z and Redish AD (2010). A reinforcement learning model of pre-commitment in decision making. *Frontiers in Behavioral Neuroscience* 4(184):1–13.

Kurth-Nelson Z and Redish AD (2012a). Don't let me do that!—models of precommitment. *Frontiers in Neuroscience* 6:138; doi: 10.3389/fnins.2012.00138.

Kurth-Nelson Z and Redish AD (2012b). Modeling decision-making systems in addiction. In: Gutkin B and Ahmed SH (eds.), *Computational Neuroscience of Drug Addiction*. New York: Springer, Chapter 6, pp. 163–188.

Kurth-Nelson Z and Redish AD (2012c). A theoretical account of cognitive effects in delay discounting. *European Journal of Neuroscience* 35:1052–1064.

Kurzban R (2010). *Why Everyone (Else) is a Hypocrite*. Princeton, NJ: Princeton University Press.

Laing CR and Chow CC (2001). Stationary bumps in networks of spiking neurons. *Neural Computation* 13(7):1473–1494.

Lakoff G (1990/1997). *Women, Fire, and Dangerous Things*. Chicago: University of Chicago Press.

Lakoff G, Dean H, and Hazen D (2004). *Don't Think of an Elephant!* White River Junction, VT: Chelsea Green.

Lakoff G and Johnson M (2003). *Metaphors We Live By.* Chicago: Chicago University Press.

Lakoff RT (2001). *The Language War.* Berkeley, CA: University of California Press.

Langer EJ and Roth J (1975). Heads I win, tails it's chance: The illusion of control as a function of the sequence of outcomes in a purely chance task. *Journal of Personality and Social Psychology* 32(6):951–955.

Lansink CS, Goltstein PM, Lankelma JV, Joosten RNJMA, McNaughton BL, and Pennartz CMA (2008). Preferential reactivation of motivationally relevant information in the ventral striatum. *Journal of Neuroscience* 28(25):6372–6382.

Lansink CS, Goltstein PM, Lankelma JV, McNaughton BL, and Pennartz CMA (2009). Hippocampus leads ventral striatum in replay of place-reward information. *PLoS Biology* 7(8):e1000173.

Lao Tsu (6th century BCE/1997). *Tao Te Ching.* Translated by Gia-Fu Feng. New York: Vintage Books.

Laplace PS (1814/1902). *A Philosophical Essay on Probabilities.* Translated by Frederick Wilson Truscott and Frederick Lincoln Emory. Chapman / New York:Wiley.

Lashley KS (1929). *Brain Mechanisms and Intelligence: A Quantitative Study of Injuries to the Brain.* Chicago: University of Chicago Press.

Lashley KS (1931). Mass action in cerebral function. *Science* 73(1888):245–254.

Lau B and Glimcher PW (2005). Dynamic response-by-response models of matching behavior in rhesus monkeys. *Journal of the Experimental Analysis of Behavior* 84(3):555–579.

Laurent PA (2008). The emergence of saliency and novelty responses from reinforcement learning principles. *Neural Networks* 21(10):1493–1499.

Laurent V, Leung B, Maidment N, and Balleine BW (2012). μ- and δ-opioid-related processes in the accumbens core and shell differentially mediate the influence of reward-guided and stimulus-guided decisions on choice. *Journal of Neuroscience* 32(5):1875–1883.

Lauwereyns J (2010). *The Anatomy of Bias.* Cambridge, MA: MIT Press.

Layton B and Krikorian R (2002). Memory mechanisms in posttraumatic stress disorder. *Journal of Neuropsychiatry and Clinical Neuroscience* 14(3):254–261.

Lean D (1962). *Lawrence of Arabia.* Columbia Pictures.

LeDoux JE (1996). *The Emotional Brain.* New York: Simon and Schuster.

LeDoux JE (2002). *The Synaptic Self.* New York: Penguin.

LeDoux JE (2012). Rethinking the emotional brain. *Neuron* 73(4):653–676.

Lee D, Rushworth MFS, Walton ME, Watanabe M, and Sakagami M (2007). Functional specialization of the primate frontal cortex during decision making. *Journal of Neuroscience* 27(31):8170–8173.

Leeson PT (2009). *The Invisible Hook: The Hidden Economics of Pirates.* Princeton, NJ: Princeton University Press.

LeFever G, Dawson KV, and Morrow AL (1999). The extent of drug therapy for attention deficit-hyperactivity disorder among children in public schools. *American Journal of Public Health* 89(9):1359–1364.

LeGuin UK (1974). *The Dispossessed: An Ambiguous Utopia.* New York: Harper and Row.

Lehrer J (2009a). Don't: The secret of self-control. *New Yorker* 05(18). www.newyorker.com/reporting/2009/05/18/090518fa_fact_lehrer

Lehrer J (2009b). *How We Decide.* Boston: Houghton Mifflin.

Lejoyeaux M and Germain C (2012). Pyromania: Phenomenology and epidemiology. In: Grant JE and Potenza MN (eds.), *The Oxford Handbook of Impulse Control Disorders.* New York: Oxford University Press, pp. 135–148.

Lenfant C and Sullivan K (1971). Adaptation to high altitude. *New England Journal of Medicine* 284:1298–1309.

Lengyel M and Dayan P (2007). Hippocampal contributions to control: The third way. In: Platt JC, Koller D, Singer Y, and Roweis ST (eds.), *Advances in Neural Information Processing Systems 20.* Cambridge, MA: MIT Press.

Lenoir M and Ahmed SH (2007). Supply of a nondrug substitute reduces escalated heroin consumption. *Neuropsychopharmacology* 33(9):2272–2282.

Lenoir M, Serre F, Cantin L, and Ahmed SH (2007). Intense sweetness surpasses cocaine reward. *PLoS ONE* 2(8):e698.

Lesieur H (1977). *The Chase: Career of the Compulsive Gambler*. Cambridge, MA: Schenkman Books.

Leukefeld C, Gullotta TP, and Gregrich J (eds.) (2011). *Handbook of Evidence-Based Substance Abuse Treatment in Criminal Justice Settings*. New York: Springer.

Leutgeb JK, Leutgeb S, Moser MB, and Moser EI (2007). Pattern separation in the dentate gyrus and CA3 of the hippocampus. *Science* 315(5814):961–966.

LeVay S (1993). *The Sexual Brain*. Cambridge, MA: MIT Press.

Levi R and Camhi JM (2000). Population vector coding by the giant interneurons of the cockroach. *Journal of Neuroscience* 20(10):3822–3829.

Levi-Strauss C (1970). *The Raw and the Cooked*. New York: Jonathan Cape.

Levine AS and Billington CJ (2004). Opioids as agents of reward-related feeding: A consideration of the evidence. *Physiology and Behavior* 82:57–61.

Levy N (2007). *Neuroethics*. Cambridge, UK: Cambridge University Press.

Libet B (1985). Unconscious cerebral initiative and the role of conscious will in voluntary action. *Behavioral and Brain Sciences* 8:529–566.

Libet B (1993). The neural time factor in conscious and unconscious events. *Ciba Foundation Symposium* 174:123–146.

Libet B, Wright EW, Feinstein B, and Pearl DK (1979). Subjective referral of the timing for a conscious sensory experience. *Brain* 102:193–224.

Liebenthal E, Uhlmann O, and Camhi JM (1994). Critical parameters of the spike trains in a cell assembly: Coding of turn direction by the giant interneurons of the cockroach. *Journal of Comparative Physiology A: Neuroethology, Sensory, Neural, and Behavioral Physiology* 174:281–296.

Lin AC and Holt CE (2007). Local translation and directional steering in axons. *EMBO Journal* 26:3729–3736.

Linkenhoker BA, von der Ohe CG, and Knudsen EI (2004). Anatomical traces of juvenile learning in the auditory system of adult barn owls. *Nature Neuroscience* 8:93–98.

Lippert MT, Steudel T, Ohl F, Logothetis NK, and Kayser C (2010). Coupling of neural activity and fMRI-BOLD in the motion area MT. *Magnetic Resonance Imaging* 28(8):1087–1094.

Lipscombe B (1989). Expert systems and computer-controlled decision making in medicine. *AI and Society* 3:184–197.

Lisman J, Yasuda R, and Raghavachari S (2012). Mechanisms of CaMKII in long-term potentiation. *Nature Reviews Neuroscience* 13:169–182.

Liu J, Harris A, and Kanwisher N (2010). Perception of face parts and face configurations: An fMRI study. *Journal of Cognitive Neuroscience* 22(1):203–211.

Liu JL, Liu JT, Hammit JK, and Chou SY (1999). The price elasticity of opium in Taiwan, 1914–1942. *Journal of Health Economics* 18:795–810.

Ljungberg T, Apicella P, and Schultz W (1992). Responses of monkey dopamine neurons during learning of behavioral reactions. *Journal of Neurophysiology* 67(1):145–163.

Llinas R (2002). *I of the Vortex*. Cambridge, MA: MIT Press.

Loewenstein G (1994). The psychology of curiosity: A review and reinterpretation. *Psychological Bulletin* 116(1):75–98.

Loftus EF and Palmer JC (1974). Reconstruction of automobile destruction. *Journal of Verbal Learning and Verbal Behavior* 13:585–589.

Logan GD and Cowan WB (1984). On the ability to inhibit thought and action: A theory of an act of control. *Psychological Review* 91(3):295–327.

Logan JS, Lively SE, and Pisoni DB (1991). Training Japanese listeners to identify English /r/ and /l/: A first report. *Journal of the Acoustical Society of America* 89(2):874–886.

Logothetis NK (2002). The neural basis of the blood-oxygen-level-dependent functional magnetic resonance imaging signal. *Philosophical Transactions of the Royal Society B: Biological Sciences* 357:1424.

Lokhorst GJ (2011). Descartes and the pineal gland. In: Zalta EN (ed.), *The Stanford Encyclopedia of Philosophy*, summer 2011 edition. Stanford University, Center for the Study of Language and Information. plato.stanford.edu/archives/sum2011/entries/pineal-gland/.

Loomes G and Sugden R (1982). Regret theory: An alternative theory of rational choice under uncertainty. *Economic Journal* 92:805–824.

Lorenz EN (1993). *The Essence of Chaos.* Seattle: University of Washington Press.

Lorenz KZ (1952/1962). *King Solomon's Ring.* New York: Thomas Y. Crowell Publishers / New York: Time Inc.

Lovinger DM (2010). Neurotransmitter roles in synaptic modulation, plasticity and learning in the dorsal striatum. *Neuropharmacology* 5(7):951–961.

Lowinson JH, Ruiz P, Millman RB, and Langrod JG (eds.) (1997). *Substance Abuse: A Comprehensive Textbook,* 3rd ed. Philadelphia: Lippincott Williams & Wilkins.

Lucas G (1977). *Star Wars: Episode IV—A New Hope.* 20th Century Fox.

Ludwig AM (1989). *Understanding the Alcoholic's Mind: The Nature of Craving and How to Control It.* New York: Oxford University Press.

Luna B, Padmanabhan A, and O'Hearn K (2010). What has fMRI told us about the development of cognitive control through adolescence? *Brain and Cognition* 72(1):101–113.

Luo S, Ainslie G, Pollini D, Giragosian L, and Monterosso JR (2012). Moderators of the association between brain activation and farsighted choice. *NeuroImage* 59(2):1469–1477.

Luria AR (1976). *The Working Brain: An Introduction to Neuropsychology.* New York: Basic Books.

Luria AR (1987). *The Man with a Shattered World: The History of a Brain Wound.* Translated by Lynn Solotaroff. Cambridge, MA: Harvard.

Lynch D and Frost M (1990–1991). *Twin Peaks.* Republic Pictures/CBS Television.

Maandag NJG, Coman D, Sanganahalli BG, Herman P, Smith AJ, Blumenfeld H, Shulman RG, and Hyder F (2007). Energetics of neuronal signaling and fMRI activity. *Proceedings of the National Academy of Sciences, USA* 104(51):20546–20551.

MacCorquodale K and Meehl PE (1948). On a distinction between hypothetical constructs and intervening variables. *Psychological Review* 55:95–107.

Mackintosh NJ (1974). *The Psychology of Animal Learning.* New York: Academic Press.

Mackowiak PA, Wasserman SS, and Levine MM (1992). A critical appraisal of 98.6°F, the upper limit of the normal body temperature, and other legacies of Carl Reinhold August Wunderlich. *Journal of the American Medical Association (JAMA)* 268:1578–1580.

MacLean PD (1973). *A Triune Concept of the Brain and Behavior.* Toronto: Ontario Mental Health Foundation and University of Toronto Press.

MacLeod CM (1991). Half a century of research on the Stroop effect: An integrative review. *Psychological Bulletin* 109(2):163–203.

Madden G and Bickel WK (eds.) (2010). *Impulsivity: The Behavioral and Neurological Science of Discounting.* Washington DC: APA Books.

Magliozzi T and Magliozzi R (1977–2012). *Car Talk.* National Public Radio.

Maia TV and Frank MJ (2011). From reinforcement learning models to psychiatric and neurological disorders. *Nature Neuroscience* 14(2):154–1652.

Maier SF and Seligman ME (1976). Learned helplessness: Theory and evidence. *Journal of Experimental Psychology: General* 105(1):3–46.

Mainen Z and Sejnowski TJ (1995). Reliability of spike timing in neocortical neurons. *Science* 268(5216):1503–1506.

Majerus M (1998). *Melanism: Evolution in Action.* New York: Oxford University Press.

Majerus M (2002). *Moths.* New York: Harper-Collins.

Malfait N, Valyear KF, Culham JC, Anton JL, Brown LE, and Gribble PL (2010). fMRI activation during observation of others' reach errors. *Journal of Cognitive Neuroscience* 22(7):1493–1503.

Manchester W (1978). *American Caesar: Douglas Macarthur 1880–1964.* New York: Back Bay Books .

Mandelstam O (1991). *Stone.* Translated with an introduction by Robert Tracy. New York: Harper-Collins.

Manski CF, Pepper J, and Petrie C (2001). *Informing America's Policy on Illegal Drugs: What We Don't Know Keeps Hurting Us.* Washington DC: National Academies Press.

Manyam BV (1990). Paralysis agitans and levodopa in "ayurveda": Ancient Indian medical treatise. *Movement Disorders* 5(1):47–48.

Margules J and Gallistel CR (1988). Heading in the rat: Determination by environmental shape. *Animal Learning and Behavior* 16(4):404–410.

Markowitz H (1952). Portfolio selection. *Journal of Finance* 7(1):77–91.

Marr D (1969). A theory of cerebellar cortex. *Journal of Physiology* 202:437–470.

Marr D (1971). Simple memory: A theory of archicortex. *Philosophical Transactions of the Royal Society of London* 262(841):23–81.

Marr D (1982). *Vision.* New York: W. H. Freeman and Co.

Marsh EB and Hillis AE (2006). Recovery from aphasia following brain injury: The role of reorganization. *Progress in Brain Research* 157:143–156.

Marshall P (1990). *Awakenings.* Columbia Pictures.

Marshall RD, Amsel L, Neria Y, and Suh EJ (2006). Strategies for dissemination of evidence-based treatments. In: Norris FH, Galea S, and Friedman MJ (eds.), *Methods for Disaster Mental Health Research.* New York: Guilford, pp. 226–239.

Martin L (1986). Eskimo words for snow: A case study in the genesis and decay of an anthropological example. *American Anthropologist* 88(2):418–423.

Martin PD (2001). Locomotion towards a goal alters the synchronous firing of neurons recorded simultaneously in the subiculum and nucleus accumbens of rats. *Behavioral Brain Research* 124(1):19–28.

Martin TA, Keating JG, Goodkin HP, Bastian AJ, and Thach WT (1996a). Throwing while looking through prisms: I. Focal olivocerebellar lesions impair adaptation. *Brain* 119(4):1183–1198.

Martin TA, Keating JG, Goodkin HP, Bastian AJ, and Thach WT (1996b). Throwing while looking through prisms II. Specificity and storage of multiple gaze-throw calibrations. *Brain* 199(4):1199–1211.

Mateas M and Sengers P (2003). *Narrative Intelligence.* Philadelphia: John Benjamins Publishing.

Mathiak KA, Klasen M, Weber R, Ackermann H, Shergill SS, and Mathiak K (2011). Reward system and temporal pole contributions to affective evaluation during a first person shooter video game. *BMC Neuroscience* 12:66.

Matsumoto M and Hikosaka O (2007). Lateral habenula as a source of negative reward signals in dopamine neurons. *Nature* 447:1111–1115.

Matsumoto M and Hikosaka O (2009). Two types of dopamine neuron distinctly convey positive and negative motivational signals. *Nature* 459(7248):837–841.

Matsuzawa T (2008). *Primate Origins of Human Cognition and Behavior.* New York: Springer.

Mayo Clinic (2011). Chest pain. www.mayoclinic.com/health/chest-pain/DS00016

Mayr E (1998). *This Is Biology: The Science of the Living World.* Cambridge, MA: Harvard University Press.

Mazur JE (2001). Hyperbolic value addition and general models of animal choice. *Psychological Review* 108(1):96–112.

Mazzoni P, Hristova A, and Krakauer JW (2007). Why don't we move faster? Parkinson's disease, movement vigor, and implicit motivation. *Journal of Neuroscience* 27(27):7105–7116.

McCartt AT, Hellinga LA, and Bratiman KA (2006). Cell phones and driving: Review of research. *Traffic Injury Prevention* 7(2):89–106.

McClelland JL, Fiez JA, and McCandliss BD (2002). Teaching the /r/-/l/ discrimination to Japanese adults: Behavioral and neural aspects. *Physiology* 77(4–5):657–662.

McClelland JL, McNaughton BL, and O'Reilly RC (1995). Why there are complementary learning systems in the hippocampus and neocortex: Insights from the successes and failures of connectionist models of learning and memory. *Psychological Review* 102(3):419–457.

McClelland JL and Rumelhart DE (eds.) (1986). *PDP: Explorations in the Microstructures of Cognition. Vol. 2, Psychological and Biological Models.* Cambridge, MA: MIT Press.

McClure SM, Ericson KM, Laibson DI, Loewenstein G, and Cohen JD (2007). Time discounting for primary rewards. *Journal of Neuroscience* 27(21):5796–5804.

McClure SM, Laibson DI, Loewenstein G, and Cohen JD (2004a). Separate neural systems value immediate and delayed monetary rewards. *Science* 306(5695):503–507.

McClure SM, Li J, Tomlin D, Cypert KS, Montague LM, and Montague PR (2004b). Neural correlates of behavioral preference for culturally familiar drinks. *Neuron* 44(2):379–387.

McComb K, Baker L, and Moss C (2005). African elephants show high levels of interest in the skulls and ivory of their own species. *Biology Letters* 2(1):26–28.

McCorduck P (2004). *Machines Who Think.* Natick, MA: A. K. Peters.

McCusker CG (2001). Cognitive biases and addiction: An evolution in theory and method. *Addiction* 96:47–56.

McDaniel MA and Einstein GO (2007). *Prospective Memory: An Overview and Synthesis of an Emerging Field*. Newbury Park: Sage Publications.

McDannald MA, Lucantonio F, Burke KA, Niv Y, and Schoenbaum G (2011). Ventral striatum and orbitofrontal cortex are both required for model-based, but not model-free, reinforcement learning. *Journal of Neuroscience* 31(7):2700–2705.

McDermott G (1972). *Anansi the Spider: A Tale from the Ashanti*. London: Macmillan.

McDermott LC (1991). What we teach and what is learned—closing the gap. Millikan Lecture, 1990. *American Journal of Physics* 59(4):301–315.

McEwan BS (1991). Steroid hormones are multifunctional messengers to the brain. *Trends in Endocrinology and Metabolism* 2(2):62–67.

McHugh PR and Slavney PR (1998). *The Perspectives of Psychiatry*. Baltimore, MD: Johns Hopkins.

McHugh R (1980). *Annotations to Finnegans Wake*. Baltimore, MD: Johns Hopkins.

McIntyre CC, Savast M, Goff LKL, and Vitek JL (2004). Uncovering the mechanism(s) of action of deep brain stimulation: Activation, inhibition, or both. *Clinical Neurophysiology* 115(6):1239–1248.

McNally GP, Johansen JP, and Blair HT (2011). Placing prediction into the fear circuit. *Trends in Neurosciences* 34(6):283–292.

McNally GP, Pigg M, and Weidemann G (2004). Blocking, unblocking, and overexpectation of fear: A role for opioid receptors in the regulation of Pavlovian association formation. *Behavioral Neuroscience* 118(1):111–120.

McNally RJ (2000). Information-processing abnormalities in obsessive-compulsive disorder. In: Goodman WK, Rudorfer MV, and Maser JD (eds.), *Obsessive-Compulsive Disorder: Contemporary Issues in Treatment*. Hillsdale, NJ: Lawrence Erlbaum, pp. 105–116.

McNaughton BL (2003). Long-term potentiation, cooperativity and Hebb's cell assemblies: A personal history. *Philosophical Transactions of the Royal Society B* 358(1432):629–634.

McNaughton BL, Douglas RM, and Goddard GV (1978). Synaptic enhancement in fascia dentata: Cooperativity among coactive afferents. *Brain Research* 157(2):277–293.

McNaughton BL and Morris RGM (1987). Hippocampal synaptic enhancement and information storage within a distributed memory system. *Trends in Neurosciences* 10(10):408–415.

McNaughton BL and Nadel L (1990). Hebb-Marr networks and the neurobiological representation of action in space. In: Gluck MA and Rumelhart DE (eds.), *Neuroscience and Connectionist Theory*. Hillsdale, NJ: Lawrence Erlbaum, pp. 1–63.

Menon V and Levitin DJ (2005). The rewards of music listening: Response and physiological connectivity of the mesolimbic system. *NeuroImage* 28(1):175–184.

Merzenich MM and Sameshima K (1993). Cortical plasticity and memory. *Current Opinion in Neurobiology* 3(2):187–196.

Mesce K and Pierce-Shimomura JT (2010). Shared strategies for behavioral switching: Understanding how locomotor patterns are turned on and off. *Frontiers in Behavioral Neuroscience* 4:49; doi: 10.3389/fnbeh.2010.00049.

Metcalfe J and Mischel W (1999). A hot/cool-system analysis of delay of gratification: Dynamics of willpower. *Psychological Review* 106(1):3–19.

Meyer R and Mirin S (1979). *The Heroin Stimulus*. New York: Plenum.

Middleton FA and Strick PL (2000). Basal ganglia and cerebellar loops: Motor and cognitive circuits. *Brain Research Reviews* 31:236–250.

Miikulainen R, Bednar J, Choe Y, and Sirosh J (2005). *Computational Maps in the Visual Cortex*. New York: Springer.

Milad MR and Quirk GJ (2002). Neurons in medial prefrontal cortex signal memory for fear extinction. *Nature* 420:70–74.

Milgram S (1974/2009). *Obedience to Authority: An Experimental View*. New York: Harper-Collins.

Mill JS (1863). *Utilitarianism*. Project Gutenberg. www.gutenberg.org.

Miller EK and Cohen JD (2001). An integrative theory of prefrontal cortex function. *Annual Review of Neuroscience* 24:167–202.

Miller G (1956). The magical number seven, plus or minus two: some limits on our capacity for processing information. *Psychological Review* 63(2):81–97.

Miller JP, Jacobs GA, and Theunissen FE (1991). Representation of sensory information in the cricket cercal sensory system. I. Response properties of the primary interneurons. *Journal of Neurophysiology* 66(5):1680–1689.

Milner AD and Goodale MA (1995). *The Visual Brain in Action*. New York: Oxford University Press.

Milner B (1998). Retrospective. In: Squire LR (ed.), *The History of Neuroscience in Autobiography*. New York: Academic Press, pp. 276–305.

Milner B, Corkin S, and Teuber H (1968). Further analysis of the hippocampal amnesia syndrome: 14-year follow-up study of H. M. *Neuropsychologia* 6:215–234.

Milton J (1674/1975). *Paradise Lost*. New York: W. W. Norton.

Minsky M (1985). *Society of Mind*. New York: Simon and Schuster.

Mintz SW (1986). *Sweetness and Power: The Place of Sugar in Modern History*. New York: Penguin.

Mirowsky J and Ross CE (1989). Psychiatric diagnosis as reified measurement. *Journal of Health and Social Behavior* 30(1):11–25.

Mischel W, Shoda Y, and Rodriguez ML (1989). Delay of gratification in children. *Science* 244(4907):933–938.

Mischel W and Underwood B (1974). Instrumental ideation in delay of gratification. *Child Development* 45:1083–1088.

Mishkin M and Appenzeller T (1987). The anatomy of memory. *Scientific American* 256(6):80–89.

Mitchell M (1993). *Analogy-Making as Perception*. Cambridge, MA: MIT Press.

Mitchell T (1997). *Machine Learning*. New York: McGraw-Hill.

Miyawaki K, Jenkins JJ, Strange W, Liberman AM, Verbrugge R, and Fujimura O (1975). An effect of linguistic experience: The discrimination of [r] and [l] by native speakers of Japanese and English. *Attention, Perception, and Psychophysics* 18(5):331–340.

Miyazaki KW, Miyazaki K, and Doya K (2010). Activation of the central serotonergic system in response to delayed but not omitted rewards. *European Journal of Neuroscience* 33(1):153–160.

Miyazaki K, Miyazaki KW, and Doya K (2012a). The role of serotonin in the regulation of patience and impulsivity. *Molecular Neurobiology* 45(2):213–224.

Miyazaki KW, Miyazaki K, and Doya K (2012b). Activation of dorsal raphe serotonin neurons is necessary for waiting for delayed rewards. *Journal of Neuroscience* 32(31):10451–10457.

Mizunami M, Unoki S, Mori Y, Hirashima D, Hatano A, and Matsumoto Y (2009). Roles of octopaminergic and dopaminergic neurons in appetitive and aversive memory recall in an insect. *BMC Biology* 7:46; doi:10.1186/1741-7007-7-46.

Mlodinow L (2009). *The Drunkard's Walk: How Randomness Rules Our Lives*. New York: Vintage.

Mobini S, Chiang TJ, Al-Ruwaitea AS, Ho MY, Bradshaw CM, and Szabadi E (2000). Effect of central 5-hydroxytryptamine depletion on inter-temporal choice: A quantitative analysis. *Psychopharmacology* 149(3):313–318.

Mogenson GJ, Jones DL, and Yim CY (1980). From motivation to action: Functional interface between the limbic system and the motor system. *Progress in Neurobiology* 14:69–97.

Mohr JP, Lazar RM, Marshall RS, and Hier DB (2004). Middle cerebral artery disease. In: Mohr JP, Choi DW, Grotta JC, Weir B, and Wolf PA (eds.), *Stroke: Pathophysiology, Diagnosis, and Management*. Philadelphia: Churchill-Livingstone, Chapter 7, pp. 123–166.

Molewijk HE, van der Poel AM, and Oliver B (1995). The ambivalent behaviour "stretched approach posture" in the rat as a paradigm to characterize anxiolytic drugs. *Psychopharmacology* 121(1):81–90.

Molinari M, Chiricozzi FR, Clausi S, Tedesco AM, Lisa MD, and Leggio MG (2008). Cerebellum and detection of sequences, from perception to cognition. *Cerebellum* 7(4):611–615.

Moll J, Krueger F, Zahn R, Pardini M, de Oliveira-Souza R, and Grafman J (2006). Human fronto-mesolimbic networks guide decisions about charitable donation. *Proceedings of the National Academy of Sciences, USA* 103(42):15623–15628.

Montague PR (2006). *Why Choose This Book?* New York: Penguin.

Montague PR, Dayan P, Person C, and Sejnowski TJ (1995). Bee foraging in uncertain environments using predictive hebbian learning. *Nature* 377(6551):725–728.

Montague PR, Dayan P, and Sejnowski TJ (1996). A framework for mesencephalic dopamine systems based on predictive Hebbian learning. *Journal of Neuroscience* 16(5):1936–1947.

Montague PR, Dolan RJ, Friston KJ, and Dayan P (2012). Computational psychiatry. *Trends in Cognitive Sciences* 16(1):72–80.

Monti PM and MacKillop J (2007). Advances in the treatment of craving for alcohol and tobacco. In: Miller PM and Kavanagh DJ (eds.), *Translation of Addiction Science into Practice*. London: Elsevier, pp. 209–235.

Moore RD and Larson GA (2004–2009). *Battlestar Galactica*. SciFi Channel.

Moos RH and Moos BS (2004). Long-term influence of duration and frequency of participation in alcoholics anonymous on individuals with alcohol use disorders. *Journal of Consulting and Clinical Psychology* 72(1):81–90.

Moos RH and Moos BS (2006). Participation in treatment and alcoholics anonymous: A 16-year follow-up of initially untreated individuals. *Journal of Clinical Psychology* 62(6):735–750.

Morgan H (1990). Dostoevsky's epilepsy: A case report and comparison. *Surgical Neurology* 33(6):413–416.

Morris G, Nevet A, Arkadir D, Vaadia E, and Bergman H (2006). Midbrain dopamine neurons encode decisions for future action. *Nature Neuroscience* 9:1057–1063.

Morris RGM (1981). Spatial localization does not require the presence of local cues. *Learning and Motivation* 12:239–260.

Morris RGM, Garrud P, Rawlins JNP, and O'Keefe J (1982). Place navigation impaired in rats with hippocampal lesions. *Nature* 297:681–683.

Moscowitz A, Nadel L, Watts P, and Jacobs WJ (2008). Delusional atmosphere, the psychotic pro-drome, and decontextualized memories. In: Moscowitz A, Schäfer I, and Dorahy MJ (eds.), *Psychosis, Trauma, and Dissociation*. New York: Wiley, pp. 65–78.

Moss C (2000). *Elephant Memories: Thirteen Years in the Life of an Elephant Family*. Chicago: University of Chicago Press.

Moulitsas M (2010). www.dailykos.com/story/2010/01/28/831461/-Midday-open-thread.

Mountcastle VB (1997). The columnar organization of the neocortex. *Brain* 120:701–722.

Moustafa AA and Gluck MA (2011). A neurocomputational model of dopamine and prefrontal-striatal interactions during multicue category learning by Parkinson patients. *Journal of Cognitive Neuroscience* 23(1):151–167.

Mozer M (2004). Lessons from an adaptive house. In: Cook D and Das S (eds.), *Smart Environments: Technology, Protocols and Applications*. New York: Wiley, Chapter 12, pp. 273–294.

Mucha RF and Herz A (1985). Motivational properties of kappa and mu opioid receptor agonists studied with place and taste preference conditioning. *Psychopharmacology* 86:274–280.

Muenzinger KF (1938). Vicarious trial and error at a point of choice. I. A general survey of its rela-tion to learning efficiency. *Journal of Genetic Psychology* 53:75–86.

Muenzinger KF and Gentry E (1931). Tone discrimination in white rats. *Journal of Comparative Psychology* 12(2):195–206.

Munn NL (1950). *Handbook of Psychological Research on the Rat*. Boston: Houghton Mifflin.

Muraven M, Shmueli D, and Burkley E (2006). Conserving self-control strength. *Journal of Personality and Social Psychology* 91(3):524–537.

Murray JD (2003). *Mathematical Biology II. Spatial Models and Biomedical Applications*. New York: Springer.

Mushiake H, Inase M, and Tanji J (1991). Neuronal activity in the primate premotor, supplemen-tary, and precentral motor cortex during visually guided and internally determined sequential movements. *Journal of Neurophysiology* 66(3):705–718.

Mussa-Ivaldi FAS (2000). Neural engineering: Real brains for real robots. *Nature* 408:305–306.

Mussa-Ivaldi FAS, Alford ST, Chiappalone M, Fadiga L, Karniel A, Kositsky M, Maggiolini E, Panzeri S, Sanguineti V, Semprini M, and Vato A (2009). New perspectives on the dialogue between brains and machines. *Frontiers in Neuroscience* 4(1):44–52.

Myers CE, Shohamy D, Gluck MA, Grossman S, Onlaor S, and Kapur N (2003). Dissociating medial temporal and basal ganglia memory systems with a latent learning task. *Neuropsychologia* 41:1919–1928.

Myers KM and Davis M (2007). Mechanisms of fear extinction. *Molecular Psychiatry* 12:120–150.

Myers KM and Davis M (2002). Behavioral and neural analysis of extinction. *Neuron* 36(4):567–584.

Nachman M and Ashe JH (1973). Learned taste aversion in rats as a function of dosage, concentra-tion, and route of administration of LiCl. *Physiology and Behavior* 10:73–78.

Nádasdy Z, Hirase H, Czurkó A, Csicsvari J, and Buzsáki G (1999). Replay and time compression of recurring spike sequences in the hippocampus. *Journal of Neuroscience* 19(2):9497–9507.

Nadel L and Jacobs WJ (1996). The role of the hippocampus in PTSD, panic, and phobia. In: Kato N (ed.), *The Hippocampus: Functions and Clinical Relevance*. London: Elsevier, pp. 455–463.

Nadel L and Land C (2000). Memory traces revisited. *Nature Reviews Neuroscience* 1:209–212.

Nadel L and Moscovitch M (1997). Memory consolidation, retrograde amnesia and the hippocampal complex. *Current Opinion in Neurobiology* 7:217–227.

Nadel L and Willner J (1980). Context and conditioning: A place for space. *Physiological Psychology* 8(2):218–228.

Nader MA and Woolverton WL (1991). Effects of increasing the magnitude of an alternative reinforcer on drug choice in a discrete-trials choice procedure. *Psychopharmacology* 105:169–174.

Nair DG (2005). About being BOLD. *Brain Research Reviews* 50:229–243.

Najib A, Lorberbaum JP, Kose S, Bohning DE, and George MS (2004). Regional brain activity in women grieving a romantic relationship breakup. *American Journal of Psychiatry* 161:2245–2256.

Nakazawa K, Quirk MC, Chitwood RA, Watanabe M, Yeckel MF, Sun LD, Kato A, Carr CA, Johnston D, Wilson MA, and Tonegawa S (2002). Requirement for hippocampal CA3 NMDA receptors in associative memory recall. *Science* 297(5579):211–218.

Nambu A, Tokuno H, and Takada M (2002). Functional significance of the cortico-subthalamo-pallidal "hyperdirect" pathway. *Neuroscience Research* 43(2):111–117.

NASA (2011). The Apollo 15 hammer-feather drop. nssdc.gsfc.nasa.gov/planetary/lunar/apollo_15_feather_drop.html.

Nash J (1951). Non-cooperative games. *Annals of Mathematics* 54(2):286–295.

Nassar S (2001). *A Beautiful Mind: The Life of Mathematical Genius and Nobel Laureate John Nash*. New York: Simon and Schuster.

New York Times (2011). Times topics: Pentagon Papers. topics.nytimes.com/top/reference/timestopics/subjects/p/pentagon_papers/index.html

Newell A (1990). *Unified Theories of Cognition*. Cambridge, MA: Harvard University Press.

Newell A (1993). *The Last Lecture: Desires and Diversions*. Pittsburgh, PA: Carnegie Mellon University, School of Computer Science, University Video Communications.

Newell A, Shaw JC, and Simon HA (1959). Report on a general problem-solving program. *Proceedings of the International Conference on Information Processing* pp. 256–264.

Newton I (1687/1726). *Philosophiae Naturalis Principia Mathematica*. London: Royal Society.

Nicolelis MAL and Lebedev MA (2009). Principles of neural ensemble physiology underlying the operation of brain-machine interfaces. *Nature Reviews Neuroscience* 10:530–540.

Nicolle A, Symmonds M, and Dolan RJ (2011). Optimistic biases in observational learning of value. *Cognition* 119(3):394–402.

Niedermeyer E and Lopes da Silva F (eds.) (1999). *Electroencephalography: Basic Principles, Clinical Applications, and Related Fields*. Philadelphia, PA: Lippincott Williams & Wilkins.

Nijslow IM, Franken IH, and Muris P (2010). Food-related Stroop interference in obese and normal-weight individuals: Behavioral and electrophysiological indices. *Eating Behaviors* 11(4):258–265.

Nili U, Goldberg H, Weizman A, and Dudai Y (2010). Fear thou not: Activity of frontal and temporal circuits in moments of real-life courage. *Neuron* 66(6):949–962.

Nilsson NJ (1998). *Artificial Intelligence*. San Francisco, CA: Morgan Kaufmann.

NIMH (2011). Suicide in the U.S.: Statistics and prevention. *NIH Publication No. 06-4594.* www.nimh.nih.gov/health/publications/suicide-in-the-us-statistics-and-prevention/index.shtml

Nissen MJ and Bullemer P (1987). Attentional requirements of learning: Evidence from performance measures. *Cognitive Psychology* 19:1–32.

Niv Y, Daw ND, and Dayan P (2006a). Choice values. *Nature Neuroscience* 9:987–988.

Niv Y, Daw ND, Joel D, and Dayan P (2006b). Tonic dopamine: Oppportunity costs and the control of response vigor. *Psychopharmacology* 191(3):507–520.

Niv Y, Joel D, and Dayan P (2006c). A normative perspective on motivation. *Trends in Cognitive Sciences* 10(8):375–381.

Niv Y and Rivlin-Etzion M (2007). Parkinson's disease: Fighting the will. *Journal of Neuroscience* 27(44):11777–11779.

Niv Y and Schoenbaum G (2008). Dialogues on prediction errors. *Trends in Cognitive Sciences* 12(7):265–272.

Niven L (1969). Death by ecstasy. *Galaxy*. Reprinted in *The Long Arm of Gil Hamilton*, New York: Ballentine Books, 1976.

Noad MJ, Cato DH, Bryden MM, Jenner MN, and Jenner KCS (2000). Cultural revolution in whale songs. *Nature* 408:537.

Nolan C (2000). *Memento*. Summit Entertainment.

Norman DA (1988). *The Psychology of Everyday Things*. New York: Basic Books.

Nourski KV and Brugge JF (2011). Representation of temporal sound features in the human auditory cortex. *Reviews in the Neurosciences* 22(2):187–203.

Nowlis DP and Kamiya J (1970). The control of electroencephalographic alpha rhythms through auditory feedback and the associated mental activity. *Psychophysiology* 6(4):476–484.

O'Brien CP (2011). Addiction and dependence in DSM-V. *Addiction* 106(5):866–867.

O'Brien CP, Childress AR, Ehrman R, and Robbins SJ (1998). Conditioning factors in drug abuse: Can they explain compulsion? *Journal of Psychopharmacology* 12(1):15–22.

O'Brien CP, Testa T, O'Brien TJ, Brady JP, and Wells B (1977). Conditioned narcotic withdrawal in humans. *Science* 195:1000–1002.

O'Brien RC (1971). *Mrs. Frisby and the Rats of NIMH*. New York: Atheneum.

O'Doherty JP (2004). Reward representations and reward-related learning in the human brain: Insights from neuroimaging. *Current Opinion in Neurobiology* 14:769–776.

O'Doherty JP, Buchanan TW, Seymour B, and Dolan RJ (2006). Predictive neural coding of reward preference involves dissociable responses in human ventral midbrain and ventral striatum. *Neuron* 49(1):157–166.

O'Doherty JP, Dayan P, Friston K, Critchley H, and Dolan RJ (2003). Temporal difference models and reward-related learning in the human brain. *Neuron* 38(2):329–337.

O'Keefe J and Nadel L (1978). *The Hippocampus as a Cognitive Map*. London: Oxford University Press.

Olds J and Milner P (1954). Positive reinforcement produced by electrical stimulation of septal area and other regions of rat brain. *Journal of Comparative Physiological Psychology* 47:419–427.

Olds ME and Fobes JL (1981). The central basis of motivation: Intracranial self-stimulation studies. *Annual Review of Psychology* 32:523–574.

Olfson M and Marcus SC (2009). National patterns in antidepressant medication treatment. *Archives of General Psychiatry* 66(8):848–856.

Op de Beeck HP, Haushofer J, and Kanwisher NG (2008). Interpreting fMRI data: Maps, modules and dimensions. *Nature Reviews Neuroscience* 9:123–125.

O'Reilly RC and McClelland JL (1994). Hippocampal conjunctive encoding, storage, and recall: Avoiding a trade-off. *Hippocampus* 4(6):661–682.

Orwell G (1949). *1984*. London: Secker and Warburg.

Osborne MJ (2004). *An Introduction to Game Theory*. New York: Oxford University Press.

Oscar-Berman M and Marinkovic K (2003). Alcoholism and the brain: An overview. *Alcohol Research and Health* 27(2):125–134.

Ostlund SB and Balleine BW (2007). The contribution of orbitofrontal cortex to action selection. *New York Academy of Sciences* 1121:174–192.

Packard MG and McGaugh JL (1996). Inactivation of hippocampus or caudate nucleus with lidocaine differentially affects expression of place and response learning. *Neurobiology of Learning and Memory* 65:65–72.

Padoa-Schioppa C (2009). Range-adapting representation of economic value in the orbitofrontal cortex. *Journal of Neuroscience* 29(4):14004–14014.

Padoa-Schioppa C and Assad JA (2006). Neurons in the orbitofrontal cortex encode economic value. *Nature* 441:223–226.

Pagels H (1984). *The Cosmic Code: Quantum Physics as the Language of Nature*. New York: Bantam Books.

Pagels H (1991). *Perfect Symmetry: The Search for the Beginning of Time*. New York: Bantam Books.

Pagnoni G, Zink CF, Montague PR, and Berns GS (2002). Activity in human ventral striatum locked to errors in reward prediction. *Nature Neuroscience* 5(2):97–98.

Pak CW, Flynn KC, and Bamburg JR (2008). Actin-binding proteins take the reins in growth cones. *Nature Reviews Neuroscience* 9:136–147.

Paladini CA and Williams JT (2004). Noradrenergic inhibition of midbrain dopamine neurons. *Journal of Neuroscience* 24(19):4568–4575.

Pan WX, Schmidt R, Wickens JR, and Hyland BI (2005). Dopamine cells respond to predicted events during classical conditioning: Evidence for eligibility traces in the reward-learning network. *Journal of Neuroscience* 25(26):6235–6242.

Papale AE, Stott JJ, Powell NJ, Regier PS, and Redish AD (2012). Interactions between deliberation and delay-discounting in rats. *Cognitive, Affective, and Behavioral Neuroscience* 12(3):513–526.

Paré D, Quirk GJ, and Ledoux JE (2004). New vistas on amygdala networks in conditioned fear. *Journal of Neurophysiology* 92:1–9.

Parent A (1986). *Comparative Neurobiology of the Basal Ganglia.* New York: Wiley.

Parkinson J (1817/2002). An essay on the shaking palsy. *Journal of Neuropsychiatry and Clinical Neurosciences* 14:223–236. Originally published by Sherwood, Neely, and Jones, London.

Pascal B (1669). *Pensées.* Paris: G. Desprez.

Pascual-Leone A, Grafman J, and Hallett M (1994). Modulation of cortical motor output maps during development of implicit and explicit knowledge. *Science* 263:1287–1289.

Passingham RE (1993). *The Frontal Lobes and Voluntary Action.* New York: Oxford University Press.

Patterson F and Linden E (1981). *The Education of Koko.* New York: Holt, Rinehart, and Winston.

Paul O (1987). Da Costa's syndrome or neuocirculatory asthenia. *British Heart Journal* 58:306–315.

Pavlides C and Winson J (1989). Influences of hippocampal place cell firing in the awake state on the activity of these cells during subsequent sleep episodes. *Journal of Neuroscience* 9(8):2907–2918.

Pavlov I (1927). *Conditioned Reflexes.* Oxford, UK: Oxford University Press.

Payne JD, Jackson ED, Hoscheidt S, Ryan L, Jacobs WJ, and Nadel L (2007). Stress administered prior to encoding impairs neutral but enhances emotional long-term episodic memories. *Learning and Memory* 14(12):861–868.

Payzan-LeNestour E and Bossaerts P (2011). Risk, unexpected uncertainty, and estimation uncertainty: Bayesian learning in unstable settings. *PLoS Computational Biology* 7(1):e1001048.

Pearl J (1988). *Probabilistic Reasoning in Intelligent Systems: Networks of Plausible Inference.* San Francisco, CA: Morgan Kaufmann.

Pei Y, Rogan SC, Yan F, and Roth BL (2008). Engineered GPCRs as tools to modulate signal transduction. *Physiology* 23(6):313–321.

Penfield W (1946). Psychical seizures. *British Medical Journal* 2(4478):639–641.

Penfield W (1975). *The Mystery of the Mind: A Critical Study of Consciousness and the Human Brain.* Princeton, NJ: Princeton University Press.

Penfield W and Rasmussen T (1950). *The Cerebral Cortex of Man.* New York: Macmillan.

Penfield W and Steelman H (1947). The treatment of focal epilepsy by cortical excision. *Annals of Surgery* 126(5):740–762.

Pennartz CMA, Lee E, Verheul J, Lipa P, Barnes CA, and McNaughton BL (2004). The ventral striatum in off-line processing: Ensemble reactivation during sleep and modulation by hippocampal ripples. *Journal of Neuroscience* 24(29):6446–6456.

Penrose R (1980/1989). *The Emperor's New Mind.* New York: Penguin / New York: Oxford University Press.

Pepperberg I (2009). *Alex and Me: How a Scientist and a Parrot Discovered a Hidden World of Animal Intelligence–and Formed a Deep Bond in the Process.* New York: Harper-Collins.

Perkins KA (2009). Does smoking cue-induced craving tell us anything important about nicotine dependence? *Addiction* 104:1610–1616.

Perkins KA, Gerlach D, Broge M, Fonte C, and Wilson A (2001). Reinforcing effects of nicotine as a function of smoking status. *Experimental and Clinical Psychopharmacology* 9(3):243–250.

Peters J and Büchel C (2010). Episodic future thinking reduces reward delay discounting through an enhancement of prefrontal-mediotemporal interactions. *Neuron* 66(1):138–148.

Peterson D and Goodall J (2000). *Visions of Caliban: On Chimpanzees and People.* Athens, GA: University of Georgia Press.

Petry NM (2011). *Contingency Management for Substance Abuse Treatment: A Guide to Implementing This Evidence-Based Practice.* London: Routledge.

Pezzulo G and Castelfranchi C (2009). Thinking as the control of imagination: A conceptual framework for goal-directed systems. *Psychological Research* 73:559–577.

Phelps E (2008). The study of emotion in neuroeconomics. In: Glimcher PW, Camerer C, Poldrack RA, and Fehr E (eds.), *Neuroeconomics: Decision Making in the Brain.* New York: Academic Press, pp. 233–250.

Phelps EA and LeDoux JE (2005). Contributions of the amygdala to emotion processing: From animal models to human behavior. *Neuron* 48(2):175–187.

Phelps EA, O'Connor KJ, and Chi J (2001). Activation of the left amygdala to a cognitive representation of fear. *Nature* 4:437–441.

Pillutla MM and Murnighan JK (1996). Unfairness, anger, and spite: Emotional rejections of ultimatum offers. *Organizational Behavior and Human Decision Processes* 68(3):208–224.

Pinker S (2007). *The Language Instinct*. New York: Harper-Collins.

Piray P, Keramati MM, Dezfouli A, Lucas C, and Mokri A (2010). Individual differences in nucleus accumbens dopamine receptors predict development of addiction-like behavior: A computational approach. *Neural Computation* 22(9):2334–2368.

Pirolli P (2007). *Information Foraging Theory: Adaptive Interaction with Information*. New York: Oxford University Press.

Pitman RK, Gilbertson MW, Gurvits TV, May FS, Lasko NB, Metzger LJ, Shenton ME, Yehuda R, and Orr SP (2006). Clarifying the origin of biological abnormalities in PTSD through the study of identical twins discordant for combat exposure. *Annals of the New York Academy of Sciences* 1071:242–254.

Pizarro J, Silver RC, and Prause J (2006). Physical and mental health costs of traumatic war experiences among Civil War veterans. *Archives of General Psychiatry* 63(2):193–200.

Plassmann H, O'Doherty JP, Shiv B, and Rangel A (2008). Marketing actions can modulate neural representations of experienced pleasantness. *Proceedings of the National Academy of Sciences, USA* 105(3):1050–1054.

Plassmann H, O'Doherty JP, and Rangel A (2010). Appetitive and aversive goal values are encoded in the medial orbitofrontal cortex at the time of decision making. *Journal of Neuroscience* 30(32):10799–10808.

Plato (4th century BCE/2008a). *Cratylus*. Translated by Benjamin Jowett. Project Gutenberg. www.gutenberg.org.

Plato (4th century BCE/2008b). *Phaedrus*. Translated by Benjamin Jowett. Project Gutenberg. www.gutenberg.org

Platt ML and Glimcher PW (1999). Neural correlates of decision variables in parietal cortex. *Nature* 400:233–238.

Plous S (1993). *The Psychology of Judgement and Decision-Making*. New York: McGraw-Hill.

Podoll K and Robinson D (2002). The migrainous nature of the visions of Hildegard of Bingen. *Neurology: Psychiatry and Brain Research* 10:95–100.

Podoll K and Robinson D (2009). *Migraine Art: The Migraine Experience from Within*. Berkeley, CA: North Atlantic Publications.

Poe GR, Nitz DA, McNaughton BL, and Barnes CA (2000). Experience-dependent phase-reversal of hippocampal neuron firing during REM sleep. *Brain Research* 855:176–180.

Poe GR, Walsh CM, and Bjorness TE (2010). Cognitive neuroscience of sleep. *Progress in Brain Research* 185:1–19.

Politser P (2008). *Neuroeconomics*. New York: Oxford University Press.

Popper KR (1935/1959/1992). *The Logic of Scientific Discovery*. Vienna: Springer-Verlag / London: Hutchinson / London: Routledge.

Potenza MN, Kosten TR, and Rounsaville BJ (2001). Pathological gambling. *Journal of the American Medical Association (JAMA)* 286(2):141–144.

Potenza MN, Sofuoglu M, Carroll KM, and Rounsaville BJ (2011). Neuroscience of behavioral and pharmacological treatments for addictions. *Neuron* 69:695–712.

Preuschoff K, Bossaerts P, and Quartz SR (2006). Neural differentiation of expected reward and risk in human subcortical structures. *Neuron* 51(3):381–390.

Preuss TM (1995). Do rats have prefrontal cortex? The Rose-Woolsey-Akert program reconsidered. *Journal of Cognitive Neuroscience* 7(1):1–24.

Pritchard TC, Nedderman EN, Edwards EM, Petticoffer AC, Schwartz GJ, and Scott TR (2008). Satiety-responsive neurons in the medial orbitofrontal cortex of the macaque. *Behavioral Neuroscience* 122(1):174–182.

Protopoescu X, Pan H, Tuescher O, Clotre M, Goldtein M, Engelien W, Epstein J, Yang Y, Gorman J, LeDoux J, Silbersweig D, and Stern E (2005). Differential time courses and specificity of amygdala activity in posttraumatic stress disorder subjects and normal control subjects. *Biological Psychiatry* 57(5):464–473.

Puhl J and Mesce K (2008). Dopamine activates the motor pattern for crawling in the medicinal leech. *Journal of Neuroscience* 28(16):4192–4200.

Purdon-Martin J (1967). *The Basal Ganglia and Posture*. Philadelphia: Lippincott Williams & Wilkins.

Purves D, Augustine GJ, Fitzpatrick D, Hall WC, LaMantia AS, McNamara JO, and White LE (eds.) (2008). *Neuroscience*. Sunderland, MA: Sinauer Associates.

Purves D, White LE, and Riddle DR (1996). Is neural development Darwinian? *Trends in Neurosciences* 19(11):460–464.

Qi S, Ding C, Song Y, and Yan D (2011). Neural correlates of near-misses effect in gambling. *Neuroscience Letters* 493(3):80–85.

Qin YL, McNaughton BL, Skaggs WE, and Barnes CA (1997). Memory reprocessing in cortico-cortical and hippocampocortical neuronal ensembles. *Philosophical Transactions of the Royal Society, London B* 352(1360):1525–1533.

Quirk GJ (2002). Memory for extinction of conditioned fear is long-lasting and persists following spontaneous recovery. *Learning and Memory* 9(6):402–407.

Quirk GJ (2006). Extinction: New excitement for an old phenomenon. *Biological Psychiatry* 60(4):317–422.

Raby CR and Clayton NS (2009). Prospective cognition in animals. *Behavioural Processes* 80(3): 314–324.

Race E, Keane MM, and Verfaellie M (2011). Medial temporal lobe damage causes deficits in episodic memory and episodic future thinking not attributable to deficits in narrative construction. *Journal of Neuroscience* 31(28):10262–10269.

Rachlin H (2004). *The Science of Self-Control*. Cambridge, MA: Harvard University Press.

Raghunathan R (1999). All negative moods are not equal: Motivational influences of anxiety and sadness on decision making. *Organizational Behavior and Human Decision Processes* 79(1):56–77.

Rahman M, Abd-El-Barr MM, Vedam-Mai V, Foote KD, Murad GJA, Okun MS, and Roper SN (2010). Disrupting abnormal electrical activity with deep brain stimulation: Is epilepsy the next frontier? *Neurosurgical Focus* 29(2):E7.

Ramachandran VS (2011). *The Tell-Tale Brain: A Neuroscientist's Quest for What Makes Us Human*. New York: W. W. Norton.

Ramachandran VS and Blakeslee S (1999). *Phantoms in the Brain: Probing the Mysteries of the Human Mind*. New York: Harper-Collins.

Ramus SJ, Davis JB, Donahue RJ, Discenza CB, and Waite AA (2007). Interactions between the orbitofrontal cortex and hippocampal memory system during the storage of long-term memory. *Annals of the New York Academy of Sciences* 1121:216–231.

Rand MK, Hikosaka O, Miyachi S, Lu X, and Miyashita K (1998). Characteristics of a long-term procedural skill in the monkey. *Experimental Brain Research* 118:293–297.

Rand MK, Hikosaka O, Miyachi S, Lu X, Nakamura K, Kitaguchi K, and Shimo Y (2000). Characteristics of sequential movements during early learning period in monkeys. *Experimental Brain Research* 131:293–304.

Rangel A and Hare T (2010). Neural computations associated with goal-directed choice. *Current Opinion in Neurobiology* 20:262–270.

Raskind MA (2009). Pharmacologic treatment of PTSD. In: Shiromani PJ, Keane TM, and Ledoux JE (eds.), *Post-Traumatic Stress Disorder: Basic Science and Clinical Practice*. New York: Humana, pp. 337–362.

Ratcliff R and McKoon G (2008). The diffusion decision model: Theory and data for two-choice decision tasks. *Neural Computation* 20:873–922.

Rawls J (1971). *A Theory of Justice*. Cambridge, MA: Harvard University Press.

Rawls J (1985). Justice as fairness: Political not metaphysical. *Philosophy and Public Affairs* 14(3):223–251.

Read SJ, Vanman EJ, and Miller LC (1997). Connectionism, parallel constraint satisfaction processes, and gestalt principles: (re)introducing cognitive dynamics to social psychology. *Personality and Social Psychology Review* 1(1):26–53.

Reber AS (1989). Implicit learning and tacit knowledge. *Journal of Experimental Psychology: General* 118(3):219–235.

Redgrave P, Prescott TJ, and Gurney K (1999). Is the short-latency dopamine response too short to signal reward error? *Trends in Neurosciences* 22(4):146–151.

Redish AD (1999). *Beyond the Cognitive Map: From Place Cells to Episodic Memory*. Cambridge, MA: MIT Press.

Redish AD (2004). Addiction as a computational process gone awry. *Science* 306(5703): 1944–1947.

Redish AD (2009). Implications of the multiple-vulnerabilities theory of addiction for craving and relapse. *Addiction* 104(11):1940–1941.

Redish AD (2013). *The Mind Within the Brain: How We Make Decisions and How Those Decisions Go Wrong*. New York: Oxford University Press.

Redish AD, Elga AN, and Touretzky DS (1996). A coupled attractor model of the rodent head direction system. *Network: Computation in Neural Systems* 7(4):671–685.

Redish AD, Jensen S, and Johnson A (2008). A unified framework for addiction: Vulnerabilities in the decision process. *Behavioral and Brain Sciences* 31:415–487.

Redish AD, Jensen S, Johnson A, and Kurth-Nelson Z (2007). Reconciling reinforcement learning models with behavioral extinction and renewal: Implications for addiction, relapse, and problem gambling. *Psychological Review* 114(3):784–805.

Redish AD and Johnson A (2007). A computational model of craving and obsession. *Annals of the New York Academy of Sciences* 1104(1):324–339.

Redish AD and Kurth-Nelson Z (2010). Neural models of temporal discounting. In: Madden G and Bickel W (eds.), *Impulsivity: The Behavioral and Neurological Science of Discounting*. Washington DC: APA Books, pp. 123–158.

Redish AD and Touretzky DS (1998). The role of the hippocampus in solving the Morris water maze. *Neural Computation* 10(1):73–111.

Redish LC (1997). *In Another Manner of Speaking: Changes in Code Among Children in an Expert Domain*. Master's thesis, Department of Linguistics, University of Pittsburgh, Pittsburgh, PA.

Reger BD, Fleming KM, Sanguineti V, Alford S, and Mussa-Ivaldi FA (2000). Connecting brains to robots: An artificial body for studying the computational properties of neural tissues. *Artificial Life* 6(4):307–324.

Reggia JA and Montgomery D (1996). A computational model of visual hallucinations in migraine. *Computational Biology of Medicine* 26(2):133–141.

Reicher S and Haslam SA (2011). After shock? Towards a social identity explanation of the Milgram "obedience" studies. *British Journal of Social Psychology* 50:163–169.

Reid RL (1986). The psychology of the near miss. *Journal of Gambling Studies* 2(1):32–39.

Reinhardt UE (2010a). Is "more efficient" always better? *New York Times* economix.blogs.nytimes.com/2010/08/20/is-more-efficient-always-better/.

Reinhardt UE (2010b). When value judgments masquerade as science. *New York Times* economix.blogs.nytimes.com/2010/08/27/when-value-judgments-masquerade-as-science/.

Rescorla RA (1988). Pavlovian conditioning: It's not what you think it is. *American Psychologist* 43(3):151–160.

Rescorla RA (2004). Spontaneous recovery. *Learning and Memory* 11(5):501–509.

Rescorla RA and Wagner AR (1972). A theory of Pavlovian conditioning: Variations in the effectiveness of reinforcement and nonreinforcement. In: Black AH and Prokesy WF (eds.), *Classical Conditioning II: Current Research and Theory*. New York: Appleton Century Crofts, pp. 64–99.

Ressler KJ, Rothbaum BO, Tannenbaum L, Anderson P, Graap K, Zimand E, Hodges L, and Davis M (2004). Cognitive enhancers as adjuncts to psychotherapy: Use of D-cycloserine in phobic individuals to facilitate extinction of fear. *Archives of General Psychiatry* 61(11):1136–1144.

Restle F (1957). Discrimination of cues in mazes: A resolution of the "place-vs-response" question. *Psychological Review* 64:217–228.

Rhodes G (2006). The evolution of facial beauty. *Annual Review of Psychology* 57:199–226.

Rich E and Knight K (1991). *Artificial Intelligence*. New York: McGraw-Hill.

Rich EL and Shapiro M (2009). Rat prefrontal cortical neurons selectively code strategy switches. *Journal of Neuroscience* 29(22):7208–7219.

Richerson PJ and Boyd R (2005). *Not by Genes Alone: How Culture Transformed Human Evolution*. Chicago: Chicago University Press.

Rick JH, Horvitz JC, and Balsam PD (2006). Dopamine receptor blockade and extinction differentially affect behavioral variability. *Behavioral Neuroscience* 120(2):488–492.

Ridley M (1995). *The Red Queen: Sex and the Evolution of Human Nature.* New York: Penguin.

Ridley M (2000). *Genome: The Autobiography of a Species in 23 Chapters.* New York: Harper-Collins.

Ridley M (2003). *Nature via Nurture: Genes, Experience, and What Makes Us Human.* New York: Harper-Collins. Also released as *The Agile Gene: How Nature Turns on Nurture.*

Riegel J (2011). Confucius. In: Zalta EN (ed.), *The Stanford Encyclopedia of Philosophy,* spring 2011 edition. Stanford University, Center for the Study of Language and Information. plato.stanford.edu/archives/spr2011/entries/confucius/.

Rieke F, Warland D, de Ruyter van Steveninck R, and Bialek W (1997). *Spikes.* Cambridge, MA: MIT Press.

Rilling JK, Gutman DA, Zeh TR, Pagnoni G, Berns GS, and Kilts CD (2002). A neural basis for social cooperation. *Neuron* 35(2):395–405.

Rilling JK, Sanfey AG, Aronson JA, Nystrom LE, and Cohen JD (2004). Opposing BOLD responses to reciprocated and unreciprocated altruism in putative reward pathways. *NeuroReport* 15(16):2539–2243.

Ritzmann RE (1984). The cockroach escape response. In: Easton RC (ed.), *Neural Mechanisms of Startle Behavior.* New York: Springer, pp. 213–266.

Rivlin G (2004). The chrome-shiny, lights-flashing, wheel-spinning, touch-screened, drew-carey-wisecracking, video-playing, "sound events"-packed, pulse-quickening bandit. *New York Times Magazine,* published May 9, 2004. www.nytimes.com/2004/05/09/magazine/chrome-shiny-lights-flashing-wheel-spinning-touch-screened-drew-carey.html.

Rizzo A, Reger G, Gahm G, Difede J, and Rothbaum BO (2009). Virtual reality exposure therapy for combat-related PTSD. In: Shiromani PJ, Keane TM, and Ledoux JE (eds.), *Post-Traumatic Stress Disorder: Basic Science and Clinical Practice.* New York: Humana, pp. 375–400.

Rizzolatti G and Craighero L (2004). The mirror-neuron system. *Annual Review of Neuroscience* 27:169–192.

Rizzolatti G, Fadiga L, Gallese V, and Fogassi L (1996). Premotor cortex and the recognition of motor actions. *Cognitive Brain Research* 3(2):131–141.

Rizzolatti G and Sinigaglia C (2010). The functional role of the parieto-frontal mirror circuit: Interpretations and misinterpretations. *Nature Reviews Neuroscience* 11:264–274.

Robbins TW, Ersche KD, and Everitt BJ (2008). Drug addiction and the memory systems of the brain. *Annals of the New York Academy of Sciences* 1141(1):1–21.

Robbins TW and Everitt BJ (1999). Drug addiction: Bad habits add up. *Nature* 398:567–570.

Robbins TW, Gillan CM, Smith DG, de Wit S, and Ersche KD (2012). Neurocognitive endophenotypes of impulsivity and compulsivity: Towards dimensional psychiatry. *Trends in Cognitive Sciences* 16(1):81–91.

Roberson D and Davidoff J (2000). The categorical perception of colors and facial expressions: The effect of verbal interference. *Memory and Cognition* 28(6):977–986.

Robinson DA (1972). Eye movements evoked by collicular stimulation in the alert monkey. *Vision Research* 12:1795–1808.

Robinson OJ, Frank MJ, Sahakian BJ, and Cools R (2010). Dissociable responses to punishment in distinct striatal regions during reversal learning. *Neuroimage* 51(4):1459–1467.

Robinson TE and Berridge KC (2001). Mechanisms of action of addictive stimuli: Incentive-sensitization and addiction. *Addiction* 96:103–114.

Robinson TE and Berridge KC (2003). Addiction. *Annual Review of Psychology* 54:25–53.

Robinson TE and Flagel SB (2009). Dissociating the predictive and incentive motivational properties of reward-related cues through the study of individual differences. *Biological Psychiatry* 65(10):869–873.

Roddenberry G (1987–1994). *Star Trek: The Next Generation.* Warner Bros.

Rodgers RJ, Cao BJ, Dalvi A, and Holmes A (1997). Animal models of anxiety: An ethological perspective. *Brazilian Journal of Medical Biological Research* 30:289–304.

Roesch MR, Calu DJ, and Schoenbaum G (2007). Dopamine neurons encode the better option in rats deciding between differently delayed or sized rewards. *Nature Neuroscience* 10:1615–1624.

Roesch MR, Singh T, Brown PL, Mullins SE, and Schoenbaum G (2009). Ventral striatal neurons encode the value of the chosen action in rats deciding between differently delayed or sized rewards. *Journal of Neuroscience* 29(42):13365–13376.

Rogers SW (1998). Exploring dinosaur neuropaleobiology: Computed tomography scanning and analysis of an *Allosaurus fragilis* endocast. *Neuron* 21(4):673–679.

Roitman JD and Shadlen MN (2002). Response of neurons in the lateral intraparietal area during a combined visual discrimination reaction time task. *Journal of Neuroscience* 22(21):9475–9489.

Rokni D, Llinas R, and Yarom Y (2008). The morpho/functional discrepancy in the cerebellar cortex: Looks alone are deceptive. *Frontiers in Neuroscience* 2(2):192–198.

Ronson J (2011). *The Psychopath Test: A Journey through the Madness Industry*. London: Macmillan.

Ros T, Munneke MAM, Ruge D, Gruzelier JH, and Rothwell JC (2010). Endogenous control of waking brain rhythms induces neuroplasticity in humans. *European Journal of Neuroscience* 31(4):770–778.

Rosch E (1973). The nature of mental codes for color categories. *Journal of Experimental Psychology: Human Perception and Performance* 1(4):303–322.

Rose JE, Herskovic JE, Trilling Y, and Jarvik ME (1985). Transdermal nicotine reduces cigarette craving and nicotine preference. *Clinical Pharmacology and Therapeutics* 38(4):450–456.

Rose JE, Salley A, Behm FM, Bates JE, and Westman EC (2010). Reinforcing effects of nicotine and non-nicotine components of cigarette smoke. *Psychopharmacology* 210:1–12.

Rosenberg J (2011). *Balanced Justice: Cost-Benefit Analysis and Criminal Justice Policy*. Technical Report Policy Brief No. 11, Institute for Policy Integrity, New York University School of Law. policyintegrity.org/publications/detail/balanced-justice/.

Ross D (2008). Timing models of reward learning and core addictive processes in the brain. *Behavioral and Brain Sciences* 31(4):457–458.

Rudy JW (2009). Context representations, context functions, and the parahippocampal/hippocampal system. *Learning and Memory* 16(10):573–585.

Rumelhart DE and McClelland JL (eds.) (1986). *PDP: Explorations in the Microstructures of Cognition. Vol. 1, Foundations.* Cambridge, MA: MIT Press.

Rushdie S (1990). *Haroun and the Sea of Stories*. New York: Viking.

Rushworth MF, Noonan MP, Boorman ED, Walton ME, and Behrens TE (2011). Frontal cortex and reward-guided learning and decision-making. *Neuron* 70(6):1054–1069.

Rushworth MFS, Walton ME, Kennerly SW, and Bannerman DM (2004). Action sets and decisions in the medial frontal cortex. *Trends in Cognitive Sciences* 8(9):410–417.

Russell MAH (1990). The nicotine addiction trap: A 40-year sentence for four cigarettes. *British Journal of Addiction* 85:293–300.

Rutledge I (2006). *Addicted to Oil: America's Relentless Drive for Energy Security*. New York: St. Martin's Press.

Rutledge RB, Lazzaro SC, Lau B, Myers CE, Gluck MA, and Glimcher PW (2009). Dopaminergic drugs modulate learning rates and perseveration in Parkinson's patients in a dynamic foraging task. *Journal of Neuroscience* 29(48):15104–15114.

Rymer M and Saunders AC (2005). Pegasus. *Battlestar Galactica*, Episode 10, Season 2.

Sacks O (1973/1990). *Awakenings*. New York: Vintage Books.

Sacks O (1973/1999). *Migraine*. Berkeley, CA: University of California Press / New York: Vintage Books.

Sacks O (1984). *A Leg to Stand On*. New York: Touchstone Books.

Sacks O (1985/1998). *The Man Who Mistook His Wife for a Hat*. New York: Simon and Schuster.

Sacktor TC (2008). PKMζ, LTP maintenance, and the dynamic molecular biology of memory storage. *Progress in Brain Research* 169:27–40.

Sagan C (1997). *The Demon-Haunted World*. New York: Random House.

Saitz R (1998). Introduction to alcohol withdrawal. *Alcohol Research and Health* 22(1):5–12.

Salamone JD, Correa M, Farrar AM, and Mingote SM (2007). Effort-related functions of nucleus accumbens dopamine and associated forebrain circuits. *Psychopharmacology* 191:461–482.

Salamone JD, Correa M, Farrar AM, Nunes EJ, and Pardo M (2009). Dopamine, behavioral economics, and effort. *Frontiers in Behavioral Neuroscience* 3:13; doi: 10.3389/neuro.08.013.2009.

Salat DH, van der Kouwe A, Tuch DS, Quinn BT, Fischl B, Dale AM, and Corkin S (2006). Neuroimaging H.M.: A 10-year follow-up examination. *Hippocampus* 16(11):936–945.

Saletan W (2007). Chess bump: The triumphant teamwork of humans and computers. *Slate* www.slate.com/id/2166000/.

Salzman CD, Murasugi CM, Britten KH, and Newsome WT (1992). Microstimulation in visual area MT: Effects on direction discrimination performance. *Journal of Neuroscience* 12(6):2331–2355.

Samuelson PA (1937). A note on measurement of utility. *Review of Economic Studies* 4(2): 155–161.

Sanfey A and Dorris M (2009). Games in humans and non-human primates: Scanners to single units. In: Glimcher PW, Camerer CF, Fehr E, and Poldrack RA (eds.), *Neuroeconomics: Decision-making and the Brain*. London: Elsevier, pp. 63–80.

Sanfey AG (2007). Social decision-making: Insights from game theory and neuroscience. *Science* 318(5850):598–602.

Sanfey AG, Rilling JK, Aronson JA, Nystrom LE, and Cohen JD (2003). The neural basis of economic decision-making in the ultimatum game. *Science* 300(5626):1755–1758.

Sapir E (1929). The status of linguistics as a science. *Language* 5(4):207–214.

Sapolsky RM (1998a). *The Trouble with Testosterone: And Other Essays on the Biology of the Human Predicament*. New York: Scribner and Sons.

Sapolsky RM (1998b). *Why Zebras Don't Get Ulcers*. New York: W. H. Freeman and Co.

Sapolsky RM (2001). *A Primate's Memoir*. New York: Touchstone.

Sartre JP (1989). *No Exit and Three Other Plays*. New York: Vintage Books.

Sato N, Kishore S, Page WK, and Duffy CJ (2010). Cortical neurons combine visual cues about self-movement. *Experimental Brain Research* 206(3):283–297.

Savage-Rumbaugh S and Lewin R (1996). *Kanzi*. New York: Wiley.

Sayette MA, Shiffman S, Tiffany ST, Niaura RS, Martin CS, and Shadel WG (2000). The measurement of drug craving. *Addiction* 95(Suppl. 2):S189–S210.

Scanziani M and Häusser M (2009). Electrophysiology in the age of light. *Nature* 461:930–939.

Schacter DL (2001). *The Seven Sins of Memory*. Boston: Houghton Mifflin.

Schacter DL and Addis DR (2011). On the nature of medial temporal lobe contributions to the constructive simulation of future events. In: Bar M (ed.), *Predictions in the Brain: Using Our Past to Generate a Future*. New York: Oxford University Press, pp. 58–69.

Schacter DL, Addis DR, and Buckner RL (2007). Remembering the past to imagine the future: The prospective brain. *Nature Reviews Neuroscience* 8:657–661.

Schacter DL, Addis DR, and Buckner RL (2008). Episodic simulation of future events. concepts, data, and applications. *Annals of the New York Academy of Sciences* 1124:39–60.

Schacter DL and Tulving E (eds.) (1994). *Memory Systems 1994*. Cambridge, MA: MIT Press.

Schall JD, Stuphorn V, and Brown JW (2002). Monitoring and control of action by the frontal lobes. *Neuron* 36:309–322.

Schank R (1980). Language and memory. *Cognitive Science* 4(3):243–284.

Schank R and Abelson RP (1977). *Scripts, Plans, and Understanding: An Inquiry into Human Knowledge Structures*. Hillsdale, NJ: Lawrence Erlbaum.

Schilbach L (2010). A second-person approach to other minds. *Nature Reviews Neuroscience* 11:449.

Schmitzer-Torbert NC and Redish AD (2002). Development of path stereotypy in a single day in rats on a multiple-T maze. *Archives Italiennes de Biologie* 140:295–301.

Schmitzer-Torbert NC and Redish AD (2004). Neuronal activity in the rodent dorsal striatum in sequential navigation: Separation of spatial and reward responses on the multiple-T task. *Journal of Neurophysiology* 91(5):2259–2272.

Schneier FR, Neria Y, Pavlicova M, Hembree E, Suh EJ, Amsel L, and Marshall RD (2012). Combined prolonged exposure therapy and paroxetine for PTSD related to the World Trade Center attack: A randomized control trial. *American Journal of Psychiatry* 169(1):80–88.

Schoenbaum G and Roesch M (2005). Orbitofrontal cortex, associative learning, and expectancies. *Neuron* 47(5):633–636.

Schoenbaum G, Roesch M, and Stalnaker TA (2006). Orbitofrontal cortex, decision making, and drug addiction. *Trends in Neurosciences* 29(2):116–124.

Schonberg T, O'Doherty JP, Joel D, Inzelberg R, Segev Y, and Daw ND (2010). Selective impairment of prediction error signaling in human dorsolateral but not ventral striatum in Parkinson's disease patients: Evidence from a model-based fMRI study. *NeuroImage* 49(1):772–781.

Schöne H (1984). *Spatial Orientation.* Translated by C. Strausfeld. Princeton, NJ: Princeton University Press.

Schulkin J (ed.) (2003). *Rethinking Homeostasis: Allostatic Regulation in Physiology and Pathophysiology.* Cambridge, MA: MIT Press.

Schultz W (1998). Predictive reward signal of dopamine neurons. *Journal of Neurophysiology* 80:1–27.

Schultz W, Dayan P, and Montague PR (1997). A neural substrate of prediction and reward. *Science* 275:1593–1599.

Schultz W and Dickinson A (2000). Neuronal coding of prediction errors. *Annual Review of Neuroscience* 23(1):473–500.

Schwaerzel M, Monastirioti M, Scholz H, Friggi-Grelin F, Birman S, and Heisenberg M (2003). Dopamine and octopamine differentiate between aversive and appetitive olfactory memories in drosophila. *Journal of Neuroscience* 23(33):10495–10502.

Schwartz AB (2007). Useful signals from motor cortex. *Journal of Physiology* 579:581–601.

Schwartz E, Tootell RBH, Silverman MS, Switkes E, and Valois RLD (1985). On the mathematical structure of the visuotopic mapping of macaque striate cortex. *Science* 227(4690):1065–1066.

Schüll ND (2012). *Addiction by Design: Machine Gambling in Las Vegas.* Princeton, NJ: Princeton University Press.

Scorcese M (1995). *Casino.* Universal Pictures.

Scott R (1982). *Blade Runner.* Warner Bros. Pictures.

Scoville WB (1968). Amnesia after bilateral medial temporal-lobe excision: Introduction to case H.M. *Neuropsychologia* 6:211–213.

Scoville WB and Milner B (1957). Loss of recent memory after bilateral hippocampal lesions. *Journal of Neurology, Neurosurgery, and Psychiatry* 20:11–21.

Seamans JK, Lapish CC, and Durstewitz D (2008). Comparing the prefrontal cortex of rats and primates: Insights from electrophysiology. *Neurotoxicity Reseach* 14(2,3):249–262.

Searle J (1965). What is a speech act? In: *Philosophy in America.* Ithaca, NY: Cornell University Press, pp. 221–239.

Searle J (1980). Minds, brains, and programs. *Behavioural and Brain Sciences* 3:417–424.

Searle J (2006). *Freedom and Neurobiology: Reflections on Free Will, Language, and Political Power.* New York: Columbia University Press.

Seife C (2007). *Decoding the Universe: How the New Science of Information Is Explaining Everything in the Cosmos, from Our Brains to Black Holes.* New York: Penguin.

Seifert W (ed.) (1983). *Neurobiology of the Hippocampus.* New York: Academic Press.

Senju A and Johnson MH (2009). The eye contact effect: Mechanisms and development. *Trends in Cognitive Sciences* 13(3):127–134.

Servan-Schreiber D, Printz H, and Cohen JD (1990). A network model of catecholamine effects: Gain, signal-to-noise ratio, and behavior. *Science* 249(4971):892–895.

Seymour B and Dolan R (2008). Emotion, decision making, and the amygdala. *Neuron* 58(5):662–671.

Seymour B, Singer T, and Dolan R (2007). The neurobiology of punishment. *Nature Reviews Neuroscience* 8:300–311.

Shadlen MN and Newsome WT (1998). The variable discharge of cortical neurons: Implications for connectivity, computation, and information coding. *Journal of Neuroscience* 18(10):3870–3896.

Shakespeare W (1596). *A Midsummer Night's Dream.*

Shakespeare W (1597). *Romeo and Juliet.*

Shakespeare W (1601). *Hamlet.*

Shakespeare W (1603a). *King Lear.*

Shakespeare W (1603b). *Macbeth.*

Shamay-Tsoory SG, Tibi-Elhanany Y, and Aharon-Peretz J (2007). The green-eyed monster and malicious joy: The neuroanatomical bases of envy and gloating (schadenfreude). *Brain* 130(6):1663–1678.

Shamosh NA, DeYoung CG, Green AE, Reis DL, Johnson MR, Conway AR, Engle RW, Braver TS, and Gray JR (2008). Individual differences in delay discounting relation to intelligence, working memory, and anterior prefrontal cortex. *Psychological Science* 19(9):904–911.

Shannon C (1948). A mathematical theory of communication. *Bell System Technical Journal* 27: 379–423, 623–656.

Shapiro C and Varian HR (1999). *Information Rules: A Strategic Guide to the Network Economy.* Cambridge, MA: Harvard Business Press.

Sharot T (2011). *The Optimism Bias: A Tour of the Irrationally Positive Brain.* New York: Pantheon.

Sharot T, Riccardi AM, Raio CM, and Phelps EA (2007). Neural mechanisms mediating optimism bias. *Nature* 450:102–105.

Shaw GB (1903/1931). *Man and Superman.* New York: Penguin.

Shaw NA (2002). The neurophysiology of concussion. *Progress in Neurobiology* 67:281–344.

Shaw WD (1992). Searching for the opportunity cost of an individual's time. *Land Economics* 68(1):107–115.

Shay J (1994) *Achilles in Vietnam: Combat Trauma and the Undoing of Character.* New York: Scribner.

Shelton R (1988). *Bull Durham.* Orion Pictures.

Shepherd R and Metzler J (1971). Mental rotation of three-dimensional objects. *Science* 171(3972):701–703.

Sherrington CS (1906). *The Integrative Action of the Nervous System.* New Haven, CT: Yale.

Sherrington CS (1940/2009). *Man on his Nature.* Cambridge, UK: Cambridge University Press.

Sherwood L (2010). *From Cells to Systems.* Stamford, CT: Brooks/Cole.

Shiromani PJ, Keane TM, and Ledoux JE (eds.) (2009). *Post-Traumatic Stress Disorder: Basic Science and Clinical Practice.* New York: Humana.

Shizgal P (1997). Neural basis of utility estimation. *Current Opinion in Neurobiology* 7(2): 198–208.

Shohamy D, Myers C, Grossman S, Sage J, Gluck M, and Poldrack R (2004). Cortico-striatal contributions to feedback-based learning: Converging data from neuroimaging and neuropsychology. *Brain* 127(4):851–859.

Shohamy D, Myers CE, Geghman KD, Sage J, and Gluck M (2006). L-Dopa impairs learning, but not generalization, in Parkinson's disease. *Neuropsychologia* 44(5):774–784.

Shohamy D, Myers CE, Grossman S, Sage J, and Gluck MA (2005). The role of dopamine in cognitive sequence learning: Evidence from Parkinson's disease. *Behavioural Brain Research* 156(2):191–199.

Shors TJ (2004). Learning during stressful times. *Learning and Memory* 11:137–144.

Shrager Y, Levy DA, Hopkins RO, and Squire LR (2008). Working memory and the organization of brain systems. *Journal of Neuroscience* 28(18):4818–4822.

Siegert RJ, Harper DN, Cameron FB, and Abernethy D (2002). Self-initiated versus externally cued reaction times in Parkinson's disease. *Journal of Clinical and Experimental Neurology* 24(2):146–153.

Silver A (2009). Mind-control toys: The force is with you. *Time Magazine* www.time.com/time/arts/article/0,8599,1880784,00.html

Simon DA and Daw ND (2011). Neural correlates of forward planning in a spatial decision task in humans. *Journal of Neuroscience* 31(14):5526–5539.

Simon H (1955). A behavioral model of rational choice. *Quarterly Journal of Economics* 69:99–118.

Simonson I and Tversky A (1992). Choice in context: Tradeoff contrast and extremeness aversion. *Journal of Marketing Research* 29(3):281–295.

Simpson FG, Kay J, and Aber CP (1984). Chest pain—indigestion or impending heart attack? *Postgraduate Medical Journal* 60:338–340.

Simpson HB, Neria Y, Lewis-Fernández R, and Schneier F (eds.) (2010). *Anxiety Disorders: Theory, Research, and Clinical Perspectives.* Cambridge, UK: Cambridge University Press.

Singer T (2008). Understanding others: Brain mechanisms of theory of mind and empathy. In: Glimcher PW, Camerer C, Poldrack RA, and Fehr E (eds.), *Neuroeconomics: Decision Making and the Brain.* New York: Academic Press, pp. 251–268.

Singer T, Seymour B, O'Doherty JP, Stephan KE, Dolan RJ, and Frith CD (2006). Empathic neural responses are modulated by the perceived fairness of others. *Nature* 439(7075):466–469.

Singh D (1993). Adaptive significance of female physical attractiveness: Role of waist-to-hip ratio. *Journal of Personality and Social Psychology* 65(2):293–307.

Skaggs WE and McNaughton BL (1996). Replay of neuronal firing sequences in rat hippocampus during sleep following spatial experience. *Science* 271:1870–1873.

Skinner BF (1948). Superstition in the pigeon. *Journal of Experimental Psychology* 38:168–172.

Skinner BF (1971). *Beyond Freedom and Dignity*. New York: Knopf.

Skinner MD and Aubin HJ (2010). Craving's place in addiction theory: Contributions of the major models. *Neuroscience & Biobehavioral Reviews* 34(4):606–623.

Smith A (1759/1790). *The Theory of Moral Sentiments*. Project Gutenberg. www.gutenberg.org.

Smith A (1776/1904). *An Inquiry into the Nature and Causes of the Wealth of Nations*. Project Gutenberg. www.gutenberg.org.

Smith AC, Frank LM, Wirth S, Yanike M, Hu D, Kubota Y, Graybiel AM, Suzuki WA, and Brown EN (2004). Dynamic analysis of learning in behavioral experiments. *Journal of Neuroscience* 24(2):447–461.

Smith C (1995). Sleep states and memory processes. *Behavioural Brain Research* 69:137–145.

Smith C (2001). Sleep states and memory processes in humans: Procedural and declarative memory systems. *Sleep Medicine Reviews* 5(6):491–506.

Smith V (2009). *Rationality in Economics: Constructivist and Ecological Forms*. Cambridge, UK: Cambridge University Press.

Smuts B (1985). *Sex and Friendship in Baboons*. Piscataway, NJ: AldineTransaction.

Snodgrass MM (1989). Measure of a man. *Star Trek: The Next Generation*.

Sober E and Wilson DS (1998). *Unto Others: The Evolution and Psychology of Unselfish Behavior*. Cambridge, MA: Harvard.

Sokolof L (1978). Local cerebral energy metabolism: Its relationships to local functional activity and blood flow. In: Elliott K and O'Connor M (eds.), *Cerebral Vascular Smooth Muscle and Its Control*. New York: Wiley, Ciba Foundation Symposium 56, Chapter 10.

Sokolof L (1981). The deoxyglucose method for the measurement of local glucose utilization and the mapping of local functional activity in the central nervous system. *Journal of Cerebral Blood Flow and Metabolism* 1:7–36.

Solomon RL and Corbit JD (1973). An opponent-process theory of motivation. II. Cigarette addiction. *Journal of Abnormal Psychology* 81(2):158–171.

Solomon RL and Corbit JD (1974). An opponent-process theory of motivation. I. Temporal dynamics of affect. *Psychological Review* 81(2):119–145.

Soltesz I and Staley K (eds.) (2008). *Computational Neuroscience in Epilepsy*. London: Elsevier.

Somerville LH and Casey BJ (2010). Developmental neurobiology of cognitive control and motivational systems. *Current Opinion in Neurobiology* 20(2):236–241.

Somerville LH, Jones RM, and Casey BJ (2010). A time of change: Behavioral and neural correlates of adolescent sensitivity to appetitive and aversive environmental cues. *Brain and Cognition* 72(1):124–133.

Sonnenfield B (1997). *Men in Black*. Columbia Pictures.

Soon CS, Brass M, Heinze HJ, and Haynes JD (2008). Unconscious determinants of free decisions in the human brain. *Nature Neuroscience* 11:543–545.

Sophocles (429 BCE/1991). *Oedipus the King, Oedipus at Colonus, Antigone*. Translated by David Grene. Chicago: University of Chicago Press.

Southwick CH (1963). *Primate Social Behavior*. Princeton, NJ: D Van Nostrand.

Sozou PD (1998). On hyperbolic discounting and uncertain hazard rates. *Journal of the Royal Society London B* 265:2015–2020.

Sparks DL and Mays LE (1983). Spatial localization of saccade targets. I. Compensation for stimulation-induced perturbations in eye position. *Journal of Neurophysiology* 49(1):45–63.

Sparks DL and Nelson JS (1987). Sensory and motor maps in the mammalian superior colliculus. *Trends in Neurosciences* 10(8):312–317.

Spear LP (2000). The adolescent brain and age-related behavioral manifestations. *Neuroscience and Biobehavioral Reviews* 24(4):417–463.

Spielberg S (1981). *Raiders of the Lost Ark*. Paramount Pictures.

Spielberg S (1993). *Schindler's List*. Universal Pictures.

Spielberg S (1998). *Saving Private Ryan*. DreamWorks.

Spielberg S (2002). *Minority Report*. DreamWorks.

Squire LR (1987). *Memory and Brain*. New York: Oxford University Press.

Squire LR (2004). Memory systems of the brain: A brief history and current perspective. *Neurobiology of Learning and Memory* 82:171–177.

Squire LR (2009). The legacy of patient H.M. for neuroscience. *Neuron* 61:6–9.

St-Laurent M, Moscovitch M, Tau M, and McAndrews MP (2011). The temporal unraveling of autobiographical memory narratives in patients with temporal lobe epilepsy or excisions. *Hippocampus* 21:409–421.

Stalnaker TA, Roesch MR, Franz TM, Burke KA, and Schoenbaum G (2006). Abnormal associative encoding in orbitofrontal neurons in cocaine-experienced rats during decision-making. *European Journal of Neuroscience* 24(9):2643–2653.

Stein BE and Meredith MA (1993). *The Merging of the Senses*. Cambridge, MA: MIT Press.

Steinberg L (2005). Cognitive and affective development in adolescence. *Trends in Cognitive Sciences* 9(2):69–74.

Steiner A and Redish AD (2012). The road not taken: Neural correlates of decision making in orbitofrontal cortex. *Frontiers in Decision Neuroscience* 6:131; doi: 10.3389/fnins.2012.00131.

Stephens DW (2008). Decision ecology: Foraging and the ecology of animal decision making. *Cognitive, Affective, and Behavioral Neuroscience* 8(4):475–484.

Stephens DW and Krebs JR (1987). *Foraging Theory*. Princeton, NJ: Princeton University Press.

Stephenson N (2002). *Cryptonomicon*. New York: Harper-Collins.

Stephenson N (2008). *Anathem*. New York: William Morrow.

Sterelny K (2006). Meme's revisited. *British Journal for the Philosophy of Science* 57:145–165.

Stevenson RL (1886). *The Strange Case of Dr. Jekyll and Mr. Hyde*. Project Gutenberg. www.gutenberg.org.

Stickgold R, Malia A, Maguire D, Roddenberry D, and O'Connor M (2000). Replaying the game: Hypnagogic images in normals and amnesics. *Science* 290(5490):350–353.

Stitzer M and Petry N (2006). Contingency management for treatment of substance abuse. *Annual Review of Clinical Psychology* 2:411–434.

Stout LA (2008). Taking conscience seriously. In: Zak PJ (ed.), *Moral Markets*. Princeton, NJ: Princeton University Press, pp. 157–172.

Strauss JL, Calhoun PS, and Marx CE (2009). Guided imagery as a therapeutic tool in post-traumatic stress disorder. In: Shiromani PJ, Keane TM, and Ledoux JE (eds.), *Post-Traumatic Stress Disorder: Basic Science and Clinical Practice*. New York: Humana, pp. 363–374.

Stray-Gundersen J and Levine BD (2008). Live high, train low at natural altitude. *Scandinavian Journal of Medicine and Science in Sports* 18:21–28.

Strick PL, Dum RP, and Picard N (1995). Macro-organization of the circuts connecting the basal ganglia with the cortical motor areas. In: Houk JC, Davis JL, and Beiser DG (eds.), *Models of Information Processing in the Basal Ganglia*. Cambridge, MA: MIT Press, pp. 117–130.

Striedter GF (2005). *Principles of Brain Evolution*. Sunderland, MA: Sinauer Associates.

Stroop JR (1935). Studies of interference in serial verbal reactions. *Journal of Experimental Psychology* 18:643–662.

Strum S (1987). *Almost Human*. New York: Random House.

Suddendorf T and Corballis MC (2007). The evolution of foresight: What is mental time travel, and is it unique to humans? *Behavioral Brain Sciences* 30:299–313.

Suddendorf T and Corballis MC (2008). Episodic memory and mental time travel. In: Dere E, Easton A, Nadel L, and Huston JP (eds.), *Handbook of Episodic Memory*. London: Elsevier, pp. 31–42.

Sugrue LP, Corrado GS, and Newsome WT (2004). Matching behavior and the representation of value in the parietal cortex. *Science* 304(5678):1782–1787.

Sun Tzu (5th century BCE/1910/1994). *The Art of War*. Translated by Lionel Giles. Project Gutenberg. www.gutenberg.org.

Surowiecki J (2005). *The Wisdom of Crowds*. New York: Anchor.

Sutherland GR and McNaughton BL (2000). Memory trace reactivation in hippocampal and neocortical neuronal ensembles. *Current Opinion in Neurobiology* 10(2):180–186.

Sutherland RJ, Sparks F, and Lehmann H (2010). Hippocampus and retrograde amnesia in the rat model: A modest proposal for the situation of systems consolidation. *Neuropsychologia* 48(8):2357–2369.

Sutton RS and Barto AG (1998). *Reinforcement Learning: An Introduction.* Cambridge, MA: MIT Press.

Swanson LW (2000). Cerebral hemisphere regulation of motivated behavior. *Brain Research* 886(1–2):113–164.

Sweeney J and Sweeney RJ (1977). Monetary theory and the great capitol hill baby sitting co-op crisis. *Journal of Money, Credit and Banking* 9(1):86–89.

Swets JA (1996). *Signal Detection Theory and ROC Analysis in Psychology and Diagnostics.* Hillsdale, NJ: Lawrence Erlbaum.

Symms M, Jäger HR, Schmierer K, and Yousry TA (2004). A review of structural magnetic resonance neuroimaging. *Journal of Neurology, Neurosurgery, and Psychiatry* 75:1235–1244.

Taibbi M (2010). The truth about the Tea Party. *Rolling Stone* www.rollingstone.com/politics/news/matt-taibbi-on-the-tea-party-20100928.

Takahashi H, Kato M, Matsuura M, Mobbs D, Suhara T, and Okubo Y (2009). When your gain is my pain and your pain is my gain: Neural correlates of envy and schadenfreude. *Science* 323(5916):937–939.

Talarico JM and Rubin DC (2003). Confidence, not consistency, characterizes flashbulb memories. *Psychological Science* 14(5):455–461.

Talmi D, Seymour B, Dayan P, and Dolan RJ (2008). Human Pavlovian-instrumental transfer. *Journal of Neuroscience* 28(2):360–368.

Tanaka S (2006). Dopaminergic control of working memory and its relevance to schizophrenia: A circuit dynamics perspective. *Neuroscience* 139(1):153–171.

Tanaka SC, Shishida K, Schweighofer N, Okamoto Y, Yamawaki S, and Doya K (2009). Serotonin affects association of aversive outcomes to past actions. *Journal of Neuroscience* 29(50):15669–15674.

Tanji J and Hoshi E (2007). Role of the lateral prefrontal cortex in executive behavioral control. *Physiological Reviews* 88(1):37–57.

Telushkin J (2010a). *Hillel: If Not Now, When?* NPR, interview by Robert Siegel, September 7, 2010. www.npr.org/templates/story/story.php?storyId=129706379.

Telushkin J (2010b). *Hillel: If Not Now, When?* New York: Random House.

Teng E and Squire LR (1999). Memory for places learned long ago is intact after hippocampal damage. *Nature* 400:675–677.

Thinus-Blanc C (1996). *Animal Spatial Cognition.* Singapore: World Scientific.

Thorndike E (1932). *The Fundamentals of Learning.* New York: Columbia University Teachers College Press.

Thrun S, Burgard W, and Fox D (2005). *Probabilistic Robotics.* Cambridge, MA: MIT Press.

Tiffany ST (1990). A cognitive model of drug urges and drug-use behavior: Role of automatic and nonautomatic processes. *Psychological Review* 97(2):147–168.

Tiffany ST and Conklin CA (2000). A cognitive processing model of alcohol craving and compulsive alcohol use. *Addiction* 95(Suppl. 2):S145–S153.

Tiffany ST and Wray J (2009). The continuing conundrum of craving. *Addiction* 104:1618–1619.

Tinbergen N (1951). *The Study of Instinct.* New York: Oxford University Press.

Tindell AJ, Smith KS, Berridge KC, and Aldridge JW (2009). Dynamic computation of incentive salience: "wanting" what was never "liked." *Journal of Neuroscience* 29(39):12220–12228.

Titus E (1958/1989). *Basil of Baker Street.* New York: Pocket Books.

Tobler PN, Fiorillo CD, and Schultz W (2005). Adaptive coding of reward value by dopamine neurons. *Science* 307(5715):1642–1645.

Tobler PN, O'Doherty JP, Dolan RJ, and Schultz W (2007). Reward value coding distinct from risk attitude-related uncertainty coding in human reward systems. *Journal of Neurophysiology* 97(2):1621–1632.

Tolkien JRR (1965). *The Lord of the Rings.* Boston: Houghton Mifflin.

Tolman EC (1932). *Purposive Behavior in Animals and Men.* New York: Appleton-Century-Crofts.

Tolman EC (1939). Prediction of vicarious trial and error by means of the schematic sowbug. *Psychological Review* 46:318–336.

Tolman EC (1948). Cognitive maps in rats and men. *Psychological Review* 55:189–208.

Tomassello M (1999). *The Cultural Origins of Human Cognition.* Cambridge, MA: Harvard University Press.

Tomassello M (2005). *Constructing a Language: A Usage-Based Theory of Language Acquisition.* Cambridge, MA: Harvard University Press.

Tomassello M (2008). *The Origins of Human Communication.* Cambridge, MA: MIT Press.

Tomasello M and Bates E (eds.) (2001). *Language Development.* Blackwell.

Tomasello M and Call J (1997). *Primate Cognition.* New York: Oxford University Press.

Tootell RBH, Silverman MS, Switkes E, and Valois RLD (1982). Deoxyglucose analysis of retinotopic organization in primate striate cortex. *Science* 218(4575):902–904.

Touitou Y and Bogdan A (2007). Promoting adjustment of the sleep–wake cycle by chronobiotics. *Physiology and Behavior* 90(2–3):294–300.

Treisman A and Gormican S (1988). Feature analysis in early vision: Evidence from search asymmetries. *Psychological Review* 95(1):15–48.

Treisman AM and Gelade G (1980). A feature-integration theory of attention. *Cognitive Psychology* 12:97–136.

Tremblay L, Hollerman JR, and Schultz W (1998). Modifications of reward expectation-related neuronal activity during learning in primate striatum. *Journal of Neurophysiology* 80:964–977.

Tremblay L and Schultz W (1999). Relative reward preference in primate orbitofrontal cortex. *Nature* 398(6729):704–708.

Tsao DY, Moeller S, and Freiwald WA (2008). Comparing face patch systems in macaques and humans. *Proceedings of the National Academy of Sciences, USA* 105(49):19514–19519.

Tse D, Langston RF, Kakeyama M, Bethus I, Spooner PA, Wood ER, Witter MP, and Morris RGM (2007). Schemas and memory consolidation. *Science* 316(5821):76–82.

Tse D, Takeuchi T, Kakeyama M, Kajii Y, Okuno H, Tohyama C, Bito H, and Morris RGM (2011). Schema-dependent gene activation and memory encoding in neocortex. *Science* 333(6044):891–895.

Tsujimoto S, Genovesio A, and Wise SP (2011). Frontal pole cortex: Encoding ends at the end of the endbrain. *Trends in Cognitive Sciences* 15(4):169–176.

Tuchman BW (1962). *The Guns of August.* New York: Random House.

Tulving E (1983). *Elements of Episodic Memory.* New York: Oxford University Press.

Tulving E (1984). Précis of elements of episodic memory. *Behavioral and Brain Sciences* 7:223–268.

Tulving E and Madigan SA (1970). Memory and verbal learning. *Annual Review of Psychology* 21:437–484.

Turchin P (2003). *Historical Dynamics: Why States Rise and Fall.* Princeton, NJ: Princeton University Press.

Turing A (1937). On computable numbers, with an application to the entscheidungsproblem. *Proceedings of the London Mathematical Society* s2-42(1):230–265.

Turing AM (1950). Computing machinery and intelligence. *Mind* 59(236):433–460.

Tversky A and Kahneman D (1981). The framing of decisions and the psychology of choice. *Science* 211(4481):453–458.

Tyler CW (1978). Some new entoptic phenomena. *Vision Research* 18(12):1633–1639.

Uchibe E and Doya K (2008). Finding intrinsic rewards by embodied evolution and constrained reinforcement learning. *Neural Networks* 21(10):1447–1455.

Ungerleider LG and Pessoa L (2008). What and where pathways. *Scholarpedia* 3(11):5342.

Ungless MA (2004). Dopamine: The salient issue. *Trends in Neurosciences* 27(12):702–706.

Ungless MA, Argilli E, and Bonci A (2010). Effects of stress and aversion on dopamine neurons: Implications for addiction. *Neuroscience & Biobehavioral Reviews* 35(2):151–156.

Ungless MA, Magill PJ, and Bolam JP (2004). Uniform inhibition of dopamine neurons in the ventral tegmental area by aversive stimuli. *Science* 303(5666):2040–2042.

Unoki S, Matsumoto Y, and Mizunami M (2005). Participation of octopaminergic reward system and dopaminergic punishment system in insect olfactory learning revealed by pharmacological study. *European Journal of Neuroscience* 22(6):1409–1416.

U.S. Department of Justice (1992). *Drugs, Crime, and the Justice System.* National Reports: DIANE.

U.S. National Academy (2001). *Climate Change Science: An Analysis of Some Key Questions.* Washington DC: National Academies Press.

Uylings HBM, Groenewegen H, and Kolb B (2003). Do rats have a prefrontal cortex? *Behavioural Brain Research* 146(1–2):3–17.

Vallabha GK and McClelland JL (2007). Success and failure of new speech category learning in adulthood: Consequences of learned Hebbian attractors in topographic maps. *Cognitive, Affective, and Behavioral Neuroscience* 7(1):53–73.

van der Horst FCP, LeRoy HA, and van der Veer R (2008). "When strangers meet": John Bowlby and Harry Harlow on attachment behavior. *Integrative Psychological and Behavioral Science* 42(4):370–388.

van der Meer MAA, Johnson A, Schmitzer-Torbert NC, and Redish AD (2010). Triple dissociation of information processing in dorsal striatum, ventral striatum, and hippocampus on a learned spatial decision task. *Neuron* 67(1):25–32.

van der Meer MAA, Kalensher T, Lansink CS, Pennartz CMA, Berke J, and Redish AD (2010). Integrating early results on ventral striatal gamma oscillations in the rat. *Frontiers in Neuroscience* 4(28):1–12.

van der Meer MAA, Kurth-Nelson Z, and Redish AD (2012). Information processing in decision-making systems. *The Neuroscientist* 18(4):342–359.

van der Meer MAA and Redish AD (2009). Covert expectation-of-reward in rat ventral striatum at decision points. *Frontiers in Integrative Neuroscience* 3(1):1–15.

van der Meer MAA and Redish AD (2010). Expectancies in decision making, reinforcement learning, and ventral striatum. *Frontiers in Neuroscience* 4(1):29–37.

van der Meer MAA and Redish AD (2011a). Theta phase precession in rat ventral striatum links place and reward information. *Journal of Neuroscience* 31(8):2843–2854.

van der Meer MAA and Redish AD (2011b). Ventral striatum: A critical look at models of learning and evaluation. *Current Opinion in Neurobiology* 21(3):387–392.

van Duuren E, Escámez FAN, Joosten RNJMA, Visser R, Mulder AB, and Pennartz CMA (2007). Neural coding of reward magnitude in the orbitofrontal cortex of the rat during a five-odor olfactory discrimination task. *Learning and Memory* 14(6):446–456.

van Duuren E, van der Plasse G, Lankelma J, Joosten RNJMA, Feenstra MGP, and Pennartz CMA (2009). Single-cell and population coding of expected reward probability in the orbitofrontal cortex of the rat. *Journal of Neuroscience* 29(28):8965–8976.

Van Essen DC, Anderson CH, and Felleman DJ (1992). Information processing in the primate visual system: An integrated systems perspective. *Science* 255(5043):419–423.

van Veen V and Carter CS (2002). The anterior cingulate as a conflict monitor: fMRI and ERP studies. *Physiology and Behavior* 77(4–5):477–482.

Vanderschuren LJMJ and Everitt BJ (2004). Drug seeking becomes compulsive after prolonged cocaine self-administration. *Science* 305(5686):1017–1019.

Vanderwolf CH (1971). Limbic-diencephalic mechanisms of voluntary movement. *Psychological Review* 78(2):83–113.

VanRullen R, Guyonneau R, and Thorpe SJ (2005). Spike times make sense. *Trends in Neuroscience* 28(1):1–4.

Vargha-Khadem F, Gadian DG, Watkins KE, Connelly A, Van Paesschen W, and Mishkin M (1997). Differential effects of early hippocampal pathology on episodic and semantic memory. *Science* 277(5324):376–380.

Velliste M, Perel S, Spalding MC, Whitford AS, and Schwartz AB (2008). Cortical control of a prosthetic arm for self-feeding. *Nature* 453:1098–1101.

Verbruggen F and Logan GD (2009). Models of response inhibition in the stop-signal and stop-change paradigms. *Neuroscience and Biobehavioral Reviews* 33:647–661.

Verfaellie M and Cermak LS (1994). Acquisition of generic memory in amnesia. *Cortex* 30(2):293–303.

Verfaellie M and Vasterling JJ (2009). Memory in PTSD: A neurocognitive approach. In: Shiromani PJ, Keane TM, and Ledoux JE (eds.), *Post-Traumatic Stress Disorder: Basic Science and Clinical Practice*. New York: Humana, pp. 105–130.

Vico G (1725/1984). *The New Science of Giambattista Vico*. Translated by Thomas Goddard Bergin and Max Harold Fisch. Ithaca, NY: Cornell University Press.

Vincent A, Ahnesjö I, Berglund A, and Rosenqvist G (1992). Pipefishes and seahorses: Are they all sex role reversed? *Trends in Ecology and Evolution* 7:237–241.

Vinogradova OS (2001). Hippocampus as comparator: Role of the two input and two output systems of the hippocampus in selection and registration of information. *Hippocampus* 11(5):578–598.

Vohs KD and Baumeister RF (eds.) (2010). *Handbook of Self-Regulation, 2nd Edition: Research, Theory, and Applications.* New York: Guilford.

Vohs KD and Faber RJ (2007). Spent resources: Self-regulatory resource availability affects impulse buying. *Journal of Consumer Research* 33:537–547.

Vohs KD and Heatherton TF (2000). Self-regulatory failure: A resource-depletion approach. *Psychological Science* 11(3):249–254.

Volkow ND, Fowler JS, and Wang GJ (2002). Role of dopamine in drug reinforcement and addiction in humans: Results from imaging studies. *Behavioral Pharmacology* 13(5):355–366.

Volkow ND, Wang GJ, and Baler RD (2011). Reward, dopamine and the control of food intake: Implications for obesity. *Trends in Cognitive Sciences* 15(1):37–46.

von Frisch K (1974). *Animal Architecture.* San Diego, CA: Harcourt Brace Jovanovich.

von Neumann J (1958/2000). *The Computer and the Brain.* New Haven, CT: Yale.

von Neumann J and Morganstern O (1944/2004). *Theory of Games and Economic Behavior.* Princeton, NJ: Princeton University Press.

Voon V, Mehta AR, and Hallett M (2011). Impulse control disorders in Parkinson's disease: Recent advances. *Current Opinion in Neurology* 24(4):324–330.

Voon V, Potenza MN, and Thomsen T (2007). Medication-related impulse control and repetitive behaviors in Parkinson's disease. *Current Opinion in Neurology* 20(4):484–492.

Voorn P, Vanderschuren LJMJ, Groenewegen HJ, Robbins TW, and Pennartz CMA (2004). Putting a spin on the dorsal-ventral divide of the striatum. *Trends in Neurosciences* 27(8):468–474.

Vulkan N (2000). An economist's perspective on probability matching. *Journal of Economic Surveys* 14(1):101–118.

Wade NJ (2005). *Perception and Illusion: Historical Perspectives.* New York: Springer.

Waelti P, Dickinson A, and Schultz W (2001). Dopamine responses comply with basic assumptions of formal learning theory. *Nature* 412:43–48.

Wagenaar WA (1988). *Paradoxes of Gambling Behavior.* Hillsdale, NJ: Lawrence Erlbaum Associates.

Wagner FA and Anthony JC (2002). From first drug use to drug dependence: Developmental periods of risk for dependence upon marijuana, cocaine, and alcohol. *Neuropsychopharmacology* 26(4):479–488.

Wallis JD (2007). Orbitofrontal cortex and its contribution to decision-making. *Annual Review of Neuroscience* 30:31–56.

Wallis JD, Anderson KC, and Miller EK (2001). Single neurons in prefrontal cortex encode abstract rules. *Nature* 411(6840):953–956.

Walters P (2012). The bad show. First broadcast January 9, 2012. *RadioLab.* Season 10, Episode 5. www.radiolab.org/2012/jan/09/whos-bad.

Walton ME, Kennerley SW, Bannerman DM, Phillips PE, and Rushworth MF (2006). Weighing up the benefits of work: Behavioral and neural analyses of effort-related decision making. *Neural Networks* 19:1302–1314.

Wang GJ, Volkow ND, Logan J, Pappas NR, Wong CT, Zhu W, Netusll N, and Fowler JS (2001). Brain dopamine and obesity. *Lancet* 357(9253):354–357.

Warren E (2011). There is nobody in this country who got rich on his own. www.youtube.com/watch?v=htX2usfqMEs.

Wassermann EM (1998). Risk and safety of repetitive transcranial magnetic stimulation: Report and suggested guidelines from the International Workshop on the Safety of Repetitive Transcranial Magnetic Stimulation, June 5–7, 1996. *Electroencephalography and Clinical Neurophysiology* 108:1–16.

Wassermann EM, Walsh V, Epstein CM, Paus T, Ziemann U, and Lisanby SH (eds.) (2008). *The Oxford Handbook of Transcranial Stimulation.* New York: Oxford University Press.

Wassum KM, Cely IC, Balleine BW, and Maidment NT (2011a). μ-opioid receptor activation in the basolateral amygdala mediates the learning of increases but not decreases in the incentive value of a food reward. *Journal of Neuroscience* 31(5):1591–1599.

Wassum KM, Ostlund SB, Balleine BW, and Maidment NT (2011b). Differential dependence of Pavlovian incentive motivation and instrumental incentive learning processes on dopamine signaling. *Learning and Memory* 18:475–483.

Waters AJ, Marhe R, and Franken IHA (2012). Attentional bias to drug cues is elevated before and during temptations to use heroin and cocaine. *Psychopharmacology* 219:909–921.

Watkins CJCH and Dayan P (1992). Q-learning. *Machine Learning* 8(3–4):279–292.

Watson J (1913). Psychology as the behaviorist views it. *Psychological Review* 20:158–177.

Watson JB (1907). Kinaesthetic and organic sensations: Their role in the reactions of the white rat to the maze. *Psychological Review* 8(2):43–100.

Watson R (2002). *Cogito, Ergo Sum: The Life of Rene Descartes.* Boston: David R. Godine.

Wegner DM (2002). *The Illusion of Conscious Will.* Cambridge, MA: MIT Press.

Weiland JD, Liu W, and Humayun MS (2005). Retinal prosthesis. *Annual Review of Biomedical Engineering* 7:361–401.

Wells MJ (1962). *Brain and Behavior in Cephalopods.* Palo Alto, CA: Stanford University Press.

Werheid K, Zysset S, Müller A, Reuter M, and von Cramon DY (2003). Rule learning in a serial reaction time task: An fMRI study on patients with early Parkinson's disease. *Cognitive Brain Research* 16(2):273–284.

Whishaw IQ (1985). Cholinergic receptor blockade in the rat impairs locale but not taxon strategies for place navigation in a swimming pool. *Behavioral Neuroscience* 99(5):979–1005.

Whishaw IQ and Brooks BL (1999). Calibrating space: Exploration is important for allothetic and idiothetic navigation. *Hippocampus* 9:659–667.

Whishaw IQ and Kolb B (2004). *The Behavior of the Laboratory Rat: A Handbook with Tests.* New York: Oxford University Press.

White AM (2003). What happened? Alcohol, memory blackouts, and the brain. *Alcohol Research and Health* 27(2):186–196.

White EL (1989). *Cortical Circuits.* Boston: Birkhauser.

White JA, Klink R, Alonso A, and Kay AR (1998). Noise from voltage-gated ion channels may influence neuronal dynamics in the entorhinal cortex. *Journal of Neurophysiology* 80(1):262–269.

White LE and Fitzpatrick D (2007). Vision and cortical map development. *Neuron* 56(2):327–338.

White-Traut R, Watanabe K, Pournajafi-Nazarloo H, Schwertz D, Bell A, and Carter CS (2009). Detection of salivary oxytocin levels in lactating women. *Developmental Psychobiology* 51(4):367–373.

Whitman W (1900). *Leaves of Grass/Song of Myself.* Boston: Wentworth.

Whittle P (1988). Restless bandits: Activity allocation in a changing world. *Journal of Applied Probability* 25:287–298.

Whorf BL (1956). *Language, Thought, and Reality.* Cambridge, MA: MIT Press.

Wickens J, Reynolds JNJ, and Hyland B (2003). Neural mechanisms of reward-related motor learning. *Current Opinion in Neurobiology* 13(6):685–690.

Wiener J (1995). *The Beak of the Finch: A Story of Evolution in Our Time.* New York: Vintage Books.

Wiener N (1948). *Cybernetics, or Control and Communications in the Animal and the Machine.* Cambridge, MA: MIT Press.

Wikenheiser AM and Redish AD (2013). The balance of forward and backward hippocampal sequences shifts across behavioral states. *Hippocampus* 23:22–29.

Wikman TS, Branicky MS, and Newman WS (1994). Reflex control for robot system preservation, reliability, and autonomy. *Computers and Electrical Engineering* 20(5):391–407.

Willingham DB (1999). The relation between implicit and explicit learning: Evidence for parallel development. *Psychological Science* 10(6):531–534.

Willingham DB, Nissen MJ, and Bullemer P (1989). On the development of procedural knowledge. *Journal of Experimental Psychology: Learning, Memory, and Cognition* 15(6):1047–1060.

Wills WD (2002). Long-term potentiation in spinothalamic neurons. *Brain Research Reviews* 40(1–3):202–214.

Wilson DS (2002). *Darwin's Cathedral: Evolution, Religion, and the Nature of Society.* Chicago: University of Chicago Press.

Wilson DS, Wilczynski C, Wells A, and Weiser L (2000). Gossip and other aspects of language as group-level adaptations. In: Hayes C and Huber L (eds.), *The Evolution of Cognition.* Cambridge, MA: MIT Press.

Wilson EO (1980). *Sociobiology.* Cambridge, MA: Harvard University Press.

Wilson HR and Cowan JD (1973). A mathematical theory of the functional dynamics of cortical and thalamic tissue. *Kybernetik* 13:55–80.

Wilson MA and McNaughton BL (1993). Dynamics of the hippocampal ensemble code for space. *Science* 261:1055–1058.

Wilson MA and McNaughton BL (1994). Reactivation of hippocampal ensemble memories during sleep. *Science* 265:676–679.

Winawer J, Witthoft N, Frank MC, Wu L, Wade AR, and Boroditsky L (2007). Russian blues reveal effects of language on color discrimination. *Proceedings of the National Academy of Sciences, USA* 104(19):7780–7785.

Winstanley CA, Balleine BW, Brown JW, Büchel C, Cools R, Durstewitz D, O'Doherty JP, Pennartz CM, Redish AD, Seamans JK, and Robbins TW (2012). Search, goals, and the brain. In: Hills T, McNamara J, Raaijmakers J, Robbins T, and Todd PM (eds.), *Cognitive Search*. Cambridge, MA: MIT Press, Ernst Strüngmann Forum Discussion Series, pp. 125–156.

Winstanley CA, Cocker PJ, and Rogers RD (2011). Dopamine modulates reward expectancy during performance of a slot machine task in rats: Evidence for a "near-miss" effect. *Neuropsychopharmacology* 36:913–925.

Wise RA (2004). Dopamine, learning, and motivation. *Nature Reviews Neuroscience* 5:1–12.

Wise RA (2005). Forebrain substrates of reward and motivation. *Journal of Comparative Neurology* 493(1):115–121.

World Health Organization (2011). Cholera. www.who.int/topics/cholera/treatment/en/.

Wright R (1995). *The Moral Animal: Why We Are the Way We Are: The New Science of Evolutionary Psychology*. New York: Vintage Books.

Wu GK, Arbuckle R, Liu BH, Tao HW, and Zhang LI (2008). Lateral sharpening of cortical frequency tuning by approximately balanced inhibition. *Neuron* 58(1):132–143.

Wunderlich K, Dayan P, and Dolan RJ (2012). Mapping value based planning and extensively trained choice in the human brain. *Nature Neuroscience* 15(5):786–791.

Wurtz RH and Duffy CJ (1992). Neuronal correlates of optic flow stimulation. *Annals of the New York Academy of Sciences* 656:205–219.

Wyler AR and Herman BP (eds.) (1994). *The Surgical Management of Epilepsy*. Boston: Butterworth-Heinemann.

Xu J, DeVito EE, Worhunsky PD, Carroll KM, Rounsaville BJ, and Potenza MN (2010). White matter integrity is associated with treatment outcome measures in cocaine dependence. *Neuropsychopharmacology* 35:1541–1549.

Yehuda R and Ledoux J (2007). Response variation following trauma: A translational neuroscience approach to PTSD. *Neuron* 56(1):19–32.

Yin HH, Knowlton B, and Balleine BW (2004). Lesions of dorsolateral striatum preserve outcome expectancy but disrupt habit formation in instrumental learning. *European Journal of Neuroscience* 19:181–189.

Yin RK (1970). Face recognition by brain-injured patients: A dissociable ability? *Neuropsychologia* 8:395–402.

Yu A and Dayan P (2005). Uncertainty, neuromodulation, and attention. *Neuron* 46(4):681–692.

Yu VL, Fagan LM, Wraith SM, Clancey WJ, Scott AC, Hannigan J, Blum RL, Buchanan BG, and Cohen SN (1979). Antimicrobial selection by a computer. *Journal of the American Medical Association (JAMA)* 242:1279–1282.

Zak PJ (ed.) (2008). *Moral Markets: The Critical Role of Values in the Economy*. Princeton, NJ: Princeton University Press.

Zak PJ, Stanton AA, and Ahmadi S (2007). Oxytocin increases generosity in humans. *PLoS ONE* 2(11):e1128.

Zald DH and Rauch SL (eds.) (2008). *The Orbitofrontal Cortex*. New York: Oxford University Press.

Zeki S (1993). *A Vision of the Brain*. New York: Oxford University Press.

Zeng FG (2004). Trends in cochlear implants. *Trends in Amplification* 8(1):1–34.

Zeng FG, Rebscher S, Harrison WV, Sun X, and Feng H (2009). Cochlear implants: System design, integration and evaluation. *IEEE Review of Biomedical Engineering* 1(1):115–142.

Zhang K (1996). Representation of spatial orientation by the intrinsic dynamics of the head-direction cell ensemble: A theory. *Journal of Neuroscience* 16(6):2112–2126.

Zhang K, Ginzburg I, McNaughton BL, and Sejnowski TJ (1998). Interpreting neuronal population activity by reconstruction: Unified framework with application to hippocampal place cells. *Journal of Neurophysiology* 79:1017–1044.

Zhou X, Panizzutti R, de Villers-Sidani E, Madeira C, and Merzenich MM (2011). Natural restoration of critical period plasticity in the juvenile and adult primary auditory cortex. *Journal of Neuroscience* 31(15):5625–5634.

Zimbardo PG (2007). *The Lucifer Effect: Understanding How Good People Turn Evil.* New York: Random House.

Zisapel N (2002). Melatonin–dopamine interactions: From basic neurochemistry to a clinical setting. *Cellular and Molecular Neurobiology* 21(6):605–616.

Zuckerman M and Kuhlman DM (2000). Personality and risk-taking: Common biosocial factors. *Journal of Personality* 68(6):999–1029.

INDEX

CHARLES JAMES

PORTRAIT OF AN UNREASONABLE MAN

From a photo shoot for Eleanor Lambert's 1954 press release
about Charles James's Coty Award for his coat designs for
Dressmaker Casuals when Charles was at the height of his fame.

CHARLES JAMES

PORTRAIT OF AN UNREASONABLE MAN

FAME, FASHION, ART

———————

MICHÈLE GERBER KLEIN

Rizzoli
ex libris

First published in the United States of America in 2018
by Rizzoli Ex Libris, an imprint of
Rizzoli International Publications, Inc.
300 Park Avenue South
New York, NY 10010
www.rizzoliusa.com

© Michèle Gerber Klein

2018   2019   2020   2021 / 10   9   8   7   6   5   4   3   2   1
Distributed in the U.S. trade by Random House, New York
Printed in China
ISBN-13: 978-0-8478-6145-3
Library of Congress Catalog Control Number: 2017958943

To Roger Webster, who suggested I write about Charles James.

And to my mother, who taught me to read.

All progress depends on the unreasonable man.

—GEORGE BERNARD SHAW[1]

CONTENTS

Foreword

BY HAROLD KODA

CHARLES JAMES WAS a man of breathtaking contradictions. Small and slightly built, he had an outsized persona and personality. For most of his life he identified unapologetically as a homosexual, but astonished his friends when in his forties he married a woman for love and had a family. He could be selfless, a nurturing mentor to many, and generous to the point of extravagance, but perceived betrayals could spark from him cruel and acerbic critiques, litigation, and a sustained and consuming rage. He was a dismissive critic of the American fashion system that celebrated his exceptional talents with numerous awards and bridled at the perceived systemic flaws that contributed, in his mind, to the eventual destruction of his career. A prescient innovator of commercial strategies ahead of his time, he was confounded again and again by the demands and responsibilities of the business of fashion. Above all, he was an artist whose fate was determined when he chose to pursue the expression of his creativity and genius within the unforgiving and delimiting commercial parameters of fashion.

In the pantheon of great twentieth-century fashion innovators, James should be included in a small subset of creators who, by challenging the structural conventions of apparel design, expanded the tectonic possibilities of cloth and clothing. Like Paul Poiret, Madeleine Vionnet, Cristóbal Balenciaga, Issey Miyake, Geoffrey Beene, and Azzedine Alaïa, James introduced modes of patternmaking and construction that transformed his métier. Any assessment of James establishes him as their equal. His influence stretches from the modernism of the 1920s and 1930s, the New Look, to the post-modern, historicist revivals of the 1980s to the present. For someone whose work has inspired so much contemporary fashion, whether or not it is explicitly cited, his renown is relatively thin. James, despite periods of great creative achievement and acclaim, was never able to sustain a commercially viable career and thus secure the more enduring visibility of his peers. To the end, surrounded by the chaotic accumulation of legal documents, paper and muslin patterns, sculpted mannequins, original designs for a sofa, jewelry maquettes, and couture samples, James continued to revisit and revise his masterworks. Nothing from the James atelier was completed until it conformed to the designer's rigorous conceptual and perfectionist standards. As a result, it has been estimated that his complete oeuvre might be as few as 250 to 300 independent designs over three decades. While that falls short of the demands of a viable fashion house, it is more than sufficient to establish his significance as a couturier. That James has been the subject of numerous museum exhibitions is hardly surprising, as everything he produced was marked by a consistent maturity and distinctive originality.

Until now, monographs on James have focused primarily on the virtuosity of his work, with relatively spare acknowledgment of the challenges of his life. This book, for the first time, colors more fully the personal aspects of James the man. By describing the significant people throughout his life, Michèle Gerber Klein establishes a faceted view of a very complicated individual. His family, beloved client-muses, the intimate circle of creatives drawn to him, even some friends and associates who betrayed him, all contribute to this portrait of the artist and the singularity of his life.

In the comprehensive Charles James archives transferred from the Brooklyn Museum to the Costume Institute of the Metropolitan Museum of Art are a number of the designer's most celebrated works. Sadly, many of them are in states of irretrievable disrepair, not through neglect or abuse, but because of a condition conservators describe as "inherent vice," the presence of a pernicious structural element intrinsic to the work. Today, these gowns of once unparalleled glamour, in their state of poetic devastation, might be the most evocative metaphor for James himself. They are beautiful ruins, still redolent of a heroic, wildly creative ambition and unfettered, self-destructive genius.

Charles James's last blouse design, the "Butterfly," was rejected by Henri Bendel.

How I Met Charles

MY FIRST INTIMATION of the Anglo-American couturier Charles James came in 1977, when he had only a few months left to live. It was the year Jimmy Carter had just pardoned almost all of the Vietnam draft evaders, and Fleetwood Mac's *Rumors* hit the top of the charts. Studio 54 and Max's Kansas City were alight with superstars, druggies, and debutantes.

Just out of Bryn Mawr—a bluestocking, Seven Sisters college, where I had lived in Katharine Hepburn's old room—I was very wet behind the ears. I had a beginner's job in the Manhattan Fashion Office of Neiman Marcus. This meant that I wrote scouting reports on new designers for Stanley Marcus, the company's president, which I illustrated with little stick figures wearing clothes that caught my eye, and chiefly answered the telephones.

The exclusive, intimate second floor of Henri Bendel, where the air always smelled vaguely of roses and sandalwood, was one of my favorite haunts. Of course, Bendel's, which specialized in what its president Geraldine Stutz called "dog-whistle fashion...clothes with a pitch so high that only the thinnest, most sophisticated women could hear their call," was the place all fashion girls loved the best. Located in a bewitchingly narrow 1920s limestone building at Ten West Fifty-seventh Street—coincidentally, in the same neighborhood as several of Charles James's old stomping grounds—it was the jewel in the crown of luxury retailing. Like Holly Golightly with her nose pressed against Tiffany's window, I couldn't afford much, but loved admiring the ever-changing display of carefully curated, beautifully made, frequently one-of-a-kind pieces. Recognizing my passion, Geraldine Stutz's partner, Jean Rosenberg, who oversaw almost everything and merchandized the entire store, occasionally asked my opinion. One afternoon,

I found Jeanie standing in the middle of the floor, clutching something and looking as though she had just seen a spider: "He's so...," she mumbled mysteriously. "This is perhaps too elaborate. We don't want to offend him, but I don't think we should take it." She inhaled and then, as though exposing some dark scandal, she showed me what she was holding. It was a square box made of clear plastic, tied with a lanky, silk bow. It had arrived, just for her, from the decadent, very cool Chelsea Hotel. Inside, folded with exacting precision into the shape of a large origami insect, was a diaphanous blouse. The box reminded me unpleasantly of the kind that inexpensive florists kept in their big, glass refrigerators, with unwieldy orchid corsages trapped inside.

I recoiled. "No. *I* wouldn't wear it," I said.

"Then we'll tell him it's too special," Jeanie decided, relieved.

The "it" I had just rejected was the historic "Butterfly Blouse," an iteration of which Henri Matisse had immortalized in a famous drawing. And it was one of the last designs that the iconic iconoclast—Charles James, "the greatest couturier in the Western world"—would ever complete.

What strikes me now is the unspoken shiver of understanding that whoever had sent it was either so famous, or so infamous, that Jeanie couldn't bring herself to even whisper his name.

My second intimation of Charles James came from Christophe de Menil, eldest child of the world-famous philanthropists John and Dominique de Menil—"millionaire radicals" who donated to the city of Houston a small constellation of museums, including the Rothko and the Byzantine Fresco chapels, as well as their unsurpassed collection of surrealist painting and sculpture, and a Renzo Piano building to house it all. Christophe, a leading figure in the art world, early patron of Twyla Tharp, and friend to Philip Glass, John Cage, Robert Rauschenberg, and Willem de Kooning, began collecting contemporary art when she was very young. She is also a brilliant designer, who invented costumes for Robert Wilson's theater pieces for over twenty years.

At the suggestion of Madeline Ewing, a mutual acquaintance, Christophe had invited me to her wonderfully spare East Side town house for an early fall lunch to talk about the possibility of my licensing her designs. We were sitting beside her narrow lap pool on some gray flannel Frank Gehry cushions, discussing clothes and eating cold chicken, when she announced very proudly in her authoritative voice, sounding as though she had grown up speaking several languages (which she had), that Charles James (as if, of course, I knew all about him) had created the gown she had worn to her coming-out party. "And," she added enigmatically, had taught her "a thing or two" as well.

She then proceeded to lend me an eye-catchingly original, beautifully deconstructed, black silk, Charles James-inspired dress she had made. At the time, I had been too proud and too shy to ask her who Mr. James was, but the dress was delightful. Simultaneously demure and revealing, it narrowed at the waist to grow wide at the hem, where it floated around me like a cloud. I wore it to a charity dance, where it received a lot of deserved attention and was much photographed.

That was in 1982, when fashionable women were all dressing in extravagantly wide-shouldered "power" jackets like the ones Joan Collins modeled in the television soap *Dynasty*—shapes that had been invented in the 1930s by Charles James and Elsa Schiaparelli. But it was the first time I had heard Charles James's name. And I still didn't know who he was.

This book is the result of a serendipitous meeting and a gift. By 2000, I was a professional writer and had started a large fashion company, "joan vass, USA." That year, I hired the New York-based society columnist and publicist R. Couri Hay to work on a successful "Art and Fashion" benefit for the Bronx Museum of the Arts, which I chaired. As we got to know each other better, Couri and his partner, Roger Webster—it was really Roger—decided that I was precisely the sort of person Charles would want to tell his story. They both had been close to and were very supportive of Charles in his last years, when he was living at the Chelsea Hotel. Couri, who had also written about Charles James for Andy Warhol's magazine *Interview*, had, with Roger's help, conducted over twenty hours of videotaped interviews with the legendary couturier just before his death in 1978. The interviews were filmed by artist Anton Perich as segments for his own cable television show, and were intended as a resource for the biography Charles James had long contemplated but never realized.

Roger and Couri asked Perich to give me this last and only set of interview videotapes that Charles James ever made. They hoped I might complete the project they had started with him over twenty years before. And Perich agreed.

The Charles James that I finally met through those tapes was a hauntingly mixed metaphor. Into his seventies and visibly fragile, he wore an impeccable jacket with the oversized black velvet bow tie of a consummate dandy, and his trendy boots had small Cuban heels. But he used a rubber band for a face-lift, and his too-dark, glistening hair looked as though it might have been boot blacked to cover the gray. The expression in his beautifully tilted eyes, under thick, very bushy eyebrows, was often bemused.

The decadently aristocratic clutter of Charles James's rooms in the Chelsea Hotel, where the interviews were conducted, was a mésalliance of bric-a-brac and mementos. Collections of waxes for jewelry jostled elegances—like his grandmother's Tiffany box—and piles of books, many of which appeared to be first editions. A large bronze of a penis ("Halston would put that to bad use," Charles James joked) could be seen, employed as an innocent paperweight. There were storyboards and sketch pads, patterns, mannequins, calipers, and, suspended from the ceiling, a whip of stays, to be applied in the infrastructure of dresses. His bed (where he dined) was a wash of rumpled linen, accented with crumbs. Michael Vollbracht, the famous fashion illustrator, told me later that when he went to visit Charles in the Chelsea, he was shocked: "The combined smells of Sputnik, Charlie's old beagle, and the powder used to kill off the cockroaches, were so strong, that as soon as I got there, I needed to run."[2]

The videotaped tête-à-tête with R. Couri Hay was a collection of gossipy, disparate anecdotes that were just distant and naughty enough to be enticing. And Charles's patrician, British-accented voice drawled and drooped at the end of his sentences as though he were deliberately making his words difficult to hear, so that watching it all made me feel like a curious child up past bedtime, straining to catch snatches of conversation from a grown-up party through the crack of a door.

Evoking the style and manner of the 1930s, Charles was almost consistently snobby and sardonic. Wryly noting that the famous French

artist and set designer Christian Bérard, who created the décor for Jean
Cocteau's film classic, *Beauty and the Beast,* came from a family of rich
undertakers, Charles added smugly, "which fact he would have preferred to conceal." He described former *Vogue* editor in chief (then special consultant to the Metropolitan Museum of Art) Diana Vreeland as
"the queen of perversity": "I don't know anyone less informed than Mrs.
Vreeland. She is one of the parlor maids of fashion," he confided. And
he breezily dismissed a historically very close friend and supporter, the
brilliant photographer Cecil Beaton, as a slightly addled self-aggrandizer
who invented a liaison with Greta Garbo. "There are many versions of
what a love affair is," an amused Charles noted sarcastically before he
went on to deep-six his former protégé, the fashion designer Halston, as
"a middle-of-the-road man who would be better as a buyer in the store
or a stylist. He knows how to select good things but his passion has been
to put his name on it. The word plagiarism is correct," he softly hissed.[3]

With a dramatic switch of tone, he became starry-eyed as he
remembered buying up a street vendor's entire supply of violets for
stage star Gertrude Lawrence, because she found them so beautiful.
And he was heart-wrenching, as well. Showing off the exquisitely sensual Matisse sketch of Clive Bell's mistress, Mary Hutchinson, in one of
his ethereally sheer blouses, (a precursor to the one I rejected at Henri
Bendel), Charles worried at the same time about going on welfare to
pay for his own medicine. "Sometimes I feel quite desperate," he said.

Gathering enough money to start a school for "true" couturiers—"I only teach dropouts," Charles whispered—was a wistful dream.
Because most of all—although he made it very clear how much he
loved and was proud of his mother's patrician American family—he dis-
agreed with the American attitude toward creativity and mourned the
increasing commercialization of fashion in the United States. "What
the market takes up the market destroys," he explained.[3]

In a brilliant 1954 press release, written on the occasion of his second special Coty American Fashion Critics' Award, Eleanor Lambert,
who invented fashion publicity, succinctly described Charles James
as a dressmaker whose "clients are the most distinguished women in
Europe and in America...When he deserted a job with a utility company to set up a hat shop," she continued, "his friends promptly became

his customers, and it is his boast that he never had an uninteresting client. It is James' passionate conviction that all real fashion has its origin in personality." And his objective, she concluded, was "to maintain in America the standards of workmanship learned in Paris which are demanded by the distinguished women throughout the world who make fashion."[4]

Couri Hay once told me, "Many people took one look at Charles James and decided he was nuts." More likely, the truth of it was that by the end of the 1970s Charles had simply outlived his world. In today's fragmented, high-speed universe—where red-carpet fashions last as long as the click of a camera, the largest luxury markets are in Korea and China, and the realms of style, art, and music only rarely and randomly coincide—it would be impossible to have or even imagine a career like the one Charles James enjoyed. When Charles came of age in the interwar period, Great Britain was at the height of its power. England controlled Canada, India, Australia, New Zealand, a good piece of Africa, and bits of China and South America as well. London and Paris, where all the "somebodies" were friends, or at least knew each other, were the only real hubs of world culture. All the arts were closely intertwined, and style really was set by a handful of exceptional and sometimes also beautifully educated women, not all of whom were film stars. Even then, it was unreasonable to expect anyone to achieve what Charles James did.

Somewhere between fact and miracle, icons like Charles James incarnate their era. Charles was born with entrée to society on two sides of the Atlantic, and he used it well. He became an intimate of the most powerful cultural pacesetters of his lifetime. And for over forty years, from the 1930s through the 1970s—in collaboration with his friends Elsa Schiaparelli, Jean Cocteau, Oliver and Anne Messel (later Countess of Rosse), Cecil Beaton, Étienne de Beaumont, Christian Dior, Millicent Rogers, Dominique de Menil, Eleanor Lambert, Salvador Dalí, and Halston, to name a handful—Charles James authored the sequence of fashion and set the standard for style in the Western world. He was the sum of the people he knew and those he impacted.

Charles, who described himself as "a legend because my work is too little known,[5]" was the ultimate éminence grise.

Supremely individualistic and self-promoting, Charles James paradoxically defined his métier as a partnership. For him, couture was the result of the relationship between distinctive and experimental women and the people who invented their clothes. Dressmaking was lovemaking. "I am not a designer," he said. "Designers are only hired help that copy what is in the wind. They don't create fashion. Only the couturier does, with his *client* as inspiration!"[6] In his 1974 autobiographical article, "A Portrait of a Genius by a Genius," Charles announced: "A book is now planned in which James will tell the stories of the clients who inspired his work."[7] That plan, however, never materialized.

Accordingly, when I began to piece together the complexities of Charles James's life and character, I looked to the women who influenced him most—women whose separate (although not necessarily sequential) stories when taken together span forty years in Europe and America and are a cultural and social history of the evolution of style. I found Elsa Schiaparelli, queen of modernist fashion in the 1930s, who was an early inspiration to Charles; Anne, Countess of Rosse, née Messel, his most important personal client of that period, whose unique romantic sensibilities helped him define a vision that would carry him beyond World War II; Elizabeth Arden, who set him up in America; and Millicent Rogers, his favorite and most important patron, with whom he shaped his first museum retrospective. Dominique de Menil took Charles beyond fashion to co-create her brilliant home in Houston, Texas; Austine Hearst enabled his greatest, most resplendent design; and Eleanor Lambert, who "invented" the business and the buzz of fashion in post–World War II America, provided the backdrop for it all. His wife and last muse, Nancy James, not only gave Charles immortality through his children, but inspired some of his most prophetic, minimal designs—adaptations of which are still worn today. This book is accordingly about Charles James, as seen through the women with whom he fashioned his life and his life's work.

The work is astounding. There were never more than a handful of Charles James matrix designs. But each one is a masterpiece, developed with painstaking care and slowness, and so beautifully calibrated that one small change could throw everything off balance. So Charles became almost as notorious for his endless ripping up and resewing as he was famous for his perfectly finished pieces.

Each of these precious Charles James creations dazzles because each one is an original invention, a realized experiment with something new: a new fabric, new fastenings, a new way of moving, and always new cuts in new shapes. And the shapes are all visceral, sculptural, poetic renderings of sexuality and sex appeal. James was the Ovid of fashion.[8] He put lust into dresses. There are coats like cocoons, ball gowns like butterflies, and even an evening dress, just for Millicent Rogers, with tantalizing frontal draping that pays homage to Georgia O'Keeffe's pastel colored portraits of vagina like seashells.

Charles James who wrote, "My seams are sentences. They all have meaning," explained that "cut in dressmaking is like grammar in language." He called his deliberately provocative and evocative designs "theses."[9]

Effectively, they're conceptual "think pieces" made, unlike any clothes that came before them, to be displayed in museums. Showcased at a remove from the personal and the utilitarian, they can be studied, analyzed, and admired with wonder for their beauty and their engineering as virtual works of art. Thus Charles James conceived a new way of looking at fashion. He literally set it apart.

Amanda Harlech, Karl Lagerfeld's creative consultant, who describes James's designs as having "rhythm inside them," is taken by "the sensuality of their textures: the rough with the smooth," and the melodic "resolution of polyphony" in their seams.[10]

Zac Posen was impressed with "the emotion expressed by the colors in the dresses," which, he believes, can "stand alone."[11]

Bill Cunningham called Charles James "the poet laureate of fashion."[12]

Salvador Dalí decided the work was "soft sculpture."[13]

Harold Koda and Sir Francis Rose described Charles James as "an artist whose medium was cloth."[14]

"He's a genius,"[15] exclaimed Virginia Woolf.

Charles James, who exemplified the individuality of creative expression, was also an innovator in broad-scale marketing. In this vein, he invented and experimented with many groundbreaking ideas for marrying affordable pricing to refined taste.[16] His theories of fashion were seminal. But unlike every other designer in America, he never even contemplated producing multiple, commercially viable, yearly collections. And unfortunately, in his attempts to dress the mainstream, he chose to stand apart from, and above, common industry practices. Charles James was raffish, unyielding, belligerent, and above all, a foreigner on both sides of the Atlantic. He paid the price for his heresy.

Oliver Messel wryly described "Charlie" James as an "extraordinary character who immediately bit the hand that fed him and insulted his most important customers."[17]

"Charlie's got every talent. The only talent he lacks is getting along with people. He thinks it's rather cute," Diana Vreeland snorted.[18]

More sympathetically, and perhaps accurately, Austine Hearst wrote that he was: "a selfish egoist, a Renaissance man, and a [wonderfully] complex genius who 'broke his heart and his health' wanting to become financially successful in the mass market of clothes."[19]

Certainly, Charles James was an unreasonable dreamer. But then, to paraphrase F. Scott Fitzgerald in *The Rich Boy*, the geniuses of the world are different from you and me.

Charles James, budding designer, circa 1930, by his friend Cecil Beaton.

CHAPTER 1

In the Beginning

Between Europe and America

SIX YEARS AFTER the turn of the last century, and four years after Edward VII's coronation and the end of the Boer War, the British Empire was near the height of its power. For the first time, the Dow Jones closed above 100, while in England, Prime Minister Harry Bannerman's cabinet, which included Sir Winston Churchill, embarked on sweeping social reforms. And on July 18, 1906, Charles Brega James was born in Camberley, Surrey, England to a life of advantage, aestheticism, wealth, patronage, idleness, and all the loneliness such a social station can entail.

On Charles's father's side, the Jameses were an aristocratic and eminent military family. His paternal grandfather, Colonel Walter Haweis James, the "very small pugnacious, charming and eccentric"[20] second son of Cornish landholders, had been one of the founders of the Royal Military Academy at Sandhurst. Colonel James also personally tutored Winston Churchill, who had failed his entrance examinations twice, and made sure the future prime minister was accepted by the Royal Military Academy when he applied for the third time.[21] Walter's own son, Charles's father Captain Ralph Ernest Haweis James, had been educated at Eton.[22]

Charles's beautiful, stylish, and talented mother, Louise (née Brega), was a much-loved only child. She grew up in Chicago where her father, a self-made Great Lakes shipping magnate, had built a real estate empire. Her parents were prominent philanthropists, and Charles Brega was a founding board member of Chicago's prestigious St. Luke's Hospital.[23] The society columns called Louise "the tuneful Miss Brega,"[24] because she had been trained as an opera singer. And in the tradition of many romantic and upwardly mobile American heiresses of the era, she fell in love during a world tour with her parents, while sailing across the

11

Atlantic aboard *The Empress of Japan*.[25] Her shipboard romance ignited when Ralph—all dressed up in blindingly colorful full Indian regalia to accompany his military unit from China to England—met and courted the elegant Miss Brega who, as the Chicago papers also reported, could have married many other titled Englishmen.

Their high-society wedding on December 29, 1903, lit up Chicago's Christmas season, where it was incandescent enough to make all the style columns in the bride's hometown. Louise wore a spellbinding dress of handmade Brussels rose-point lace fittingly designed by Charles Frederick Worth, the world's first haute couturier. After the wedding, Ralph and Louise settled into Agincourt House, a present from the bride's parents and one of the largest and most imposing mansions in Camberley, an affluent small town close to London that had its roots in the Royal Military Academy where Ralph, following his own father's footsteps, was an instructor. This was where Charles, the only son and heir apparent, was born. Named after his recently deceased maternal grandfather, Charles was a middle child whose sisters Frances and Margaret were respectively two years older and fourteen months younger than the exquisite little boy.[26]

Elfin, precocious, stubborn, rebellious, mischievous, oppositional, multi-talented, and wildly creative, Charles was cosseted and adored by his mother, whom he took after. The opposite was true of his father. A photograph of Captain James[27] with his regiment, discovered in the Sandhurst archives, reveals a very fashionable, uniformed, and decorated officer with a fierce mustache and cruel, dangerous eyes. Ralph James had a violent and brutal temper, which Charles ceaselessly and probably deliberately provoked. It's easy to imagine that the rigid, truculent captain would have preferred a more conventional child and was jealous and pitilessly judgmental of his son, who would later describe Ralph as a sadist who enjoyed beating him when he was four and five.[28] Charles also remembered being deliberately humiliated by his father; forced to carry coal and shine shoes.[29] He wrote, "My father always made me feel that I was an impostor, so my life has been a succession of acts to prove I was, through my work, a real person, not a straw man."[30]

When Charles was four, the family moved to London, first to Sloane Street and then to a gracious red-brick, seventeenth-century

Dutch–style house at Thirty-nine Egerton Gardens in Chelsea, where they lived in "Upstairs Downstairs" Edwardian opulence, with a butler and a staff of five. The following year Charles, who was a musical prodigy, began private lessons in composition and piano. His knowledge and love of this art form would color the rest of his life.

After speculative investments made by Ralph James during the 1906–15 bear market went bad, Charles's grandmother Fanny, who had inherited the entire Brega fortune, left America for England so she could live with and support her daughter's family. Such living arrangements were common in the early 1900s. There was, however a very conspicuous imbalance between Ralph's small income and the considerable inherited money on Louise's side of the family. And the Chicago society columns—which had already been faintly critical of Louise's choice of marriage partners—reported, after Charles Brega's death, that Louise had been disinherited.[31] So Fanny's move, which may well have been the Bregas' way of protecting their fortune from Ralph, probably also contributed to the family's malaise.

At the outbreak of World War I in 1914, Ralph, who had been promoted to the rank of lieutenant colonel, was transferred to the War Office. And Charles was shuffled off to boarding school at Sevenoaks in Kent, where he was deposited for the duration of the war. Although there is no record of how the eight-year-old little boy enjoyed his first school away from home, Elizabeth de Cuevas, whose mother Margaret Strong, a Rockefeller heiress, had had a similar upbringing, and in whose outer circles Charles later traveled, confirmed that in most cases these schools were hotbeds of abuse. Writing about a similar environment, Winston Churchill's comments on his first experience at boarding school are telling: "Flogging with birch was a great feature of the curriculum... I had such wonderful toys, now it was to be all lessons."[32]

When Charles's grandmother Fanny died in 1919, the family moved back to the United States for a few months to settle their affairs. Charles was shunted off yet again, this time to the luxe Lake Placid School, where Chicago's elite educated their children. There he spent a solitary summer trimester at the Adirondacks property, followed by a dreary winter term at the school's Florida campus in Coconut Grove. It's not surprising that, by the age of thirteen, Charles had become a

*Cecil Beaton's first photograph of his lifelong friend Charles James,
when they were both at Harrow. Charles is holding his performance
flowers, after appearing as Puck in* A Midsummer Night's Dream.

defensively independent, attention-seeking, and "obnoxious little boy," according to Florence Miller, (a close family friend whose father was then governor of Illinois.)

Back in England after the American visit, Charles's home atmosphere grew increasingly tense. As a very young and sarcastic Evelyn Waugh noted in his diary, "I took tea *en famille* with Charles James and found him restless and his sisters noisy and his father's butler in pince-nez."[33]

At fourteen, Charles was sent away again. It was 1920, the beginning of the Jazz Age, a time that his friend and schoolmate Cecil Beaton would later describe in *The Glass of Fashion*:

> For all of the deleterious values that are generally associated with the decade of the Green Hat and Our Dancing Daughters, bathtub gin, speed, the precipice-bound excitement of youth, gangsters, and immorality, some people seem to forget that it was also a period of immense creativeness. Since then we can point to few writers, actors, artists, or cinema stars whose personal contributions have been so great. Literature produced Huxley... Fitzgerald, Faulkner, Hemingway, and Thornton Wilder; the films created stars—Garbo, Gloria Swanson, Charlie Chaplin— of a magnitude never since equaled. Art yielded Dadaism, the post-cubist period of Picasso, Klee, the German expressionists, and Brancusi; sport was represented by Suzanne Lenglen, playing incredible tennis and looking hideously chic in a knee-length shift, her head bound up in a sunset-coloured turban. In the theatre, Noel Coward, Gertrude Lawrence, Helen Hayes, Pirandello, and Eugene O'Neill were exercising their literary or dramatic talents.[34]

Over three crucial years—from 1920 to 1923—at Harrow, Eton's counterpart as one of the two best and most famous preparatory schools in England, Charles honed his creative focus. He wrote, illustrated, and published a book of poems. One of his musical compositions was played in the school chapel.[35] And he won a prize in theater for acting the role of Puck in *A Midsummer Night's Dream*.[36] After the play, he was brilliantly photographed by Cecil Beaton, his best friend at school, who would become one of the most famous fashion and portrait photographers of the 1930s through the 1970s, and go on to produce some of his best work in collaboration with Charles. This is Cecil's first photograph of Charles James—shown on page 14 looking the part of Puck perfectly, carefully groomed and in costume, cradling his performance flowers, and showing off his shapely legs.[37]

It was also at Harrow that Charles James, less than a generation after Oscar Wilde's death, chose to openly call himself a homosexual. James, who lived throughout his life in what he would define as a "double-gated" society, was attracted to both men and women. But as he would explain to Couri Hay in the 1970s, Charles viewed homosexuality as "a natural state of being," adding bluntly, "You're either sexual or you're not."

With other theater students at Harrow, and off-campus friends like Sir Francis Rose, Charles had a wonderful time dressing up and wearing makeup. This was quite common for young upper-class men of Charles's circle, many of whom had, like Rose, been raised in grand mansions surrounded by venerable portraits of famous ancestors proudly posed for posterity bewigged, bejeweled, powdered, and wearing high heels.[38] Cecil wrote of himself, "I always used to powder and put red stuff on my lips...I must have been rather awful at Harrow, and I used to think I was so marvelous...subtle and interesting."[39]

In May 1923 during Charles's third and last term, Ralph, disapproving of his son's "sloppy," and artistic[40] friendships in general (Cecil, for example, was the son of a timber agent and, therefore, socially inferior; as was Evelyn Waugh, not a schoolmate, whose father was Charles Dickens's literary agent; and the elegant baronet Sir Francis Rose was simply too decadent), withdrew him from Harrow before the school term was over. Charles glamorized the wretched situation by telling everyone his exit was the result of "a sexual *escapade*."[41] But years later he would write that at approximately this time his father had actually had him raped (by someone in Ralph's military command) "so as to make a man of me."

After Harrow, Charles was exiled to France, where in preparation for university he was enrolled in a six-month prebaccalaureate music tutorial at the University of Bordeaux. He was unable to complete the curriculum.

Even though this was the end of his career in music, Charles's love for and visceral understanding of musical theory never left him. It would imbue the fugues and counterpoints in his design compositions, as he played Brahms at top volume during his fittings. And the Romantics (particularly Debussy and Ravel, who were special favorites), along with harp music by Satie and Afro-American jazz from Chicago's South Side, accompanies his fashion shows.

In a last-ditch attempt to prepare Charles for secondary school his parents sent him to study oil painting in the North West Highlands of Scotland. But when his applications to Oxford and Yale were rejected, they gave up[42] and his lessons were terminated.

Although he never attended college, Charles James was described by Elizabeth de Cuevas as "beautifully educated" and extensively well-read. "He quoted Walter Pater, spoke French fluently, could play the piano wonderfully, had a real understanding of architectural construction and he knew exactly how a medieval knight's armor was built."[43] *New York Times* columnist Virginia Pope, "Dean of Fashion Editors," thought Charles never stopped learning, and believed that he "acquired his knowledge of fashion architecture through his continual study of the human form."[44] Certainly, Charles never abandoned his quest for knowledge or his intellectual curiosity. He routinely quoted Shakespeare and the Romantics, and adored Emily Dickinson's poems. Well into his seventies, he enjoyed giving de Cuevas (and all his other friends) lists of the books he thought they should read.

In the last tapes, Charles grumbled to Couri Hay about being sent by his parents from Scotland to Chicago, where they managed to get him a clearly unsustainable job with their friend Samuel Insull. The British-born Insull, who established Commonwealth Edison Co., was famous for catalyzing the creation of an integrated electrical infrastructure in the United States, where he used holding companies to purchase railroads and utilities. He agreed to mentor Charles; and since he had begun his own career as Thomas Edison's secretary, he took the eighteen-year-old under his wing as a personal assistant.

This honor in no way deterred Charles from disrupting Insull's entire front office by prancing around in the hand-dyed batiks he'd made to wear at the beach. When he was reassigned to the architectural department, he enjoyed learning the architectural and engineering concepts he would later, in an attempt to distinguish himself from all other designers, famously apply to his couture.[45] But when Ralph was recruited to "help Insull solve a coal problem" in 1925, Charles once again shamed and angered his father by abruptly leaving the company.[46]

Finally, choosing to make a career doing something he actually enjoyed, in "a business of which my father disapproved,"[47] and where Ralph couldn't compete with him, Charles took a leaf from a chic and socially prominent acquaintance in London, the son of a duke[48] who had made a nice *social splash* as a milliner after his aristocratic family fell on hard times. From what he later described as a "temporary hide-out" in a friend's basement, he began to make hats.[49]

At nineteen, in his first formal attempt to design for a living, Charles used a bit of cash he'd inherited from his godfather, John T. Pirie, of the famous Carsons, Pirie, Scott retail establishment, to open a small store at 109 North Street in Chicago, where he planned to promote himself by selling his handmade wares to the society women and heiresses in his family's circle of friends. In an attempt at simultaneous sabotage and face-saving, Ralph James cut Charles off from family and money and refused to let him use his own name on his creations. Louise, however, remained sympathetic, and Florence Miller remembered that Charles's hats weren't bought because of their striking and amazing design[50] but because the Jameses' family friends—including Edith Rockefeller, whose husband Harold Fowler McCormick owned International Harvester, Ada Moor, whose family had founded Nabisco, and Mrs. Edward Ryerson of Ryerson Steel—wanted to help Louise's boy. And as Elizabeth Ann Coleman, the author of *The Genius of Charles James*, notes, they probably also had a very good time visiting the new shop—which Charles called Boucheron after Louis Boucheron, his friend from the famous French jewelry family—where they savored the novelty of having "Charlie" mold bespoke felt hats *individually*, cutting the (daringly) lop-sided brims to suit each particular face.

A perfect blend of beautiful manners and dreadful behavior, Charles remained an escort at high-society balls until, according to Coleman, he enjoyed the notoriety of getting kicked off the "debutante list." At the same time he was widening his sexual experiences in

Charles was constantly revisiting earlier designs.
This hat sketch by Antonio Lopez from the 1970s is of a Charles James
felt helmet that was on the cover of Vogue *in 1952. It was a variant*
of one of Charles's 1930s hat designs and it prefigured Courrèges.

the famously louche South Side of Chicago, and managed to generate even more local gossip when early the following year, after a botched suicide over a passade, he was "hauled off to be saved" in St. Luke's, the hospital his grandfather had founded. He confided to Couri he'd put his head in an oven, but romanticized the story for Cecil Beaton, who wrote in his diaries that "in a mirror-lined room lit only with candles," Charles "soused his handkerchief with ether and was sinking away when suddenly the ether burned his nose. He screamed in acute agony..."[51]

On the advice of Fowler McCormick, who lent him twenty-eight dollars, (and in one of the moves that Sir Francis Rose described as "escaping from the chores of life by episodes that were like the acts of trapezists [*sic*] in the circus"), Charles piled his belongings into "a secondhand Pierce-Arrow roadster," which he had "bought off the street" in the South Side, and headed straight for New York.[52]

It was only a matter of months before America's prophet of prosperity Herbert Hoover would sweep the 1928 presidential elections. The

Dow was spiraling upward. And Ralph James, who had just been promoted to vice president of State Line Generating, one of Insull's holding companies, invested most of his wife's money in Commonwealth Edison.

When Charles arrived in chic Southampton, Long Island, he indulgently squandered his last pennies on an image-perfecting manicure (a must in his edgy circle of friends) and was soon spotted by Diana Vreeland (later editor in chief of *Vogue*), who described him as "running up and down Southampton Beach in beautiful robes, wearing his millinery on his head."[53]

Probably through the oddly beautiful stage star Gertrude Lawrence (Cecil called her "a combination of remarkable contrasts"),[54] who was dramaturge Noel Coward's favorite actress and partner (and who had gone boating with Charles and Cecil at Harrow),[55] Charles managed to quickly establish a new New York headquarters in Coward's repurposed nineteenth-century stable in Sniffen Court, next door to the Murray Hill Amateur Comedy Club. Here he sublet two rooms from poet and playwright Mercedes de Acosta, who had been Isadora Duncan's lover and, as Cecil described it, "Greta Garbo's very best friend."[56]

In a first use of interior decoration to astonish his clients and brand his own image, Charles painted one of his showrooms cobalt blue (for his lighter clothes) and the other stark white with brilliant yellow (for his darker ones).[57] Both were cluttered with tangles of wildflowers and filled with the scattering light of crystal chandeliers.[58]

That November, when Cecil Beaton, who had just signed his first writing and photography contracts with *Vogue*, arrived in Manhattan, the two schoolmates reunited. And Cecil, who had built his career by orchestrating his own magazine publicity, helped Charles evolve what would become a lifelong habit of publicly linking his fashions to the remarkable and original women of his era.

Cecil also provided introductions. Through Cecil, Charles met golden-haired Rosamond Pinchot, known as one of the loveliest women in the world. Pinchot was a socialite, a stage and film star, and Edie Sedgwick's much older cousin. Her elegant suicide by carbon monoxide (she was discovered dead in her country garage, dressed in a white satin gown, an ermine stole, and silver slippers) would make newspaper headlines in nine years. One of the most famous stage stars of the 1930s, the almond-eyed Austrian ballerina and seductress Tilly Losch was another introduction of Cecil's. Losch was so cruel to men that Beaton called her "That Serpent of the Old Danube."[59] Even so, her first husband, Edward James, a very rich gay poet, a collector of surrealist art (and a godson of Edward VII), would underwrite George Balanchine's Les Ballets dance company, and star her in Brecht's *The Seven Deadly Sins*, where she worked with Pavel Tchelitchew, who designed the sets.

These discriminating ladies became clients of "Charles Boucheron," and, several months later, in his first *Vogue* columns, Beaton featured Pinchot[60] and Losch wearing Boucheron's intrepidly tucked and beribboned cloches and dome-crowned hat inventions, whose new, irregular brims in flattering shapes were pulled down at the back or up at the rims. That year *Vogue* also published its first sketch of a Charles James design: an asymmetrical blue felt hat by Boucheron.[61] The following year Losch would again be photographed by Cecil for *Vogue* in a Boucheron turban.[62]

Soon Mercedes's sister, Rita Lydig de Acosta, a world-famous beauty who had been painted by Boldini and dressed by the Callot Sisters (whom she financed), became a New York client.[63] And when Gertrude Lawrence, who loved Charles's eye, set a trend by commissioning and paying in advance for one of his first clothing designs,[64] a divided skirt in soft cotton he'd invented while towel-drying his thighs at the beach,[65] Charles James was on a roll.

Simultaneously, Charles was also establishing himself with the moneyed and prominent women connected to one of the world's first and largest multinational companies, Standard Oil. Isabel de Rivas (then Mrs. Oliver Burr Jennings Jr.), a well-known Paris-born coffee heiress, whose exotic good looks turned the head of the grandson of Standard Oil's former director, would remain a client well after the end of World War II in 1945. Charles also met Princess Laura Rospigliosi, a Standard Oil heiress from Cincinnati and an all-American beauty. (By 1930, Charles would be selling through Laurina, Inc., her exclusive hat and scent shop, nestled on the third floor of Thirty-five East Fifty-seventh Street in Manhattan.) And the most famous Standard Oil heiress of all, the artistic and adventuresome Millicent Rogers, went out of her way to meet Charles James in New York.[66]

By September, through Elsie de Wolfe's longtime partner, international literary agent Bessie Marbury, Charles had also met Elizabeth Arden, Bessie's new protégée.

Then in October 1929, Charles's sister Frances, who had made her London ballet debut in Frederick Ashton's *A Tragedy of Fashion, or The Scarlet Scissors*, married into dance world royalty.[67] Her husband was ballet photographer Gordon Anthony, whose images would popularize and define modern dance. Gordon's sister and partner, the famous Ninette de Valois, went on to found Sadler's Wells Theatre and direct the iconic Royal Ballet. Crucially for Charles, both Gordon Anthony and Ninette—who had trained as a soloist (*Les Biches, Le Train Bleu*) in ballet impresario Sergei Diaghilev's trendsetting dance company (Cocteau would write "Les Ballets Russes splashed Paris with color")[68]—understood and cared about the importance of style.

So, when after a five-year hiatus, Charles returned to London to design the wedding gown and bridesmaid dresses for his sister Frances's wedding on October 18,[69] the party became a platform for his fashions and an important link to the stage. And even though his father attended the wedding ceremony, it was Charles who, in a small victory, gave the bride away.[70]

But back in America, just two days after Frances's wedding, it was Black Tuesday.

On October 29, 1929, the stock market crash flagged the onset of the Great Depression. Samuel Insull, who had just finished building a magnificent new opera house as a gift to the city of Chicago, staked his reputation to unload $100 million in new securities.[71] It was only a matter of time before his empire would implode. Questionable brokerage fees had taken assets. Padded payrolls had favored relatives and friends.[72] Insull was accused of profiting personally by selling worthless stock; he fled the country. And Ralph James had lost much of his wife's inheritance.[73]

Charles's leap across the Atlantic was lucky, indeed. Without knowing what was coming, and unlike his father, he escaped the worst of the stock market crash. In Europe, fashion provided glamour and diversion, in the same way that Hollywood films popularized elegance with stars like Greta Garbo, Marlene Dietrich, and Joan Crawford.

Like painting, sculpture, music, and dance, all of which it impacted and reflected, haute couture was seen as an art—and as a passport to a spangled, transatlantic society.

London—where electric streetlights were beginning to replace gas lamps, and motor vehicles were starting to do the work of horse-drawn delivery wagons—was a propitious place to be at the onset of a worldwide depression. It had a high proportion of so-called "sunrise" industries based on new technology and, after 1933, the beginnings of a boom in the housing industry. Unlike in New York, there were jobs to be had. London also harbored small enclaves of the well-born, intellectual, and artistic society who'd somehow held on to a piece of their wealth. So, at least in patches, England was able to evade much of the worst of the economic depression that flattened the United States. Plus, prices were so low during the 1930s that one could actually live stylishly and have a very good time with a relatively small amount of cash.

Paris, too, was at a glamorous high. For the artists and expatriates, socialites, aristocrats, and arrivistes who swarmed the French capital in the 1930s, Paris was the epicenter of fashion and a hub of magical allure. At salons, galleries, cafés, and palaces, Christian (Bébé) Bérard, Max Ernst, Jean Michel Frank, Coco Chanel, Eric Satie, Nancy Cunard, Elsie de Wolfe, and Salvador Dalí joined illustrious exiles of the 1920s, like Pablo Picasso and Man Ray, or Rockefeller heiress Margaret Strong and her ballet-impresario husband, the Marquis de Cuevas. Jazz orchestrated the city's nights. Surrealism flourished. Publicized and subsidized by famous trendsetters like Daisy Fellows, Millicent Rogers, and Mona Williams, haute couture reinvented itself. And Cole Porter, another famous American in Paris, famously lyricized it all when he wrote: "What do I care if Mrs. Harrison Williams is the best dressed woman in town?"[74]

Elsa Schiaparelli, T. S. Eliot, the Windsors, Niki de Gunzburg, Jean Cocteau, and Compte Étienne de Beaumont (who threw Paris's most glittery parties), as well as a host of other celebrities, art patrons, and intellectual luminaries, were shaping a decade that fostered a creative revolution and the expat epoch in gold-rich, belle France.[75]

Naturally, though, not everyone was celebrating. In 1934, Winston Churchill, who had been out of office and "in the wilderness" for four

One of Charles's early experiments with wrapping. This is Antonio Lopez's rendering of a
dress first designed for Lady Leucha Warner and later perfected in Paris through 1937.

miserable years, wrote in the *Daily Mail*: "I marvel at the complacency
of ministers in the face of the frightful experiences through which we
have all so newly passed. I look with wonder at the thoughtless crowds
disporting themselves in the summer sunshine, and upon the unheed-
ing House of Commons, which seems to have no higher function than
to cheer on a Minister, [and all the while, across the North Sea,] a terrible process is astir. *Germany is arming.*"[76]

Of course, in the end Churchill was right. The 1930s were such
a wash of political dithering, corruption, and, above all, myopia, in
both France and England, that it is easy to think of *"La guerre de Troie
n'aura pas lieu,"* [77]—playwright Jean Giraudoux's elegantly expressed
1935 polemic against blinkered world leaders—as an icon of the ten

years of governmental denial that would end, ineluctably, with the 1940 German invasion of Paris.

Charles would find all of this easy to ignore from London, where he gracefully landed in 1930, at age twenty-four.

Heedlessly underfinanced by the profits from his New York enterprises, he established his showroom almost next door to the Queen's anointed designer, Norman Hartnell, at 1 Bruton Street,[78] in the fashionable Mayfair neighborhood. And he wickedly named the new venture "E. Haweis" after his father's middle names.

Though short on cash, Charles did manage to arrive in England with a growing reputation, a publicity-padded portfolio and an already-established venue for selling his designs. In New York, he had made a new friend: Mary Lewis, who bought for Best & Co. and was an early, important and faithful backer of his young career. Best & Co. was the first department store to carry and promote Charles's designs where, in a totally original marketing innovation, James had allowed them to promote store copies that retailed for $17.50 next to the couture millinery, which was twice as expensive. This experiment in "high-low" merchandising was his first experience with mass retailing, which in turn would lead to Charles's licensing career.

When, concomitant to his arrival in London, an advertisement for nine "slightly wicked" Boucheron hats (for sale at Best & Co.) appeared in the *New York Times*, Charles finally had written proof of his commercial viability as well. He was described in the copy (which reads as though he'd written it personally to heighten his own mystique) as "erratic, picturesque, amusing," and as possessing "a rare spark of genius and the talent for expressing the spirit of his times."[79]

In addition to the already well-publicized hats, the first London collection included one or two investigational designs for dresses—chiefly tryouts of new ideas in lengths, draping, and wrapping. An example was the silk "Scarf" evening gown he designed for an influential London client, Lady Leucha Warner, and fashioned with a diagonal neckline that sweeps into a cape, over the bias-cut body.

These experiments were planned to help Charles capitalize on the Insull experience and launch himself as a "sartorial structural architect"[80] (a title he invented) to the trade and to the circle of clients and friends through whom he would now define himself, and with whose support he would begin to establish a tripartite career in London, Paris, and across the Atlantic in New York.

In this regard at least, Charles's planning was ingenious. First he would approach fabric manufacturers to finance his "research" into new fashions. They would pay him (though never enough) to invent designs featuring their fabrics or notions, which he would, then, (as a boon to all involved), arrange to have photographed for the press on one of his socially prominent friends.

These very social, "singular people," members of young London's "gratin," many of whom Charles met through Evelyn Waugh and Cecil, were a community of intellectually and culturally influential peers, all of whom seemed to know one another. They matched Charles's upper-class upbringing and his dandified and unorthodox proclivities. Their extravagant, dramatic company empowered and encouraged his naturally eccentric, opulent perfectionism, while their inbred aristocratic condescension underscored his conviction that the best of life was his by right. For both better and worse, they played a formative role in the creation of his brilliant, arrogant, outspoken, and larger-than-life persona.

Importantly, this high-octane group viewed Charles as he wanted to see himself—as much more than a mere dressmaker. Their empathetic encouragement nurtured his passion for inventing his own brand of beauty, and their mind-set fostered a different kind of elitism, one that spared no expense or energy to realize an ideal. As Marit Guinness-Aschan, artisan, banking heiress, client, and friend from Charles's childhood, explained: "It was always accepted by my family that Charlie was a genius."[81]

At the time of Charles's sister Frances's wedding, Cecil was very involved in cultivating his own image, taking portraits of glamorous, brainy, publicity-seeking, and influential young ne'er-do-wells called "the Bright Young Things."

These stars of London's social and cultural firmament included the artist and war hero Rex Whistler, who illustrated Waugh's novels; the poet Siegfried Sassoon; and the six stylishly notorious Mitford sisters, whose brother Tom was one of Tilly Losch's lovers.

Nancy, the eldest, achieved celebrity when, with Evelyn Waugh's encouragement, she published *Love in a Cold Climate,* a roman à clef scandalously brimming with thinly disguised characters from English high society. The youngest, Deborah—"Debo" to her loved ones—would become the Dowager Duchess of Devonshire, Dame Commander of the Royal Victorian Order, and would raise pet chickens in her spare time.

Then, there were the three flamboyant Sitwell siblings, self-proclaimed descendants of the House of Plantagenet, who founded a literary circle that prefigured Bloomsbury. Osbert, who described himself as having "the remote air of legend," would, according to the composer William Walton, "do absolutely anything for publicity" and kept his press clippings on public display in a silver bowl on his drawing-room table. Sacheverell, the shyest of the three, was an art and music critic. Lady Edith Sitwell was the eldest and most gifted. She was also the most complicated, not the least because she was *so* ugly as a child that her vain and beautiful mother forced her to wear a veil in public (to avoid embarrassment) and essentially abandoned her to her governess, Helen Roothman. Edith was educated in isolation at Renishaw Hall—the forbiddingly Gothic, six-hundred-year-old family estate in Yorkshire (which would become the model for the mansion in D. H. Lawrence's *Lady Chatterley's Lover*).

Escaping to London, Edith made a name for herself with a new style of poetry, which referenced jazz by mixing its syncopated rhythms with a confusion of visual and tactile images:

Jane, Jane
Tall as a crane
The morning light creaks down again[82]

In town she quickly became even more famous for her ostentatious dresses and turbans, her magnificent jewelry (some of which Millicent Rogers designed and gave to her), and her aquiline nose than she was for her verse. Her choice of Waugh as godfather when she converted to Catholicism, and her well-publicized romantic love for Charles's soon-to-be-friend, the gay, Russian-born, surrealist painter Pavel

Tchelitchew—who Charles later claimed influenced him more than any other artist he had ever met—fueled her notoriety as well.

The "brightest" of these aristocratically iconoclastic "Brights" was Lord Stephen Tennant. He was the pampered youngest son of a Scottish baronet, a good friend of Cecil's, and he took an immediate liking to Charles.

Gorgeously narcissistic (he was self-described as possessing "the fatal gift of beauty"),[83] Stephen defined eccentricity as a "kind of innocent pride." He dusted his dyed hair with gold powder, rouged his bee-stung lips to look like his favorite film star, Mae Murray, and by flagrantly doing as little as possible, became incredibly important to the literature of his time. He was the model for the gay charmer Cedric Hampton in Nancy Mitford's *Love in a Cold Climate*, as well as Evelyn Waugh's most famous character, Lord Sebastian Flyte, in *Brideshead Revisited*. In 1929, the year of Frances James's wedding, Stephen ordered a small wardrobe from Charles to wear on an excursion to Italy with the poet and war hero Siegfried Sassoon, who, old enough to be his father, sentimentally commemorated the trip:

> Let us be true to what we have shared and seen,
> And as our amulet this idyll save.
> And since the unreturning day must die,
> Let it forever be lit by an evening sky
> And the wild myrtle grow upon its grave.[84]

The romantic wardrobe included, in Stephen's own words, "the stunningest (*sic*) fancy dress black trousers, that seem glued to every fissure and ripple of thigh and bottom and an ineffably limp shirt of creamy satin like ultra-ultra Devonshire crème mixed with mother of pearl."[85] In a photograph by Cecil, taken in Syracuse, he is costumed in pale silk custom-made Charles James lounging pajamas. Seated on the ground with his caged parrot beside him, and leaning back against an ancient wall, he turns his delicate profile toward the Italian sun.[86]

Together with Cecil, Stephen Tennant, who also personally enjoyed wearing Charles's dresses, would become, as Charles described it, his "key to the English clientele of note, which in turn impressed the (rich and international) American clientele, which longed to meet the English clientele."[87] In other words, he was an enormous help in developing a celebrity client base of aristocrats, royals, theater professionals, and associates of the literarily influential Bloomsbury Group, who were all also friends.

Centered around Virginia Woolf, E. M. Forster (whose *Passage to India* was one of the finest books to come out of the era), Virginia's sister Vanessa Bell, and Vanessa's husband, the noted artist Clive Bell, the Bloomsbury Group was an informal assemblage of generally well-heeled, left-leaning intellectuals, writers, artists, pleasure-seeking philosophers, feminists, pacifists, and believers in sexual freedom. Many had gone to school together and lived or worked near London's Bloomsbury district.

Stephen's friend Lady Ottoline Morrell—the wife of the emotionally unstable liberal member of Parliament Philip Morell and an accomplished art patron and famous literary hostess—is an example of the type of woman to whom Charles James was drawn and whom he liked to dress. She entertained fellow pacifists, including Clive Bell, Lytton Strachey, D. H. Lawrence, and T. S. Eliot, in her town house at 44 Bedford Street in Bloomsbury, and was famously photographed by Cecil. She was six feet tall, with brilliant red-gold hair, turquoise eyes, and a peculiar, ungainly, horsey face, which was also somehow notoriously irresistible to both men and women, including the portrait painter Augustus John. One of her lovers was the family gardener, and she became the model for D. H. Lawrence's Lady Chatterley. Obstinately idiosyncratic, Morrell favored clothing copied from medieval and Renaissance drawings, and she taught Charles, as he later wrote, "the importance of disregarding current fashion trends."[88] Her close friend Virginia Woolf, who stood at the center of the Bloomsbury Group, ordered hats from Charles, and according to Coleman, decided he was a "genius" when he cut them for her "right on her head."

Another very financially supportive friend and patron was Lady Leucha Warner. Described as having "exemplary elegance of figure and carriage," and being "one of the most open-minded and deeply unconventional human beings ever,"[89] Leucha was also a famous society hostess, and the daughter of another Liberal MP, "the first and last Earl de Montalt of Dundrum."

Finally, there was Ottoline's protégée and sometime lover, the wealthy Indian-born artist and writer Mary Hutchinson, who was Lytton Strachey's cousin, a close friend of T. S. Eliot and Aldous Huxley, and Clive Bell's mistress, all at once. Woolf, who also wrote for *British Vogue*, described Mary as "worldly, elegantly fashionable, ugly, charming, with a wonderful taste in clothes, patina, and interior decoration," and regarded her as "a paragon."[90]

It was in this circle, and with their tutelage, that Charles would develop his theory of style. Individuality was an absolute prerequisite for what he would come to define as elegance, which for him always had more to do with character and intelligence than symmetrical shape. Fashion, which was the outgrowth of "a melding of personalities,"[91] Charles theorized, represented a process of becoming, and the tension between interiority and form.

Thus Charles never tried to build a traditional business. Setting himself apart from other designers, he was focused on dressing and being a member of his social milieu of aristocrats and intellectuals, all of whom were distinguished by their unique personalities and idiomatic sense of self. As Philippe Jullian later remarked in the *The Snob Spotter's Guide*, "Charles James made only ten dresses a year."[92] Each one, crucially, was an important design that allowed a woman to stand out in a society notable for "standing out" in general. Being dressed by Charles would quickly become a way to be recognized as a person of substance and originality.

Unfortunately, despite his growing group of friends and rapidly burgeoning reputation, on March 23, 1931, scarcely nine months after he opened E. Haweis, Charles James filed for bankruptcy.[93] It was the first of a myriad of financial collapses that would become the hallmark of his business practices.

With his own ineffable blend of aristocratic offhandedness, bad-boy insouciance, and denial, Charles celebrated his misfortune by throwing a large party for his clients and friends. He sold the hats he had managed to rescue from the sheriff to Best & Co., and, as the police were lugging off the last contents of his studio, he was introduced to Elsa

Schiaparelli by Cecil and another designer in their circle, the Princess Dilkusha de Rohan. Schiaparelli, who would over the next few years be Charles's colleague, co-creator, and sometime employer, helped him load up a car with left-behind lamps, sewing machines, and miscellaneous bric-a-brac. Then, they all decided, it was time for tea.[94]

Elsa Schiaparelli, by Cecil Beaton, photographed in London. During the shoot a chandelier crashed to the floor, narrowly missing her head.

CHAPTER 2

Art and Invention:

Elsa Schiaparelli

LIKE CHARLES, ELSA SCHIAPARELLI ("That Italian artist who makes clothes,"[95] as Chanel invidiously called her) was a self-taught designer. And she was as wild—if not wilder—than he.

Born in 1890 in the Palazzo Corsini in Rome, Elsa was the younger of two daughters, the baby of the family. Her half-Scottish mother was Neapolitan nobility. Her father, whom she invariably described as kind,[96] was dean of the faculty at the University of Rome as well as a prominent medieval scholar specializing in Islamic manuscripts. And her beloved great uncle, Giovanni Schiaparelli, was senator of the kingdom of Italy and the astronomer who discovered the "canals" on Mars.[97]

In her autobiography, *Shocking Life*—in which she frequently refers to herself in the third person as an "alter ego" character named Schiap—Elsa painted her personality as independently quirky, passionately inventive, and calamitous. She had an unpredictable sense of humor and illimitable creativity: talents she used endlessly to amuse herself and her clients.[98]

Saucer eyed and raven haired, Elsa claimed to have been born ugly, or at least not as pretty as her elder sister. She told the story of how, as a little girl, she had the idea to improve her looks by covering her face, mouth, and ears with soil in which she planted flower seeds, hoping that a beautiful garden would sprout. Her parents were indulgent, and her only punishment was her disappointment when the experiment failed. On another occasion, she jumped out of a window, holding an open umbrella to see if it would work as a parachute. It didn't. But she landed unhurt in a large pile of manure.

At thirteen, totally lacking in any kind of sexual experience, Elsa managed to publish a collection of riotously imaginative poems of erotic love, loss, and sorrow in a little book called *Arethusa*. Her parents were hugely embarrassed. They tried to discipline her by sending her off to a convent school in Switzerland. There, at odds with the cold and hypocritical nuns, who would not let her undress for her baths, she promptly went on a hunger strike until her father gave in and brought her back home.[99]

At twenty-three, with her formal education permanently disrupted by her mercurial behavior, Schiaparelli finally found a way to escape from the shelter of her family when she decided to attend a talk in London given by the indolent and apparently penniless French Swiss theosophist, Count William de Wendt de Kerlor. She introduced herself to him after the lecture. And to the dismay of her parents, she married him the next day. After a simple ceremony, the newlyweds returned to the small mews house de Kerlor had been renting, where the new countess discovered that all seven mirrors in the house had been mysteriously smashed. This, wrote Schiaparelli, was "a sinister beginning."[100]

At William's insistence, the couple moved to New York. There they lived on her dwindling dowry. The following year, Schiap's only daughter—nicknamed "Gogo," for the gurgling sounds she made as an infant—was born. In 1922, when the count deserted her and his baby for other women, including Isadora Duncan, Elsa discovered that Gogo, who at fifteen months walked "like a crab,"[101] had infantile paralysis. She decided to move to Paris, which was much cheaper than New York, in search of medical treatment for her child. She filed for divorce and renewed her passport in her maiden name.

The move changed everything for her. "If I have become what I am," she wrote in *Shocking Life*, "I owe it to two things: poverty and Paris. Poverty forced me to work, and Paris gave me a liking for it."[102]

In Paris, she met and was mentored by the great couturier Paul Poiret, known to all France as "Le Magnifique." Poiret had established the canon of modern dress in Europe and America (where his innovations were so unscrupulously copied that he was forced to invent licensing). He was the fashion revolutionary who liberated women from the corset. He also introduced harem pants, which he advertised by throwing glamorous theme parties based on dreams of the Orient. At his "Thousand and Second Night" costume ball, he exhibited his beautiful model wife, dressed like an Arabian concubine, in a huge, gilded cage. Later, he experimented successfully with a variety of other exotic silhouettes, such as his iconic "lampshade" tunic, as well as with color, prints, and lavish fabrics. Poiret was also one of the first fashion designers to collaborate with artists. The young Fauvist painter Raoul Dufy was commissioned to create printed textiles for his designs.

When Elsa and Poiret met in his "maison de couture," as she was trying on a tubular coat of brightly striped black velvet, lined with dazzling blue crepe de chine, Schiaparelli wrote, "The great Poiret himself was looking at me. I felt the impact of our personalities." He asked her if she wanted to buy the coat. She replied that she couldn't begin to afford it and had nowhere to wear it, even if she could. "Don't worry about money and you can wear anything anywhere,"[103] he replied. This was the beginning of a heady friendship, full of delicious food, cheap white wine, and wonderful conversations. Poiret very generously helped Elsa—who, because of her background, had easy entrée to Paris society—become a fashion leader by giving her a fabulous wardrobe of his extravagant clothes. He was equally supportive of her talent, and encouraged her to begin designing for herself. So she did.[104]

Giddy with modernity, and ambitious to create the "look" of the 1930s, Schiap rang out the 1920s by—to paraphrase Yves Saint Laurent—slapping, torturing, and bewitching Paris[105] until it fell in love with her. By 1931, the year of her unceremonious introduction to Charles James, the French capital was the unquestionable center of the fashion world, and Elsa its queen.

Riffing on Chanel's knitted sportswear she had already invented her famous black-and-white "trompe-l'oeil sweater," which, after several attempts to get it right, had been produced for her by Armenian refugees, who managed to make a flat bow design look dimensional. She had also devised the first pointy woolen "mad cap," so attitudinal that it became a sensation all across the United States. And she was about to create an uproar by dressing the Spanish tennis player Lili de Alvarez for Wimbledon in the culottes she dreamt up for her (they actually looked like pantaloons wrapped with an apron—it was illegal for women to wear trousers in France). Importantly, she had also begun to develop her American market. She had a fan in *Women's Wear Daily*, which praised her individuality, and Strauss (later Macy's) and other

35

American department stores had placed significant orders and were paying promptly.

Befriended by Man Ray and Gaby Picabia, wife of painter Francis Picabia, while she was a down-and-out countess in New York, Elsa had by this time also made friends with Francis (Gaby was his ex-wife by then), Pablo Picasso, Eric Satie, Coco Chanel, Jean Cocteau, and the whole gang at Cocteau's small den of iniquity—a nightclub and in spot of the moment called Le Boeuf sur le Toit. She knew Pavel Tchelitchew and was fascinated by Dalí. She had met Jean Michel Frank, who would design her famously simple, famously all-black (Chanel said it made her "shudder as though passing a cemetery") Parisian studio at 21 Place Vendôme. She was also close to Elsie de Wolfe, with whom she would join forces in creating the most spectacular circus-themed fancy dress parties of the decade.

Like Charles James, Elsa was interested in selling internationally, and around the time that she met him she began flirting with the idea of a boutique in London, the brainchild of one of her English beaus who, as she recorded in her quirky reminiscences, "Followed me wherever I went and…was an incorrigible dreamer. He had 'la manie des grandeurs,' and persuaded me to open a house in London. Thus [in 1934] No. 36 Grosvenor Square was born."[106] (One wonders if the "beau" might have really been Charles.)

Once ensconced in Great Britain, Schiap, who complained that her English employees' mania for taking tea every afternoon nearly drove her mad, was contrapuntally thrilled to discover that the contrast between the femininity of Paris and the masculinity of London stimulated her brain "to give out ideas like a fireworks show."[107] She thoroughly enjoyed her social life in England as well, and bragged that "the names of famous people who flocked to Upper Grosvenor Street would make a small *Who's Who.*"[108]

Elsa was gratified when Cecil Beaton asked to photograph her, although, "He made Schiap sit for hours turning first this way and then that…a huge chandelier moved perhaps by the exasperation surging in Schiap's mind crashed down from the ceiling just missing her head…. Poor Cecil was so frantic that he took a magnificent photo [of her], the next second."

Sadly, like Charles, Schiaparelli was unable to achieve commercial success on the island side of the Channel: "The London experiment proved highly entertaining, afforded me excellent publicity, and allowed me to form wonderful friendships but as far as cash was concerned, I quickly came up against a well-established English custom—that one has to wait for people to die in order to get paid."[109]

On the upside, she was able to use the British adventure to generate wonderful new fabrics—"I became intensely interested in British textiles"—and visited all kinds of factories in England and Scotland. "The Isle of Skye, which at that time was greatly patronized by the Duke and Duchess of York (later king and queen), remains vivid.... in Scotland I first saw black sheep. I had them shorn, and the wool was made up into the most startling materials slightly reminiscent of the heavy Arab wools....I have always loved materials and I worked more closely with the textile people than any of my colleagues,"[110] she reminisced.

Schiap also became increasingly experimental with colors and shapes as she moved from wrapping to construction, declaring, "Never fit the dress to the body, but train the body to fit the dress." [111] Mae West, who was intrigued by such a concept, promised to travel to Paris. She wanted to be personally measured by Schiaparelli even though she had already sent all the most intimate details of her famous figure in advance to Elsa's atelier, along with a life-size plaster statue of herself "quite naked and posed like the Venus de Milo."[112]

Schiap, who had styled Katharine Hepburn's way to celebrity for her breakout screen role in the 1932 film *A Bill of Divorcement*, finally decided to visit Hollywood. In southern California, Elsa (who unlike Charles had the money to travel speculatively) discovered perfect martinis, was unnerved by unexpected earthquakes, and found to her dismay that the exaggerated shoulders she had developed to give women slimmer waists had preceded her. "They proved to be the mecca of the manufacturers." She reminisced about those broad shoulders: "Joan Crawford [much later] adopted them and molded her silhouette on them for years to come....[the designer] Adrian took them up with overwhelming enthusiasm."[113] When Elsa was invited to Adrian's villa in Los Angeles, she remembered, he had "as a surprise all of the big stars of the moment to model his clothes for me. I wore that day a black coat with very wide shoulders and it was fringed with monkey fur, and I left it in the cloakroom downstairs. In the middle of the show, an undulating blond starlet appeared with what looked like my coat and made for me in a straight line. 'Don't you think it is divine? What a genius the dear boy is.'"[114]

Americans were mad for and about Schiaparelli's pyrotechnical fashion ideas, but although she tried repeatedly, business practices in the United States made it impossible for her ever to establish a successful venture in either California or New York. The rampant American practice of unabashed copying wasn't the only problem. American luxury import taxes were prohibitive. And the costs to manufacture in the United States were worse, particularly since, unlike the French fabric makers, the Americans demanded advance payment together with bulk orders, and would not let her sample their wares.

In revenge, Elsa's boutique, Schiap Shop, which was already one of the sights of Paris, became the go-to haute couture house for film costumes and the glamorous international movie star set. She dressed Marlene Dietrich, who tried on hats, "her famous legs crossed, smoking a perennial cigarette as if she were posing for the movies, and like nobody else does. Claudette Colbert, mischievous and twinkling... Merle Oberon perfumed like the Queen of Sheba...Lauren Bogart with her aristocratic face and Brooklyn vocabulary saying a deep long *bonjour* that sounded like a high note...Simone Simon tearing a dress to pieces in the face of the fitter because she did not wish to wear it in spite of Sacha Guitry's wish...and Gloria Swanson."[115] All flickered in the constantly moving picture of Schiaparelli's imagination.

Elsa, who had decided that "as soon as a dress is born it becomes a thing of the past,"[116] banned the word "creativity" from her showroom.[117] In her hands, fashion became an ongoing stream of self-expression that took its inspiration from prevailing art trends as she decorated her designs with visual jokes whose cleverness veered on absurdity. She sent embroidered ants scurrying along on a hat brim, painted black gloves with shiny pink fingernails, and peered at the world through cabana-awning sunglasses. Then she made a hat in the shape of a lamb chop with a white paper frill on it, and an otter's fur bathing suit. It was a sensibility that had much in common with surrealist expression. By the second half of the decade, Elsa was specifically engaging her artist friends to, as she articulated it, "lift her out" of "the crude boring reality of merely making dresses only to sell."[118]

Christian Bérard, for example, designed (and illustrated for *Vogue*) a Medusa head in the shape of a sun that adorned the back of a cape in her Zodiac collection. Dalí first dyed an enormous stuffed teddy bear shocking pink and put real little drawers in its round, fat tummy for Schiaparelli to use as a display prop in her Place Vendôme store, where it was dressed up in an orchid-colored satin coat and loaded with jewels. Then, in 1936, he was commissioned to paint an outrageously phallic lobster design (surrounded by very edible looking sprigs of green parsley) all down the front of a pure white silk chiffon evening dress for Wallis Simpson. Wallis fell in love with the lobster and insisted on being officially photographed in it by Cecil during the summer of 1937, just before she became the Duchess of Windsor. That same year, Elsa showed twin full-length evening coats, on which François Lesage's delicate trompe l'oeil embroidery traced a romantic Jean Cocteau sketch of two faces in profile looking into each other's eyes. The matching heads were crowned with blooming roses, which, because of the shape made by the profiles, could also be seen as an overflowing urn. Finally, in 1938, Dalí developed the controversial "skeleton dress." Decorated with padding that looked like bones, it was the specter of death in Elsa's Circus Collection.

"A frock from Schiap," wrote Janet Flanner in the *New Yorker,* "ranks like a modern canvas."[119]

And although Mae West's plaster figure was never used to make any dresses, Elsa gave it to the artist Leonor Fini, who reproduced it for the "Shocking" perfume bottle.

Adventuresome, inspiring, and sympathetic, Schiaparelli was a perfect connection for Charles, who liked her very much personally as well. They admired each other, he said, as colleagues and as co-innovators of style.[120] Elsa was a great impetus for Charles to cross the Channel, and a great support to him in Paris. And even though he continued to develop his private clientele by showing in England in smaller spaces lent to him by the faithful Cecil and Oliver Messel, Cecil's friend and rival, after 1931 he would spend longer and longer blocks of time in France.

At the beginning of the 1930s, with Schiap in the City of Lights, Charles gave up the Boucheron and E. Haweis imprints in favor of his own name on his labels. His Parisian focus was on really learning how to make clothing. He studied couture methods, soaked up French aesthetics, and perfected his nascent technique. And Charles would get to know almost Schiap's entire circle, although he didn't necessarily meet all of them through her. (His friend and admirer, the baronet Sir Francis Rose, for example, who was also an artist, probably introduced him to Christian Dior.)

He, too, would be mentored by Poiret. And he would exchange ideas and sketches with Chanel and Balenciaga. Over the next several years, Charles and Elsa would work together on couture for the excruciatingly rich and internationally admired Millicent Rogers. In London they both designed for the "Coronation Review," a stage spectacular mounted by impresario C. B. Cochran, London's greatest theatrical producer at the time. In Paris they whipped up fancy dress costumes for world-famous party-givers like Elsie de Wolfe and art and music patron Étienne de Beaumont, who was Charles's great friend. They would trade inspirations, patterns, and ideas and for a time their practices would evolve— albeit very differently and personally—along parallel paths.

In 1931, the year of their meeting, just after the debut of Charles's first "clothing collection," Charles and Schiap both experimented with wrapping. Schiaparelli created wrap skirts that evolved into wrap day dresses and the "most successful dress"[121] of her career, an uncomplicated long sheath made of black crepe de chine under a soft white crepe de chine jacket, with long sashes that crossed over the back and tied in the front.

Equally tired of the shapeless, tubular dresses that had been all the rage in the 1920s, before he began dress designing, and hungry for new design "inventions," Charles started, with the encouragement of Elsa's equivalent vision, to focus increasingly on rethinking the rules of dressmaking in order to accomplish a leaner, closer-fitting line, like the one he had been able to achieve for men with his friend Stephen Tennant's travel clothes. (He would return throughout his life to "body hugging," in the form of various restatements of cut and binding.) He continued the experiments he had initiated with his designs for Leucha Warner

Antonio Lopez's rendering of the first wrap dress. Charles had the idea for this dress in 1929 when he came to New York, where he fantasized a dress so simply sexy that it could be put on—or taken off—in the back seat of a taxi. He perfected this famous design in the early 1930s and named it the "Taxi Dress."

and Gertrude Lawrence. He also played with the placement of darts and seams, moving them from the sides of patterns toward the front, to make what he would call a "false profile." In some cases, he eliminated them altogether. In the first of his original techniques (which he christened "theses" because each of these "inventions" would become part of a personal, ever-evolving design vocabulary), he tested a "semi-bias" and found that by cutting cloth diagonally to the grain of the fabric, he was able to mold it all around breasts, waist, and hips, allowing the material to cling to the body and move with the wearer.

He named a first radically new design the "Taxi Dress," which, using this technique, coiled sinuously around the figure from left to right, to fasten at the right hip with Bakelite clips. It was invented in

1929 during Charles's trip to New York, when the intensity and speed of Manhattan made him dream of a dress that was so easy it could be put on—or sexily taken off—in the back of a taxi. Mary Hutchinson immediately bought the infamous wrap, which she described in a letter to her fan Virginia Woolf as "symmetrical, diabolical, and geometrically perfect."[122] She added, "I think he [Charles] has a romantic gift...he makes women look exciting and strange."[123]

Closer in thinking to Schiaparelli's creations, another Jamesian improvisation on the "wrapping" theme was a straightforward sheath dress with an integrated shoulder scarf, made of two long pieces of fabric which could be bound around the waist and tied at the back for an individual fit.

Charles, like Schiap, was also indelibly influenced by the surrealists Pavel Tchelitchew, Salvador Dalí, and Jean Cocteau, with whom he would collaborate. And, like them, he used his creativity to explore the "unconscious," the irrational, and the daring. But Charles, who at the time had little to do with Hollywood glitter, was much less interested in whimsy and ornamentation than Schiaparelli. It was surrealist theory and the techniques of the surrealist artists—their displacements, transpositions, illusions, and distortions of *form;* he called them "morphology"—that inspired him. And through his career these practices would inflect the shape and drape of his designs.

Schiap and Charles both played with soft suiting and widely exaggerated shoulders (which Hollywood was so happy to copy). In Charles James's 1933 "Incroyable (Incredible) Suit," the jacket had puff shoulders and an attenuated waistline, which were deliberately suggestive of the exaggeratedly elongated lines of fashions worn by the Incroyables: famously rule-flaunting French Directoire dandies. But the narrow sleeves were cut on the bias, and Charles sewed the long jacket tails together to create a graceful and suggestively fluid, low-back cowl, like a half hobbled skirt, a collapsed bustle, or beetle wings at rest.

In further experimentation with motion, fit, and shifts of draping and structure that worked against and away from the body, a black silk viscose evening dress featured an elegantly narrowed bias-cut skirt. The folds of the skirt were pulled up at the front of the waist to form drapes on each side. These pointed, pocket-like shapes dramatically

Antonio Lopez's version of a 1937 Charles James experiment with draping.
The silhouette is formed by pulling up the front waist to create side-drape pockets.

mirrored the deep "V" of the dress's décolletage and the triangular cutouts between the sleeves and the shoulders.

Not all of his experiments were successful, however. Even Mary Hutchinson, who was one of his favorite clients, particularly because she understood that by buying from Charles she was "not so much ordering clothes as patronizing the arts," would write, "Charlie was sometimes so entranced by the shape he was 'sculpting' over one's own shape that when the dress arrived finished, it was impossible to get into it. It existed on its own. Much time was then spent in discerning the proper relationship between shapes."[124]

Again in tandem with Elsa, who was the first to use cutting-edge materials like rayon, latex, and cellophane in her couture, Charles enjoyed pushing the envelope by implementing new technology and experimenting with wonder fabrics, which were the latest rage. He was sponsored by fabric manufacturer William Hollins & Co. to try out dresses in unusual color combinations and color blocks made of Viyella, a new synthetic material, and published his resulting designs in *Vogue* and *Harper's Bazaar.*

Charles found anatomical references almost as sensually appealing as the latest fasteners and newest "fake" fabrics. If he could have both at the same time, he was doubly gratified. In 1933, when he took a collection of his designs to the United States branches of Dunhill and Fortnum & Mason, he made sure the American press noticed one dress with dark angora on its bodice, which looked "like hair on the chest."[125] And he was thrilled with the growing "international-ness" of his reputation when both British and American *Harper's Bazaar* published a sketch of him, looking quite suave with one fist on a hip, gazing slant eyed at a graceful woman in an evening wrap he'd made of a new, uncut white velvet that (reads the insinuating copy) "looks like *wet* feathers."[126]

Many of Charles's new designs were also three-dimensional illustrations of sexuality, sensuality, and sex appeal. He began to define fashion as "a rehearsal for propagation."[127]

In collaboration with Lightning Fasteners Ltd. of England he created his "Zipper Dress," which was an evolved, even more suggestive version of the Taxi Dress design, in which the zipper that slithered around the figure was both decorative and functional.

"He made my sister-in-law [Sheila Hill] her going-away dress," wrote Derek Hill, Oliver Messel's friend, who remembered Charles as a prime-time eccentric. "And it was the first ever dress with a zip. It went around her like a bandage, and at the bottom he ended the zip with a little clasp. And Charlie gave my brother a key to that clasp as a wedding present."[128]

In a historically defining moment, Henri Matisse, who was preparing to sketch her, asked Mary Hutchinson to model one of Charles's famously transparent, filmy, curvilinear wrap blouses. As he turned in the finished charcoal portrait, the artist confessed, *"Madame, votre blouse m'a beaucoup aidé."*[129] That year, Charles's childhood friend lovely Marit Guinness was forbidden by her parents to wear his (suggestive) tops.

"Fashion" Charles James wrote, is "that which is rare, correctly proportioned, and though utterly discrete, libidinous."[130] Gertrude Lawrence, a lifelong customer, concurred. She described Charles's clothes as "the most respectable I have ever bought, though utterly indecent."

Unlike Schiaparelli, who would turn her fashion shows into whimsically themed theatrical festivals with names like "Stop, Look and Listen,"[131] "The Metamorphosis Collection" (whose symbol was the butterfly, a surrealist image of change), and, much later, "Zodiac" and "Circus," Charles, who worked very slowly, tended to treat his designs as individual pieces, giving each its own name. Nonetheless, when he was still only twenty-six and had been making clothes for less than three years, Charles decided, either bravely or shamelessly, that when all the American retailers (including Marshall Field's from Chicago, where he had connections) were in town for the *French* haute couture shows, he would show a small collection of his *American* work in *Paris*.[132] It was something only Mainbocher had dared do before.

The February show was an artistic triumph. And he scooped the French designers by selling to the American retailers original dress designs for duplication (in much the same way as he had been providing Best & Co. with couture hats, which he allowed them to copy), something the more-established couture houses wouldn't do.[133] So the show was a financial success, too. His retail clients included the House of Tappé and, naturally, Best & Co. in New York, as well as Marshall Field's in Chicago. In London, he sold to Harrods and Victoire, an exclusive dress shop on London's fashionable Sloane Street.

Once again, one has the impression that Charles was writing his own headlines when the dispatch from *Women's Wear Daily*'s Paris bureau reads: "Charles James, a Former Architect, Uses Structural Idea in Designing. Exponent of Erotical Theory of Fashion Shows Collection in Paris after Varied Career Here and Abroad."[134]

In a brief interview, Charles informed *WWD* that because "increased exercise had toned the modern woman's body and made her posture and movement more athletic,"[135] he was planning to develop new dressmaking techniques that showed off the figure and provided what he called the "erotical it."[136] This was the first published articulation of the emphasis that the designer of "slightly wicked" hats for Best & Co. would continue to place on sex appeal, not just in the making, but *also in the marketing*, of his clothes—and of himself.

That summer, when fashion publicist Eleanor Lambert went to see him for the first time in his rooms at the Plaza Athénée, he greeted her lying recumbent on a couch. "I was taken into a sitting room," Eleanor related, "and I waited and waited. And finally, the doors were opened dramatically. He'd taken white tulle and made a great whoosh of it all over the sofa, and he was lying down in it!"[137]

This was to be a pattern. Charles would welcome others to the roof terrace of his elegant suite, posed by the balustrade in tiny, revealing bathing trunks. Later, he would have himself theatrically photographed in his hotel room for British *Harper's Bazaar*; again very bare legged, in the shortest of short shorts, musing, with the point of his scissors tantalizingly held up to his lips, in what the copy dramatically called "creative agony."[138]

By June 1933, Charles James had amazingly gathered enough money to open a new "grand salon" in London (where Elsa would join him the next year). And here at 15 Bruton Street, in his old neighborhood, he would begin to work with a new muse, his most significant client of the 1930s: Anne Armstrong-Jones, née Messel, and later the Countess of Rosse.

The following year he accrued even more capital when, in a triumphant homecoming, he took a collection to Marshall Field's in Chicago, where his mother and his friend Mary Slaughter Field personally sent hand-engraved invitations to a small, exclusive tea and a showing of Charles's "Parisian" designs in the Wedgwood Room. It was, Charles remembered, one of the "biggest successes I have ever had."[139]

In 1935 Elsa traveled to Copenhagen and visited the fish market, filled with old wives who sat for hours on the banks of the canals surrounded by silver fish scales wearing "on their heads newspapers twisted into the queer shapes of hats."[140] As soon as she got back to Paris she called her friend the cloth manufacturer Jean Colcombet, "the most daring of the textile men."[141] She clipped newspaper articles about herself, stuck them together like a puzzle, and had Colcombet print them on silk and cotton "in all sorts of colors," which she turned into a wide variety of products from blouses to bathing suits and cases for toiletries. "The man," as Schiap called Colcombet, sold "thousands and thousands of yards."[142] And, she noted later, one could still, in the 1960s, buy tobacco pouches made from her pattern in England.

By 1936, when (according to Millicent Rogers's granddaughter, Christina Peralta Ramos) Charles and Elsa were both making clothes for Millicent's Tyrolean period,[143] Colcombet, whose company was known for its military and ribbon fabrics, gave Charles some eighteen-inch-wide grosgrain that had been woven during World War I, and Charles developed the rigid fabric into a group of evening capes so spectacular in their simplicity that after they appeared in Harrods's windows, Cecil Beaton chose them for a surrealist photograph spread.[144] In Cecil's famous image the models are arranged like chess pieces, staged against drawings by Christian Bérard. The stark black and white of the shapes and the long shadows they had created echoed Dalí's own long shadows and Man Ray's plays with, and against, "dark and light." The photographs were successfully published on both sides of the Atlantic.

A few months later, Cecil made a twin set of surrealist dress photographs for Schiaparelli. In this series, models wearing Schiap's "Desk Suits," festooned with multiple pockets—some real and some false—were posed like dancers, either dramatically shading their eyes or holding up empty boxes. The imagery is a clear reference to Salvador Dalí's *The Burning Giraffe*.

Charles James and Colcombet continued to create various textile projects for street and high fashion, including blends of cotton and silk. And Paul Poiret, whose family had been in the fabric business, suggested to Charles that he might also work with some of the softer vintage prewar Colcombet ribbons they discovered together in a junk shop. With Poiret's help, Charles began a now legendary sequence of wraps and dresses created in conversation with the surrealist obsession: trompe l'oeil.

Echoing Marcel Proust on remembrance and desire, Charles wrote that the first cape was "made of fanned ribbons—the colors were pale and creamy, meringue pink, banana, pistachio, Greuze blue—all alternating, but in an irregular color order, so as to mystify eye and memory."[145] It was such a perfect realization that when Poiret saw the finished design at a dinner held in his honor, he scribbled a note on the menu to Charles. It read: "I pass you my crown; you do for cut what I have done for colors."[146]

In Paris, Beaton's friend Dilkusha de Rohan rented Charles a formal space in which to show his expanded "ribbon" collections, which were a huge social and commercial success.[147] Private clients like Cecil's mother, who bought (and was photographed in) a ribbon gown, Mona Williams, and Marit Guinness snapped up the dresses while *Vogue* swooned ecstatic, and Hattie Carnegie, Bonwit Teller, Lord & Taylor, and Milgrim placed orders for them.[148]

Schiap's colleague Jean Cocteau, who enjoyed playing a paternal role in guiding young talent (Raymond Radiguet and Francis Rose are two well-known examples), also took an interest in Charles, who to compensate for his habit of living above his means had become an expert at skipping out on Paris hotel bills by putting his Vuitton trunks with the luggage of other departing guests.[149] (Then, instead of actually checking out, he would take his Alsatian, Zampa, for a short walk. On his return he would coolly collect his belongings after the porters had placed them on the sidewalk outside the hotel and simply move on.)

In 1934, however (in conjunction with Jean Cocteau), Charles was able to settle more or less permanently at the Hotel Lancaster, where they lived on the same floor.[150] Cocteau, who insisted on describing himself as a poet, was really a natural polymath. He wrote novels, published his diaries, was active in the worlds of theater, dance, and music, and made unforgettable films. His fine line drawings, clearly inspired by Picasso's classical period, had "a suggestive magic."[151] And when he chose to venture into the world of fashion, the subtle embroideries he sketched for Schiaparelli coats and jackets retained their lyrical edge.[152] He was also a wonderful friend. When, in a second attempt at killing himself, Charles tried hanging, it was Cocteau, whose own father had committed suicide, who saved Charles by cutting him down and rushing him to the nearest hospital.[153]

At his first meeting with Charles James, in a café near the Arc de Triomphe, Cocteau tried to sketch Charles and failed, because, as he told him, "your front face and profile are two different people."[154]

Charles James explained the white eiderdown jacket he created in 1938
as "an experiment with quilting." Salvador Dalí called it a soft sculpture.
Sketch by Antonio Lopez.

Perhaps as a rejoinder, Charles, who almost always worked with solid color fabrics, decided to "translate" Cocteau into fashion. He printed patterns on silk from the artist's sketches and also established a prize at the Paris branch of Parsons School of Design, for the best print-on-silk adaptations of the artist's motifs. Then, in 1938, Charles James took it all one step further, by making his own sensuous, flowing dresses decorated with small-scale surrealist configurations—Jean Cocteau's doodles of women's profiles and stars.[155] (These very rare garments are now in the collection of the Victoria and Albert Museum in London.)

The same year, in another nod to surrealism—he said it was a response to Elsa Schiaparelli's rather menacing "Commonplace Short Bulky Jacket," a hallucinatory, boxy creation in hairy black monkey fur that is reminiscent of the Wicked Witch of the West in *The Wizard of Oz*—Charles designed his famous "puffer," a voluptuously curved and quilted bed jacket that was made to be worn *out* in the evening where its pearl-colored satin would shimmer softly like the jewel of a Chinese princess.[156] Charles said it was only "a technical challenge and

49

fantasy."[157] But Salvador Dalí called it soft sculpture. (Perhaps Dalí was thinking of the plump lascivious lushness of his own Mae West Lip Sofa, commissioned by Tilly Losch's husband, the collector Edward James.)

Two other new Charles James models were engineering innovations: A pioneering strapless ball gown (perhaps the first ever) would, in Charles's hands, become a grosgrain confection, intended to be worn with full-length gloves that reached to the armpits, so that gleaming shoulders and décolletage were emphasized. Charles named it the "Umbrella Dress," because, to add an element of contrapuntal eroticism and underscore the effect of the décolletage, he had replicated the spokes of an umbrella to create a supporting structure for the skirt that, imitating and exaggerating the natural sway of a woman's hips, would undulate with the gait of the wearer. This was also a nod to the "parachute" shaped skirts Schiap had discovered on a trip to Russia.

Charles referenced Tchelitchew in his greatest trompe l'oeil masterpiece—a chef d'oeuvre of juxtaposed "attraction" and "repulsion"— which he named La Sirène (mermaid). It has been called Charles James's most surreal creation and is alternately known as the "Lobster" dress because it was also conceived in conversation with Schiaparelli's (and Dalí's) skeleton and lobster designs. Only this time, instead of merely *putting on* the painting of a lobster, the wearer *becomes* a sea creature. In Charles's sartorial essay on death and sexuality, fine silk tucks, delicate as little fish bones, radiate from a ruched, spine like panel that runs down the center of the ankle-length evening dress and give the impression of an X-rayed fish. But these tucks also cling seductively to the figure as they bind the torso and legs of the wearer into the enticingly curvaceous shape of the alluring and deadly mermaid's long tail.

Nineteen thirty-eight was the height of the "surrealist fashion period" in Paris. It was also the pinnacle of Elsa's fame. By 1939 the political situation in Europe was so tense that everyone who could was dreaming up ways to escape. Even Max Ernst married poor rich Peggy Guggenheim (he never loved her) so he could stay in New York.

Schiap, who was back and forth between France and America during the early 1940s in an effort to raise money for the orphans of Paris, also spent time in Manhattan, where she maintained her friendship with Charles but did not design. Instead she volunteered for the Red Cross. To keep her workers alive, Elsa continued to pay them during the Occupation, but did almost no business in England or on the Continent during that time.

When, in 1945, she reopened her showroom in Paris, conditions had changed. And despite glowing reviews of her early postwar collections, all her attempts to reignite former successes were dismal fizzles. Frightened and highly superstitious, Schiap tried everything she could think of, including two exorcisms in Bahia, Brazil, to rid herself of what she perceived as a plague of bad luck—to no avail.[158]

Finally, on an Italian train traveling to Rome, her birth city, she reached a place of peace. Gogo had married, and as Elsa wrote in *Shocking Life:* "I realized that a circle had been closed....Having thus decided I felt a great deliverance....I saw myself holding the fluttering hands of my small granddaughters, Marissa and Berynthia [Berenson]...ready for what the future would hold."[159]

In 1954, the year Charles completed the Clover Leaf ball gown (his penultimate "thesis"), Elsa finally closed up her Paris businesses. She retired in luxury to write her autobiography at her adored villa Hammamet in Tunisia and died quietly in Paris in November 1973.

Anne Armstrong-Jones in fancy dress with her brother Oliver Messel,
photographed by Cecil Beaton (who disliked her intensely) in 1932, the year
before she became Charles James's client and mentor.

CHAPTER 3

Fairy Tales for the Future:

Anne, Countess of Rosse

IN PARIS CHARLES'S practice centered on modernity and surrealism. But in London, his friendship with Oliver Messel's sister, Anne Armstrong-Jones—later the Countess of Rosse—who was his most significant client from 1933 through 1939, opened his imagination to a new level of fantasy.

In her essay for the catalog of the Brooklyn Museum's 1982 show "The Genius of Charles James," Anne described her first impressions of Charles:

> He seemed to blow into the London orbit and he must have been very young then. My most vivid memories are of the time he had a grand salon in Bruton Street, luxuriant with gilt furniture and crystal chandeliers. How it was ever financed I cannot imagine! But a faithful friend, Miss Barnes, wielded what discipline there existed— she was so kind, efficient and calm. I remember her tenderly. So far from the platform of today—when one rushes into a mass production store that accommodates every lady with replicas of great houses—to suit the tall and the short, the fat and the thin, the young and the old. Charlie's creations were specialties for special people— all masterpieces.

Charles James's magnificent "grand salon" in London on Bruton Street, an elegant eighteenth-century house in his old neighborhood, was "all white," according to Derek Hill, with "dyed pampas grass in great vases,"[160] and a glitter of chandeliers, on walls made of mirrors. It had gilt Second Empire chairs, modern tables, tall doors upholstered with tufted blue satin, orchid plants on tables, and fur rugs on the floor. A painting of a nude hung over the mantle.

When he was in London, this was where, Charles would live, work, and host his much-publicized Thursday afternoon salons and midnight suppers. His guests were select clients and the friends who would impress them, including Cecil; Lady Ottoline Morell (who had been Oscar Wilde's friend); Virginia Woolf; Lady Mosley (Cynthia Curzon), who introduced Charles to Pavel Tchelitchew; Diana Mitford (the Honorable Mrs. Bryan Guinness); Queen Ena, in exile from Spain; and Stephen Tennant. And, as was noted in the newspaper columns, which praised him for his idiosyncratic originality, on these very exclusive occasions, Charles stashed his liquor in an ice-packed bathtub-turned-bar.

Since being dressed by Charles James was quickly becoming a way to be recognized as a person of substance, originality, and elegance, it goes without saying that Charles was incredibly picky about who he would allow to wear his clothes. As Anne recalled:

> So little did he seem to care about the niceties of encouraging a wide and wealthy clientele, or indeed good business at all, that he could be downright difficult with some of his much-needed customers—that was his honesty. I remember with misery—embarrassment, yet amusement as my thoughts go back—a very rich and charming American hostess in London whom I took to see him; though he looked up, there was silence as we came in. "Charlie, I've brought my friend Mrs. X who so admires your beautiful clothes," I ventured. "What do you want?" he asked her bluntly. "Oh well, I'd like to see what you've got," the dear fat middle-aged lady replied. "Well, I couldn't possibly make anything for a frump like you. Why you can't even walk properly!" Oh the despair of helping to bring lucrative customers! But there were no ill feelings at all—we all just laughed.[161]

Utterly unlike the dear, frumpy American, Anne Messel was very "special" indeed. Small, lithe, and graceful, with debonair charm and occasionally gilded hair, she was frequently referred to as "the most beautiful woman in London" by her friends and acquaintances and in the newspaper columns in which she was also described as having "beautiful manners." Anne was passionate about romance, history, and flowers.

Early on she developed a unique, personal style and was much praised for having "a rare genius for wearing strange and original clothes." She also came from exactly the sort of rich, cultured, and sophisticatedly eclectic background to which Charles instinctively cleaved.

With the exception of her father's brother Alfred Messel, a famous architect who built the Wertheim department store and designed the Pergamon Museum in Berlin, the members of Anne's father's family were all prominent German-Jewish bankers and stockbrokers from Darmstadt who established themselves in England in the 1870s. On her mother's side, her grandfather Edward Linley Sambourne, a distinguished member of London's artistic community, was the principal cartoonist for *Punch* magazine, and even more famously, the illustrator of Charles Kingsley's best-selling fairy tale, *The Water Babies*. And somewhere in Anne's ancestry a great aunt, the exquisite Elizabeth Linley, whose portrait Gainsborough had frequently painted, married the eighteenth-century Irish MP and writer Richard Brinsley Sheridan, whose play *School for Scandal* took Reformation London by storm.

Anne, the middle child, born on February 8, 1902, three years after her elder brother, Linley, grew up inseparable from Oliver, the dark and beautiful baby of the family, who was three years younger than she and had "eyes like a fawn." They all shared an enchanted childhood spent traveling through Europe to Italy, France, and Germany in the company of intellectuals, esthetes like Philip Agnew, artists like William Morris, and writers like Bram Stoker and Max Beerbohm.

In London, the Messel family lived regally at 104 Lancaster Gate, an ornate, six-story stucco house overlooking Hyde Park. In the country, Anne and Oliver played outdoors at their family's expansive estates, Glovers and especially Nymans, in Sussex, where they were surrounded by six hundred acres of superb wild-style gardens luxuriant with exotic specimens that had been specially imported from China and Tasmania. Here, the Messels were country gentry, but not exclusively of the "hunting, fishing and dog-loving" kind.[162]

"The people who came to [our family's houses]" Anne wrote of her parent's social circle, which also included the Duchess of Marlborough, "were [mostly] collectors and by and large museum people. And therefore museums came into our lives very early on. Oliver and I started being taken to the V&A as small children which," Anne explained, "was my only real schooling"[163] She also described her upbringing as "most eccentric; laced with the whims and wisdom of rare parents."[164]

The children did have a traditional governess, who specialized in discipline and manners. And Anne learned to hunt and fish well enough to be featured in 1931 on the cover of a magazine called *The Field* dressed in full fishing gear and holding up her catch. While Linley and Oliver were sent to Eton, she was tutored at home in music, languages, and weaving. (Anne's mother, Maud, was a connoisseur and collector of textiles and a virtuoso at embroidery.) So her formal education as she described it was an "endless stream" of experts and foreign private tutors or "masters" who "came and went:"

> Our teacher was an eccentric old woman dressed as a shepherd, smock leggings and all and speaking as a man in brogue...How vividly these escapades linger in my mind: the collecting of dirty sheep's wool from the hedges, the washing, the carding, the spinning and finally the weaving...Every form of needle work was a joy, from lace making taught by a nun to Umbrian needle point from a charming Italian. And woven through it all was the whirl of languages, music and signing.[165]

Two mornings every week, when the weather permitted, there were also lessons in gardening at Nymans. Anne, who had a natural affinity for plants, became very skillful and zealous. She knew about botany, soils, and planting conditions as well as landscape gardening esthetics and plant breeding. And she later developed new varieties of flowers, including two in honor of her parents: a Leonard Messel magnolia and a Maud Messel camellia for the gardens at Nymans.

Although Oliver was generally supposed to be away at school, he was very indulged by his mother, who adored him. When he suffered from "bouts of illness real or imaginary" he was kept home with Anne for long periods. And every day Maud read fairy tales to the children. All of Oliver and Anne's leisure time was built around a fairyland imagination and their shared love for making objects like the ones they discovered at the V&A. As Anne fondly remembered, "There were months when we were in bed. We both had a bit of tuberculosis. At least we thought we had. And that was really when we made so much with our hands. We'd sit up in bed making things like maquettes, perhaps a chapel. Little candlestick altars and a tiny bishop, all dressed up because we both adored sewing."[166]

"Oliver was a great perfectionist. We loved the thing of being ill in bed. *Pretending* to be ill in bed. Wallowing in it. If we had a mouse that died we'd have a lovely funeral and make wreaths for it and Oliver would make a glorious coffin out of a soap box."[167]

Dressing up in fancy costumes, a pastime that paralleled their love of make-believe, became another favorite game for the siblings and was encouraged by their parents, especially since costumes and costume balls were very much part of the way of life of the older Messels. In one well-documented example, Maud and Anne's father, Leonard, attended the Chelsea Arts Ball in 1911 disguised as beautiful Linley and the playwright Sheridan. (Anne's mother enjoyed playing up the connection because it highlighted the artistic qualities of the family.)

The children followed suit: "The first thing I ever remember," wrote Oliver, "when I was about four years old at Balcombe. I was dressed up as a little French soldier in a fancy dress that belonged to my father."[168] And a charming photograph of Anne and Oliver together shows an eight-year-old Anne turned out like a little girl in a Renoir portrait, with white satin ribbons in her hair and a white muslin dress with full crinolines. She is tenderly kissing very sweet, small Oliver, who is costumed as Cupid, with crepe-paper wings.[168]

Anne's mother also taught Anne about collecting and preserving clothing. Maud was a connoisseur of ancient textiles and embroideries, which she bought on trips wherever she could find them, and she also acquired exotic garments, including two original Chinese Han dynasty jackets from the late 1800s. Her own mother, Marion Sambourne, had saved her most beautiful dresses. And carrying on what would become a family tradition, Maud carefully kept all her most exceptional and spectacular evening ensembles, particularly the ones she herself had embroidered by hand.

Anne made her debut in 1920, at eighteen. Then, in 1922, the year Oliver entered the Slade School of Fine Art, she was presented at court.

Her official photograph shows her looking just like a Pre-Raphaelite princess in a wide-necked, ankle-length, embroidered crème satin dress with a short train. She is wearing a jeweled headband tied at the back with wide ribbons and cradles a bunch of white lilies with very long stems.

That year, Anne attended all the parties, dances, and events that were part of the social season, where "small, enchanting, and lively, indulged by doting parents and with everything money could buy, [she] was soon surrounded by a host of admirers."[169] At the same time, she worked at Victoire, where she learned to cut and sew professionally. A press clipping from the period described how she made "clothes as other women might paint portraits or collect miniatures. I know no one smarter or more individual in her dress,"[170] continued the columnist, "and the designing and making of these delectable garments is her great interest." "She was," her nephew Thomas Messel said, "just enormously creative."[171]

At twenty-two, following her mother's example, Anne also started to carefully conserve her own clothes. She began to imagine the collection she was assembling as a kind of autobiography, in which the dresses—which she poetically defined as tangible memories, or material fragments of her existence—would, when preserved all together, tell the story of her life.

The next year, she married Ronald Armstrong-Jones, a career barrister and good friend of her older brother, Linley, from Eton. The wedding took place on July 22, 1925, at St. Margaret's, the celebrated Gothic church in Westminster, and was performed by the Archbishop of Wales. Anne's pale crème silk satin wedding dress, embroidered with roses, was sewn at home by her mother. The bridesmaids and child attendants also wore crème dresses, made of chiffon with leaf green sashes and wreathes of green leaves in their hair. These were designed by Oliver.

Oliver Messel had a charmed sensibility. A favorite memory of Anne's son, Lord Snowdon (Anthony Armstrong-Jones, Princess Margaret's husband), is of walking through his uncle's tangled London garden when he was eight years old and discovering a beautiful bird's nest. When he looked more closely, it turned out that the nest had been made by Oliver and held hand-painted china eggs.[172]

Although both Oliver and Anne could be forceful, Anne had perhaps the stronger personality. Anne's nephew Thomas described her as a delightful if sometimes intimidating combination of fanciful imagination and down-to-earth practicality, who cooked beautifully, mended exquisitely, gardened expertly, and could create perfect flower arrangements as well.[173] She was, he said, very "hands on,"[174] and "she was the sort of person who when you were sick was the first one to immediately call the doctor. She didn't like what she called 'Yahoos,'[175] and if you displeased her you could certainly feel it, but if you were at all creative or artistic, she was very supportive. My young friends were always welcomed warmly and wholeheartedly by her."[176] Her niece Victoria Messel, who as a very little girl visited Birr Castle in Ireland, where Anne lived after she had become the Countess of Rosse, remembers her as "absolutely terrifying and always immaculately dressed."[177]

In 1925, while Oliver was still a student at the Slade, Sergei Diaghilev asked him to "do some work for him for the new ballet, *Zephyr et Flore*," which was to have décor by Georges Braque. So Oliver, for whom design was "making as much magic as possible,"[178] and who could conjure chandeliers out of sticky paper and headdresses from pipe cleaners, constructed a papier-mâché helmet and lyre for the production. He was credited for his work in the program and received a note of thanks from Diaghilev himself. This success was followed by a series of spectacular masks and costumes for stage producer C. B. Cochran's music and dance reviews. Anne helped him with all of them, as well as with the costumes for Tilly Losch, which launched Oliver into the theater and a swift rise to fame. She was her brother's muse as well as his sometime co-designer and seamstress. As he was embraced by fashionable society, Anne became his frequent companion as well.[179]

Unsurprisingly, brother and sister particularly enjoyed attending fancy dress balls in dreamy, historical costumes, where they posed together for a number of photographs, including as "Bacchus and Ariadne" at the Pageant of Great Lovers, and "Poseidon and Aphrodite," snapped by Cecil Beaton[180] at Bryan and Diana Guinness's ball in 1932. In both images, Anne in wide skirts, lush with pattern and embroidery, looks like an Edmond Dulack Cinderella. Oliver is down on one knee at the feet of the belle of the ball.

Unfortunately, after eight years of marriage and two children—Anthony (later Lord Snowdon) and Susan (later Vicomtesse de Vecci)—Ronald Armstrong-Jones revealed himself to be a bit of a "Yahoo," in Anne's terms. He was serious, very ambitious, and spent most of his time working. When he wasn't, his preferred leisure pursuits involved hunting and fishing with what Anne referred to as the "rather small pool"[181] of the British upper-class sporting world. He had very little interest in parties or the theatrical, artistic, and intellectual milieu Anne so enjoyed. In 1933, they separated. With Oliver, she continued to mix in a world where fashion designers, artists, photographers, actors, and musicians mingled with "old money" and were accorded celebrity status. In this environment, in the year of her separation, Anne—who seemed to remember being introduced by the Baroness d'Erlanger (an interior decorator and a great patron of young artists, who lived in Lord Byron's old home)—met Charles James.

Anne adored creative characters and Charles could be very warm, compelling, and amusing as well. They shared many interests, including her romantic passion for history and flowers.[182] Their friendship was instant, easy, natural, and fluent.

At that time it was widely accepted in London that the French haute couture houses were the originators of trends. Worth, Schiaparelli, Irté, and Chanel had all opened shops on the streets of the capital. But Anne chose independence. Sure of her own taste, and proud of her country, she patronized the English couture houses as well as, if not instead of, the French competition. Following her pregnancies, Anne had had two ribs removed (ostensibly for medical reasons), which made her figure "tiny" and svelte. So she had become an ideal fashion model as well. And she was exercising her keen eye for groundbreaking design.[183]

That year, Anne's initial Charles James acquisitions were in the most cutting-edge, body-hugging style.

Her first purchase was one of his famous bias-cut Zipper dresses. Anne's was made in textured-weave black linen, with a metal zip that spun around the body one and a half times.

She also had Charles specially design for her a floaty, limpid, late-afternoon dress of pastel organza, with short, handkerchief-drape sleeves and a fitted décolleté bodice over a bias-cut midi skirt. (At the time, women still changed ceremonially several times a day, so there would be one dress for the morning, a new one for teatime, and formal wear at night.) And Cecil famously photographed Anne in her brother's Yeoman's Row house wearing her new, form-fitting tea dress with a side-slanted,[184] wide-brimmed Ascot hat in front of a white-on-white Oliver Messel-designed plaster relief of two singing, dancing angels from the production of *Helen!* a 1932 London stage triumph about Helen of Troy, for which Oliver made all the sets and costumes. (These all-white mise-en-scènes received a standing ovation every night of the show's run. And Oliver became famous throughout the 1930s for inventing "white-on-white" design.)[185]

Two years later, for a Cecil Beaton photograph in British *Harper's Bazaar,* Anne allowed Charles (who delighted in smudging the fine line between himself and his clients) to wrap her all up like a bonbon in an evening stole made of strips of pink and black tulle like the ones he wore for Eleanor Lambert. He also improvised Anne's coiffure: blackening her usually lighter locks he piled her hair high on her head, and pinned it all up with a contrasting, pale pink flower. In the resulting Beaton image, styled by Charles and shot in the Bruton Street salon, beautiful Anne is posed as stiffly as a little china doll in an antique gilded armchair next to Charles's wall of mirrors.[186]

"Charlie James was unpredictable to say the least," wrote Oliver:

...and immediately bit the hand that fed him, insulted his most influential customers by telling them their figures were lopsided or grotesque, or at a fitting he would cut through their underwear, leaving them naked, with their clothes in shreds.

His work however was so brilliant that a small group, including my darling sister and one or two others, [including another Anne Messel, who was Linley's wife] determined to prop him up and try to help reorganize him.

It seems that Anne resolved to do more than just commission dresses. She tried to improve Charles's living quarters as well. "I was *not* rude to Anne," Charles wrote plaintively to Cecil (who never liked her) after Anne had fired the maid for incompetence so there was no one to look after his domicile.[187]

Oliver gleefully reported on the consistent turmoil in his friend's existence and Anne's growing personal involvement with Charles's life and designs:

> With buckets of soap and water we scrubbed the premises on Bruton Street while he constructed fabulous dresses. The trouble was the bailiffs were constantly at the door and there were never enough skilled hands available to help him stitch together the specially cut pieces ingeniously created by the master hand. As soon as Charlie cut his patterns and fitted them roughly for Anne, she would snatch them away, and being immensely talented with a needle, she would finish them off herself superbly at home.[188]

Notoriously particular about everything having to do with his designing, Charles trusted Anne's craftsmanship completely. "He always sent the dresses the morning before the ball," wrote Anne's niece Victoria Messel, "with a note: 'Darling, I am in such a rush. I know you wouldn't mind finishing the hem?'"[189]

"Charlie James was totally chaotic," Thomas confirmed, "and Anne and Oliver would work with him late into the evening. When it came to Charlie's designs, Anne could make them herself and help him improve them."[190]

At Anne's behest, Charles James also began to design for the theater with Oliver. In 1934, the Messels recommended Charles to C. B. Cochran, who had discovered the Dolly Sisters and worked with Cole Porter and Noel Coward. He was also the father of the grand music hall review in England, and a great admirer and patron of Oliver.[191]

Charles James's first production with Cochran was *Streamline*—a splashy four-hour spectacular in twenty-six acts—which opened to a roar in the East End that September. He contributed a draped dress with vast batwing sleeves and a diagonally cut torso. It was designed for Tilly Losch's grand solo number and showcased his knowledge of fabric in motion. Perhaps even more significantly, he also designed all the costumes for the dance chorus's glitzy finale.

Then in 1935, at the request of Oliver, who was doing the sets but didn't enjoy working with contemporary clothing, Charles was employed to make the "modern dress" costumes for *Glamorous Night*, an over-the-top, saccharine, and wildly popular Ivor Novello (one of the "Brights" and Tennant's lover) extravaganza planned to open with much fanfare in May.

For this production, Charles continued his exploration of modernity by dressing the dance chorus in tubular sheaths decorated with diagonal black zippers and trimmed with crinkly broad collars of clear cellophane. And in a signature blurring of street life (and his personal and couture design) with the theater, he swathed them all in stoles made out of tulle.[192]

Shortly before the opening, Cochran, who had financed everything, complained that he hadn't yet seen the costumes, and so it was arranged that he, his wife, and Oliver would visit Bruton Street after the salon had closed, at midnight. Oliver remembered:

> As we approached the building, strains of music and billows of chiffon floated through the first floor windows. But it was Charlie who danced and modeled the dresses himself, insisting the model girls didn't know how to move. And so the two girls sat huddled quite nude on a sofa with only some dove's wings to shroud them.

"Charlie won out in the end," Oliver continued, "and the dresses were a huge success."[193]

In 1935, again at Anne's urging, Charles also designed most of the costumes for Cochran's *Follow the Sun*, starring Clare Boothe Luce. Here, he experimented with "the stiffest and most gentlemanly of materials," including grosgrain, gentleman's pique, and military fabric.[194] (This was also the beginning of his relationship with Colcombet, which would result in Cecil's surrealist photos and the famous "ribbon" capes and evening dresses.)

Meanwhile, according to Sir Harold Acton, the beautiful Anne Armstrong-Jones who "was at every party and every ball [and] was photographed by every society photographer," became reacquainted ("because of everyone knowing everybody")[195] with Michael Harvey Parsons, the Sixth Earl of Rosse and an old friend of Oliver's from Eton days. And almost immediately, they were engaged. "Since [Oliver's] sister had divorced Armstrong-Jones and was engaged to marry the Earl of Rosse, their names and photographs were continually in the press," Mary Ellis, who was Ivor's leading lady in *Glamorous Night*, recalled.[196]

On September 19, 1935, just three weeks after her marriage to Armstrong-Jones ended in divorce, and very quietly to avoid further publicity, Anne and Michael were married at the Church of St. Ethelburga the Virgin in Bishopsgate. Their union, which in Acton's words "proved to be a most favorable match for all concerned," became a lifelong romance.

The luxuriously lavish twelve-month honeymoon to Paris, Munich, Berlin, Warsaw, Moscow, Colombo, Jakarta, Bali, and Peking made up for the small size of the wedding in spades. And Anne famously commissioned her elegant trousseau from Charles James: "I still have among my treasured collection," she wrote in her essay for *The Genius of Charles James* in 1982, "simple yet not really simple dresses for the tropics and Far East, stout thick wear for mid-winter China and Russia, unique designs for desert wear and also dresses for embassy dinners."

One of these, a bouclé dress, was called the "Bali Dress" because it referenced the Balinese *kamen*. It was dyed the bright yellow that young Balinese girls wore to their feasts, and tied at the back with bold red asymmetrical sashes, like the ones Balinese women used.[197] It mirrored another dress in Anne's collection that was from Schiap's February 1935 "Stop, Look and Listen" show, a wrapped crème silk evening "sari" with bright blue panels—a present from Michael that Anne also wore on her honeymoon.

"But the zenith of delight to me," Anne continued "was the designs 'en grand tenue'—challenging and exquisite."[198]

For formal dinner parties and grand balls, Anne experimented with Victorian styles made modern, which Charles designed with and especially for her. Like stage costumes, these featured corsetry and stiff underpinnings, which were softened for personal use with unusual mixes of glistening shell-pale colors and seductive draping (to hide the inner construction), and then combined with bustle-style or crinoline skirts.

In 1936, Charles created an evening dress for Anne to wear to the Holland House Ball that was inspired by an 1874 portrait of her grandmother Marion Sambourne. It's a deceptively uncomplicated, exquisitely feminine, and highly sophisticated unexpected mix of silk satins in ice blue, amber, and pale rose, with an up-to-the-minute, sensually draped and flared parachute skirt, and a back-laced bodice that's held up by the frailest of pale, ultramodern "shoestring" shoulder straps.

The next year, Anne commissioned another new design named "La Sylphide." It was inspired by Fokine's romantic 1909 ballet's dance dresses and a costume Oliver had made for a 1934 Merle Oberon film called *The Private Life of Don Juan*.[199] The Charles James remix is of crème-colored satin with starkly contrasting black underskirts and a contemporary external corselet in frothy black lace with a black floral corsage. There is a later version of this design in canary yellow and also one in lilac organza that appeared in 1937 in American *Vogue*.[200]

Another 1937 creation designed especially for Anne, "Coq Noir," fuses surrealism and history. A typically suggestive Jamesian play on form and displacement, the gown had an asymmetrical front, plunging "V" back and an obscenely gorgeous, labial (neo-Edwardian) bustle— but in this case the bustle is provocatively set to one side and supported with a meshed nylon interlining.

That year Charles James and Schiap both created costumes for Cochran's riotous "feast of fashion," the "Coronation Review: Home and Beauty," which was a showcase of eight hundred dresses for a galaxy of stage stars and intended to be the inspiration for designs for the forthcoming coronation of King George IV.[201]

Charles was very proud to be able to claim that some of his "Coronation Review" costumes stimulated "a rekindling of Edwardian fashion in mainstream style"—particularly the dress he designed for Gitta Alpar of cellophane lamé with an undulating bustle over a double-draped skirt, which mirrors work he had been making with and for Anne.[202]

Oliver, who understood the sequence of fashion, would in a much later interview (where he also pointed out that many of Charles's dresses were in American museums) draw a parallel between the gowns Charles James designed with his sister Anne and Christian Dior's "New Look." As he told Charles Castle: "Like Dior's dresses after, Charlie's dresses were constructed on a boned corset foundation that held the diaphragm firmly in place and the gossamer fabric would be draped and secured to the base with a fine silk thread."[203]

By 1937, Charles found himself in an uncomfortably incongruous position. He was revered by his peers. He had developed friendships and business relationships with the best-dressed women in the world. He was selling his designs to the most exclusive retailers in England and America. And his finances were in shreds.[204]

Charles not only misunderstood money, he was (perhaps in response to the tensions in his family surrounding the subject) utterly unable to hold onto it. As he vividly expressed to Florence Miller, "I have never been sure about wealth, in that money never seems to have the same value day by day, and sometimes having a loose five dollar bill allows one some tremendous intellectual luxury, while at other times having quite a lot of loose cash makes me feel poor because I can't buy something very rare." Additionally, as Derek Hill pointed out, Charles was also a quintessentially distrustful and ungrateful loner who couldn't help being "rude to the people who rescued him so they eventually withdrew their support."[205] Thus his hand-to-mouth operations consisted of a continual finagling of loans and juggling of expenditures. And, as Anne noted, "cheques could be lost or torn up even in hard times."[206] Yet he could never stop whining about cash. In 1937 he wrote to a friend: "I missed the extra $1000 off Lady L [Leucha Warner], and couldn't pay Sally & G [his workroom helpers]...but, poor dears, they are tired of asking."[207] By the end of the year Charles had once again lost control of his budgets. His fiscal difficulties in England became overwhelming. And in 1938, he was forced to leave London for good.

"Understandably," Anne wrote, "there came a day when the bailiffs came into Bruton Street and his beautiful collection was quickly thrown into taxis for me to find piled up on the floors of my little dining room as I was preparing a luncheon party. Such was his generosity that he wanted to give me the lot in the end."[208]

Charles retreated quickly to Paris, which was still all asparkle before the looming military storm. Here, with Edith de Beaumont as his client and Schiap as his friend and his guide, Charles was close to *le Tout-Paris*, whose hosts and hostesses were determined to throw fantastical parties that would not only provide their guests with an excuse to dress up as whomever they dreamt of becoming, but be talked about not for days, but for many years to come.[209]

In 1930, Elsa Maxwell—a fat, ugly, and poor American spinster who had, by means of her irresistible joie de vivre and her shrewdness in getting things underwritten, become a toast of the town—had kicked off the decade with her "Come As You Are" party.[210] Guests were told they would be picked up by a bus sometime in the late afternoon or early evening. As soon as they heard the horn honking, they were supposed to drop everything and come exactly as they were. "The Marquis de Polignac," Elsa remembered with satisfaction, "was attired in full dress, except he wasn't wearing his trousers. Daisy Fellowes was carrying her lace panties in her hand. Six women arrived in slips that were definitely not shadow proof. And Bébé Bérard wore [only] his dressing gown."[211]

Schiaparelli's friend Elsie de Wolfe, now Lady Mendl, loved to entertain at the Villa Trianon, a flawlessly rehabilitated ruin at 57 Boulevard Saint-Antoine, almost next door to the royal Porte de Versailles, where Marie Antoinette used to play at being a milkmaid. There Elsie received, rather more grandly, hundreds of costumed guests (including Charles) who, under the stars or outside pavilions, danced to the strains of several orchestras from dusk, when dinner was served, to dawn, when breakfast appeared, all the while quaffing countless flutes of champagne.[212]

Charles was additionally a constant guest at the lavish fêtes of his close friend Comte Étienne de Beaumont (whose niece, Jacqueline, Comtesse de Ribes, became a member of the International Best Dressed List in the 1960s and was celebrated at the Metropolitan Museum in 2015 as "The Last Queen of Paris.")

The count, the model for the main character of Raymond Radiguet's novel *Le Bal du Compte d'Orgel,* was very tall, very thin, and very mannered.[213] He embodied a near-perfect union of money and glamour. He was a generous patron of the arts, an early supporter of Cocteau and Satie. And a summons to one of the famous balls in his exquisite *hôtel particulier* on rue Duroc—where he was one of the first to hang Picassos on the walls of his salon—was *the* coveted invitation in Paris. Accordingly, Étienne, who frequently said that parties were given to annoy the uninvited,[214] always sent his invitations out late on purpose to make everyone as nervous as possible about whether or not they were on his list. As the intellectual lifestyle publication *Le Journal Inutile*[215] (*The Useless Newspaper*) recorded, guests could include an aging Marcel Proust, who habitually made his New Year's Eve entrances just when the clock was chiming twelve; the duelist and ballet impresario Marquis de Cuevas, whose beautiful daughter, artist Elizabeth Strong de Cuevas, would became Charles's client in the 1970s; Maurice Chevalier; and Charles's favorite, Pavel Tchelitchew. Also to be found at the de Beaumont parties were Coco Chanel's lover, the Slavic beauty Misia Sert; artist Marie Laurencin, who had illustrated the sapphic Edith, Comtesse de Beaumont's translation of Sappho's poems; surrealist painter Francis Picabia; and Sergei Diaghilev. Other familiar faces were Pablo Picasso, Coco Chanel, Christian Bérard, and, of course, Jean Cocteau, whose musical revues at "Le Boeuf sur le Toit" Étienne had helped organize.[216]

De Beaumont, for whom Charles designed costumes, was a consummate dandy. He loved to shock and very much enjoyed making appearances in an array of garments designed for astonishment. At his Sea Ball, he dressed as a devilfish. At another party, he welcomed his guests first in "classic drag," then later—at one o'clock in the morning, when only close friends were left—reappeared as Cupid, in a pink leotard with tulle wings, and pranced around pretending to fling arrows at his guests.

In elevated 1930s society smaller dinner parties also frequently demanded costumes. And when in 1938 Anne and Michael traveled to South Carolina, Mexico, and New York, Anne had several new Charles James dresses for the trip. In Manhattan, Cecil invited them to dinner at his apartment in the Waldorf Astoria, where Horst photographed her wearing one of her latest Charles James acquisitions, a rich white satin ball gown.[217]

"Decidedly Victorian…" reads the May 15, 1938, American *Vogue* copy, "are the evening dresses worn by the Countess of Rosse.…This white satin one, all lace flounces, velvet bows, and padded bustle, was made—as are all her clothes—by Charles James." [218]

That summer in Paris, observing that "in difficult times fashion is always outrageous,"[219] Schiap had produced the Circus Collection. It was her most splendiferous show to date, in which printed silk dresses, covered with storybook drawings of prancing horses and white rabbits by the artist Marcel Vertès, danced down the runway, accompanied by wool jackets sporting rearing-horse buttons made especially from cast metal and painted by hand.[220]

In kindred spirit, the same season, Elsie de Wolfe, after months of planning, threw an elaborately themed Circus Ball at Villa Trianon. A specially built striped canvas pavilion, lit with Basquès chandeliers and decorated with eighteenth-century sculptures of Blackamoors frolicking with leopards, was filled with 150 "special people" dancing the night away. Entertainment was provided by a bevy of clowns in full circus costume, and cavorting ponies with plumes on their heads. There were tumblers and acrobats, and a blind accordionist who sported little round sunglasses. A quick glance at the party pictures shows Chanel arriving in tiers of white lace and a "statement" necklace of gold, pearl, rubies, and emeralds. Daisy Fellowes and the Princess Jean Poniatowska were dressed by Schiaparelli. And the Brazilian fashion plate Aimée Lopez covered her Chanel dress with a ribbon cloak by Charles James.[221]

In the first months of 1939, Charles made Anne one more astonishingly beautiful, François Boucher-like dress for the Duchess of Marlborough's Blenheim Ball. It was delicately cut from the palest silk faille and flesh-toned organza with a form-fitting bodice and contrasting crossover shoulder straps. The eighteenth-century-style wide skirt is of bouilonne swags draped over stiff tulle underskirts. And the "bouilonnes" are all looped, bedecked, and picked out with a bright array of multicolored bow-tied ribbons that look, from a distance, like tiny bouquets. Anne and Charles named it the "Ribbon Dress." And as the writer John Cornforth would note at her funeral, Anne had to be sewn into it for the ball, and then cut out again at the end of the evening.[222]

Simultaneously, Charles was inventing costumes for de Beaumont's Racine Ball, planned for June 28 of that year. Since Jean Racine was one of the seventeenth century's greatest tragedians, who spent his life writing about the fates of queens, kings, princesses, and princes, with many other characters thrown in on the side, this theme gave the guests a wide range of personalities from which to choose.[223] And, as *Vogue's* editor Edna Chase commented, "Fortunes were spent on costumes."[224]

A real-life fairy tale come true, Anne, Countess of Rosse, with her children Anthony Armstrong-Jones (later Earl of Snowdon), Susan Armstrong-Jones (later Viscountess de Vesci), and William Brendan (Lord Oxmantown, later Earl of Rosse). Anne is wearing the last dress Charles James ever designed for her. It is printed with Walt Disney drawings of Snow White.

Handsome Jean Marais, who was Cocteau's lover, made his entrance in boots and a one-shouldered leopard-skin leotard. Serge Lifar was Louis XIV's dancing master. Chanel cross-dressed as "L'Indifférent," from a painting by Watteau. Schiap's daughter, Gogo, wore metallic pantaloons and was an ambassador of Siam. And one guest even paid Balanchine to choreograph her entrance. [225] But although *L'Officiel* reported that

70

the masquerade "for one night made the privileged guests forget the troubled hours of present times,"[226] a terrible thunderstorm drowned out the fireworks planned for de Beaumont's beautiful garden. It was an omen of what was to come.

Perhaps the last dress Charles ever designed for Anne, another unique piece, highlights her fairy-princess persona and circles back to the long afternoons she and Oliver spent when they were children, reading Perrault and playing at make-believe together in the gardens at Nymans. In 1939, the year the animated cartoon *Snow White* was released, in one of perhaps only two examples of uses of patterned fabrics in all of his clothing, Charles made a day dress for Anne from a print of Walt Disney's drawings of Snow White as a little princess.[227] Like a fairy tale made real, the result is simultaneously enchanting, edgy, eminently wearable, and also deeply romantic, a symbol of what, and how very much, Anne meant to Charles James.

By September, the Nazis had invaded Poland and the war winds were blowing. For Charles, Europe was over. It was America's turn.

In New York, he stopped designing for the Countess of Rosse, who was spending more of her time at Birr Castle, where she worked almost exclusively with Irish designers. But Anne always remembered her friend. In the 1982 catalogue for the Brooklyn Museum's exhibition, "The Genius of Charles James," she wrote lovingly: "Charlie James was one of the greatest masters of 'le plus grand Couture.' Whimsical and impetuous, he was a true genius of line and originality and a perfectionist. Everything he designed was a masterpiece of style and elegance. He laced daring originality with unfailing flair of the best possible taste for the occasions for which the dresses had to be worn....I treasured everything he ever made...and the golden memories they recalled."[228]

Anne's "autobiographical" clothing collection was presented to the Brighton Museum & Art Gallery, where it is currently housed. It includes some of the most beautifully conceived and sophisticated designs of the 1930s and beyond. A multitude of these are by Charles James.

Elizabeth Arden in the infamous Cecil Beaton portrait she so detested that she ripped the proof into little pieces and flung them at him.

CHAPTER 4

Setting up Shop:

Elizabeth Arden

AS WAR SWIRLED over the continent, a flock of international society figures migrated from Europe to the United States, where the economy had been transformed into what President Roosevelt called the "Arsenal of Democracy." By 1944, the gross national product would grow to $135 billion, from $88.6 billion in 1939.

Gliding in from London on the tailwind, Charles alighted in Manhattan in October 1939, his entry sponsored by Best & Co.'s Mary Lewis. He opened a showroom in the elegant Gothic limestone town house at Sixty-three East Fifty-seventh Street, a most stylish address.[229]

Among his first patrons were the glamorous Parsee brother and sister, Edulji and Bachoo Dinshaw, who were fellow war refugees.[230] Their fortune came from investment in cement manufacturing, as well as the largest private land holdings in an area near Bombay. Pavel Tchelitchew would later paint a wide-eyed, pale-skinned, elegantly, gracefully, and erotically half-naked Edulji, propped up Roman–style on one elbow, with his elongated body curving and stretched sideways over striped and rolling lands that look like a tiger-skin rug. Charles stayed at their extravagant town house at 851 Fifth Avenue, which had recently been redecorated to include a Louis XV paneled room from the 1750s,[231] Marie Antoinette's cylinder desk from Fontainebleau, and rock crystal chandeliers.[232] (Edulji's private study had walls encrusted with mother-of-pearl, and a Puranic period sculpture of the Indian bull god Nandi, which he liked to say looked like his mother.)

The war years were a wonderful time to be in New York, where the social whirl was at a seductively giddy high. Many members of Charles's own international set—Noel Coward, Salvador Dalí, and Mona Williams, as well as a bevy of Rothschilds—had just arrived. So, too, Gypsy Rose Lee, the sophisticated star stripper who read Schopenhauer in her bathtub and whom Charles met in 1942. (Charles would design personal as well as stage wear for Gypsy for over a decade, and in 1954 she became the matron of honor at his wedding to heiress Nancy Lee Gregory.) Even the "Dollar Princess," Millicent Rogers, had finally packed up her dachshunds, waved good-bye to her chalet in Austria, and settled in between a new estate in Virginia named Claremont and a Dorothy Draper-designed apartment with lacquered black walls in Manhattan, where she would sit out her third divorce. Elsie de Wolfe, unwilling to abandon her beloved Villa Trianon for Hollywood, lingered in France until after Germany had invaded Luxembourg on May 10, 1940, and was one of the last to leave. Others, like Duke Fulco di Verdura, the Princess Natalia Paley, and Baron Niki de Gunzburg—who, after spending his last *sou* throwing parties in Paris, had comfortably entrenched himself in the editorial department of *Harper's Bazaar,* where he was teaching Diana Vreeland "everything" she knew—were already there. Only Schiaparelli was still back and forth across the Atlantic.

Meanwhile, Manhattan nightlife sizzled with celebrities. The Stork Club at Three East Fifty-third Street (where one night in 1940 Ernest Hemingway drunkenly tried to pay his bar bill with the $100,000 check he had just received for the screen rights for *For Whom the Bell Tolls,* and its Mob-funded owner, Sherman Billingsley, was actually able to cash it) was the center of café society's activity. Hearst journalist Walter Winchell's column was the basic medium for recording that mad world, where poet Carl Sandburg, his friend Leonard Lyons (Winchell's rival), Al Jolson, Errol Flynn, Rita Hayworth, Claudette Colbert, Oona O'Neill, Fred Astaire, Robert Benchley, Balanchine, celebrity debutante Brenda Frazier, and Gloria Vanderbilt (who later would famously not wear Charles James because he had ripped up her dress) could all be found in one room.[233] Farther east, at El Morocco on East Fifty-fourth Street, Hollywood gossip columnist and queen of mean Hedda Hopper, Steve Reeves, Moss Hart, John O'Hara, Hearst correspondents Austine and Igor Cassini (whose nom de plume became Cholly Knickerbocker), Niki de Gunzburg, Mona Williams, still more Vanderbilts, and Salvador Dalí all posed for society photographer Jerome Zerbe, perched on the famous zebra-striped banquettes.

Even more important for Charles, since luxury goods were for all intents and purposes unavailable from Europe, and Paris was in such turmoil that even Chanel was forced to close her showroom for the duration of the war, fashion's focus had turned to the United States. American-made clothes were now the pinnacle of chic.

Leading figures in American fashion spearheaded this trend. Chief among these were: Morris de Camp Crawford, the editor of *Women's Wear Daily*; star publicist Eleanor Lambert, who had pioneered the promotion of American art at the Whitney Museum and was married to *New York Journal-American* publisher Seymour Berkson; and the black-haired, impeccable Dorothy Schaver, who accelerated her own fast track to becoming the first woman president of Lord & Taylor by introducing the American Beauty rose as a symbol of the store and the Signature of American Style. The new American avant-garde included Hollywood's most famous costume designer, Adrian; sportswear designers Bonnie Cashin and Claire McCardell; milliners like Lilly Daché, who would later mentor Charles's acolyte-turned-enemy, Halston; couturiers such as the Russian-born Valentina, who was an intimate of Greta Garbo; and American couturier Mainbocher, who was James's neighbor on East Fifty-seventh Street. Like Charles, Mainbocher had roots in Chicago and had recently relocated from Europe, where, at Elsie de Wolfe's recommendation, he designed Wallis Simpson's trousseau for her marriage to Edward, now Duke of Westminster. (It was Mainbocher who named the duchess's favorite shade "Wallis blue.") His other famous clients included C. Z. Guest, Bunny Mellon, Adele Astaire (an old flame of Cecil's), and that American original, Millicent Rogers.

In a more academic but equally powerful vein, Charles's new friend and collaborator at the Brooklyn Museum, Michelle Murphy,[234] had begun offering educational and research services to the design community, centered in Brooklyn at that time.

Charles, with his wonderful English manners, impressively elite American background, and ferocious talent for creating unexpected beauty, was perfectly positioned to ride the crest of this trend. His old friend Virginia Pope, the influential *New York Times* fashion editor, featured him in her widely read reports on New York's best couturiers for two years running. And in 1941, the year America finally entered the war, the top-drawer Fifth Avenue department store B. Altman devoted an entire fashion show and window front to twelve versions of James's avant-garde trouser-skirt designs.[235]

Then in 1942, cosmetic tycoon Elizabeth Arden, "the richest little woman in the world,"[236] commissioned Charles to make the entire trousseau for her splashy second marriage to Prince Michael Evlanoff—a swindling, high-profile, blue-blooded Russian émigré. It would be a seminal episode in a friendship that had begun in 1929 and lasted the rest of Elizabeth's life.[237]

Historians have not always been kind to Elizabeth Arden. Her own biographers characterized her as "conservative, uninformed, a...little girl of a woman."[238] Alfred Allan Lewis, author of *Ladies and Not-So-Gentle Women,* dismisses her in seven words as "Ruthless and provincial, with a porcelain complexion."[239] And in his last tapes, a more subtle and crueler Charles conjures mixed emotions when he describes her as "more charming than Eleanor Roosevelt."[240]

"She was a totally professional client. And she had no beauty at all. She was a small, gray robin-like creature, as tough as could be, with a terrible temper that frightened everybody," said Laurel Cutler, who wrote advertising copy for Elizabeth Arden in the 1960s and later became head of McCann Erickson. Cutler added:

> I took my lessons from her on how to apply makeup and what creams were for which purpose. She insisted that anybody who worked on the brand be totally knowledgeable, and expert. She never bothered to say, "This shade of red lipstick would look really good on you." She could have cared less about me. I was a tool. And I certainly had no intimate time with her other than the lessons, which were quite intimate.
>
> We called her Mrs. Graham. I suppose everyone wanted to be thought of as Mrs. in those days.[241]

Elizabeth, christened Florence Nightingale Graham, was born to poverty in Woodbridge, Ontario, Canada, where there are no records of that birth. She was the fourth of five children. Her mother, who like Charles was of Cornish descent, died while she was still a little girl. Her father, a tenant farmer, loved to bet on the horses, and spent too much time at the track.[242]

While she was still in her teens, Elizabeth met and was inspired by a clinician who was treating acne in Woodbridge, and she began boiling up experimental face unguents in the stone fireplace of her family's old farmhouse. Then, in 1910, with a loan of six thousand dollars from her older brother, she opened her first Red Door salon in Manhattan and ironically renamed herself Elizabeth Arden, after Enoch Arden, an Odysseus-like Tennyson hero who journeys to save his family fortune and sacrifices his own well-being for their happiness and security.

Elizabeth also traveled. In 1914, with money borrowed from the bank, she took her younger sister, Gladys (soon to become the Vicomtesse de Maublanc, and later head of the Arden operations in Europe), to France. Oblivious of the danger of World War I, which had just broken out all around them, Elizabeth "had a facial" in "every salon in Paris."

There also, while watching the graceful courtesans in a fashionable Parisian restaurant, she noticed how attractive they looked with their eyes lined with kohl and their blackened eye lashes. It was her discovery of mascara. She was the first to import eye makeup to the United States, where it had never before been used by respectable women. Shortly thereafter, in 1915, she married Thomas Jenkins Lewis, the banker who had authorized the loan she used to travel to Paris. He gave up banking to come and work with her. By the 1920s, the robin-like Ms. Arden was rich and determinedly upwardly mobile.

In 1926, Elizabeth was taken to one of Bessie Marbury's famous Sunday teas at Irving House. Built at the intersection of Irving Place and Seventeenth Street, Irving House had been Bessie's family home, and with the help of Elsie de Wolfe (Bessie's lover, who in 1926 had surprised everyone by marrying Lord Charles Mendl), she had totally redesigned it in 1897 as a Parisian–style salon and a heaven of "light, air, and comfort." It served as a stage set for the formidable Brahmin— Cecil would later describe Bessie as "A huge old Buddha with a personality as grandiose as her figure." Marbury, who had discovered Cole Porter, produced Jerome Kern, and was the first woman to become a literary agent (she represented, among others, George Bernard

Shaw, Oscar Wilde, Edmond Rostand, W. Somerset Maugham, Edith Wharton, Alexander Dumas *fils*, Eugene O'Neill, and James M. Barrie, who wrote *Peter Pan*), also regularly entertained. The mix at one of her teas might include Toscanini listening to George Gershwin at the piano, Al Smith talking politics with Edward, Prince of Wales, and Groucho Marx flirting madly with anyone who would pay attention.[243]

Improbably, Elizabeth and Bessie hit it off. And, guided by Marbury, who took her under her large and sheltering wing, a frequently balking Elizabeth buffered her own image. She took up charities: the Opera Guild, the Friends of the Philharmonic. And she began to collect art, acquiring work by Georgia O'Keeffe, Marie Laurencin, and Mary Cassatt,[244] while her luminous, multi-terraced apartment at 834 Fifth Avenue, with exciting views of Central Park, was transformed into a flower-filled masterpiece of modern elegance.[245]

In 1929, to top off her new friend's newfound style, Bessie introduced Elizabeth to the sophisticated young milliner Charles James. It was the beginning of a profitable, histrionic, and highly complicated, but very long, friendship. "We always respected each other," quipped Charles.[246]

Bessie also decided that Elizabeth should glamorize herself by commissioning her own portraits. And after Cecil Beaton arrived at one of Bessie's teas (on the occasion of his first visit to New York in 1930, impressively equipped with a letter of introduction from Osbert Sitwell), Marbury determined that Beaton was the one to take Elizabeth's photograph. Arden agreed, but then hated the proofs (which made her look bovine) so much that she tore them all up into little pieces, which she flung at Cecil's head. "You'll still have to pay for them,"[247] Beaton replied.

Eight years later, Bessie finally convinced Elizabeth to commission another portrait, this time by the flamboyant, mustachioed, and bearded Augustus John, Ottoline Morrell's admirer, who (though seldom remembered now) was the most popular artist on the Continent at that time, and world famous for his vivid, attitudinal paintings of literary luminaries: T. E. Lawrence, Thomas Hardy, and W. B. Yeats, as well as that flame-haired seductress, the Marchesa Casati, who, apart from being Fascist-poet Gabriele d'Annunzio's sometime mistress, was not literary at all. Charles James, who was chosen to create

Elizabeth's "look" for the painting, styled her as a Georgian beauty. She had a little top hat, rakishly tilted high atop an unruly mop of curls, and a strictly fitted bodice cut to a blushingly deep "V." For the second time, Elizabeth found her own image personally embarrassing. When she saw the completed work, she forced John to totally redesign the portrait and paint in a dowdy, puritanical, turtleneck blouse where the Charles James décolletage had previously been. "You could stick a knife into that cleavage," commented James.[248]

Somehow, perhaps because Ms. Arden was acutely aware of Charles James's prestige, the two remained on good terms. And after his return to New York she liked to use him as an escort to social affairs. Charles later enjoyed telling the story of how they went to a formal dinner given by Mr. and Mrs. William H. Moore, friends of Charles's from Chicago who owned Nabisco and had a brilliant collection of museum-quality porcelain. As Mrs. Moore was introducing her to the other guests and showing her around the house, Elizabeth allegedly swooped down on a wonderfully elegant, eighteenth-century, bone-china cachepot. Turning it over and holding it up to the light, she exclaimed with delight: "It's so beautiful! It would make a lovely little jar for [my face cream] Joie de Vivre."[249]

Although Elizabeth's 1942 marriage to the Russian prince failed rapidly, dissolving into lawsuits as soon as she discovered that the royal Evlanoff was stealing from her and might actually be no prince at all, Charles James's trousseau for her wedding was a big success. One of Arden's archrivals, the delicate, fine-boned, Austrian-born luxury retailer Hattie Carnegie, had begun promoting her own brand of cosmetics in her eponymous East Forty-ninth Street clothing boutique. To offset this competition, Elizabeth decided that she would start selling *her own* line of clothing: American haute couture, designed by the genius who had made her trousseau.[250] And so, ridding herself of one aristocrat, Elizabeth turned to another. In 1943, Elizabeth Arden offered Charles James "partnership for life." Charles, who was keenly aware of what such solid business support could mean to him, went wild with enthusiasm. Over the next two years he would use his position and Elizabeth's backing to strengthen his customer base and concretize his mystique.[251]

James had been hired specifically to direct a new initiative for a custom fashion collection within Arden's cosmetics empire, and to redesign the second-floor showroom at 691 Madison Avenue, which was to be his domain. He wanted more. Reimagining Arden's own business plan, he borrowed money from his mother and expanded the project (at his own expense) to include workrooms, and a fitting room, too.

With Elizabeth's endorsement, Charles also went in search of new clients. And he fixed his sights on someone he had first met when she had sought him out in 1929: Standard Oil heiress and media darling Millicent Rogers, who at that moment was the patron of ne plus ultra American couturier Mainbocher. The ethereal, esthetic, and intellectually curious socialite, who had nearly died of and never properly recovered from rheumatic fever as a child, was in New York recuperating from the most recent of a lifelong series of small strokes. So James decided to woo her with something beautiful for her boudoir; his first recorded piece for Millicent is a tantalizing, pale gold organdy "dishabille" trimmed with spider web-fine lace and biscuit-colored ribbons.[252] "I hoped it might tempt her to leave her bed,"[253] he explained. As their relationship solidified, she became his muse, close friend, and important benefactor. "I remember when Millicent Rogers definitively left Mainbocher for Charles James in 1944," Ruth Gordon's son, Jones Harris, said. "It was a very big deal."[254]

During the next two years Charles would also acquire for the House of Arden several other important, and importantly visible, patrons: tall, slim, vivacious Austine McDonnell (Mrs. Igor) Cassini, later Mrs. Randolph Hearst II; the exquisite and ubiquitously photographed Babe Mortimer, née Cushing ("She wasn't all that nice but she wanted her picture in my dress and knew enough to ask me which one she should wear," observed Charles),[255] whose second husband, William Paley, was the head of CBS; and Babe's sister Minnie, who was Mrs. Vincent Astor at that time. (When he and Elizabeth parted ways, Charles continued to design for these star customers throughout his career.)

Elizabeth also demanded publicity. "Dear, if you want to get into the papers, take the pictures and stories to the newspapers, yourself, and sit there, until they see you if only to get rid of you. It works. I know. I've done it myself,"[256] she advised. But Arden's tactics were far from infallible. At 102, the legendary *Vogue* editor Babs Simpson could still remember Charles, in the midst one of his many feuds with *Vogue* magazine, encamped in the Condé Nast foyer waiting for Edna Wollman Chase, who was editor in chief at the time. "He thought he would just sit it out because he had her cornered," Ms. Simpson recalled. "Little did he know there was a back door. We all used it to sneak out when it was time to go home. And he didn't know it. He was left in the empty offices—just waiting—all alone."[257]

In April 1944, Charles's old friend and mentor, Paul Poiret, died quietly, in obscurity and Charles chose to upgrade his own image. He got Cecil to promise to sketch his new workroom in the Elizabeth Arden town house.[258] He also moved into the exclusive Hotel Delmonico on the corner of Fifty-ninth Street, where he lived in style for four years, in a suite of two rooms with nine-foot ceilings, overlooking Park Avenue, and ordered his dinners delivered from their restaurant downstairs, one of the most famously elegant establishments in New York.[259]

James also began to work intensely with the dynamic, art-trained Michelle Murphy, who was the curator of the Brooklyn Museum's Design Laboratory,[260] and whose educational passion and mission was to originate and nurture new ideas in fashion design. His first collaboration with Michelle was a germinal multi-year project (completed in 1951) to create patterns using a consistent standard of measurements he devised, relating to body proportions that do not change over the years.[261] Then, just months after their meeting, in a watershed, career-defining action, Charles James made his first move toward creating and preserving his artistic legacy by having three of his most important designs—a gleaming dressing gown made of satin ribbons from one of his celebrated Paris collections in the late 1930s, a 1940s bodice with a Charles James wraparound scarf from the early 1930s attached to it, and a satin wrap trouser skirt from 1940—donated to the Brooklyn Museum. These are perhaps the first examples of a living designer's work to enter any museum collection.

Icing the cake, Charles and Elizabeth came up with the idea of promoting "their" clothes (the label was supposed to read *Charles James* but it was known he would be designing exclusively for Elizabeth Arden) through a series of "society benefits." Putting the designs on

*This Antonio Lopez sketch shows a 1945 version of Charles James's work
with bias cutting and draping that was featured in the famous Modess
advertisement and is also an example of the kinds of designs produced in the
1930s that Charles James included in his first collection for Elizabeth Arden.*

the right runway would get lots of press in the intensely-studied society columns of the day.

In April they introduced their precious new collection at a fashion-show fund-raiser for the Red Cross, to be publicized by Eleanor Lambert. Grandiloquently named "One Touch of Genius: A New Posture in Fashion Created by Charles James," the event was staged at the Ritz-Carlton Hotel, where an unknown pianist, Leonard Bernstein, played the music that accompanied the parade of socialites and willing customers dressed in the newest James-Arden Couture gowns.[262] Charles James's sketch for the invitation—an attenuated "S"-shaped woman's profile, with a long, narrow waist that widens gently to a slightly rounded stomach and sensual rear, expressed a contemporary, lithe, and curvilinear female fashion form. It was the promise of what an Arden customer could become.[263] And it predicted the standard that would define the style of the 1950s around the world.

Most of the fashion show dresses were reiterated variations of Charles James's sinuous "erotical it" 1930s designs. These were followed by a sampling of newer ideas that included asymmetrical draping and emphasized yards of fabric puffed out into ample, petticoat-filled skirts.

Women's Wear Daily, repeating that Charles had "created a new posture...With lengthened bodies that are molded over the hips and scooped out at the hollow of the back," heaped high praise on the collection. But (probably because it was still wartime and there were governmental restrictions on extravagant uses of fabric in the United States) they found the truly groundbreaking, more voluminous dresses, which anticipated the "New Look," contradictory to his general premise and "difficult to understand."

Discussing *Women's Wear Daily*'s difficulty with Charles's first full-skirted designs for Elizabeth Arden, Babs Simpson, who knew Charles and was an editor at *Vogue* in the 1940s, also noted that "Charles James brought America a level of luxury we'd just never seen before."[264]

In the summer of 1944, one of Hollywood's favorite femme fatales, the blond Venus Marlene Dietrich, (Tilly Losch's lover) was persuaded to pose in Arden's salon for a *Vogue*[265] shoot wearing a clinging satin dinner sheath that was one of Charles's pet Parisian designs from the previous decade, which he had reintroduced in the Red Cross extravaganza. It wrapped snugly, left over right, and to heighten the sensory dimension Charles had slit the ice-blue fabric diagonally from shoulder to hip, fastening it with small matching ties, and draping the satin to loop away from the slightly floppy closures, letting sexy little glimpses of skin peek through.

The day of the shoot was unbearably hot, and Marlene was in such a bad mood that Charles improvised an air-conditioning system for the salon. Using what he would later characterize as an "old restaurant trick," he had a greengrocer deliver large blocks of ice. He placed the ice in front of Marlene and positioned an electric fan behind them to blow the cooled air toward the star. The scheme must have fallen through because, in the now-iconic Rawlings photograph, Dietrich's body is uncharacteristically rigid and her expression is tense. Charles kept a copy of that photograph pinned to one of his storyboards in his

Chelsea Hotel rooms in the 1970s, but he had snipped off the star's head. "I decapitated Dietrich, because I didn't like the way she did her hair. And Elizabeth didn't like her either. She thought she was vulgar"[266] he said, adding that Elizabeth refused to sell her the dress. Nonetheless, when the little blue number appeared in *Vogue* (Charles James's first mention in the magazine in nearly three years),[267] it created a buzz.

In the flurry of press that followed, another celebrity, Mrs. Vincent Astor (Babe Mortimer's sister and the head of the Women's Division of the New York War Fund) also posed for the "People Are Talking About" section of the October 15, 1944, *Vogue*.[268] In the photograph, which is an archetypal Charles James mixed metaphor—Minnie, with her hair pulled back by a classic "wasp" head band, and her torso propped up sphinxlike on fat cushions to reveal her long neck and the low-cut neckline of a forest-green, T-shirt-sleeved Charles James dress—somehow manages to be totally preppy and unforgettably provocative at the same time.

At long last, Cecil Beaton's dreamy sketch of Charles's own workroom—where rich fabrics are piled on table and bench, the "La Serine" dress is draped in a slouch on a dressmaker's model, and the exaggeratedly long, slim torsos of the dummies lend an air of unstudied elegance to the work area's artful disarray—finally and famously appeared in the December 15, 1944 *Vogue*.[269]

Meanwhile, inside the actual Arden showrooms, the contractors were progressing at a finicky snail's pace.[270] In Charles's recherché and exquisite design scheme, the walls were to be painted the pink of the youngest rose petals. The grand plaster moldings were to be plated with hammered gold leaf. Crystal chandeliers scattered variable light on the deep, soft, carpets, and one could barely sense the hum of Madison Avenue through a curved wall of windows sheathed in gossamer drapes.

Arden, who was becoming increasingly unhappy with the preciousness of it all, watched her relationship with Charles, who squirmed under what he called "her tyranny,"[271] literally "fray at the seams."

Charles later complained to Elizabeth's biographer, Constance Woodworth, that Ms. Arden, whose favorite motto was "It's my business. You just work here," became incredibly domineering and hard to please. Worse, according to Charles, she had no taste at all (except for the little he had been able to teach her).

The satin he chose was too heavy. The decoration process was too slow. And the bills were miles too high. Elizabeth loved blaming him: "You're too temperamental"[272] was another favorite catch phrase. Moreover, she hated his pranks. When, after Charles had impishly lit a fire in one of the town house's false fireplaces and smoked out several floors of the Arden establishment, the building manager tried, but failed, to strangle him to death. "Too bad he didn't try again,"[273] was all she would say.

Charles and Elizabeth had planned to introduce the flawless first collection in Chicago, where Arden was banking on the social prominence of his mother's family to open many doors. Their venue was to be another fashion-show benefit, this time for "the Cradle" at St. Luke's Hospital,[274] which Charles Brega had funded nearly a hundred years before. But on October 27, 1944, Charles's mother, who had been organizing the event from her hospital bed, died. (His father, as Charles later recorded, had withheld from him information about his mother's final illness and had deliberately neglected to pass on to his dying wife correspondence from their son.)[275]

Tragically, Charles had lost his only emotional mainstay. As he wrote afterward, "Since mother died, Daddy has become very strange and sits alone in his apartment dressed in [the] Chinese robes [he wore when he met her]. Mother was the heart of our family, and when she died, it sort of fell apart."[276]

At the same time, Charles finally had enough inheritance money to be independent—at least for a while.

Charles later remembered that just days after his mother's funeral he was emotionally unable to stage a fashion show, particularly one in Chicago. But Arden doggedly insisted on going through with the plan. In the commotion of newspaper articles that followed the Cradle benefit, however, Elizabeth Arden's existence was largely ignored. "Even without being there, I got all the credit for the success. She was barely mentioned," crowed Charles. "She got so furious, she wanted to take my name out of the clothes and only use her own label."[277]

The third Charles and Elizabeth fashion show was scheduled for the beginning of 1945, to benefit the March of Dimes fight against infantile paralysis. Planned for a maximum of publicity, it was sponsored by Eleanor Lambert's New York Dress Institute. This benefit would become an annual event attended by New York's splashiest high society. In all there would be fifteen March of Dimes fashion shows, and Charles would participate in the first twelve.

Gypsy Rose Lee, "stunningly clothed to the teeth"[278] in a dark fern satin Charles James evening gown with a spectacularly slashed skirt that revealed the top of her stocking and "fitted her like the skin of a banana,"[279] was the scandalous star of the first March of Dimes lunch, at which Charles was very noticeable by his absence.

There are at least three versions of the theatrical backstory. One is that Charles walked out of the March of Dimes show dressing rooms after throwing a temper tantrum, when Eleanor Lambert didn't want Gypsy Rose Lee to model his dress. As Charles described the incident to John Duka, he crumpled up a bunch of white orchids intended for the stripper and hurled them at Eleanor. Lambert later apologized. "After, at the lunch, she told Marietta [Tree] that I was sweet and had given her flowers,"[280] he smirked.

In a Lambert version, as told to publicist Jon Marder, she had to ban Charles James from the backstage of the March of Dimes show because "Charlie was annoying the models. So I told him that if he didn't stop I'd have him removed. He didn't so I had the guards walk him out. About twenty minutes later there was a knock and there he was again. He said, "Don't worry, I'm not coming in. I just wanted to bring some flowers,' and he told a guard, 'These are for Mrs. Berkson [her married name]. But before you give them to her please crush them a little.'"[281]

A third version is that, in revenge for the Chicago debacle, when Arden had "gone on with the show" in his absence, Charles decided to exacerbate an already tense situation by mischievously putting an enormous, backlit, and very expensive ruby-red crystal vase in the window of Elizabeth's exclusive Red Door salon. Elizabeth's friend Sam Riddle, who thought it was funny, told her the vase made her fancy establishment look like a bordello in the red-light district of Amsterdam. That was the last straw. By this time, Arden was so angry and tired of Charles's "high-handedness and untrammeled extravagance" that she fired him on the spot and wouldn't let him come near the first March of Dimes lunch in New York.

In a flamboyant denouement to this cumulative minidrama, Charles is said to have crashed the March of Dimes after-party Arden had originally arranged in his honor. He made a dramatic late entrance, accompanied by his black maid, who was wearing one of Elizabeth's own Charles James dresses, which she had sent back to him for some minor repairs. And, according to Lindy Woodhead, author of *War Paint*, "The maid was holding a writ for wrongful dismissal and breach of contract."[282]

By the beginning of 1945, the year World War II finally ended and the world waited to see how the future would look—just two years after Charles James and Elizabeth Arden had announced their lifelong collaboration —the two strong personalities dissolved their agreement.

Arden would try, and fail, to get Charles to come back to her, but she would also go on to work with a series of brilliant, European-trained designers, including Oscar de la Renta, who, after his apprenticeships in the ateliers of Balenciaga and Lanvin, came to her on Diana Vreeland's recommendation. "She's not a clothing designer and she will promote you,"[283] Vreeland, thinking of Charles, is said to have advised. All on her own, Elizabeth Arden not only developed a very successful couture business for her salons, but—vindicating her father's bad habits—built wildly successful racing stables as well. In 1946, Mr. Graham would probably have been very proud to see his daughter, Florence Nightingale, featured on the coveted cover of *Time* magazine, for her wonderful racehorses and many wins at the track.[284]

Even Elizabeth's relationship with Charles had a happy ending. In 1956, despite their tabloid quarrels and their theatrical breakup, she became the godmother to his son, little Charles.

And when she died on October 12, 1966, her businesses were grossing an estimated $60 million a year. Elizabeth Arden was still the richest little woman in the world.

Charles's severance was only $6,000, but his association with Elizabeth Arden had proved priceless. It had given him weight in the American fashion community. Even more, it had yielded him a treasure trove of supporters and patrons, and a mission that would define his life and the legacy he would work so hard to memorialize.[285]

Millicent Rogers in one of the blouses she was famous for "accumulating,"
photographed here at Falcon Lair, Rudolph Valentino's old mansion in
Hollywood where she was pursuing Clark Gable. Photographer unknown.

CHAPTER 5

Immortality:

Millicent Rogers

CHARLES JAMES CELEBRATED his newfound freedom by invest-ing some of the money his mother left him in an impressive new show-room, just a stone's throw from the Arden salon at 691 Madison Avenue. The décor of this new space, where he would work for the next seven years, was even *more* inventive than anything before. The salon fea-tured indigo and puce walls, furniture covered in beige satin, Charles's signature crystal chandeliers, a vast framed mirror, and a very white, tall, curvaceous, and elaborate antique alabaster urn.[286]

For the first publicity shot in December 1945, the young, lissome *Washington Times-Herald* columnist Austine McDonnell—who was also the Countess Cassini—modeled one of Charles's body-clinging designs.[287]

In the richly layered chiaroscuro photograph, Charles has posed her for the camera so she is glimpsed in profile, leaning backward, fac-ing the urn. Her arms are raised provocatively as she lifts her hands behind her head, hips swaying forward and sideways, like an ancient Chinese porcelain figure of a dancing princess.

The next year, Charles decided to hire Japanese Americans, recently released from the American internment camps, to work in his atelier, where he had famously placed a sheer, curtained window between the workroom and the showroom, so that his customers could delight in the view of the wonderfully skilled and exact work-ers gorgeously sewing his beautiful designs. "My most important bigger clothes, ball dresses and such, were made in the Japanese workroom, the Japanese having a special quality of precision," he later explained.[288]

After the loss of his mother and the six years of professional uncer-tainty that had followed his exodus from Europe, Charles began to relax into the luxury of working like a true French couturier in America.

He turned his atelier into a self-styled laboratory of fashion, where he would experiment with new inventions of patterns, shapes, and techniques, with which he intended to remake the fashion industry and recreate the look of his world.[289]

He perfected his sculptural parachute skirt and its stand-away volume, and invented the "Trapeze" coat—a new shape that much later, in 1958, would make Yves Saint Laurent's career. He began research on the first of his famous "perfect" sleeves, which legendarily took him two years and twenty thousand dollars to achieve. (The matrix of his concept was to widen the back of the jacket and set the sleeve in a new, anatomically correct, softly rounded shoulder, which would allow the lowering and raising of the arm without bunching up the surrounding fabric.) He also created "a bouquet of important evening dresses" with diminutive waists and full, crinoline-lined skirts.[290]

Then, on February 12, 1947, Charles's old friend from his Parisian days, Christian Dior, made history when he launched his first solo collection in the company's Paris headquarters at 30 Avenue Montaigne. Taking a leaf from Charles's sensual, sexual, organic allusions, Dior had named the collection "Corolle," a French word for the corolla that surrounds the ovule of an opened blossom. His debut fashion show was intended to evoke a parade of flowers in full bloom.

In a eureka moment *Harper's Bazaar*'s celebrated editor in chief, Carmel Snow, renamed it all. To her American eye, the opulent, exaggeratedly female shapes were simply revolutionary. So she called them: "the New Look."

And the new name swept the world.

Whatever its allusions and derivations, this "New Look" aesthetic—with its wasp waists and flamboyantly voluminous skirts, puffed out with layer upon layer of petal like petticoats—not only made transatlantic headlines but became the yardstick of fashion and beauty that would define the 1950s, and set a standard for style that would reach far beyond.

Somehow, and clearly also on merit, Charles James got and took recognition as "the New Look's" muse. Sir Francis Rose—artist, aristocrat, and Charles's childhood friend and admirer from Paris—wrote (and told everyone) that Dior had confided to him that the inspiration for "the New Look" had come from "Charlie James." Dior corroborated the statement. And Charles also set out to prove this himself. In an interview with Eileen Callahan called "Nothing New in New Look, Says Designer, Proving It," published in in the *Daily News* on Sunday, April 4, 1948, and illustrated with sketches of the progression of his own designs over a ten-year period, Charles observed: "There is no such thing as a new look. What people have been going mad for in the last year is nothing more than the summation of ten years of dressmaking development." Cristóbal Balenciaga, the eminence grise of midcentury fashion, following suit commented later that Charles James was not only the greatest American designer, but "the greatest couturier in the world."[291]

Having thus established his identity, Charles accepted invitations to go back to Europe. With all the pomp of returning royalty, he journeyed across the Atlantic with twenty-five of his most ceremonious gowns. His first stop was London, where Hardy Amies, couturier to the Queen of England, gave Charles his Bruton Street atelier to display his designs, and complimented him after the show. From England, Charles traveled on to Paris, where the city's most eminent host, his old friend the Comte Étienne de Beaumont, insisted on organizing the Charles James event, which he cohosted with iconic set designer Christian Bérard. Bérard personally designed the invitations to what everyone decided should be a fashion défilé at midnight in the grand Hotel Plaza Athénée.[292]

In the ballroom, whose walls were decorated with shining floor-to-ceiling mirrors set into seventeenth-century boiserie, the elite of Paris society were seated on small gold-backed chairs around little white circular tables, lit by long narrow tapers in three-pronged silver candelabras, to watch the languorous parade of Charles James ball gowns, as they listened to harp music by Satie and sipped vintage champagne. In an unprecedented gesture of friendship, Christian Dior, Elsa Schiaparelli, Coco Chanel, and Jacques Fath all lent Charles their best models for the night. It was a great homage to "the American." The crown that Poiret had deeded to Charles was now firmly in place. No buyers were invited. This was "prestige."[293]

During all this period Charles was working closely with Millicent Rogers, a true soul mate,[294] on a project they hoped would further promote both their images, while reinforcing their fame.

Millicent, four years older than Charles, was born February 1, 1902. She arrived in the world beautiful, rich, multitalented, and destined for celebrity. Her notorious grandfather, Henry Rogers, "the Hell Hound of Wall Street," had amassed his fortune in transactions with U.S. Steel and Anaconda Copper and was a major Standard Oil trustee. When he died in 1909, he was worth $75 million, the equivalent of $2 billion today.

Mary Rogers, Millicent's exquisitely dressed and extravagant mother, with whom Millicent remained close all her life, was born Mary Benjamin. Her father had helped establish the *New York Herald Tribune.* She was one of Mark Twain's famous twenty-five "adopted nieces." And she is the subject of a famous book: *Mark Twain's Letters to Mary,* a compilation of her correspondence with the iconic author, which began when she was twenty-five and he seventy-one.[295] Millicent's father, Henry Huttleson Rogers, whom everyone called "the Colonel," inherited a quarter of Henry Rogers's fortune, and was what the family described as "a controlling personality."

Millicent's childhood was cultured, cosseted, and horribly marred. When she almost died from rheumatic fever as little more than a toddler, the family doctors thought she would not live to be ten.[296] And although she outlived the date of her prophesized demise by forty-one years, the near-fatal illness left her heart with permanent scars. As a little girl she was frequently in great pain.[297] And she remained a beautiful invalid for the rest of her life. Her granddaughter, Christina Peralta-Ramos, remembers her own father telling her that he and his brothers lived under a constant cloud of worry that "something" would happen, and their mother would die in in the night. When they came home from school they would tiptoe around the house to avoid disturbing her rest.[298]

Mary decided that education would be the best cure for her fretful, convalescent daughter. As a diversion from the nightmare of the lingering sickness (and the tension of her parents' unhappy marriage), Millicent was taught to speak effortless French, Spanish, and German. She particularly enjoyed translating Rainer Maria Rilke's lyrical, mystical writings. She knew Greek, was widely read in the classics and conversationally fluent Latin, which became the "secret language" she spoke with her little brother, Harry, in their nursery in the New York town house and on the beach at their Southampton estate. (The John Russell Pope–designed Italianate villa, called the "Port of Missing Men," was situated on 1,200 acres of meadows, ponds, woods, and wetlands; the actual gardens were designed by Frederick Law Olmsted.) Millicent loved art classes, and could draw beautifully, too. Like Frida Kahlo, another invalid-turned-artist who painted to while away her solitude, Millicent made wonderful sketches: portraits of people, and self-portraits. She was, her granddaughter Christina explained, "trained to be visual."

Unsurprisingly, Millicent began to create and recreate herself as a kind of "art object," which was easy to do. (Her proportions were so perfect that until Charles started making clothes for his wife, Nancy, he would use Millicent's measurements as the standard for all his design prototypes.) She was five foot nine inches tall, unusual, and strikingly beautiful. Her neck and shoulders were elegant. She had divinely high cheekbones and the wonderfully, long, slanted eyes "of a deer," as Serge Obolensky later described them.[299] She moved languidly, in slow motion, which men found incredibly alluring. And she knew how to turn heads, which she thoroughly enjoyed.

At sixteen, Millicent proved her natural talent for making head-lines when, as the *Washington Post* reported with wonder, she wore a Chinese headdress bought in Chinatown and long scarlet fingernails to a friend's debutante ball (she was probably taking a leaf from the exotic costumes for Nijinsky's Ballets Russes—all the rage in the Parisian style sheets that year). After that, almost all her romantic and dramatic gestures—together with the clothes she wore to make them—would receive maximum publicity.[300]

The Rogerses, who were left out of Mrs. Astor's fabled Four Hundred, were essentially and splashily bohemian and intellectual. But they were very social, all the same. When seventeen-year-old Millicent made her debut at the Ritz-Carlton, the headline-grabbing coming-out party was crowded with 1,300 guests, including Brigadier General and Mrs. Cornelius Vanderbilt Whitney.[301] Almost immediately afterward, Millicent was again all over the newspapers, this time for dancing with Edward, Prince of Wales, at multiple festivities during his grand tour of the United States.

Over the next several years, the Rogerses traveled widely in Europe and China. In Naples, the youngest son of the king of Italy wanted to marry Millicent. Then, Prince Serge Obolensky trekked to Scotland to propose to her at Cortachy Castle, which her parents had rented for the season. Around this time, Lela Emery, a family friend, wrote in her diary that the Rogerses couldn't stay in a town for more than two weeks because Millicent kept getting engaged. But none of her suitors suited her father.[302]

Just back in New York, and only three years after her debut, Millicent eloped with penniless Count Ludwig Salm von Hoogstraten,[303] who at forty years old was exactly twice her age. As she waved good-bye to the reporters who went to the dock to see her off on her honeymoon, she announced that she was going to Africa to watch her husband play tennis, and get a very big new monkey. She was pregnant with her first son, Peter Salm when, five months later, her father, who traveled to Paris to retrieve her, had the marriage dissolved. Six months after her first divorce, she married Arturo Peralta-Ramos, a well-born Argentinian, with whom she had two other boys: Paul Jamie and Arturo Harry Peralta-Ramos. Then, in January 1936, just a month after her divorce from Ramos, Millicent married again, this time to an American—the handsome stockbroker Ronald Balcom, who had also dated film stars Norma Shearer and Claudette Colbert. The boys were all sent to Swiss boarding schools, and the couple moved to Europe to be nearer to them. In Italy, Millicent entertained Noel Coward, Valentina, and poor little rich girl Barbara Hutton, the dime-store heiress, at her palazzo in Venice.

In Austria her life was even more stylish and spectacular. Millicent kept a pack of eight matching red-haired dachshunds at Shulla House, the Tyrolean chalet she built in the shadow of the Arlberg Mountains, which was variously published for its mix of Biedermeier furniture and Austrian peasant charm. And she matched the eclecticism of her clothing to her Austrian décor. Her combinations of Schiaparelli and peasant accessories, or vests and/or dirndl skirts (which, according to Christina, she had had made by Charles James, who was working in conjunction with Elsa at the time), turned Millicent into an international style sensation. "Many have acquired taste. She has it by instinct,"[304] decreed Diana Vreeland in *Harper's Bazaar*. "In a winter of pretty frou-frou, she passes up the houps and bouffants for her own soigné school of dressing. Schiaparelli suits are her uniform,"[305] purred *Vogue*. "She is the first real American woman with any style," stated Horst. In her memoirs, *In My Fashion,* Bettina Ballard described Millicent as a style icon who "made fashion." Elsa Schiaparelli went a step further. "Had she not been so incredibly rich...she might have been a great artist,"[306] Schiaparelli wrote when Millicent briefly partnered with the (terrible snob) Princess Baba de Faucigny-Lucinge to open a successful shop in Paris, which specialized in Austrian clothes.

After being arrested twice right after the Anschluss, "she had a huge American flag made in Switzerland and flew it from this bloody tall pole. And when Hitler's henchmen ordered her to take it down, she refused. 'Whatever for?' she inquired. 'We're not at war with you,'" is her youngest son Paul's version of the story.[307] Millicent returned to America, and in 1939 she bought Claremont, a historic mansion on the James River in Virginia, which she fastidiously restored, with the help of architect William Lawrence Bottomley and Parsons School of Design director Van Day Truex. Claremont's sumptuous decorations included hand-painted wallpapers and a mix of her Austrian Biedermeier furniture and Empire antiques, which created an atmosphere that *Architectural Digest* would define as "rich and romantic."[308] Inside these palatial walls—hung with her collection of Watteau, Boucher, Renoir, Fragonard, and Cézanne—Millicent wore ornately upholstered dresses, commissioned from Mainbocher in deep rich shades of velvet and satin, to match the mood and hues of her house.

In the early 1940s, Millicent also immersed herself in the war effort, offering her Virginia showplace as a rehabilitation center for shell-shocked war veterans. And during the war she was frequently in Washington, at the heart of the action. Like her acquaintance, Clare Boothe Luce, she liked to talk with the men, and she was also a member of the high-flying Washington social set, which encompassed Oatsie Charles, Mrs. Stanley Mortimer (later Babe Paley), and Bootsie (Austine) Cassini (all of whom were clients of Charles James).

In Washington Millicent also enjoyed involvements with a series of high-profile men, including: Jim Forrestal, who was at that time the United States Undersecretary of the Navy,[309] and who would rise to become Defense Secretary before committing suicide; Ian Fleming, who kept turning up from England, and whom she visited in Jamaica with Noel Coward and Cecil; and secret agent and author Roald Dahl, who wrote *Willy Wonka* and was only twenty-eight when he and Millicent had their affair.

"Her biggest problem," said her son Arthur Ramos, referring to the rapid succession of Millicent's marriages and romantic interests, "was that she was smarter than most men. Marriage was stagnation and complacency for her."[310] Christina echoed, "She was always acutely aware that she could die at any moment. So she didn't really give time to introspection. If she was unhappy, she just left and went on to the next."[311]

Millicent's last famous lover was Hollywood's leading man, Clark Gable, to whom she had been introduced years before by her friends Rocky and Gary Cooper at the Port of Missing Men. Setting her cap, she moved to California to be near Clark, who, ever since his role as Rhett Butler in *Gone with the Wind*, was in his own galaxy as America's male sex symbol.

In Hollywood, she lived at Falcon's Lair, silent screen idol Rudolph Valentino's old estate, or at a bungalow at the Beverly Hills Hotel, which she had redecorated by film set designer Tony Duquette, who was Elsie de Wolfe's protégé.

She pursued Clark in a wardrobe made for her by her friend, film costume designer Adrian. (He was famous for dressing Rudolph Valentino, among others, and creating the costumes for *The Wizard of Oz.*)

And she caught Clark—for a second time—in bed with starlet Virginia Gray. In her good-bye letter to Gable (which she sent to Hedda Hopper, who published it instantly), Millicent tellingly and generously wrote: "I have always found life so short, so terrifyingly uncertain.... Allow yourself happiness. There is no paying life in advance for what it will do to you."[312]

Through all the seismographic changes of her last years, her work and friendship with Charles James was a constant for Millicent. Christina described their relationship as that "of very, very close friends—they fought like brother and sister," adding that they understood each other and could talk to each other intimately: "It was harder," said Christina, "for her to have real friends than most people knew."[313]

During one of Millicent's more severe health episodes, Charles wrote to her on United Airways stationery:

> I'm more than worried about you. I'm so damned inhibited I can't make plausible my feelings to you and somehow always feel just around the corner from where I want to be. In life you have given more happiness than you have perhaps received. There is a credit balance due you. Physically in looks and in shape you are at your peak…you seem to have lost ten years.[314]

And again, from 699 Madison Avenue: "I have missed you very much, you and your very sweet sense of reason and poetry all tangled up in Emily Dickinson and Mark Twain." And then, "That special quality of bringing out people's work at its best is what gave you special rating."[315]

For her part, Millicent was so seduced by her own appearance in Charles James clothing that she literally "accumulated" his designs. In *The Glass of Fashion,* Cecil Beaton tells the story of how, after Charles had just delivered an order for four dozen satin blouses to Millicent, her maid telephoned for more. "She's nothing but a hoarder," grumbled Charles, who was worried that all his beautiful work might end up in storage. "Not a hoarder, a collector!"[316] the maid retorted. According to Christina, "When Millicent found something she liked, she simply bought it in every color."[317] Then she invented some new shades.

There were the usual money issues as well. Millicent, who, to avoid overspending, paid her bills only once a year, had a platinum, diamond, and 84.81-carat sapphire ring signed over to Charles to secure one of her orders. When Charles pawned it to cover expenses, there was a small row.[318]

And, true to form, Charlie came up with a typically ingenious scheme that would, he hoped, actually allow her to save money, by buying his clothes and donating them to museums, where they would be accorded the homage and audience they deserved. He planned to charge Millicent twice the normal price for a dress he made to be given to the Brooklyn Museum. She could then donate the dress in question and take a tax deduction for twice the real amount, as a charitable contribution. Then Charles would replicate the donated dress, so she could actually wear it, and just give it to her—free of charge.[319] Naturally, he got full payment for both the dresses he made, but he accounted for the price of the dress he had "given" to Millicent as "business expenses for publicity." This was "in the French way."[320]

"I have simply arranged a contribution to the museum of $6,000 which is entirely payable out of your untaxed income and should not cost you more than one thousand dollars; therefore save you five grand," he wrote to her. "What's all this business about my owing you $10,000," she wrote back to him. "If you are going to double your client's accounts you won't have them very long."[321] Of course Charles was examined and fined by the IRS.

"They bickered like brother and sister," says Christina, "but she had the money, so she always won. She knew exactly what she wanted to look like, and they fought over the smallest of details, over hemlines, over the width of a lapel. People frequently comment on how much he did for her, but she did a huge amount for him, too. She was a muse who co-designed with him." As Nancy Gregory, Charles's wife explained it, "Millicent inspired him more than anyone. He felt she could help him resolve a design when he wasn't certain how to finish it."

CHARLES'S VERY SENSE of self was entwined with Millicent. A couturier only creates "with his client as inspiration,"[322] he explained. But for Charles, Millicent was even more than a muse. She was his guide to immortality through the designs she would help him memorialize. "We are working quite seriously on this project and the Museum are [sic] delighted to have it. They feel you are one of the most representative figures of today and best able to stand for the development of taste," he added self-consciously. The project Charles referred to was assembling an unparalleled collection of twenty-four original dresses, to be shown at the opening of the Brooklyn Museum's Design Laboratory. It was Charles James's first one-man retrospective. He called it "A Decade of Design." The show would exclusively feature dresses he had made for Millicent in the 1940s (together with patterns and sewn muslins created to explain the design process). It was a turning point in Charles's life.

Antonio Lopez's impression of Charles James frontal vagina-like draping in a version of "Homage to Georgia O'Keeffe." Millicent ordered the dress in flesh-colored faille over delicate peach taffeta.

Charles was at a height of fluster during the preparations. He threatened nonpayment to the poor mannequin maker in Chicago (some of the mannequins were Millicent's likeness; even the ones without heads had to be her exact proportions). He received pleading letters saying that without the money there would be nothing, because the manufacturer would go out of business.[323] He fretted over the special bust of Millicent she had commissioned from Lillian Greneker for display in the exhibition. And he demanded perfect flowers for the dinner. Despite, or perhaps because of all this, the grand opening was a huge success. The mannequins[324] looked as though they were dancing, and the lush fabrics of the dresses seemed to sway with them. And exquisite Millicent flew in for the evening from New Mexico, where she had moved after the Clark Gable episode.

The press was triumphant. In her column on the show, Austine reminded everyone that it was Charles who had inspired the New Look.[325] The *Daily News* called the party "The smartest, most unusual function of the year." And Charles James, who now considered himself the highest-priced dressmaker in the world, toyed with the idea of capitalizing on his preeminence by reopening a studio in Paris. "I am not a designer," he wrote, "designers are hired help who only copy what's in the wind…all my seams have meaning. They emphasize something about the body." He added, "They give the form a variation of physical appeal."[326] Sir Francis Rose described him as, "This great artist, Charley James who chose silks and furs instead of stone and paint for his media."[327] And *Vogue* underscored the triumph by publishing Cecil's most famous photograph. It's of eight models—wearing some of Charles's most provocative gowns, designed over a period of ten years, in the showroom of French & Co., a recherché dealer in eighteenth-century furniture that Charles had scouted for the shoot.[328]

Then, in 1949, Millicent Rogers concretized the entire operation by donating all the materials and all the dresses that had been in the retrospective to the museum. She mailed the check from her new house, Turtle Walk, in Taos, where she was working with Charles to create her latest (and last) look—"Southwestern Style."

New Mexico, with its astonishing wide desert mesas, bright mountain light, and fine fragrant air, was a place where artists and rich bohemians congregated. Georgia O'Keeffe, Carl Jung, Igor Stravinsky, and Thornton Wilder all lived or spent time there, as did the prototypical American photographer Ansel Adams, whose early work is deeply inflected with the desert's magic and who published some of his most famous images in *Taos Pueblo*, his first book.

Claude Anderson, a Kodak heiress-turned-rancher, was one of Millicent's neighbors. Mabel Dodge (who had been a much-fêted debutante in Buffalo as well a friend of Gertrude Stein and André Gide in Paris, and was now married to a Pueblo Indian) lived literally next door, at Luhan House where she entertained Marsden Hartley, Edward James, and Cecil's old friend Willa Cather, and enjoyed a fraught relationship with D. H. Lawrence, who lived as her guest in a homesteader's cabin on the property, while writing fragments of what he hoped would become his great American novel, including this description of a shiver in the Taos winter night:

> It has snowed, and the nearly full moon blazes…risen like a were-wolf over the mountains. So there is a faint hoar shagginess of pine trees, away at the foot of the alfalfa field, and a grey gleam of snow in the night, on the level desert, and a ruddy point of human light, in Ranchos de Taos.
>
> And beyond, you see them even if you don't see them, the circling mountains, since there is a moon.
>
> So, one hurries indoors, and throws more logs on the fire.[329]

Millicent's reaction to "the Land of Enchantment" was simpler. She described it as being "like a time stop to falling in love."

Turtle Walk had been an ancient and sprawling adobe fort. Millicent, who used local workers to restore it, also hand-mixed the colors for the walls in empty tin cans, and painted some of the decorations on the *vigas* of the library herself.[330] Her sofas were now covered with solid, bright cottons. She drove around buying up windows from the old Arroyo Hondo chapel far up the road and Spanish doors native to the region. She slept in her golden-canopied bed from Claremont, which she draped with Hopi fabrics, and placed so that while lying in it she could watch the big sky from her bedroom window, which was the length of the wall. She hung her Cézannes in the guest bedrooms. And she lived surrounded by Spanish Colonial furniture, Native American textiles, pottery, jewelry, baskets, *santos*, tinwork, and paintings that she lovingly amassed to create a cluttered, slightly unfinished, unconventional bohemian atmosphere.

Millicent, who would occasionally take one of the woven Indian rugs off the floor and wrap it, shawl-like, around her shoulders, also made friends with the Native Americans and gave money to their causes. (She traveled to Washington to campaign for Native American rights.) And she adapted their silver, coral, and turquoise, as well as their smithing techniques, to jewelry she made for herself. She had successfully and originally designed jewelry since the 1930s, and had worked with masters like Jean Schlumberger (Dominique de Menil's cousin) to create her own designs. The poet Edith Sitwell fell in love with an oversize necklace Millicent gave her.[331] And later, Niki de Gunzburg had himself photographed wearing one of her rings on his little finger. (Millicent had made it for him out of a twenty-four-karat gold Louis.)

In New Mexico, her taste ran to the barbaric. She wore vast tangles of necklaces; all mixed together, and piled her bangles and bracelets high to her elbows. Christina suggested that sometimes these bracelets were worn to hide the withering and paralysis that strokes had caused in one of her arms. Whatever the motive, the effect was electric, particularly when she worked with Charles to mix it all in with his blouses over the fiesta skirts that he interpreted for her, and under the dark Navajo jackets he redesigned.[332]

The Santa Fe look was Millicent's life, and Charles worked obsessively to produce her new costumes. In September 1951, he wrote to her from the Sherry-Netherland Hotel where he lived in New York: "After you left Wednesday evening I stayed until midnight to rebuild your stand. In the morning it was taken over and readied for work.... The skirt will be delivered late this afternoon in time to take with you. The red blouse went out without delay."[333]

In the Taos Museum archives there is a photograph of Millicent (styled by Charles who, to please her, flew a hairdresser in from Hollywood). She is wearing one of his boho fiesta skirts as she stands on a stool, wrapped in an apron and bent over a tub of indigo, looking up, slightly startled, into the camera—as if caught by surprise in the act of hand dyeing some of the fabrics herself. There is another image, in *Harper's Bazaar*, of Millicent in Charles James and her own mix of jewels. For *Town & Country*, Niki de Gunzburg covered the look.[334]

"That year we all wore a black sateen skirt with ten petticoats," said Polly Mellen, a top editor at *Vogue*. "It wasn't the head to toe matching of that time," as Harold Koda, chief curator of the Fashion Institute at the Metropolitan Museum of Art, explained to one of Millicent's biographers, Cherie Burns. "Millicent incorporated Southwestern style into American dress."[335]

The fusion look Millicent and Charles co-created was a dramatic, eclectic, personal statement that inflected the fashion world of the 1950s. It foreshadowed the haute hippies of the 1960s and the nomad chic of the 1970s. And it remains a strong reference point of style to this day.

As the winter of 1952 approached, the "Dollar Princess" was in clear decline. "She had dizzy spells and began to walk with a stick. Her chief activity was wandering in her garden. Then, the week before Christmas, she wrote to her son Paul, "I am tired of fighting." On the last day of December, she fell while dyeing fabric in her tub, hit her head on a doorjamb, and was rushed to St. Joseph's Hospital in Albuquerque, a hundred miles away.[336] At 7:15 the following evening, she was dead. Millicent had spent almost all of her money. In 1954, the *New York Times* calculated her estate at $137,184—just over a million dollars today.

Schiaparelli, who wasn't there, wrote of her funeral:

The whole Pueblo of Taos, New Mexico, asked to go to the cathedral. It had never happened before. She had understood and helped them and they wanted to give her one last message of gratitude. They stood against the white sacred mountains banked with flowers, at the foot of which rose a huge scintillating Christmas tree. The Indians came wrapped in their colorful blankets. They stood in rigid silence and faced the mountains and the rising sun.[337]

Millicent's mother, Mary Rogers, and two of her sons—the Peralta-Ramos brothers—created a foundation in her name and opened the Millicent Rogers Museum (on historic Ledoux Street in Taos), where the thousands of pieces of the finest Navajo, Hopi, and Zuni silver objects Millicent owned, together with the Native American jewelry that she discovered and collected and some of her own jewelry designs, are now visited and admired by thousands of people each year.

In an obituary for *Women's Wear Daily*, Charles James called Millicent "someone who has not only inspired my whole work for a decade but that of every artist she knew. The columns carried the story of her death. They did not carry the story of an imagination that would live on through others...nor the story of a legend that retirement from public life caused to strengthen. Her influence on fashion in general, in my opinion, transcended that of any other woman I ever knew—perhaps because in part she was never aware of it."[338]

Dominique de Menil on the chaise longue Charles James invented for her famous Philip Johnson-designed house in Houston.

CHAPTER 6

Beyond Fashion:

Modess, Andy Warhol, and Dominique de Menil

THE RETROSPECTIVE AT the Brooklyn Museum in 1948 was a watershed event for Charles James in more ways than one.

Charles had, to borrow a term from the art world, "taken a displacement." In other words, by disconnecting the dresses he made for Millicent Rogers from the arena of daily life and displaying them in the context of a museum, he had invented a new way of looking at fashion. From this remove, his designs, "objectified" and "intellectualized" by their environment, could be viewed and admired at leisure, as special pieces created to be thought about, analyzed, and commented on. In "A Decade of Design," Charles James had moved fashion beyond the borders of an applied art form. He was also the first fashion designer to link his own fashion rules to worlds outside of clothing by exploring the application of fashion design techniques to advertising and interior design.

While he was planning the Brooklyn Museum retrospective, Modess (a maker of sanitary napkins, owned by the Johnson & Johnson Company) hired Charles, as America's outstanding designer, to become the creative director for their advertisements. In this brief role, Charles not only produced a trailblazing advertising campaign but, unknowingly, catalyzed the career of one of America's most significant artists.

To enhance the debut Modess advertisement, Charles decided to overlook already famous models and—in a wonderful "coup de foudre"—chose instead to "star" an unknown aristocrat, British-born beauty Maxime de la Falaise, who was the daughter of Sir Oswald Birley, portrait painter to the Court of St. James's. Charles met Maxime when she was working for his old friend Elsa Schiaparelli as "a sort of muse who was supposed to promote sales to the rich English."³³⁹ He

105

then hired Cecil (who was still in the process of rebuilding his American career after the war) to photograph her.

Standing beside the windows of the sumptuous, gold-flocked Rococo state room in a Venetian palazzo (typically, Charles had spent some of his own money to spectacularly refurbish the brocade-covered walls), Maxime is sheathed in ice-blue charmeuse. Her eyes are demurely downcast. But the resulting message is anything but bashful: the shimmering skirt of the dress James has made for her gathers in an achingly suggestive, central front "V" fold placed just below Maxime's hipline—from which it literally *flows* around her thighs before erotically slithering down to the floor.[340]

In the resulting advertisement, the glamorous film-still–like, multilayered image—which, on the surface, had nothing whatsoever to do with menstruation—was accompanied by only six enigmatically allusive words: "Think of the softest...Modess....because."[341] Charles's obliquely brilliant insider reference aligned sexuality, sensuality, and elegance in a way that only those who bought the product could understand.

By connecting the raw, sometimes unpleasant edge of sex with the provocatively enticing mystery of "sex appeal," Charles had elevated something previously viewed as an unmentionable necessity that no one wanted to think about to the aspirational. Think of all the ten-year-old girls yearning for puberty, so they could buy the product and become as fascinating as Maxime.[342] Or as Charles wrote later, "The spice of the campaign is that every woman, at a 'difficult time,' can imagine herself a duchess."[343]

Charles made three of these advertisements during his contract with Johnson & Johnson. They ran nationally beginning in June 1948, and although neither Charles James nor Cecil Beaton received "credits" for them, they were the nucleus of a hugely successful campaign that lasted more than twenty years. Charles not only branded Modess;he put it at the top of its field.

After Charles James's Modess contract had completed and was not renewed, Cecil—who was by far more charming, more businesslike, and infinitely less temperamental than Charles—took over the account (along with his friend Charlie's idea) and, as Beaton's biographer Hugo

Vickers explained, "made a good lot of money from it"[344] over the ensuing years.

In a 2001 interview for *Shūz* magazine, Tom Sokolowski, who was then head of the Andy Warhol Museum, spoke about how Andy began his career in advertising. Andy, said Sokolowski, was "a very well-known and highly paid illustrator, for whom commerce was *haut* art."[345]

In 1964, Warhol submitted a Modess campaign idea, with a playful drawing of little butterflies wafting tampons in the air, which was turned down—"*flat*"—for a Cecil Beaton photograph that involved couture ball gowns and "some sort of evasive copy about sanitary napkins freeing women to be themselves. *Instantly*," as Tom described it, Andy stopped making his fanciful illustrations:

> Andy saw the writing on the wall. He embraced *photography* as the new medium, and re-invented it. This was the birth of the Marilyn (and the Jackie and the Liz). He abandoned whimsy for *sex appeal*. Appeal always fascinated Andy. When he put all those different colors on the Marilyn image, he was talking about the creation of beauty: it's what you add to nature to make art.

As Charles James expressed it "Art steps in where nature fails"[346]

According to Tom (who didn't actually name Charles because he didn't know who had invented the Modess ball gown advertisements), the famous silkscreen portraits that are the beginning of Andy Warhol's career as an artist, were Andy's answer to Charles James.

Leaving no Jamesian inspiration unexplored, Warhol would go on to cast Maxime de la Falaise as part of *Andy Warhol's Nothing Serious*, a 1971 video project he made for television. Andy also included Maxime, with Candy Darling and Brigid Berlin, in his 1973 black-and-white video *Phony*. And the following year Maxime played a victim in the 1974 Warhol cult film *Dracula*.[347]

One of Charles James's last memories of his protégée Maxime was at Desmond Guinness's ball in the 1970s. He described her in an interview as "the only really funny person there...dancing very wildly with a young man who might have been somewhat under half her age, pretty-faced, with a touch of hair on his *not* casually exposed chest."[348]

❁

CHARLES'S SECOND VENTURE beyond fashion came a little less than a year after the Modess contract had lapsed. French-born Dominique de Menil, one of the most individualistic heiresses in America, and her husband, John, asked Charles to design the interior of their controversial new "modernist" house in Houston, Texas.

The rarified coterie of haute couture customers in the 1940s and 1950s were largely members of the conventional upper class, whose narrow interests ran to society balls, ladies' luncheons, and obligatory annual treks to the traditional watering holes of the very rich, like Newport, Rhode Island; Biarritz; and the French Riviera. Generally they were listed in the Social Register—or in England, Debrett's.

Naturally, Charles's favorite customers were the cream of this crop. Vivid and original, like Charles himself, these women considered themselves stars of their own life-stories. Still, in that era one hardly expected a member of the social elite to choose as her life's mission the collecting and championing of unknown modern and unrecognized primitive art. But that is precisely what Dominique de Menil, one of Charles's richest clients, did.

Her interests were as uncommon as Charles's designs, and her work would define the city she lived in long after she was dead. In Houston at the time, culture in general and the visual arts in particular were about as low as you could go on the list of priorities of the "good ol' boy" nouveau oil-rich clique that dominated the town. "I remember John [as Dominique's messenger] going to the Museum of Fine Arts [in Houston] and begging, pleading with them to let him hang some modern art," said private investor Aaron Farfel, an old de Menil family friend. "He would have taken space anywhere; he begged them to let him have the basement even, but he was refused every single time."[349] Like Millicent Rogers, Dominique's money came from oil. The second of three daughters of Conrad and Louise Schlumberger, Dominique was born in 1908 in Paris. Her Huguenot family, who could trace their roots back to the fifteenth century and had made their first fortune in the textile industry, had immigrated to France from their home in the iron-rich northwestern province of Alsace when the Prussians annexed it in 1871.

Dominique's father, a physics professor at the Paris School of Mines, sold his shares in the family fabric business to finance his invention, a "sonde," or sounding tool, that could be suspended by cables in a borehole to send up electronic, sonic, or nuclear analysis of the makeup of that hole. Until the late 1930s, the family held the exclusive patent on the invention. Any time anyone drilled an oil well anywhere in the world, Schlumberger was called in. Within ten years of its founding, the company was a huge global concern. Today, long after the patent has expired; it is still the world's largest oil services company. And the process of well logging is still called "running a Slumberjay" in oil fields, no matter whose equipment is being used.

Conrad Schlumberger's family was sophisticated and hardworking, but they did not enjoy spending their money. "We had no fine rugs, no antiques, no rare books; no great art in our home," Dominique de Menil told Dominique Browning in a 1983 interview for an article aptly titled "What I Admire I Must Possess." "Spending money was frowned upon. We entertained only once or twice a year. That was only for family. My parents were very strict puritanical Protestants."

Dominique herself was highly educated, intellectual, and strong-willed. She studied physics and math at the Sorbonne, where she received an advanced degree in mathematics. She rode her horse in the Bois de Boulogne every morning and vacationed every summer at the family chateau in Normandy. After completing her studies at the Sorbonne, Dominique worked in Berlin as script assistant to Josef von Sternberg on his production of *The Blue Angel*, starring Marlene Dietrich. She published serious articles on film technology in the French *La Revue du Cinéma*. She also studied art history and years later would chair the art department at the University of St. Thomas in Houston.

She met her husband, John (born Jean) de Menil, a banker and descendant of Napoleonic nobility, in 1930 at a ball in Versailles they had both dreaded attending. After they married the next year, Dominique converted to John's Catholicism and began to leave behind the restrictions of her parents' way of life.

In 1934, the surrealist painter Max Ernst, who had originally been commissioned by the de Menils to decorate a wall in their first apartment with frescos of birds, painted Dominique's head on a small canvas instead. It was the first work of art she acquired, and it made her uncomfortable. The portrait shows Dominique's face and neck in three-quarter profile. Her short blond hair curls softly around her temples and behind her ears.[350] Her skin is very smooth and pale and her limpid blue eyes are focused, catlike, on the invisible distance as her lips curve almost imperceptibly in an enigmatic smile. The truncated head appears to be floating on an orange, red, and royal blue background, surrounded by an orbit of ambiguous shapes that could be either seashells or pottery shards. "I didn't like the painting at all," she said. "I thought I looked very stiff." When the couple fled the war and France for America in 1941, the portrait, which had been bundled up in brown paper and stuffed out of sight on top of a tall armoire in the bedroom, was left behind in the Paris apartment.

Dominique and John's collecting began in earnest in 1945, when they bought Paul Cézanne's *Montagne*, under the guidance of the Dominican priest Marie-Alain Couturier, and became interested in the intersection of art and spirituality. They were tutored in the wonders of surrealist and modern art (including Max Ernst's work) by Egyptian-born New York art dealer Alexander Iolas. To her joy, Dominique acquired the ability to judge painting, appreciate it, and feel its magic—in other words, she developed her "eye."

When she returned to Paris in the late 1940s to retrieve her belongings, Dominique rediscovered the Max Ernst portrait. Later, she remembered that when she unwrapped the bundle containing the long-discarded work she was stunned by the beauty of the colors and the originality of its composition. Staring at it with new eyes, she suddenly realized how profoundly her interaction with art had changed her, or, as she expressed it, "how much my eyes had been opened."[351] It was as if she had been born again.

By the end of the 1940s, Dominique and John's collecting had become their passion. "I would have never started buying so much art if I had not moved to Houston," Dominique explained. "When I arrived in Texas there was not much you could call art. Houston was a provincial, dormant place, much like Strasbourg, Alsace. That is why I started buying. That is why I discovered the physical need to acquire."[352] In the end, Dominique's vast holdings would range from modern European art to major American postwar movements, including Abstract Expressionism, Pop Art, and minimalism.

The Cy Twombly Gallery would become a significant part of the Menil Collection complex; a Dan Flavin site-specific installation would be established at Richmond Hall, Houston; and the Rothko Chapel, built in central Houston, provided intimate sanctuary to people of all faiths. Dominique and John also broadened their scope to include pieces from classical Mediterranean and Byzantine cultures, as well as objects from Africa, Oceania, and the Pacific Northwest. The collection finally included fifteen thousand paintings, photographs, sculptures, objects, prints, drawings, photographs, and rare books. A wide variety of the artists who created these objects became Dominique and John's close friends.

The de Menils' true love, however, was always for the surrealists. According to architectural planner Peter Wolf, their collection of René Magritte is the most distinguished in the world. It includes master-pieces like *The Dominion of Light* (1954) and *The Meaning of Night* (1927).[353]

Understandably, John and Dominique wanted their home to represent the cutting edge of contemporary architecture. "Always aiming high,"[354] as Christophe, the eldest of their five children, would characterize it, the couple, at the suggestion of sculptor Mary Callery, asked the legendary Mies van der Rohe—widely recognized as one of the pioneering masters of modern architecture—to design their home. Mies said he thought he would be too expensive and recommended instead one of his disciples, a brilliant young curator at the Museum of Modern Art in Manhattan, Philip Johnson.

Forty-two at the time, Johnson had founded the Department of Architecture and Design at MoMA in 1930, before graduating from Harvard's Graduate School of Design in 1943. John and Dominique commissioned Johnson to develop their project in 1948–49, just as he was beginning his Glass House in Connecticut, which would make him famous. The de Menil house, which unnerved tradition-bound Houston, was one of America's first great modernist structures.

In Dominique de Menil's words, with the advent of international modernism, "the rectangle reigned supreme." And, following Mies's famous dictum, "less is more," Johnson built a plain (and for Houston, relatively small) 5,600-square-foot International Style structure. It's a one-story box of glass, brick, and steel, with a flat roof that leaked.[355]

"Most people in Houston knew nothing about Philip Johnson or Mies van der Rohe or Le Corbusier," a local architect commented. "This wasn't a house—it was a dental office or a Laundromat," he added.[356] The meandering, tree-lined drive through the grounds also disoriented guests and delivery people, who became confused and mistook the front door for the service entrance.

Located in the city's fashionable River Oaks neighborhood, the home is situated on two lots. It encloses a planted interior courtyard and is surrounded by a dense, jungle like jumble of twenty trees and fifteen varieties of tropical plants.

Philip Johnson's design was bordered by ersatz-Plantation and Tudor-style mega mansions, all with no grass around them at all. Imagine a glass rectangle inside a terrarium encircled by antebellum houses built right next to the road. The de Menil architecture didn't exactly fit in.

The couple's five children were unhappy. "I was very embarrassed," said Christophe de Menil. "It was just so different. And my sister Adelaide speaks of being too embarrassed to have friends over."[357]

"As a teenager I longed to live in a 'normal' house like everyone else," Adelaide added recently. "[There] were all these weird paintings hanging on the walls," she continued. "For instance, there was a big purple and yellow canvas by Léger, and I hated to take my friends through the hall where they could see it. And I loathed the black tile floor. I wanted a wooden one." The youngest brother, François, now himself an architect, remembers that he grew up thinking architects were people whose job was to fix leaky roofs.[358]

Johnson planned to complete his building with stark Mies Van der Rohe furniture. But Dominique and John balked at the concept. Dominique said she wanted something "voluptuous." And John, whose eye, although not as educated as his wife's, was as refined and more instinctive than hers, suggested that Charles James could design the interiors. Insulted that he wasn't allowed to complete his own project, Johnson was angry at their violation of his vision. "I admire [Charles James's] work as a dress designer tremendously," he wrote to Dominique on May 2, 1950, "but you can imagine the disappointment of an architect when someone else finishes his work."[359] Charles was delighted when he heard about the letter. "Let's have a little Turkish patio. It will be quite Oriental,"[360] he chuckled wickedly. For years, Philip Johnson deliberately omitted the house from surveys of his architecture. And in fact it wasn't until 1954, when he was selected to make buildings for Houston's Menil-supported St. Thomas University, that Johnson relented and claimed that "he was delighted with what Charles James did."[361]

Charmingly, the de Menil choice was essentially intuitive. Dominique got to know Charles James practically by accident in the late 1940s when, according to Christophe, the princess Donna Maria Ruspoli, who had had an affair with Charles, sent Dominique to his atelier to deliver a "Dear John" letter.[362]

Dominique was just coming into her own as an art collector, and her modesty was legendary. She was one of the richest people in America, but she ran her vast affairs from a tiny, nondescript, one-chair table, nestled almost invisibly in the corner of her bedroom. And she was totally oblivious to the fanfare of fashion. She preferred "old clothes," in subdued mousy colors, because, as Christophe told me, "These made her feel as though she were saving her money for art."[363] She liked the brush of fur against her skin and wore her mink coat inside out, and she was well known for showing up time and again to fancy art openings in the same (slightly tatty) black dress with mismatched shoes, one green and one blue, because their mates had been abandoned in a closet in some other city.

But when she met Charles, Dominique's art-trained eye immediately recognized, understood, and admired his work. He was able to make fashion interesting to her. Christophe remembers that the two spent long hours discussing clothing design. "She loved his ideas. They talked a little bit about literature."[364] (Charles, who enjoyed giving books as presents, gave Dominique a history of the Huguenots and a biography of Oscar Wilde.)[365] But their conversations were "mostly about clothes and shapes."[366]

Both Charles and Dominique had been deeply influenced by surrealism and its practitioners. And the bond they developed was based on a passionately felt mutual aesthetic. Like Charles's London friends in the 1930s, John, who loved and understood both art and luxury, and Dominique, always thought of Charles James in terms of his vision. Dominique later wrote that she felt his ideas were a major influence on European designers. She appreciated the biomorphic forms of his ball gowns, which, for her, were closer in nature to true works of art than the oeuvre of any other couturier. And she credited Charles for teaching her about color and turning her away from the banality of "tasteful" choices. She understood that his eccentricity and his genius were linked. Charles, she wrote, "had ideas that were, in their originality considered perverse because they went against the grain but were often very remarkable." He "really taught me how to turn my back from easy things and look for more elaborate ones instead"[367]

In 1947, soon after she met Charles, Dominique ordered her first Charles James evening dress. It was a version of the "Bustle Gown" originally created for Millicent Rogers. Unlike Millicent, Dominique never worked with Charles to co-design clothing but, as a true patron, she commissioned the ones she thought were the best. Through the years, she accumulated over twenty of Charles's couture "creations," which she acquired as what she would later call "objects de collection" and loved owning, but rarely wore. These include a carefully chosen, representative spectrum of coats, jackets, suits, scarves, belts, and hats, as well as dresses for day and evening. As Susan Sutton, who organized "A Thin Wall of Air: Charles James," the de Menil Museum show, observed, the clothes, executed in idiosyncratic shades like chestnut brown or oxblood red, reflect a gamut of the surrealist palette. They are, she commented, "reflections of the art of their time."

Dominique also accrued a Charles James "model for a sculpture,"[368] a cache of his poetical, sensory fashion sketches, and, importantly, the prints of the famous Charles James ads for Modess.

"She trusted him, and that is why she could bring him into her house and let him do whatever extreme things he felt like doing,"[369] said Christophe.

Charles James came as a novice to the de Menil project.

His collaborations with Millicent Rogers on her fashion fantasies of self-presentation—the haute-Austrian outfits she had invented to complement her Austrian chalet in the 1930s, and the Native American tiered skirts and Navajo jackets she wore to offset the beauty of Turtle Walk—pointed directly to a new kind of lifestyle designing, but Charles never tampered with Millicent's interior décor. So although the splendor and startling originality of his showrooms was legendary—and though he claimed to Couri in the tapes that John and Dominique had previously hired him to decorate a small apartment on Sixty-eighth Street in Manhattan "in the palette of de Chirico"[370]—Charles, who preferred to live in hotels, was essentially inexperienced when it came to interiors. Certainly he had never designed an entire house.

Intrepid, he landed in Houston in 1951, "ready for action" and bearing a gift: an enormous, opalescent emerald-green vase so big it couldn't fit into a taxi. So Charles telephoned the de Menils from the airport and demanded a special van to pick it up. When it finally arrived, he placed it himself and filled it with a riot of pure white lilacs he'd imported from California just for the vase. "It was his symbol," Sutton explained, "for what he was going to do to the place."[371]

Charles's first outrageous move was to demolish Philip Johnson's carefully composed architectural proportions by raising the ceilings all over the house. "The most brilliant idea I think he had," Christophe remembers, "was to raise the ceiling one foot. So from being eight and a half or nine feet, it went to ten feet, which," she adds, "was a more noble space."

His work habits were equally egregious. According to Adelaide, he would arrive at the work site just before midday, when the painters, who had spent the morning waiting around for his instructions, were leaving for their lunch break.[372] Furious at their absence, Charles, who insisted on creating a different color board for each room, would don a fancy army jumpsuit in a pretty shade of khaki and retreat to the garage, where he started mixing his imported Japanese colors all by himself. This would continue for most of the afternoon and evening until, Christophe recalled, "inspiration struck." By then, sometimes as late as eleven o'clock at night, the de Menil daughter added, "my sister and I had to hold lights so he could try the paints on the walls."

There were unexpected color combinations all over the modernist box. Vibrant hues—magenta, blue, acid green, and a caramel brown, which Charles, who adored being naughty, called "goose shit"[373]—were splashed throughout the corridors, closets, and even the drawers. He introduced rich, warm colors like bubblegum pink into small dark spaces, while the living room was the most translucent of dove grays. Doors were wrapped with antique velvet. The walls of niches and halls were covered in fuchsia and butterscotch felt. In Dominique's dressing room, a checkerboard of squares in slightly variant hues of silky aqua, gray, and pale blue were painted by candlelight, and produced a luxuriously cool, elegant atmosphere that opposes and echoes the garden outside her window. The interiors of the drawers and cabinets, like the lining of a coat or a suit jacket, are in contrasting colors of olive green or butter yellow. When asked what her most vivid memory of the house was, Christophe answered: "The red. He used dark blood red for a whole couch. He put blood red on the doors in our little hall." Christophe also told me that the time she remembers her mother the happiest was when she discovered Dominique sitting on the floor, helping Charles paint a closet door with a putty knife.

Charles's use of color had the wonderful effect of adding a quirkily contrapuntal warmth and fantasy to Johnson's plain linearity. The cold, polished black Mexican tile floors were strewn with zebra-skin rugs. And in a blue bedroom, Luis Fernández's 1953 *Buste de Femme Nue,* a white profile against a cerulean background, hang vivid blue on a lilac blue wall.

The furniture Charles chose was as original as the palette. Some of it he designed. He made a double-arced, pale beige-pink couch with a scarlet cushion. Echoing Max Ernst and reminiscent of Dalí's lips sofa, its contours are molded to the curves of a human form. Charles, who later explained the shapes of his couch as "the indentations that would occur if a woman sat on wet cement," announced that "if nature could grow a sofa, it might look like this." He called it "the Butterfly," and Dominique had herself photographed for a Houston newspaper perched on it, wearing a vermilion Charles James evening gown.[374] As she grew older, the couch became, according to Christophe, her mother's favorite resting place in the afternoon.[375]

For the dining room, Charles also built a long, plump bench that winds and snuggles voluptuously the length of a wall, beckoning dinner guests to postprandial repose. And he sculpted a chaise longue for the terrace that—from a side view—resembles a woman's figure. "His ball gowns look like furniture and his furniture looks like ball gowns," a Houston socialite observed.[376]

The house's wide, angular glass entrance is dominated by a violently green, extravagantly carved Rococo Revival couch designed by German-born American violin and cabinetmaker John Henry Belter. It completely contradicts the austerity of the architecture, while perfectly mirroring the tropical tangle of the garden outside. In the tapes, Charles offhandedly mentions to Couri that he "just found" the inimitable nineteenth-century French-inspired piece in a "little shop."

The pièce de résistance, however, is the walk-in liquor closet—an enchanting surprise hidden behind the living room paneling. It is both a cabinet of curiosities and a little art installation where miniature master paintings (by the likes of Max Ernst, and Andy Warhol from) the de Menil's collection hang, jostled one next to the other, salon style, on the satin-lined walls, and the curved shelves display a gleaming collection of gem-colored goblets and decanters mixed in with the bottles of liquor.

"It's an actual room and not just a display cabinet…it's really its own little world…there's a fantasy aspect," architect Brad Cloepfil, who praised the cabinet as "a space of intense intimacy,"[377] told the *Wall Street Journal*.

In "Mrs. de Menil's Liquor Closet," an unconventional essay on collecting originally written for *Esquire,* Edward Albee describes the concept:

> Most of us who accumulate art are given to variety and have large and small paintings, drawings, prints, large and small sculpture—whatever. And since the big pieces look best in the big rooms,

Dominique de Menil in front of the "very old" grand piano Charles James personally selected for her rectilinear living room. Although Charles James was a piano prodigy, none of the de Menils played the piano.

you are (unless you've figured out, of course, that the right big painting looks super next to the right small one) stuck with the problem of what to do with the twenty or so small paintings and drawings that don't fit in

...Some small pieces just don't "work" in the overall design. Well, it's so simple—if you're a de Menil. Put them in a space almost everybody will go to from time to time—the room where the nourishment of conviviality is kept: the Liquor Closet.

Such a simple, such an elegant solution. You go to the Liquor Closet to get yourself a drink (and the hosts are happy to let you), and there you are face-to-face with a small Braque, a Victor Brauner, a Chagall, a Laurens, an Anne Ryan, a Schwitters. They are there with other pieces and with glasses and liquor bottles and stuff.

The only problem with this solution is that someday someone is going to be so happy with the art and with the liquor that a permanent house guest will have been born.

I suppose every good idea has its downside.[378]

The de Menils (who paid Charles three thousand dollars for the complete design) loved the house. They respected Charles, and were grateful for what they learned from him. "Charles James," John told *Vogue*, "has the courage...to look for the difficult solution...he taught us to meet difficult problems in taste."

"It was pretty romantic and glamorous when he was finished," Christophe observed. "It was free. Well it wasn't any historical period. It wasn't modern, it wasn't seventeenth century. It wasn't just what he would find, or what he would make. And it was always very fitting. It was what you'd feel comfortable with and useful."[379]

The furniture Charles made for the de Menils was later produced by Brierleigh, Ltd. It sold through Lord & Taylor. Christophe would herself buy two copies of the Butterfly couch her mother loved so much.

Significantly, although Poiret sold wallpaper and upholstery fabrics, Charles was the first fashion designer to professionally apply principles of clothing design to a house, but his intervention in Johnson's rectilinear structure is much more than an innovative expression of "lifestyle marketing." Charles's delightful riots of tensions amid the constraints of international modernism are an inspired interpretation of the intersection of life and art. And if surrealism is the expression of the contradiction between the austerities of the rational and the animation of the subconscious, then Charles James designed the first surrealist house.

The house was also, naturally, a stage set for parties. It was frequently filled with visiting artists, intellectuals, scientists, and civil rights leaders. Max Ernst (who had his picture taken laughing with Dominique in the garden),[380] René Magritte, Man Ray, Giorgio de Chirico (whose rusts and ochers inspired the colors in the de Menils 'New York apartment), Andy Warhol, Fred Hughes (Andy's right hand), Roberto Rossellini, sculptress Niki de Saint Phalle, Jean Tinguely, Alexander Calder, and Jasper Johns were just some of the visitors welcomed there.

René Magritte was taken to a rodeo. The existentialist film director Michelangelo Antonioni, who told John he wanted to meet some "rich Texans," was given a big celebration in his honor. When the famous photographer Henri Cartier-Bresson was invited, he slunk around silently, surreptitiously photographing the place.[381]

Perhaps the most thoughtful of the guests was architect and futurist Buckminster (Bucky) Fuller, who invented the geodesic dome. Dominique asked him to say a few words after a dinner, and while gazing beyond the artwork and the sumptuous surroundings, he hesitated a moment until the room went quiet. "Looking around your magnificent house," Bucky began, "I am reminded of my childhood…one rainy Saturday afternoon when I was ten years old my grandmother showed me some toys stored in the attic. Lined up against the back wall under the eaves, I saw a set of twelve magnificent gold-leaf dining chairs covered in red velvet. I asked, 'What are those chairs? I've never seen them before.' She told me this: 'I'm only the custodian of those chairs. They were my mother's. They will belong to someone else someday. We are guardians. We don't really own anything.'"[382]

A year after Dominique's death in 1997, the Menil Collection, housed in one of the most acclaimed designs by prize-winning Italian architect Renzo Piano, was completed. It was commissioned by her children so she could share the joys of her vast collection with the people of Houston, the city where she and her husband made their lives. It is open to the public free of charge from Wednesday to Sunday. Renzo Piano says it's a portrait of Dominique de Menil.[383]

The James/Johnson house was restored in 2004. It is a small, precious museum that can be visited by appointment, also free of charge.

In 1954, Charles James received a commission from Celanese Corporation of America to create coats in their materials and persuaded Mrs. Austine Hearst to model one of them for this advertisement in Vogue.

CHAPTER 7

Apotheosis:

Austine Hearst

BY 1952, THE UNITED STATES was the dominant world power.
Dwight D. Eisenhower, who had led the Allies to their World War II
victory, was well on his way to winning the American presidency by a
landslide. And Charles James, who was planning his grandest ball gown
to salute that inauguration, was expanding his business by leaps and
bounds.

During the previous year, Charles had put into production two new
design concepts, or "theses": the first version of the "Swan Gown," which
he originally made as an ankle-length dress for Jennifer Jones to wear to
the 1949 Venice Film Festival, and the famous "Louis-Philippe sleeve"
that legendarily took him three years and twenty thousand dollars to
perfect. He had additionally begun four years of work on his "Pagoda
Suit"—by his own admission, a chef d'oeuvre of tailoring. He was
eagerly preparing to expand into mass marketing through lower priced
duplications of his new "inventions." And to accommodate the anticipated increase in his workload, Charles had closed 699 Madison Avenue
and opened a much larger atelier at 716 Madison Avenue. He had also
re-designed his showroom space at the elegant Sherry-Netherland
Hotel on Fifth Avenue and Sixtieth Street, where he now lived.[384]

His handpicked private clients were a star-studded group, positioned to receive full media coverage as the "Who's Who" of Lambert's
syndicated best-dressed list. They included: Jennifer Jones, who was
also Mrs. David O. Selznick at the time; opera singer Eleanor Searle
Whitney, who had modeled for Elizabeth Arden and married Cornelius
Vanderbilt Whitney; Babe Paley, now wife of CBS chairman William
Paley; and Slim Keith, who was Mrs. Leland Hayward. Hayward produced *The Sound of Music*, *South Pacific*, and *Gypsy* (which was based
on the life of Gypsy Rose Lee, another Charles James devotée).[385]

123

Most significant, Charles was in the midst of inventing his favorite thesis, his most lavish and famous creation of all time: the "Clover Leaf" ball gown. Originally intended as an homage to Eisenhower's inauguration, it would be purchased, promoted, and incarnated by his most loyal, loving, and important couture client of the 1950s, Austine Hearst.

Mrs. Hearst was tall, auburn-haired, slim, empathetic, and vivacious, and managed with seemingly effortless charm to strike just the right note with everyone she met. Liz Smith, who worked for the Hearsts in the early 1960s, when she was taken to some of Austine's parties by Charles James's old apprentice Arnold Scaasi, explained that Austine "was spirited, down to earth, and lovely to everyone, even those who were young and not socially important—like me."[386] Austine was also, as her sons, Will and Austin, confirm, a marvelous mother and a connoisseur of the arts of fashion and of life. Austin, the youngest (who doesn't remember Charles), describes himself as having "spent a lot of [his] happy childhood playing on the fitting-room floor."[387]

The daughter of Southern gentry, Austine Hearst was born Austine McDonnell in 1920 (the year Charles was sent to Harrow), in Warrenton, her mother's hometown at the heart of the Virginia hunt country, where her father was a major stationed at the U.S. Army base there. Both her parents' families traced their ancestry back to the English subjects who fought to have King John sign the Magna Carta, and whose descendants came to Maryland and Virginia in the seventeenth century and served as officers during the Revolutionary War.[388]

Later, Austine often said that she had been lucky to be born in such a sophisticated little place. The town was well known for its white sulphur springs that attracted people from neighboring states, and had been as much a resort as a farm community during the eighteenth and nineteenth centuries, when a visit to one of these "spa" towns was considered a great luxury. (In *Gone with the Wind*, Mr. O'Hara promises Scarlett a trip to a similar location as a reward for obeying him.) So, even though its population was less than ten thousand, Warrenton, the Fauquier county seat, had "high life, entertaining, and reasons to dress up."

When Austine went out with her mother she was showered with attention "like royalty," and recognized everywhere she went. As she remembered: "In the kind of community I grew up in, [you walk] into a store, down the street, [and] everyone you pass knows you. Everyone knows who you are. And in a small southern town in particular, where they're interested in genealogy, everyone knows who your great-grandmother was.…That, I think, is one of the problems of young people today. They have a feeling they are not known. They're not appreciated. They're lost in crowds."[389]

Austine, who was pretty, beloved and indulged, was brought up by her parents and grandmother to be a professional Southern belle, "which was something of a cross between a geisha girl and a duchess."

She grew up in what she describes as "a big old house with an enormous attic with trunks of elegant old clothes," which, to her delectation, she was allowed to play with, try on, and "parade around in." She loved poking around the old cedar chests and discovering what was inside the "band boxes," or hatboxes, made out of tin so people could travel without crushing their hats. One hat "even had curls in it, false curls so that when you put on the hat your hair was all done, too."[390] (In 1978, at the romantic height of hippy eclecticism in fashion, Austine remembered those marvelous old clothes in her mother's attic. And observed that: "all those lace shirtwaists and velvet mantels and lace hats" had come back into style.) Dressing up was an exciting experience. Every new getup was like a new personality. For Austine, inventing different outfits was a wonderful way to discover who she was and what she could become.

"I think one of the prime functions of adornment, self-adornment," she continued, "[is] to make you feel better. Often the question is asked: 'Do people dress for men? Or do they dress for women?' There is no doubt. People dress for themselves." Back in Warrenton, where big stores weren't really accessible, every lady had a dressmaker. "Even if you knew how to sew for yourself you would work with a dressmaker. She would either come to your house or you would go to hers." The dressmaker acted as a sounding board, helping to choose what looked best, and to develop one's own taste. Like Charles James, Austine enjoyed reworking dress designs:

"Sometimes in my family, they remade old clothes over and over. They would go up in the attic, choose an outmoded dress, and restyle it: take the buttons off one thing and put them on another. In the South in that period before and following the Civil War, when the attic began being filled, they saved everything, so that in my girlhood there were just endless resources: pieces of ribbon, bolts of lace, boxes of feathers, and pieces of fur, buttons, and buckles. Nothing was ever thrown away."[391]

Her first party dress, of pale yellow organdy, was made out of another dress. "There is nothing sadder to me," Austine said, "than women who are afraid to touch a dress because it was made by a famous designer. A woman who doesn't adapt things to suit herself, and her own styles, and her own taste, misses a lot of fun, a lot of creativity. Outstanding leaders of fashion have always done that. I was taught to value manners and externals. I remember my grandmother's [saying] 'if you have a black lace dress and a ham in the ice box you're ready for any emergency.' Now that may sound frivolous but there's a kernel of wisdom in believing it that if you cover your body gracefully, you can cover whatever upsets your heart. If you look presentable, people will believe you are in control."[392]

When she was twenty, Austine, who as a little girl wanted at various times to "run fast, ride well, be popular with boys, and become an actress," ended up—just as many Southern belles might—marrying young. She met her first husband, the Russian count Igor Cassini, just after her debut, when she was attending junior college in Washington, DC. She was nineteen; he was a twenty-one-year-old junior columnist who had recently been hired by the *Washington Times-Herald* to report on social life in the capital and its conurbations in Virginia. Igor describes his first impression of Austine, who everyone called "Bootsie," as "a vision of yellow chiffon: titian hair, flawless skin, and a high forehead of perfect proportion. We fell in love," Igor wrote, "although there was a rival I had to overcome, Miguel Quirno Lavalle, an attaché at the Argentinian embassy."[393]

Bootsie offered to become Cassini's "informant" for local society gossip. Their affair, which wreaked havoc with her studies, also resulted in the near-death by lynching of Igor when local "good ol' boys," purportedly incensed by the tone of the foreigner's reportage of their town's affairs, hauled him out of a country club dance they claimed he had crashed, tarred and feathered him, and beat him up so badly that he landed in a local hospital. The police became involved. The story was front-paged by the *Washington Times-Herald* and quickly picked up by the wire services. Cassini was fired over the incident, but Austine, who could have, as he commented, "dropped him fast,"[394] remained loyal despite anonymous phone calls and other harassments. The columnist Walter Winchell stuck up for him, too, defending Igor in print and on the air.

There had never been a lynching in Warrenton, and it turned out, as Austine discovered, that the assailants had recently emigrated from England and weren't real Southerners at all. The *Times-Herald* demanded a court hearing. Igor was the prime witness for the prosecution, and all three of the attackers were found guilty of assault. Cassini was reinstated, promoted, and given his own column.

During this time Austine had been acting in local playhouses and auditioning for the movies, so when Howard Hughes offered her a contract and an airplane ticket to Hollywood in 1940, Igor unsurprisingly decided he couldn't live without her, and the couple eloped.

Igor's employer, Elinor "Cissy" Patterson, owner of the *Times-Herald,* was "the most powerful woman in America."[395] As a debutante in the 1920s, Cissy, an unconventional beauty with a pug nose and vivid red hair, was an heiress from the McCormick family in Illinois (the McCormicks were friends of Charles's parents), and had been a member of a very socially prominent group in Washington, known in the newspaper columns as "the Three Graces." It included Alice Roosevelt Longworth and Marguerite Cassini, the daughter of the Russian ambassador to Washington at that time. (He was Igor's uncle as well). Her grandfather Joseph Medill had been mayor of Chicago and owned the *Herald Tribune.* She was said to have "printer's ink in her veins," and according to Austine was a "woman's libber well before the time."[396]

"Her own family would not give her a position on the *Herald Tribune,*" Austine remembered. "So [through his right hand and chief reporter, Arthur Brisbane] she got William Randolph Hearst to give her a job and he made her the publisher of the [papers] he owned in Washington."[397] Cissy, who was the first woman editor in chief of a major newspaper, bought both papers from Hearst in 1930. There is no equivalent for what this would mean today—unless one thinks in terms of developing and managing a major television news channel in conjunction with owning the *Huffington Post.*

At the turn of the last century, competitors William Randolph Hearst and Joseph Pulitzer, both of whom had newspapers in the American West, decided to expand into New York City at the same time. During the ensuing "circulation wars," they individually and simultaneously pioneered a more accessible, personalized, and interpretative style of reporting, in the hopes of widening their audience appeal. This practice spread to many other newspapers, and columnists gained increasing importance and power in the daily life of America. By 1926, when Arthur Brisbane was Hearst's star correspondent, *Time* magazine reported:

> *The New York American*, the *Chicago Herald-Examiner*, the *San Francisco Examiner* and many another newspapers owned by Publisher Hearst, to say nothing of some 200 non-Hearst dailies and 800 country weeklies which buy syndicated Brisbane, all publish what Mr. Brisbane has said. His column is headed, with simple finality, "Today," [and is] a column that vies with the weather and market reports for the size of its audience, probably beating both.
>
> It is said to be read by a third of the total U.S. population—"Today" and every day.[398]

In a similar vein, more juicy journalism flourished as well. Walter Winchell's column, which ran in two thousand newspapers from the 1920s to the early 1950s, had an estimated fifty million daily readers, while his radio broadcasts were calculated to have twenty million listeners each. By the 1940s and 1950s, gossip columnists like Earl Wilson, Leonard Lyons, Louella Parsons, Cholly Knickerbocker (which was first Maury Paul's, then in 1945 Igor Cassini's "nom de plume"), and Eileen Mehle, who detailed the doings of high society as *SUZY*, ruled public opinion. A sentence, or just a word, from them could make or break a Broadway show, a marriage, even a lifetime career. It was no accident that Hedda Hopper, who was Louella's rival for the throne of "Queen of Hollywood," called her Beverly Hills mansion "the House that Fear Built."[399] Everyone— media, critics, those with a reputation, and those without one—was afraid of these columnists even as they daily devoured their words.

According to Austine, "Cissy believed in giving women a chance so she hired me to work for her newspaper. When I knew Cissy she already had a damn good newspaper…It was like a daily magazine.…[And] it was very exciting being part of the team."[400] Austine ended up doing "everything for the paper," which included fashion layouts and—under the byline "Austine"—writing two front-page gossip columns: "These Charming People" and "Under My Hat." She also wrote a diet book and many series of articles, one of which was about the world's most beautiful women, beginning with Helen of Troy and ending with Grace Kelly.

Then in 1945, Austine took over Igor's job as chief gossip columnist at the *Times-Herald* when he moved to Manhattan to write the "Cholly Knickerbocker" column for Hearst at the *New York Journal-American*. As a result their marriage rapidly deteriorated to what Igor would later describe as "a weekend commuter stage."[401] Upset that Austine wouldn't give up her own front-page column to come to New York to work as his assistant, and "left to my own devices during the week," as he wrote in his biography, *I'd Do It All Over Again,* Igor was "invited everywhere on [his] own because of [his] by-line…and [he] began to prefer it that way." [402]

If Igor was self-involved and distractible, William Randolph Hearst Jr.—who won a Pulitzer Prize in 1956 for his reporting on the Soviet Union and would become editor in chief of all the Hearst newspapers—respected Austine. He was willing to give her the freedom to work as she wanted and appreciated her talents. William considered her an excellent newspaperwoman and a helping hand in a great deal of what he and other journalists reported. "Without her encouragement and sharp mind some of us would have faltered along the way," he wrote in his memoir, *The Hearsts: Father and Son.* "William was so crazy about her," Liz Smith, who became Igor's assistant for the "Cholly Knickerbocker" column in 1959, told me, "that he couldn't bear to have her leave the room if he was in it."[403]

They first met in passing at a lavish party in the Stanford White-designed Patterson mansion in Washington during the war. William saw Austine for a second time in 1945, when he had just returned home from the service and his own marriage was on the rocks. He was on what he called a "busman's holiday" to San Francisco, where Austine was covering a story for Cissy Patterson. In his book he remembers being surprised and pleased:

She was as thin and as wispy as ever and retained her fresh look and beautiful smile. She had established herself as a first rate columnist, writing about everything from people to politics to Washington parties. Austine was among the first to blow the whistle on Alger Hiss, a member of the American diplomatic delegation at the U.N.'s founding. Hiss was later convicted of perjury in connection with Communist associations.[404]

Patterson, who thought it was a good match, did everything she could to foster and promote the relationship. And, as a Charles James client and admirer who knew what he could do for a woman, she sent Austine to interview Charles. Although Austine would later compare Charles to Leonardo da Vinci—because the patron who paid Leonardo for the *Mona Lisa* never got it and it ended up in the Louvre instead[405]— she liked Charles right away and understood him instinctively. For his part, he loved dressing her.

> He was very good to me when I was working on the paper because he allowed me to pay for the clothes on the installment plan. His clothes were very expensive, even then. Suits were $2,500 and in the '40's [when an average suit cost $12] that was very expensive. Evening dresses were $2,500 to $4,000. A simple dress would be $950 to $1,000. Well, that would take months to pay. But that was always my philosophy. Buy the best.[406]

Austine reciprocated by including Charles in her widely read columns. Thus her *Times-Herald* audience learned that Charles's fashion theories, which reached beyond fashion, were taken as seriously by the Brooklyn Museum as by the glamorous women who wore his clothes. Similarly, she quoted Mona (Mrs. Harrison) Williams as saying that Charles's new collection kindled "for the first time the same enthusiasm she used to feel in Paris, where discovery and execution came before the desire to make money and a name."[407] And Austine also noted that Mainbocher had sparked "a storm of French protest" when he reported that ever since Charles James left France for America, "Paris—as a fashion center—was *dead*."[408]

When Charles opened his own showroom at 699 Madison Avenue, Austine was one of the first to model his clothes. In the famous December 1945 *Vogue* photograph, she is sheathed in a black Charles James evening dress fitted along the curves of her figure. It has thin shoulder straps that are cut of the same piece as a deep front yoke in pale Benedictine satin which dips down the dress's center to snuggle past the waist of the black velvet skirt and end in a taper where her torso meets her legs.

Again on October 16, 1946, the *Times-Herald* headlined: "Our Austine Models Gown": "Austine took time from her colummning [*sic*] yesterday to model a [cobalt gros de Londres] Charles James gown at the St Luke's Hospital fashion show in Chicago. Countess Cassini wears her own heirloom gems."[409] And once more on July 17, 1947, the *Washington Times-Herald* reported that Austine was as "lovely as a flower in this fragile-looking dinner gown created by American designer Charles James.…A medieval look is achieved."[410]

Austine's relationship with William progressed a little more slowly than her relationship with Charles. It took another two years after the San Francisco sighting, but when William ran into her for a third time in West Virginia during a week of extravagant celebrations for the relaunching of the historic and luxurious Greenbrier Hotel—a 1771 "sulphur springs spa" that had just been completely remodeled by Dorothy Draper[411]—Austine's divorce was underway and William's was finalized. During the soft Southern nights filled with endless grand dinners and giddy dancing parties that followed one after another at the festival, William finally decided that Austine was the perfect mélange of beauty and brains. Before the year was over he had proposed.[412]

They were married in June 1948 at a candlelight ceremony in the boxwood gardens of Austine's parents' "rambling old house" in Warrenton, Virginia. In the wedding picture, the beautiful couple is posed in front of a bower of lilies. William looks ecstatic. Twenty-eight-year-old Austine is soigné and wide-eyed, and crowned in tube roses. She is dressed in a virtuosic Charles James concoction, cut along Victorian proportions, with an elongated wasp waist and a wash of lilac organza that emphasizes the narrowness of her rib cage by draping just exactly at her hipline to float cumulus-like over the flowing net skirt.[413] William would later write that marrying Austine was the best decision he had ever made, adding: "Austine and my father are the two most important persons I have known in my life."[414]

At the time of the marriage, Mr. Hearst was employed as the publisher of the *New York Journal-American,* and the newlyweds set up twin residences in New York and Washington. They would visit each other midweek and weekends in a Washington-New York "commuter" relationship. This time, it worked. Austine continued reporting and modeling, and her partnership with Charles flourished. In December 1948, Louise Dahl Wolfe photographed her for Hearst-owned *Harper's Bazaar* in "a dinner dress by Charles James who designed her winter wardrobe. It's in two parts—a myrtle green top of faille and satin and a pale blue satin skirt.... Made to order in Ben Mann fabrics, available at Carson Pirie Scott, The Fashion House [Houston],"[415] the copy reads.

Behind and beyond the endless stream of publicity, Austine and Charles also mentored each other. Austine, who admiringly described Charles's brain as "a magic loom, weaving ideas, shifting harmonies and patterns," remembered "hours of discussion with him about the arts, history and politics.... In conversations," she wrote, "he could skillfully combine, in exquisite detail, the social scientist's analytical insight with the historian's perspective."[416] Loving the history of fashion as much as Charles did, Austine enjoyed supporting his fashion experiments, which were frequently based on historical precedent. It was Austine who bought him the antique nineteenth-century Directoire and Empire dresses that he studied, replicated, and used as the foundation of his signature high bust line.

As was his wont, Charles also gave Austine books (in particular *Fallen Woman* by his friend Willa Cather),[417] as well as recommendations to other designers whose techniques he found interesting. When Austine, who had read about and dreamt of visiting Europe, was taken to Paris for the first time by William, she went to Charles for advice and shopping recommendations. He sent her to Dior, and also suggested she visit newer designers. "He recommended Grès and that was the first time I went to Mme. Grès,"[418] Austine remembered gratefully.

(After Charles died, Madame Grès, who had been trained as a sculptress and whose skillful, dramatic use of weight and natural draping in fabric was unequaled, became Mrs. Hearst's favorite designer.)

Austine's first son, William Randolph Hearst III, was born in July 1949 in Washington DC, and she carefully and lovingly preserved William's first pictures and doings in her baby scrapbook.[419]

In December of that year, the *New York Daily Mirror*—clipped and pasted into another of her scrapbooks—lists Austine as a Charles James client, and along with Millicent Rogers, as one of the nine "repeaters" on Eleanor Lambert's list of the world's ten best-dressed women.[420]

Three years later, in January 1952, another photo of Austine in the *Times-Herald* highlights her black-tie ensemble by Charles James and the copy reports, "she swept in to also do a repeat in the New York list of the 'best dressed 14.'"[421]

When John Augustus Clinton (Austin) Hearst, her second son, was born in October 1952, she gave up writing to spend more time with her husband and her boys, but she continued supporting, wearing, and being photographed in Charles James.

It was Austine's generosity that rescued Charles James's most famous design, which wasn't anywhere near finished in time for Eisenhower's 1953 inauguration, from the cutting-room floor.

The "Clover Leaf" ball gown, as Charles explained to Couri in the tapes, was ordered in 1952 by Patricia Nixon, who intended to wear it to the inauguration. But when Charles sent the muslins to Washington for a first fitting, Pat (who was a strict Quaker) rejected them out of hand as much too "fancy" for her. And she didn't offer to pay him for his efforts either, apparently.[422]

Austine, on the other hand, had a vivid, Southern belle's imagination. She found the concept of a satin skirt that was an astounding eight feet in diameter exciting. She was happy to finance Charles's extravagant design experiment, and she was equally happy to model it for him.

In one of his essays on Charles James, Bill Cunningham describes the impression created by the immaculate gown when Austine finally did wear it for the first time, on the runway of the 1954 March of Dimes Fashion Show:

At the apotheosis of his career he reshapes Mrs. William Randolph Hearst Jr., making her body something it wasn't. He lifted her breasts, pushed her hips and abdomen forward, dropped her back waistline, and achieved a posture like a breast of a swan for his black and white strapless gown. The dress weighed nearly 15 pounds, yet the enormous skirt moved with the grace of a feather, balanced perfectly on the separately constructed bodice and the undulating waistline that distributed the weight over the hip bone. Over the gown she wore a short jacket completely covered with five dozen fresh gardenias, attached five hours before the gala and then stored in the refrigerator of her... hotel.[423]

The scent of the gardenias was intoxicating. And Austine, in an unforgettable gesture, flung the jacket to her awestruck audience.

As the designer Mary McFadden—whose mother, Marie Josephine Cutting, was a good friend of Austine's—pointed out, by this time Mrs. Hearst had access to any press as well asall the designers she desired, not to mention "hundreds of dresses."[424] It was Charles who needed Austine and not the other way around. But Austine wasn't finished. She went on to turn the Clover Leaf into an international sensation when she "fittingly" wore it to the coronation of Queen Elizabeth II in June[425] and then later that year at a ball at Versailles. ("My dinner partner had to sit on his seat sideways to make room for my skirts," she remembered.)

The calibration of its weight and the audacity of its size made the Clover Leaf gown into an instant sensation among Charles James's fellow designers, too. And they studied it as a technical feat of construction. A 1958 *New York Times* photograph shows a group of America's "most original" taste makers, Pauline Trigère, James Galanos, and Norman Norell, lined up by the edge of a runway scrutinizing the ball gown's calculated proportions, as the model wearing Charles's chef d'oeuvre of engineering edges past them.[426]

The Clover Leaf, whose alternate name is "Abstraction"—a double nod to a dominant art movement of the time, as well as the refinement of favorite techniques Charles employed in making it—has since become a symbol of midcentury couture and, by James's own evaluation, his pinnacle in dressmaking.

*Antonio Lopez's rendering of the lilt and sway of Charles James's most famous dress,
the "Clover Leaf." Charles James said of his work, "You can't really tell why it's erotic—
it's the mystery that makes it good. It has to do with the movement of a dress."*

"The garment," according to Coleman, who diagrammed it in
her catalog, "is constructed from thirty pattern pieces, twenty-eight
of which are cut in duplicate, the remaining two singly."[427] These are
pieced together to create the four irregularly shaped lobes of the gown's
skirt, which taken together form a perfect circle.

In notes on the Clover Leaf's architectural shaping, Harold Koda
points out:

> [the] supporting underskirts are not the usual boned hoops of flex-
> ible wands but multilayered canopies of boning, net, buckram,
> Pellon, and canvas sandwiched into shape. James treated the fixed
> contours of these engineered understructures as an architectural
> form that he ornamented without constraint, like a milliner trim-
> ming a hat. He pieced together a gown's surface by juxtaposing mate-
> rials that are not especially compatible with each other or with the
> cantilevered and form-retaining volumes he desired. In the Clover
> Leaf gown, for example, the wide band of black velvet encircling the

skirt is a separate piece attached to ivory satin at the top and faille at
the bottom, despite the fabric's different tensions, weights, grains,
and hand. The gown's graphic power is [only] possible because the
seams that join the textiles are freed from structural requirements
by the ingenious support system below. In this masterwork James
thus elevated fashion to a fine art, merging the science of engineering with aesthetics.[428]

And while the graphic power of the Clover Leaf's contrasts in
color and textural juxtapositions is astonishing, it is equally important to note that the rippling, to-and-fro movement of the wavy skirts
made possible by the dress's engineering, which allowed the skirts
to sway when the wearer walked and, as Metropolitan Museum
of Art curator Jan Reeder described, "lift like an ice skater's skirt
in pirouette"[429] when she danced, are as important to the design's
integrity as the yin-yang of its form.

In the end, Austine wasn't the only celebrity to model the
Clover Leaf in 1953. Charles got it out and about as much as he
could. Gloria Vanderbilt (then Mrs. Leopold Stokowski), for one,
wore it to the opening of Ringling Brothers and Barnum & Bailey
Circus in April.[430] But Austine was the most important because
she was the one who had made it possible. It became as much her
emblem as it was Charles's.

Explaining Austine's intense relationship to fashion, Austin said
recently that his mother "understood the potential of designers and
appreciated craft and artists and artists' craft."[431] She saw life as they
did. She recorded her impressions and opinions of fashion for future
students at the Fashion Institute of Technology and also invented her
own clothes. If Austine was, as Liz Smith described her, "very much of
her moment—a symbol of the style of her time," it was also because
of her multidimensionality. Austine, who made a point of conducting
her daily life with flair and ceremony, celebrated all facets of what the
French call "Living as Art."

Her attention to and care for the simple rituals of living mirrored her intense empathy for creativity in design. In the same way
that Austine delighted in the memory of her grandmother personally

picking the vegetables for that night's dinner in her back garden, she considered planning menus for her own dinners a pleasure, and kept a lovingly detailed archive of each party she gave in a diary reserved for those records. A page in the notebooks reads:

Dinner at 810 Fifth Avenue
Thursday February 7, 1963
Followed by movie: "To Kill a Mockingbird"
445 Park Avenue

Acceptances include: Mr. and Mrs. Hearst, Mr. and Mrs. Bancroft, Mr. Baskerville, Mr. and Mrs. Conniff, Mr. Craig Mitchell, Mrs. Frances Baker, Mr. and Mrs. Frost, Mr. and Mrs. Watson Blair.

Menu:
In Dr. Room:
Quail eggs
Pickled beans
Green pepper and carrot stix [sic]

At table:
Caviar w. lemon,
Sour cream
Ch. Onion, egg
Black bread and toast
Chicken soup with dash almond
w. Sputniks
Scaloppini—Madera
Rice & peas—white wine
String beans with bacon garnish & cherry tomatoes
Apple dessert

She also kept detailed notes on which silver was used, together with table seating charts, to avoid possible repeats in the future. The reminder card, which is taped to the page, mentions that the dress is "Black tie."

The parties she threw for her children are recorded with similar devotion:

At Austin Hearst's Birthday on October 26, 1963 a lunch of:
Spaghetti with sauce and cheese
Carrots
Celery
Milk and Pepsi
Ice cream with Choc [*sic*] Sauce; Butter Scotch Sauce
Cake—candles

—is served to six lucky little boys and four adults (including the nanny and Austin's parents) before a private screening of Walt Disney's *The Sword in the Stone* at Radio City Music Hall.

"Willie's" rather larger party in February, to see *101 Dalmatians,* is logged with the same care, as are endless telegrams of congratulations on the birth of both boys, their personal invitations to presidential inaugurations, adorable photographs of them at San Simeon taken by Diana Vreeland, and on.[432]

And every occasion required its own costume. In a 2014 *Harper's Bazaar* article on Charles James and Austine's collaboration with the designer, in which Austin remembers his mother dressed for the evening, "floating out of the house like a swan about to take flight,"[433] he is quoted as saying, "My mother had the most beautiful dresses [Charles] created—I don't want to be prejudiced." As he explained recently, "Fashion was my mother's passport to everything that was current. It was a world that was hers alone. My father understood and got out of the way. She could see James's potential as a designer. She appreciated his uniqueness and universality as well."[434]

Austine's patronage of James continued through to the end of the 1950s. For her 1956 "best dressed" photograph she chose Charles's tulle and satin Butterfly gown. And he even convinced her to be his model in a commercial advertisement for Du Pont,[435] where she is photographed wearing a peacock-blue acetate slipper-satin theater coat.

In addition to the Clover Leaf and the Butterfly, Austine's immaculate collection of Charles James designs from the 1950s included: the

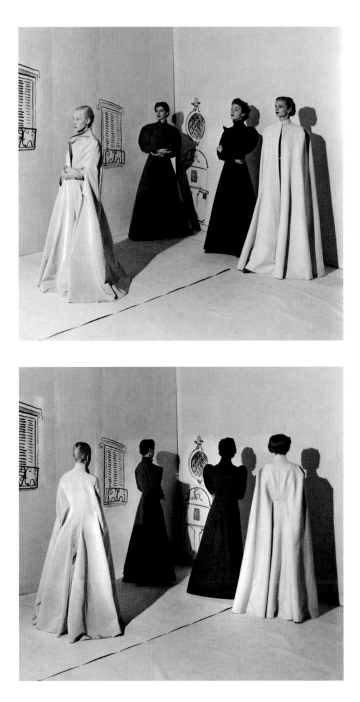

Charles James's first experiments with capes, photographed by Cecil Beaton with backdrops by Christian Bérard, appeared in the November 1, 1936 issue of Vogue *where they were described as "Poetic Mantels."*

Cecil Beaton's elegant sketch of Charles James's workroom at Elizabeth Arden appeared in the December 15, 1944 Vogue *shortly before Charles and Elizabeth dissolved their partnership.*

In 2012, Robert Polidori was commissioned to photograph the de Menil archives. This image appropriately juxtaposes Dominique de Menil's red Charles James jacket with a René Magritte painting in the de Menil collection. The jacket's sleeve channels the shape of a discarded elbow pipe Charles and Dominique discovered by a street curb while out taking a walk together.

*Charles's favorite photograph of his designs by Louise Dahl-Wolfe
appeared in* Harper's Bazaar *December 1948.*

This iconic Louise Dahl-Wolfe image of a blue Charles James ball gown was published in the April 1947 issue of Harper's Bazaar.

*This dress was first made in blue velvet for Austine Hearst to wear
to the March of Dimes ball in 1955. And Austine supplied Charles
with the Empire gowns on which the elevated bust line is based. This
iteration appeared in an advertisement for the American Rayon
Institute published by in the September 1956 issue of* Harper's Bazaar.

In 1948, the year Charles invented his first Modess advertisement and the Brooklyn Museum staged its retrospective of the dresses he had made for Millicent Rogers, Vogue hired Cecil Beaton to take a series of photos of Charles fitting a model. Here he is on the floor (possibly with Kate Peil, who ran his work rooms) pinning the hem of one of his suits.

This Horst P. Horst photograph appeared in the March 1, 1940 issue of Vogue *and shows one of the Charles James ribbon capes famous for combining spectacular coloration and mathematically precise seaming of unusual fabrics— in this case, rare World War I ribbons discovered in a Parisian street market.*

"Pouf"; "Swan"; "Rose," in deep wine satin and bittersweet faille; a pink and white "Umbrella"; a bright plaid coat; and a black satin trousseau coat, to name a few. "She really did appreciate these things," Austin said, "not just like dresses, but like jewelry or pieces of art." And she relived the delight she first experienced as a little girl "parading around" in her big Virginia attic, whenever she wore Charles James's marvelous clothes.

"I didn't see him in his last years," Austine wrote of Charles in her essay for the 1982 catalogue of his retrospective at the Brooklyn Museum:

> Better to think of Napoleon robed resplendently for his Coronation as Emperor than in pain and despair at St. Helena.
>
> I will always remember the magic of wearing one of Charles James's ravishing, romantic ball gowns, remember being transformed by him like Cinderella into a radiant princess.
>
> Everyone turns when I sweep into a room, the gentlemen with admiration, the ladies with envy. I'm the sensation of the evening, a triumphant opera star, showered with bouquets and a standing ovation, a prima ballerina bringing down the house.
>
> I'm a star!

Austine died at Memorial Sloan Kettering Hospital in Manhattan on June 23, 1991, with her family around her. The *New York Times* noted that she had worked for charitable causes, including the Girl Scouts, the endowment fund of Mount Vernon, and the Abigail Adams Smith Museum in Manhattan for the last forty years.[436] During this time she had worn the clothing of many designers: Arnold Scaasi, Pauline Trigère, James Galanos, Hubert de Givenchy, Madame Grès, and Mary McFadden were a few she admired.[437] But Charles James, whom she described as "a man of pugnacity and passion,"[438] was her personal favorite.

There is a full-page reproduction of her formal portrait in *The Hearsts: Father and Son*. Austine is wearing a Charles James creation. And in the credits for the photo William Randolph Hearst Jr. reports, proudly: "She was famous for modeling Charles James."[439]

Fair-haired, round-eyed, and incredibly spunky Eleanor Lambert, photographed by her longtime friend and client Cecil Beaton in the 1930s, when they were both starting out together.

CHAPTER 8

Nemesis:

Eleanor Lambert

IF CHARLES WAS the ne plus ultra of exclusivity, he was also—at least conceptually—an advocate and pioneer of mass marketing. Like Frank Lloyd Wright with his beloved Usonian houses, Charles was esthetically obsessed with the idea of creating universal design in both image and pattern. And he enjoyed conducting many experiments in that vein. He was additionally, particularly as he neared his fifties, interested in expanding beyond his beautifully established couture base and finding quick ways to get rich.

Of course, from the beginning, Charles had dabbled in mass-market retail, supplementing his income and increasing his visibility by selling couture designs to department stores for copying. His first newspaper advertisement in1929 with middle-of-the-road retailer Best & Co. was a highly remunerative early investigation of high/low of marketing. In 1933 Charles scooped the Parisian haute couture by again authorizing the copying of his originals by the American department stores. It was Best & Co. who sponsored his return to America in 1939. And in the 1940s Charles enjoyed some of his greatest successes working with Marshall Field's, during which time he also sold designs to Roberts Dresses, a midlevel American clothing manufacturer.[440]

In Charles's view, the greatest clothing design in history was the blue jean, because it's universal, utilitarian, and sexy at the same time.[441] And the end goal of his "scientific" design investigations begun in 1944, when he initiated his collaboration with Michelle Murphy and the Brooklyn Museum's Design Laboratory, was to organize and clarify the concept of a generic "one size fits all" standard in clothing by determining which body measurements change and which remain consistent over time. With the help of his students, he measured over 100 dress bodices, spanning 150 years of design, and learned that some measurements related to bone structure never change. He discovered, for example, that the distance from the nape of the neck to the pivot point at the front of the armhole is almost consistently ten and a half inches for women. And this statistic became essential to his experiments with sleeve patterns. By 1946, Charles had developed a perfectly designed suit sleeve that allowed the jacket to remain still when the arm was in motion.

Again and again throughout his career—in conversation, in his writings, and later in the classroom—Charles James reiterated that the study and understanding of the structure of the human body is central to what he called "the continued creativity of design."[442]

In 1944, Charles had also started selling original designs that he made for copying to Lord & Taylor through Dorothy Shaver.[443] Dorothy was his personal couture client as well as the first woman president of the Lord & Taylor chain. She was not only a star of American retailing but one of the most enlightened pioneers of American design. During the resulting ten-year association, her widespread, supportive, and head-turning advertisements of Charles's designs—and his coats in particular—were instrumental to him in promoting his name and his own design services to other manufacturers.

In search of the key to perfect fit in mass-produced clothing, Charles also worked to develop a standardized dress form that would reflect the lines of the modern woman's body. In 1949, during several months of self-imposed seclusion, he perfected the "Jennies," which were papier-mâché dress forms based on a compilation of measurements from Millicent Rogers, Jennifer Jones,[444] and the constant measurements discovered at the Brooklyn Museum four years earlier. The Jennies were produced in 1951 by the Cavanaugh Form Company and sampled by Schiaparelli and Hardy Amies, as well as a handful of small manufacturers of less expensive clothing.[445] The National Bureau of Standards even adjusted one of its measurements for dress forms downwards to accord with Charles James's dimensions. But even though the likes of Eugenia Sheppard in the *New York Herald-Tribune* trumpeted "the potential" of the Jennies to revolutionize the fit of American women's clothes, the concept was too far ahead of its time and too few of the Jennies were sold to make manufacturing them a profitable venture.[446]

While he was marketing his mannequins, Charles, who was also looking for new ways to expand his business into the broader, more remunerative markets of middle-priced dress and coat manufacturing, started a company called Charles James Services Inc. Working through this company—which controlled the Charles James name for all non-couture products—he planned to advise manufacturers of less expensive, more widely-distributed clothing and revise and improve the patterns they used. The new company was financed by Mrs. William H. Moore—the porcelain collector whose cachepot Elizabeth Arden had so admired—and Charles's future wife, heiress and artist Nancy Lee Gregory. (At the time, Nancy was still married to Keith Cuerdon, who was also Charles's lover and employee.)

Light years ahead of its time, Charles James Services was a precursor of the modern licensing office. No other designer had yet created anything like it. Unfortunately, like many of Charles James's business adventures, some of its projects were of the highly iffy and definitely hit or miss variety. Nor was the new company instantly profitable. Charles—who calculated that it took $500,000 a year (slightly under $5 million in today's money) to run a couture operation—reported an income to Charles James Services of only $125,000 for the first year.[447]

In 1950, through Charles James Services, Charles partnered with Orbach's, a specialty store on Fourteenth Street in Manhattan famous for its line-for-line copies of the crème de la crème of French couture. James's contract with them was for twenty designs of suits, coats, and dresses, whose manufacture for mass market he agreed to personally supervise.[448] One of the blouses in the new collection would even feature his just perfected Louis-Philippe sleeve. Charles announced to the newspapers that he "had been waiting twenty-four years for an opportunity such as this." Both Charles James and Orbach's stressed that the reproduction of James models would not be mere "copying" but would incorporate ideas inspired by Charles James in garments now priced within the reach of Orbach's customers. In some cases only one particular feature, such as a sleeve or a neckline, would be adapted, with the designer's approval, of course.

At a celebratory launch of the collaboration held in California, Charles purportedly wrecked a grand piano by filling it with water so he could float orchid arrangements in it. And although Orbach's paid him $20,000, there is no record that the designs contemplated for the store were ever produced.[449]

The same year he also put into production a dolman coat he had designed in 1947 for opera star Lily Pons (who had famously held up the departure of a transatlantic ocean liner until it was delivered to her in her stateroom). He would successfully distribute this design through high-end stores for the next seven years.

Then—fatefully—in 1952, Charles signed agreements with two manufacturers, William N. Popper, an upscale coat manufacturer, and Samuel Winston, who was running an inexpensive blouse business with a troubled bottom line. Charles planned to use his upgraded work-spaces at the elegant Sherry-Netherland and at 716 Madison Avenue to train workers in his style of patternmaking, cutting, and sewing, so they in turn could supervise his licensees. He was optimistic, and for good reason. He had been introduced to Samuel Winston by his great friend and longtime supporter Eleanor Lambert, the most powerful woman in American fashion. She had blessed their union.

It's safe to say that Eleanor Lambert created the American fashion world as we know it. And certainly, the career of Charles James was ineradicably marked by his friendship with her.

Petite, round-eyed, blonde, and incredibly spunky, Eleanor came into the world on August 10, 1903, in the small town of Crawfordsville, Indiana. Her father, Henry Clay Lambert, was an ex-newspaper writer who, deserted his family for the bright lights of Broadway, and ran off to become an advance man for Ringling Brothers circus just a few months before she was born.[450] Eleanor described her mother as "feckless,"[451] but luckily, her two adored older brothers—Kent, who was twelve years older than Eleanor and grew up to be a much decorated cavalryman, and Ward, fifteen years her senior and later a legendary basketball coach nicknamed "Piggy" Lambert, after whom the stadium at Purdue University is named—pitched in to raise her as de facto parents.

When she was still a little girl, her brothers took her to a gypsy who told her she would have a long life filled with interesting people, and from that time forward, Eleanor, who believed in fate, did everything she could to make her gypsy's prediction come true.

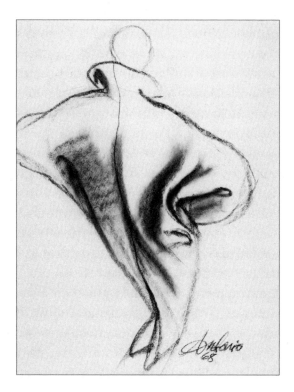

In 1954, Charles won Eleanor Lambert's Coty Award for his coat designs. Antonio Lopez's sketch of one of the famous Charles James coat shapes.

She was very active in school. At Crawfordsville High School she worked on the *Athenian Yearbook* staff and acted in the school play, *Blundering Billy,* in which she played Woyo San, a Japanese maid. She cooked and packed picnic baskets for the boys at Crawfordsville's Wabash College to earn enough money to study sculpture in Indianapolis's John Herron Art Institute. While moonlighting in Indianapolis as a shopping writer for the Fort Wayne *Journal Gazette* and the *Indianapolis Star,* she finally met her "ticket out of town": an architecture student named Willis Connor, with whom she quickly eloped to Chicago, where she studied at the Art Institute and was miserable.[452]

In 1925, the year Charles went to work in Chicago for Samuel Insull, the newlyweds, who were equipped with a $250 nest egg, lit out for New York. Eleanor claimed she left Chicago because she was a failure as an artist and, as she confided to John Tiffany, the assistant who worked for her at the end of her life, "all she ever wanted to do was get to the big city." But Eleanor's son, the poet and art critic Bill Berkson, told me he thought she just wanted to be where her father was.[453]

Effectively, as soon as she got to Manhattan she looked up her father—whom she later described as "an aloof, self-contained loner."[454] He had by this time actually produced an ephemeral Broadway show called *Twin Beds*. There's no record of what Mr. Lambert thought of his long-lost child when he finally met her, but he sternly informed her that "New York was no place for a young lady" and tried to pack her back to Crawfordsville on the earliest train, which, according to Berkson, "she exited smartly on the next track."[455]

Adding to the disappointment, almost as soon as Eleanor arrived in the Big Apple her marriage to Willis began to fall apart. He turned out to be a leech, and Eleanor, who according to her son was determined to "be the best at whatever she did even if she had to invent a new profession," soon found herself living alone in Astoria, Queens, miles away from the hubbub she craved.

It was a long subway ride into Manhattan, where she was working two jobs. For a total of $32 a week she wrote for a fashion newsletter called "Breath of the Avenue" and designed book covers for Franklin Spear, a publicist and book cover designer with a small office in midtown. After work, Eleanor enjoyed having dinner at the Automat and hanging around the Algonquin, where, as she told Amy Fine Collins, she liked to "study the crowd. One night I ended up joining Dorothy Parker and some actors—they were drunk—and they dragged me downtown to a tattoo parlor in the Bowery. I wanted to be a good sport—I was too young and scared to say no. So I ended up with a small blue star on my right ankle."[456] According to another friend of Eleanor's, Dorothy got her tattoo on her midriff. And Eleanor liked to tell that her "date" for the evening, one of the actors (whose name always escaped her), would never forget her for the rest of his life. He got his left arm tattooed "Eleanor"![457] Eleanor re-told the same story to her biographer, John Tiffany, who interpreted it as an example of how she could make the best of anything.[458]

The artist Alex Katz, who met Eleanor through Bill and the writer John O'Hara, confirmed the reality of this storied talent. "Even though she was very unhappy in art school and dropped out eventually, Eleanor was beautifully educated," he told me. Explaining that "art school is a trade school, so if you want to learn you have to teach yourself," Alex said that despite her misery in Chicago, "Eleanor had taught herself so well she could hold her own with Virgil Thompson or even John Ashbery—and on their terms."[459]

According to Bill, while she was still working as a book publicist, Eleanor, who was in charge of getting quotes for the book covers, made cold calls to a number of opera singers (and actresses like Mary Pickford), with whom she got along very well, and seeing her aptitude, her employer Frank Spear suggested she start her own business with an artistic clientele. It was an excellent idea. While Eleanor may have been an uninspired sculptor, she loved and understood art and artists especially well.

According to Lambert lore, Eleanor, who was making $10 a week in 1925 working for Spear, began by walking up and down East Fifty-seventh Street in Manhattan, where all the chic art galleries were located. In a record five business days she had signed up ten of those galleries as clients for $10 a week each. When one of her first events was held at the Carston Gallery and included Cecil Beaton and Salvador and Gala Dalí she quickly discovered that she liked promoting personal talent as much as she enjoyed marketing businesses.

John Curry, George Bellows, Thomas Hart Benton, Jacob Epstein, and Isamu Noguchi—who sculpted a bust of Eleanor as payment for some of her services—and later Jackson Pollock and Walt Kuhn as well as Beaton and Dalí, became loyal clients of Eleanor Lambert, the first publicist for the arts.[460]

In 1929, she helped Abby Aldrich found the Museum of Modern Art. Then, in 1930, after the Metropolitan Museum of Art had haughtily rejected the proposed gift of nearly seven hundred works by American artists, Gertrude Vanderbilt Whitney established the Whitney Museum of American Art to house her collection.[461] And Juliana Force, the Whitney Museum's first director, asked Eleanor Lambert, who was still the world's only arts publicist, to become the museum's first director of public relations.

In 1933 the Whitney sent Eleanor to Europe for the tenth Venice Biennale, where, at her suggestion, the museum had sponsored the American Pavilion. Her route led through Paris, where she had her first audience with a tulle-swathed Charles James at the Plaza Athénée. Then, passing through Rome on her way to Venice, she met Seymour Berkson, who would become the man in her life.

But it wasn't love at first sight. Jon Marder, an Eleanor admirer and acolyte, told me that Seymour's first thought when he saw Miss Lambert was, "Who's that woman in the God-awful hat?" And Eleanor and Seymour were on opposing teams.[462] She had been dispatched by the Whitney to keep a portrait of William Randolph Hearst's mistress Marion Davies out of the Peggy Guggenheim Museum in Venice. But Seymour was the general manager of the Hearst Corporation's International News Syndicate. And it was his job to see that the painting—which in Juliana Force's words "was not American, not art; not desirable in any way"—was prominently displayed. The resulting entanglement nearly caused an international incident and would have made a wonderful plot for a 1930s Hollywood romantic comedy. Still, Eleanor, as was her wont, somehow managed to win out. Berkson invited her out to dinner and they fell madly in love. The happy ending arrived two years later when both their divorces were finalized and the couple was wed. They became New York's first working "power couple."[463] She wrote about the talent she discovered, and he published what she said.

As Amy Fine Collins wrote in *Vanity Fair*: "In 1932 a fashion designer [Annette Simpson], impressed by a newspaper interview Lambert had engineered for one of her artists, phoned to inquire if it was possible to get similar press coverage for herself. 'She was my first designer client,' Lambert recounted. 'I never got paid however. She was very crazy.'"[464]

Still, the episode with Simpson turned out to be incredibly profitable, because it gave Eleanor the dramatic insight that she might be able to legitimize American fashion in much the same way as the Whitney Museum was championing American art. American designers could get credit for their creations—and adulation, just as their Parisian counterparts did. Of course, the business of fashion in Europe was vastly different from the business of fashion in America. Still,

Eleanor felt she could package American creativity and turn American designers "into personalities and give them rounded appearances."[465] The American fashion industry and individual American designers, she believed, deserved to be treated as equals on the world stage. One day over lunch, she confided her dream to Diana Vreeland, who was at *Harper's Bazaar* at the time. "Eleanor, you're such an amateur,"[466] Vreeland allegedly replied.

Diana's disdain notwithstanding, by the time Charles arrived in New York in 1939, Eleanor—who by now had New York department stores as her clients—was adding up as a fashion force to be reckoned with as she went about reorganizing the Metropolitan Museum of Art and Seventh Avenue.

In 1937, Lambert had joined with colleagues to help form the Costume Institute at the Metropolitan Museum, "so that America could have its own collection of fashion history."[467] She asked her friends to give all their best pieces to the museum and donated her own most elegant dresses as well. Then, in 1939, as Germany marched into Poland, the American government began rationing fabric. The International Ladies' Garment Workers' Union worried that women would stop buying dresses. It joined forces with the New York dress manufacturers in a new society called the "New York Dress Institute," created to stimulate business, and began a propaganda campaign to increase dress sales. They asked Eleanor to represent them. She insisted they expand their membership to coat and suit manufacturers—who had complete collections, which would interest the press—and create a "Couture Group" that would promote individual designers as well. When they agreed, Eleanor became executive director of the Institute.

Eleanor's next move was to take over the International Best Dressed List.

In the 1930s, when Mainbocher had his couture salon in Paris, the "Directrice"[468] of his operation had begun, at the end of each December, to send out—with the help of a friendly journalist—unsigned wire-service stories from Paris, listing the results of an alleged Paris couturiers' poll of their best-dressed clients. This "Best Dressed List" was all about marketing. The top awards always went to Mainbocher customers, with a couple of other names sprinkled in to "make it look real." Wallis Simpson, for example—whose wedding dress for her marriage to the Duke of Windsor in 1937 had been designed by Mainbocher—was prominently featured from 1937 to 1939, and by January 1940, the last time the list was sent out from France, the duchess had the number one spot. A few months later—when the German occupation had effectively shut down the Parisian couture houses—Lambert, who understood its enormous publicity value, simply commandeered the list for the United States.

In the fall of 1940 she mailed out fifty mimeographed ballots to fashion experts, including the milliner Lilly Daché, Sophie Gimbel, Valentina, the design staff at Bergdorf Goodman, editors at *Vogue* and *Harper's Bazaar,* and other key members of the fashion press. When the results came in, she promptly added them all up and sent them out in a press release on the Dress Institute's stationery. On December 27, 1940, the *New York Times* proudly proclaimed that Mona Williams, the aquamarine-eyed Kentuckian who had married the richest man in America (and was also a Charles James client), was the number-one best-dressed woman in the world. And the poor Duchess of Windsor had only received two out of the fifty votes cast by New York fashion authorities. "The selection just announced was for many years compiled in Paris, but was taken over this Winter for the first time by the key designers, fashion authorities, and members of the fashion press in New York, as the world's new style center," the triumphant *New York Times* copy read. From then on, almost all of Charles's favorite clients—Millicent Rogers, Austine Hearst, Babe Mortimer (later Paley), Slim Keith, Mrs. Lucien Lelong (the lovely Princess Natalie Paley), Clare Boothe Luce, Jennifer Jones, Diana Vreeland, as well as would-be client Marlene Dietrich, to name a few—were on that list, recorded and publicized across the United States and in Europe as wearing Charles James clothes. Eleanor herself would of course become a Charles James client, as well.

Fashion Week was another of Eleanor's ideas, created to promote the Couture Group of the New York Dress Institute by organizing scheduled fashion presentations for the press. Outside of New York, fashion reporting focused on what was available in the department and specialty stores, but Eleanor wanted local journalists from everywhere in the United States to meet the new American designers and see their fashion shows in person. Hoping that increased fashion coverage would result in more fashion advertising and more sales, Eleanor personally telephoned publishers and asked that they send their fashion and life-style writers to Manhattan to cover the collections. With funds from the New York Dress Institute, she even offered the most important editors all-expenses-paid trips to the shows.

In January 1943—the year the Great Depression was officially over, and Charles James went to work with Elizabeth Arden—fifty-three editors from across the United Sates came to Fashion Week for the first time. The collections were all to be shown in the glorious, million-square-foot neo-Rococo Plaza Hotel, which, standing at the intersection of Fifth Avenue and Fifty-seventh Street in Manhattan, dominates Grand Army Plaza and overlooks the tangle of Central Park. Here, in the hotel's majestic, gilded ballrooms, the writers and editors were given a privileged look at the newest styles six months in advance of the upcoming season.

At the on-site press room, photographs and press releases for each of the collections were distributed, and Eleanor put together a different package for each editor so that no two publications received the same pictures.

She also made sure to entertain—all day, every day. Eleanor socialized with designers and she took newspaper people to fancy restaurants and the theater, where they were invited backstage to meet Broadway stars.

With New York Fashion Week, Eleanor had established the biannual fashion shows that are still followed zealously all over the world today.

Later that year, Mayor Fiorello La Guardia presented the first Coty Award—popularly known as a "Winnie," or more formally as the American Fashion Critics' Award—to Norman Norell, one of Eleanor Lambert's clients, at a black-tie ceremony hosted by the Metropolitan Museum of Art.

These awards were initiated by Jean Despres, husband of Lily Daché. Despres, a founder of the Fragrance Foundation, collaborated with Grover Whalen, a maestro of political public relations who was a member of the New York City Mayor's Committee on Receptions to

Distinguished Guests and had just become chairman of Coty Fragrances. Their purpose was to promote and celebrate American fashion and encourage design during World War II. And they were—predictably— invented by Eleanor Lambert, who was Coty's publicist at the time.

Eleanor was also the publicist for the awards themselves, and for the forty-two years they were presented, the Cotys were the ulti- mate stamp of approval. Being a "Coty Award Winner" would be the first entry on a designer's résumé, and the headline of his obituary as well. The Cotys, which were given exclusively to American designers, became the most exclusive award in the entire fashion world.

Charles made *Life* magazine (the headline read "An Unknown Wins 'Winnie'") when he received his first Coty in 1950 for "great mastery of color and artistry of draping."[469] He also won a special Coty Award (a Winnie), which cited his expertise in cutting and shape, in 1954. He was the first designer to win the Coty Award in two different categories.

While American fashion was flexing its muscle, Franklin Delano Roosevelt, whose personal struggle with polio had led him to create the National Foundation for Infantile Paralysis—better known as "the March of Dimes"—was busy convincing Smith College graduate Elaine Whitelaw—a "great dame,"[470] as one of the patients she person- ally helped later described her—to join the March of Dimes National Women's Committee. Miss Whitelaw, whose understanding of the phil- anthropic potential of Middle America was instant and instinctive, soon became the general of Roosevelt's volunteer army. Then, in 1944, in the middle of the second-worst polio epidemic in our country's history, which that year had affected twenty thousand people, Whitelaw discov- ered Lambert. It was kismet. The two can-do do-gooders immediately started talking about a fund-raising event that would be the biggest fashion show on earth.

The "grand-scale" fashion show, as we know it, is essentially an American invention. John Wanamaker staged the first one in Philadelphia in 1910,[471] and by the mid-1920s, heavily attended, elab- orate, and often theatrically themed fashion extravaganzas were being used coast to coast by American retailers as a way to amuse and bedaz- zle their clients, while selling them the latest designs copied from Paris.[472] Just a few months before Eleanor and Elaine got together, a charity fashion show for the American Red Cross at the St. Regis had won Charles praise and publicity for his first Elizabeth Arden collection and the brilliant "new posture" of fashion he had created with his designs. So the idea of using fashion to raise money for charity wasn't entirely new. As far as Eleanor was concerned, however, the January 24, 1945, March of Dimes Benefit Luncheon would outperform all the fashion and charity benefits that had gone before.

Eleanor not only persuaded the Dress Institute to underwrite the event but, according to the archives of the March of Dimes, she secured the participation of America's leading designers, established a selections committee of leading fashion experts from the press, convinced Coty to promise a big contribution in return for doing the makeup, and handled all the publicity—which was excellent. At the first March of Dimes spectacular (when Charles was quarrelling with Elizabeth Arden), Gypsy Rose Lee (dressed in a Charles James gown with a side slit that went almost up to her waistline) was photographed next to the donation box showing off a very fat roll of dollar bills that had been given to help the sick children. It was tucked into the top of her silk stocking.

There were a total of fifteen March of Dimes shows. And in 1957, the last year Charles participated, *Life* magazine described the annual event as "an extravagant intermingling of Park Avenue, Seventh Avenue, and Broadway, the biggest, most glamorous fashion show in the world."[473] That year, the mix of 145 models included socialites and stars from television, Hollywood, and eleven Broadway shows. They pranced up and down the Waldorf Astoria runway for over two hours, wearing a million dollars' worth of clothes, furs, and jewels. Over the years, Marilyn Monroe, Bette Davis, Eartha Kitt, Grace Kelly, Judy Garland, Jane Fonda, Kitty Carlisle Hart, Walter Cronkite, Helen Hayes (who was a perennial), and Audrey Hepburn had all modeled for polio. And Eleanor made sure the best photographers, illustrators, and artists contributed to the cachet of the March of Dimes as well: Grandma Moses, Salvador Dalí, Alexander Calder, Cecil Beaton, Louise Dahl Wolfe, Ludwig Bemelmans, and Joe Eula had all designed the shows' sets and back drops.[474] The finale was always the March of Dimes poster children on crutches or in their wheelchairs. One year they were accompanied by Jimmy Durante.

The annual extravaganzas were so popular they lasted five years after Dr. Jonas Salk had famously stemmed the tide of the epidemic by discovering his vaccine against polio.

By the boom years of the 1950s, Eleanor ruled American fashion. As Fine Collins reported:

> Says illustrator Joe Eula, who helped Lambert produce charity fashion shows for the March of Dimes in the 1940s and 1950s, "Eleanor was tougher than any man I knew. She was the grandmother of the Fashion Mafia! There wasn't a soul on Seventh Avenue who didn't have Eleanor behind her. If you couldn't afford her and you wanted her she'd work for free."
>
> To his lasting regret, Oleg Cassini [Igor Cassini's older brother] made himself the exception to this rule. "When I arrived in town in 1950 she came to me and offered me her services," Cassini says. "But I hired a fellow called Al Davidson. What a huge mistake! I paid dearly for it. Eleanor never forgave me. It was a long exile."
>
> The nerve center for one of the city's biggest industries, Lambert's office relayed exclusive preview photos to newspapers (the *Times* got first pick, the *Daily News* last), set up interviews on early television's daytime programs, and controlled admission to the Press Week shows that were staged to "on-the-minute perfection," as the *San Francisco Examiner* marveled. "Miss Lambert really looked after the out-of-town press," Lepselter [Clare Lepselter was one of Eleanor's six staff members] says."In 1952 she arranged for them to see Audrey Hepburn in her first play, *Gigi,* and then took them backstage to meet her afterwards...Although Bill Berkson remembered her as demanding and felt she must have been sometimes difficult to work for, her staff apparently loved her and Lepselter's letter reminisced to Amy Fine Collins about summer visits to Eleanor's house in Port Jefferson and how handsome her husband, Seymour Berkson, was."[475]

Eleanor was apparently incredibly nurturing as well. When a friend's teenage daughter came to New York on her own, Eleanor regularly put her up in the guest bedroom. (Eleanor was Liza Minnelli's

This Antonio Lopez rendering of a Charles James funnel necked coat emphasizes the protective "cocoon-like" quality of Charles' design.

godmother, and confidante, too.)[476] She was instrumental in the career of Kenneth Jay Lane, who enjoyed a lifelong friendship with her and Billy—and said she never charged him one cent. "She was like a mother to me and I called her 'mom.'"[477] Eleanor came up with unexpected ideas like trimming an entire Christmas tree with KJL baubles and had a wonderful sense of humor as well. "I was supposed to talk at a fashion breakfast for out-of-town press and I had a license to design for Marvella," he said, "so I showed up with a tall, dark, and handsome male model dressed in a tiny black bikini and fifty strands of pearls in varying lengths and sizes. I walked in with my arm around him. And my entire speech was 'I love pearls.' And Eleanor laughed her head off!"[478]

It was just at the time that Audrey Hepburn was making her stage debut in *Gigi* and Charles James was beginning work on his masterpiece

Clover Leaf dress that Eleanor suggested to Charles in her motherly way that he might like to team up with William N. Popper and Co., an upscale coat manufacturer, and Samuel Winston, a failing but street-smart manufacturer of cheap blouses. Even if he had wanted to (which he certainly didn't) Charles was in no position to refuse.

The Popper Company collaboration—which was for one year only—was a success at retail, as Lord & Taylor rapidly snapped up ten of the Popper designs Charles had created for the mid-price coat department. The problem was that Charles could sell his *own* haute couture designs directly to Lord & Taylor for their private label and get over $1,250 for one design (approximately $13,000 in today's dollars). But Charles's revenues from Popper for twenty coat designs—modified at his own expense for the mass market—were only $10,000 total,[479] or $500 per design. And even though the coats were to be sold exclusively to Lord & Taylor, a Charles James client of long standing, the concept of Charles receiving any kind of royalties based on sales or on his retail connection doesn't seem to have entered into the contract. The num-bers simply didn't make sense. And the agreement with Popper was never renewed.[480]

The document Charles signed with Samuel Winston was much more complicated, and closer in format to today's licensing agreements. The arrangement (again for selling designs exclusively to Lord & Taylor) was for multiple years, and required Charles to produce thirty designs per annum, for which he would receive an up-front minimum guarantee of $15,000 against royalties.

It was an instant success. In 1953, the first year of the busi-ness, Winston reported an increase of 60 percent in revenues.[481] Unfortunately for Charles, he and Samuel Winston were so completely different that their enmity was probably a predestined fait-accompli.

Winston, a native New Yorker, had cut his teeth on the grit of Seventh Avenue, where he had been variously employed as a "piece goods" buyer, a dress salesman, and the vice president of a defunct company called Milmont Gowns, which he had organized. He was clever, streetwise, totally business oriented, and deployed every trick of the trade. As soon as he signed Charles James as his designer, he hired Roxane Kamenstein, a housewife who had worked for a big buying office and was currently married to one of his business partners, as Charles's assistant on another dress collection that would pay Charles royalties but not carry his name.

Charles, who was all airs and graces, had learned couture in France, where "fashion" had been legally classified as "an applied art" since 1793 and where the broad system of copyright still extends to "any original work of the mind." His entire reason for being was his creations, and he didn't understand Seventh Avenue business practices. He knew how to wheedle money out of friends and could raise funds for new ventures, but was terrible at keeping existing ones going. He treated going bankrupt as a celebration. And it amused him to receive his creditors in bed, swathed only in furs—claiming he was too poor to pay for pajamas. He disdained taxes and, because of his elaborate and fanciful accounting practices, was under constant surveillance by the IRS. Moreover, he worked meticulously and at the pace of dripping molasses, so he just wasn't equipped to come up with the thirty new designs a year he'd signed up for.

Meanwhile, as his couture suits were being bought for more than $2,500 by his personal clients— he simply started turning over already bought and produced couture clothes to his licensee, instead of to the clients who had actually paid for them. He then competed openly with his own Winston collection by selling couture dress designs directly to Winston's retail accounts. Both Lord & Taylor and Neiman Marcus (who gave Charles James their prestigious Design Award "for distinguished service to the industry" in 1953) were buying dresses for copying directly from Charles, who was additionally making maternity and plus-size designs for specialty retailer Lane Bryant to use in their promotions—which he then tried to take back and resell to Lord & Taylor.

In short, Charles James's pioneering (and successful) new licensing venture was quickly morphing into a perfect Jamesian muddle. By 1954, the second year of the contract, Winston was courting Charles's assistant Arnold Scaasi—(who spoke Winston and Roxane's language and was easily able to work closely with them)—and selling variations of the designs Charles James had delivered to him under two labels: "*Samuel Winston/by Charles James,*" as the contract specified; and *Roxane*—a collection that existed outside the Charles James agreement and that Charles had never authorized. Charles received neither money nor credit for the Roxane dresses, which were based on designs he had supplied in the expectation of receiving royalties.

When Charles, who was getting married and had other things on his mind, discovered the deception, he simply stopped sending new designs to Winston. By the end of the year he had produced only twelve of the thirty contractually required designs.

In 1954, the year Charles won his second Coty and Austine jubilantly modeled the Clover Leaf dress on the March of Dimes runway, Samuel Winston sued Charles James. He publicly (and damningly) accused him of breach of contract and demanded recovery of $61,341.52.

Charles had publicized his successes in *Women's Wear Daily* by taking out double-page ads that listed all his licenses and awards.[482]

But now, "Samuel Winston, Inc. Sues Charles James for $61,341 on Pact," the November 4, 1954, headlines in *Women's Wear Daily* screamed:

> Winston alleges the date for delivery of the first set of models was extended to May 21 but defendants [Charles James Services] failed to deliver any of them.
>
> It is further charged that defendants, in further violation of the contract, the defendants [Charles James Services, Inc.] caused Mr. James to design dresses for Lane Bryant for the fall season of 1954. Because of this, according to Winston, the exclusive nature of the designs created by Mr. James for designs to be manufactured by Winston was destroyed.
>
> Winston avers it cancelled the contract as of last June 10.

And completely ignoring the fact that without Charles James Winston would not have been in the dress business in the first place, "Complaint avers Winston has been damaged in its business reputation and good will," the slanted, incriminatory, and pejorative copy read.[483]

Charles, whose entire mass-marketing plan depended on his ownership of the design inventions he had so laboriously developed over the course of his twenty-three-year career, countered. He (accurately) charged Winston, Winston's wife, Mildred, and Roxane with conspiracy to supplant his name with Roxane's on unauthorized adaptations and reproductions of his own designs and asked for damages in the amount of $500,000.

Then overlooking the obvious point that since Winston had signed a contractual agreement to pay Charles for the Charles James designs he copied, he was obliged to do so, Charles instead argued (oddly and self-defeatingly) that this was not technically a piracy suit, but rather a test to see if the same laws that governed the correct labeling of other nationally sold commercial products applied to fashion markets as well. "I couldn't bear to see all the experimental cuts and personal convictions [*sic*] which had cost me fortunes attributed to those hired to exploit them," he later explained.[484]

Eleanor, who represented Samuel Winston and was a great proponent of Charles's, was caught between the two, and canny enough to smell disaster. She rightly perceived that the best course of action was to make the litigation disappear. In private talks with both Charles James and Samuel Winston, Eleanor tried to smooth things over by getting Winston to withdraw his suit—which he did.

But Charles had found unexpected and heady emotional support from his father for what had by now become a point of honor and his cause célèbre. He refused to listen to Eleanor. He blamed her for siding with Winston. And he wouldn't give in.

Nerve-wracking, draining, and seemingly endless, the trial dragged on and on. The same questions were posed and repeated ad infinitum. Homer Layne, Charles's last assistant, showed me piles of fat, dusty scrapbooks filled with depositions. Over and again, Roxane was asked if a certain element in one of her dresses—a button, a collar, or a sleeve—reminded her of one designed by Charles James. Her designs always did remind her of Charles James's designs—because that's exactly what they looked like—but then, she could never remember where her ideas came from.[485]

Eleanor, who was called as an expert witness, was extremely uncomfortable and equally evasive. She couldn't remember if press releases with her name on them had actually been written by her, and (probably because she often didn't charge for her services) she needed to check her records to see who had been her client at which date. Pushed into a corner by Charles James's attorneys, who tried to make it look as though she were on Winston's payroll, she finally came down against Charles: "I would say Mr. James's interpretation, which certainly is great, and has been reflected in many collections as well as Winston—was present in the 1954 collection, but it is impossible to say that the 1954 Roxane collection could have been in any direct [way] copies of the James 1954 collection,"[486] she coolly and intelligently concluded.

In contrast, Charles, who was unluckily so anxious and angry that he could neither articulate his complaints nor verbalize his damages with any real clarity, was at a histrionic high. As Eleanor later remembered, "Charlie" leapt at her, "his fingers like claws,"[487] when she got down from the stand.

Two dark, anxiety-ridden years after the first filings, the litigation ended at last. The final verdict awarded Charles $22,018.48, and he received a settlement of $19,018.48. In his decision, the judge noted that Roxane's "overnight metamorphosis from a recent housewife to…a publicized designer taxes one's credibility." But tragically, Charles lost his battle against piracy, which the judge pointed out "could have been successful, absent so much temperament and balderdash," and with "more constructive marshaling of the facts." After which the IRS immediately seized all the award money for back taxes. (By Charles's own accounting, the costs of his action added up to $300,000.)

To make matters worse, the *New York Times* announced that Charles James had lost.[488]

Charles's relationship with Eleanor Lambert was over. He never forgave her for testifying against him. In later years he would try to return his two Cotys. He also threatened to sue her as an accessory to plagiarism. And he considered her a dehumanizing "double dealer" to the end. "We used to have personalities, now we have press agents," Charles drawled dismissively when Couri mentioned her name.

But of course the sad truth was that in alienating Eleanor, Charles *had* lost a crucial backer and a key friend. After the trial there was virtually no support for Charles in the press. "If you're not copied, you're nobody,"[489] Diana Vreeland, who knew which side of her bread was buttered, snapped unsympathetically. Employees of Charles

James Services deserted en masse to work with Winston. And even Cecil, who Sir Francis Rose later described as "manipulating [fashion] as a stock broker does shares,"[490] joined the band of turncoats. In what Charles would always consider unspeakable treachery, Cecil Beaton (who according to Hugo Vickers "could be quite spikey about money"[491])signed a yearlong contract with Samuel Winston to design dresses for him.

For Charles, the encounter with his enemy Samuel Winston marked a turn to chill in the wind. Things would never be the same again for Charles, as a man or as a designer. It was the beginning of an end.

Not so for Roxane. She happily continued her relationship with Winston, and won her own Coty Award in 1960 for the embroidered evening dresses she designed for him. Ever unsinkable, Eleanor moved on to represent every well-known designer in America and some famous foreigners as well. But she never stopped respecting Charles's talent. She donated all her Charles James dresses to the Metropolitan Museum of Art's Costume Institute, and the Met was, according to John Tiffany, very happy with the present.

Eleanor founded "the Party of the Year" at the Metropolitan Museum of Art and organized the "Battle of Versailles"[492] in 1973. There (with the help of Liza Minnelli, who performed for the evening), five American designers—Halston, Bill Blass, Oscar de la Renta, Anne Klein, and Stephen Burrows, all Lambert clients—outdid Yves Saint Laurent, Ungaro, Pierre Cardin, Dior, and Givenchy in the fashion show charity splash of the decade, which raised $250,000 for the preservation of Versailles.

And, despite a lifelong habit of eating eight strips of bacon for breakfast every morning,[493] Eleanor fulfilled her gypsy's prophecy. She lived to be 100. Her life had been filled with (many) interesting people and she died, honored and fêted, as the Empress of Fashion.

But perhaps not without some regrets: "There is nobody now," Eleanor, who was famous for never looking back, lamented uncharacteristically in her last interview on the state of fashion in America. "There is nobody now that forces us to change the way we look. That is what we are missing…someone to give fashion a *shape*."[494] It's easy to imagine she was thinking of Charles James.

As his wedding present to the Jameses, Cecil Beaton made a series of photographs of Nancy in Charles's studio at Twelve East Fifty-seventh Street in New York. Here she is, pregnant, in front of the famously romantic "Pellon" curtains Charles designed. She is wearing the "Swan Gown."

CHAPTER 9

The Last Muse:

Nancy James

IN THE EARLY SUMMER of 1954 Charles James—unconventional as always—surprised practically everyone who knew him by marrying a woman he loved.

The new Mrs. James was born Nancy Lee Gregory on St. Valentine's Day, 1926, in Kansas City, Missouri, into an affluent, unusual family. Her father, Riddelle Gregory (named after the French doctor who delivered him), was from Alabama but was raised in Kansas City, where he founded the Postal Life and Casualty Insurance Company in 1927 and was well known about town for his skill at golf and polo, and piloting his own planes. He loved stunting and night flying and went on to develop the Commercial Airways Airport to the east of Kansas City.

Nancy's mother, a London-born beauty named Rowena Nancy Masten Brown, had been raised by her aunt and uncle, who was president of Traders Gate City National Bank in downtown Kansas City. Rowena, who preferred to be called Nancy, was strong minded, civically active, a member of the Junior League and the Arts Club, and a cofounder of the Ozanam Home for Boys.

Nancy Lee was the eldest of the three Gregory children. Riddelle Jr., or Rocket, was born in 1927. He would have a brief but well-documented career as a race-car driver and take a third at Pebble Beach in 1954 before settling down at the sales and engineering firm Smith & Loveless in Missouri. Her youngest brother Masten's birthday was on Leap Year Day, February 29, 1932. Like Riddelle, Masten would go on to have a (much more successful) career racing cars.[495]

When the children were still very young (Masten was about two), their father divorced their mother to marry a twenty-three-year-old named Marion Hovey. In 1935, two months after Nancy's ninth birthday and very shortly after his second wedding, Riddelle Sr. died suddenly of pneumonia. He was thirty-eight. "Gregory died intestate last April, six months after his marriage to Miss Marion Hovey," the *Kansas City Star* reported in July. "Probate Judge Mitchell J. Henderson, however, appointed a trust company as co-administrator, announcing that his personal investigation had convinced him the widow was incompetent to serve alone because of her youth and inexperience....A fourth of the Gregory estate, also, was settled on each child, with the remainder going to the second wife."[496]

As a result of this very public tragedy, Nancy, Riddelle, and Masten collectively owned three fourths of Postal Life and Casualty and Rowena, as their guardian, became president of the insurance company and later chairman of the board. Even as a little girl, Nancy had her own trust fund and was independent financially.

Rowena, who after seeing the children off to school went to work every day, later wrote about how difficult it had been for her to raise a family without a husband. Luckily, she said, Nancy had "taken a motherly interest" in Masten. They all lived in a big, five-bedroom Tudor–style, half-timber house with a large front yard at 6056 Mission Drive, one of the nicest streets in the city.

Nancy attended the exclusive Barstow School for Girls, which had been founded on the English model in 1884.[497] Her schoolmates called her "Nance," voted her (rather ambiguously) "Editor's Daughter," and described her as "monopolizing the freshman ads." Nancy, who was tall for her age, with a narrow face, curly hair, and a thoughtful expression, was not at all pretty. She was sensitive and very visual and she liked writing poetry. She wrote this in her seventh-grade Barstow yearbook:

MOUNTAINS
(Word Picture)
There is nothing that can equal the mountains. They are very beautiful at all times, but they seem to me most beautiful in the evening when the glowing red sun goes down behind their snow slopes and their color fades from purple to grey, as the twilight deepens into dusk. At last they stand like silent black sentinels until the moon comes up and bathes them in mystic silver.[498]

Nancy left Missouri as soon as she could. In 1946 she enrolled in the luxurious Bennett Junior College in Millbrook, New York. Its main building, Halcyon Hall, a sprawling, James E. Ware-designed, two-hundred-room Queen Anne-style manor, was set on twenty-seven and a half rambling acres and housed approximately one hundred and fifty female students from prominent American families. There was a faculty of twenty-nine. The campus also included a chapel, riding stables, and an outdoor theater. The girls, who graduated with a two-year degree, were offered majors in art, fashion and interior design, music, modern languages, literature, history, dance, drama, child development, domestic science, and equine studies. Sports were riding, gymnastics, golf, tennis, and skiing. Nancy majored in art, enjoyed painting, and later took classes at the Art Students League in Manhattan, too.[499]

Meanwhile, Riddelle Jr., at odds with his mother and the man she had hired to run the family business, became increasingly impatient with the management of the company. In 1951 he was finally able to orchestrate its sale, which resulted in all the members of the family receiving what Masten's biographer, Michael Cox, calls "a considerable amount of money."[500]

Masten, who was nineteen at the time (and had allegedly been expelled from the prestigious Pembroke Country Day School for trying to drop a bowling ball on the head of a teacher who had given him a bad grade), decided, instead of going to college, to buy his first race car, a Mercury-powered Allard, which he ordered specially from Sidney Allard in England. He managed, despite his terrible eyesight and "Coke bottle-thick" eyeglasses, to be one of the first Americans to race a Formula One sport car. In 1965 he won first place in the twenty-four-hour Le Mans and became known throughout Europe and America as "the Kansas City Flash."[501]

When Nancy (who had voted alongside her mother to keep the insurance company) received her share of the money from the sale, she married Keith Cuerdon, four years her junior. It was Keith who introduced Nancy to Charles, who had recently received his first Coty Award and was just finishing up his work on the de Menil house in Houston. They met at the Sherry-Netherland Hotel, and Nancy remembered that "[Charles] said I was the only person who ever told him he was shy."

Nancy and Keith had a house on Fire Island, which Charles visited frequently. And although Nancy was less affluent than most of his clients, she became Charles James's customer and his muse long before she actually married him. "She looked like a refined version, a quiet version of him,"[502] said costume designer Miles White.

"Wearing a Charles James gown made me feel special," Nancy remembered in a 2013 interview with a fashion blog. "Before I married him I owned several of his cocktail dresses, and a black silk faille coat that belted and flared out, in the back. They came from the department store Lord & Taylor. I had a black seal coat made (like the silk faille one) with a bronze silk lining."[503] (This was made to Charles's specifications by furrier Gunther Jaeckel, a one-year licensee whom Charles, in an attempt to collect monies owed him, later threatened with an open jar of moths.)[504]

According to Charles, Nancy's Lucas Cranach-style figure catalyzed a radical change in his work, which up to this time had been built around Millicent Rogers's elongated hourglass shape and characterized by his signature corseted waists and the abundant, full skirts that had inspired the "New Look" worn by everyone in the 1950s.

Charles was fascinated by the contrast between Nancy's small, high breasts set on a narrow rib cage and the wide forward thrust of her ample pelvis and hips. He was equally captivated with the fact that a perfect plumb line could be dropped from the mid shoulder point of her back. Her silhouette inspired him to invent a totally new mannequin in Nancy's proportions, made out of bound muslins stuffed with newspapers and rags which he built layer by layer into a sculptural form, and finished with a whalebone casing.

Significantly, the first iteration of Nancy's elevated breasts in his tailoring is expressed in the maternity clothes Charles designed for Lane Bryant (which he began in 1951, while he was developing a suit for Nancy named the "Pagoda," that was finally perfected four years later). In 1953 Nancy's figure also inspired the sheath or empire dress that emphasized a raised bust line, but narrowed Nancy's torso by bypassing her waist. It was a seminal design, and was picked up the next year by Parisian designers. Eventually, it influenced the new shape of fashion in the early 1960s. (And as late as 1967, even Andre Courrèges took a leaf from Charles James's yoke seaming.)

These inventions were then collectively transformed by Charles into a flock of groundbreaking, award-winning coat shapes, which are considered by many, including Bill Cunningham and William Ivey Long, the Tony Award–winning costume designer who apprenticed with Charles in the 1970s, to be Charles James's best and most influential designs.

Nancy additionally became—probably at the suggestion of Keith (from whom she would be amicably divorced by the end of 1952), but perhaps also because she missed being connected to her family company—an investor in Charles James Services. She had total faith in Charles's talent. "There were no fashion designers he looked up to. He stood alone. In Paris years ago, there was a book called 'The Dictionaire of Snobbisme.' It said: 'At the top there is only Charles James,'" she later explained.[505] Charles gave Nancy a new style and a venue for self-expression. She was willing to underwrite his experiments in licensing and mass market. They were partners. And he loved children.

They were married on June 8, 1954. It was a chic, beautiful ceremony at St. Bartholomew's, the bronze, gold, and silver Byzantine Revival Episcopal church at Park Avenue and Fiftieth Street. Amazingly, Charles, who choreographed everything, had finished the ankle-length wedding dress of pale blue-gray silk quickly and on time. Patrick O'Higgins, beauty tycoon Helena Rubinstein's tall, witty, and sophisticated aide-de-camp, was the best man. Gypsy Rose Lee was matron of honor. And Nancy's brother Riddelle Jr. had traveled all the way from Kansas City to give away the bride. When the service was over, guests repaired to a champagne reception a few blocks away at the elegant Sherry-Netherland, where the newlyweds were in residence.

Cecil's wedding present, delivered the following year, was a series of photographs. The most famous of these is a full-length image of the newly pregnant bride turned at a three-quarter angle to the camera. She is dressed in a floor-length Charles James Swan ball gown. The pale, tight, strapless bodice clings to her Northern Renaissance-like figure as the exaggerated, festooned bustle flows out behind her and into the dark cloud of a vast, softly layered tulle skirt. Gentle light from the tall windows of her husband's Fifty-seventh Street salon halos her short, fair, upswept curls and caresses her profile. In a pose reminiscent of a Howard Chandler Christy nymph, she reaches dramatically, bare arms outstretched, to steady herself on an unadorned white windowsill between two colossal transparent white draperies that billow romantically from ceiling to floor. In the background, an extravagant Rococo urn carved in white marble rests on its white marble pedestal.

Predictably, the couple raised a few eyebrows. Charles, who had won the Neiman Marcus Award just eleven months before his wedding for being the American designer who "touches genius and immortality,"[506] was an urbane forty-eight-year-old avowed homosexual at the peak of his career and transatlantic reputation. Twenty years younger than her husband, Nancy was wealthy, divorced, and Midwestern. There was an (unsubstantiated) rumor that Keith came along on the honeymoon.

Popular opinion to the contrary, through to the end of his life Charles vehemently insisted that Nancy's inheritance was never the motive for their union. He told John Duka, "I stupidly married Nancy because I loved her. I should have married her for her money, she would have been happy, I would have been happy, and everyone would have gotten along beautifully,"[507] he told the artist Harold Stevenson. "The wife knew I was homosexual when we married, that I had lived with her husband," he explained. "All of society is double gaited; Proust said that. Lady [Leucha] Warner told me that no man goes into society unless he is looking for an heiress or a lover. Otherwise they'd be out on the moors shooting grouse. I wanted to be married. That's not so special. No one could believe I could love a woman. The remarkable thing about marriage is that the same woman appears to be every day a different woman. You play the field with your own sex; each one becomes the same."

By 1954, Charles James Services was virtually bankrupt, and so—as the marriage brought in new funding—Charles, who would never dissolve any of his companies, created a feeder corporation called Charles James Associates Ltd., which he merged with Charles James Services, Inc. He moved out of his showroom at 699 Madison Avenue and without closing it, he dropped Charles James Proprietorship, Inc.—which owned the exclusive rights to his name, in association with his haute couture—from his books.

The new company, Charles James Associates, Inc., was financed by Nancy, the de Menils, and Josephine Abercrombie Robinson, all of whom were to receive stock in Charles James Services in exchange for their investment. As soon as it was incorporated, Charles signed an additional three-year lease for a 3,500-foot space at Twelve East Fifty-seventh Street (where Cecil photographed Nancy), to be used as a new, elegant showroom, atelier, and wholesale manufacturing facility for CJ Services. Here, he intended to maintain quality control of his less expensive clothing by personally overseeing all production, from color dyeing fabric to his precise specifications, to having his personal assistant involved in the operation. The new label for the clothes produced there, which were intended to be sold to both retail stores and private customers, read: "An Original Design by Charles James."

Meanwhile, Charles continued to dress his private clientele. In 1954, his haute couture production averaged approximately three garments a month. And that year, he completed three important new designs. The Pagoda suit inspired by Nancy[508]—which he had been working on since 1951—is the most notorious. Echoing shapes of the Far East, its impeccable hip-length jacket flares out into an equally impeccable cone created by elegant diagonal seams that almost merge, ever so slightly off center, in the front at the closure. Diana Vreeland hired Lillian Bassman to photograph the "Pagoda" in profile for *Harper's Bazaar*,[509] and infuriatingly, in the resulting, now-iconic image, the cone juts forward, not sideways. Charles would never forgive Mrs. Vreeland for making his best tailoring "look," as he claimed, "like the cow catcher on a locomotive."[510]

The Butterfly ball gown made its debut soon after at the March of Dimes Fashion Show, where it was modeled by Austine Hearst. The dress is sculpted with what Charles bragged was "the highest bust line in 125 years."[511] Its ankle-length form-hugging sheath mimics the butterfly's body. The gloriously shimmering multilayered and multi-hued broad tulle, floor-length bustle represents the butterfly's wings. The third 1955 design, "Tree Gown," was made for and named after Marietta Tree, and, like the Jennies, Charles composed it in clay before it was executed in fabric. The Tree's strapless, delicately tucked, gauzy sheath outlines the figure until it reaches mid-calf, where, unexpectedly,

In 1955, Charles designed the "Tree Dress" for Marietta Tree. He was extremely proud of the fluidity of its flounce. This rendering is by Antonio Lopez.

a fluid, floor-length flounce flairs out from under the overskirt, down to the floor. "My structures look as if the body were no more ambulatory than a mermaid's yet permit large reckless movement," wrote Charles, who was very proud of the lightness of that flounce.

Despite his anguish over Samuel Winston, who'd sued him less than a month after his marriage to Nancy, Charles continued to ambitiously invent and sign new licensing agreements. In 1954, he contracted with Albert Weiss, the costume jeweler, to make twenty designs, including tiered and festooned rhinestone necklaces sculpted to contour to the shape of the neck. He also was hired by the Celanese Corporation to create a double-spread advertisement featuring a garment in their fabric. (Austine Hearst modeled the coat he designed for *Vogue*.) And he entered into a new license with Dressmaker Casuals, a company set up—ironically, at Samuel Winston's suggestion—by Robert Winter-Berger and Robert Lang, to manufacture and market informal day-wear suits and coats under the Charles James label (this time under the designer's direct supervision from the Charles James showroom on East Fifty-seventh Street). It was an instant sensation. Lord & Taylor advertised one of Charles's coats in *Vogue's* October issue as the "shape-of-the-future,"[512] while the *New York Times* described the collection as "a perfect balance of 'design in the round'—almost architectural perfection."[513] A few months later, Charles received his second Coty Award—a special citation for "giving a new life to an industry through his sculptured, ready-to-wear-coats, designed for Dressmaker Casuals."[514]

He also inaugurated a new "Gothic" coat, evolved from the "Pagoda" jacket created for Nancy. It's distinguished by, and named for, the high seam that arches over the top of its raised bust line and the elongated pyramid shape of its skirts. And he launched the "Pear" dress, a variation of the sheath, also inspired by Nancy, but which adds curves to the hips.

Twelve East Fifty-seventh Street was an astonishing workspace. It had soaring ceilings and tall, wide windows, and was filled with light and beautiful art. Charles had signed a contract with Pellon, Inc. to make designs from its fabrics, so the capacious and seductively flowing translucent draperies were made from a synthetic interfacing manufactured by them. The walls were flocked a lingerie pink. The shining floors were pale gray, polished cement. Shimmering silks in a prism's spectrum of colors were crammed into cases that stretched from ceiling to floor. The furnishings, which included Louis XV chairs covered in yellow satin and Charles's famous Butterfly sofa, were simply superb. On either side of the entrance, padded mannequins of Charles's world-famous clients stood lined up against the walls in receiving line-like formation. Mary Ann Crenshaw, former lifestyle reporter for the *New York Times,* who began working for Charles as an intern while she was still studying fashion, recalled that the first time she walked into the atelier she was "simply amazed."[515]

The atmosphere in the showroom was not, however, always so lovely. By the end of 1954, the poisonous lawsuit with Samuel Winston was only one of Charles's many litigations. Bruno Belts, with whom he had signed the previous year, was also a target of his ire. Charles, who had designed two personally supervised belt collections for this company (one was sold exclusively to Lord & Taylor, the other went to a variety of retailers, including Saks Fifth Avenue), sued its parent, Vogue Belts, for breach of contract and pilfering his designs. Vogue Belts promptly declared bankruptcy, and Bruno Belts was dissolved. Then, because payments owed him were late, Charles also obtained an injunction against Dressmaker Casuals, less than a year after entering into his agreement with them. By December 1954, Dressmaker Casuals was out of business, too.

On a brief publicity tour to his mother's hometown of Chicago—where he staged a grand retrospective show for hundreds of attendees at a convention of dry cleaners—Charles made a visionary, down-to-earth, and impassioned speech in favor of explicit fabric content labels and cleaning directions in garments. The show received full-page coverage in the *Chicago American,* where an aerial photograph of the resplendent "Clover Leaf" shows it radiating its allure down the runway.

Finally, in June 1955, Charles James Services presented its first full fashion collection. The company, however, was again almost asphyxiated by financial and tax liabilities.

On August 2, Charles met with Arturo Peralta-Ramos Jr., Millicent Rogers's son, "to devise a system whereby the various phases of the [Charles James] organization could be put on a profitable basis." With Arturo's help, Charles established another feeder company, called Charles James Manufacturers Co. "The Charles James legend," Charles and Arturo had decided, "must be aggressively and methodically turned to profit by means of Charles James Manufacturers Co. and its offshoots—Charles James Services, in particular." Essentially, the purpose of the new company was to keep the old one afloat. Between 1955 and 1957, Charles James Manufacturers Co. received loans totaling $180,000. James's business receipts from April 1954 through March 1955 totaled $112,963. His expenditures were $310,266.

Inaugurating a tumultuous year, Charles and Nancy's first child—who would be christened Charles Brega Haweis James at New York's Cathedral of Saint John the Divine, where he was attended by his godmother, Elizabeth Arden, and Gypsy Rose Lee—was born in January 1956, a few months before the *New York Times* announced that Charles had lost his case against Winston and the federal government had attached Charles's $19,018.48 settlement from Winston for back taxes.

That January was also Mary Ann Crenshaw's inauguration as Charles's intern. "I grew up in Alabama and spent a lot of time looking at fashion magazines. My mother adored reading about Millicent Rogers, and Charles James was a hero of hers, too. In 1956, I was enrolled in Parsons and hating every minute of it. So I went to study with Charles James," Mary Ann remembers. "In the beginning, you paid Charles for the internship. He got your work for free. In return, you learned everything you needed to know: how to make patterns, cut fabric, roll a perfect collar and stitch a straight seam on chiffon. It was a much better education than going to school. Kate Peil, who had been with him forever, ran the workrooms. I always thought she had a secret crush on Charles James. She would have had to—to be as loyal as she was. It was a dangerous lifestyle, even if she did die at 103. Once, in a rage, he pinned her arm to the cutting-room table. There was a bodyguard called Thomas, who was six foot five inches tall. Thomas's main job was to restrain Charles when he flew into one of his tantrums. Towards the end, I believe Charles was taking drugs. This made things much worse. Sometimes, just to stay out of the way, I would go hide on the fire escape."[516]

Nancy James claimed that she never saw her husband's temper. "He could be volatile, but I did not see that side of him, as it only occurred in the workroom. I wouldn't say he was a manic perfectionist. He was an artist. And artists find it hard to realize their vision,"[517] she explained in her 2013 interview.

After Mary Ann had studied in the workrooms for six months, "Charles started to pay me fifty dollars a week. I stayed with Charles for two and a half years and he always paid me on time. I think someone had told him I was a cotton heiress—which wasn't true. Perhaps that was why he was so nice to me. When my mother came to visit, he took us out to lunch across the street from the workrooms. I don't remember the name of the restaurant. I only remember that it had only Chinese waiters and only American food, and that Charles wouldn't let them check his overcoat because he didn't want to tip the coat-check girl.

"Charles was a very attractive man: small, wiry, and hyper intense, with seductive eyes and a very tight mouth. I don't think I ever saw him relaxed. Everyone who could afford it wanted something by Charles James. His clients adored him. He had them in thrall. He made them feel that they were the most important people in the world."[518]

"It's hard to say about his character," Nancy equivocated. "He had very polished manners and speech....He remained a true Englishman....He loved to read the classics, which is different to the American approach. When he was working I would serve tea at a certain time in the afternoon, with his favorite Lapsang Souchong tea from Twinings, and toast with ginger marmalade. He was so proud of his British nationality that in his will he specified that the British embassy should be notified of his death....He never became an American citizen. He lived in America on a permanent resident visa obtained through the influence of his Aunt Enders—because he gave employment to people without making money."[519]

"He was constantly borrowing from Peter to pay Paul," Mary Ann remembered. "He had a huge overhead. There were three leases. And he paid an entire retinue. Some did nothing. Then he was always suing someone. There were a lot of lawyers on call. Charles always said he didn't care about money. He once tipped a cab driver with a hundred dollar bill. He'd thought it was a single. We were all regularly evicted from East Fifty-seventh Street for nonpayment of rent. It became my job to stand on the corner of Fifth Avenue, in view of the Plaza, and guard all our possessions: chairs, art, silk, mannequins—which had been thrown out onto the street—until Dominique de Menil's check arrived and we could be reinstated again," Mary Ann said, describing a scene better played out in Hell's Kitchen.

"I didn't know [Nancy] well. I always felt she just missed being a beauty. It was the length of her jaw. She was very polite and very timid, almost apologetic. In the workrooms we all thought of her generally as a rich little mouse. But she had very pretty upswept hair and she was very stylish. Of course she was stylish; she was dressed by Charles James."[520]

"After our wedding, two suits were made for me, and several versions of the sheath dress,"[521] said Nancy. "Charles always decided on the colors and fabrics! In addition, I wore coats and ball gowns from the collection, as well as a black velvet cocktail suit and skirts from the salon."

"He was very faithful to her, very devoted," said Harold Stevenson. "But he revamped her into this terribly sophisticated mannequin, which wasn't terribly suited to Nancy." [522]

"He made the Pagoda suit, with variations for Nancy when she was pregnant," Mary Ann remembered. "Balenciaga lived for the rest of his career off that design. I always felt sorry for her because her jewelry kept disappearing. Charles made her pawn it or sell it to pay off his debts. He also sold the art from his walls. After the baby was born, they were constantly moving to new addresses—very fancy ones—to avoid paying their bills. They were borrowing other people's chic apartments."[523] A list of the James family residences in 1956 includes the Sherry-Netherland Hotel, Thirty Beekman Place, 830 Park Avenue, and 340 East Seventy-fourth Street.[524]

Strained by the continual relocations, Nancy began to visit Dr. Max Jacobson, whose clients included Marilyn Monroe, Yul Brynner, Cecil B. DeMille, and, later, John F. Kennedy. The chic set also called him "Dr. Feelgood," or "Miracle Max." And his "tissue regenerator" injections, which were a concoction of amphetamines, animal hormones, bone marrow, enzymes, human placenta, painkillers, steroids, and multivitamins, were very popular in stylish circles before his license to practice medicine was revoked in 1975.

Charles worked like a dervish—all over the lot. At the Supermarket Institute Convention in Cleveland that year, he personally presented a smock he had contracted for and devised as the uniform of 100,000 supermarket checkout people. When the design didn't go into production, he evolved it into a couture coat that was part of a wardrobe he made for the artist Lee Krasner to wear to Paris that year for husband Jackson Pollock's internationally publicized mid-career retrospective.

In celebration of the birth of his son, Charles the younger, and encouraged by Ellen Engel in the New York office of Christian Dior, he invented a collection of clothing for babies "from birth to eighteen months,"[525] which he later expanded to include designs for toddlers. Charles negotiated a five-year contract with a children's wear manufacturer based in Atlanta, Alexis Corporation, a subsidiary of Warren Featherbone Company, in which he agreed to supply designs and patterns. All the fabrics were to be chosen and approved by Charles James. The labels were specified as either "Shaped by Charles James" or "Designed by Charles James."[526]

Charles was, as always, attuned to anatomy. The pride of the collection, his personal favorite, was a miniature "opera" cape taken from a Belle-Époque, dolman-cut "manteau de visite." It is made of pale-blue wool flannel lined in white satin. And its snug, short sleeves and egg-shaped armholes were specially designed to move his little boy's arms forward and prevent them from flailing (which Charles found unattractive). Similarly ingenious straps on infant rompers were rounded and contoured to keep them from slipping off tiny shoulders. The press release photograph shows a plump, crowing baby Charlie, all buttoned up in the cape he inspired, basking in the delighted admiration of both his proud parents.[527]

To display the diminutive outfits, Charles (the elder) also sculpted little papier-mâché children's torsos—perfectly proportioned, with flat buttocks and rounded tummies—which he flocked a bright cherry red. At the elaborate launch in early October, at Twelve East Fifty-seventh Street, a chorus line of white-capped "nurses" carried the little dressed dummies into the showroom. And baby Charles again modeled his opera cape, as his mother and father danced attendance in matching suit jackets that flared like minarets. Nancy's tunic suit was in deep purple; Charles's was rough wool tweed.

The first production of the children's clothing for Alexis was exquisite and (although Mary Ann Crenshaw believes Charles gave them to her) the columns reported that Princess Grace of Monaco—the former Grace Kelly—bought up eighteen of Charles's infant designs for the layette of Princess Caroline, who was almost exactly little Charles's age. By the end of 1956, thirty-one specialty and department stores were selling Alexis Infant Wear. And for the two years the agreement actually lasted, Charles James received a royalty of three quarters of a percent of gross sales in return for his work and the exclusive use of his name.

(By the 1980s, seven percent of gross sales to the designer had become an industry standard.) In love with the marvelous baby cape, Charles translated it into an adult design—and slyly renamed the grown-up version "Cocoon." It's a short, wide, cozy cloak in plush wool, with bent sleeves whose shape was taken from an elbow pipe that Charles and Dominique de Menil had salvaged from a New York City sewer.

Then, in a further muddling of the lines between all his design endeavors, from 1956 on, Charles also designed single-garment stage costumes—including a two-piece strip ensemble for Gypsy Rose Lee, a strapless leotard for Janet Gaynor, and a gown Marguerite Piazza wore for her act in Las Vegas—that were adaptations of original patterns created for his couture clientele. These were produced through CJ Services.

In 1957, Charles James's family moved back and forth between the Hotel Ambassador on West Forty-fifth Street in the theater district in Manhattan and the Sulgrave Hotel in Chicago. The New Year rang in with another brilliant new evening shape, made for Mrs. Byron Harvey Jr. and named the "Diamond Dress." Its hourglass fit echoes fin-de-siècle fashions, but the dress is a composition of untraditional juxtapositions in which facet-like marquise shaped panels of smooth ivory silk satin and rough beige silk twill are pieced together in a symphony of curves and angles in which some of the seams are sensuously highlighted with black rayon velvet cords that exaggerate the round of the buttocks, viewed from the rear, to create an enticingly abstracted female form. Accessorized with a large De Beers diamond pinned between two layers of the cantilevered bodice to scatter light in the cleavage, the dress made its debut in Chicago in 1957 at a lavish dinner and fashion show given by the diamond industry. "I have sometimes spent twelve hours working on one seam, utterly entranced and not hungry or tired till finally it had, as if of its own will, found the precise place where it should be placed," wrote Charles James, who reveled in his own ceaseless creativity and was as ever in love with his work. But the price of constant legal embroilment was taking its toll.

A tiny redheaded daughter, the couple's second child—named Louise Brega James, after the mother Charles idolized—came into the family at an unhappy time. Just days before she was born in July 1957,

IRS agents had seized the premises and contents of Twelve East Fifty-seventh Street for nonpayment of $80,000 in withholding taxes (about $660,000 today). Probably because Charles complained of it to her, Eugenia Sheppard reported in the *New York Herald Tribune* that ten of Charles James's original designs had been stolen from his showroom while he was waiting at the hospital to see his new child. Nancy became sick from anxiety and postpartum depression. And for several months, "to prevent a complete nervous breakdown," Charles had also been visiting Dr. Jacobson regularly. He would be drug dependent for the rest of his life.

Charles and Nancy fought on. They visited Rowena, Nancy's mother, in Missouri, where a photograph in the *Kansas City Independent* showed the elegant couple enjoying a Stork Club Party given by Austine. The photograph's caption advertised Charles as the trendsetting designer who was responsible for the "best dressed" status of the glamorous Mrs. Hearst.[528] In an ongoing act of legacy building, John and Christophe de Menil bought and gave to the Brooklyn Museum a group of Charles James's most beautiful current designs, including the Diamond dress, the infant mannequin, and the opera cape. Simultaneously, Charles persuaded two childhood friends from Chicago (one an heir to the Ryerson Steel fortune) to not only buy more than three hundred of his sketches from him but give them to the Brooklyn Museum as well.

Evolving his interest in unusual fabrics (including novelty synthetics like the "hairy white fabric that looks like wet feathers" of his well-publicized 1933 vamp evening cape), Charles designed a collection made out of Borgana, a synthetic fur version of Dynel. The coats were licensed by E. Albrecht & Son, a St. Paul corporation. "Borgana is synthetic NOTHING," Charles enthused, "but one of the most beautiful fabric inventions of the last decade...warm, crushproof, indefeatable [*sic*]—plush."[529] By early September he had even cajoled the IRS into letting him (temporarily) show the coats at the Twelve East Fifty-seventh Street space they had appropriated. Sadly, the fake fur (which would be all the rage ten years later) was too far ahead of its time. Sales were disappointing. In less than a year, by March 1958, the agreement was canceled. It was the last substantive contract Charles James would ever have.

"As [Charles] took Charles James Services deeper and deeper into debt, defaulted on taxes, negotiated (and renegotiated) loans, failed to deliver on contracts and, in the end, merged (and merged again) the finances of CJ Services with company after company, ownership of his name became an unresolvable question. What had begun as a commercial asset of high potential became an unredeemable element in the tangled web of James's business complications,"[530] wrote Elizabeth Ann Coleman in her catalog, *The Genius of Charles James*, for the eponymous 1982 retrospective at the Brooklyn Museum.

Charles, who continued despite everything to resolutely pursue short-term agreements, embarked on a creative attempt to reduce his tax liability by reorganizing himself into a nonprofit corporation—the Charles James Foundation, Inc., which he chartered in March in Illinois. The concept involved selling Charles James Services at a huge loss to a big (unspecified) corporation, which would then—for a tax deduction—donate it back to the Charles James Foundation.

Unfortunately, under the daily threat of subpoenas, both Charles James and his family were on the run. In 1958, their residences, in chronological order, included the Ambassador East Hotel, the Lake Shore Club, and the Lake Shore Drive Hotel in Chicago, the Sulgrave Hotel in Chicago, the Westbury Hotel, the Gotham Hotel, the Beekman Towers Hotel, the Plaza Hotel, the Barbizon Plaza Hotel, and the Manhattan Hotel (where Charles registered under an assumed name, Chester Johnson of 700 North Michigan Avenue, Chicago) in New York, the Roosevelt Hotel in New Orleans, the Hotel Muehlebach in Kansas City, the Hotel Alrae and the Hotel Gladstone in New York, and, back in Chicago, the Allerton Hotel and the East Oak Hotel.

No buyers for Charles James Services surfaced. The Charles James Foundation failed to attract donations. Suitable space to house it could not be found. Its project, "Floodlight," a series of "educational" fashion shows, was aborted. Negotiations with Dansant, Inc., a Broadway-based manufacturer of prom dresses, fell apart; so did a new coat license with Ranone, Inc. A commission from Eileen Farrell for a stage production of *Medea* was unprofitable. His couture business had dwindled from thirty-six pieces in 1954 to five in 1958. Charles discarded his foundation (again) in a matter of months.

Then things started to look up. In May of 1958, a *New York Times* article decrying rampant copying that was destroying America's fashion industry, named Charles James, James Galanos, Pauline Trigère, and Norman Norell as the most original of the American designers.[531]

That autumn, Charles was featured in the University of Chicago Service League show at the Shoreland Hotel. Nancy was one of his models. Mrs. Cornelius (Eleanor Searle) Vanderbilt Whitney, who had also modeled his coats for *Town & Country*, sent Charles her entire collection of twenty of his dresses for the show with a maid to take care of it for him. And Margaret "Peg" Zwecker, the fashion editor of the *Chicago Daily News*, introduced Charles to Roy Halston Frowick, a handsome young milliner who became his apprentice, adoring disciple, and friend.

Charles began to dream of setting up his family's first home in Chicago, which, he felt, had "wider horizons and more vision" than New York. "Friends there," he hoped, "would mean position, appreciation, warmth, music, pictures; travel." He had his sights on Mies van der Rohe's newly finished, luxurious apartment building, "the Glass House." He imagined an apartment with walls and ceilings covered in oxblood red felt and one little room lined with navy Borgana, "together with nylon carpets, Pellon curtains, a very old Steinway, and some personal magic." He thought he could get the results published for payment in a magazine called *Living*.[532]

Ralph James, who was again working with Samuel Insull in Chicago (after Insull had been cleared of all the charges against him in 1934), had been sympathetic at the time of the first IRS seizure. So Charles went to his father for a sum roughly equal to the value of the jewelry his mother had left him, but which (because he was homosexual) he had never received. He was instantly refused. His father was not interested in helping him out of "the appalling mess...into which your folly and your immeasurable conceit have brought you and your unfortunate family....You are," Ralph James wrote to his son, "totally unrepentant, [you] show no intention, wish, or inclination to live within your income and you brazenly assert that your PRESTIGE demands you live on a scale beyond any reasonable prospect of any income you may earn."[533] In New York, officials seized the contents of James's last office at 716

Madison Avenue, to satisfy creditors' judgments against him. And the steadfast Kate Peil finally resigned.

The collapse of the Madison Avenue office was kept from Nancy, who was still struggling with depression and had exhausted almost all her capital financing Charles's businesses and paying his legal fees. The strain of constantly moving with two babies in tow had become unendurable, and by the end of the year, she went back to Kansas City, to be with her mother.

In 1959, the year of his separation from Nancy, Charles split his time between the Hotel Gladstone in New York, and Chicago, where he stayed at the Lake Shore Drive Hotel and sketched the last of his famous coat shapes. He named it the "Great Coat" and its form has been taken as an expression of his emotional state at the time. Its back is humped like the back of a turtle. Curved and pointed seams swoop around the breasts—like the markings on the shell of a Japanese beetle—to, in the words of Jan Reeder, coauthor of the Metropolitan Museum of Art's catalog *Charles James: Beyond Fashion,* "confront each other at acute angles" at the front closure. And its oddly truncated dolman sleeves are squat, wide, and impeccable, like the arms of samurai armor. The Great Coat is a static garment, statuesque but uncomfortable. And as Reeder notes, Charles in his rendering has drawn and redrawn the angles "obsessively…with muscular strokes."[534] A publicity photograph of the finished product reveals uncharacteristically lumpy hems.[535]

The year of the Great Coat was filled with disappointments for Charles James. Negotiations with Ivan Obolensky for a biography to be titled *Beyond Fashion* had gone nowhere.[536] Plans to make twenty-five original designs for the Chicago International Fair & Exposition and participate in the opening celebrations for the St. Lawrence Seaway failed to materialize. Then Charles incorporated Non Plagia, Inc. (from the Latin verb *plagiare* meaning "to plagiarize"), which was the last of his wildly ambitious and idiosyncratically creative companies. The monies were to come from a group of former clients: Gloria Case, Jane Doggett, Muriel Bultman Francis, Marit Guinness Aschan (whose parents had been friends of Charles's parents), Herbert T. Cobey of the Perfection Steel Body Company, and Mary Ellen Hecht, Gertrude

Stein's niece and a department store heiress who was to be the principal investor.

In Charles's scheme he would create and fit seven garments for each of his shareholders. Collectively, these clothes would become a segment of a broader collection of original designs owned by the corporation—which would present them for business promotion. The problem was that businesses interested in using Charles James designs for self-promotion were becoming scarcer and harder to find.

In an article for *Vogue* in 2011, Mary Ellen Hecht described Charles as "a restless elf of a man with dark hair swept back from sharp features" and "a graceful, dancelike way of moving and working" even though he was frequently "hung over" in the mornings from drinking vodka the night before. She wrote that she had met Charles that year through Keith Cuerdon and remembered fondly: "Charlie taught me what we now call 'pushing the envelope.'" But she said when the directors of her trust fund told her she had to "stop supporting him,"[537] she pulled out. And Non Plagia, Inc. imploded.

In 1960 Charles relocated to the child-friendly, upper-middle-class New York suburb of Scarsdale where Nancy and the children came to be with him. But the marriage was essentially over. The attempted reconciliation lasted less than a year. And, once again, Nancy and the children home went home to her mother. The protracted divorce was finalized in 1966.

In Kansas City, Nancy would never be close to her brothers, who loved her but with whom she had failed to fully reconcile after the sale of the Postal Life and Casualty Insurance Company.

"She was considered to be 'a kind of an odd bird'—a bit eccentric,"[538] Michael Cox, Masten's biographer, explained.

Nonetheless she was able to raise Charles Jr. and little Louise II in a stable environment. And Jan Reeder gives her high marks for being a caring mother. Charles Jr. went on to a career as a computer expert in Pennsylvania and Louise involved herself with real estate in California. Although neither of them married, they each had a child. Charles's little girl is Ann James, and Louise's daughter is Rio James.

Even after the divorce Nancy's faith never faltered: "I always thought [Charles] was a good businessman, but he never found any one to capitalize him in the French manner,"[539] she reaffirmed loyally in 2013. And Charles, who bitterly blamed Rowena for the splintering of his marriage, would refer to Nancy as his wife for as long as he lived. For the next twelve years he received regular domestic updates on his family from Nancy and sent presents and letters to both his children, who also visited him in New York. "Our marriage has been successful, as marriages go," he wrote when they separated. "Happier by far than most.... Nancy and I have retained what others so often lose, complete faith in each other. I do not know if I did right to marry and ruin Nancy, but the advice to save [money] was in our case not the solution. The necessity of success and achievement came first.... You must never forget that, for me, Nancy is an absolute star, and she has given me life through becoming the mother of my children."[540]

When Charles James attended the opening of Studio 54 in April 1977,
a photograph of him in this black hat made the New York Post.
Photograph by Anton Perich.

CHAPTER 10

After All

WHEN HIS RECONCILIATION with Nancy failed, Charles abandoned Westchester.

He retreated to Manhattan in 1961, where he lived in dreary circumstances in a middle-of-the-road residential hotel at 70 Park Avenue near Grand Central Station, and worked for two years on a groundbreaking and brilliant but underappreciated project for the discount store chain E. J. Korvette. It was meant to be just an "off the rack" collection of pieces priced to retail from twenty to two hundred dollars, with the label "From a Charles James Design." But instead of the expected sequence of "watered down for the masses" costumes, Charles surprised his licensee with a magical capsule collection containing the coded components of one coat, one suit, and three dress patterns, which—like a wonderful series of ingenious jigsaw puzzle pieces—could be inexpensively assembled in an assortment of ways by Korvette's factories, to make over twenty different garments.[541]

Charles also returned to jewelry design in 1963 and with the help of the now-famous artist Ron Gorchov cast a group of what Harold Koda would call "wild," and Bill Cunningham "fascinating," organically shaped adornments for Corocraft, Inc. One design in particular, a huge, free-form, curved knuckle ring—in an organic shape that Charles later identified to Couri as "important"—mixed poured plastic with encrusted mother-of-pearl and proved that Charles's imagination was still undaunted, untamed, and way over the head of his business partners.[542]

"I introduced him to Coro and in the end he got a small contract, perhaps for one year. But he hardly gave them anything—just one little shape," Kenneth Jay Lane remembered. No matter the details, the single-year jewelry contract wasn't renewed. And Charles, now

185

fifty-eight years old, was out in the cold of the fashion design world. "He used to show up at interviews with his dossier of litigation papers,"[543] Kenny explained.

Finally, Charles had a stroke of good luck. In 1964 he was given a home and (with Keith Cuerdon and a baby beagle named Sputnik) finally settled into the Chelsea Hotel at 222 West Twenty-third Street in Manhattan, where—courtesy of Stanley Bard, its artist-centric manager—he lived, essentially rent free, for the rest of his life.

The Chelsea's idiosyncratic glamour was ideal for Charles James. It had been built by Hubert & Pirsson in 1884 (when, at twelve stories, it was the tallest building in Manhattan), and planned as a haven for artists of all kinds. Its landmarked, ornate, redbrick structure, decorated with elaborate cream-colored moldings and New Orleans-style balconies of pieced, lacy, wrought iron, was filled with ghosts of what Edgar Lee Masters called "ancient grandeur." Its walls were hung with paintings. It had marble stairs. And it was inhabited by a hard-partying crowd of eccentrics, ne'er do wells, and the disaffected offspring of the excessively rich (who unwittingly paid the rent for themselves *and* the artists in residence). According to Miloš Forman, it also had the slowest elevator in the whole country.[544]

As New York's bohemian outpost, the Chelsea had housed, housed, and would house, a parade of the iridescently famous, ranging from Edgar Allan Poe and Mark Twain (who had loved Millicent Rogers's mother), to Jackson Pollock (who married Lee Krasner), Nobel Prize winner Bob Dylan (who composed there), Dylan Thomas (who died there), Arthur Miller, Robert Mapplethorpe, Patti Smith, Sid Vicious, Rufus Wainwright, Betsey Johnson, R. Crumb, Andy Warhol and Valerie Solanas, the radical feminist who famously shot him. Additional celebrity residents, in no particular order, were Sherwood Anderson, Edie Sedgwick, Frida Kahlo and Diego Rivera, Yves Saint Laurent (but only in transit), Jane Fonda, Stanley Kubrick, Thomas Wolfe, Jasper Johns, Leonard Cohen, Willem de Kooning, Tennessee Williams, and Jonas Mekas.

Charles enjoyed the cult figure distinction of being the Chelsea's lone "haute couturier." Many old friends, however, were dismayed by the disarray of his living conditions when they visited the rooms on West Twenty-third Street, where he worked in his double bed, surrounded by bookshelves of his own making, filled with thousands of books (all of which he had read), precious mementos of past loves and successes, photos of his designs on Millicent Rogers, Marlene Dietrich, Ruth Ford, and Gypsy Rose Lee, not to mention patterns, mannequins, calipers, papers, and half-eaten sandwiches.

In her book on the Chelsea, Charles's neighbor Florence Turner described the apartment as "so untidy that the maids refused to clean it. The result was chaos—and a kind of awful charm."[545] And William Ivey Long—who moved to the Chelsea after he graduated from Yale Drama School to meet Charles and ended up spending a lot of time as an unpaid apprentice in Charles James's chambers, sprinkling powder to kill the roaches—explained that "[Charles] didn't like anyone straightening things up because he knew where everything was."[546] Mary Ann Crenshaw commented that she was shocked by how far he had fallen, but actually, in many ways, Charles's lifestyle, though deflated, was quite similar to that of his contemporary and friend of long standing, the blue-blooded aesthete Lord Stephen Tennant, who had retired to the tattered luxury of Wilsford, his ancestral English country manor in Avon. There, amidst peeling, hand-painted pink and gold wallpaper, zebra rugs, and forgotten mouse traps, Tennant reworked his interminable novel *Laskar* and received friends like Cecil Beaton and David Hockney, reclining, fully clothed, perfumed, and perfectly made-up, on his unmade bed. In brief, Charles's was a thoroughly aristocratic decline.

After Nancy, his last muse, left, Charles's design years were essentially over. But at least he had found a (semi) safe place where he could receive remaining clients, battle old enemies, nurse unhealed wounds, try to make sense of his life, memorialize his work—and teach what he had so painstakingly learned.

Of course, revisiting the past was important to him. And during his years at the Chelsea, Charles would regularly pop into museums to review and admire the examples of his work that were kept there. Harold Koda, who was interning at the Met during one of these visits in the 1970s, was told, "'Hide! Charles James is coming!' Otherwise, if Charles saw you, your whole afternoon would be taken up by talking about his dresses," Koda explained, adding, "What a missed opportunity."[547]

And Charles always liked gossiping. He particularly enjoyed chatting about the progression of fashion, its history, and the history of famous people who wore it. "I remember saying one day, 'Charlie, what do you think is the average age of the people we have been talking about?'" Elizabeth de Cuevas remembered affectionately. "And it turned out to be 103."[548]

During this time, Charles, who once wrote, "My designs are not luxuries. They represent fashion research,"[549] continued to rework and clarify the principles of fashion he had first recorded in 1960. In conjunction with Robert Riley, who was a curator at the Brooklyn Museum, he shaped these theories into a series of experimental college-level courses.

An exploratory first syllabus was tentatively titled "The Calculus of Fashion." Since fashion is change, it was supposed "to be to a fashion student what advanced calculus [the mathematical study of change] is to a math student."[550] The multidisciplinary curriculum's goal was to create "fashion engineers," or artisans, with the facility to translate "the ideas of artists efficiently and inexpensively into mass-produced clothes."[551] In Charles's mind, mass production without highly trained, skilled craftspeople was impossible. And it was important "to have thinking minds among them.... After all, knocking off is a science," he wrote. And although this first attempt turned out to be too complicated for the students at RISD and Pratt, where it was tested, it would later be revised and retaught.

As he was moving into his new home at the Chelsea, Charles was also (appropriately) invited to participate in a historical fashion show and fundraiser at America's oldest public art museum, the Wadsworth Atheneum in Hartford, Connecticut, which had been founded in 1842. (His friend Samuel Wagstaff—who was poised to become one of the most influential figures in contemporary art in America, and was an early and revered collector of photography, as well as Robert Mapplethorpe's lover and patron—was the museum's curator of contemporary art at that time, and probably influenced Charles's invitation.) It was a significant moment, almost exactly when the pendulum of art (and fashion) appreciation was tipping toward minimalism, in large part because of Wagstaff's influence.[552]

The show positioned Charles as a most modern designer. In a January 1964 letter to Wagstaff, Charles, who had been given an official title as the "Fashion History Commentator" (a very Jamesian name) of "The Sculpture of Style" show scheduled for that April, described the line of its narrative to his friend: "The chronological clothes," he explained succinctly, "have a pictorial relationship to each other."[553]

With Charles's approval, the Women's Committee of the Wadsworth Atheneum and J. Herbert Callister, acting curator of costume and textiles, organized a carefully chosen sequence of rarely seen Victorian and Edwardian dresses from the museum's own clothing collection for the gala's fashion show. The grand finale was a bouquet of Charles James's sleekly clean-cut dresses and tailored coats.

Typically, after months of preparation, Charles, gripped by stage fright, locked himself in the curator's office for the whole day before the event and refused to come out until he could hear the roar of his audience's ecstatic applause.[554]

The show's catalogue, whose entire cover consisted of one of his most recent, gracefully abstracted "minimal" coat sketches—adorned by Charles's very large signature—was exquisitely conceived. With Charles's customary care for detail and the "rounding out" of an experience, a loose-leaf insert to the booklet was devoted to the menu for the opening night's celebratory dinner in the museum's Avery Court: Crevettes Rose (pink shrimp), Consommé Madeleine, Filet de Boeuf Rôti Suprême, Broccoli à la Dauphinoise, Tomates Farcies, Riz Sauvage, a special salad, then strawberries with Kirsch and whipped crème, all downed with champagne, followed by coffee and liqueurs. *And* there were table favors.

Each catalogue page was sponsored, many by supporters of Charles. His friend Elizabeth Arden underwrote a page with the photograph of a French wedding dress from 1870 that was Louis Havemeyer's gift to the museum. The Chelsea Hotel shared its paid-for page with an exquisite pink satin reception dress overembroidered with white lilies—made in 1903 by Walker Brothers in Salt Lake City—a gift from Lawrence Lee. Neiman Marcus sponsored a photograph of Charles's 1947 dolman coat, designed for Lily Pons. An image of Charles's Great Coat was underwritten by Nan Duskin, while Vera Maxwell presented the Pear Sheath "to salute the Wadsworth Atheneum and the Designs of Charles James."[555] Charles James, we learn from the copy, "is represented in great museum costume collections across the country." His clothes "have perfect proportion, grace and almost a life of their own."[556]

"My entire career," Charles wrote in summation to Sam Wagstaff, "has pointed to the relation between industry and art."[557]

Later that year, Charles met Antonio Lopez by chance in a Greenwich Village bistro, and Antonio and his partner, Juan Ramos, became important new friends. Antonio had grown up on the streets of Spanish Harlem, attended FIT on scholarship, and was only twenty-one, but his erotically charged illustrations would introduce youth culture to the haute fashion of glossy magazines *Vogue* and *Harper's Bazaar,* setting a new tone for the imagery of style over the next thirty years.

Antonio invited Charles into his excitingly young world of "gossip, gorgeous people, designer clothes, groovy tunes, art, kitsch, and street culture."[558] An anonymous 1964 photograph shows Charles James cozily piled into the illustrator's palm-tree-lined studio, lounging on fat Indian print pillows with Juan and Antonio, and surrounded by blond beauties Kathleen and Ingeborg Marcus and Cathee Dahmen.[559] Charles is looking quite pleased with himself.

Lopez was entranced by the shapes of Charles's clothes; he asked permission to sketch them. And André Leon Talley remembers frequently visiting Charles in his rooms at the Chelsea on Sunday after church, where there always seemed to be some sort of party going on. "Marathon drawing sessions would start midafternoon and last until two or three in the morning,"[560] Talley reported. And "in the middle of this glorious mayhem and detritus of his life, Charles would regale [us] with anecdotes about everyone he hated in the fashion universe."

In the drawings made during these gatherings of students, clients like Mrs. Fritz (Jean) Bultman, the wife of the Abstract Expressionist painter (who were willing to pose in their Charles James designs), beautiful boys pulled off the street to wear dresses only they could fit into, photographers, celebrities, and assorted groupies shimmer with life. Their lines whirl and zip across the page, emphasizing the musicality and movement inherent in Charles James's work.

In Antonio's rendering, the famous ribbon cape inspired by Paul Poiret reaches across broad shoulders to swirl giddily from right to left, while the curves of James's "soft sculpture," the one-of-a-kind eiderdown jacket, spin around to apparently flip backward, as the Tree Dress's flounce kicks up its heels. Imbued with attitude, a pouf slinks elegantly away from the viewer. But an angular, jacketed sheath glides forward with intention—as if stalking the runway. Over the next ten years there were hundreds of these beautiful drawings interpreting and documenting the body of Charles's life work. "[Lopez] forced designers to actually think—about their own clothes,"[561] Rosita Missoni commented to Karin Nelson at *W Magazine.*

For an adoring Pat Cleveland, Antonio was simply "the Gauguin of our time."

At the end of 1964, Ralph James, who was eighty-seven, died without making any effort to say goodbye to his son. After Ralph's death, Charles discovered that he had been cut out of his father's will. Charles Jr. and little Louise II received the portion that would have been due him. And, more generous by far than his father had ever been to him, Charles James—who had no trouble suing anyone for anything at any time—accepted Ralph's decision. He consoled himself by composing poetry and wrote tenderly of the man who had so badly hurt him: "It may well have been that I alone knowing all there was to know…bad and good, loved my father the best."[562]

By 1966, Charles had found a new groove, and his sixtieth birthday was cause for celebration. Friends old and more recent—including Salvador and Gala Dalí, Juan and Antonio and their entourage, Halston, and pal Bill Cunningham—threw a bash for him at Max's Kansas City, which, thanks to regulars David Bowie, Roger Vadim (who had just married Jane Fonda), and Andy Warhol and his entourage of superstars, had become a new hub of glam. Anton Perich (who bussed in the famous back room when he wasn't taking pictures of the celebrities or making pictures with the painting machine he invented) said it was the most vibrant restaurant and one of most exciting meeting places in Manhattan at that time.[563]

Re-reviewing his practice, Charles began to evolve his theories on the constant of change. He supplemented "The Calculus of

Fashion" with a new concept: "Meta-morphology," which he related to the sequence of his own fashion practices and the theory of fashion in general. "Meta-morphology" was based on an idea borrowed from the eighteenth-century German poet, novelist, alchemist, and scientific theorist, Johann Wolfgang von Goethe, who had observed the inexorable evolution natural to plants, in particular—and by extension, all living things.

"The ever-changing display of plant forms, which I have followed for so many years, awakens increasingly within me the notion: The plant forms which surround us were not all created at some given point in time and then locked into the given form, they have been given...a felicitous mobility and plasticity that allows them to grow and adapt themselves to many different conditions in many different places," Goethe wrote in *The Story of My Botanical Studies.*[564]

"[Charles] attempted to create...ideals of the female figure....He continued to work on even his most perfected designs, tweaking them, sometimes completely redesigning them. The metamorphosis part of 'Meta-morphology' is [Charles's] constant revisiting of a shape and evolving it without end," Harold Koda explained in a 2014 interview with Cindi di Marzo.[565]

But, for Charles James, this concept of endless (organically mutating) variety applied not only to the continuous evolution that is fashion, but additionally to the varied uses to which one cut or piece of a pattern or even a single drapery technique could be put—thus birthing an infinite diversity of forms. Contrapuntally, Charles also used the term "Meta-morphology" to describe the variety of techniques that can be used to achieve the same structural shape. He would later offer an elective class on this subject at the Pratt Institute in 1970.[566]

In conjunction with the Art Students League, Charles additionally began to experiment with evolving his Jennie into what he described as a "flexible sculpture"—essentially a sliced-up dress form whose horizontal segments were held together by a bendable backbone like rod running vertically down its center. The "sculpture" was a mannequin that could be twisted into many postures and was designed to help manufacturers create clothes that move easily with the wearer and fit better as a result.

In the last project of his sixtieth year Charles recorded the observations, thoughts, and impressions on the subject of his fashions of fourteen friends, clients, and students. He wanted to create "a live documentation of Charles James's work, which will become a permanent record for the students of fashion design, and after an interval of years, to writers who may desire to do research on the same." He called these tapes "The Sound of Shape and Design."[567]

Then, in December 1969, Halston—whose designs would become not only the style signature of America but the incarnation of fashion in the 1970s, when they placed the United States preeminently on the world's fashion map—decided to produce a Charles James retrospective spectacular.

Roy Halston Frowick had been a Charles James acolyte ever since the two had been introduced in Chicago eleven years earlier.[568] And as Halston's friend and Fire Island roommate, Arthur Williams, described it, "[Halston] fed off Charlie."[569]

According to Steven Gaines, one of Halston's biographers, Charles James "was most of all an *artiste* and Halston was enthralled with him. For a long period, they had dinner one or two times a week and James became a confidant and mentor to the young milliner. James was grand; Halston became grander. James's favorite champagne was Möet et Chandon; it became Halston's favorite. James's favorite flowers were orchids; orchids would not only become Halston's favorite flower, they became his trademark bloom. Halston also began to look at cut and construction through James's eye."[570]

"Charles James played a very important part in my life," Halston admitted dryly. "He introduced me to a 'higher' element in fashion."[571] Charles himself described Halston as "one who much admired my creativity [and] envied my position in fashion." According to Gaines, Charles "would later claim credit for most of the important points in Halston's career, including bringing him to New York and getting him employed by the famous hat maker, Lilly Daché, and subsequently, Bergdorf Goodman's hat salon."[572]

"Making hats is a tremendously good training for being a dress designer," Halston, who left Bergdorf Goodman in 1968 to go off on his own (and open an orchid-filled "couture" showroom), recited, parroting what Charles James had taught him. "You learn to think in three dimensions, so your dresses have a sculptural quality. Also, you think in terms of small details."[573] Lilly Daché recollected, "Halston learned a great deal from Charles James about designing and the world of style and society, and probably other things too."

And Halston, who was Eleanor Lambert's client and had won his second Coty Award two months earlier, in October 1969 (for "the total look" of his first solo collection), wanted to link his image to the Charles James legend. So staging the retrospective was a very political move for him. "I'm producing this show because Charles James has always been one of my heroes,"[574] he proclaimed in a press interview about the event, which was organized as a fund-raiser for Pratt Institute's Engineering Department, to reflect Charles's belief that his work was applicable to the world beyond style.

Halston selected Manhattan's latest nightclub du jour, the Electric Circus, as the venue for his extravaganza. Located at 19–25 St. Mark's Place in the East Village, the discotheque advertised itself as a hedonist's paradise—the embodiment of the wild and creative side of club culture and "New York's ultimate mixed media pleasure dome." Inside the "Circus," strobe lights scanned the dance floor while multiple projectors flashed images from home movies to the beat of experimental bands like the Grateful Dead or the Velvet Underground. There were sofas and armchairs for lounging and enjoying the performances of flamethrowers, jugglers, and acrobats between musical sets. Unlike Max's Kansas City, which catered to a culture-centric downtown crowd, the Electric Circus, with its psychedelic appeal, was a mecca "for every sector of New York Society."[575]

For the event's poster, Halston chose one of Charles's drawings, which, in keeping with the circus theme, was a figure with a whip lying on it, and was interpreted knowingly—by those who knew things—as a private joke between Halston and Charles James. [576]

"This kinky combination—the grand *couturiers* Halston and James giving a fashion show in the East Village—turned the benefit into one of the great reverse-chic events of the Christmas season,"[577] Gaines wrote. All of Halston's (and some of Charles's) fashionable celebrity and society ladies—Catherine Deneuve, Babe Paley, Alexis Smith,

Bianca Jagger, Ali McGraw, Liza Minnelli, Raquel Welch, Mrs. Averell (Katherine) Harriman, Doris Duke, Amanda Burden, Lee Radziwill, and Lily Auchincloss—were invited to attend. The expensive (forty dollars) tickets sold out. Anonymous patrons bought 100 extra tickets, which were distributed free to students who couldn't afford them. Mrs. Michael (Betsy Pickering) Kaiser, who had been a *Vogue* cover girl and was a Charles James patron and benefactor, underwrote the event.[578] Halston offered to lend his best models.

From across the Atlantic, legendary clients like the Countess of Rosse and Mary Hutchinson sent some of Charles's fragile, earliest pieces. Other contributors included Dominique de Menil and Oatsie Charles, a Washington customer from the war years and close friend of Scottie Fitzgerald and Millicent Rogers.

Keith Cuerdon, Nancy's first husband, who was living with Charles at the Chelsea and had worked as a production assistant for plays like *Strange Interlude* in 1963 and *The Three Sisters* in 1964, choreographed the show. He also helped Antonio Lopez with the sets.[579]

In the midst of all the commotion over the party, which had taken on a life of its own, Charles felt neglected. So, adding to the drama, he announced he would boycott the pre-event cocktail that socialite Mrs. William F. (Pat) Buckley was hosting in her flamboyant Keith Irvine-designed East Seventy-third Street maisonette.[580] But in the end he capitulated and made an entrance, even later than usual, with Couri Hay, chair of the benefit's junior committee and his escort for the evening, in tow. At which point, according to Gaines, "Charles and Halston stood on either side of the room" and made "snide remarks."[581]

Then, everyone, including supermodel Verushka, designer Giorgio di Sant'Angelo, and Mrs. John (Veronica) Converse, Gary Cooper's blond widow, piled into one of the two private buses that Pat Buckley had provided for the night, and made their way to the Electric Circus.[582]

Inside the club, gigantic blowups of Antonio's vivid drawings flashed on the walls as rock music crashed and celebrity models like Naomi Sims and Elsa Schiaparelli's granddaughter Berry Berenson pranced and danced down the runway to a rotating platform glittering with mosaic mirrors, where they struck still poses to provide a 360-degree view of each design.

And 100 wildly appreciative students, who had never seen anything like them, gave a standing ovation to Charles James classics from the 1930s: the "Ribbon Cape" and the "Taxi Dress."[583]

The next year, 1970, Halston decided to outdo himself by hiring Charles James. Halston's first collections when he opened his boutique in 1968 got outstanding reviews, but were so badly made that most of the wholesale orders were returned from the stores.[584] So it became Charles's mission to help Halston with the shape and fit of his clothes. He was given a new title: "Fashion Consultant Engineer." And Halston, who had a history of not sharing credit with other people, promised Charles the new label would read "Shaped by Charles James."

When Charles moved into the third floor of Halston's offices where he had a little studio (described by Bernadine Morris in the *New York Times* as a cross "between a doctor's office and an artist's workroom with anatomical drawings on the walls—some headless forms of the human body and a surgical white décor"[585]), he began examining Halston's collections and immediately recognized that Halston's problem was that he had been fitting (for effect) on extraordinary, extraordinarily tall, rawboned models instead of "ordinary people or the shape of ordinary people." But it took a long time to correct Halston's proportions. And, by spring, Charles, who was slow as always, had only been able to produce a handful of new designs. "Of course," he explained to Morris, "once you get the structure right the things can be reproduced quickly." In the end, Halston's June fashion show was a composite of Halston's and Charles James's designs.

Morris, who devoted almost a full page to the luminescent partnership, reported:

> Some of the shapes that stepped quietly, elegantly into Halston's heavily curtained showroom are the kind you don't see around much anymore. They looked sculptural rather than pasted together and they were the work of Charles James, erstwhile couturier, [and] now "fashion consultant engineer" to Halston Frowick. "He helped shape the collection like Balenciaga helped Givenchy," Halston [loftily] explained....

Mr. James, who Halston likens to Leonardo da Vinci, has only turned out a few styles, but then he's only been ensconced there a few weeks. He's working out the basic shapes on which endless variations can be played....

Jamesian notes were the gently flaring, wrapped evening skirts that turned out to be pants and the Hans Brinker pants that were like ankle-length bloomers..."[86]

Immediately following Bernadine Morris's praise in the *New York Times*, the "New Fashion Team," as she called it, fell apart. "Halston was basically very jealous and understood the superiority of Charles,"[587] Elsa Peretti—whose silver jewelry also made its debut appearance in Halston's June 1970 show—said in a 2014 interview.

"Halston became Halston after the Charles James show," the designer Clovis Ruffin told Gaines, "because he realized he was just as good as Charles James."[588]

Now that they were on a semi-equal footing, Halston stopped wanting to give Charles so much credit and became irritated with him. He had no interest in Charles's high goals and painstaking methods, or in the slow process of inventing new fashions. On a fast track to richness and stardom, Halston just wanted to repackage pretested designs. Charles caught his drift. "One day Halston walked into the showroom he had given me, which wasn't all that nice, and said, 'You're too old to design. How much do you want to stop being in this business and just live forever?' He offered me $250 a week for the rest of my life. I declined. I knew he just wanted to steal my work and claim it as his own, of course," Charles told Gaines.

Fred Rottman, another of Halston's biographers, who worked for both Charles and Halston, confided that the first time Halston became angry with him, "I got fired. (You really weren't part of Halston's team until you were fired.)" He remembered, "That was when Halston sat me down and gave me a lecture on the principles and meaning of fashion. He started talking about things like 'posture' and 'plumb line' and each word of that lecture was something I had heard about from Charles James. I actually wanted to write my book about how the impetus of everything designed by Halston was an evolution of Charles's work in the 1930s, but my publishers didn't think that would be a very good idea."[589]

Jan Reeder, co-curator of the Metropolitan Museum's retrospective, agrees that Halston's world-famous signatures—his bias cuts, tubular dresses, angular necklines, and bifurcated skirts—all bear the stamp of Charles James.

According to Charles's last assistant, Homer Layne, Charles "felt he didn't get his due recognition from Halston. [Halston] used a lot of his ideas and silhouettes and shapes, like the figure-eight skirt, the wraparound pants, and the bubble top. All of those things were Charles James and the one-sided neckline, which [Charles] did in the 1930s. And Halston, you know, that was his big thing, the asymmetric neckline. And [Charles] felt he didn't get recognition. That's all he wanted was recognition."[590]

In the end, Halston never bothered to fully pay or properly recognize Charles James for his services, and after the breakup Charles hated him. As Halston became more and more rich and famous, "James would...call Myrna Davis [the accessories editor for *McCall's* and a close friend of Halston's] on the phone and complain about Halston to her for hours," wrote Gaines. Charles additionally and obsessively made lists of every design element Halston had stolen from him. He may also, as Gaines implies, actually have stalked his ex-protégé on Fire Island.

In R. Couri Hay's works on paper collection, there's a Charles James drawing called "Halston." It's the sketch of a very big cockroach.

As the fiasco chez Halston was unfolding, Homer Layne—a self-effacing scholarship student from a large family on a small farm in Tennessee, who was one of four students with the talent, intellectual curiosity, and endurance to complete the Charles James's twelve-session seminars at Pratt Institute's University Without Walls in 1970—became Charles's perfect apostle and his final and most trusted right hand.

"I was a student at Pratt Institute in Brooklyn in 1970; he came over and gave one-semester seminars once a week. [At] the first meeting...it was standing room only, all the chairs were filled, and people were standing around the wall," Layne told Alina Cho in 2014. "By the end of the twelve or thirteen sessions, there were only four students left, and I was one. He tends to go off on tangents. I think it was hard for a lot of students to follow along," he recalled. "[But] the first time he brought around the spiral wrap dress from 1929, I'd never seen anything quite that simple, yet it looked complicated.... So, on one side of the bodice, the whole skirt wraps around the body. It's all cut from one pattern piece. Then it has a back and sleeves on another side of the bodice and you just wind it around and hook it....I got more interested, seeing his patterns....In school, they really teach you just the basics. You know, you have bust darts, side darts, [and] waist darts. But his were somewhere else, or no darts at all, so it really fascinated me. He saw more than I thought of myself in me, I guess. And he wanted me to stop school and come and work with him and I said no, I wanted to get my degree. So I worked with him on weeknights, on days that I didn't have classes, which was either one or two days a week, depending on the schedule, and weekends. And I would go in, like one o'clock in the afternoon and come home at midnight or something, back to Brooklyn. The first thing was the dog, Sputnik. He had to have a walk. So you walked Sputnik, or rather he walked you, because he was a huge, big beagle. And usually, before I went home, another walk, and then in between, you know, I did patterns. He would draw and we would make patterns together. And I was able to follow along and sort of jump ahead of what he was doing, and I guess he liked that. We would talk about resolutions of things that we were working on, the way he wanted it. And if it were sewing, he wanted it sewn a certain way."[591]

Homer was Charles's perfect "fashion engineer," and with Layne at his side, Charles James was able to revisit designing. He looked back to the fluidity of his first shapes, which his new work infused with fresh meaning as he embraced the androgyny and eclecticism of the 1970s.

By 1972, after some years of research and experimentation, which included molding clay sculptures to determine the exact influence of the penis on the fit of soft trousers, Charles was able to complete a new design. It was a pair of slimming, unisex pants derived from the ones he first made for Stephen Tennant. The trousers cling to the hips and mold the buttocks, while their diagonal waistline slants from back to front, making waists appear smaller and flattening the stomach. These trousers are cut to fit a range of sizes and can accommodate waists from twenty-four to twenty-nine inches.

I was [his] model at [that] moment…and then, little by little, I got to be a friend of him," confided Elsa Peretti, who became a member of a small coterie that made it their business to support Charles during the last years of his life.

A fitting with Charles James, fitting a pair of pants, [lasted] two hours and [included] listening to Brahms and other classical music. And to have Charles pinning on me [meant that] sometimes the pin will go into my body. But I learned a lot listening to this spirit. He made me a lot of pants…this [one] pair of pants I gave…to my mother. And she [asked], "Who did these pants? She told me they were the best pair of pants she had in her life.

He [was cutting] a shape on me…And he said, "Elsa, don't get so thin because people, they should design around you…you should not make any sacrifice…" Charles would make maybe a model suffer, but *women were comfortable in [his] clothes.*

One time…I arrive[d] very late…[And he said,] "I'm sure you spent a lot of time choosing what you are wearing." [This was] true. And he knew…I was late because [I had spent a lot of time deciding on my] necklace. At that time I had only two necklaces, the amber one and the other one. And he said, "It's good you choose the amber."[592]

[Charles] understood women very well," said Elsa, who still remembered, with longing, a perfect little black dress Charles had made for her and then taken back.[593]

Branching out into sportswear, Charles also removed the sleeves from the cropped top he had made for his 1930s culottes. Merging it with a "sports bra" he had invented in the 1950s for Mary Ellen Hecht, who was a passionate golfer, he developed a seamless, perfectly smooth, cup-less bra that supports the breast through its bias cut rather than traditional bra construction. This top could be worn over his new pants, as a piece by itself, or under a sheer top.

*In the late 1970s Charles James experimented with trans-gender design and
by re-working the pants pattern he originally created for Stephan Tennant in
the 1930s created a design that could be worn by both men and women as well
as a seamless "sports bra." Drawing by Antonio Lopez.*

"He came out to the country," the sculptress Elizabeth Strong de Cuevas recounted in 2014. "And Lee Krasner, who was dressed by Charles James when she went to Paris…[and] was a funny lady [was also my guest]….[Charles] wanted to show off. We were in the middle of summer and he had a green bra. (And nothing was made for me but he insisted on showing this off.) I was cooking dinner and he was pinning, in the kitchen, a green satin bra, made for somebody like Gina Lollobrigida. I *mean, enormous.* And he was clumsy with his fingers; whenever he pinned anything, it was clumsy. So I would go, 'Ouch, Charlie, be careful. Ouch!'…Lee Krasner said to me later, 'I dined out on that for one year….There you were holding up a plate of fish… [and] he's following you, trying to pin.'"[594]

Elizabeth remembered Charles as simultaneously passionate and jealous. "We were friends but he imagined, you know, more than that....We both came from unusual backgrounds," Elizabeth (who, like Charles, was born of an American heiress mother into the prewar Parisian beau monde, where her father, the Marquis de Cuevas, was, like Charles's sister-in-law, a famous ballet impresario) recalled. "So we had a sense of being outsiders. That was a shared memory and a common bond." It was an intensely felt, genuine connection. "We had a [sardonic] little joke together about our feelings—that our feelings were only skin deep. What I always admired about Charlie was that he told the truth *in art*. He was very generous with other artists. And he was always very encouraging to me." [595]

Charles's last completed design was a poetic restatement of the blouse he had made for Mary Hutchinson, famously sketched by Matisse in the 1930s. It's the gossamer wrap with floating sleeves, like vast wings, that so startled and frightened me on Henri Bendel's second floor. R. Couri Hay told Alina Cho the story of how, during this period, Charles "created one of his last garments. It was astonishing. It was a 'Butterfly' top, totally transparent. And it, again, [had] that famous point [of sexual tension] at the décolletage...And then out to butterfly sleeves. And then he put it in a cellophane box, a clear plastic box, and sent it to Henri Bendel's to, was it Geraldine Stutz, or whoever was there. And I remember, you know, there was no reception to it and Charles was very hurt by that." [596]

Unfortunately for Charles, his reputation of being, as Harold Koda (quoting Caroline Lamb) put it,[597] "mad, bad, and dangerous to know" and often more of a "monstre" than "sacré," preceded him, so that during the 1970s many people avoided him. Or perhaps they simply couldn't deal with his pathos.

When Diana Vreeland was beginning her preparations for the Metropolitan Museum of Art's "American Women of Style" show, scheduled to open in 1975 to honor Millicent Rogers, Elizabeth de Cuevas asked Diana, "just as any friend might," if she would include Charles James's designs. "I will if you don't tell him," Diana, who hated prodding, snapped back. In the end, Diana simply omitted Charles and his work from her show. Joan Kron, who had asked her about the exclusion, wrote about Vreeland's reaction in a 2014 article for *Allure*: "I didn't look for his clothes. And I didn't see them…the whole Charles James thing is despairing,"[598] Vreeland replied.

Much of Charles's time at the Chelsea was spent battling these "wrongs." And, in much the same way as he crafted his dresses, Charles wrote, amended, revisited and re-construed, over and over, the most painful episodes of his life.

William Ivey Long, who eventually worked his way up from collecting pins off the floor to being allowed to "thread mark" a dress so Homer could "come in and take it in or out a quarter of an inch," told how

A third of my time was spent on maintenance and a third on privileged work on the dresses, and the other third was writing hate mail.

I would type letters on my typewriter, continuing his feuds with stores. He whined about Wanamaker's stealing his patterns. I found out years later he had been paid for them. He was known for borrowing back clothes and selling them to someone else. I just assumed he was telling the truth. That Halston had stolen his patterns and that people refused to pay him for things he had done. How would I know otherwise?…Within a month or two of listening to all this, I thought, *Oh my goodness, he's a British citizen, wouldn't it be nice if the Queen put him on one of her honors lists?* So, of course, I wrote a note to elicit support from Sir Cecil himself, and almost within a week, by return mail I received a response. "Dear Mr. William Ivey Long, Thank you for the information. I am not close to it at all as I used to be, I'm afraid I'm not able to do anything. Please give Charlie my very best and I hope you will understand."[599]

Effectively, Charles and Cecil's relationship had already been severed. When, in a book of diaries published with much fanfare in 1973, Cecil described Charles James as "embittered," Charles (who liked to write with a quill and sometimes sealed his letters with paraffin) bombarded him with a series of tortuously revised and reworded epistles, complaining at length to his old schoolmate of his misuse of their friendship.

In the first communiqué (with a note at the top explaining it was originally planned as a night letter, before telegramming turned out to be too expensive), Charles wrote:

Dearest Cecil,
But I am not embittered as you write in your book which I received today, and have a remarkable facility for forgetting grievance which others would remember. It's true that I fall into despair from time to time for weeks on end, when finding myself exploited, and other[s] making a profit out of work that has cost my life's blood. But this state of mind changes, and again I am twenty one and setting out again towards battles and victories rather than defeats despite the fact that reason would suggest the latter.

The brightest part of early life was our time together in New York when I had Ilka Chase's flat. I'm sending you a long letter, which may not entirely please you, but you will recognize true when presented....

[I]n a bad moment in your financial situation it was I who brought you back into the advertising field, never expecting to lose the account [Modess] to you, the jamor [*sic*] part of which, as usual, I had to finance myself.

You should remember the sort of thing you wrote could drive capital badly needed away from a friend...."[600]

In the promised "long letter" Charles continued:

Our lives and vocations have been different, yours consisting of the visual reportage of what others made, with [your] every expense born [*sic*] by theirs...while mine has been that of some-one who created...at my own expense, what may have brought me reclaim but no money; money going always to those who exploited my work.

...My wife and I both thought that, in the role of a friend, you should never have accepted money [$10,000] for doing a few drawings for a collection [of Samuel Winston who] instigated a suit which any could assume would both ruin me and keep me out of the market.

It is something I would not have done to you.

You see I do not come from a commercial background as your father did; so I am bound to be a loser in sharp deals, thinking only of the concepts I want to work out which certainly have benefited the business world as much as private clients.

You have never viewed my situation fairly or realistically....

For my money you are the best photographer I ever knew. And one who, in his simpler work has done beautiful things for the stage. But you have had the means to do all this placed at your disposal....

You thought nothing of using the double page photograph I had suggested taking [the famous photograph of eight of Charles James's ball gowns published in *Vogue* in 1948] for VOGUE magazine at French and Co; in imitation of the scene which met our eyes on leaving the dining room after Mona Williams' dinner for Bérard, for the cover of one of your books without giving me credit. The [Charles James] designs had been delivered to VOGUE, as the slip I signed showed, purely for use in [the *Vogue* "book"]. This [use of the photograph of *my* work for *your* own book cover] was an act of provocation [on your part]...

...for by no stretch of the mind could I have benefited by YOUR use of MY work.

...You are no longer the older boy at school.

You are simply someone joined to me through long years by links of admiration and love; someone [who when I was in need] I felt let me down out of greed.

...Contrary to your belief that I have few friends, there are many who have shown love and respect...(not always together) and among them are many quite "important" people who do not feel well towards yourself for reasons it is inappropriate and useless to bring up, but which I am sure you know.

It is more I who turn down invitations, and do not want to go into the world which lies far beyond the vestibule of this shabby hotel.

However, as with many between whom and myself there have been passages of extreme unpleasantness, were you to come UNannounced to visit me…quite simply and without pose…I would be *bird happy*…[601]

This second longer version of the letter is signed, "With love always, Charlie."

Cecil (who Cocteau called "Malice in Wonderland") responded to the entirety of these tortured outpourings by countering meanly: "Such a pity he is so difficult because I would like to like him…he's a genius manqué."

When, in a similar vein, Eleanor Lambert, in a 1973 *Esquire* magazine interview with Patricia Bosworth, entitled "Who Killed High Fashion," described Charles as "traumatized" by the litigation with Samuel Winston, Charles's reaction to her was much harsher.

He wrote to Eleanor in a previously unpublished, undated, five-page letter shared by Bill Berkson, which was probably begun in 1973, but finally mailed in 1975:

This is not the first occasion on which you have represented my character as deranged by "mental trauma" following the law action brought against me by Samuel Winston (to whom you introduced me) when he was a partner in a small blouse house "Milmont," when I had provided national press contacts and retail interests which drew the world to his door….

There was no question that you instigated this law suit against me, and subsequently passed off in the women's page press (over which you secured a strangle-hold) as one brought against the Winston firm, contrary to the record, by myself….

You came to tea with my wife and my-self two weeks before the trial to assure us that you were willing and able to have the action withdrawn, in the belief that it could disgrace the manufacturing industry and one of your clients from whom you received double revenue….

No less than eight contracts between Charles James Services and manufacturers of many different varieties of apparel later waited finalization. Negotiations were in each case discontinued, on my agent being informed of your having said things about my mental condition which would have made any business with me a dangerous venture....

Shortly after the court's decision in my favor, you procured... a Coty award for [my opponent] Mrs. Roxane Kamenstein's embroideries [which everyone knows she buys ready-made].... Thus you mulcted the Coty Award of any valid claim to reward creativity in fashion....

I consider you and those you have persuaded to work to your advantage as the prime factor in the continuing disintegration of the apparel manufacturing industry in New York City....

With regard to damaging remarks you are credited with having made about me...My record of achievement proves that I have never been or am out of my mind....

The missive is signed "Yours truly, Charles James," and there is a postscript:

P.S. Your business, as many see it, consists of publicizing plagiarism, a different form of piracy; where when proven, the damages are up to the court to assess—and when the guilty is shown to act in collaboration with two other persons for the gain of all concerned, they are automatically tripled.[602]

Eleanor had been advised by her lawyers to discourage Charles by ignoring his attacks. And there is no copy of a response.

"I think the anger," William Ivey Long concluded, "somehow kept him alive. There was always talk of scores of lawyers on call though I never saw any. But Charles was highly competitive at all levels, and it could be wearing,"[603] William continued, remembering a lunch to which Charles arrived an hour late, announcing that he had already eaten at White Castle, and then spent the rest of the time praising White Castle hamburgers as his friends (perforce) ate something else.[604]

In a further, more public attempt to redress his "tarnished" reputation, Charles also decided to write his own version of his character and history and published the autobiographical article, "A Portrait of a Genius by a Genius" in the July 1974 issue of *Nova,* a "politically radical, beautifully designed, intellectual" British women's magazine.[605] Subtitled "Charles James as Seen by Himself and His Friends," the article is accompanied by photographs, including the one Cecil took of Nancy for their wedding present, and Antonio's drawings of some of Charles's greatest designs.[606]

This career summary is peppered with praise and also disarmingly charming, frank comments and little funny stories by those who knew him well. Philippa Barnes, a former assistant in 1930s London, is quoted as saying, for example:

> Charles was a genius, but impossible. He had his own ideas for designs and fitted them to the customers whether they liked them or not. He had rows with everyone. One of the cutters in the workroom of the Bruton Street salon said to me, "Il s'appelle une maison de couture mais c'est une maison de torture." Once I went with Charles to get some special feathers for costumes he was making for Ivor Novello, and the supplier was explaining how this type of feather came from the female hummingbird, the other from the male. Charles said, "Please, Mr. Botibol, do not confuse me with the sex of hummingbirds. I have enough difficulty myself." He loved shocking people. He used to get terrible hiccups, and once when he had them for two days he thought he was going to die. So he had his bed brought into the small salon surrounded by flowers, with Charles in the middle hiccupping away as if it were a gangster's funeral.[607]

Mrs. Vere French, a journalist and model, reported:

> Dior told me he considered him the greatest talent of his generation. But he was impossible in every possible way. I went to Paris for a George VI visit there in the 1930s. I was covering it for a newspaper, but going to all the parties as well, so Charles had lent me a dress to wear for the big reception. When I unpacked it I found it was unlined and had no petticoat, so instead I wore a dress by Victor Stiebel. Charles was furious. I told him I couldn't wear it because

it was see-through and had no petticoat. He said it was *meant* to be see-through. Only Charles could envisage someone going to a royal reception…in a completely transparent dress.[608]

In 1975, the year he was so conspicuously omitted from Diana Vreeland's "American Women of Style" show, Charles James became the only designer in history to receive a Guggenheim Fellowship.

The award of fifteen thousand dollars was granted to him for a book about his dressmaking techniques, which Charles never finished. But his proposal, in which he imagined a "mathematical & geometric analysis of the shape of apparel as it relates to the body in movement," was spectacular. Upon reading it, Richard Oldenburg, then president of the Museum of Modern Art in Manhattan and one of the judges, noted, "His extraordinary talents, as well as his special devotion and commitment to his profession, have been pioneering in a field in which commercial considerations sometimes obscure the essential qualities of extraordinary creativity, [Charles James's] invention of form…raises craftsmanship to the level of art." (Richard later admitted he had met Charles only once, "but he seemed very nice."[609])

The New York School artist Robert Motherwell, who served with Oldenburg on the Fellowship Committee, remarked, "I have never met him—I don't particularly need to—but I think Charles James is a genius…the drawings which he submitted are more powerful and more to the point than any of the works submitted by 'regular artists,' that is, painters and sculptors."[610] William Segal, publisher of *American Fabrics and Fashions*, also wrote in support of the Guggenheim.

That June, with Homer Layne's help, Charles James opened a comprehensive retrospective at the Everson Museum of Art in Syracuse, New York, which included over two hundred of Charles's original drawings, fifty of Antonio's beautiful sketches, together with photographs of Charles's dresses, his sculpted jewelry molds, and the famous Butterfly sofa.

Elaine Louie, then a young fashion editor, was invited by Juan and Antonio to escort Charles to the June 20 opening. She wore a black silk bias-cut dress that Charles had designed in the 1930s, with short kimono sleeves and a back that was cut into a deep V. Black silk sashes attached at the waist fluttered behind her when the wind blew. "It was the most beautiful erotic dress. The fabric slithered over the body, just barely touching the skin,"[611] she remembered thirty-nine years later. Charles wore a navy blue blazer and tan pants. Her "job," as Louie wrote in the *New York Times,* was "to flatter him on his drawings and smile benevolently as people came up to congratulate him. I was to prevent him from mentioning either Halston or Ms. Vreeland." Juan, Antonio, Homer Layne, the artist Paul Caranicas, Jerry Hall, and Sputnik, the beagle, were all part of Charles James's entourage.

But when Charles went by the museum early to preview the show, he was unhappy. Charles was very specific about how he wanted everything hung. "It was very hard for him to accept the fact that other people thought they knew better," Paul Caranicas told Alina Cho.

[T]he curator of the show—I remember her name, Trop Blumberg, Mrs. Trop Blumberg, because he enunciated it in disdain to her, when he saw she had hung something in the wrong place. It was a drawing she had hung in the entrance as you came into the museum and he felt it shouldn't be there because it was drawn by Antonio. So he took it off the wall. It was the opening night that night and he walked out of the museum with it. He said, "This is mine, and I'm not having it here," and we had to chase him down the road and convince him that he should take it back and they would put it in another place. And he said, "Mrs. Trop Blumberg did it." It went back up, but not where she put it.[612]

Finally, the party for the opening got going, and everyone was in a much better mood. "Ms. Hall, tall, lithe and bubbling," wrote Elaine Louie, "with that outsized Texas charm, swanned about the museum wearing another Charles James dress, under a glamorous white eiderdown jacket from 1938. I gaped at the jacket and said how wildly beautiful it was. Halfway through the dinner as plates were being cleared from the table, Charles said, 'I think you should wear that jacket now.' He went over to Ms. Hall and asked her for that jacket. Then he held it out for me to slip on. It was my first and last time wearing haute couture. It was a singular moment, to be clothed in pure silk, inside and out, head to toe, a white puff of a jacket over a slink of a black dress. I was in a state of bliss."

By 1976 Charles seemed to be taking the decade in stride. "The 1970s, particularly the 1970s in Manhattan," reminisced Beauregard Houston-Montgomery, a neighbor of Charles's at the Chelsea who remembers being groped in the elevator by Jean-Paul Sartre for Simone de Beauvoir's amusement, "were pretty wild. And everyone was doing drugs. So Charles didn't stand out in any particular way for that—if there was that." Beauregard said, "Given the general state of affairs there, Charles's habits didn't seem at all bad."[613]

"There was always someone, usually someone famous, stopping by," reminisced Rory Denis,[614] whom Charles hired as an errand boy after meeting him in the urinal at Mr. Chow's. William Ivey Long remembered the same: "Elsa Peretti would drop by—this is when she was in her heyday at Tiffany—Paloma Picasso, and some of the de Menils: fancy ladies coming in with dark glasses. He didn't like many people."[615]

"We had a very up and down relationship," Rory recalled. "I locked Couri Hay's fiancée, Zandra Rhodes, in or out, by accident, when she came by, I think it was for a fitting. I can't remember which. And then there was this party for Salvador Dalí's wife, Gala, at the St. Regis and I was supposed to present Gala with sunflowers. Instead, I ended up having a fight with Dalí. We got into a tug of war over the bouquet. Charles was pretty good about it. He took me to a French restaurant to calm me down afterwards." Rory remembered that Charles paid him "sporadically."

"He was generous and he was kind. He even bought a fur coat for himself when I was in school, a brown bearskin coat. And he insisted that I take it. I didn't know what I did to deserve it, but he actually insisted. You know, he would not take it back. I still have it to this day. He was kind and considerate. A lot of people don't...you know, the stories that go around. I don't think they have that image of him," Homer Layne insisted.[616]

"Charles was a very warm and caring person. I think that is often overshadowed by the number of feuds and lawsuits,"[617] Barbara Hodes, an apprentice, wrote. To Barbara, Charles was always very supportive.

After he lent her a dress to wear on a date with the artist Larry Rivers to an opening at the Beaubourg, Charles sent her a letter requesting details. He wanted to know "what I felt like wearing the 'exceedingly fitted and stiffened brocade…that was so comfortable to move in.'" He said he was planning to put her response in a book of endorsements and that he was very proud of her appearance and poise "that was emphasized by the knowledge that you looked better than any of the women present….Mrs. Birley McKendry [Maxime de la Falaise], who chooses to call herself by the name of a husband she never ceases betraying, must have been FURIOUS, just as I think you were correct in assuming Mme. de Menil was at the realization that you out-shone her in looks, youth and silhouette….Larry should have been proud."

And when Barbara found herself despondent between jobs, in a note that he headed "[from the] Chelsea bordello," he wrote to her:

> Your real love, I've found out in knowing you better: is work…curiosity and craftsmanship. If you are not working for someone else right now work for yourself. Later you will sell the results….[D]on't give way to self-indulgence in any way.
>
> Come to me when you want. Do spend time in my workroom doing your thing. This will encourage me to my own thing; too….A job will come to you.[618]

"Charlie always believed in what I was doing. He was the one who pushed me and gave me the courage to make my work LARGE,"[619] remembered the sculptress Elizabeth Strong de Cuevas gratefully.

Charles also enjoyed simple pleasures. "He liked architecture," said Homer. "We would drive all over the city. And if a new building went up, he could tell me what building was there before, and maybe the one before that. And he liked the South Street Seaport. A member of his family, like a great-great-grandfather, actually had a business there, in shipping….We spent a lot of time there."[620]

Rory remembered, "Lou Reed worked for Charles briefly as an errand boy before I got there, and Charles loved playing 'Walk on the Wild Side' over and over on the jukebox of the neighborhood greasy spoon on Twenty-third Street where we would go to order his eggs.

Charles also had another little ritual: every Christmas, he would go down to Carnegie Hall to exchange gifts with a black elevator man there—whose name was also Charles James."[621]

Charles remained very au courant. "When I saw Charles in the lobby of the Chelsea," Anton Perich remembers, "I thought he was the youngest person I had ever seen. Charles was the youngest person. And Sputnik was the oldest dog."[622] Rory added, "Charles was very fashionable—I think I will remember him forever, lying in the bathtub, shaving carefully, but always without a mirror. He liked to dress simply: a T-shirt and a leather jacket, but he was also very up-to-date. He wore hip boots with little Cuban heels and he loved musk from Caswell-Massey."[623]

When Couri took him to the opening of Studio 54 in 1977—well after he stopped being at all famous—it was Charles James's picture that the *Post,* which was covering the party, published in a full-page black-and-white shot. Charles was wearing a wonderful big-brimmed hat. It was the *way* he wore his hat, his friend Couri, who had started filming the last twenty hours of video of Charles in 1975, remembered: "He had great natural style."[624]

"Mr. James was a shortish man who loved wearing trendy clothes, which, at the time, were silk shirts, hip hugger pants, and Cuban heels," Ivey Long told Eve MacSweeney, who interviewed him for *Vogue.* "I would pin the hems of his pants and adjust his cuffs and his collars. He had white skin and black eyebrows and it looked as though he dyed his hair with shoe polish. I later realized that he used the type you were meant to wash out. But he left it in, so it would drip and drool down his neck like Gustav von Aschenbach in *Death in Venice.*"[625]

Ivey Long tried to cook for and feed Charles, but all Charles really enjoyed eating was "corned beef sandwiches."[626] "He ate lots of eggs," Rory also reported, admitting that food was always an issue, "and when we went out for brunch on Sunday to a place like David's Potbelly, he would always order the omelet."[627] "He didn't take care of himself at all," William Ivey Long remembered. "He didn't eat well, never saw a doctor. I felt he was daring his body, as well as the world, to appreciate him."[628]

Charles, who had been complaining to Couri in the tapes about his bad colds and inadequate temperature control at the Chelsea, wrote in the summer of 1978, "My room has closed on me. During the heat wave I virtually lived in the dark between the crippled air conditioner and a fan, the sweat drying on me as soon as it poured forth to inundate me.... My great soporific was to re-read over and over again the records of 'A Lady in Waiting' during the last days of Queen Victoria, feeling by doing so that disasters do not belong to any one period.... Now all faces are tinged with gloom and despair."[629]

In the early fall of 1978, weak from drug misuse and irregular living, Charles fell ill. After several days, on the evening of September 22 he was taken by ambulance to the Cabrini Medical Center —but not before keeping the ambulance attendants waiting as he adjusted his makeup to freshen his appearance. When they asked him to identify himself, he answered, "It may not mean anything to you, but I am what is popularly regarded as the greatest couturier of the Western world." It was the last title he invented, and he bestowed the crown on himself.

By two o'clock the next morning, Charles James, racked with bronchial pneumonia and arteriosclerosis, was dead.

Homer Layne, who took care of the funeral services, had the body cremated and arranged visiting at Frank E. Campbell, on Madison Avenue and Eighty-Second Street, near the Metropolitan Museum of Art. There was a press strike on September 23, and the *New York Times* never published his obituary, but Charles's good friend Bill Cunningham wrote of him in a tribute for the *SoHo Weekly News*, "Charles James was the poet laureate of fashion."[630]

True to character, Charles James, who had intended to leave all of his estate to the care of Homer Layne, had also insisted on writing his own will, which did not pass probate. His assets went instead to his children, who gave them to their mother. And Nancy, wishing to carry out Charles's intentions, returned everything to Homer Layne.

Homer personally preserved Charles James's archives, including ninety pieces of clothing and 1,600 drawings, for over thirty-five years. In 2013, he donated the bulk of this material to the Costume Institute at the Metropolitan Museum of Art in advance of the 2014 Charles James retrospective, "Beyond Fashion."

Charles James's work has perhaps been the subject of more one-person museum shows than that of any other fashion designer.

These include: "A Decade of Fashion" at the Brooklyn Museum, in 1948; "Charles James" at the Everson Museum of Art in Syracuse, in 1975; Homer Layne's "Collection of Charles James Fashions" at MoMA PS1, in 1981; "The Genius of Charles James" at the Brooklyn Museum, in 1982; "Charles James, Genius Deconstructed" at the Chicago History Museum, in 2011; "Charles James: Beyond Fashion" at the Metropolitan Museum of Art, in 2014; and "Charles James: A Thin Wall of Air" at the Menil Collection in Houston, in 2014.

If his work remains ongoing, mysterious, and fascinating, it is because Charles James was, as Austine Hearst correctly described him, someone who inspired. "[He] trained Scaasi, Adolfo, Halston, many others," she remembered.[631] "They all went to school with Charles James. He influenced a lot of young people. He gave out a lot of ideas... he was a wellspring, his place [is] secure."[632]

"In reflection," Charles James wrote of his own legacy, "it seems to me that every man has in him a dream, the realization of which may or may not cost him his all; and....it is the dream that is remembered—rather than facts."

CREDITS

ACKNOWLEDGMENTS

I would especially like to thank my agent, Andrew Wylie, and my editor, Alessandra Lusardi. Without their help this book would not be.

AUTHOR'S NOTE

THE PRIMARY SOURCE for information on Charles James is Charles James himself, through the archives he created, the tapes he made with R. Couri Hay and Anton Perich, and information he provided to Alfred Allan Lewis, Constance Woodworth (*Miss Elizabeth Arden*, 1972), and Elizabeth Ann Coleman (*The Genius of Charles James*, 1982) for their published work on his life. I am also very grateful to Jan Glier Reeder for the invaluable timeline she provided in *Charles James: Beyond Fashion*, 2014, and to the Victoria & Albert Museum and Elsa Schiaparelli for her colorful and spirited self-portrait, *Shocking Life*, 1954.

BIBLIOGRAPHY

BOOKS

Albee, Edward. "Mrs. De Menil's Liquor Closet." In *Stretching My Mind: The Collected Essays of Edward Albee*. New York: Da Capo Press, 2009.

Ballard, Bettina. *In My Fashion*. New York: D. McKay, 1960.

Baxter-Wright, Emma. *The Little Book of Schiaparelli*. London: Carlton Books, 2012.

Beaton, Cecil. *The Glass of Fashion*. Garden City, NY: Doubleday, 1954.

_____. *The Strenuous Years: Diaries, 1948–1955*. Worthing, UK: Littlehampton Book Services Ltd., 1973.

Beaton, Cecil, and Hugo Vickers. *The Unexpurgated Beaton: The Cecil Beaton Diaries as He Wrote Them, 1970–1980*. New York: Knopf, 2003.

Beaton, Cecil, Walter Hardy, and Hugo Vickers. *Cecil Beaton: Portraits and Profiles*. London: Frances Lincoln, 2014.

Bernier, Olivier. *Fireworks at Dusk: Paris in the Thirties*. Boston: Little, Brown, 1993.

Blumenthal, Ralph. *The Stork Club: America's Most Famous Nightspot and the Lost World of Café Society*. Boston: Little, Brown, 2000.

Bluttal, Steven, and Patricia Mears. *Halston*. London: Phaidon, 2001.

Burns, Cherie. *Searching for Beauty: The Life of Millicent Rogers*. New York: St. Martin's Press, 2011.

Cassini, Igor, and Jeanne Molli. *I'd Do It All Over Again: The Life and Times of Igor Cassini*. New York: Putnam, 1977.

Castle, Charles. *Oliver Messel: A Biography*. New York: Thames and Hudson, 1986.

Churchill, Winston. *The Gathering Storm*. Boston: Houghton Mifflin, 1948.

Churchill, Winston, and William Manchester. *My Early Life, 1874–1904*. New York: Scribner, 1996.

Cocteau, Jean. *The Journals of Jean Cocteau*. Bloomington: Indiana University Press, 1956.

Cocteau, Jean, and Pierre Chanel. *Past Tense: Diaries*. Vol. 1. San Diego: Harcourt Brace Jovanovich, 1987.

_____. *Past Tense: Diaries*. Vol. 2. San Diego: Harcourt Brace Jovanovich, 1987.

Coleman, Elizabeth A. *The Genius of Charles James*. New York: The Brooklyn Musuem, 1982.

Coudert, Thierry. *Café Society: Socialites, Patrons, and Artists, 1920–1960*. Paris: Flammarion, 2010.

Cox, Michael J. *Masten Gregory: Totally Fearless, Two Decades of Motorsport through the Spectacles of the Kansas City Flash*. n.p.: MTCA Creations, 2004.

Crimp, Douglas. "Way Out on a Nut." In *Before Pictures*. Chicago: University of Chicago Press, 2016.

Crosland, Margaret. *Jean Cocteau: A Biography*. New York: Knopf, 1956.

Davis, Mary E. *Ballets Russes Style: Diaghilev's Dancers and Paris Fashion*. London: Reaktion Books, 2012.

de la Haye, Amy, Lou Taylor, and Eleanor Thompson. *A Family of Fashion: The Messels: Six Generations of Dress*. London: Philip Wilson, 2005.

de Rohan, Dilkusha. "Panorama: Dilkusha by Dilkusha," manuscript autobiography, 1945-53. National Art Library, Victoria and Albert Museum, London.

Fitzgerald, F. Scott. *The Rich Boy*. London: Hesperus, 2005.

Gaines, Steven S. *Simply Halston: The Untold Story*. New York: Putnam, 1991.

Gross, Elaine, and Fred Rottman. *Halston: An American Original*. New York: Harper Collins, 1999.

Hawes, Elizabeth. *Fashion Is Spinach*. New York: Random House, 1938.

Hay, R. Couri. *Charles James Beneath the Dress*. New York: National Arts Club, 2014.

Hearst, William Randolph. *The Hearsts: Father and Son*. San Simeon: San Simeon Books, 2013.

Hearst, Jr., Mrs. William Randolph, *The Horses of San Simeon*. San Simeon: San Simeon Books, 1985.

Helfenstein, Josef, and Laureen Schipsi. *Art and Activism: Projects of John and Dominique de Menil*. New Haven: Yale University Press, 2010.

Hoare, Philip. *Serious Pleasures: The Life of Stephen Tennant*. London: H. Hamilton, 1990.

Koda, Harold, Jan Glier Reeder, Sarah Scaturro, Glenn Petersen, and Ralph Rucci. *Charles James: Beyond Fashion*. New York: Metropolitan Museum of Art, 2014.

Lawrence, D. H. *Mornings in Mexico*. New York: Knopf, 1927.

Lewis, Alfred Allan, and Constance Woodworth. *Miss Elizabeth Arden*. New York: Coward, McCann & Geoghegan, 1972.

Lewis, Alfred Allan. *Ladies and Not-So-Gentle Women*. New York: Viking, 2000.

Lobenthal, Joel. *Radical Rags: Fashions of the Sixties*. New York: Abbeville Press, 1990.

Long, Timothy A., and Leonie Davis. *Charles James: Designer in Detail*. UK: V & A Publishing, 2015.

Martin, Richard. *Charles James*. Paris: Assouline, 2006.

McKinney, Megan. *The Magnificent Medills: America's Royal Family of Journalism During a Century of Turbulent Splendor*. New York: HarperCollins, 2011.

Messel, Thomas, Stephen Calloway, and Sarah Woodcock. *Oliver Messel: In the Theatre of Design*. New York: Rizzoli International Publications, 2011.

Nasaw, David. *The Chief: The Life of William Randolph Hearst*. Boston: Houghton Mifflin, 2000.

Nicolson, Nigel, and Joanne Trautmann, eds. *The Letters of Virginia Woolf, Volume 5, 1932–1935*. New York and London: Harcourt Brace Jovanovich, 1979.

Niemeyer, Daniel Charles. *1950s American Style: A Reference Guide*. Boulder: Fifties Book Publishers, 2013.

Obolensky, Serge. *One Man in His Time: The Memories of Serge Obolensky*. New York: McDowell, Obolensky Inc., 1958.

Philippe, Jullian. *The Snob Spotter's Guide*. London: Weidenfeld and Nicolson, 1958.

Radiguet, Raymond. *Le Bal Du Comte D'Orgel*. France: LGF-Livre De Poche, 1980.

Richardson, John. *Sacred Monsters, Sacred Masters: Beaton, Capote, Dalí, Picasso, Freud, Warhol, and More*. New York: Random House, 2001.

Rose, Francis Cyril. *Saying Life. The Memoirs of Sir Francis Rose*. London: Cassell, 1961.

Schanke, Robert A. *"That Furious Lesbian": The Story of Mercedes de Acosta*. Carbondale: Southern Illinois University Press, 2003.

Scheips, Charlie. *Elsie de Wolfe's Paris: Frivolity Before the Storm*. New York: Harry N. Abrams, 2014.

Schiaparelli, Elsa. *Shocking Life*. London: Dent, 1954.

Shaw, George Bernard. *Man and Superman*. Cambridge, MA: The University Press, 1903.

Sicherman, Barbara, and Carol Hurd Green. *Notable American Women: The Modern Period: A Biographical Dictionary*. Cambridge, MA: Belknap Press, 1980.

Sinclair, David. *Snowdon: A Man for Our Times*. London: Proteus, 1982.

Sitwell, Dame Edith. *Taken Care Of: An Autobiography*. London: Bloomsbury, 2012.

Smith, Amanda. *Newspaper Titan: The Infamous Life and Monumental Times of Cissy Patterson*. New York: Knopf, 2011.

Smith, Jane S. *Elsie de Wolfe: A Life in the High Style*. New York: Atheneum, 1982.

Tapert, Annette, and Diana Edkins. *The Power of Style: The Women Who Defined the Art of Living Well*. New York: Crown, 1994.

Teichmann, Frank. "The Emergence of the Idea of Evolution at the Time of Goethe." Translated by Jon McAlice. In *Interdisciplinary Aspects of Evolution*. Stuttgart: Urachhaus, 1989.

Thin Wall of Air: Charles James. Houston: The Menil Collection, 2014.

Tiffany, John A. *Eleanor Lambert: Still Here*. New York: Pointed Leaf Press, 2011.

Turner, Florence. *At the Chelsea: A Personal Memoir of New York's Most Famous Hotel*. London: Foruli Classics, 2013.

Untermeyer, Louis, ed. *A Treasury of Great Poems*. n.p.: Galahad Books, 2001.

Vickers, Hugo. *Cecil Beaton: A Biography*. Boston: Little, Brown, 1985.

Wadsworth Atheneum. *The Sculpture of Style*. Hartford: Wadsworth Atheneum, 1964.

Ware, Susan, and Stacy Lorraine Braukman. *Notable American Women: A Biographical Dictionary Completing the Twentieth Century*. Cambridge, MA: Belknap Press, 2004.

Waugh, Evelyn. *The Diaries of Evelyn Waugh*. Edited by Michael Davie. Boston: Little Brown, 1976.

Wiser, William. *The Twilight Years: Paris in the 1930s*. New York: Carroll & Graf Publishers, 2001.

Wolf, Peter M. *My New Orleans, Gone Away: A Memoir of Loss and Renewal*. Harrison, NY: Delphinium Books, 2013.

Woodhead, Lindy. *War Paint: Madame Helena Rubinstein and Miss Elizabeth Arden: Their Lives, Their Times, Their Rivalry*. Hoboken, NJ: John Wiley & Sons, 2003.

ARTICLES

1900

"Chum of Lady Curzon Disinherited by Father," *Washington Times*, May 13, 1906, 5.

1910

"Tea Table Talk." *The Teesdale Mercury* (Barnard Castle, UK), March 1, 1911. Accessed May 9, 2016, Teesdale Mercury Archive.

1920

"A Midsummer Night's Dream." *The Harrovian* (Harrow), May 28, 1921, 32.

Time, August 16, 1926, 24.

"The New Hats." *Vogue*, March 2,1929, 54.

"Beauty." *Vogue*, May 25, 1929, 64.

Thalia. "Mrs. C. Barnes Writes Novel on Vacation." *Chicago Daily Tribune*, July 12, 1929, 17.

John, Augustus. "Interior Decoration." *Vogue*, August 3, 1929, 59, 88.

1930

"Boucheron!" *New York Times*, February 16, 1930.

"Polka Dots." *Vogue*, May 10, 1930, 62.

Evening News, London, February 1, 1931.

"On Her Dressing Table." *Vogue*, August 15, 1931, 76.

Flanner, Janet. "Comet." *New Yorker*, June 18, 1932.

Perkins, B. J. "Charles James, a Former Architect, Uses Structural Idea in Designing." *Women's Wear Daily*, February 21, 1933, 17.

"Charles James, London Designer, Presents Models to Trade and English Notables." *Women's Wear Daily*, April 12, 1933, 2.

"Elizabeth Arden Lives in This Charming Setting." *Vogue*, September 15, 1933, 60–61.

"The Living Image." *Vogue*, October 1, 1933, 40–41.

"Daring Surplice Used on Pastel Jersey Gown." *Washington Post*, December 9, 1933, 15.

"Life's Problems Solved." *Harper's Bazaar*, January 1934, 48.

"Summer Siesta Chez Elizabeth Arden in Maine." *Vogue*, June 15, 1934, 66–67,78.

Column, Churchill, Winston. *Daily Mail*, July 1934. www.historynet.com/winston-churchills-prewar-effort-to-increase-military-spending.htm.

Associated Press. "Widow Fights to Operate Big Risk Company." *Southeast Missourian*. July 2, 1935.

"Youthful Widow Fights for Control of Insurance Firm." *Jefferson City Post*, July 2, 1935, 1.

"Shop-Hound Gives and Gives." *Vogue*, December 15, 1936, 74.

"Hair-Raising News." *Vogue*, November 1, 1937, 70.

Column, *Vogue*, May 15, 1938, 62.

Thalia. "Thanksgiving Teas Aid Presbyterian Hospital: Teas Benefit Presbyterian Hospital Fund." *Chicago Daily Tribune*, November 21, 1938, F1.

"Mrs.Ronald Balcom Goes Her Own Sleek Way," *Vogue*, January 1, 1939, 38–39.

"Discoveries in Beauty." *Vogue*, April 1, 1939, 104.

"Elizabeth Arden in Paris." *Vogue*, April 15, 1939, 130–31.

1940

"In You Go…Midriff Bare." *Vogue*, June 1, 1940, 45.

"The Pompadour by Day." *Vogue*, September 14, 1940, 82–83.

Pope, Virginia. "New Pajama-Skirt Is Exhibited Here." *New York Times*, January 3, 1941.

"Color Collaborators." *Vogue*, February 15, 1941, 52–53.

"Mrs. Howard Linn Invites Windsors to Victory Roundup." *Chicago Tribune*, October 5, 1941, 2.

Pope, Virginia. "Formal Fashions by New York Couturiers." *New York Times*, November 9, 1941.

"Marlene Dietrich." *Vogue*, October 11, 1944, 126.

"People Are Talking About. *Vogue*, October 15, 1944, 114–15.

Cass, Judith. "All Tickets Sold for Annual St. Luke's Style Show Today." *Chicago Tribune*, October 18, 1944.

"Mrs. L. B. James, A Belle of Old Chicago, Dies." *Chicago Daily Tribune*, October 28, 1944.

Cassini, Austine. "These Charming People." *Times-Herald* (Washington, DC), November 28, 1944.

"On Elizabeth Arden's New Fashion Floor." *Vogue*, December 15, 1944, 52–55.

Cassini, Austine. "These Charming People." *Times-Herald* (Washington, DC), December 17, 1944.

"Charles James Introduces Original Ideas in Madison Avenue Salon and Workroom." *Women's Wear Daily*, August 20, 1945, 3.

Time, May 6, 1946. Cover.

"Our Austine Models Gown." *Times-Herald* (Washington, DC), October 16, 1946.

"Society Parades at St. Luke's Fashion Show." *Chicago Times*, October 17, 1946, 30.

"Cassini's Sister U-I 'Doll' Choice." *The Hollywood Reporter*, November 21, 1946.

Gabbett, Harry. "Typewriter Given to 'Bootsie,' But Gabbett Grabs It." *The Times-Herald* (Washington DC), November 30, 1946.

"Our Austine Broadcasts from Sickbed." *Times-Herald* (Washington, DC), April 18, 1947.

"Chiffon and Hoops." *Vogue*, July 1, 1947, 69.

Rundvold, Inga. "The Flower Silhouette." *Times-Herald* (Washington, DC), July 17, 1947.

"Lady Leucha Warner," *Times* (London), August 17, 1947, 6.

Porter, Amy. "Young Man of Fashion." *Collier's*, September 20, 1947, 100–1,104.

"Take Another Change." *Vogue*, October 1, 1947, 208–11.

Callahan, Eileen. "Nothing New in New Look, Says Designer, Proving It." *New York Daily News*, April 4, 1948.

"High Priestess of Beauty." *Women's Wear Daily*, April 1948, 6.

Thalia. "Women's Aid of Passavant Plans Painless Benefit." *Chicago Daily Tribune*, May 23, 1948, D1.

"Present Neiman-Marcus Fashion Awards on Sept. 6." *Women's Wear Daily*, August 1948, 6.

"British Weddings." *Life*, August 9, 1948.

Pignatelli, Princess Conchita Sepulveda. "Couple Feted at Reception." *Los Angeles Examiner*, September 7, 1948.

Robin, Toni. "Women in Black." *Holiday*, October 1948.

"Charles James Designs for Millicent Rogers in Museum Display." *Women's Wear Daily*, October 29, 1948, 4.

Pope, Virginia. "Created by Distinguished Designers." *New York Times*, November 10, 1948.

Column, *New York Daily News*, November 12, 1948.

Column, *Harper's Bazaar*, December 1948.

Geare, Mildred Kahler. "Women of Press Visit First Lady." *Baltimore News-Post*. December 8, 1948.

"The World's Best-Dressed Women." *New York Journal-American*, December 26, 1948.

Thalia. "Governor's Inaugural Ball to Be Highlight of Week." *Chicago Daily Tribune*, January 9, 1949, F1.

"Salon Discoveries." *Vogue*, April 1, 1949, 200.

"9 Repeaters on List of 10 Best-Dressed Women." *New York Daily Mirror*, December 27, 1949.

1950

Sheppard, Eugenia. "Charles James Advocates New Lines in Styles." *New York Herald-Tribune*, January 3, 1950, 17.

Cass, Judith. "Fashions and Fancy." *Chicago Daily Tribune*, March 26, 1950, E4.

Fowler, Glenn. "Ohrbach's Will Launch James Fashion Nov. 1." *Women's Wear Daily*, September 13, 1950.

"An Unknown Wins a 'Winnie': Fashion Critics Pick Charles James Who Has Small Public, Big Influence." *Life*, October 23, 1950, 129–30, 132.

"Get New Duties." *Women's Wear Daily*, February 1951, 37.

Cass, Judith. "Recorded at Random." *Chicago Daily Tribune*, August 1, 1951, A1.

Thalia. "Gold Diggers Ball Scheduled for Aug. 24." *Chicago Daily Tribune*, August 12, 1951, E1.

Thalia. "Frontier Nursing Head Typifies Spirit of Yule." *Chicago Daily Tribune*, December 23, 1951, E1.

Hearst, Austine. Column in *The Times-Herald (Washington D.C)*, January 6, 1952.

"Quick Course in Fall Silhouettes." *Vogue*, August 1, 1952, 64.

Thalia. "Junior League to Hear Famed Dress Designer." *Chicago Daily Tribune*, November 30, 1952, F6.

Thalia. "Form Chicago Group to Save Historic Sites." *Chicago Daily Tribune*, December 14, 1952, G2.

James, Charles. "A Designer Pays Tribute to a Fashion Inspiration." *Women's Wear Daily*, January 8, 1953, 3.

James, Charles. "The Romantic Life and Tragic Death of Millicent Rogers." *American Weekly*, March 22, 1953, 12.

"1953 Neiman Marcus Award Winners." *Women's Wear Daily*, August 10, 1953, 4.

Thalia. "Fire Scars Fail to Dim Floral Show." *Chicago Daily Tribune*, August 16, 1953, D8.

Thalia. "Style Show Wednesday Aids Cradle." *Chicago Tribune*, November 15, 1953.

"Tribune Prize Fashions." *Chicago Daily Tribune*, November 29, 1953, G42.

Fowler, Glenn. "Charles James Has New Setup for Wholesale." *Women's Wear Daily*, January 1954, 2, 50.

McCormick, Maryland. "The Distaf Side." *Chicago Daily Tribune*, February 28, 1954, E3.

"Successories." *Vogue*, August 1, 1954, 109.

"They Are Wearing in Chicago: Red and Feather Hats at Tea." *Women's Wear Daily*, September 20, 1954.

"One-Color Costumes at Lunch." *Women's Wear Daily*, September 20, 1954, 5.

Hawkins, Dorothy. "Californian Gets a Fashion Trophy." *New York Times*, October 12, 1954.

"Samuel Winston, Inc. Sues Charles James For $61,341 on Pact." *Women's Wear Daily*, November 4, 1954, 10.

Page, Eleanor. "Charles James' Initial Designs Led to Scandal." *Chicago Tribune*, November 12, 1954, B5.

Pope, Virginia. "Fashion Designer Marks 25th Year." *New York Times*, January 4, 1955, 22.

Hughes, Alice. "A Woman's New York." *Reading Eagle* (Reading, PA), February 7, 1955.

Thalia. "Gala Fetes Blossoming with Spring." *Chicago Daily Tribune*, March 13, 1955, L9.

"Discoveries in Beauty." *Vogue*, April 15, 1955, 136.

"The Beret: New Fashion-Slant." *Vogue*, August 15, 1955, 73.

"White Fur Berets; Tunics." *Women's Wear Daily*, September 15, 1955, 5.

"Harry T. Johnson Joins Corday." *Women's Wear Daily*, November 1955, 19.

Hopper, Hedda. "Looking at Hollywood: Hedda Tells of Celebrities at Convention in Frisco." *Chicago Daily Tribune*, August 22, 1956, B4.

"Charles James Designing Infants' Wear Collection." *Women's Wear Daily*, August 31, 1956, 4.

"Of Things and People." *Women's Wear Daily*, October 1956, 22.

"Fashion Group Spring Show." *Women's Wear Daily*, February 1957, 5.

"Three Ring Benefit." *Life*, February 11, 1957, 119.

Livingstone, Evelyn. "This Is Charles James—Truly a Designer's Designer." *Chicago Tribune*, July 21, 1957, B4.

Cass, Judith. "Charles James Back Home—To Set Up Style Studio." *Chicago Tribune*, April 2, 1958.

Levin, Phyllis Lee. "Paris Sets Pace, But Creative Fashion Talent, Critics Agree, Exists in U.S." *New York Times*, May 20, 1958.

Page, Eleanor. "Cradle Society Presents an 'Angel' for 10 Years of Style Show Benefits." *Chicago Daily Tribune*, June 16, 1959.

1960

Schulz, Barbara. "Well-Known Hair Stylist Will Be Wed." *Chicago Tribune*, September 5, 1960.

"They Are Wearing in Chicago: Wool and Crepe Dresses." *Women's Wear Daily*, September 27, 1960, 4.

"The Calculus of Fashion to Be Taught," *New York Herald Tribune*, October 17, 1960, 16.

"Charles James Launches College Fashion Seminars." *Women's Wear Daily*, October 17, 1960, 4.

"The Ruffle—Its New Private Life." *Vogue*, July 1962, 100.

"American Sports Clothes in Italy." *Vogue*, August 1, 1964, 100–3.

"The Look of Summer Wherever You Are." *Vogue*, June, 1965, 122–23.

"Mrs. Gertrude Dominick Was Banker's Widow Creampuff." *Kansas City Times*, October 13, 1966, 59.

"Of Things and People." *Women's Wear Daily*, September 1967, 23.

Fairfield, John. "Out of Her Time, Lady Ottoline." *Vogue UK*, September 1969, 442–43.

"Lady Ottoline." *Vogue UK*, September 1969, 446–47. Vogue.

1970

Morris, Bernadine. "At Halston, New Fashion Team." *New York Times*, June 6, 1970, 36.

"Miss Elizabeth Arden." *Women's Wear Daily*, September 22, 1972.

Hay, R. Couri. "Charles James" *Interview*, November 1972.

"Charles James, the Majority of One." *American Fabrics and Fashions*, Fall 1973, 19.

Bosworth, Patricia. "Who Killed High Fashion?" *Esquire*, May 1973, 124.

"Top Female Exec at Arden in U.K. Earned Her Perch." *Women's Wear Daily,* June 14, 1974, 14.

James, Charles, et al. "A Portrait of a Genius By a Genius. Charles James as seen by himself and all his friends." *Nova*, July 1974, 44.

"First Lady to Attend Sept. 7 Gala Benefit as Honored Guest." *Sarasota Herald Tribune*, August 30, 1974.

"The Elsa Peretti Phenomenon." *Vogue,* December 1974, 206.

Cunningham, Bill. "Is the New Sub-culture Getting You Down?" *New York Daily News*, February 3, 1975.

Nancy Masten Brown obituary, *Kansas City Times*, March 17, 1975.

Talley, André Leon. "Thoroughly Modern Millicent." *Women's Wear Daily*, April 16, 1976, 16–17.

Cunningham, Bill. "Charles James." *SoHo Weekly News*, September 28, 1978, 33–34.

Lane, Jane F. "Grès Matter." *Women's Wear Daily*, October 6, 1978, 28.

Duka, John. "The Ghost of Seventh Avenue." *New York Magazine*, October 16, 1978, 81–88.

1980

Browning, Dominique. "What I Admire I Must Possess." *Texas Monthly*, April 1983. www.texasmonthly.com/articles /what-i-admire-i-must-possess/.

Turner, Florence. "Remembering Charles James." *Vogue UK*, May 1983.

Esterhazy, Louise J. "Love-'em and Leaf-'em." *Women's Wear Daily*, June 21, 1983, 6.

Moin, David. "De Ribes for Scouts." *Women's Wear Daily*, May 8, 1986, 20.

Glueck, Grace. "The De Menil Family: The Medici of Modern Art." *New York Times*, May 18, 1986. www.nytimes.com/1986/05/18/maga-zine/the-de-menil-family-the-medici-of-modern-art.html?pagewanted=all.

"Girl Scout Green." *Women's Wear Daily*, January 22, 1987, 24.

Morris, Bernadine. "Diana Vreeland, Editor, Dies; Voice of Fashion for Decades." *New York Times,* August 23, 1989. www.nytimes .com/1989/08/23/obituaries/diana-vreeland -editor-dies-voice-of-fashion-for-decades .html?pagewanted=all.

1990

Waters, John. "The Man Who Stayed in Bed." *New York Times*, February 3, 1991. www.nytimes.com/1991/02/03/books/the-man -who-stayed-in-bed.html?pagewanted=all.

"Austine Hearst, of Newspaper Family." *Chicago Daily Tribune*, June 24, 1991, A7.

"Austine M. Hearst, 72, Newspaper Columnist." *New York Times*, June 25, 1991, www.nytimes.com/1991/06/25/obituaries /austine-m-hearst-72-newspaper-columnist.html.

O'Neill, Molly. "Elaine Whitelaw, 77, March of Dimes Backer, Dies." *New York Times,* December 17, 1992. www.nytimes .com/1992/12/17/nyregion/elaine-whitelaw-77 -march-of-dimes-backer-dies.html.

Fine Collins, Amy. "The Powerful Rivalry of Hedda Hopper and Louella Parsons." *Vanity Fair*, April 1997. www.vanityfair.com /hollywood/2016/02/rivalry-hedda-hopper -louella-parsons-gossip-columnists.

Colacello, Bob. "Remains of the Dia." *Vanity Fair*, September 1996. www.vanityfair.com /magazine/1996/09/colacello199609.

Jacobs, Laura. "Gowned for Glory." *Vanity Fair*, November 1998. www.vanityfair.com /news/1998/11/charles-james-couture.

Viladas, Pilar. "Style; They Did It Their Way." *New York Times Magazine*, October 10, 1999. www.nytimes.com/1999/10/10/magazine/style -they-did-it-their-way.html?pagewanted=all.

2000

Cox, Michael. "'The Kansas City Flash': The Lives & Times of Masten Gregory." *Atlas F1.* 2000. Volume 6, Issue 29. www.atlasf1 .com/2000/aut/cox.html.

Owens, Mitchell. "Desert Flower." *New York Times*, August 19, 2001. www.nytimes .com/2001/08/19/magazine/desert-flower.html.

Gerber Klein, Michèle. "With Andy Warhol, Shoes Were Somehow At the Bottom of It All: An Interview with Tom Sokolowski the Director of the Andy Warhol Museum in Pittsburgh" *Shūz*. Fall 2001. Vol. IV, No. 3, 28–31.

Collins, Amy Fine. "The Lady, The List, The Legacy." *Vanity Fair*, April 2004. www.vanityfair.com/news/2004/04/eleanor-lambert200404.

Middleton, William. "A House That Rattled Texas Windows." *New York Times*, June 3, 2004. www.nytimes.com/2004/06/03/garden/a-house-that-rattled-texas-Windows.html.

Franklin, Ruth. "A Life in Good Taste." *New Yorker*, September 24, 2004. www.newyorker.com/magazine/2004/09/27/a-life-in-good-taste.

Muir, Kate. "The Greatest Magazine of All Time." *The Times (UK)*, April 22, 2006. www.thetimes.co.uk/tto/life/article1750562.ece.

Collins, Nancy. "Remembering Dorothy Draper's Legendary Interior Design Style." *Architectural Digest*, May 1, 2006. www.architecturaldigest.com/story/draper-article-052006.

Fuller, Martin. "The Real Menil." *Magazine Antiques*, September 2008. www.themagazineantiques.com/articles/the-real-menil/.

Fox, Margalit. "Maxime de la Falaise, Model, Designer and Muse, Is Dead at 86." *New York Times*, May 1, 2009. www.nytimes.com/2009/05/02/nyregion/02falaise.html?_r=0.

"Maxime de la Falaise." *The Telegraph*, May 3, 2009. www.telegraph.co.uk/news/obituaries/culture-obituaries/5268584/Maxime-de-la-Falaise.html.

2010

Hecht, M. E. "The Cutting Edge." *Vogue*, April 2011, 145.

Slonim, Jeffrey. "Remembering Eleanor Lambert." *Gotham*, March 13, 2012. gotham-magazine.com/remembering-eleanor-lambert.

Trebay, Guy. "Drawn Again to His Shining Light." *New York Times*. August 29, 2012. www.nytimes.com/2012/08/30/fashion/drawn-again-to-the-images-of-the-illustrator-antonio-lopez.html?_r=0.

Nelson, Karin. "Shooting Star." *W Magazine*, September 2012. www.wmagazine.com/fashion/2012/09/antonio-lopez-fashion-illustrator.

Renzi, Jen. "A Pint-Sized Wonder Bar." *Wall Street Journal*, October 5, 2012. www.wsj.com/articles/SB10000872396390444004704578030421178258986.

Janjigian, Robert. "Former model, '92 Ballinger Winner Betsy Kaiser Dies." *Palm Beach Daily News,* March 30, 2013. www.palmbeachdailynews.com/news/news/national/former-model-92-ballinger-winner-betsy-kaiser-dies/nW7X7/.

Karim, Reed. "How the De Menils and Their Art Museum Changed Houston." *Architect Magazine*, June 19, 2013. www.architectmagazine.com/awards/aia-honor-awards/how-the-de-menils-and-their-art-museum-changed-houston_o.

Hay, R. Couri, and Emily McDermott. "New Again: Charles James." *Interview*, September 11, 2013. www.interviewmagazine.com/fashion/new-again-charles-james/.

Rich, Nathaniel. "Where the Walls Still Talk." *Vanity Fair*, October 8, 2013. www.vanityfair.com/culture/2013/10/chelsea-hotel-oral-history

Talley, André Leon. "André Leon Talley Previews Zac Posen's Charles James-Inspired Fall 2014 Collection." *Vogue*, February 2014. www.vogue.com/866720/andre-leon-talley-previews-zac-posens-charles-james-inspired-fall-2014-collection/.

"Transactions." *New York Social Diary*, February 26, 2014. www.newyorksocialdiary.com/social-diary/2014/transactions.

Louie, Elaine. "Charles James and Me." *New York Times*, April 23, 2014. www.nytimes.com/2014/04/24/fashion/charles-james-and-me.html?_r=0.

"The One and Only." *Vogue*, May 1, 2014. 212–17, 266.

Owens, Mitchell. "The Inspiring Style of Millicent Rogers." *Architectural Digest*, May 1, 2014. www.architecturaldigest.com/gallery/millicent-rogers-iconic-style-decorating-slideshow/all.

Fortini, Amanda. "He Was the Einstein of Fashion." *Harper's Bazaar*, May 2, 2014.

www.harpersbazaar.com/culture/features/a1451/charles-james-couture-profile-0214/.

Kron, Joan. "Difficult Genius: My Afternoon with Charles James." *Allure*, May 6, 2014. www.allure.com/beauty-trends/blogs/daily-beauty-reporter/2014/05/charles-james-couturier-remembered.html.

di Marzo, Cindi. "Unravelling the Mystery and Mastery of America's First Couturier." *Studio International*, May 26, 2014. www.studiointernational.com/index.php/unravelling-the-mystery-and-mastery-of-america-s-first-couturier.

"The National Arts Club Presents Charles James: Beneath the Dress." *The Kinsky*, September 4, 2014. www.thekinsky.com/fashion/the-national-arts-club-presents-charles-james-beneath-the-dress/.

"Pictures, Before and After—An Exhibition for Douglas Crimp, Galerie Bucholz, Berlin." *Mousse*, October 15, 2014. moussemagazine.it/for-douglas-crimp-buchholz/.

MacSweeney, Eve. "The Apprentice." *Vogue Met Gala Special Edition*, 2014.

Simon, Stephanie. "The New Whitney: A Look Back." Transcript. *New York 1 News*, April 27, 2015. www.ny1.com/nyc/all-boroughs/the-new-whitney/2015/04/24/the-new-whitney--a-look-back.html.

Bernstein, Jacob. "'Battle of Versailles' Relives 1973 Win for American Fashion." *New York Times*, March 4, 2016. www.nytimes.com/2016/03/06/fashion/battle-of-versailles-relives-1973-winfor-american-fashion.html.

INTERVIEWS

Michèle Gerber Klein would like to thank the following people, who were willing to share with her some of their memories and knowledge of Charles James and/or the most influential people in his world.

Berkson, Bill. Telephone interview. February 2015.

Cox, Michael. Telephone interview. December 2015.

Crenshaw, Mary Ann. Telephone interview. October 2015.

Crimp, Douglas. Telephone interview. December 2014.

Cutler, Laurel. Interview. November 2014.

de Cuevas, Elizabeth. Interviews. March 2008, September 2014, March 2015.

Denis, Rory. Telephone interview. September 2015.

Elia, Ariele. Interview. February 2015.

Gorchov, Ron. Interview. June 2016.

Harris, Jones. Interview. May 2013.

Hartmann, Celia. Interview. May 2015.

Hay, R. Couri. Interview. January 2008.

Hearst, Austin. Interview. March 2015.

Hearst, William R., III. Telephone interview. March 2015.

Hodes, Barbara. Interview. October 2015.

Houston-Montgomery, Beauregard. Telephone interview. September 2015.

Katz, Alex. Telephone interview. February 2015.

Koda, Harold. Interview. February 2015.

Lane, Kenneth Jay. Interview. June 2015.

Layne, Homer. Interview. March 2005.

Long, William Ivey. Interview. January 2015.

Marder, Jon. Interview. August 2015.

McFadden, Mary. Interview. June 2015.

Messel, Thomas. Telephone interview. March 2016.

Messel, Victoria. Telephone interview. March 2016.

Oldenburg, Richard. Telephone interview. April 2015.

Parsons, Brendan, Earl of Rosse. Telephone interview. February 2016.

Peralta-Ramos, Christina Lucia. Telephone interview. February 2015.

Perich, Anton. Interview. January 2008.

Posen, Zac. Telephone interview. June 2015.

Puncher, Sebastian. Telephone interview. June 2015.

Reeder, Jan G. Several interviews. 2015.

Rottman, Fred. Telephone interview. September 2015.

Simpson, Babs. Interview. June 2015.

Smith, Liz. Telephone interview. March 2015.

Steele, Valerie. Several interviews. 2015.

Sutton, Susan. Telephone interview. November 2015.

Vickers, Hugo. Telephone interview. September 2015.

Vollbracht, Michaele. Interview. May 2008.

Webster, Roger. Interview. January 2008.

Whitney, Sondra. Interview. March 2015.

Wolf, Peter. Interview. June 2010.

IMAGES FROM WEB SITES

Chicago History Museum. "Dress." Digital Collection. www.digitalcollection.chicagohistory .org/cdm/ref/collection/p16029coll3/id/117

Chicago History Museum. "Hat." Digital Collection. www.digitalcollection.chicagohistory .org/cdm/ref/collection/p16029coll3/id/1237

Chicago History Museum. "Infanta." Digital Collection. www.digitalcollection.chicagohistory .org/cdm/ref/collection/p16029coll3/id/513.

Chicago History Museum. "Petal." Digital Collection. www.digitalcollection.chicagohistory .org/cdm/ref/collection/p16029coll3/id/103.

Chicago History Museum. "Pouff." Digital Collection.

www.digitalcollection.chicagohistory.org/cdm /ref/collection/p16029coll3/id/556/rec/122.

PAINTINGS

Ernst, Max. *Portrait of Dominique de Menil.* 1934. The Menil Collection, Houston.

John, Augustus. *Portrait of Elizabeth Arden.* 1930.

Matisse, Henri. *Portrait of Mary Hutchinson.* 1936.

PHOTOGRAPHS

Beaton, Cecil. Courtesy of the Cecil Beaton Studio Archive at Sotheby's, London. 1921.

Beaton, Cecil. Courtesy of the Cecil Beaton Studio Archive at Sotheby's, London. 1932.

Beaton, Cecil. Courtesy of The Cecil Beaton Studio Archive at Sotheby's, London. 1933.

Beaton, Cecil. Courtesy of The Cecil Beaton Studio Archive at Sotheby's, London. 1934.

Beaton, Cecil. Courtesy of Menil Archives, The Menil Collection, Houston.

Beaton, Cecil. *Vogue,* June 1, 1948, 98–99, 112–13, 136–37.

Beaton, Cecil. *Harper's Bazaar,* April 1950.

Celanese Corporation of America, 1954.

Cooke, Jerry. 1947.

Courtesy of the Earl of Rosse, Birr Castle Archives, Birr, Ireland.

Courtesy of the Hearst Corporation and Margaret and William Hearst III.

de Meyer, Adolph. *Portrait of Comte Étienne de Beaumont.* 1910.

Hoyningen-Huene, George. *Vogue,* May 15, 1938, 62.

New York Herald-Tribune, 1956.

Parkinson, Norman. *Harper's Bazaar UK,* 1937.

Rawlings, John. *Vogue,* October 1, 1944, 126.

Rawlings, John. *Vogue,* December 1, 1945, 134.

Unknown, 1964. thegenealogyofstyle.files .wordpress.com/2013/05/clockwise-from -bottom-antonio-lopez-kathleen-ingeborg -marcus-cathee-dahmen-and-friend-charles -james-and-juan-ramos-in-1966-photo-by-dick -balarian.jpg.

WEB SITES

Alston, Gary. "Charles James: 'A Personal Memoir with Nancy James' As Told to Gary Alston." House of Retro. 2013. houseofretro .com/index.php/2013/01/25/charles-james-a -personal-memoir-with-nancy-james-as-told-to -gary-alston/.

"At a Glance." The Barstow School. Accessed April 6, 2016. www.barstowschool.org/Page /About.

"Charles James and Johnson & Johnson at the Metropolitan Museum of Art." Kilmer House (blog). May 8, 2014. www.kilmerhouse .com/2014/05/charles-james-and-johnson -johnson-at-the-metropolitan-museum-of-art/.

Chenier, Elise. "Elizabeth Arden." GLBTQ Archive, 2004. http://www.glbtqarchive.com/ssh /arden_e_S.pdf.

Hay, R.Couri. "Charles James: Beneath the Dress." Charles James Designer. 2014. www .charlesjamesdesigner.com/charles-james -beneath-the-dress.html.

"History." The Menil Collection. Accessed May 9, 2016. menil.org/about/history.

"John Wanamker: Who Made America?" PBS.org. Accessed May 9, 2016. www.pbs .org/wgbh/theymadeamerica/whomade /wanamaker_hi.html.

"Lady Leucha Diana Warner (née Maude)." National Portrait Gallery. Accessed May 9, 2016. www.npg.org.uk/ collections/search/person/mp136428/ lady-leucha-diana-warner-nee-maude.

"A Louis XV Cream-Painted Panelled Room." Sale May 20, 2008, Christie's, Rockefeller Plaza, New York. www.christies.com/lotfinder /furniture-lighting/a-louis-xv-cream-painted -panelled-room-four-5065821-details.aspx.

"Lyric Opera—Civic Opera House History." Lyric Opera. Accessed July 11, 2016. www .lyricopera.org/about/history/civicoperahistory.

"Pavel Tchelitchew (1898–1957) Portrait of Edulji Dinshaw." Sale April 24, 2009, Christie's, Rockefeller Plaza, New York. www.christies .com/lotfinder/drawings-watercolors/pavel -tchelitchew-portrait-of-edulji-dinshaw-5195800 -details.aspx.

Sutton, Susan, Harold Koda, Amanda Harlech, Lady, and William Middleton. "Dangerous Ideas: Charles James and the de Menils." Lecture, the Menil Collection, Houston, May 31, 2014. www.menil.org/exhibitions/36 -a-thin-wall-of-air-charles-james.

VIDEOS

Caranicas, Paul. "Recalling Charles James: Paul Caranicas." Interview by Alina Cho. Metropolitan Museum of Art. www .metmuseum.org/metmedia/audio/exhibitions /recalling-charles-james-paul-caranicas.

Devon Dikeou: Not Quite Mrs. De Menil's Liquor Closet. Directed by Heinrich Schmidt. Vernissage TV. December 18, 2012. vernissage .tv/2012/12/18/devon-dikeou-not-quite-mrs-de -menils-liquor-closet-nada-miami-beach-2012/.

de Menil, Christophe. "Recalling Charles James: Christophe de Menil." Interview by Alina Cho. Metropolitan Museum of Art. www .metmuseum.org/metmedia/audio/exhibitions/ recalling-charles-james-christophe-de-menil.

Eleanor Lambert: Defining Decades of Fashion. Produced by Look TV. Performed by Eleanor Lambert. November 21, 2013. youtu.be/inaLhwknn0g.

Hay, R. Couri. "The Charles James Story 1 with R. Couri Hay." Interview by Michèle Gerber Klein. YouTube. January 16, 2008. www.youtube.com/watch?v=jxGHaR5QXp0.

Hay, R. Couri. "Recalling Charles James: R. Couri Hay." Interview by Alina Cho. Metropolitan Museum of Art. www.metmuseum.org/metmedia/audio /exhibitions/recalling-charles-james-r-couri-hay.

Hecht, Mary Ellen. "Recalling Charles James: Mary Ellen Hecht." Interview by Alina Cho. Metropolitan Museum of Art. www .metmuseum.org/metmedia/audio/exhibitions /recalling-charles-james-mary-ellen-hecht.

Layne, Homer. "Recalling Charles James: Homer Layne." Interview by Alina Cho. Metropolitan Museum of Art. www .metmuseum.org/metmedia/audio/exhibitions /recalling-charles-james-homer-layne.

Peretti, Elsa. "Recalling Charles James: Elsa Peretti." Interview by Alina Cho. Metropolitan Museum of Art. www .metmuseum.org/metmedia/audio/exhibitions /recalling-charles-james-elsa-peretti.

Strong-Cuevas, Elizabeth. "Recalling Charles James: Elizabeth Strong-Cuevas." Interview by Alina Cho. Metropolitan Museum of Art. www .metmuseum.org/metmedia/audio/exhibitions /recalling-charles-james-elizabeth-strong-cuevas.

Tiffany, John. "Eleanor Lambert: Still Here." Library of Congress. www.youtube.com /watch?v=1W4JOF0NHLc.

YEARBOOKS

Barstow School. 1938 Yearbook. Kansas City, MO: Graduating Class of 1938, 1938. Barstow School Archives.

Barstow School. 1939 Yearbook. Kansas City, MO: Graduating Class of 1939, 1939. Barstow School Archives.

Barstow School. 1940 Yearbook. Kansas City, MO: Graduating Class of 1940, 1940. Barstow School Archives.

Barstow School. 1941 Yearbook. Kansas City, MO: Graduating Class of 1941, 1941. Barstow School Archives.

Barstow School. 1943 Yearbook. Kansas City, MO: Graduating Class of 1943, 1943. Barstow School Archives.

SPECIAL COLLECTIONS/ PRIVATE ARCHIVES

"Anne, Countess of Rosse: 'The Eccentric Upbringing of a Collector's Daughter,'" unpublished document, early 1980s. A/33/2, Nymans Archive.

Beaton, Sir Cecil. Photographer AAD/1986/13, Volume I–XLVIII. Circa 1922–1980, Special

Box 1, Folder 28, Samuel J. Wagstaff Papers, ca. 1932–985, Archives of American Art, Smithsonian Institution.

Charles James Papers, page 1. The Menil Archives, The Menil Collection.

"Cholly Knickerbocker Says: Society Sees N.Y. Dress Institute's Scintillating Fashion Show for Polio Benefit, Tots in Braces Lend Poignancy." *New York Journal-American*, clipping, 1945. Series 3: Fashion Show, 1945–1970; Publicity,1945, March of Dimes Archives, Fundraising Collection, White Plains, New York.

Collections, National Art Library. Victoria and Albert Museum, London.

Cornforth, John. Address at Anne Countess of Rosse's Funeral, 1992. Privately held by Thomas Messel.

Eleanor Lambert Papers circa 1950–70. Folder F1-7, Spec Coll X 56. Fashion Institute of Technology, State University of New York.

Eleanor Lambert Papers circa 1950–70. Spec Coll X 56, Ruth Preston. Fashion Institute of Technology, State University of New York.

Eleanor Lambert Papers circa 1950–70. Spec Coll US. NNFITSC.214.319-321,330. Fashion Institute of Technology, State University of New York.

Eleanor Lambert Papers circa 1950–70. Spec Coll US. NNFITSC.214.2348-50. Fashion Institute of Technology, State University of New York.

Dominique de Menil about Charles James. Interviewed by Adelaide de Menil, February 14, 1933. The Menil Archives, The Menil Collection.

Gregory, Nancy (Cuerdon). Records ca. 1952–54, Art Students League.

An Interview with Arnold Scaasi. Interviewed by Mildred Finger, May 3, 1989. "Oral History Collection at the Fashion Institute of Technology." Spec Coll TT 139.O73 v 108. Fashion Institute of Technology, State University of New York.

An Interview with Austine Hearst. Interviewed by John F. Touhey, May 15, 1980. "Oral History Collection at the Fashion Institute of Technology." Spec Coll TT 139.O73 V.12. Fashion Institute of Technology, State University of New York.

An Interview with Eleanor Lambert. Interviewed by Phyllis Feldkamp, May 1, 1980. "Oral History Collection at the Fashion Institute of Technology." Spec Coll TT TT139. O73 v.13. Fashion Institute of Technology, State University of New York.

Hay, R. Couri, and Anton Perich. Videotapes of Charles James, ca.1975. Privately held by R. Couri Hay and Anton Perich.

Hearst, Austine. Scrapbook, ca.1930–80. Privately held by Mr. and Mrs. Austin Hearst, New York.

Hodes, Barbara. E-mail to author. October 2015. Privately held by Michèle Gerber Klein, New York.

James, Charles, "Chicago papers were all full of Paul Poiret's imminent visit…" Typescript memoir, Layne gift, James Collection, Metropolitan Museum of Art.

James, Charles, and Jean Cocteau. "Evening Dress." Printed Silk Evening Dress 1938–1939, T.274–1974, T& F Collection, Victoria and Albert Museum, London.

James, Charles. Letter to Barbara Hodes, ca. 1973. Privately held by Barbara Hodes.

Charles James. Letter to Cecil Beaton, July 29, 1973. Cecil Beaton Collection. Special Collections, St. John's College. Cambridge University.

Charles James. Letter to Cecil Beaton, July 30, 1973. Cecil Beaton Collection. Special Collections, St. John's College. Cambridge University.

James, Charles. Letter to Eleanor Lambert. n.d. Privately held by Bill Berkson.

James, Charles. Letter to Marilyn Bender, n.d. Layne Gift, Charles James Collection, Metropolitan Museum of Art.

James, Charles. Letter to Millicent Rogers, January 3, 1951. Millicent Rogers Museum. Taos, NM.

James, Charles. Letter to Millicent Rogers, n.d. Millicent Rogers Museum. Taos, NM.

James, Charles. Letter to Philippa Barnes. n.d. Transcription #0019, 1939, archive of letters written by Charles James to his London assistant, Philippa Barnes, between August and April 1939, Victoria and Albert Museum, London.

James, Charles. Manuscript for autobiography, *Beyond Fashion*, 1978. MS, Gift of Homer Layne, Charles James Collection, Metropolitan Museum of Art, p. 7.

James, Charles. Manuscript for autobiography, *Beyond Fashion,* "TEXTILE SUBSIDY," 1978. MS, Gift of Homer Layne, Charles James Collection, Metropolitan Museum of Art.

James, Charles notes on designs drawn by Antonio Lopez prior to Electric Circus show, ca. 1969. Charles James donor files, Victoria and Albert Museum, London.

James, Charles. Sketch. "One Touch of Genius: A New Posture in Fashion Created by Charles James." Layne Gift, Charles James Collection, Metropolitan Museum of Art.

James, Charles. Telegram to Millicent Rogers. August 11,1950. Millicent Rogers Museum.

James, Charles. Telegram to Millicent Rogers. September 26,1951. Millicent Rogers Museum.

James, Charles. "Working Title of a Program Being Worked Out with the Institute of Sound," early proposal for "Sound of Shape and Design." Brooklyn Museum Gift, Charles James Collection, Metropolitan Museum of Art.

Johnson, Philip. Letter to Dominique de Menil, May 2, 1950. The Menil Archives, The Menil Collection.

Kansas City Independent, 1957. The Independent Magazine, Kansas City, MO.

Lodwick, Keith. Assistant Curator, Theatre Collections, "The Film Work of Stage Designer Oliver Messel." V&A Online Journal, Issue No.1, Autumn 2008. Victoria and Albert Museum, London. www.vam.ac.uk /content/journals/research-journal/issue-01 /the-film-work-of-stage-designer-oliver-messel/.

Marder, Jon. E-mail to Michèle Gerber Klein, July 2016. Privately held by Michèle Gerber Klein.

"A Memoir of Charles James' Years in London by Mary St. John Hutchinson: London 1932 to 1938." Typescript memoir. Layne gift, Charles James Collection, Metropolitan Museum of Art.

de Menil, Dominique. Letter to Simone Swan, October 7, 1978. The Menil Archives, The Menil Collection.

Messel, Victoria. Letter to Michèle Gerber Klein, March 2016. Privately held by Michèle Gerber Klein.

Program and Radio broadcast, March of Dimes fashion show cue sheet notes, 1945. Series 3: Fashion Show, 1945–1970, March of Dimes Archives, Fundraising Collection, White Plains, New York.

"Sensational Frocks," *Manchester* (England) *Evening Chronicle.* December 10, 1935. C. B. Cochran Archive. Scrapbook, THM/97, Box 95. Theater and Performance Department, Victoria and Albert Museum, London.

"Sound of Shape and Design: An Educational Project Conceived by Charles James," audiotape collection. "European Reminiscences," interview between Charles James and Princess Helene Obolensky, ca.1966. Layne Gift, Charles James Collection, The Metropolitan Museum of Art.

"Sound of Shape and Design: An Educational Project Conceived by Charles James," audiotape collection. "European Reminiscences," interview between Helene Obolensky and Anne, Countess of Rosse, ca.1966. Layne Gift, Charles James Collection, The Metropolitan Museum of Art.

"Sound of Shape and Design: An Educational Project Conceived by Charles James," audiotape collection. "European Reminiscences," interview between Helene Obolensky, Robert Fraser, Daintrey, and Mary St. John Hutchinson, ca.1966. Layne Gift, Charles James Collection, The Metropolitan Museum of Art.

NOTES

INTRODUCTION

1   George Bernard Shaw, *Man and Superman* (Cambridge, Mass.: University Press, 1903).

2   Michael Vollbracht, interview by author, May 2008.

3   R. Couri Hay and Anton Perich, videotapes of Charles James, ca.1975. Privately held by R. Couri Hay and Anton Perich.

4   John A. Tiffany, *Eleanor Lambert: Still Here* (New York: Pointed Leaf Press, 2011), 119.

5   Hay and Perich, videotapes, 1975.

6   John Duka, "The Ghost of Seventh Avenue," *New York Magazine*, October 16, 1978, 81–88.

7   Charles James, "A Portrait of a Genius By a Genius." *Nova*, July 1974, 45.

8   Richard Martin, *Charles James* (Paris: Assouline, 2006), 7.

9   Duka, "The Ghost of Seventh Avenue," *New York Magazine,* 81–88.

10 Susan Sutton, Harold Koda, Lady Amanda Harlech, and William Middleton, "Dangerous Ideas: Charles James and the de Menils," Lecture, the Menil Collection, Houston, May 31, 2014, www.menil.org/exhibitions/36-a-thin-wall-of-air-charles-james.

11 Zac Posen, telephone interview by author, June 2015.

12 Bill Cunningham, "Charles James," *SoHo Weekly News*, September 28, 1978, 34.

13 Elizabeth A. Coleman, *The Genius of Charles James* (New York: The Brooklyn Musuem, 1982), 23.

14 Harold Koda, Jan Glier Reeder, Sarah Scaturro, Glenn Petersen, and Ralph Rucci. *Charles James: Beyond Fashion* (New York: Metropolitan Museum of Art, 2014), 59. Also Francis Cyril Rose, *Saying Life: The Memoirs of Sir Francis Rose* (London: Cassell, 1961), 74.

15 Nigel Nicolson and Joanne Trautmann, *The Letters of Virginia Woolf, Volume 5, 1932–1935* (New York and London: Harcourt Brace Jovanovich, 1979), 158.

16 Coleman, *The Genius of Charles James*, 11.

17 Charles Castle, *Oliver Messel: A Biography* (New York: Thames and Hudson, 1986), 97.

18 Duka, "The Ghost of Seventh Avenue," *New York Magazine*, 81–88.

19 Coleman, *The Genius of Charles James*, 112.

CHAPTER ONE

20 Ibid., 77.

21 Winston Churchill and William Manchester, *My Early Life, 1874–1904* (New York: Scribner, 1996), 39.

22 Coleman, *The Genius of Charles James*, 77.

23 Koda, et al., *Charles James: Beyond Fashion*, 18.

24 "Mrs. L. B. James, A Belle of Old Chicago, Dies." *Chicago Daily Tribune*, October 28, 1944.

25 Hay and Perich, videotapes,1975.

26 Coleman, *The Genius of Charles James*, 77.

27 Courtesy of Sebastian Puncher at Sandhurst.

28 R. Couri Hay, interview by author, January 2008.

29 Ibid.

30 Laura Jacobs, "Gowned for Glory," *Vanity Fair*, November 1998, http://www.vanityfair.com/news/1998/11/charles-james-couture.

31 "Chum of Lady Curzon Disinherited by Father," *Washington Times*, May 13, 1906, 5.

32 Churchill and Manchester. *My Early Life, 1874–1904,*.

33 Evelyn Waugh, *The Diaries of Evelyn Waugh*. From an unpaginated manuscript.

34 Cecil Beaton, *The Glass of Fashion* (Garden City, NY: Doubleday, 1954), 163.

35 Coleman, *The Genius of Charles James*, 78.

36 "A Midsummer Night's Dream," *The Harrovian* (Harrow), May 28, 1921, Harrow School, 32.

37 Cecil Beaton photograph, 1921. Cecil Beaton Studio Archive at Sotheby's.

38 Rose, *Saying Life*, 358.

39 Hugo Vickers, *Cecil Beaton: A Biography* (Boston: Little, Brown, 1985), 23.

40 Ibid., 22.

41 Coleman, *The Genius of Charles James*, 78.

42 Ibid.

43 Elizabeth de Cuevas. interviews by author, March 2008, September 2014, March 2015.

44 Virginia Pope, "Fashion Designer Marks 25th Year," *New York Times*, January 4, 1955.

45 Coleman, *The Genius of Charles James*, 78.

46 Ibid.

47 Koda, et al., *Charles James: Beyond Fashion*, 17.

48 Hay and Perich, videotapes, 1975.

49 B.J. Perkins, "Charles James, a Former Architect, Uses Structural Idea in Designing." *Women's Wear Daily*, February 21, 1933, 17.

50 Coleman, *The Genius of Charles James*, 78.

51 Vickers, *Cecil Beaton: A Biography*, 116.

52 Hay and Perich, videotapes, 1975.

53 Coleman, *The Genius of Charles James*, 8.

54 Beaton, *The Glass of Fashion*, 184.

55 Jacobs, "Gowned for Glory." *Vanity Fair*, November 1998.

56 Robert A. Schanke, *"That Furious Lesbian": The Story of Mercedes de Acosta* (Carbondale: Southern Illinois University Press, 2003), 164.

57 Koda, et al., *Charles James: Beyond Fashion*, 21.

58 Coleman, *The Genius of Charles James*, 111.

59 "Transactions," *New York Social Diary*, February 26, 2014, www.newyorksocialdiary.com/social-diary/2014/transactions.

60 "Beauty," *Vogue*, May 25, 1929, 64.

61 "The New Hats," *Vogue*, March 2, 1929, 54.

62 "Polka Dots," *Vogue*, May 10, 1930, 62.

63 Duka, "The Ghost of Seventh Avenue," *New York Magazine*, 81–88.

64 Koda, et al., *Charles James: Beyond Fashion*, 21.

65 Harold Koda, in a panel discussion at the Menil Collection, Houston, in 2014, in support of the exhibition "A Thin Wall of Air: Charles James."

66 Cherie Burns, *Searching for Beauty: The Life of Millicent Rogers* (New York: St. Martin's Press, 2011), 131.

67 Coleman, *The Genius of Charles James*, 78.

68 Jean Cocteau, *The Journals of Jean Cocteau* (Bloomington: Indiana University Press, 1956), 50.

69 Coleman, *The Genius of Charles James*, 79.

70 Koda, et al., *Charles James: Beyond Fashion*, 21.

71 "Lyric Opera—Civic Opera House History," Lyric Opera,,accessed July 11, 2016, www.lyricopera.org/about/history/civicoperahistory.

72 William Randolph Hearst, *The Hearsts: Father and Son* (San Simeon: San Simeon Books, 2013), 131.

73 Koda, et al., *Charles James: Beyond Fashion*, 21.

74 "Ridin' High," Cole Porter, 1936.

75 William Wiser, *The Twilight Years: Paris in the 1930s* (New York: Carroll & Graf Publishers, 2001), 34.

76 Winston Churchill, *Daily Mail* (UK), July 1934.

77 Olivier Bernier, *Fireworks at Dusk: Paris in the Thirties* (Boston: Little, Brown, 1993), 8.

78 Coleman, *The Genius of Charles James*, 79.

79 "Boucheron!," *New York Times*, February 16, 1930.

80 Perkins, "Charles James, a Former Architect, Uses Structural Idea in Designing," *Women's Wear Daily*, 17.

81 Coleman, *The Genius of Charles James*, 9.

82 Louis Untermeyer, ed., *A Treasury of Great Poems* (n.p.: Galahad Books, 2001), 1143.

83 John Waters, "The Man Who Stayed in Bed," *New York Times*, February 3, 1991.

www.nytimes.com/1991/02/03
/books/the-man-who-stayed-in
-bed.html?pagewanted=all.

84 Philip Hoare. *Serious Pleasures: The Life of Stephen Tennant* (London: H. Hamilton, 1990), 149.

85 Ibid., 148.

86 Cecil Beaton photograph, in Philip Hoare, *Serious Pleasures: The Life of Stephen Tennant.*

87 "Sound of Shape and Design: An Educational Project Conceived by Charles James," audiotape collection. "European Reminiscences," interview between Charles James and Princess Helene Obolensky, 1966, Metropolitan Museum of Art, Layne Gift, Charles James Collection.

88 Charles James, "A Portrait of a Genius By a Genius," *Nova*, 45.

89 "Lady Leucha Warner," *Times* (London), August 17, 1947, 6.

90 Hermione Lee, *Virginia Woolf* (New York: Alfred A. Knopf, 1996), quoted by John Simkin, "Mary Hutchinson" in *Spartacus Educational*: wwwspartacus-schoolnet.co.uk/ARThutchinson.htm.

91 Ibid.

92 Jullian Philippe, *The Snob Spotter's Guide* (London: Weidenfeld and Nicolson), 1958, 55.

93 Koda, et al., *Charles James: Beyond Fashion*, 22.

94 Princess Dilkusha de Rohan, "Panorama: Dilkusha by Dilkusha," manuscript autobiography, 1945–53. National Art Library, Victoria and Albert Museum, London.

CHAPTER TWO

95 Emma Baxter-Wright, *The Little Book of Schiaparelli* (London: Carlton Books, 2012), 71.

96 Paraphrased from Elsa Schiaparelli, *Shocking Life* (London: Dent, 1954), 5, 6.

97 Ibid., 14.

98 Baxter-Wright, *The Little Book of Schiaparelli*, 9.

99 Schiaparelli, *Shocking Life*, 9.

100 Ibid., 30.

101 Ibid., 39.

102 Baxter-Wright, *The Little Book of Schiaparelli*, 15.

103 Schiaparelli, *Shocking Life*, 42.

104 Ibid.

105 Baxter-Wright, *The Little Book of Schiaparelli*, 27.

106 Schiaparelli, *Shocking Life*, 65.

107 Ibid., 66.

108 Ibid., 67.

109 Ibid., 65.

110 Ibid., 66.

111 Ibid., 230.

112 Ibid., 95.

113 Ibid., 62.

114 Ibid.

115 Ibid., 99.

116 Baxter-Wright, *The Little Book of Schiaparelli*, 17.

117 Ibid., 7.

118 Schiaparelli, *Shocking Life*, 96.

119 Janet Flanner, "Comet," *New Yorker*, June 18, 1932.

120 Hay and Perich, videotapes.1975.

121 Baxter-Wright, *The Little Book of Schiaparelli*, 28.

122 Nicolson and Trautmann, *The Letters of Virginia Woolf, Volume 5*, 158.

123 "Sound of Shape and Design: An Educational Project Conceived by Charles James," audiotape collection. "European Reminiscences," interview between Robert Fraser, Adrian Daintrey and Mary St. John Hutchinson, circa 1966, Metropolitan Museum of Art, Layne Gift, Charles James Collection.

124 "Sound of Shape and Design: An Educational Project Conceived by Charles James," audiotape collection. "European Reminiscences," interview between Helene Obolensky and Anne, Countess of Rosse, circa 1966, Metropolitan Museum of Art, Layne Gift, Charles James Collection.

125 "Daring Surplice Used on Pastel Jersey Gown," *Washington Post*, December 9, 1933, 15.

126 "Life's Problems Solved," *Harper's Bazaar*, January 1934, 48.

127 Koda, et al., *Charles James: Beyond Fashion*, 107.

128 Bernier, *Fireworks at Dusk*, 97.

129 "A Memoir of Charles James' Years in London by Mary St. John Hutchinson: London 1932 to 1938," Typescript memoir. Layne gift, James Collection, Metropolitan Museum of Art.

130 Koda, et al., *Charles James: Beyond Fashion*, 116.

131 Schiaparelli, *Shocking Life*, 71.

132 Coleman, *The Genius of Charles James*. 80.
133 Koda, et al., *Charles James: Beyond Fashion*, 25.
134 Perkins, "Charles James, a Former Architect, Uses Structural Idea in Designing." *Women's Wear Daily*, 17.
135 Koda, et al., *Charles James: Beyond Fashion*, 22.
136 Perkins, "Charles James, a Former Architect, Uses Structural Idea in Designing." *Women's Wear Daily*, 17.
137 Jacobs, "Gowned for Glory," *Vanity Fair*, November 1998, 111.
138 Norman Parkinson, *Harper's Bazaar UK*, 1937.
139 Coleman, *The Genius of Charles James*, 80.
140 Schiaparelli, *Shocking Life*, 74.
141 Ibid.
142 Ibid.
143 Christina Lucia Peralta-Ramos, telephone interview by author, February 2015.
144 Coleman, *The Genius of Charles James*, 16.
145 Charles James, "Chicago papers were all full of Paul Poiret's imminent visit," typescript memoir, Layne gift, James Collection, Metropolitan Museum of Art.
146 Ibid.
147 Koda, et al., *Charles James: Beyond Fashion*, 22.
148 Coleman, *The Genius of Charles James*, 81.
149 Ibid.
150 Hay and Perich, videotapes.1975.
151 Bernier, *Fireworks at Dusk*, 146.
152 Ibid.
153 Coleman, *The Genius of Charles James*, 81.
154 Hay and Perich, videotapes.1975.
155 Charles James and Jean Cocteau, "Evening Dress," Printed Silk Evening Dress 1938–1939, T.274-1974, T& F Collection, Victoria and Albert Museum, London.
156 *Harper's Bazaar*, October 1938, 67.
157 Charles James notes on designs drawn by Antonio Lopez prior to Electric Circus show, circa 1969, Charles James donor files, Victoria and Albert Museum, London. Also Koda, et al., *Charles James: Beyond Fashion*, 30.
158 Schiaparelli, *Shocking Life*, 218.
159 Ibid., 228.

CHAPTER THREE
160 Castle, *Oliver Messel*, 97.
161 Anne Messel, essay, in Coleman, *The Genius of Charles James*, 111–12.
162 Thomas Messel, telephone interview by author, March 2016.
163 Amy de la Haye, Lou Taylor, and Eleanor Thompson, *A Family of Fashion: The Messels: Six Generations of Dress* (London: Philip Wilson, 2005), 94.
164 "Anne, Countess of Rosse, 'The Eccentric Upbringing of a Collector's Daughter,'" unpublished document, early 1980s,
165 Ibid.
166 Ibid.
167 Castle, *Oliver Messel*, 20.
168 Ibid., 19.
169 de la Haye, et al., *A Family of Fashion*, 95.
170 *Evening News*, London, February 1,1931.
171 Thomas Messel, telephone interview by author, March 2016.
172 Keith Lodwick, Assistant Curator, Theatre Collections, "The Film Work of Stage Designer Oliver Messel," V&A Online Journal, Issue No.1 Autumn 2008, Victoria and Albert Museum, London, www.vam.ac.uk/content/journals/research-journal/issue-01/the-film-work-of-stage-designer-oliver-messel/.
173 Thomas Messel, telephone interview by author, March 2016.
174 Ibid.
175 Ibid.
176 Ibid.
177 Victoria Messel, telephone interview by author, March 2016.
178 Castle, *Oliver Messel*, 43.
179 de la Haye, et al., *A Family of Fashion*, 99.
180 Cecil Beaton, courtesy of the Cecil Beaton Studio Archive at Sotheby's, London, 1932.
181 Thomas Messel, telephone interview by author. March 2016.
182 Ibid.
183 de la Haye, et al., *A Family of Fashion*, 109.
184 Beaton, Cecil. Courtesy of The Cecil Beaton Studio Archive at Sotheby's, London. 1933.
185 Castle, *Oliver Messel*, 56.
186 Cecil Beaton, courtesy of the Cecil Beaton Studio Archive at Sotheby's, London, 1934.

187 Sir Cecil Beaton, Photographer
AAD/1986/13, Volume I–XLVIII, circa
1922–1980, Special Collections, National
Art Library, Victoria and Albert Museum,
London.
188 Castle, *Oliver Messel*, 97–98.
189 Victoria Messel, letter to Michèle Gerber
Klein, March 2016. Privately held by
Michèle Gerber Klein.
190 Thomas Messel, telephone interview by
author, March 2016.
191 Castle, *Oliver Messel*, 92.
192 Koda, et al., *Charles James: Beyond
Fashion*, 29.
193 Castle, *Oliver Messel*, 98.
194 "Sensational Frocks," *Manchester*
(England) *Evening Chronicle*, December
10, 1935, C. B. Cochran Archive,
Scrapbook, THM/97, Box 95, Theater and
Performance Department, Victoria and
Albert Museum, London.
195 Castle, *Oliver Messel*, 31.
196 Ibid., 99.
197 de la Haye, et al., *A Family of Fashion*,
180.
198 Anne, Countess of Rosse, essay, in Coleman, *The Genius of Charles James*, 111.
199 Castle, *Oliver Messel*, 86.
200 George Hoyningen-Huene, *Vogue*, May
15, 1938, 62.
201 Koda, et al., *Charles James: Beyond
Fashion*, 29.
202 Ibid.
203 Castle, *Oliver Messel*, 98.
204 Koda, et al., *Charles James: Beyond
Fashion*, 30. Also, Charles James to
Philippa Barnes, Letter, date unknown,
Transcription #0019, 1939, Archive
of letters written by Charles James to
his London assistant Philippa Barnes
between August and April 1939, Victoria
and Albert Museum, London.
205 Castle, *Oliver Messel*, 97.
206 Coleman, *The Genius of Charles James*,
112.
207 Koda, et al., *Charles James: Beyond
Fashion*, 90.
208 Coleman, *The Genius of Charles James*,
112.
209 Bernier, *Fireworks at Dusk*, 3.
210 Ibid., 52.
211 Ibid.
212 Charlie Scheips, *Elsie De Wolfe's Paris:
Frivolity Before the Storm* (New York:
Harry N. Abrams, 2014), 70.
213 Adolph de Meyer, *Portrait of Comte
Étienne De Beaumont*, 1910.
214 Bernier, *Fireworks at Dusk*, 69.
215 Thierry Coudert, *Café Society: Socialites,
Patrons, and Artists, 1920–1960* (Paris:
Flammarion, 2010), 32.
216 Scheips, *Elsie De Wolfe's Paris*, 9.
217 de la Haye, et al., *A Family of Fashion*,
136.
218 *Vogue*, May 15, 1938, 62.
219 Baxter-Wright, *The Little Book of
Schiaparelli*, 57.
220 Ibid.
221 Scheips, *Elsie De Wolfe's Paris*, 56–77.
222 John Cornforth's Address at Anne
Countess of Rosse's Funeral, 1992.
Privately held by Thomas Messel.
223 Bernier, *Fireworks at Dusk*, 312.
224 Scheips, *Elsie De Wolfe's Paris*, 84.
225 Ibid., 86–87.
226 Ibid., 90.
227 Courtesy of the Earl of Rosse, Birr Castle
Archives, Birr, Ireland.
228 Anne, Countess of Rosse, essay, in
Coleman, *The Genius of Charles James*,
111.

CHAPTER FOUR
229 Coleman, *The Genius of Charles James*,
82.
230 Elizabeth de Cuevas, interviews by
author, March 2008, September 2014,
March 2015.
231 "A Louis XV Cream-Painted Panelled
Room," Sale May 20, 2008, Christie's,
Rockefeller Plaza, New York, www.
christies.com/lotfinder/furniture-lighting
/a-louis-xv-cream-painted-panelled-room
-four-5065821-details.aspx.
232 "Pavel Tchelitchew (1898–1957) Portrait
of Edulji Dinshaw," Sale April 24, 2009,
Christie's, Rockefeller Plaza, New York,
www.christies.com/lotfinder/drawings
-watercolors/pavel-tchelitchew-portrait
-of-edulji-dinshaw-5195800-details.aspx.
233 Ralph Blumenthal, *The Stork Club:
America's Most Famous Nightspot and
the Lost World of Café Society* (Boston:
Little, Brown, 2000), 13.
234 Koda, et al., *Charles James: Beyond
Fashion*, 30.
235 Pope, "Fashion Designer Marks 25th
Year," *New York Times*, January 4, 1955.
236 Alfred Allan Lewis and Constance
Woodworth, *Miss Elizabeth Arden* (New

York: Coward, McCann & Geoghegan, 1972), 27.

237 Ibid., 224.

238 Ibid., 128.

239 Alfred Allan Lewis, *Ladies and Not-So-Gentle Women* (New York: Viking, 2000), 400.

240 Hay and Perich, videotapes.1975.

241 Laurel Cutler, interview by author, November 2014.

242 Lewis and Woodworth, *Miss Elizabeth Arden*, 28.

243 Ibid., 127.

244 Ibid.

245 "Elizabeth Arden Lives In This Charming Setting." *Vogue*, September 1933, 60-61.

246 Hay and Perich, videotapes.1975.

247 Lewis and Woodworth, *Miss Elizabeth Arden,* 130.

248 Hay and Perich, videotapes.1975.

249 Lewis and Woodworth, *Miss Elizabeth Arden*, 213.

250 Ibid., 224.

251 Coleman, *The Genius of Charles James*, 82.

252 Ibid., 135.

253 Charles James, "The Romantic Life and Tragic Death of Millicent Rogers," *American Weekly*, March 22, 1953, 12.

254 Jones Harris, interview by author, May 2013.

255 Hay and Perich, videotapes.1975.

256 Lewis and Woodworth, *Miss Elizabeth Arden*, 231.

257 Babs Simpson, interview by author, June 2015.

258 "On Elizabeth Arden's New Fashion Floor," *Vogue*, December 15, 1944, 52–55.

259 Coleman, *The Genius of Charles James,* 93.

260 Ibid., 83.

261 Ibid.

262 Lewis and Woodworth, *Miss Elizabeth Arden*, 232.

263 Koda, et al., *Charles James: Beyond Fashion*, 33.

264 Babs Simpson, interview by author, June 2015.

265 John Rawlings, *Vogue*, October 1, 1944, 126.

266 Hay and Perich, videotapes.1975.

267 Koda, et al., *Charles James: Beyond Fashion*, 33.

268 "People Are Talking About," *Vogue*, October 15, 1944, 114–15.

269 "On Elizabeth Arden's New Fashion Floor," *Vogue*, December 15, 1944, 55.

270 Lewis and Woodworth, *Miss Elizabeth Arden*, 229.

271 Ibid., 232.

272 Ibid.

273 Ibid.

274 Judith Cass, "All Tickets Sold for Annual St. Luke's Style Show Today," *Chicago Tribune*, October 18, 1944.

275 Coleman, *The Genius of Charles James*, 82.

276 Ibid.

277 Lewis and Woodworth, *Miss Elizabeth Arden*, 232.

278 Program and Radio Broadcast, March of Dimes Fashion Show cue sheet notes, 1945. Series 3: Fashion Show, 1945–1970, March of Dimes Archives, Fundraising Collection, White Plains, NY.

279 "Cholly Knickerbocker Says: Society Sees N.Y. Dress Institute's Scintillating Fashion Show for Polio Benefit; Tots in Braces Lend Poignancy," *New York Journal-American*, date unknown, clipping, 1945. Series 3: Fashion Show, 1945–1970, March of Dimes Archives, Publicity, 1945, Fundraising Collection, White Plains, NY.

280 Duka, "The Ghost of Seventh Avenue," *New York Magazine*, 81-88.

281 Jon Marder, e-mail to Michèle Gerber Klein, July 2016. Privately held by Michèle Gerber Klein.

282 Lindy Woodhead, *War Paint: Madame Helena Rubinstein and Miss Elizabeth Arden: Their Lives, Their Times, Their Rivalry* (Hoboken, NJ: John Wiley & Sons, 2003), 293

283 Bernadine Morris, "Diana Vreeland, Editor, Dies; Voice of Fashion for Decades," *New York Times*, August 23, 1989, www.nytimes.com/1989/08/23/obituaries/diana-vreeland-dies-voice-of-fashion-for-decades.html?pagewanted=all.

284 *Time* cover, May 6, 1946.

285 Lewis and Woodworth, *Miss Elizabeth Arden*, 233.

CHAPTER FIVE

286 "On Elizabeth Arden's New Fashion Floor," *Vogue*, December 15, 1944, 134.

287 John Rawlings, *Vogue,* December 1, 1945, 134.

288 R. Couri Hay, "Charles James," *Interview*, November 1972.

289 Coleman, *The Genius of Charles James*, 83.
290 Koda, et al., *Charles James: Beyond Fashion*, 194.
291 Eileen Callahan, "Nothing New in New Look, Says Designer, Proving It," *New York Daily News*, April 4, 1948.
292 Hay, "Charles James" *Interview*, November 1972.
293 Koda, et al., *Charles James: Beyond Fashion*, 34.
294 Christina Lucia Peralta-Ramos, telephone interview by author, February 2015.
295 Burns, *Searching for Beauty*, 13.
296 Ibid., 18.
297 Christina Lucia Peralta-Ramos, telephone interview by author, February 2015.
298 Ibid.
299 Serge Obolensky, *One Man In His Time: The Memories of Serge Obolensky* (New York: McDowell, Obolensky Inc., 1958).
300 Burns, *Searching for Beauty*, 31.
301 Ibid., 34.
302 Ibid., 57.
303 Ibid., 59.
304 "Mrs. Ronald Balcom Goes Her Own Sleek Way," *Vogue*, January 1, 1939, 38–39.
305 Ibid.
306 Schiaparelli, *Shocking Life*, 109.
307 Mitchell Owens, "Desert Flower," *New York Times*, August 19, 2001, www.nytimes.com/2001/08/19/magazine/desert-flower.html.
308 Mitchell Owens, "The Inspiring Style of Millicent Rogers," *Architectural Digest*, May 1, 2014, www.architecturaldigest.com/gallery/millicent-rogers-iconic-style-decorating-slideshow/all.
309 Ibid.
310 Owens, "Desert Flower," *New York Times*, August 19, 2001.
311 Christina Lucia Peralta-Ramos, telephone interview by author, February 2015.
312 Burns, *Searching for Beauty*, 240.
313 Christina Lucia Peralta-Ramos, telephone interview by author, February 2015.
314 Charles James, letter to Millicent Rogers, Millicent Rogers Museum, Taos, New Mexico.
315 Ibid.
316 Beaton, *The Glass of Fashion*, 227.
317 Christina Lucia Peralta-Ramos, telephone interview by author, February 2015.
318 Burns, *Searching for Beauty*, 135.
319 Coleman, *The Genius of Charles James*, 83.
320 Ibid., 82.
321 Burns, *Searching for Beauty*, 135.
322 Duka, "The Ghost of Seventh Avenue," *New York Magazine*, 81–88.
323 Author's research 2006–7, letter from mannequin maker to Charles James, demanding payment, Brooklyn Museum Archives.
324 Jerry Cooke, photograph, 1947, in Coleman, *The Genius of Charles James*, 83.
325 *New York Daily News*, November 12, 1948.
326 Duka, "The Ghost of Seventh Avenue," *New York Magazine*, 81–88.
327 Rose, *Saying Life*, 328.
328 Cecil Beaton, *Vogue*, June 1, 1948, 98–99, 112–13, 136–37.
329 D. H. Lawrence, *Mornings in Mexico* (New York: Knopf, 1927), 175.
330 Owens, "The Inspiring Style of Millicent Rogers," *Architectural Digest*, May 1, 2014.
331 Christina Lucia Peralta-Ramos, telephone interview by author, February 2015.
332 Ibid.
333 Charles James, telegram to Millicent Rogers, September 26,1951, Millicent Rogers Museum.
334 Christina Lucia Peralta-Ramos, telephone interview by author, February 2015.
335 Burns, *Searching for Beauty*, 236.
336 Ibid.
337 Schiaparelli, *Shocking Life*, 109.
338 Charles James, "A Designer Pays Tribute to a Fashion Inspiration," *Women's Wear Daily*, January 8, 1953, 3.

CHAPTER SIX
339 "Maxime de la Falaise." *Telegraph* (London), May 3, 2009, www.telegraph.co.uk/news/obituaries/culture-obituaries/5268584/Maxime-de-la-Falaise.html.
340 Cecil Beaton, *Harper's Bazaar*, April 1950.
341 Ibid.
342 Jacobs, "Gowned for Glory," *Vanity Fair*, November 1998.
343 Charles James, Manuscript for autobiography, *Beyond Fashion*, "TEXTILE SUBSIDY," 1978, gift of Homer Layne, Charles James Collection, Metropolitan Museum of Art, 7.

344 Hugo Vickers, telephone interview by author, September 2015.

345 Michèle Gerber Klein, "With Andy Warhol Shoes Were Somehow At the Bottom of It All: An Interview with Tom Sokolowski, the Director of the Andy Warhol Museum in Pittsburgh," *Shūz,* Fall 2001, Volume IV, No. 3, 28–31.

346 Coleman, *The Genius of Charles James,* 100.

347 Margalit Fox, "Maxime de la Falaise, Model, Designer and Muse, Is Dead at 86," *New York Times*, May 1, 2009, www.nytimes.com/2009/05/02/nyregion/02falaise.html?_r=0.

348 Hay, "Charles James," *Interview,* November 1972.

349 Dominique Browning, "What I Admire I Must Possess," *Texas Monthly*, April 1983, www.texasmonthly.com/articles/what-i-admire-i-must-possess/.

350 Max Ernst, *Portrait of Dominique De Menil*, 1934, The Menil Collection, Houston.

351 Browning, "What I Admire I Must Possess," *Texas Monthly*, April 1983.

352 Ibid.

353 Peter Wolf, interview by author, June 2010.

354 Pilar Viladas, "Style; They Did It Their Way," *New York Times Magazine*, October 10, 1999, www.nytimes.com/1999/10/10/magazine/style-they-did-it-their-way.html?pagewanted=all.

355 Sutton, et al., "Dangerous Ideas: Charles James and the de Menils."

356 William Middleton, "A House That Rattled Texas Windows," *New York Times*, June 3, 2004, www.nytimes.com/2004/06/03/garden/a-house-that-rattled-texas-Windows.html.

357 Ibid.

358 Ibid.

359 Philip Johnson, letter to Dominique de Menil, May 2,1950, The Menil Collection, Menil Archives.

360 Sutton, et al., "Dangerous Ideas: Charles James and the de Menils."

361 Philip Johnson, letter to Dominique de Menil, May 2,1950, The Menil Collection, Menil Archives.

362 This information was requested and received from Christophe de Menil.

363 Christophe told the author this at a dinner party circa 2013.

364 Christophe de Menil, "Recalling Charles James: Christophe de Menil." interview by Alina Cho, Metropolitan Museum of Art, www.metmuseum.org/metmedia/audio/exhibitions/recalling-charles-james-christophe-de-menil.

365 Susan Sutton, telephone interview by author, November 2015.

366 Christophe de Menil, "Recalling Charles James: Christophe de Menil," interview by Alina Cho, Metropolitan Museum of Art.

367 "Thin Wall of Air: Charles James," The Menil Collection, Houston, 2014.

368 The Menil Collection, The Menil Archives, Charles James Papers, Page 1.

369 Christophe de Menil, "Recalling Charles James: Christophe de Menil," interview by Alina Cho, Metropolitan Museum of Art.

370 Hay and Perich, videotapes.1975.

371 Susan Sutton, telephone interview by author. November 2015.

372 William Middleton. "A House That Rattled Texas Windows." *New York Times*, June 3, 2004.

373 Christophe de Menil, "Recalling Charles James: Christophe de Menil," interview by Alina Cho, Metropolitan Museum of Art.

374 Courtesy of the Menil Archives, The Menil Collection, Houston.

375 Christophe de Menil in conversation with Michèle Gerber Klein 2012.

376 "Thin Wall of Air: Charles James," The Menil Collection, Houston, 2014.

377 Jen Renzi, "A Pint-Sized Wonder Bar," Wall Street Journal, October 5, 2012, www.wsj.com/articles/SB10000872396390444004704578030421178258986.

378 Edward Albee, "Mrs. de Menil's Liquor Closet," in Stretching My Mind: The Collected Essays of Edward Albee, Da Capo Press, 2009.

379 Christophe de Menil, "Recalling Charles James: Christophe de Menil," interview by Alina Cho, Metropolitan Museum of Art.

380 Courtesy of the Menil Archives, The Menil Collection, Houston.

381 Josef Helfenstein and Laureen Schipsi, *Art and Activism: Projects of John and Dominique de Menil* (New Haven, CT: Yale University Press, 2010).

382 Peter M. Wolf, *My New Orleans, Gone*

Away: A Memoir of Loss and Renewal (Harrison, NY: Delphinium Books, 2013), 291–92.

383 "History," The Menil Collection, Accessed May 9, 2016, menil.org/about/history.

CHAPTER SEVEN

384 Koda, et al., *Charles James: Beyond Fashion*, 40.

385 Ibid.

386 Liz Smith, telephone interview by author, March 2015.

387 Austin Hearst, interview by author, March 2015.

388 Hearst, *The Hearsts: Father and Son*, 308.

389 "An Interview with Austine Hearst," by John F. Touhey, May 15, 1980, "Oral History Collection at the Fashion Institute of Technology," Spec Coll TT 139.O73 V.12, Fashion Institute of Technology, State University of New York.

390 Ibid.

391 Ibid.

392 Ibid.

393 Igor Cassini, and Jeanne Molli. *I'd Do It All Over Again: The Life and Times of Igor Cassini* (New York: Putnam, 1977), 57.

394 Ibid., 63.

395 Amanda Smith, *Newspaper Titan: The Infamous Life and Monumental Times of Cissy Patterson* (New York: Knopf, 2011), 4.

396 "An Interview with Austine Hearst," by John F. Touhey, May 15, 1980, "Oral History Collection at the Fashion Institute of Technology," Spec Coll TT 139.O73 V.12, Fashion Institute of Technology, State University of New York.

397 Ibid.

398 *Time*, August 16, 1926, 24.

399 Amy Fine Collins, "The Lady, The List, The Legacy," *Vanity Fair*, April 2004, www.vanityfair.com/news/2004/04 /eleanor-lambert200404.

400 "An Interview with Austine Hearst," by John F. Touhey, May 15, 1980, "Oral History Collection at the Fashion Institute of Technology," Spec Coll TT 139.O73 V.12, Fashion Institute of Technology, State University of New York.

401 Cassini and Molli, *I'd Do It All Over Again*, 123.

402 Ibid.

403 Liz Smith, telephone interview by author, March 2015.

404 Hearst, *The Hearsts: Father and Son*, 307.

405 Austine Hearst, essay, in Coleman, *The Genius of Charles James*, 115.

406 "An Interview with Austine Hearst," by John F. Touhey, May 15, 1980, "Oral History Collection at the Fashion Institute of Technology," Spec Coll TT 139.O73 V.12, Fashion Institute of Technology, State University of New York.

407 Austine Cassini, "These Charming People," *Washington Times-Herald*, November 28, 1944.

408 Ibid., December 17, 1944.

409 "Our Austine Models Gown," *Washington Times-Herald*, October 16, 1946.

410 Inga Rundvold, "The Flower Silhouette," *Washington Times-Herald*, July 17, 1947.

411 Nancy Collins, "Remembering Dorothy Draper's Legendary Interior Design Style," *Architectural Digest*. May 1, 2006, www.architecturaldigest.com/story /draper-article-052006.

412 Hearst, *The Hearsts: Father and Son*, 308.

413 Courtesy of the Hearst Corporation and Margaret and Will Hearst III, in Hearst, *The Hearsts: Father and Son*, 397.

414 Ibid., 309.

415 *Harper's Bazaar*, December 1948.

416 Austine Hearst, essay, in Coleman, *The Genius of Charles James*, 113–14.

417 Ibid.

418 "An Interview with Austine Hearst," by John F. Touhey, May 15, 1980, "Oral History Collection at the Fashion Institute of Technology," Spec Coll TT 139.O73 V.12, Fashion Institute of Technology, State University of New York.

419 Austine Hearst, Scrapbook, circa 1930–1980. Privately held by Mr. and Mrs. Austin Hearst, New York.

420 "9 Repeaters on List of 10 Best-Dressed Women," *New York Daily Mirror*, December 27, 1949.

421 Austine Hearst, *Washington Times-Herald*, January 6, 1952.

422 Hay and Perich, videotapes.1975.

423 Bill Cunningham, essay, in Coleman, *The Genius of Charles James*, 108.

424 Mary McFadden, interview by author, June 2015.

425 Koda, et al., *Charles James: Beyond Fashion*, 43.

426 Phyllis Lee Levin, "Paris Sets Pace, But Creative Fashion Talent, Critics Agree, Exists in U.S.," *New York Times*, May 20, 1958.

427 Coleman, *The Genius of Charles James*, 88.

428 Koda, et al., *Charles James: Beyond Fashion*, 193.

429 Ibid., 226.

430 Ibid., 229.

431 "An Interview with Austine Hearst," by John F. Touhey, May 15, 1980, "Oral History Collection at the Fashion Institute of Technology," Spec Coll TT 139.O73 V.12, Fashion Institute of Technology, State University of New York.

432 Austine Hearst, Scrapbook, circa 1930–1980. Privately held by Mr. and Mrs. Austin Hearst, New York.

433 Amanda Fortini. "He Was the Einstein of Fashion," *Harper's Bazaar*, May 2, 2014, www.harpersbazaar.com/culture /features/a1451/charles-james-couture -profile-0214/.

434 Austin Hearst, interview by author, March 2015.

435 Celanese Corporation of America, 1954, in Coleman, *The Genius of Charles James*, 68.

436 "Austine Hearst, of Newspaper Family," *Chicago Daily Tribune*, June 24, 1991, A7.

437 "An Interview with Austine Hearst," by John F. Touhey, May 15, 1980, "Oral History Collection at the Fashion Institute of Technology," Spec Coll TT 139.O73 V.12, Fashion Institute of Technology, State University of New York.

438 Coleman, *The Genius of Charles James*, 114.

439 Celanese Corporation of America, 1954, in Coleman, *The Genius of Charles James*, 68.

CHAPTER EIGHT

440 Coleman, *The Genius of Charles James*, 80.

441 Hay, "Charles James" *Interview*, November 1972.

442 Koda, et al., *Charles James: Beyond Fashion*, 44.

443 Coleman, *The Genius of Charles James*, 175.

444 Ibid., 77

445 Ibid., 91.

446 Sheppard, Eugenia, "Charles James Advocates New Lines in Styles," *New York Herald-Tribune*, January 3, 1950, 17.

447 Coleman, *The Genius of Charles James*, 87–95.

448 Ibid., 93.

449 Ibid., 96.

450 Tiffany, *Eleanor Lambert: Still Here*, 9.

451 Collins, "The Lady, The List, The Legacy," *Vanity Fair*, April 2004.

452 Ibid.

453 Bill Berkson, telephone interview by author, February 2015.

454 Ibid.

455 Collins, "The Lady, The List, The Legacy," *Vanity Fair*, April 2004. Also Bill Berkson, telephone interview by author. February 2015.

456 Collins, "The Lady, The List, The Legacy," *Vanity Fair*, April 2004.

457 As told to the author by Sondra Whitney.

458 Tiffany, *Eleanor Lambert: Still Here*, 281.

459 Alex Katz, telephone interview by author, February 2015.

460 Tiffany, *Eleanor Lambert: Still Here*, 17.

461 Adam Weinberg, Whitney curator quoted in Stephanie Simon, "The New Whitney: A Look Back," *New York 1 News*, April 27, 2015, www.ny1.com/nyc/all-boroughs /the-new-whitney/2015/04/24/the-new -whitney--a-look-back.html.

462 Jon Marder, interview by author, August 2015.

463 Tiffany, "Eleanor Lambert: Still Here." The Library of Congress. https://www .youtube.com/watch?v=1W4JOF0NHLc.

464 Collins, "The Lady, The List, The Legacy," *Vanity Fair*, April 2004.

465 Ibid.

466 Ibid.

467 Tiffany, *Eleanor Lambert: Still Here*, 75.

468 Collins, "The Lady, The List, The Legacy," *Vanity Fair*, April 2004.

469 "An Unknown Wins a 'Winnie': Fashion Critics Pick Charles James Who Has Small Public, Big Influence," *Life*, October 23, 1950, 129–30, 132.

470 Molly O'Neill, "Elaine Whitelaw, 77, March of Dimes Backer, Dies," *New York Times*, December 17, 1992, www.nytimes.com/1992/12/17/nyregion /elaine-whitelaw-77-march-of-dimes -backer-dies.html.

471 Daniel Charles Niemeyer, *1950s American Style: A Reference Guide*

(Boulder: Fifties Book Publishers, 2013), 25.

472 "John Wanamaker: Who Made America?," PBS.org, accessed May 9, 2016, www.pbs .org/wgbh/theymadeamerica/whomade /wanamaker_hi.html.

473 "Three Ring Benefit," *Life*, February 11, 1957, 119.

474 Tiffany, *Eleanor Lambert: Still Here*, 29.

475 Bill Berkson, interview by author, December 2015.

476 Sondra Whitney, interview by author, March 2015.

477 Kenneth Jay Lane, interview by author, June 2015.

478 Ibid.

479 Coleman, *The Genius of Charles James*, 93.

480 Koda, et al., *Charles James: Beyond Fashion*, 43.

481 Coleman, *The Genius of Charles James*, 93.

482 Jacobs, "Gowned for Glory," *Vanity Fair*, November 1998.

483 "Samuel Winston, Inc. Sues Charles James for $61,341 on Pact," *Women's Wear Daily*, November 4, 1954, 10.

484 Charles James, letter to Marilyn Bender, date unknown, Metropolitan Museum of Art, Layne Gift, Charles James Collection.

485 Homer Layne, interview by author, March 2005.

486 Fashion Institute of Technology, State University of New York, Eleanor Lambert Papers circa 1950–1970, Spec Coll US. NNFITSC.214.2348-50.

487 Duka, "The Ghost of Seventh Avenue," *New York Magazine*, 81–88.

488 Ibid.

489 Ibid.

490 Rose, *Saying Life*, 150.

491 Hugo Vickers, telephone interview by author, September 2015.

492 Tiffany, *Eleanor Lambert: Still Here*, 75.

493 Ibid., 292.

494 "Eleanor Lambert: Defining Decades of Fashion," produced by Look TV, performed by Eleanor Lambert. November 21, 2013, youtu.be/inaLhwknn0g.

CHAPTER NINE

495 Michael J. Cox, *Masten Gregory: Totally Fearless, Two Decades of Motorsport through the Spectacles of the Kansas City Flash* (n.p.: MTCA Creations, 2004), 15.

496 "Youthful Widow Fights for Control of Insurance Firm," *Jefferson City Post*, July 2, 1935, 1.

497 "At a Glance," Barstow School, accessed April 6, 2016, www.barstowschool.org /Page/About.

498 Barstow School. 1938 Yearbook. Graduating Class of 1938. Barstow School Archives, Kansas City, MO.

499 Nancy (Cuerdon) Gregory Records, circa 1952–1954, Art Students League.

500 Michael Cox, telephone interview by author, December 2015.

501 Michael Cox, "'The Kansas City Flash': The Lives & Times of Masten Gregory," *Atlas F1*, 2000, Volume 6, Issue 29, www.atlasf1.com/2000/aut/cox.html.

502 Jacobs, "Gowned for Glory," *Vanity Fair*, November 1998. Duka, "The Ghost of Seventh Avenue," *New York Magazine*, 81–88.

503 Gary Alston, "Charles James: 'A Personal Memoir with Nancy James' As Told to Gary Alston," House of Retro, 2013, houseofretro.com/index.php/2013/01/25 /charles-james-a-personal-memoir-with -nancy-james-as-told-to-gary-alston/.

504 Coleman, *The Genius of Charles James*, 60.

505 Alston, "Charles James: 'A Personal Memoir with Nancy James' As Told to Gary Alston," House of Retro, 2013.

506 "1953 Neiman Marcus Award Winners," *Women's Wear Daily*, August 10, 1953, 4.

507 Jacobs, "Gowned for Glory," *Vanity Fair*, November 1998.

508 Mary Ann Crenshaw, telephone interview by author. October 2015.

509 Koda, et al., *Charles James: Beyond Fashion*, 42.

510 Hay and Perich, videotapes,1975.

511 Ibid.

512 *Vogue*, October 1,1954. 15.

513 Dorothy Hawkins, "Californian Gets a Fashion Trophy," *New York Times*, October 12, 1954.

514 Tiffany, *Eleanor Lambert: Still Here*, 119.

515 Mary Ann Crenshaw, telephone interview by author, October 2015.

516 Ibid.

517 Alston, "Charles James: 'A Personal Memoir with Nancy James' As Told to Gary Alston," House of Retro, 2013.

518 Mary Ann Crenshaw, telephone interview by author, October 2015.

519 Alston, "Charles James: 'A Personal Memoir with Nancy James' As Told to Gary Alston," House of Retro, 2013.

520 Mary Ann Crenshaw, telephone interview by author, October 2015.

521 Alston, "Charles James: 'A Personal Memoir with Nancy James' As Told to Gary Alston," House of Retro, 2013.

522 Jacobs, "Gowned for Glory," *Vanity Fair*, November 1998.

523 Mary Ann Crenshaw, telephone interview by author, October 2015.

524 Coleman, *The Genius of Charles James*, 94–95.

525 Ibid., 97.

526 Ibid., 95.

527 Ibid., 97.

528 *Kansas City Independent*, 1957. The Independent Magazine, Kansas City, Missouri.

529 Coleman, *The Genius of Charles James*, 97.

530 Ibid., 87.

531 Levin, "Paris Sets Pace, But Creative Fashion Talent, Critics Agree, Exists in U.S.," *New York Times*, May 20, 1958.

532 Coleman, *The Genius of Charles James*, 98.

533 Ibid.

534 Coleman, *The Genius of Charles James*, 100.

535 Wadsworth Atheneum. *The Sculpture of Style* (Hartford: Wadsworth Atheneum, 1964).

536 Coleman, *The Genius of Charles James*, 99.

537 M. E. Hecht, "The Cutting Edge," *Vogue*, April 2011, 145.

538 Michael Cox, telephone interview by author, December 2015.

539 Alston, "Charles James: 'A Personal Memoir with Nancy James' As Told to Gary Alston," House of Retro, 2013.

540 Coleman, *The Genius of Charles James*, 98.

CHAPTER TEN

541 Ibid., 85.

542 Hay and Perich, videotapes, 1975.

543 Kenneth Jay Lane, interview by author, June 2015.

544 Nathaniel Rich, "Where the Walls Still Talk," *Vanity Fair*, October 8, 2013, www.vanityfair.com/culture/2013/10/chelsea-hotel-oral-history.

545 Florence Turner, *At the Chelsea: A Personal Memoir of New York's Most Famous Hotel* (London: Foruli Classics, 2013).

546 William Ivey Long, interviews by author, January 2015.

547 Harold Koda, interview by author, February 2015.

548 Elizabeth de Cuevas, interviews by author, March 2008, September 2014, March 2015.

549 Hay and Perich, videotapes.1975.

550 "The Calculus of Fashion to Be Taught," *New York Herald-Tribune*, October 17, 1960, 16.

551 "Charles James Launches College Fashion Seminars," *Women's Wear Daily*, October 17, 1960, 4.

552 Smithsonian Institution, Archives of American Art, The Wadsworth Atheneum, Samuel J. Wagstaff Papers, circa 1932–1985, Box 1, Folder 28.

553 Ibid.

554 Cunningham, "Charles James," *SoHo Weekly News*, 33–34.

555 *The Sculpture of Style,* Hartford: Wadsworth Atheneum, 1964, 6.

556 Ibid.

557 Smithsonian Institution, The Archives of American Art, Samuel J. Wagstaff Papers, circa 1932–1985, Box 1, Folder 28.

558 Karin Nelson, "Shooting Star," *W Magazine*, September 2012, www.wmagazine.com/fashion/2012/09/antonio-lopez-fashion-illustrator.

559 Unknown, 1964. thegenealogyofstyle.files.wordpress.com/2013/05/clockwise-from-bottom-antonio-lopez-kathleen-ingeborg-marcus-cathee-dahmen-and-friend-charles-james-and-juan-ramos-in-1966-photo-by-dick-balarian.jpg.

560 André Leon Talley, "André Leon Talley Previews Zac Posen's Charles James-Inspired Fall 2014 Collection," *Vogue* February 8, 2014, www.vogue.com/866720/andre-leon-talley-previews-zac-posens-charles-james-inspired-fall-2014-collection/.

561 Nelson, "Shooting Star." *W Magazine*, September 2012.

562 Koda, et al., *Charles James: Beyond Fashion*, 48.

563 Anton Perich, in conversation with the author. Elizabeth de Cuevas, interviews by author, March 2008, September 2014, March 2015.

564 This is also the description of a common artistic practice, in which the artist sets himself a group of problems and evolves the solutions over the years.

565 Cindi di Marzo, "Unravelling the Mystery and Mastery of America's First Couturier," *Studio International*, May 26, 2014, www.studiointernational.com /index.php/unravelling-the-mystery-and -mastery-of-america-s-first-couturier.

566 Virginia Pope, "New Pajama-Skirt Is Exhibited Here," *New York Times*, January 3, 1941.

567 "Working Title of a Program Being Worked Out with the Institute of Sound," early proposal for "Sound of Shape and Design," Brooklyn Museum Gift, Metropolitan Museum of Art, Charles James Collection.

568 Steven S. Gaines, *Simply Halston: The Untold Story* (New York: Putnam, 1991), 57.

569 Ibid., 59.

570 Ibid.

571 Ibid.

572 Ibid.

573 Ibid., 99.

574 Ibid., 126.

575 Florence Turner, "Remembering Charles James," *Vogue UK*, May 1983.

576 Gaines, *Simply Halston*, 127.

577 Ibid.

578 Robert Janjigian, "Former model, '92 Ballinger Winner Betsy Kaiser Dies," *Palm Beach Daily News,* March 30, 2013, www.palmbeachdailynews.com/news /news/national/former-model-92 -ballinger-winner-betsy-kaiser-dies /nW7X7/.

579 Koda, et al., *Charles James: Beyond Fashion*, 48.

580 Turner, "Remembering Charles James," *Vogue UK*, May 1983.

581 Gaines,. *Simply Halston*, 127.

582 R. Couri Hay, "The Charles James Story 1 with R. Couri Hay," interview by Michèle Gerber Klein, YouTube. January 16, 2008, www.youtube.com /watch?v=jxGHaR5QXp0.

583 Gaines, *Simply Halston*, 128.

584 Homer Layne in conversation with the author.

585 Gaines, *Simply Halston*, 128–29.

586 Bernadine Morris, "At Halston, New Fashion Team," *New York Times*, June 6, 1970.

587 Elsa Peretti, "Recalling Charles James: Elsa Peretti," interview by Alina Cho, Metropolitan Museum of Art, www.metmuseum.org/metmedia/audio /exhibitions/recalling-charles-james-elsa -peretti.

588 Gaines, *Simply Halston*, 130.

589 Fred Rottman, telephone interview by author, September 2015.

590 Homer Layne, "Recalling Charles James: Homer Layne," interview by Alina Cho, Metropolitan Museum of Art, www.metmuseum.org/metmedia/audio /exhibitions/recalling-charles-james -homer-layne.

591 Ibid.

592 Elsa Peretti, "Recalling Charles James: Elsa Peretti," interview by Alina Cho, Metropolitan Museum of Art.

593 Ibid.

594 Elizabeth Strong Cuevas, "Recalling Charles James: Elizabeth Strong-Cuevas," interview by Alina Cho, Metropolitan Museum of Art, www.metmuseum.org /metmedia/audio/exhibitions/recalling -charles-james-elizabeth-strong-cuevas.

595 Elizabeth de Cuevas in conversation with the author.

596 R. Couri Hay, "Recalling Charles James: R. Couri Hay." Interview by Alina Cho, Metropolitan Museum of Art, www.metmuseum.org/metmedia/audio /exhibitions/recalling-charles-james-r -couri-hay.

597 Sutton, et al., "Dangerous Ideas: Charles James and the de Menils."

598 Joan Kron, "Difficult Genius: My Afternoon With Charles James," *Allure*, May 6, 2014, www.allure.com /beauty-trends/blogs/daily-beauty -reporter/2014/05/charles-james -couturier-remembered.html.

599 Eve MacSweeney, "The Apprentice," *Vogue Met Gala Special Edition*, 2014.

600 Charles James, letter to Cecil Beaton, July 29, 1973, Cecil Beaton Collection. Special Collections, St. John's College. Cambridge, UK.

601 Ibid.

602 Charles James, letter to Eleanor Lambert. Privately held by Bill Berkson.

603 William Ivey Long, interview by author, January 2015.

604 Ibid.

605   Kate Muir, "The Greatest Magazine of All Time," *Times* (UK), April 22, 2006, www.thetimes.co.uk/tto/life/article1750562.ece.

606   James, "A Portrait of a Genius By a Genius," *Nova*, July 1974, 44.

607   Ibid.

608   Ibid.

609   Richard Oldenburg in conversation with the author.

610   "Charles James, the Majority of One," *American Fabrics and Fashions*, Fall 1973.

611   Elaine Louie, "Charles James and Me," *New York Times*, April 23, 2014, www.nytimes.com/2014/04/24/fashion/charles-james-and-me.html?_r=0.

612   Paul Caranicas, "Recalling Charles James: Paul Caranicas," interview by Alina Cho, Metropolitan Museum of Art, www.metmuseum.org/metmedia/audio/exhibitions/recalling-charles-james-paul-caranicas.

613   Beauregard Houston-Montgomery, telephone interview by author, September 2015.

614   Rory Denis, telephone interview by author, September 2015.

615   William Ivey Long, interviews by author, January 2015.

616   Homer Layne,."Recalling Charles James: Homer Layne," interview by Alina Cho, Metropolitan Museum of Art.

617   Barbara Hodes, e-mail to author, October 2015. Privately held by Michèle Gerber Klein, New York.

618   Charles James, letter to Barbara Hodes, circa. 1973. Privately held by Barbara Hodes.

619   Elizabeth de Cuevas, interviews by author, March 2008, September 2014, March 2015.

620   Homer Layne, interview by author, March 2005.

621   Rory Denis, telephone interview by author, September 2015.

622   Anton Perich, interview by author, January 2008.

623   Rory Denis, telephone interview by author, September 2015.

624   R. Couri Hay, interview by author, January 2008.

625   MacSweeney, "The Apprentice," *Vogue Met Gala Special Edition*, 2014.

626   William Ivey Long, interview by author, January 2015.

627   Rory Denis, telephone interview by author, September 2015.

628   William Ivey Long, interviews by author, January 2015.

629   Turner, "Remembering Charles James," *Vogue UK*, May 1983.

630   Cunningham, "Charles James." *SoHo Weekly News*, 34.

631   Coleman, *The Genius of Charles James*, 113.

632   "An Interview with Austine Hearst," by John F. Touhey, May 15, 1980, "Oral History Collection at the Fashion Institute of Technology," Spec Coll TT 139.O73 V.12, Fashion Institute of Technology, State University of New York.

INDEX